Big business and the wealth of nations

Written in nontechnical terms, *Big Business and the Wealth of Nations* explains how the dynamics of big business have influenced national and international economies in the twentieth century. A path-breaking study, it provides the first systematic treatment of big business in advanced, emerging, and centrally planned economies from the late nineteenth century, when big businesses first appeared in American and West European manufacturing, to the present. Large industrial enterprises have played a vital role in developing new technologies and commercializing new products for over a century in all of the major countries. How such firms emerged and evolved in different economic, political, and social settings constitutes a significant part of twentieth-century world history. This historical review of big business is particularly valuable at the present time, when the viability of large enterprises is being challenged by small firms, networks, and alliances. These essays, written by internationally known historians and economists, help one to understand the essential role and functions of big businesses, past and present.

Big business and the wealth of nations

Edited by

ALFRED D. CHANDLER, JR.
Harvard University

FRANCO AMATORI
Bocconi University

TAKASHI HIKINO
Massachusetts Institute of Technology and Harvard University

CAMBRIDGE
UNIVERSITY PRESS

PUBLISHED BY THE PRESS SYNDICATE OF THE UNIVERSITY OF CAMBRIDGE
The Pitt Building, Trumpington Street, Cambridge, United Kingdom

CAMBRIDGE UNIVERSITY PRESS
The Edinburgh Building, Cambridge CB2 2RU, UK   http: //www.cup.cam.ac.uk
40 West 20th Street, New York, NY 10011-4211, USA   http: //www.cup.org
10 Stamford Road, Oakleigh, Melbourne 3166, Australia

First published 1997
Reprinted 1998, 1999
First paperback edition 1999

Printed in the United States of America

Typeset in Sabon

A catalogue record for this book is available from the British Library

Library of Congress Cataloguing-in-Publication data is available

ISBN 0 521 48123 6 hardback
ISBN 0 521 66347 4 paperback

Contents

Acknowledgments

The essays in this volume are the fruits of a project, Global Enterprise: Big Business and the Wealth of Nations in the Past Century, 1880s to 1980s, for the Eleventh International Economic History Congress at Milan in 1994. The authors of most papers had originally submitted their draft versions to a workshop in Florence in 1992 and subsequently revised them for the Congress meeting in 1994. Then they rewrote them for this book in light of conference exchanges.

Many individuals and institutions made significant contributions to the making of this volume. The editors would like to thank all who took part in the discussions at various conferences and workshops where the authors, individually or collectively, presented their papers. Some people played particularly important roles in various capacities. Those include Alan Gold, Max Hall, Russell Hahn, Leslie Hannah, Peter Hertner, Shirley Kessel, David Landes, Aldo De Maddalena, Guilio Sapelli, Paola Subacchi and Herman van der Wee. The complicated and time-consuming word-processing job was performed by Jane Barrett, Aimee Hamel, Eileen Heath and particularly Anne O'Connell. We are indebted to Frank Smith of Cambridge University Press for his enthusiastic encouragement and patient cooperation. We thankfully acknowledge ASSI Foundation, Bocconi University, European University Institute and Gruppo Dioguardi for their generous financial support of the project.

Tables and figures

Tables

viii

Figures

Contributors

Franco Amatori, Istituto di Storia Economica, Università Bocconi, Milan, Italy.

Alice H. Amsden, Department of Urban Studies and Planning, Massachusetts Institute of Technology, Cambridge, USA.

María Innés Barbero, Departament de Ciencias Sociales, Universidad de Luján, Luján, Argentina.

Albert Carreras, Department of Economics and Business, Universitat Pompeu Fabra, Barcelona, Spain.

Alfred D. Chandler, Jr., Graduate School of Business Administration, Harvard University, Boston, USA.

Giovanni Dosi, Dipartimento di Scienze Economiche, Universitá 'la Sapienza' di Roma, Rome, Italy.

Jeffrey R. Fear, Department of History, University of Pennsylvania, Philadelphia, USA.

Patrick Fridenson, Centre de Recherches Historiques, École des Hautes Études en Sciences Sociales, Paris, France.

Takashi Hikino, Center for International Studies, Massachusetts Institute of Technology, Cambridge, and Graduate School of Business Administration, Harvard University, Boston, USA.

Geoffrey Jones, Department of Economics, University of Reading, Reading, England.

William Lazonick, Center for Industrial Competitiveness, University of Massachusetts at Lowell, Lowell, USA, and INSEAD, Fontainebleau, France.

Thomas K. McCraw, Graduate School of Business Administration, Harvard University, Boston, USA.

Hidemasa Morikawa, Department of Management and Information, Toyohashi Sozo College, Toyohashi, Japan.

Harm G. Schröter, Faculty of Philosophy, University of Konstanz, Konstanz, Germany.

Mary O'Sullivan, INSEAD, Fontainebleau, France.

Xavier Tafunell, Department of Economics and Business, Universitat Pompeu Fabra, Barcelona, Spain.

Alice Teichova, Girton College, University of Cambridge, Cambridge, England.

Ulrich Wengenroth, Central Institute for the History of Technology, Technical University of Munich, Munich, Germany.

Andrei Yu. Yudanov, Financial Academy, The Government of Russian Federation, Moscow, Russia.

Part I

Overview

1

Historical and comparative contours of big business

ALFRED D. CHANDLER, JR., FRANCO AMATORI, AND TAKASHI HIKINO

This book aims to understand how "The Wealth of Nations" during the past century has been influenced by the dynamics of big business. All the authors recognize big business, particularly large industrial enterprises, as a key microeconomic agent that employs such productive assets as raw materials, machinery and equipment, human resources, and technological knowledge on a vast scale. How such firms emerged and evolved in various economic, political, and social settings constitutes a significant part of the modern development of international as well as national economies (whose "wealth" we consider as equivalent to "national income" in modern economic terms). This historical review of the contributions of large industrial enterprises seems particularly valuable at this time when significant scholarly work has analyzed the role of small firms, networks, and alliances. The essays in this collection help to relate such analyses to the contributing and complementary roles and functions of the large firm, past and present.

The collection consists of an introductory part (Part I), the central section on country experiences (Part II), and a segment of commentaries on the country papers (Part III). The introductory part consists of this overview (Chapter 1) and a chapter on the contributions of the large industrial enterprises to modern economic growth (Chapter 2). The two chapters provide a point of reference, a setting to which the reader can relate the narratives told, the interpretations made, and the insights offered in this wide-ranging, perceptive set of chapters that deal with the historical evolution of large firms and their place in national economies. Subject to the overall goals of the project, the contributors of the country chapters (3 to 14) of Part II wrote to reflect their own viewpoints as

3

well as the different experiences of individual nations. Part III consists of five short subject chapters (15 to 19), which, in the form of commentary on the chapters of Part II, deal with critical economic and institutional issues related to the functions and operations of large industrial enterprises.

The chapters on the national experiences of Part II fall into four groups, each related to the timing of the coming of industries based on the new capital-intensive, scale-dependent technology that large firms dominated. First are the chapters on the United States, Britain, and Germany, nations that made up the initial core of the modern industrial global economy dating from the late nineteenth century, and the smaller countries whose economies were closely related to their large neighbor, Germany – Switzerland, Holland, Belgium and the Scandinavian nations (Chapters 3 to 6). The second group deals with three European countries – France, Italy, and Spain (Chapters 7 to 9) – where the emergence of large industrial enterprises was slower compared with that in the first set of nations. The third group then takes up three of the late-coming non-European countries – Japan, South Korea, and Argentina (Chapters 10 to 12) – in which the development of large firms, particularly those in capital-intensive industries, was further behind relative to the first and second groups. The fourth group reviews the impact of the transformation from market to planned economies in the USSR and Czechoslovakia (Chapters 13 to 14) on the functions and, therefore, the organizations of the large industrial enterprises, and the effect of that impact on economic growth.

The twelve chapters that make up Part II on the national experiences provide the historical data for the five commentaries of Part III, "Economic and Institutional Environment of Big Business." The first, Chapter 15, relates the historical stories to economic theory by focusing on the impact of the evolution of organizational competences through organizational learning on different nations' abilities to produce and accumulate wealth. Chapter 16 analyzes the key role of learned organizational knowledge from different perspectives of large industrial enterprises and capital markets. Chapter 17 concentrates on the comparable impact of organizational learning on the formation of work force skills. Chapter 18 deals more with the broader environment in which the force of government policies influences the performance of large enterprises and their national economies. The final chapter considers the corporation as a cultural expression of broader national attitudes and values and how the enterprise or enterprise system is conceived as a unified whole.

THE CHRONOLOGY OF ECONOMIC GROWTH

This overview of the diverse experiences of large enterprises – big business – in twelve chapters must first be placed in the briefest of reviews of the broader macroeconomic developments during the century covered in this book. From the 1880s to the 1980s the national income of all twelve countries grew thanks to rapid technological change and rising economic efficiency, particularly industrial productivity.[1] As is illustrated in Table 1.1 and Table 1.2, each one of those nations has enjoyed a substantial level of economic growth which was historically unprecedented, although growth performance varied by individual countries and fluctuated by time periods.[2] Growth economists and historians concerned with the evolution of national economies agree that technological change has been a major force in the sustained economic growth of nations' wealth during the century covered by these essays.[3] Large industrial enterprises have thus been a substantial part of this economic achievement mainly through the

---

[1] For diverse viewpoints of modern industrialization processes in general, see Jonathan R. T. Hughes, *Industrialization and Economic History: Theses and Conjectures* (New York: McGraw-Hill, 1970); Simon S. Kuznets, *Economic Growth of Nations: Total Output and Production Structure* (Cambridge, Mass.: Harvard University Press, 1971); Charles P. Kindleberger, *Economic Response: Comparative Studies in Trade, Finance, and Growth* (Cambridge, Mass.: Harvard University Press, 1978); Sidney Pollard, *Peaceful Conquest: The Industrialization of Europe, 1760–1970* (Oxford: Oxford University Press, 1981); Michael J. Piore and Charles F. Sabel, *The Second Industrial Divide: Possibilities for Prosperity* (New York: Basic Books, 1984); Nathan Rosenberg and L. E. Birdzell, Jr., *How the West Grew Rich: The Economic Transformation of the Industrial World* (New York: Basic Books, 1986); Angus Maddison, *Dynamic Forces in Capitalist Development: A Long-Run Comparative View* (Oxford: Oxford University Press, 1991); William J. Baumol, Richard R. Nelson, and Edward N. Wolff, eds., *Convergence of Productivity: Cross-National Studies and Historical Evidence* (New York: Oxford University Press, 1994).

[2] For the detailed statistical data of various aspects of economic growth, see Brian R. Mitchell's compilations: *International Historical Statistics: Europe, 1750–1988*, 3rd ed. (New York: Stockton Press, 1992); *International Historical Statistics: The Americas, 1750–1988*, 2nd ed. (New York: Stockton Press, 1993); *International Historical Statistics: Africa and Asia* (New York: New York University Press, 1982).

[3] For the relationships between technology and industrialization, see David S. Landes, *The Unbound Prometheus: Technological Change and Industrial Development in Western Europe from 1750 to the Present* (Cambridge: Cambridge University Press, 1969); David F. Noble, *America by Design: Science, Technology, and the Rise of Corporate Capitalism* (New York: Knopf, 1977); Joel Mokyr, *The Lever of Riches: Technological Creativity and Economic Progress* (New York: Oxford University Press, 1990); Thomas P. Hughes, *American Genesis: A Century of Invention and Technological Enthusiasm, 1870–1970* (New York: Viking, 1989); Giovanni Dosi, Renato Giannetti, and Pier Angelo Toninelli, eds., *Technology and Enterprise in a Historical Perspective* (Oxford: Oxford University Press, 1992); Nathan Rosenberg, Ralph Landau, and David C. Mowery, eds., *Technology and the Wealth of Nations* (Stanford, Calif.: Stanford University Press, 1992); Nathan Rosenberg, *Exploring the Black Box: Technology, Economics, and History* (Cambridge: Cambridge University Press, 1994).

Table 1.1. *Economic growth of nations, 1820–1992 (Gross domestic product per capita in 1990 international dollars)*

	1820	1870	1913	1950	1973	1992
Prime drivers in North America and Western Europe						
United States	$1,287	$2,457	$5,307	$9,573	$16,607	$21,558
Great Britain	1,756	3,263	5,032	6,847	11,992	15,738
Germany	1,112	1,913	3,833	4,281	13,152	19,351
Belgium	1,291	2,640	4,130	5,346	11,905	17,165
The Netherlands	1,561	2,640	3,950	5,850	12,763	16,898
Sweden	1,198	1,664	3,096	6,738	13,494	16,927
Switzerland	—	2,172	4,207	8,939	17,953	21,036
Followers in Western Europe						
France	1,218	1,858	3,452	5,221	12,940	17,959
Italy	1,092	1,467	2,507	3,425	10,409	16,229
Spain	1,063	1,376	2,255	2,397	8,739	12,498
Late industrializers in East Asia and South America						
Japan	704	741	1,334	1,873	11,017	19,425
South Korea	—	—	948	876	2,840	10,010
Argentina	—	1,311	3,797	4,987	7,970	7,616
Centrally planned economies in Eastern Europe						
USSR/Russia	751	1,023	1,488	2,834	6,058	4,671
Czechoslovakia	849	1,164	2,096	3,501	7,036	6,845

Source: Compiled from Angus Maddison, *Monitoring the World Economy, 1820–1992* (Paris: Development Centre, OECD, 1995), table 1.3, p. 23.

commercialization of new products and processes which embodied innovating technologies.[4]

[4] Useful previous volumes of comparative perspectives on the rise of big business in developed market economies include Herman Daems and Herman van der Wee, eds., *The Rise of Managerial Capitalism* (Louvain: Louvain University Press, 1974); Keiichiro Nakagawa, ed., *Strategy and Structure of Big Business: Proceedings of the First Fuji Conference* (Tokyo: University of Tokyo Press, 1975); Harold F. Williamson, ed., *Evolution of International Management Structures* (Newark: University of Delaware Press, 1975); Leslie Hannah, ed., *Management Strategy and Business Development: An Historical and Comparative Study* (London: Macmillan, 1976); Norbert Horn and Jürgen Kocka, eds., *Law and the Formation of the Big Enterprises in the 19th and Early 20th Centuries: Studies in the History of Industrialization in Germany, France, Great Britain, and the United States* (Göttingen: Bandenhoeck & Ruprecht, 1979); Alfred D. Chandler, Jr., and Herman Daems, eds., *Managerial Hierarchies: Comparative Perspectives on the Rise of Modern Industrial Enterprise* (Cambridge, Mass.: Harvard University Press, 1980); Kesaji Kobayashi

Table 1.2. *Rates of economic growth of nations, 1820–1992*
(Average compound annual growth rate of GDP per capita
in 1990 international dollars)

	1820–1870	1870–1913	1913–1950	1950–1973	1973–1992
Prime drivers in North America and Western Europe					
United States	1.3%	1.8%	1.6%	2.4%	1.4%
Great Britain	1.2	1.0	0.8	2.5	1.4
Germany	1.1	1.6	0.3	5.0	2.1
Belgium	1.4	1.0	0.7	3.5	1.9
The Netherlands	1.1	0.9	1.1	3.4	1.4
Sweden	0.7	1.5	2.1	3.1	1.2
Switzerland	—	1.5	2.1	3.1	0.8
Followers in Western Europe					
France	0.8	1.5	1.1	4.0	1.7
Italy	0.6	1.3	0.8	5.0	2.4
Spain	0.5	1.2	0.2	5.8	1.9
Late industrializers in East Asia and South America					
Japan	0.1	1.4	0.9	8.0	3.0
South Korea	—	—	−0.2	5.2	6.9
Argentina	—	2.5	0.7	2.1	−0.2
Centrally planned economies in Eastern Europe					
USSR/Russia	0.6	0.9	1.8	3.4	−1.4
Czechoslovakia	0.6	1.4	1.4	3.1	−0.1

Source: Compiled from Angus Maddison, *Monitoring the World Economy, 1820–1992*
(Paris: Development Centre, OECD, 1995), table 3.2, p. 62.

and Hidemasa Morikawa, eds., *Development of Managerial Enterprise: Proceedings of the Fuji Conference* (Tokyo: University of Tokyo Press, 1986); Alice Teichova, Maurice Levy-Leboyer, and Helga Nussbaum, eds., *Multinational Enterprise in Historical Perspective* (Cambridge: Cambridge University Press, 1986); Mansel G. Blackford, *The Rise of Modern Business in Great Britain, the United States, and Japan* (Chapel Hill: University of North Carolina Press, 1988); Alfred D. Chandler, Jr., with the assistance of Takashi Hikino, *Scale and Scope: The Dynamics of Industrial Capitalism* (Cambridge, Mass.: Harvard University Press, 1990); William Lazonick, *Business Organization and the Myth of the Market Economy* (Cambridge: Cambridge University Press, 1991); Geoffrey Jones, ed., *Transnational Corporations: A Historical Perspective* (London: Routledge, 1993). Important journal articles on the development of big business are collected in several volumes in Geoffrey Jones, series editor, *The International Library of Critical Writings in Business History* published by Edward Elgar, Aldershot, Hants., England. Particularly relevant are Mira Wilkins, ed., *The Growth of Multinationals* (1991); Barry E. Supple, ed., *The Rise of Big Business* (1992); Geoffrey Jones, ed., *Coalitions and Collaboration in International Business* (1993); William Lazonick and William Mass, eds., *Organizational Capability and Competitive Advantage* (1995); Steven W. Tolliday, ed., *The Rise and Fall of Mass Production* (forthcoming).

During the later decades of the nineteenth century, the completion of the new transportation and communication systems based on steam power and electricity led to a recurrent wave of technological innovations in the industrial processes and their products. The potential of these technologies for growth rested on the unprecedented volume of production and distribution made possible by the new railroads, steamships, telegraphs, and cable networks. The new industrial technologies, in turn, brought impressive increases in productivity, value-added in manufacture, and other indices of economic growth. In this sense, this transformation of technologies and their impact on national and international economies have been aptly labeled the "Second Industrial Revolution," whose economic effects became even more pervasive than those of the First Industrial Revolution of the late eighteenth and early nineteenth centuries.[5]

The commercialization of the new high-volume, capital-intensive industrial technologies transformed existing industries and created new ones. The effective exploitation of those technologies demanded new forms of production and distribution and of management and business organization. They called for much greater investment in physical capital than had earlier industrial technologies. So the resulting industries became more capital-intensive, that is, they had a higher ratio of capital per worker than their predecessors. The commercializing of these technologies required the creation of industrial enterprises to mobilize the necessary capital and employ the large number of workers and managers needed. It also demanded the corporate structures essential to coordinate the flow of goods through the processes of production and distribution and to monitor the different functional activities involved.

The significant impact of those new technologies was not narrowly limited to the industrial centers of the United States and Western Europe, where the Second Industrial Revolution originated. The large industrial enterprises commercializing the new technologies critically affected the rest of the world economy by playing a dual role. They functioned as

---

[5] Alfred D. Chandler, Jr., *The Visible Hand: The Managerial Revolution in American Business* (Cambridge, Mass.: Harvard University Press, 1977), and Chandler with Hikino, *Scale and Scope*, give an overall perspective of the Second Industrial Revolution which constitutes a starting point of the present book. For different European outlooks, see Alan S. Milward and S. B. Saul, *The Development of the Economies of Continental Europe, 1850–1914* (Cambridge, Mass.: Harvard University Press, 1977); T. Ivan Berend and Gyorgy Ranki, *The European Periphery and Industrialization, 1780–1914* (Cambridge: Cambridge University Press, 1982); Leslie Hannah, *The Rise of the Corporate Economy* (London: Methuen, 1983); Tom Kemp, *Industrialization in Nineteenth-Century Europe* (London: Longman, 1985).

technology transfer agents through diverse diffusing mechanisms, such as the export of manufactured goods embodying new knowledge, the licensing of technology to foreign firms, and the establishment of overseas manufacturing facilities. For emerging indigenous industrial firms, on the other hand, those large enterprises from the global industrial centers often created entry barriers in international markets. The Second Industrial Revolution thus transformed the ways in which industrial firms interacted with each other and how the industrial nations dealt with the rest of the world.[6]

The timing and extent of the development of large industrial enterprises and their commercialization of the new capital-intensive technologies varied from nation to nation. Because the United States was favored by an abundance of raw materials and a large and growing population, it took the lead in commercializing the new technologies as its railroad system and telegraph networks neared completion. In the smaller West European nations where resources were less abundant and markets of more modest size, capital accumulation of new corporate organizations came more slowly and in fewer industries than in the United States. By 1914 American firms had become the leaders in technological innovation

---

[6] Foreign business activities and relations of large enterprises have been extensively researched. Particularly useful theoretical examinations in the context of the present book include Charles P. Kindleberger, *American Business Abroad: Six Lectures on Direct Investment* (New Haven: Yale University Press, 1969); Raymond Vernon, *Sovereignty at Bay: The Multinational Spread of U.S. Enterprises* (New York: Basic Books, 1971); Stephen Hymer, *The International Operations of National Firms: A Study of Direct Foreign Investment* (Cambridge, Mass.: MIT Press, 1976); Richard E. Caves, *Multinational Enterprise and Economic Analysis* (Cambridge: Cambridge University Press, 1982); John H. Dunning, *Multinational Enterprises and the Global Economy* (Wokingham: Addison-Wesley, 1993). A few examples of empirical works are Mira Wilkins and Frank E. Hill, *American Business Abroad: Ford on Six Continents* (Detroit: Wayne State University Press, 1964); John P. McKay, *Pioneers for Profit: Foreign Entrepreneurship and Russian Industrialization, 1885–1913* (Chicago: University of Chicago Press, 1970); Mira Wilkins, *The Emergence of Multinational Enterprise: American Business Abroad from the Colonial Era to 1914* (Cambridge, Mass.: Harvard University Press, 1970); Mira Wilkins, *The Maturing of Multinational Enterprise: American Business Abroad from 1914 to 1970* (Cambridge, Mass.: Harvard University Press, 1974); D. K. Fieldhouse, *Unilever Overseas: The Anatomy of a Multinational, 1895–1965* (London: Croom Helm, 1978); Charles E. Harvey, *The Rio Tinto Company: An Economic History of a Leading International Mining Concern, 1873–1954* (Penzance, Cornwell: A. Hodge, 1981); Fred V. Carstensen, *American Enterprise in Foreign Markets: Studies of Singer and International Harvester in Imperial Russia* (Chapel Hill: University of North Carolina Press, 1984); Mark Mason, *American Multinationals and Japan: The Political Economy of Japanese Capital Controls, 1899–1980* (Cambridge, Mass.: Harvard University Press, 1992); Geoffrey Jones and Harm G. Schröter, eds., *The Rise of Multinationals in Continental Europe* (Aldershot, Hants.: Edward Elgar, 1993); Geoffrey Jones, ed., *Transnational Corporations: A Historical Perspective* (London: Routledge, 1993).

particularly in those markets which stimulated the new capital-intensive industries. But in several of such industries European enterprises were not far behind, and in some they had taken the lead.

Then came World War I followed by a sharp recession, a temporary economic recovery with continuing political instabilities, the Great Depression, and finally World War II – events that radically dissipated the opportunities for growth based on technological advance in Europe and also in Japan where initial large-scale industrialization had only begun.[7] As a result, in the words of Moses Abramovitz and Paul David, "During the 37 years from 1913 to 1950 the forces making for catch-up and convergence vis-à-vis the United States were overwhelmed."[8]

A dramatic period of catch-up came in the 1950s. Indeed, this unique "Golden Age of Capitalism" was universal for all industrial-advanced economies.[9] During this phase, as Moses Abramovitz and Paul David point out, "the pace of catch-up was achieved in spite of rapid American productivity growth which was at least as fast, it may have been even faster, than in any previous period of comparable duration."[10] Much of this American growth rested on the exploitation by large industrial firms of the new knowledge-intensive as well as capital-intensive technologies in chemistry, pharmaceuticals, aircraft, and electronics – technologies that had been force-fed by wartime demands.

Europe, in particular, reflected the dynamics of the utilization of the technological backlog which had resulted from macroeconomic and

---

[7] For a survey of this turbulent period, see Ingvar Svennilson, *Growth and Stagnation in the European Economy* (Geneva: United Nations Economic Commission for Europe, 1954); Milton Friedman and Anna J. Schwartz, *The Great Contraction, 1929–1933* (Princeton: Princeton University Press, 1965); Herman van der Wee, *The Great Depression Revisited* (The Hague, Leuven University Press, 1972); Derek H. Aldcroft, *From Versailles to Wall Street, 1919–1929* (Berkeley: University of California Press, 1977); Alan S. Milward, *War, Economy, and Society, 1939–1945* (Berkeley: University of California Press, 1977); Charles P. Kindleberger, *World in Depression, 1929–1939*, rev. and enl. ed. (Berkeley: University of California Press, 1986); Peter Temin, *Lessons from the Great Depression* (Cambridge, Mass.: MIT Press, 1989).

[8] Moses Abramovitz and Paul David, "Convergence and Deferred Catch-Up: Productivity Leadership and the Warning of American Exceptionalism," Center for Economic Policy Research, Stanford University, Working Paper no. 401, August 1994, p. 10.

[9] For a balanced survey of the growth of the international economy since the 1950s, see Herman van der Wee, *Prosperity and Upheaval: The World Economy, 1945–1980* (New York: Viking, 1986). For a different view, see Stephen A. Marglin and Juliet Schor, eds., *The Golden Age of Capitalism: Reinterpreting the Postwar Experience* (Oxford: Oxford University Press, 1990).

[10] Abramovitz and David, "Convergence and Deferred Catch-Up," pp. 9–10. Their observation is based on Angus Maddison's data, the latest and most comprehensive version of which is published in his *Monitoring the World Economy, 1820–1992* (Paris: OECD Development Centre, 1995).

microeconomic disturbances in the interwar years. Indeed, according to Angus Maddison, "The post-war boom in Western Europe was not due to an acceleration of technical change but was in large part the extent of a catch-up phenomenon. . . . The long post-war boom in Europe was due, in large part, to the exploitation of once-for-all opportunities that had been missed earlier because of two wars and the protectionist, dirigiste, and otherwise defensive policies of the interwar years." The boom was propelled by the Marshall Plan, increasingly liberal trade policies, the coming of the European Economic Community in 1958, and comparable international institutions for economic cooperation, and overall macroeconomic stability. "By the end of the boom the productivity gap between the advanced European countries and the United States was considerably reduced."[11]

Then, in the 1970s, came the breakdown of the postwar international monetary system, an unprecedented jump in energy costs, a period of a leveling-off of productivity and growth that reflected a basic slowdown in technological innovations, and intensified domestic and international competition, particularly in the capital-intensive industries. Since 1973, Abramovitz and David note, "Catch-up has been distinctly slower – only 1.3 percent a year in spite of the severe slowdown in the United States, growth rates in Europe and Japan fell even more (in percentage points) than in this country."[12]

Even during the Golden Age of capitalism, however, the convergence of productivity among national economies and the resulting catch-up to the world economic frontier was not uniform or even across countries. Particularly beyond a small set of advanced industrial nations which William Baumol has called "the Convergence Club" the catch-up process remained confined and irregular.[13] Only a few East Asian countries managed to achieve a notable performance in terms of industrial development and export through the successful exploitation of the Gerschenkronian economies of backwardness. These represented the extensive commercialization, in large part by large industrial enterprises, of the accumulated and

---

[11] Angus Maddison, "Explaining the Economic Performance of Nations, 1820–1989," in William Baumol, Richard R. Nelson, and Edward N. Wolff, eds., *Convergence of Productivity: Cross-National Studies and Historical Evidence* (New York: Oxford University Press, 1994), p. 34.

[12] Abramovitz and David, "Convergence and Deferred Catch-Up," p. 9.

[13] William J. Baumol, "Productivity Growth, Convergence, and Welfare: What the Long Run Data Show," *American Economic Review* 76 (1986): 1072–1085. For a comprehensive summary of the convergence controversy see Baumol et al., *Convergence of Productivity*.

available international pool of technological knowledge.[14] Oil-producing nations, despite their huge natural-resource base, did not transform their economies into modern manufacturing powers. Latin American economies, after a promising start toward industrial development, seriously suffered from macroeconomic troubles and government policy mistakes, although possibly Brazil has resumed its ascent.[15] In centrally planned economies government bureaus took over the strategic functions of commercializing, coordinating, and monitoring that in market economies are usually carried out in technologically advanced industries by large private firms. The resulting system did not permit its industrial enterprises to improve existing technologies and develop new ones in ways that supported sustained economic growth.[16]

THE DIVERSE EXPERIENCES OF NATIONAL ECONOMIES AND THEIR LARGE INDUSTRIAL ENTERPRISES

At the beginning of the twentieth century the United States, Britain, and Germany were the world's leading industrial economies. The first group of chapters deals with their experiences and also those of Germany's smaller neighbors whose contours of growth paralleled that of Germany. Entrepreneurs and firms in these nations pioneered in the commercializing of

[14] Alexander Gerschenkron, "Economic Backwardness in Historical Perspective," in his *Economic Backwardness in Historical Perspective* (Cambridge, Mass.: Harvard University Press, 1962), ch. 1.

[15] For a convenient summary of the industrial development of the Third World, see Ian Little, Tibor Scitovsky, and Maurice Scott, *Industry and Trade in Some Developing Countries: A Comparative Study* (London: Oxford University Press, 1970); Paul Bairoch, *The Economic Development of the Third World since 1900* (Berkeley: University of California Press, 1977); United Nations Industrial Development Organization, *World Industry since 1960: Progress and Prospects* (New York: United Nations, 1979); Lloyd G. Reynolds, *Economic Growth in the Third World, 1850–1980* (New Haven: Yale University Press, 1985); Hollis B. Chenery et al., *Industrialization and Growth: A Comparative Study* (New York: Oxford University Press, 1986).

[16] For the industrial history of centrally planned economies, see Paul R. Gregory, *Socialist and Nonsocialist Industrialization Patterns: A Comparative Appraisal* (New York: Praeger, 1970); Gregory Guroff and Fred V. Carstensen, eds., *Entrepreneurship in Imperial Russia and the Soviet Union* (Princeton: Princeton University Press, 1983); M. C. Kaser, eds., *The Economic History of Eastern Europe, 1919–1975*, vol. 3: *Institutional Change within a Planned Economy* (London: Oxford University Press, 1986); Alec Nove, *The Soviet Economic System*, 3rd ed. (Boston: Allen & Unwin, 1986); Alec Nove, *An Economic History of the U.S.S.R., 1917–1991*, 3rd ed. (London: Penguin, 1992); Alice Teichova, *Central Europe in the Twentieth Century: An Economic History Perspective* (Leicester: Leicester University Press, 1993).

the new capital-intensive technologies by making the investments and creating the new corporate forms required to exploit fully their profit-making potential. As the first to dominate the resulting new or transformed established industries, these initial leaders quickly created powerful barriers to entry in terms of the price and quality of their products. They soon became a primary source for continuous learning to enhance the productivity of the existing technologies and to commercialize new closely related ones. They also became cores of networks or clusters of essential ancillary and supporting industries and their firms. Both of these roles permitted those large enterprises and their national industries to develop powerful long-term advantages, which followers in other nations had to overcome if they were to compete in global markets.

Prime drivers in North America and Western Europe

The United States, given the availability of natural resources and its large and rapidly growing market, led the way in commercializing the new capital-intensive technologies of the Second Industrial Revolution. Its entrepreneurs and firms invested in a larger number of these industries and, in most cases, more intensively than did those of other nations. These enterprises were already driving technological advance by the end of the nineteenth century and continued to do so until the onslaught of the Great Depression. In the second and third decade of the twentieth century, the powerful drivers were those firms that had grasped the opportunities created by the coming of the internal combustion engine, particularly those of the new motor vehicle industry. The depressed years of the 1930s slowed growth, although enterprises in science-based chemicals and electrical and electronics industries continued to develop new products and processes.

World War II revived the stagnant economy. Even more significant, the war forced the commercialization on an unprecedented scale of new technologies that were just emerging in the early 1940s – polymer chemicals, antibiotics, electronics, and aerospace. In nearly all these industries the commercialization was carried out by long-established enterprises. It was primarily in those industries based on the postwar innovation of the integrated circuit that new entrepreneurial firms became large by making the initial investments and creating the necessary corporate organizations. Although the stable and prosperous postwar years brought catch-up convergence to the United States in established capital-intensive industries, the successful commercialization of the new, increasingly knowledge-intensive technologies permitted the United States to remain the world's leader in productive efficiency and technological advance.

Great Britain was slow in exploiting the new technologies of the Second Industrial Revolution. For as the heir to the First Industrial Revolution and the world's nineteenth-century industrial leader, industrialists were still benefiting from the existing industrial and institutional frameworks. As the twentieth century progressed, its economic strength continued to rest on its earlier global commercial reach and its service industries, particularly retailing, banking, finance, and utilities, rather than on manufacturing. As the first industrial nation, it was also the first consumer society. Its entrepreneurs effectively commercialized new processes of production and methods of distribution in food, drink, and tobacco, as well as in glass and rayon, before 1914 and by the 1920s in oil and chemicals. But British entrepreneurs failed to make the investments in production, distribution, and corporate structures needed to develop an essential learning base and to become a core of related ancillary enterprises in primary metals, many light and heavy machinery industries, and electrical equipment.

The full implications of these failures only became apparent in the years following World War II, when the contribution of manufacturing to national income dropped dramatically, when the subsidiaries of foreign firms became the leaders in Britain's industrial growth and productivity, and when imports of high-technology products became higher than in other developed nations. On the other hand, in industries in which British firms made the investment by the 1920s to build competitive strength and thus created the learning base and nexus of related enterprises, they remained major players in global markets.

In continental Europe German entrepreneurs led the way in commercializing the new technologies of the Second Industrial Revolution. They did so primarily in the production of industrial rather than consumer goods. They quickly took the lead by making the investments and by creating the new forms of corporate organization necessary to utilize fully the economies of scale and scope in the production of metals, heavy machinery, and the new science-based chemical and electrical technologies. Indeed, Germany became the major provider of machinery and other equipment used in commercializing the new capital-intensive processes of production in continental Europe.

Between 1914 and 1925, World War I, defeat and military occupation, and then the inflation that came in their aftermath, temporarily forced

German firms out of continental and global markets. After a brief period of recovery, the coming of worldwide depression, the German economy's transformation into a command economy, and finally a disastrous war and the resulting division of the nation into two hostile states weakened Germany's industrial strength. Nevertheless, the investments made and the corporate structures that had been created before 1914 permitted West Germany to become Europe's leading industrial nation after World War II. Much of West Germany's industrial strength rested on the scientific, engineering, shop floor, and managerial skills embedded in large industrial enterprises in the chemical, pharmaceutical, electrical, and motor vehicle industries, and in more specialized machinery firms, both large and medium-sized, most of which had been created before 1914.

In Germany's smaller neighboring nations, the firms that had commercialized the new high-volume, capital-intensive technologies had to rely from the very start almost wholly on foreign markets to achieve the cost advantages of scale and scope. The removal of German competition during World War I provided an opportunity, particularly in Switzerland, Holland, and Sweden, for such firms to expand their investments and create their organizational structures in ways that permitted most of them to remain global competitors for the rest of the twentieth century under review. As was the case in Germany, cooperation at home, largely through cartelization, was seen as a prerequisite to maintaining competitive strength abroad.

Followers of Western Europe

In a second group of countries, France, Italy, and Spain, investments were made before World War I in smaller amounts and in fewer industries of the Second Industrial Revolution than occurred in the first group of nations. For each the timing of the move into these capital-intensive industries differed. France made the necessary investments in greater extent before Italy, and both did so well ahead of Spain. Because the industrialists in these countries often had to compete in national and world markets against already established enterprises from the international industrial core, they turned more toward government assistance. Compared with the countries of the first group, therefore, governments in France, Italy, and Spain played a more active and significant role in the entry of these countries into newer, more capital-intensive industries. Most public investments came during the 1914–1950 period, when wars and economic depression reduced opportunities for private firms to develop capital-intensive production capacities. This partially explains why in the three countries government had to invest directly in those strategic industries in the form of state-owned firms.

The development of large enterprises in France was relatively slow in the new and transformed industries of the Second Industrial Revolution. By the 1920s a few entrepreneurs had made extensive investments to develop large firms in such industries as metals, machinery, and chemicals. Firms such as Pechiney, Thomson-Houston, and Rhône-Poulenc remained leaders in their industries in international markets throughout the century. These large enterprises adopted growth strategies which were comparable with those of their counterparts in the United States and Germany, and they developed similar, though often smaller, administrative structures.

The early growth of large industrial enterprises in France was historically limited by two major factors: the weakness of capital markets and the nature of managerial education. First, because the country lacked a strong investment banking tradition, financial markets had difficulty in mobilizing large amounts of capital to reorganize fragmented industries and to form large enterprises through mergers and acquisitions. Second, France's central institution of higher education, the *grande écoles*, trained their students as generalists with little exposure to the study of business, economics, or applied science. Their graduates, who would become the senior managers of large industrial enterprises, had little opportunity to learn the technical and managerial skills necessary to manage firms in the capital-intensive industries.

In the postwar years the French government utilized nationalist feelings to advance state-sponsored mergers and joint ventures to create "national champions." They were to compete in international markets as defined in broad government industrial policy plans. Controversy continues over whether these strategies enhanced substantially the organizational capabilities and competitive strength of French industrial firms and the industries in which they operated. Recent cases of privatization, therefore, may mark a new era of large industrial enterprises in France.

Italy's special competitive strength in global markets is recognized to lie in medium-sized and smaller companies that have operated in the labor-intensive industries producing consumer products such as textiles and apparel, household goods, personal products, and food and beverages. Over decades and, in some cases, centuries, geographically defined clusters of these small enterprises have benefited from a long learning process as they have passed from craftsmanship to modern manufacture. Indeed, those small Italian enterprises have created a special niche or segment in the international markets to sustain their growth. Usually independent of the networks organized around large industrial firms, they have become a model of "flexible capitalism."

In capital-intensive industries, on the other hand, large industrial enterprises have played a central role in Italian industrialization. A few entrepreneurs did actually build enterprises around the turn of the century that would later become national representatives in global oligopolies such as automobiles, tires, chemicals, and light machinery. In many of these enterprises, however, the founding families such as the Agnellis at Fiat and the Olivettis have often exercised their ownership power in a way to prevent the enhancement of managerial control and accountability for the long-term growth of firms.

In the industries where private enterprises remained uncompetitive or fell into financial troubles government made key contributions. In steel, oil, telephone equipment, and petrochemicals, for instance, government established government-owned or -sponsored enterprises. Italy's government, in addition, played an important role in forming government-owned holding companies such as Istituto per la Ricostruzione Industriale (IRI) and Ente Nazionale Idrocarburi (ENI). In acquiring and then reconstructing weak companies in diverse industries, these holding companies functioned as the saviors of those firms and their industries. They thus eventually became widely diversified in many industrial areas, but the competitiveness of constituent enterprises remained mixed.

Compared with those in France or Italy, large industrial enterprises in Spain historically remained smaller in terms of their size and made a more limited contribution to the development of national economy. By contrast government played a more substantial role in organizing and controlling them. Large industrial firms originally emerged toward the late nineteenth century and grew rapidly between 1917 and 1930. Many of these firms were linked to the technologies of the First Industrial Revolution such as textiles and food processing. But then they collapsed amid the turbulence created by political instability, the depression of the 1930s, civil war, and Generalissimo Franco's autocratic policies, which collectively destroyed the assets, particularly intangible ones, of many big firms.

Spain began to reindustrialize under government control after World War II, when industrial development became an important goal of Franco's policy of autarky, which eventually separated Spain from the international economy by cutting trade and investment ties to other nations. In an extreme form of self-sufficiency, even the absorption of technological knowledge from foreign sources was severely curtailed. Instead, through a state-owned holding company, government created "national enterprises" often by nationalizing existing foreign companies. Because the main aim of state enterprises was to address domestic economic and political issues, their dominance limited the dynamic growth of many key industries. Lacking up-to-date facilities and managerial skills, government-owned enterprises did not became effective productive or learning organizations.

Only in the 1960s, after a period of strikes and food riots and the devaluation of the nation's currency, did autarkic policy begin to change. From the early 1960s to the early 1970s Spain experienced an "economic miracle" after which, starting in the mid-1970s, the country shared a period of contraction with many other economies. Since then Spain has been unsteadily feeling its way toward continued stability and growth in a rapidly changing technological and business environment.

Late industrializers in East Asia and South America

The nations in the third group of countries – Japan, South Korea, and Argentina – represent latecomers outside the North Atlantic region. Their exploitation of capital-intensive industries and their modern economic growth came mostly after World War II. Ironically Argentina, with its huge resource endowment and low population density, had the most opportunity for economic development. Actually, per capita income of the nation was much higher than that of Japan and South Korea as late as 1950, as is indicated in Table 1.1. But its growth was stunted by inadequate commitment to modern manufacturing and by inconsistent economic policies adopted by populist governments. On the other hand, Japan's and later Korea's extensive investment in physical capital and human resources made them the classic examples of latecomers exploiting existing technological knowledge. Although government again played a significant role in those three countries, the form of government intervention differed substantially. The pattern of government involvement in Argentina has been somewhat similar to that of France, Italy, and Spain, with the emphasis on the protection of the domestic market and the formation of state-owned enterprises. In Japan and Korea government has also protected the domestic market. But in addition government has encouraged international competitiveness and export by imposing monitorable performance standards. In all three of these latecomer countries, the challenges of catch-up led to the development of family and corporate groups, networks and alliances, such as *zaibatsu* and *keiretsu* in Japan, *chaebol* in South Korea, and interrelated family connections in Argentina.

Japan's industrial progress before World War II was skewed toward the labor-intensive industries, especially the textile industry. In capital-intensive industries, thanks to a small domestic market and underdeveloped technological skills, Japanese enterprises did not attain an international level of efficiency. Beginning in 1932, however, Japan's wartime economy became critical for the rapid growth of the country's heavy capital-intensive industries such as metals, machinery, and chemicals. Since the 1950s, encouraged by the industrial policy of the Ministry of International Trade and Industry (MITI), Japanese firms constructed or enlarged their production capacities with the latest available technology, which was usually purchased from the United States and Western Europe.

The private institution central to Japan's industrialization since the Meiji Restoration of 1868 was the diversified industrial group, zaibatsu, owned and controlled by such wealthy families as Mitsui, Iwasaki (Mitsubishi), and Sumitomo. The zaibatsu groups competed against each other in recruiting their future managers among college graduates and established hierarchical organizations to coordinate their various activities. As family owners of those groups became rulers in name only, senior salaried managers actively reinforced the long-term growth of the firm or group by investing in human, technological, and organizational capabilities.

After World War II many of these prewar groups reemerged as keiretsu in which individual member firms collectively came to control other enterprises of the same group mainly through intragroup shareholding. In the keiretsu groups, therefore, strategic management discretion was constrained only by managers of allied enterprises. Facilitated by intergroup competition, then, Japan's industrial organization is characterized by several diversified groups operating in a similar set of strategic industries, particularly in capital-intensive ones. This structure encouraged intergroup oligopolistic rivalry and intragroup growth drive, which in turn fostered Japan's rapid industrial development.

If Japan is historically the first real late industrializer outside the North Atlantic region to transform its economy successfully into a stable, modern industrial one, Korea subsequently achieved the same goal at a record-breaking pace after World War II. As was the case of Japan before the war, two critical players in Korean industrialization have been the large family-owned diversified group (chaebol) and an entrepreneurial government. Because a government-owned banking system prohibited business groups from establishing their own banking institutions, the chaebol (more than their Japanese counterpart, the zaibatsu) depended on government for long-term investment. Utilizing its leverage over chaebol, the Korean government bureaucracy could impose performance standards on them related to productivity and export in exchange for tariffs and other forms of protection, preferential credit allocation, and various additional assistance programs. Government, thus, successfully created the microeconomic environment in which the chaebol groups aggressively pursued product diversification and overseas expansion.

The progenitors of the chaebol were mostly entrepreneurs who fully exploited their political as well as business and organizational skills particularly during reconstruction following the Japanese occupation and the Korean War. Whatever their origins, these entrepreneurs excelled in long-term organization building and generally made the large-scale investments in manufacturing, marketing and distribution, and management. Given the rapid pace of industrialization and the low starting level of capital and technology accumulation, Korean chaebol had to integrate into the production of many basic intermediate goods in order to secure necessary inputs as well as to exploit economies of scale. Simultaneously, because of the fragmentation of indigenous small businesses, the groups often organized, controlled, and nurtured networks of suppliers, distributors, and retailers. Compared even with the situation in Japan, therefore, the presence in Korea of large enterprise groups has been economically vital, publicly visible, and politically controversial. While many of their founders still rule at the top of groups, the chaebol continue to recruit a sufficient number of salaried managers and engineers to have significant administrative hierarchies. Gradually, they have also engaged those managerial resources in strategic decision making.

Argentina's industrial evolution has illustrated an experience of continuous frustration. Since the nineteenth century the country's successful agricultural entrepreneurs often remained cautious about diversifying aggressively into manufacturing. In addition, the Argentine government failed to formulate a stable and effective micro- and macroeconomic policy through which modern industrial enterprises could grow to constitute a leading driver of the economy.

Argentina has exhibited three major types of large industrial enterprises, in part reflecting entrepreneurial conservatism and in part respond-
ing to ever changing government policies. Historically, business groups,
mostly owned by European traders and their local family branches,
emerged in the later decades of the nineteenth century. Those groups
did not evolve to a central institution in the country's economy partially
because they began to face formidable competition of two subsequent
types of large enterprises, especially in capital-intensive industries. First,
mainly since World War I, multinational enterprises from the United
States, Great Britain, and other European nations established their manufacturing facilities in Argentina. This was then followed by the creation
of government-owned enterprises operating largely in military- and
national-security-related areas such as explosives, steel, and petroleum.

Regardless of their size, ownership, or management, Argentina's large
industrial enterprises have basically oriented their operations toward the
domestic market, whose demand was limited thanks to a small population. The government continued to encourage import substitution by
instituting tariff protection and subsidizing various enterprises for political as well as economic reasons. For all of its assistance, however, the
government could not foster industrialization through import substitution-
cum-exports. The resulting industrial organization remained one of intrain-
dustry competition among various types of inefficient firms targeting a
limited domestic market.

Centrally planned economies in Eastern Europe

The chapters on the fourth group of countries, USSR and Czechoslovakia,
provide a view of the major alternative system of national production to
capitalism in the twentieth century, that of the centrally planned command
economies. Their histories thus provide a counterpoint to the development of the large industrial enterprise in the market economies narrated
in the previous groups of essays. For in the planned economies the basic
strategic function of the corporate office of large firms was handled by
government agencies. Therefore, the enterprise was unable to become, as
it did in market economies, a learning base for continuing technological
change or a core of a large industrial complex.

The history of the large industrial enterprise in the planned economies began in the USSR with Stalin's first five-year plan in 1930 and in

Czechoslovakia immediately after World War II. Russia's Gosplan was responsible for carrying out the annual plans set forth by the Central Committee of the Politburo of the Communist Party. Gosplan not only determined the investment to be made in the facilities and workers of each enterprise, but also decided its output, range of goods to be produced, wages, salaries, prices paid, and prices charged. Gossnab, the State Committee for Material-Technical Supply, became responsible for coordinating the flow of goods from the producers of raw and semifinished materials to the processing and fabricating plants, to the distribution centers, and then to the retailers or final industrial customers. Gostekhnika (Gostech) made decisions on product and process improvement and innovation.

As a result, the industrial enterprise in Russia rarely carried out more than a single function, production. At first the enterprise was usually a single production unit. As time passed it often became an "association" of production units producing the same product. This allocation of decision making between the government and the production unit made it close to impossible for the managers of enterprises to have a say in coordinating the flow of goods and information through the processes of production and distribution, starting from the processing of raw materials to the final customer. Therefore, their firms rarely became cores of intermediary networks or "communities" of closely related and ancillary businesses. As their managers were not responsible for long-term or even short-term investment in physical and human capital, they rarely had the opportunity to become a learning base to improve existing products and processes or to commercialize new ones. Surely the inability of managers of Soviet industrial enterprises to carry out the basic functions of their capitalist counterparts played a significant part in the ultimate collapse of the planned economy of the USSR.

From the establishment of Czechoslovakia in 1919 until the beginning of the Russia-dominated post–World War II years, the large Czech industrial enterprise concentrated primarily on the production of machinery and armaments. It differed from large corporate enterprises in small neighboring nations in that it had close financial and technological ties with leading French, British, and German enterprises. Czech firms developed a hierarchical corporate structure which created an institutional base for a wide range of integration and coordination at the level of national economy. By the time of the Nazi takeover in 1939, Czechoslovakia had actually developed to become one of the major emerging industrial economies. Because of their manufacturing capabilities, however, the Czech large industrial firms in heavy industry became exploited as major suppliers of Germany's war machine.

After 1945 Czech firms became the machine shop of Eastern Europe. After a brief period of experimentation with a democratic and pluralistic regime, the adoption of a Soviet-style planned economy brought an even greater forced demand for heavy machinery and armaments, which led to a large-scale misallocation of available resources and difficulty in maintaining an effective network of related enterprises. The rigid centrally planned regime, which was the closest to the inflexible Soviet system even among East European nations, continued to fail to reorganize large industrial enterprises in ways that permitted them to provide a sustained source of improved products and processes. These weaknesses hastened the regime's ultimate collapse in the late 1980s.

2

The large industrial enterprise and the dynamics
of modern economic growth

ALFRED D. CHANDLER, JR., AND TAKASHI HIKINO

Ever since the Second Industrial Revolution exploded in the last decades
of the nineteenth century, the large industrial enterprise has continuously
played a central role in the dynamic growth of the international economy
and the economic transformation of all major nations. Among the new
forms of large enterprises, manufacturing firms have been at the forefront
not only of capital formation and productivity growth but also of technological progress and knowledge augmentation. This is not simply because
modern economic growth on a global scale has taken the general form
of *industrial* development. It is also because manufacturing enterprises,
especially those in capital-intensive and knowledge-intensive industries,
have historically accounted for most of the research and development
which became essential to continuing technological innovation in the
twentieth century.

From their beginnings in the late nineteenth century large enterprises in capital-intensive industries have systematically embodied the latest
scientific and technological advances and have commercialized these into
marketable products. In industries which led the Second Industrial Revolution, "first movers" – often start-up firms which invested in manufacturing
facilities large enough to exploit economies of scale – established themselves as dominant oligopolistic players in domestic and then international markets. They invested not only in manufacturing facilities but also
in extensive marketing and distribution networks and competent managerial hierarchies. They became truly "large *industrial* enterprises," a term
broad enough to suggest their nonmanufacturing as well as manufacturing functions. Later, in the twentieth century, these same enterprises were
usually the first in their respective countries to establish systematically the
research and development facilities for nurturing their own technological

capabilities. And these capabilities became the basis for commercializing new products and processes through the use of similar materials, equipment, operating personnel, and operational information.

Large industrial enterprises thus established themselves as the fertile learning ground for technological, managerial, and organizational knowledge for an entire economy. The new technologies they developed in manufacturing were extensively adopted in nonmanufacturing sectors. This contributed to productivity improvement in a wide range of industries, especially transportation, communication, and financial services. Large industrial enterprises accelerated this diffusion process by internalizing the technology-transfer mechanism through their integration and diversification into nonmanufacturing functions. These enterprises became a rich spring of managerial and organizational information as well as technological knowledge, all of which spilled over into the wider spheres of domestic and international economies by means of networks, spin-offs and even ordinary market transactions.

The modern industrial enterprise, therefore, has not been simply scale-intensive, capital-using, and natural-resource-consuming. It has also been knowledge-augmenting and learning-enhancing. By committing to the extensive long-term investment in human and organizational resources as well as physical assets, these large enterprises could exploit the complementarity between the large-scale investment in physical capital and the sustained capital formation in such intangible assets as human resources and technological knowledge. The capabilities which resulted became the core competencies of many of the international firms. These competencies enabled such firms to maintain themselves as major global players and to exploit the dramatic technological innovations in electronics, aerospace, chemicals, and pharmaceuticals associated with what might be considered a Third Industrial Revolution after World War II.

The new technologies of the Third Industrial Revolution transformed the processes of production and distribution as effectively as the new capital-intensive technologies of the Second Industrial Revolution altered them in the late nineteenth century. But now the prime commercializers were large firms already in existence, whereas in the Second Industrial Revolution the lead had usually been taken by new firms. New firms most often took the lead in the Second Industrial Revolution because the exploitation of novel technologies required new methods of production and distribution. The enterprise that had arisen to commercialize the technologies of the *First* Industrial Revolution of the late eighteenth and early nineteenth centuries had not nurtured manufacturing and organizational capabilities that were adequate to meet the challenges of technological advances and rapidly changing markets in much more capital-intensive industries.

The major contributions of the world's large industrial enterprises to economic growth during the twentieth century appear to be four. Each reflects the nature of the origins of such enterprises in the late nineteenth century.

First, large firms substantially lowered the cost of production by investing in manufacturing facilities large enough to exploit economies of scale. This was historically a necessary condition for those firms to become oligopolistic players in capital-intensive industries. Enterprises which subsequently integrated production and distribution accounted for a significant share of physical capital formation in the new scale-dependent technologies that were prime engines of growth particularly between the 1880s and World War I.

Second, by recruiting the managers, workers, and technicians – the human capital – required to use and commercialize the new technologies, these enterprises became the locus of learning for the initial development and continued enhancement of their product-specific intangible organizational assets. And these assets were essential to maintain the industrial and competitive strength of the national industries in which they operated.

Third, the managers of the new industrial enterprises quickly realized that, if they were to maintain the cost advantages of large-scale production, they had to have an assured flow of materials and information and direct contacts with distributors in national and global markets. Thus, these firms became the core, the nexus, of a network of suppliers, equipment makers, retailers, advertisers, designers, and providers of technical and financial services.

Fourth, based on the human capital they cultivated, large industrial enterprises became a primary driver of technological advances through their heavy investment in research and development activities. This investment has become increasingly critical for the commercialization of new technology, particularly in capital-intensive and increasingly knowledge-intensive industries, in order to secure and raise market share in a domestic market, to expand into international markets, and to create barriers to entry for newcomers.

COMPLEMENTARITY BETWEEN THE ACCUMULATION OF
PHYSICAL CAPITAL AND INTANGIBLE CAPITAL

An understanding of how the large industrial firm came to play the afore-
mentioned roles requires an awareness of the complementary relationship
between investment in plant and equipment (physical or tangible capital)
and the human skills and knowledge developed in their operation (intangible capital). Extensive investments in large-scale plant and equipment
created a fertile ground for managers and other personnel to educate themselves about both the technical skills and the organizational process of a
new technology. Reciprocally the potential of the new technology could
only be realized through the trained skills acquired in the production and
distribution of past products. Yet the awareness of this dynamic mechanism between tangible and intangible capital has been slow in coming in
scholarly analyses of technological change and economic growth.

In the late 1950s, a few economists such as Moses Abramovitz, Robert
Solow and Edward Denison began to recognize that combining and analyzing inputs of land, labor, and capital only partially accounted for economic growth. They turned their attention to explaining the "residual"
or what Solow called "technical progress." Pioneering studies by Denison
indicated that part of this technical progress could be attributed to the shift
of the work force from agriculture to industry and the coming of scale
economies.[1] Even so, Denison concluded that the remaining residual, in
his terms "the advancement of knowledge," still accounted for almost
half of the source of economic growth. Even though Dale Jorgenson and
others have since then substantially reduced the size of the residual, in
Angus Maddison's words, "Technical progress is the most essential characteristic of economic growth. If there had been no technical progress, the
whole process of accumulation would have been much more modest."[2]

---

[1] Robert Solow, "A Contribution to the Theory of Economic Growth," *Quarterly Journal of Economics*, 70 (February 1956): 65–94; Edward Denison, *Why Growth Rates Differ* (Washington, D.C.: Brookings Institution, 1967).

[2] Angus Maddison, "Explaining the Economic Performance of Nations, 1820–1989," in William J. Baumol, Richard R. Nelson, and Edward N. Wolff, eds., *Convergence of Productivity: Cross-National Studies and Historical Evidence* (New York: Oxford University Press, 1994), p. 53. See also Robert M. Solow and Peter Temin, "Introduction: Inputs for Growth," in Peter Mathias and M. M. Postan, eds., *Cambridge Economic History of Europe*, vol. 7, *The Industrial Economies: Capital, Labour and Enterprise*, Part 2 (Cambridge: Cambridge University Press, 1978); and Dale W. Jorgenson, *Productivity*, 2 vols. (Cambridge, Mass.: MIT Press, 1995).

Yet for business historians searching for the dynamics of the modern industrial capitalism, one source of frustration with this conventional growth accounting approach, so well expressed by a leading growth economist, Moses Abramovitz, is its technical assumption "that the appropriate sources of growth operated independently of one another and the contribution of each could be added up."[3] The interactive dynamics of these growth factors – capital, labor, materials, and technological change – are crucial for business historians because individual firms thrive and survive on integrating all of them within their internal organizations. This has been how the large industrial firm nurtured technological progress.

Even with the recent "endogenous" growth theories, which acknowledge the importance of increasing returns to scale in such intangible resources as human capital, information, and knowledge, the treatment of growth factors as independent and separable inputs persists. While emphasizing the role of skill-enhancing investment at the national level, the new approaches still, for theoretical convenience and coherence, sidestep the issue of scale economies of physical capital.[4] They fail to recognize the interactive complementarity between physical capital investment and intangible capital formation. As long as they ignore such complementarity, the firm, particularly the large enterprise, which is the major economic agent of interaction, cannot be, and is not, incorporated as a unit of analysis.

Some economists, however, have begun to emphasize precisely the interrelatedness of technical progress and both tangible and intangible capital. Richard Nelson focuses on the interaction of education with science systems, technological development, and productivity growth, because "certain sources of growth that conventionally are considered separately ought to be considered as clusters" and "the nature of their interaction is an important part of the story."[5] Moses Abramovitz and

[3] Moses Abramovitz, "The Search for Sources of Economic Growth: Areas of Ignorance, Old and New," *Journal of Economic History*, 53 (June 1993): 218–220.

[4] Robert E. Lucas, Jr., "On the Mechanics of Economic Development," *Journal of Monetary Economics*, 22 (July 1988): 3–42; Nancy L. Stokey, "Learning by Doing and the Introduction of New Goods," *Journal of Political Economy*, 96 (August 1988): 701–717; Nancy L. Stokey, "Human Capital, Product Quality, and Growth," *Quarterly Journal of Economics*, 106 (May 1991): 587–616.

[5] Richard R. Nelson, "Where Are We in the Discussion? Retrospect and Prospect," in John W. Kendrick, ed., *International Comparisons of Productivity and Causes of the Slowdown* (Cambridge, Mass.: Ballinger Publishing, 1984), p. 405. See also Richard R. Nelson, "Recent Evolutionary Theorizing about Economic Change," *Journal of Economic Literature*, 33, no.1 (March 1995): 48–90, for the latest summary of the literature on the interactions among various input factors and technical change.

Paul David emphasize the character and bias of technical progress in capital accumulation, in particular how capital-using technological processes, by raising the marginal productivity of capital relative to that of labor, increase the demand for capital, physical and human, that replaces raw labor. Like Nelson, the two authors lay stress on the nonseparable relationships of physical (tangible) and human (intangible) capital in the exploitation of technology and thereby acknowledge the importance of the business enterprise in embodying the two.[6]

CAPITAL FORMATION AND THE SOURCES OF INCREASING RETURNS TO SCALE

The critical interrelationships between physical and human capital are inherent in the nature of what economists call "increasing returns" to the scale of invested resources, particularly those based on the economies of scale and scope of operation – economies that permitted large firms to become engines of technological progress in the new capital-intensive technologies of the Second Industrial Revolution. First came an exploitation of the economies of scale and then came an exploitation of those of scope.[7]

The exploitation of the unprecedented economies of scale inherent in the new technologies brought the firm both competitive advantage and vulnerability. For, as the rated capacity of operation rose, long-run unit costs fell to the point where plant size reached "minimum efficient scale" (i.e., until output reached the lowest cost per unit determined roughly by the state of existing technology and the size of the market). These potential cost advantages of plant size, however, could not be fully realized unless a steady flow of materials through the plant and factory was attained. If output volume fell below minimum efficient scale, then short-run unit costs would rise sharply and large firms would swiftly lose their competitive advantage. (In this sense, the new capital-intensive technology was "scale-dependent.")[8] Costs behaved this way because fixed costs and "sunk costs" (the original physical capital investment) in those capital-intensive industries were much higher than those in the established industries of the day.

---

[6] Moses Abramovitz and Paul David, "Convergence and Deferred Catch-Up: Productivity Leadership and the Waning of American Exceptionalism," Center for Economic Policy Research, Stanford University, Working Paper no. 401, August 1994.

[7] The argument in this section reorients the theory presented in chapter 2 and pp. 593–605 of Alfred D. Chandler, Jr., with the assistance of Takashi Hikino, *Scale and Scope: The Dynamics of Industrial Capitalism* (Cambridge, Mass.: Harvard University Press, 1990).

[8] Abramovitz and David, "Convergence and Deferred Catch-Up," pp. 4, 24.

The decisive economic variables in determining costs and profits, thus, were now throughput (scale) as well as rated capacity (size). Profitability became dependent on an extensive investment in nonmanufacturing functions in order to maintain throughput. Where essential supplies of raw and intermediate materials were not readily available, firms had to integrate backward into such industries and activities. The full utilization of invested resources required also the formation of national and international marketing and distribution organizations.

The full utilization of the invested physical capital did not necessarily come from the production of a single product. It was often achieved through the simultaneous manufacturing of closely related products. The economies of scope at the plant level mostly came from the cost advantages of producing different end products by using much the same materials and equipment. The simultaneous production of dyes and chemicals, refined petroleum and petrochemicals, rayon and cellophane, closely related electrical equipment, and the like are examples of such joint production. As in the case of the economies of scale, the potential of scope economies was fully realized only through the "learning by doing" in the day-to-day operations of the new production facilities.

As a result, in the new capital-intensive industries with scale-dependent technologies the long-term financial returns on investments in physical facilities and human resources required more than just building manufacturing plants of optimum size. The throughput needed to maintain the optimal scale required careful coordination not only of flows through the processes of production but also flows of inputs from suppliers and flows of output to intermediaries and final users. Such coordination did not, and indeed could not, happen automatically. It demanded the constant attention of managerial teams. Consequently, *potential* economies of *size*, as measured by the rated capacity of tangible capital invested, were based on the physical and engineering characteristics of the production facilities (tangible capital). But the *realized* economies of *scale*, as determined by capacity utilization and throughput, were operational and organizational, and depended on knowledge, skills, experience, and teamwork – that is, on organized human capabilities (intangible capital).

The first firms to make these capital investments quickly dominated the new capital-intensive industries. Yet these firms were rarely the technological inventors or innovators or necessarily even the pioneering commercializers. They were the enterprises that were first to make large-scale investments in the physical capital, human capabilities, and organizational structure essential to exploit fully the economies of scale. Challengers had to construct plants of comparable size and do so after such first movers had already begun to work out the bugs in the new production processes. Challengers had to create distribution and selling organizations to capture markets where first movers were already established. They had to recruit management teams to compete with those already well down the learning curve in the several functional and strategic activities. Given these barriers to entry, a small number of large firms soon dominated their industries.

As illustrated in Table 2.1, an embryonic pattern of oligopoly emerged in leading industrial economies by World War I. Large firms everywhere were beginning to concentrate in the same set of industries: those transformed by capital-using, scale-dependent technologies including food processing, cigarette making, chemicals, petroleum refining, primary metals, and various types of machinery making including electrical products and transportation equipment. Naturally each country shows some unique pattern. The prominence of U.S. petroleum companies reflects the resource-base growth of the country. The rich consumer society of Great Britain could support a huge number of large processors of food and beverages, while an abundance of textile firms epitomized the path-dependent legacy of the country's First Industrial Revolution. On the other hand, the eminence of labor-intensive cotton spinning firms in Japan exemplified the nation's low degree of capital accumulation and technological maturity. Yet, regardless of the differences in resource endowment, in phases of economic development, and in political environment and cultural and societal construction, large firms were beginning to dominate a new set of capital-intensive industries.

In these oligopolistic industries the basic element of market behavior shifted from price competition to nonprice competition. Although product pricing remained a significant competitive weapon, oligopolistic firms competed even more forcefully through functional and particularly strategic effectiveness: that is, by carrying out processes of production and distribution more capably; by improving both product and process through systematic research and development; by identifying more suitable sources of supply; by providing more effective marketing services; by product differentiation (in branded packaged products primarily through advertising); and by moving more quickly into expanding markets and out of declining ones. In this climate of oligopolistic competition, market share and profits changed constantly, which kept oligopolies from becoming stagnant and monopolistic. In this climate such bureaucratic tendencies

Table 2.1. *Industrial distribution of the 200 largest industrial enterprises in the United States, Great Britain, Germany, France, and Japan in the period of World War I*

SIC	Industry	United States (1917)	Great Britain (1919)	Germany (1913)	France (1912)	Japan (1918)
20	Food	30	63	26	20	31
21	Tobacco	6	3	1	1	1
22	Textiles	5	26	15	8	54
23	Apparel	3	1	1	3	2
24	Lumber	3	0	1	1	3
25	Furniture	0	0	0	0	0
26	Paper	5	4	4	3	12
27	Printing and publishing	2	5	0	7	1
28	Chemicals	20	11	30	28	23
29	Petroleum	22	3	5	2	6
30	Rubber	5	3	4	3	0
31	Leather	4	0	2	3	4
32	Stone, clay, and glass	5	2	7	8	16
33	Primary metals	29	35	49	36	21
34	Fabricated metals	8	2	5	4	4
35	Nonelectrical machinery	20	8	25	9	4
36	Electrical machinery	5	11	7	14	7
37	Transportation equipment	26	20	16	39	9
38	Instruments	1	0	2	9	1
39	Miscellaneous	1	3	0	2	1
	Total	200	200	200	200	200

Note: Ranked by total assets, except for Great Britain where ranking is based on the market value of quoted capital.
Source: The authors' calculation, except for France, whose numbers come from Bruce Kogut's preliminary lists.

as operational inefficiency and strategic ineffectiveness inherent in large hierarchical organizations – weaknesses that critics of large-scale enterprise validly emphasize – were also curbed.

Successful industrial enterprises in these oligopolistic industries historically evolved in four ways. They adopted two basic and generic strategies of corporate development: growth within the same product market (horizontal expansion) and the integration into supply sources and product outlets (vertical integration). In capital-intensive industries in particular, the continuing long-term strategy of growth for the still relatively new large enterprises was to move into distant markets (geographical expansion) and into related markets (product diversification), in which their organizational learning, based on initial product-specific and process-specific investments in production and distribution, gave them a competitive advantage.

These learned capabilities became a source of more powerful competitive advantages than merely the reduction of unit costs. Just as the capabilities that were learned by exploiting the physical economies of scale led to capital augmentation through improvement of processes and products, so the organizational skills developed in pursuing joint production at the manufacturing establishment level led not only to improvement in existing processes and products but also to the systematic commercialization of *new* processes and products. This is particularly true in the industries in which joint production rested on the systematic exploitation of chemistry, biology, or physics.

During and after World War II new technologies in chemicals, pharmaceuticals, aerospace, and electronics were developed in the United States and other advanced economies on the basis of the learned capabilities that companies had accumulated earlier in commercializing products based on these and other sciences. Just as the new technologies associated with the Second Industrial Revolution came to be dominated by large enterprises, so too the new industries associated with the Third Industrial Revolution fell under their domination. In this respect, growth has been "path-dependent." Indeed, except for electronic data-processing technologies, based on the transistor and integrated circuit, the new technologies were commercialized by large, well-established industrial enterprises rather than by start-ups, as had been the norm before the 1940s.

The growing intensity of corporate research and development reflects a general trend of investment patterns and technological developments. In Moses Abramovitz's terms, in the nineteenth century technical change was heavily biased in a "capital-using direction," a bias that "supported the high rate of capital accumulation per worker hour." In the twentieth century by contrast, "the bias shifted in intangible [human and knowledge] direction."

Technological change tended to raise the relative marginal productivity to the capital in the form of education and training of the labor force at all levels; in the form of practical knowledge acquired by deliberate investment of resources in research and development; and other forms of intangible capital, such as the creation and support of corporate managerial structures and cultures and the development of product markets, which are the infrastructure for the economies of scale and scope.[9]

During this relative shift in the orientation of technological change, the large industrial enterprise remained the primary agent to exploit the commercial potential of new products and processes.

ORGANIZATIONAL LEARNING AND CORPORATE STRUCTURE AND NETWORKS

The functional, technical, and managerial capabilities, honed by oligopolistic competition, provided a dynamic not only for the continuing growth of the firm but also for the industries which they dominated and the national economies in which they operated. These capabilities were initially created during the learning process involved in manufacturing and marketing the products of a new technology for national and international markets. They resulted from solving problems related to the following: scaling up the production process; acquiring knowledge of customers' needs and altering products and process to service them; getting to know the sources of supplies and the reliability of suppliers; and becoming knowledgeable in the ways of recruiting, training, and motivating workers and managers. Such learned capabilities manifested themselves in augmenting the productivity of a firm's facilities, its tangible capital. They were even more evident in enhancing a firm's product-specific and process-specific human skills, its intangible capital.

The knowledge and skills of both managers and workers were further developed by learning through trial and error, feedback and evaluation – that is through learning by doing within the enterprise. Thus, the skills of individuals mostly depended on the organizational setting in which they were developed and used. Such learned skills and knowledge were often company-specific and even more often industry-specific. They were not, of course, marketable or patentable. They were difficult to transfer from one industry to another, or even from one company to another, precisely because they had been learned within a specific organizational context.

If these company-specific and industry-specific organizational capabilities continued to be enhanced by constant learning about products,

---

[9] Abramovitz, "The Search for Sources of Economic Growth," pp. 224–229.

processes, customers, suppliers, and relationships between workers and managers within the firm, then enterprises in capital-intensive industries were usually able to remain competitive and profitable. If not, and this was often the case, then typically these enterprises lost out in domestic and international markets to those firms that did continue to learn. In addition, because the development of these highly specific capabilities created powerful barriers to entry, new entrants in oligopolistic industries were rarely start-up firms. Instead, they were those enterprises that had developed comparable capabilities in technologically related industries or in the same industry in other nations.

One critical outcome of oligopolistic rivalry was the search for, and the development of, various organizational designs suitable to large firms' strategic needs. Large industrial firms first established managerial hierarchies toward the end of the nineteenth century along functional lines. At the lower level were the managers of the operating units, that is, the factories and the offices for sales, purchasing, and finance. At the middle level were managers responsible for each of the functional departments. At the top were the heads of departments, along with the president and sometimes full-time chairman of the board. These executives met regularly to monitor the current operations and to allocate resources, both physical and human, for the future of the enterprise.

As large enterprises in capital-intensive and particularly science-based industries grew by moving into new geographical and product markets, the initial centralized structure (in economists' terms, the unitary or U-form) became increasingly ineffective. Senior managers became acutely aware that they did not have the time or the competence to coordinate and monitor – or to devise and implement – long-term strategies for their units operating in different geographical and product markets. To meet their broader responsibilities more effectively, they began during the interwar years in the United States and to a lesser degree in Europe to adopt a decentralized structure (the multidivisional structure or M-form). In the M-form, corporate headquarters coordinated and monitored current operations and planned and allocated resources for the future activities of several units ("divisions" or "subsidiaries," as legal and tax requirements determined) that operated, usually through U-form structure, in different product and/or regional markets. After World War II variations of this multidivisional form were widely adopted throughout the United States and Europe. Yet the organizational structure was rarely viable unless it was employed to implement a strategy of growth through diversification into new regional and product markets based on competitive strengths that rested on a firm's learned internal organizational capabilities.[10]

In addition to implementing these internal corporate structures, a large industrial enterprise also became the nucleus of a network of firms in closely related industrial activities. These networks resulted from the need to assure the flow of materials and information to, through, and from the firm's core production facilities. As large industrial enterprises moved into international markets, this network of related enterprises also expanded. With the growth in the number of reliable material suppliers, and of producers of specialized equipment and parts, and of distributors, dealers, and other franchised outlets, the core firms increasingly relied on independent enterprises for many of their nonstrategic needs, although they usually continued to own and operate their own wholesale marketing and distribution activities.

As the scientific and other knowledge bases of product technology often reached beyond the technical capabilities and business necessities of industrial firms, they also began to integrate specialists in product research and design into their networks. For, as has been emphasized, from their very beginnings large industrial firms concentrated, not on basic research but on development, not on inventing new products and processes, but on commercializing them, for national and global markets. As the sources of technological advance increasingly rested on the commercialization of science-based technologies, these networks were expanded to include knowledge-producing institutions – universities, private foundations, and a variety of governmental agencies.

As networks expanded, the relationships between core firms and their allied and related enterprises and other institutions became defined in many ways – contractual arrangements, joint ventures, variations of control through equity purchases, and strategic alliances. As a result, the boundaries of the core firms and even of their operating divisions or subsidiaries became blurred. Finally, because scale-dependent technologies of core firms required greater standardization of production for national and often international markets, the opportunity for independent niche firms to move into more specialized yet sizable product and regional

---

[10] Bruce Kogut, "Diffusion of American Organizing Principles to Europe," in Bruce Kogut, ed., *Country Competitiveness*, pp. 116–145; Mauro F. Guillen, *Models of Management: Work, Authority and Organization in a Comparative Perspective* (Chicago: University of Chicago Press, 1994), ch. 6; Chandler, *Scale and Scope*; Alfred D. Chandler, Jr., "Corporate Strategy, Structure and Control Methods in the United States during the 20th Century," *Industrial and Corporate Change*, 1 (1991): 263–284.

markets grew. Indeed, a number of successful challengers started as niche firms.

In this evolutionary manner large industrial firms came to contribute to economic growth in the four ways that were stated at the beginning of this chapter: (1) They provided the initial financial, physical, and human capital necessary to exploit the new capital-intensive, scale-dependent technologies. Their retained earnings soon became a primary source for an industry's continuing expenditures on physical capital. (2) They became the locus of learning in which the transformation of new technologies into commercial products and processes was carried out, and so became the seedbed for the further commercialization of improved product and processes of that technology. (3) They became the initial core of a network of ancillary enterprises essential to the volume production and distribution of products whose number and variety expanded as markets became global. (4) The intensive effort of research and development within large industrial enterprises made them a core of technological progress for the whole economy. As the existing technologies matured and new ones appeared, the role of large enterprises for and economy as technological and organizational learning bases and cores of industrial networks became more significant than the original role of investing in and utilizing physical capital.

THE UNITED STATES AS THE LEADER OF THE SHIFT FROM TANGIBLE TO INTANGIBLE CAPITAL

As the twentieth century wore on, this shift in roles reflected a shift in the bias of growth in the United States from capital-intensive technologies to more knowledge-intensive ones. Because the United States led the world in industrial productivity and national income, that shift had global implications. As Angus Maddison writes, "In the analysis of technical progress, the leader–follower dichotomy is, in my view, fundamental. . . . We can therefore get some idea of the changing pace of technical advance only by close inspection of performance in the lead country. Followers continue to draw upon the lead country's fund of technology by building up their own stock through physical and human capital, opening their economies to facilitate trade, and by possessing institutions which nurture absorptive capacity."[11]

---

[11] Angus Maddison, "Monitoring the World Economy, 1820–1999," in his *Explaining the Economic Performance of Nations: Essays in Time and Space* (Brookfield, Vt.: Edward Elgar, 1995), p. 20.

Through the massive exploitation of new capital-intensive technologies, the United States had become by 1913 the world's economic leader in terms of gross domestic product. The nation was blessed with an exceptional potential for utilizing these technologies which propelled it into the lead. It had a much larger amount of sources of energy and easily available raw materials – agricultural and mineral – than most other nations had. Its fast growing and assimilated population assured the standardized market needed to consume the high output of the new technologies at a level necessary to maintain maximum efficiency. Finally, by the 1880s the United States had a high-volume, low-cost intercontinental transportation system that was as efficient as any in the world. Indeed, by 1890, cumulative investment in railroads was greater than that in all nonagricultural industries combined and comprised more than 40 percent of the nonresidential capital formation to date.[12] Only after modern transportation and communication technologies made possible the unprecedented speed, volume, and regularity essential for high-volume production and distribution could large industrial enterprises play a critical role in exploiting the new scale-dependent, capital-using technologies.

In the twentieth century, particularly after World War II, as has been noted, a major source of growth became the systematization and utilization of science to commercialize new products, processes, and occasionally basic new technologies – a source that was enhanced in the United States by the federal government's investments in industrial research, particularly in defense and health, and by its support of basic research, particularly in universities. Table 2.2 shows a general trend of the continuing significance of U.S. research and development activities since the 1960s. Except for a sudden and short-term slump of R&D efforts in the early 1970s related to the first oil shock, the number of R&D scientists and engineers substantially increased, with the private business sector, mostly manufacturing enterprises, playing a dominant role. R&D expenditures, too, have steadily increased since the second half of the 1970s. Private businesses have continuously performed around 70 percent of the total U.S. R&D activities with the remainder being carried out by such nonprofit entities as universities and government agencies.

Tables 2.3 to 2.8 provide documentation for these historical developments in the United States. They permit a close examination of general

---

[12] Simon Kuznets, *National Product since 1869* (New York: National Bureau of Economic Research, 1946), table IV-2, p. 202.

Table 2.2. *Research and development in the United States, 1965–1992*

	R&D scientists and engineers (thousands)		R&D scientists and engineers per 10,000 labor force population	R&D expenditure (thousands of 1987 dollars)		R&D expenditure as a percentage of GNP
	Total	Business		Total	Business	
1965	494.2	348.4	64.7	$70,643	$49,930	2.9%
1970	543.8	375.6	64.1	74,722	51,429	2.6
1975	527.4	363.9	55.3	72,256	49,171	2.2
1980	651.1	469.2	60.0	87,666	62,062	2.3
1985	841.6	646.8	71.8	120,624	89,265	2.8
1989	949.3	726.0	75.6	129,888	93,944	2.7
1990				129,545	92,446	2.7
1992				130,361	91,346	2.6

Note: R&D scientists and engineers represent full-time employees and the full-time equivalent of part-time employees.
Source: Compiled and calculated from National Science Foundation, *National Patterns of R&D Resources, 1992* (Washington, D.C., 1992), table B-1, p. 46, table B-4, p. 49, and table B-16, p. 63.

Table 2.3. *Distribution of the 200 largest industrial enterprises in the United States, by industry, ranked by assets, 1917–1988*

Group	Industry	1917	1930	1948	1973	1988
20	Food	29	31	27	22	18
21	Tobacco	6	5	5	3	3
22	Textiles	6	4	8	3	2
23	Apparel	3	0	0	0	1
24	Lumber	3	4	2	3	7
25	Furniture	0	1	1	0	1
26	Paper	5	8	6	10	9
27	Printing and publishing	2	2	2	1	9
28	Chemicals	20	20	23	28	40
29	Petroleum	22	26	22	26	18
30	Rubber	5	5	5	5	1
31	Leather	4	2	2	0	0
32	Stone, clay, and glass	5	8	6	8	6
33	Primary metals	31	23	23	18	10
34	Fabricated metals	11	10	6	4	5
35	Machinery	17	19	23	13	13
36	Electrical machinery	5	5	7	15	21
37	Transportation equipment	24	23	29	22	20
38	Instruments	1	2	1	2	4
39	Miscellaneous	1	2	2	1	1
—	Conglomerate	0	0	0	16	11
	Total	200	200	200	200	200

Sources: For 1917, 1930, 1948, and 1973, Alfred D. Chandler, Jr., *Scale and Scope: Dynamics of Industrial Capitalism* (Cambridge, Mass.: Harvard University Press, 1990), p. 19, with some modifications for the 1973 figures based on new information. For 1988, compiled, classified, and calculated from the *Fortune 500*, 1988 in *Fortune*, 24 April 1989, pp. 345–399. Industrial classification for individual companies is checked against information in *Moody's Industrial Manual*.

trends and performance in the lead country which is critical to understand the changing pattern and pace of technological progress in the follower nations. Table 2.3 indicates that in the United States, in spite of the emergence and development of new industries, large industrial firms throughout the twentieth century have concentrated in the similar industry categories decade by decade. Using the U.S. Standard Industrial Classification (SIC), the representative industry groups include food (SIC 20), tobacco (SIC 21), chemicals (SIC 28), petroleum (SIC 29), primary metals (SIC 33), and three machinery classifications (SIC 35, 36, and 37). A somewhat smaller number of large enterprises is also found in paper (SIC 26), rubber (SIC 30), and stone, clay, and glass (SIC 32). In 1988 close to 75 percent of the largest manufacturing companies were in SIC groups 20, 21, 26, 28, 29, 33, and 35–37. Eight more companies were in the high-tech industries, glass, and scientific instruments.[13]

The industry groups in which the large firms clustered were created or transformed by the capital-intensive, scale-dependent technology of the Second Industrial Revolution. But their significance in terms of capital expenditures and value-added in manufacturing changed during the century. And that change reflected the basic nature of their processes of production. Tables 2.4, 2.5, and 2.6 illustrate this trend. Tables 2.4 and 2.5 illustrate historical changes in capital intensity for three groups of industries classified by the basic characteristics of manufacturing processes. They are, in the overall decreasing order of capital intensity, chemical processes, metal working and machinery processes, and mechanical processes.

The new industries at the turn of the century were primarily those commercializing technologies based on *chemical processes* – chemicals, petroleum, primary metals, glass, paper, and rubber. As Table 2.6 shows, at the turn of the nineteenth century, more than 40 percent of the value-added in U.S. manufacturing already came in SIC categories where chemical processes dominated.[14] That proportion stayed roughly the same until the 1980s.

Industries where relatively simple *mechanical processes* were more dominant – textiles, apparel, leather, lumber, furniture, publishing and printing, and some fabricated metals – remained the nation's most labor-intensive. As such only a few large firms appeared in these industries. Expansion came mainly by the widening of capital, that is, increasing the number of both machines and workers tending them. Although machines gradually reduced the number of operators required per machine, the ratio of capital to labor did not dramatically change. The share of

---

[13] Alfred D. Chandler, Jr., "The Competitive Performance of U.S. Industrial Enterprises since the Second World War," *Business History Review*, 68 (Spring 1994): 60–69.

[14] These data indicate only broad general trends, for individual SIC groups at the two-digit level often cover a wide range of diverse industries. Industries whose production technologies are chemical processes, for instance, sometimes include a small number of mechanical ones.

Table 2.4. *Production processes and capital intensity in U.S. manufacturing industries, 1899, 1937, and 1957 (total capital stock per production worker in thousands of 1987 dollars)*

SIC	Industry	1899	1937	1957
Chemical processes				
29	Petroleum	$54	$449	$956
28	Chemicals	48	105	167
20/21	Food and tobacco	38	74	88
33	Primary metals	—	70	—
26	Paper	38	62	70
32	Stone, clay, and glass	25	54	62
30	Rubber	16	50	72
Metalworking and machinery processes				
37	Transportation equipment	—	45	60
35	Machinery	—	50	58
36	Electrical machinery	34	31	51
38	Instruments	—	—	—
34	Fabricated metals	—	34	—
Mechanical processes				
27	Printing and publishing	32	57	42
22/23	Textiles and apparel	22	25	31
24/25	Lumber and furniture	27	32	24
31	Leather	26	20	23
39	Miscellaneous	—	—	—
	Manufacturing average			

Note: Total capital represents the sum of fixed capital and working capital. Deflators are those for private non-residential investment. Figures are not available for all industries for all years.
Source: Calculated from U.S. Bureau of the Census, *Historical Statistics of the United States: From Colonial Times to 1970* (Washington, D.C., 1975), part 2, series P123–176, p. 685, and series P58–67, pp. 669–680.

the total value-added of manufacturing steadily declined from close to 40 percent in 1899 to less than 20 percent in 1991.

But in industries employing *metalworking and machinery processes* for the production of fabricated metals and increasingly complex machines and instruments (SIC 34–38), the technologies and their commercialization became more capital-intensive. These industries differed from the

Table 2.5. *Production processes and capital intensity in U.S. manufacturing industries, 1962 and 1987 (fixed capital stock and annual expenditure in thousands of 1987 dollars)*

SIC	Industry	1962		1987	
		Fixed assets per production worker	Expenditure per production worker	Fixed assets per production worker	Expenditure per production worker
Chemical processes					
29	Petroleum	$328.2	$15.2	$647.0	$30.6
28	Chemicals	135.1	10.0	271.1	18.8
281/286	Industrial chemicals	218.9	14.6	—	25.8
282	Plastics materials	136.7	12.0	—	22.7
283	Drugs and pharmaceuticals	80.8	5.7	—	22.0
20	Food	48.1	3.9	78.6	7.0
21	Tobacco	33.0	2.6	187.7	14.2
211	Cigarettes	43.0	3.8	—	17.4
33	Primary metals	93.4	4.4	134.5	7.1
331	Steel rolling and finishing	131.3	5.9	—	8.5
26	Paper	79.2	5.7	157.0	12.4
262	Paper mills	126.6	8.9	—	27.8
32	Stone, clay, and glass	61.4	4.1	87.9	6.0
321	Flat glass	99.2	6.2	—	12.8
324	Cement	262.9	11.4	—	11.5
30	Rubber	39.3	3.9	56.1	5.3
301	Tires	71.4	6.3	—	6.4
Metalworking and machinery processes					
37	Transportation equipment	35.4	2.7	73.7	8.9
371	Motor vehicles	49.6	3.2	—	10.8
372	Aircraft and parts	21.7	2.5	—	7.8
35	Nonelectrical machinery	35.6	2.4	70.0	6.1
357	Office machines	38.6	4.1	—	18.1

Table 2.5. (*cont.*)

SIC	Industry	1962 Fixed assets per production worker	1962 Expenditure per production worker	1987 Fixed assets per production worker	1987 Expenditure per production worker
36	Electrical machinery	25.0	2.2	66.6	6.9
361–362	Industrial apparatus	26.9	2.0	—	3.9
366	Communication equipment	31.8	2.8	—	9.7
38	Instruments	27.2	2.9	71.2	7.7
382	Scientific devices	6.1	2.6	—	6.0
384	Medical devices	27.1	3.2	—	6.0
34	Fabricated metals	30.5	2.2	49.0	4.5
Mechanical processes					
27	Printing and publishing	31.8	2.7	57.4	6.2
22	Textiles	24.2	1.7	40.9	3.5
23	Apparel	5.2	0.3	8.7	0.8
24	Lumber	24.9	2.1	39.8	3.1
25	Furniture	13.6	1.1	21.8	2.2
31	Leather	6.0	0.4	12.5	0.9
39	Miscellaneous	11.5	1.8	27.7	2.6
	Manufacturing average	43.0	3.0	75.3	6.4

Note: Fixed assets represent the gross book value in original cost of fixed depreciable assets (structure and machinery and equipment). Expenditure represents the annual expenditure on new fixed depreciable assets (structure and machinery and equipment). Fixed assets figures for the 3-digit industries are not available for 1987. Deflators are those for private nonresidential investment.

Source: Compiled and calculated from U.S. Bureau of the Census, *Annual Survey of Manufactures, 1962* (Washington, D.C., 1964), ch. 2, table 1, pp. 32–49; U.S. Bureau of the Census, *Annual Survey of Manufactures, 1964–65* (Washington, D.C., 1968), ch. 7, table 1, pp. 150–169; U.S. Bureau of the Census, *Census of Manufactures, 1987* (Washington, D.C., 1992), Subject Series, General Summary, table 3, pp. 1-4–1-21, table 3d, pp. 1-95–1-96.

Table 2.6. *Production processes and value-added by manufacture, 1899–1991*

	Industries based on chemical processes (million current dollars)		Industries based on metalworking and machinery processes (million current dollars)		Industries based on mechanical processes (million current dollars)		Total (million current dollars)	
1899	$2,110	43.7%	$911	18.8%	$1,810	37.5%	$4,831	100.0%
1937	10,817	44.2	7,142	29.1	6,638	26.7	24,497	100.0
1957	60,576	41.8	53,946	37.1	30,432	21.0	144,954	100.0
1970	119,611	40.5	118,371	40.1	57,162	19.4	295,114	100.0
1991	536,657	40.8	542,089	41.2	236,084	18.0	1,313,829	100.0

Source: For 1899, compiled and calculated from U.S. Bureau of the Census. For 1937, 1957, 1970, compiled and calculated from U.S. Bureau of the Census, *Historical Statistics of the United States.* For 1991, compiled and calculated from U.S. Bureau of the Census, *Statistical Abstract of the United States, 1994,* table 1235, pp. 753–757.

other industries using labor-intensive mechanical processes in that the equipment required was much more costly. They differed from industries with chemical processes in that they required a much larger labor force. In these industries with metalworking and machinery processes the incentives were highest to develop production technologies that increased daily throughput by replacing labor with capital equipment. So while the proportion of U.S. manufacturing value-added in chemically processed industries remained much the same, and that in the labor-intensive mechanical processes dropped by a half between 1899 and 1991, the portion of industries with metalworking and machinery processes more than doubled from less than 20 percent to more than 40 percent.

Table 2.7 emphasizes the importance of the large industrial firm for U.S. economic performance after World War II. Since the 1960s the largest 200 manufacturing companies accounted for 42 to 44 percent of total manufacturing value-added and approximately one-half of new physical capital expenditures committed in manufacturing in the United States. Given the capital-intensive and labor-saving characteristics of the technologies which these enterprises use, the percentage of the total work force they employed was relatively small. Nevertheless, for their number of employees, the 200 largest industrial enterprises consistantly accounted for a disproportionally high proportion of total payroll. Thus, employees in the largest industrial enterprises are paid on average better than their counterparts in smaller firms. This most likely indicates a high level of education and training of employees, which reflects the concentration of these firms in capital-using and increasingly knowledge-intensive industries.

Table 2.8 shows the industrial distribution of investments in research and development in the United States. Manufacturing enterprises account for 90 percent of industrial R&D expenditures and R&D intensity substantially varies by industry even within the manufacturing sector. In 1990 such industries as chemicals, pharmaceuticals, office machinery, electronics, aircraft, and scientific instruments had the highest proportion of R&D expenditures. On the other hand, other capital-intensive industries whose technological trajectories became at least temporarily stagnant – food and tobacco, and paper, petroleum refining, primary metals – were investing less in developing their technological capabilities.

Figure 2.1 illustrates the relationships between physical capital intensity (based on Table 2.6) and R&D efforts (based on Table 2.8). Figure 2.1 and Table 2.3 combined suggest that the clustering of large industrial enterprises has been historically shifting toward the industries (those

Table 2.7. *Aggregate concentration shares of the 200 largest manufacturing companies in the United States, 1947–1987*

	1947	1958	1967	1977	1987
Value-added by manufacture					
50 largest firms	17%	23%	24.6%	24.4%	24.9%
100 largest firms	23	30	32.8	33.4	34.4
200 largest firms	30	38	41.6	43.7	43.2
Number of employees					
50 largest firms	—	—	20.2	17.9	16.8
100 largest firms	—	—	26.4	25.0	22.5
200 largest firms	—	—	33.7	33.4	30.6
Total payroll					
50 largest firms	—	—	25.2	24.8	24.1
100 largest firms	—	—	32.4	32.9	31.0
200 largest firms	—	—	40.3	42.1	39.8
New capital expenditures					
50 largest firms	—	—	27.4	28.0	27.2
100 largest firms	—	—	40.3	38.5	36.4
200 largest firms	—	—	51.5	49.2	46.6

Note: Figures for 1947 and 1958 are available for value-added only.
Source: U.S. Bureau of the Census, *Historical Statistics of the United States, Colonial Times to 1970* (Washington, D.C., 1975), part 2, series P177–180, p. 686; U.S. Bureau of the Census, *Census of Manufactures, 1987: Concentration Ratios in Manufacturing* (Washington, D.C., 1992), tables 1 and 2.

in the upper right corner) which are capital-using *and* R&D-intensive. This gradual shift reflects the changing technical bias toward intangible capital, particularly technological knowledge resulting from research and development. In the U.S. economy large firms are concentrated more and more in such industries, examples being chemicals, pharmaceuticals, office machinery, electronics, and aircraft. Therefore, firms in such established capital-intensive industries as food, tobacco, rubber tires, and iron and steel have been replaced in the top 200 list by firms in the more R&D-intensive industries. The only notable exception to this rule has been petroleum refining, which symbolizes the long-lasting legacy of the natural-resource-base growth of the U.S. economy.

Table 2.8. *Research and development investment in U.S. industries, 1990*

Industry	R&D expenditures (million dollars)	R&D expenditures as a percentage of net sales	Number of R&D and engineers (thousands)
Food, kindred, and tobacco products	$1,308	0.5%	8.8
Textiles and apparel	242	0.4	
Lumber, wood products, and furniture	160	0.7	
Paper	715	0.8	
Chemicals	12,277	5.6	78.9
Industrial chemicals	4,272	4.7	
Drugs and pharmaceuticals	5,366	9.3	33.5
Other chemicals	2,646	3.7	22.4
Petroleum refining and extraction	2,113	1.0	10.2
Rubber products	730	1.7	
Stone, clay, and glass products	894	2.4	8.6
Primary metals	801	1.0	
Ferrous metals and products	245	0.5	
Nonferrous metals and products	556	1.5	3.4
Fabricated metal products	644	1.0	
Machinery	13,780	8.3	112.3
Office, computing and accounting machines	11,073	15.3	88.6
Other machinery, except electrical	2,707	2.9	23.7

Industry			
Electrical equipment	12,131	4.7	138.0
Radio and TV receiving equipment	93	3.1	0.6
Communication equipment	5,932	4.3	74.2
Electronic components	4,709	8.5	48.5
Other electrical equipment	1,397	2.3	
Transportation equipment	14,992	3.6	183.7
Motor vehicles and motor vehicle equipment	8,548	3.9	49.6
Aircraft and missiles	6,140	3.5	128.5
Other transportation equipment	304	1.8	
Professional and scientific instruments	6,095	7.6	
Scientific and mechanical measuring instruments	2,086	9.4	
Optical, surgical, photographic, and other instruments	4,009	6.9	
Other manufacturing industries	472	1.1	
Nonmanufacturing industries	6,588		
Total	73,980	4.7	720.3

Note: Because of disclosure restrictions, figures on the number of R&D scientists and engineers are not available for many industries.

Source: Compiled from National Science Foundation, *Selected Data on Research and Development in Industry, 1991* (Washington, D.C., 1993), tables SD-4, SD-9, pp. 8–9, 18; National Science Foundation, *National Patterns of R&D Resources, 1992* (Washington, D.C., 1992), table B-32, p. 80.

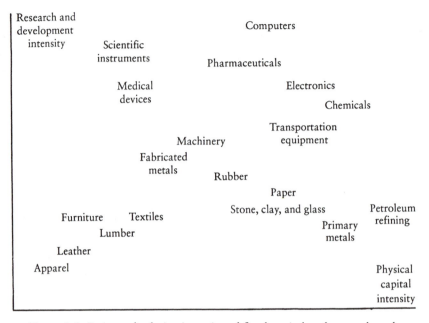

Figure 2.1. Estimated relative intensity of fixed capital and research and
development around 1980s.
Source: Based on Tables 2.5 and 2.8.

THE ROLE OF LARGE INDUSTRIAL FIRMS IN CATCH-UP AND CONVERGENCE

The development of capital-intensive and knowledge-intensive industries, and the role of the large industrial enterprise in driving technological change and in playing a critical role in the catch-up process in these industries, was a global as well as an American phenomenon. Table 2.9 shows the industrial distribution of the world's 500 largest industrial firms during the post – World War II era. It suggests that large firms worldwide clustered in the same capital-intensive industry groups. Their industrial location historically also remained remarkably stable. Furthermore, the table indicates declining numbers of firms in such established industries as textiles (the labor-intensive prime mover of the First Industrial Revolution), primary metals, and nonelectrical machinery – industries in which international demand and/or technological trajectories do not promise high growth of large firms. By contrast, the table shows increasing numbers in industries related to the major new technologies, including chemicals, pharmaceuticals, electronics, computers, and scientific instruments, as well

Table 2.9. *Industrial distribution of the 500 largest industrial enterprises in the world, 1962 and 1993 (ranked by sales)*

SIC	Industry	1962	1993
20	Food	53	47
208	Beverages	10	16
21	Tobacco	9	5
22	Textiles	24	8
23	Apparel	0	2
24	Lumber	0	0
25	Furniture	0	0
26	Paper	22	23
27	Printing and publishing	5	12
28	Chemicals	36	53
283	Drugs and pharmaceuticals	23	26
29	Petroleum	36	48
30	Rubber	9	11
31	Leather	0	0
32	Stone, clay, and glass	14	21
33	Primary metals	79	39
34	Fabricated metal products	10	8
35	Nonelectrical machinery	39	26
357	Office and computing machines	9	18
36	Electrical machinery	44	39
37	Transportation equipment	62	59
38	Instruments	1	10
39	Miscellaneous	11	4
—	Conglomerates	0	12
—	Diversified groups	1	13
	Total	497	500

Note: Enterprises, including private and state-owned, are from market economies only and are ranked by sales. Firms included are manufacturers which often engage in such related activities as mining and distribution. Because of the lack of adequate data 497 companies are listed for 1962. The companies of late industrialization may be underrepresented thanks to different corporate structures and disclosure standards.
Source: For 1962, adopted and reorganized from John H. Dunning and Robert D. Pearce, *The World's Largest Industrial Enterprises, 1962–1983* (New York: St. Martins Press, 1985), pp. 51, 171–180. For 1993, compiled and reorganized from "Fortune's Global 500," *Fortune*, 25 July 1994.

as petroleum refining. In such major capital-intensive industries as food, paper, electrical machinery (where electronics replaced electromechnical processes), and transportation equipment, the number of companies represented has hardly changed at all.

Behind this extraordinary stability in the industrial representation of large firms was the postwar convergence of productivity and the resulting catch-up of follower nations to the technological and economic leadership of the United States. For while *industrial* representation remained the same, Table 2.10 shows that the *geographical* location of the world's largest 500 industrial firms has changed dramatically. Between 1962 and 1993, the number of U.S. firms in the top 500 dropped from 296 to 160. The number in the top 500 in the four European leading nations fell off slightly. In part, the U.S. and Western European drop-off reflected macroeconomic factors such as fluctuating exchange rates. In part, it resulted from microeconomic and organizational factors such as unproductive competitive strategies, particularly those of unrelated diversification, adopted by many of the large established industrial enterprises. But the underlying cause of the shift was the emergence of new global competitors in the industries in which American and European companies had dominated since the Second Industrial Revolution. Some new competitors came from the smaller European countries, but most notable were from Pacific Rim economies, particularly those of late industrializers such as Japan and South Korea.

A stability in the *industrial* representation and a shift of *geographical* location of large industrial enterprises support one key hypothesis of Alexander Gerschenkron's economies of backwardness, namely, latecomers rapidly industrialize their economies by effectively exploiting an international pool of existing technology.[15] As the overall pattern of the geographical shift of large industrial enterprises indicates, less technologically advanced nations have become internationally competitive in established capital-intensive industries, rather than by suddenly assuming the technological and economic leadership of the new industries of the Third Industrial Revolution.

This particular pattern in the international shift of large industrial enterprises after World War II is in sharp contrast to the catch-up process of the United States and Germany in the Second Industrial Revolution. In

---

[15] Alexander Gerschenkron, "Economic Backwardness in Historical Perspective," in his *Economic Backwardness in Historical Perspective* (Cambridge, Mass.: Harvard University Press, 1962), ch. 1.

Table 2.10. *Country distribution of the 500 largest industrial enterprises in the world, 1962 and 1993 (ranked by sales)*

Country	1962	1993
Developed market economies (except Japan)		
United States	298	160
Great Britain	55	43
Germany	36	32
France	27	26
Sweden	8	12
Australia	2	10
Switzerland	6	9
The Netherlands	5	9
Canada	13	7
Italy	7	7
Belgium	3	4
Spain	0	3
Norway	0	3
Finland	0	3
Austria	1	2
Others	0	3
Total	462	333
Japan	31	135
Late-industrializing countries		
South Korea	0	11
South Africa	2	4
India	1	5
Mexico	1	3
Turkey	0	3
Others	0	6
Total	4	32
Total	497	500

Note: Enterprises, including private and state-owned, are from market economies only and are ranked by sales. Firms included are manufacturers which often engage in such related activities as mining and distribution. Because of the lack of adequate data 497 companies are listed for 1962. The companies of late industrialization may be underrepresented thanks to different corporate structures and disclosure standards. Country identification is based on the location of the headquarters, not the legal address of incorporation. Schulumberger for 1962 and McDermott International for 1993, therefore, are both classified as U.S. corportions.
Source: For 1962, adopted and reorganized from John H. Dunning and Robert D. Pearce, *The World's Largest Industrial Enterprises, 1962–1983* (New York: St. Martins Press, 1985). For 1993, compiled and reorganized from "Fortune's Global 500," *Fortune*, 25 July 1994.

the late nineteenth and early twentieth centuries American and German large industrial firms leapfrogged over their British counterparts by investing on a large scale in physical and human capital and by exploiting emerging scale-intensive technology in new industries. These enterprises were usually start-up firms which had been established to exploit certain new technologies of the Second Industrial Revolution. After World War II, by contrast, large industrial enterprises in the United States and other leading nations continued to be in command in the commercialization of the technology of the Third Industrial Revolution. The only viable path for latecomers thus became securing a position as global players in existing industries, particularly capital-intensive ones. This is because in capital-intensive industries, enterprises in catch-up economies could gain international competitiveness through exploiting scale economies, employing lower-cost labor, introducing incremental improvements in production processes, and improving customer services, most of which resulted from learned and accumulated capabilities. These capabilities, in turn, derived from highly complementary investments in tangible capital such as manufacturing facilities large enough to exploit economies of scale *and* in intangible assets such as human capabilities and organizational innovations.[16] This explains why, with a notable exception of South Korea, in catching-up nations those firms which became international players in capital-intensive industries often had had a long history in other industries and businesses before they invested on a large scale in existing scale-oriented technologies.

The most important outcome of the catch-up of more nations is a more fierce international competition in industries which are capital-intensive and increasingly knowledge-intensive. International rivalry has thus increasingly become based on investments in intangible capital, particularly research and development expenditures to enhance technological capabilities. Table 2.11 shows that in R&D expenditures as a percentage of GNP, Japan and Germany have moved slightly ahead of the United States, with Great Britain and France a good bit behind. On the other hand, assuming substantial increasing return to overall R&D investment, the United States still has the advantage of much larger total expenditures,

---

[16] Takashi Hikino and Alice H. Amsden, "Staying Behind, Stumbling Back, Sneaking Up, Soaring Ahead: Late Industrialization in Historical Perspective," in Baumol et al. *Convergence of Productivity*, pp. 285–315; Alice H. Amsden and Takashi Hikino, "Project Execution Capability, Organizational Know-How and Conglomerate Corporate Growth in Late Industrialization," *Industrial and Corporate Change*, 3, no.1 (1994): 111–147.

Table 2.11. *Research and development investments and high-technology trade*

	United States		United Kingdom		West Germany		France		Japan	
	1965	1987/88	1965	1987/88	1965	1987/88	1965	1987/88	1965	1987/88
National R&D expenditures in constant 1982 U.S. billion dollars	59.3	111.5	8.4	13.8	6.7	20.8	5.8	14.5	6.1	42.3
R&D expenditures as a percentage of GNP	2.8	2.8	2.3	2.2	1.4	2.9	1.6	2.3	1.4	2.9
R&D scientists and engineers (in thousands)	494.6	949.2	49.9	101.4	61.0	165.6	42.8	109.4	117.6	441.9
R&D scientists and engineers per 10,000 labor force	64.7	76.9	19.6	35.9	22.6	53.7	21.0	44.9	24.6	72.9
World export share of technology-intensive products (percentage)		20.6		8.7		16.4		8.5		18.9
Import share of domestic market for high-technology products, 1992 (percentage)		28.5		81.5		67.4		77.7		18.7

Source: Compiled from various publications of the U.S. National Science Foundation.

while those of Japan are twice those of Germany and three times those of Britain. The same pattern holds for investments in human capital in R&D, where Japan is only slightly behind the United States in R&D scientists per thousand labor force.

The significance of this catch-up cannot be overstated. If American firms had somehow continued to dominate the capital-intensive industries based on the monopolized knowledge of advanced technology, and had thereby ruled the global economy beyond the 1950s, economic growth through technological progress would have been much more modest in Europe and East Asia, and the new age of capitalism far less golden.

CONCLUSION

A rise in a nation's economic efficiency and improvements in its national income have reflected the nature of its resource endowment, educational system, political and legal heritage, micro- and macroeconomic policies, financial markets, and cultural configurations as well as large-scale firms. Other forms of enterprise have been also essential to economic progress. Small and medium-sized firms have probably been of more significance than large ones in stimulating growth in labor-intensive and service industries. Furthermore, as we have stressed, small firms have been vital ingredients in the clusters and networks organized around large industrial firms in the capital-intensive industries.

Yet, the large industrial enterprise has remained *a* central institution in the dynamics of modern economic growth. Its essential role has been to drive technological advance. Large industrial enterprises have performed this function through the commercialization of new technologies on a global scale and then the maintenance and enhancement of their potential. The large industrial enterprise became an instrument of technological progress by making the primary investment in physical and human capital which was necessary to exploit fully the potential of new technologies. These firms transformed the processes of production and distribution by providing the corporate organizations fundamental to enhance existing technologies and commercialize new ones. As such, the large industrial enterprise became an engine of modern economic growth in the century spanning the 1880s to the 1980s, an era of industrial capitalism when technological advance provided the most powerful dynamic for the sustained growth of nations and the global economy.

Acknowledgments

The authors thank Moses Abramovitz, Angus Maddison, and all the participants of this project, particularly Alice H. Amsden, for their constructive criticism of earlier drafts of this chapter.

Part II

National experiences of big business

Group 1

Prime drivers in North America and
Western Europe

3

The United States: Engines of economic
growth in the capital-intensive and
knowledge-intensive industries

ALFRED D. CHANDLER, JR.

As emphasized in the previous chapter, a nation's economic growth and
competitive strength rest on more than natural resources, labor and managerial skills, available capital, or even the size of internal markets. The
wealth of nations during the past hundred years has been based more on
organization and technology – on how technologies of production have
been created or improved. It rested on the ability of industrial enterprises
to adopt and to develop these technologies and to devise administrative
structures to coordinate the flow of materials from the raw materials
through the processes of production and distribution to the final consumer.

The United States story is a place to begin a study of the impact of "big
business" in the form of the large industrial enterprise on the economic
performance and growth of nations. During the century from the 1880s
to the 1980s the United States was the world leader in terms of per capita
income, output per worker, and, most important of all, technical change.
In the United States large industrial firms developed – that is, brought to
market – the products and processes of more new technologies in a broader
variety of industries than in any other nation. As the world's leader, the
history of its large industrial enterprises provides an essential introduction to those of other nations. And according to Angus Maddison, "We
can get some idea of the changing pace of technical change only by close
inspection of performance in the lead country." This chapter divides into
three historical periods that follow the chronology of economic growth
worldwide outlined in Chapter 1.

The first covers the years from the 1880s to 1914, when unprecedented
capital accumulation in the new capital-intensive, scale-dependent technologies helped to propel the United States into a position of world
leadership. In this period, firms made the investments large enough to

utilize fully the productivity of the new technologies and recruited workers and managers essential for that utilization. These firms became the initial learning bases for the development of product-specific skills and organizational capabilities in these new technologies and the seedbeds of related industrial activities.

The second period covers the interwar years, when such learning continued and led to further augmentation of capital – that is, the more intensive use of existing equipment and facilities – in the industries created before World War I. In these years too, science-based industries became increasingly a major source of commercializing new products and processes closely related to their initial core technologies. The most important source of new capital accumulation and technical progress during the interwar years, however, was the new set of technologies based on the internal-combustion engine, particularly in motor vehicles. Again, those new firms that made the largest investment in tangible goods and most rapidly embodied the needed skills and capabilities into their organizational routines quickly dominated their industries, became essential sources of learning as well as cores of networks of small, medium, and large firms in ancillary industries.

In the third period, from the end of World War II until the 1980s, as the bias of technical progress shifted from the accumulation of tangible capital to that of intangible capital, the primary sources of growth came in new, knowledge-intensive, science-based technologies. In those the essential large-scale investments in both tangible and intangible capital were made not by new enterprises as they had been in the past, but primarily by well-established firms whose existing learned organizational capabilities were critical in developing and commercializing the potential of the new technologies on a global scale. This was true of aerospace, polymer chemicals, antibiotics, telecommunications, consumer electronics, and mainframe computers. And those that made the largest investments, particularly in intangible capital, quickly dominated the commercializing of these new technologies. Large industrial enterprises also played a major role in the exploitation of the two major postwar technologies, those based on electronic integrated circuits and recombinant DNA.

This review only outlines the historical narrative, identifying the beginning and continuing existence of the major players in the capital-intensive and increasingly knowledge-intensive industries. I make little attempt here to detail the processes by which intangible capital came to embody physical capital and how the resulting organizational capabilities were developed through "learning by using" and "learning by doing." I do, however, point out the continuing interaction between tangible and intangible capital as being absolutely essential to economic growth through technical progress.

CAPITAL-INTENSIVE, SCALE-DEPENDENT INDUSTRIES BEFORE WORLD WAR I

First wave – chemical processes

The exploitation of the new capital-intensive technologies had to wait until the completion of modern transportation and communication networks – those powered by steam and electricity. Only as the railroad, steamship, telegraph, and cable systems were nearing completion in the late 1870s were manufacturing establishments assured the steady, scheduled, high-volume flows of materials *in* and finished products *out* that were essential to maintain close to the potential minimum efficient scale of each new technology. Such firms initially appeared primarily in technologies where the transformation processes were primarily chemical – such industries as primary metals, glass, paper, rubber, and oil. In these industries, as pointed out in Chapter 2, the economies of scale were much greater in terms of daily throughput and value-added than they were in the mechanical industries. There the ratio of machine tenders to machines remained much the same. Only in tobacco and some food-processing industries did high-speed mechanical processes come quickly.

In tobacco, continuous production came with the development in the 1880s of two machines – one producing cigarettes and the other simultaneously packing them. Those machines immediately reduced production costs to one-sixth of their previous level. In 1890 the four firms acquiring these machines joined the first mover, James B. Duke, to form the American Tobacco Company, which immediately competed in Europe and Asia with Wills, the first user of this production technology in Britain and the dominant leader in the 1901 merger that formed Imperial Tobacco. In 1911 American Tobacco was broken up by antitrust action into four firms. These four plus one other continued to be the American industry's leaders at least until 1964 when the report of the U.S. Surgeon General on the health hazard of cigarette smoking pushed these companies into new lines of products.

In the processing of grains, vegetables, fruit, and dairy products, comparable integrated mechanical processes appeared in the same decade of the 1880s. In grains new technologies, both European and American, were embodied in the "automatic, all-roller, gradual-reduction" mills into which carloads of wheat and oats entered and bags of flour or boxes of cereals emerged. Here the first firms to use this technology, such as Pillsbury in flour and Quaker Oats in cereals, remained leaders throughout most of the next century. The invention of high-speed canning equipment in the 1880s and comparable machinery in bottle making somewhat later led to the quick rise of such large food-processing firms as Heinz, Campbell Soup, California Packing (Del Monte), Corn Products Refining, Borden (powdered milk), and also such brewers as Anheuser-Busch and such soft-drink makers as Coca-Cola. In the same decade of the 1880s the modern meat-packing industry was created and was dominated until after World War II by Swift, Armour, and three smaller firms. These leaders built large "disassembling plants" next to stockyards in Chicago and other mid-western cities and shipped their chilled products over their own national and international refrigerated transportation networks throughout the United States and Europe.

These large food firms, unlike those in tobacco, rarely drove out smaller ones. The rapid growth of markets, the multitude of farmers that provided the supplies, and the seasonal and perishable nature of the products provided continuing opportunities for the smaller producers. In 1921, the first time the U.S. Census listed the number of establishments in food and related products (SIC 20), that group had 51,502 establishments, far more than any other two-digit SIC classification. But those firms that did make the investment in capital-intensive, high-volume production and in national distribution networks quickly moved into international markets. By World War I such firms as Quaker Oats, Heinz, and Coca-Cola, had built factories abroad, while Armour's and Swift's meat-packing plants dominated their industry in Argentina and Uruguay.

In glass the new capital-intensive, chemically processed technology – the Siemens continuous-process, gas-heated, electrically controlled tank furnaces – transformed the production of heavy plate and lighter window glass, but not of tableware or specialty glass. The development of the Owens bottle-making machinery in the next decade did the same for glass bottles. In plate glass, the first to make essential investments in the new technology, Pittsburgh Plate Glass formed in 1893, quickly dominated. In 1911 Michael Owens, the inventor of the bottle-making machine, developed a new process for producing flat glass. In the 1920s, each firm used its learned capabilities to move into the other's product markets.

Before World War I, Pittsburgh Plate Glass had established plants in Europe, and Libby-Owens did so in 1921. In abrasives the new scale-dependent electrolytic production technologies required a more massive amount of energy. So the two firms, Norton and Carborundum, that built plants at Niagara Falls in the 1890s followed the same route as the glass-makers. By 1910, Carborundum had plants in Germany and Britain, and Norton in Germany. On the other hand, in the production of SIC 32 products other than glass and abrasives – these included bricks, tiles, ceramics, pottery, chinaware, kitchenware, and stone products – labor-intensive, customized, small-batch processes of production continued to thrive.

The transformation of the paper industry came in the 1880s and 1890s with the adoption of a German-developed technology that made paper from wood rather than rags, one that required a great amount of energy and wood pulp. The first companies to commercialize these new processes merged in 1900 to form International Paper Company. But the merged enterprise failed to rationalize its activities by consolidating production facilities and creating a single national marketing organization. So smaller challengers were able to become firmly established before International Paper carried out the rationalization essential to obtain the scale economies required to maintain its competitive position. Because the production processes required a steady flow of pulp, 80 percent of the producers of newsprint, paperboard, and other paper packaging products had their own pulp mills by 1930. Those that did not integrate backward were nearly all producers of stationery and other high-grade paper, using specialized, more labor-intensive processes of production.

In primary metals, the new Bessemer Steel making technology was introduced in the 1860s, but the potential of scale economies came only after the several processes of production were placed within a single works that included coke ovens, blast furnaces, and rolling and shaping mills that turned out rails, beams, bars, and structural steel. Andrew Carnegie became the new American steel industry's first mover in the 1880s when he completed a carefully designed "greenfield" works in Pittsburgh that went into full production in 1879 when its battery of blast furnaces was completed. Carnegie then acquired and reshaped two other nearby works. In one he placed the first open-hearth furnaces to be operated in the United States. In 1894 the output of these three establishments was 1.7 million tons of steel – more than was produced in all of the United States six years before.

The massive increases in output drove down costs and prices. Between

1880 and 1889 the price of steel rails at Pittsburgh plummeted from $67.50 to $29.25 a ton. By 1898 it was $17.63. By the mid-1890s the four works of Carnegie's leading competitor, Illinois Steel, had an annual output of two million tons, even larger than Carnegie's. Such vast increases in throughput brought backward and forward integration. The two scale-dependent giants purchased coal mines and then large ore deposits, primarily in Lake Superior's Mesabi Range. The two also quickly built marketing organizations to sell to railroads, building contractors, machinery makers, and other industrial customers.

At the end of the century came a series of mergers that culminated in combining Carnegie Company with Federal Steel, the successor of Illinois Steel, and with a number of producers of secondary products – wire, tin plate, hoops, and sheet steel – into a huge combination, the United States Steel Corporation, the world's first billion-dollar firm. However, like International Paper, the Steel Corporation failed to rationalize its facilities quickly. Moreover, its explicit policy of not utilizing scale economies to reduce prices (generated by fear of federal antitrust actions), gave independent firms the time to make investments in facilities and personnel to assure them the benefits of scale economies. After 1910 these leaders competed oligopolistically, not on price, but functionally and strategically. In this competition U.S. Steel continually lost market share.

In nonferrous metals the coming of an electric generator powerful enough to provide for the electrolytic reduction of smelted copper and refined aluminum completely transformed the processes of production in the first and in the second turned a semiprecious metal into a mass-produced one. In 1891 five new electrolytic copper smelters went on stream. Their minimum efficient scale was so high that only twelve more copper smelters were built in the United States during the next ninety years, and seven of these were in operation by 1910. Four American firms and one German firm dominated global as well as U.S. copper markets from the 1890s until well after World War II. In 1896 the predecessor of the Aluminum Company of America built a plant at Niagara Falls to provide the electric power needed to mass-produce aluminum and formed a marketing organization to distribute and sell a wide range of new products – tubes, rods, castings, wire and cable, containers, foil, and kitchenware. The result was that Alcoa completely dominated the U.S. aluminum industry until World War II.

In the 1880s rubber and oil were still new industries. Both had come into full production after the civil war. The initial products of the rubber industry provide an early example of the cost advantages of the economies of scope in the utilization of physical capital (i.e., the economies gained by producing a number of different products in a single manufacturing establishment using the same raw materials and many of the same intermediate processes). The use of different admixtures and accelerators in the vulcanizing process, and of different machines to mold, extrude, and further process the finished rubber, made possible the production within a single plant of a wide variety of apparel (boots, gloves, and rainwear) and of industrial goods (hoses, belting, flooring, and insulating materials). By 1899 the average number of workers in a rubber establishment was 125 as compared to 9 in the production of apparel made from natural fibers. By that time the rubber apparel industry was dominated by B. F. Goodrich and industrial rubber by United States Rubber Company (created by a 1893 merger). In 1905 as Goodrich moved into the production of industrial rubber, U.S. Rubber expanded into apparel. In a few years, however, the coming of the motor vehicle enormously expanded the demand for rubber and altered the structure of the firms so that they could exploit the economies of scale as well as those of scope.

John D. Rockefeller's Standard Oil Company has long been identified as the classic example of a giant integrated multinational enterprise of that era. From the start, its process of refining was one of close to steady flow. Then the building of pipelines permitted crude oil to flow from the oil fields to the refineries. In the twentieth century pipelines came to carry the refined product to distribution centers throughout the nation, and those pipelines acted as inventory reservoirs as well as conduits of flow. By the time the Standard Oil Company consolidated its control over the oil industry by acquiring its major competitors, that industry had achieved the nation's highest ratio of capital to labor. (See Table 2.4.)

Standard Oil achieved its initial dominance in the early 1870s by building the nation's largest refinery in Cleveland and by vastly increasing the company's throughput (a word first used in the oil industry). During the 1870s the throughput of Standard's refineries rose from 500 to 2,000 barrels a day, thus reducing the cost of a gallon of kerosene from 5¢ to 3¢ and then to 2½ ¢. As the lowest-cost producer by far, Standard Oil acquired about 90 percent of the industry during that decade. And from 1879 to 1881 Standard Oil and other companies it controlled built over 4,000 miles of pipelines to replace railroads as shippers.

In 1881 Rockefeller and the heads of the acquired companies formed the Standard Oil Trust to consolidate into a single enterprise the many companies' operating units. Their aim was to capture the cost potentials of the oil-refining technology by rationalizing their industries – their rationalization became the model for comparable mergers in capital-intensive industries, particularly at the turn of the century. Between 1881 and 1886 the trust reduced the number of its refineries from fifty-six to twenty-three, concentrating production of its primary product, kerosene, in three 6,000-barrel refineries and converting other refineries into production of such specialties as lubricants, paraffins, wax, and vaseline. By 1884 the cost of refining a gallon of kerosene had dropped from 1.5¢ to 0.45¢. In that same year the purchasing of crude oil was centralized into a single department. By the end of the decade Standard Oil had completed its nationwide marketing organization at home, had built a comparable one abroad, had begun to own and operate oceangoing tankers and scores of railroad cars, and was beginning to integrate backward into the production of crude oil in the newly opened fields on the Ohio–Indiana border.

By then its middle managers at corporate headquarters, 26 Broadway in New York, were supervising and coordinating the several functional activities and the flow of products. Its top managers monitored the work of the operating departments and planned the strategies and allocated the resources to maintain and expand the operations of this global empire. By then Standard's competition consisted mainly of two or three small U.S. competitors, the powerful Nobel and Rothschild enterprises in Europe, and Royal Dutch Shell in Asia.

Nevertheless, with the opening of the huge Texas and California oil fields at the turn of the century and, at almost the same moment, the coming of the swiftly growing markets created by the automobile, challengers immediately appeared. The U.S. industry was quickly transformed into a modern oligopoly. Before 1911, when the U.S. government dismembered the Standard Oil Company of New Jersey (the successor to the trust), for violations of the antitrust laws, seven other integrated oil companies were listed among the nation's largest 200 enterprises.

By 1899 the industries based on the first wave of the new technologies, primarily those using chemical processes of production, became the most capital-intensive in the nation and already accounted for approximately 40 percent of the value-added in U.S. manufacturing, as stated earlier. The relatively few firms which made the large investments needed to capture the scale economies had contributed a substantial share of the capital accumulation in these industries that drove economic growth at the turn of the century. By embodying the physical facilities of the new technologies with the human skills needed to exploit their potential, these firms became the initial learning bases from which much of the new organizational capabilities and new organizational structures would evolve.

Metalworking and machinery-making industries

Raising output, adding value, and increasing productivity by speeding up the flow of materials through the processes of production and distribution came more slowly in the metalworking and machinery-making. Here the increase in output per worker was more the result of capital augmentation than of capital accumulation. For in these same years these industries were still a locus of small shops making custom-ordered goods or a single line of equipment in small batches or small-bulk production processes, or making different products from the same set of individual craft skills. But, as the demand for specific products grew with the nation's expanding industrialization, machinery-making firms increasingly focused on producing standardized equipment for those markets. Here firms moved toward volume output by fabricating and assembling standardized parts in large batches and in some cases by what became close to continuous sequential line production. As they concentrated production in large capital-using works, the coordination of flows within and to and from the production establishment came to be increasingly essential to competitive strength and continuing profits. Such coordination required the development of complex skills and capabilities in the allied activities of purchasing, marketing, and distribution.

The metalworking industries grouped by the Census in SIC 34 (fabricated metals) remained far less concentrated and more labor-intensive and continued to rely much more on craft and small-batch production methods than did the machinery industries classified in SIC 35, 36, 37, and 38. (The United States Standard Industrial Classifications are listed on Table 2.9.) In 1937, SIC 34 had 493,000 production workers in 8,688 establishments for an average of 56.7 workers per establishment. In 1948 only 6 of the 200 largest U.S. firms were listed in SIC 34. Only in the making of metal cans and canning machinery, standardized plumbing and heating equipment, and safety razors (Gillette) did the cost advantages of scale bring large integrated enterprises in SIC 34.

In nonelectrical machinery (SIC 35), more enterprises had moved into higher-volume production of standardized machines through fabricating and assembling of standardized parts, making for greater accumulation of capital and greater employment. In 1937 the number of production workers in nonelectrical machinery (654,000) was 31 percent more, and the capital expenditures of $4,097 million were closer to twice the amount than in fabricated metals. Although the number of establishments in nonelectrical machinery, 7,327, was only a little less than in fabricated metals, those small establishments were concentrated in two three-digit subindustry categories, called metalworking (SIC 354) and unclassified industrial machinery (SIC 359).

In the other SIC 35 three-digit categories, companies during the last decades of the nineteenth century had begun to move toward producing standardized machinery used in major labor-intensive industries – textiles, shoes, lumbering, woodworking, printing, mining, and construction. Others concentrated on one major line of products such as pumps and other hydraulic equipment, steam boilers, conveyors and transmission equipment, or even elevators – that is, things used in many industries and businesses. Here products were produced in large batches or in large-bulk units with their final forms shaped to customers' needs. These machinery companies built extensive sales forces that included engineers and other trained personnel to install and help maintain the industrial equipment sold and to make arrangements with customers for financing purchases. But they made little attempt to acquire either their suppliers or the makers of their own capital equipment. By 1914 such leaders as United Shoe Machinery, Mergenthaler Linotype, Babcock & Wilcox, Otis Elevator, Chicago Pneumatic Tool, Worthington Pump, Crown Cork & Seal, and Westinghouse Air Brake, had built plants abroad to support their international marketing activities. Indeed, by that time SIC 35 included more American multinationals than any other SIC category.

It was, however, in the light-machinery industries with the most standardized products that the processes of manufacturing moved closest to the continuous process developed in the chemically processed industries. In harvesters, reapers, and other agricultural equipment; in typewriters, cash registers, adding machines, and other business equipment; and in sewing machinery, American companies had acquired a near monopoly in international markets by 1914. They were operating some of the largest manufacturing works in Britain, Germany, France, and Russia.

Their factories were designed to facilitate sequential line production. Materials moved from the foundry and the receiving areas to the departments making the different parts and then to the final assembly process, so as to assure a smooth and continuing flow of throughput. The production process was not yet fully continuous. The movement of materials through the factory remained relatively slow, and the final finishing and assembling of parts still required their individual filing and other hand work by fitters. Parts were standardized but not yet fully interchangeable.

As these light-machinery producers moved into volume production, they created national and then worldwide wholesale organizations. They quickly discovered that existing jobbers were unable to assure that the retailers who sold their products to the final customers provided essential marketing services including demonstrations and after-sales service and repair. Nor were the jobbers able to supply the retailers with the credit needed by housewives, farmers, and small businessmen to pay for the products. Moreover, independent jobbers were slow in forwarding payments from the retailers to the company's corporate office – payments that were needed to meet current operating costs. In the management of the costs of production the coordination of financial flows was as critical as the coordination of materials. Therefore, most of these companies used their wholesale organizations to provide these services through a network of exclusive franchise dealers – retailers who handled their products exclusively but could also sell related products made by other companies. Thus, a McCormick Harvester dealer sold plows, seeders, and mowers of other companies, lines which McCormick did not produce.

Of the three other machinery groups (SIC 36, 37, and 38), transportation equipment (SIC 37) was still relatively labor-intensive in the early part of this century, producing locomotives, ships, and wooden horsedrawn vehicles. Its capital-intensive, scale-dependent technologies would come with the development of the internal-combustion engine. SIC 38, instruments and related products, also was small, in fact still in its infancy with only 85,000 employees in 1909. Employment in the third (SIC 36, electrical equipment) in 1909 had not yet become large. But its high ratio of capital investment to labor (see Table 2.4) and its technological sophistication indicate its importance for economic growth through technological progress.

The new science-based industries – electrical equipment and chemicals

In the years before World War I, the electrical equipment industry had a far more profound impact on American industry and American life, especially urban living, than had the other science-based industry, chemicals. In SIC 36, the processes of production were technologically far more sophisticated than those in other industries and its marketing and distribution more complex. Its manufacturing works produced systems made up of the many products essential to the generation, transmission, and uses of electric power, and these products were made by different methods. Turbines, generators, and transformers were large, indeed massive, pieces of equipment. They and large electrical motors, streetcars, and subway trains were made by large-batch processes and then customized to purchasers' needs. On the other hand, smaller equipment such as small motors, connectors, circuit breakers, switches, relays, fuse boxes, sockets, light bulbs, and other lighting fixtures lent themselves to more coordinated sequential volume production. Thus, production was concentrated in a very small number of large works designed so that the different shops or factories within the works benefited both from the economies of scope, by using the similar materials and machines, and the economies of scale, by maintaining a steady throughput in the making of small standardized products. Here the coordination of flows to assure delivery of whole systems on schedule was therefore more challenging than in volume-produced light machinery.

The first companies to make the large investment in plant and equipment and to recruit the substantial number of workers and managers required to produce electric-power systems quickly dominated the industry. By the mid-1890s, little more than a decade after Thomas Edison completed the nation's first central electric power station at Pearl Street in New York in 1882, four enterprises – two American and two German – already dominated world markets and would continue to do so until well after World War II. The American firms were General Electric (GE), an 1892 merger of Thomson-Houston and Edison General Electric, and Westinghouse. The German ones were Siemens and Allgemeine Elektricitäts Gesellschaft (AEG).

A marketing organization was more essential to this new industry than to any others, for the installation and initial operations of electrical equipment by untrained workers could bring death or serious injury by electrocution. Thus, the first movers immediately created the national sales forces not only to market but also to install and service. Thomson-Houston, even before its merger with Edison General Electric in 1892, had built production plants in Britain and France. Westinghouse followed with works in Britain in 1899 and then in France, Germany, and Russia.

Because its products were so costly, General Electric, following the model of Siemens and AEG, formed a credit company – Electric Bond & Share – to take payment in shares of the new utility companies it equipped.

The technology of producing of electrical equipment, based as it was on physics and mathematics, was so sophisticated that it quickly led to the creation of the nation's first industrial research and development organization. General Electric, after setting up laboratories at its primary works in Lynn, Massachusetts, and Schenectady, New York, established in 1901 a research laboratory headed by an MIT professor, Willis R. Whitney. Within a decade Whitney's team developed vacuum tubes, tungsten filaments for better lighting, x-ray equipment, improved plastics for insulation, and metal alloys for better-performing equipment. All became major lines in the company's product portfolio, thus providing a foretaste of the potential of the economies of scope in the science-based industries where a firm would commercialize new products on the basis of its learned organizational capabilities.

By the turn of the century, the science-based electrical equipment industry was already a driving force in the growth and transformation of the American economy. Not only did new works create a multitude of new jobs, but as the industry grew, smaller regional and niche firms began to produce specialized equipment, replacement parts, or both. The products of the first movers provided a brand-new source of light (replacing kerosene) and power (replacing steam) in many of the mechanical and chemical processes of production; a new form of urban transportation (streetcars and subways); and the new electrolytic process of producing chemicals, aluminum, and abrasives.

Also in the last two decades of the century another electrical product, the telephone, began to transform communications. The telephone industry was quickly dominated by a single enterprise – Bell Telephone and its successor, American Telephone & Telegraph (AT&T) – which built a huge production plant outside Chicago and set up a research organization comparable to that of GE. By 1914 its manufacturing subsidiary, Western Electric, had plants in Great Britain, Germany, France, Austria, Italy, Russia, and Canada.

In this same initial period of rapid growth, the other major science-based industry, chemicals, was on the rise. The rapid expansion of the chemical-processed industries – glass, paper, primary metals, oil, and rubber – had brought comparable expansion and output for the chemicals used in their production. This swelling demand led to more continuous-process methods and the resulting scale economies to the production of chemicals themselves. However, modern capital-intensive, scale-dependent chemical industry only began in the United States with the introduction of the new electrolytic process. Dow, American Cyanamid, and forerunners of Union Carbide and Allied Chemical had their start at the turn of the century producing inorganic chemicals with this high-volume process. It required so much energy that Niagara Falls became for the making of those chemicals (and also aluminum and abrasives) what the Merrimack River had been sixty years earlier for the mechanized production of textiles.

By World War I the major players in the capital-intensive industrial oligopolies had established themselves. Many of these firms remained the leaders in their industries for the next half century. Some would disappear by merger, and others would drop off the list of the top 200 as new technologies brought new industrial leaders to the top. Because of continuing oligopolistic competition, rankings in terms of sales, market share, and profit within an industry rose and fell. Nevertheless the first movers, those that made the large initial investment in capital equipment, continued during the following decades to make large-scale investments in physical capital, in most cases funded by retained earnings, and to be among the nation's major employers of industrial workers. The barriers to entry became so high that few challengers entered the oligopoly. These enterprises thus became learning bases for further development of products and processes. They remained at the core of a network of suppliers, dealers, and other related firms.

CAPITAL ACCUMULATION AND AUGMENTATION, 1914–1950

During the years from 1914 to 1950 – the period when global wars, depressions, and international turmoil dissipated the opportunities for continuing growth and productivity in Europe – such opportunities continued in the United States until the coming of the Great Depression in 1930. Continuing capital accumulation and "learning by doing" increased output per worker and value-added in manufacturing in the capital-intensive and scale-dependent industries that had been created earlier. But the major dynamic for growth through technical progress during the interwar years came from the new and improved technologies based on the internal-combustion engine. The motor vehicle industry had the most profound impact.

The impact of the internal-combustion engine

As the twentieth century opened, the gasoline-driven internal-combustion engine was just beginning to be a source of energy that competed with steam and the new electric power. Its most immediate and most profound effect was on transportation and on the mechanical processes of production. After 1900, the year Ransom E. Olds demonstrated the commercial viability of the automobile by producing and selling 500 of his Oldsmobiles, the auto industry grew exuberantly. A decade later, in 1911, 200,000 passenger cars were sold; by 1919, 1.5 million; by 1929, 4.5 million. Then, with the Depression, the industry suffered a staggering sales drop to 1.1 million in 1932. It recovered to 3.9 million in 1937 and fell back to 2.9 million in 1939. The three-digit SIC industry, motor vehicles and equipment (SIC 371) had not been listed in 1899. By 1914 it was still fifteenth among all three-digit classifications in number of workers, seventh in wages, sixth in value-added, and ninth in value of products. By 1935, however, it ranked first in all but number of workers, where it ranked third.

This massive growth marked the culmination of the capital-augmenting sequential production line that had begun with the processors of grain and the makers of agricultural equipment and other light machinery in the 1880s. The moving assembly line that went into operation at Henry Ford's Highland Park plant in the summer of 1913 incorporated the most advanced materials, metalworking machinery, and plant design developed during the two previous decades. With the completion of the assembly line, throughput soared. Work hours expended on the production of an automobile fell from 12 hours and 8 minutes in 1913 to 1 hour and 35 minutes in April 1914. By then Highland Park was producing 1,000 cars a day. The resulting scale economies of throughput permitted Ford to sell his cars at far lower prices than any competitor, to pay the highest wages in the industry, and to acquire within a decade an enormous personal fortune.

In distribution Ford followed the earlier light-machinery companies by setting up exclusive franchise dealers supported by the company's international wholesale network. That organization scheduled deliveries of cars and monitored dealers' service and repair facilities, advertising, and payments to the corporate office. In distribution the Ford Motor Company carried out another impressive innovation, the branch assembly plant which assembled "knocked-down kits," thus reducing shipping costs while maintaining the cost advantages of scale. By 1913 Ford had already built thirteen assembly plants in the United States and one in Manchester, England. Other manufacturers soon followed Ford's example in both production and distribution. By 1929 over 6,500 franchised dealers were selling the output of the leading automobile manufacturers.

In the 1920s two companies – General Motors and Chrysler – began to challenge Ford's dominance. They did so by developing a full line of cars and commercial vehicles – in the terms of General Motors' advertising slogan, a vehicle for "every purse and purpose." This strategy permitted the companies to exploit the economies of scope by having their different end products and their parts and accessories made of much the same materials and by much the same machinery. In time this strategy also drove single-line, middle-price producers out of business – companies such as Packard, Studebaker, Hudson, and Nash. In 1935 the "Big Three" held 90.9 percent of the domestic market. By then Ford's share had dropped to 28 percent. General Motors had risen to 39.2 percent and Chrysler 23.7. Well before that date the U.S. manufacturers dominated world markets. In 1928, 72 percent of all cars exported from one country to another were American, 6 percent French, 5 percent British, and 1 percent German. In the 1930s the subsidiaries of General Motors and Ford were major producers in Britain, Germany, and Japan.

The "Big Three" concentrated on cars and light commercial vehicles. In the production of heavier, more specialized trucks and trailers, both the output and value of production were much smaller (882,100 units produced in 1929 as compared with 4.5 million cars and value-added of $62 million as opposed to $2,790 million). Here sequential, usually large-batch, production remained the mode. Here too niche companies throve, but by exploiting the economies of both scale and scope, some truck companies did become large. By World War II, White Motors, Mack Truck, and Fruehauf Trailer were listed among the 200 largest U.S. industrial enterprises.

The industry producing motor vehicle parts and accessories (SIC 3714) became one of the nation's largest four-digit industries. This occurred because of the zooming requirements of the truck and automobile firms and also because the makers of agricultural, industrial, construction, and mining machinery needed comparable equipment. By 1935 the number of employees hired and the amount of wages paid in SIC 3714 were even greater than in the production of the motor vehicles alone (SIC 3711). The leading parts makers – Borg-Warner, Bendix, Dana, and Thompson Products – were among the nation's largest companies.

During the 1930s the internal-combustion engine became the source of motive power for ships and railroads, and reshaped agricultural and construction equipment. It also became the essential ingredient in the creation of the aircraft industry. One of General Motors' major achievements in the 1930s was the commercialization of the diesel locomotive, which within a decade made the steam locomotive obsolete. In the early 1920s both International Harvester and John Deere had developed all-purpose farm tractors. Caterpillar Tractor commercialized and continued to improve the tracked (as differentiated from wheeled) tractor for highway and building construction. These companies and a handful of smaller competitors quickly diversified into each others' markets as well as remaining leaders in international markets.

The new demands created by the internal-combustion engine made existing capital-intensive industries still more capital-intensive and often brought an increase in the number of players in their respective oligopolies. For example, the unprecedented demand for gasoline and lubricating oil brought a series of technological innovations that increased refinery output by 270 percent between 1919 and 1929, while the number of refining establishments was rising only 22 percent and the number of employees 29 percent. By the 1930s the petroleum industry was by far the most capital-intensive in the United States and the third largest (after food and primary metals) in expenditures for capital goods. Increased throughput brought more vertical integration. By 1939 the twenty largest companies in the industry held 96.5 percent of the U.S. crude oil stocks. The opening of new fields at home and abroad, as well as the huge new markets created by motor vehicles, enlarged the size of the global oil oligopoly. But the reduction of demand during the Great Depression reduced the number of major players. By the coming of World War II the so-called Seven Sisters – five American firms, one British, and one Anglo-Dutch – dominated global markets. Over the past half century this pattern of oligopoly has changed little.

In rubber (SIC 30) the swift expansion of demand for pneumatic tires turned production from exploiting the economies of scope to those of scale. In tires (SIC 301), production per man-hour rose 433 percent, between 1914 and 1935, the largest increase of any three-digit industry. By World War I two new tire makers, Firestone and Goodyear, together with the existing leaders, U.S. Rubber and Goodrich, dominated the industry. They all went abroad in the 1920s where they competed with a French firm, Michelin; a British firm, Dunlop; and a German firm, Continental.

In glass and primary metals the impact of motor vehicle production was less, as that new market took a smaller portion of their industries' total output than was the case with oil and rubber. Nevertheless, by creating a huge new demand for glass, the industry added two more members to the international glass oligopoly. And the new demand for primary metals stimulated innovations in light metals and alloys and the development of hot (and also cold) continuous-strip steel mills. The independents quickly took up these innovations and so strengthened their market positions vis-à-vis U.S. Steel.

The science-based industries – electrical equipment and chemicals – 1914–1950

Second only to the internal-combustion engine in contributing to increased productivity and growth through technical progress during the war and interwar years was the rapid expansion of the two major American science-based industries, electrical equipment and chemicals. They led the way both in the employment of highly skilled nonproduction workers and the creation of large research and development organizations. In chemicals (SIC 28), scientific personnel in 1921 accounted for 30.4 percent of total scientific personnel employed in U.S. manufacturing, followed by primary metals with 8.2 percent and electrical equipment with 7.2 percent. By 1946 the figure for chemicals remained almost exactly the same, 30.6 percent. Electrical had risen to 15.5 and metals had dropped to 5.3.

During these years the electrical industry moved along the trajectory it had begun before 1900, and the chemical industry for the first time came into its own. Both benefited from the forced departure of the German first movers from global markets during the four years of World War I, then followed by five years of military occupation of the industrial Rhineland and Ruhr and explosive inflation.

With the removal of the Germans, General Electric became the industry's dominant firm in global competition, with Westinghouse a good bit behind. In 1929 GE's Associated Electrical Industries was the second largest electrical manufacturer in Britain. It held 25 percent of the voting shares of Germany's AGE and had a controlling interest in leading electrical manufacturers in France, Mexico, South Africa, and Japan. At home its research and development laboratories gave it first-mover advantages in x-rays and other medical equipment, in electrical household appliances and radio, and made it a major player in the production of alloys, plastics, and other man-made materials. The new product lines required substantial investment in both new production facilities and marketing organizations. In appliances, where rapid growth came through the use of assembly-line production, the company set up a separate "merchandising" department. Of particular importance was the development, production, and distribution of radio receiving and transmitting equipment carried out by the Radio Corporation of America (RCA), which had been formed in 1919 as a joint venture of GE, Westinghouse, and AT&T's Western Electric. In 1930 these owners sold off their interests in RCA, which then set up its own laboratories, which, besides improving radio and other electronic products, pioneered in the development of television.

In these same years the R&D departments at GE, Westinghouse, and Western Electric continued to improve existing products and develop new ones. At GE, for example, the number of product lines (the ones whose operating results were accounted for separately) rose from 10 in 1900, to 85 in 1920, to 193 in 1930, to 281 in 1940. In these years GE, Westinghouse, and AT&T's Bell Laboratories laid much of the technological base for the electronic technologies that so transformed their industry after World War II.

In chemicals the dislodgment of the Germans who had dominated the organic chemical branch since the 1880s permitted the leading American firms to move into the production of dyes, pharmaceuticals, agricultural and other chemicals. These firms included the previously mentioned leaders in inorganic chemicals produced through the highly capital-intensive electrolytic processes. They also included Du Pont, which, after an industry-wide merger in 1903, dominated the explosives industry. After World War I all these firms built large research and development organizations following the example of Du Pont, which had established the industry's first formal R&D department in 1902.

During the 1920s each of the major producers of chemicals improved its existing products and commercialized new ones on the basis of the highly product-specific organizational capabilities that had evolved from the production and distribution of its initial product line. Du Pont, for example, used its strength in nitrocellulose organic chemistry to move into the production of rayon, cellophane, photographic film, refrigerants, and pigments, as well as making synthetic ammonia by new high-pressure technology. For the new automobile market, the firm began producing quick-drying paints, antifreeze, and ethyl gasoline additives. Another company, Dow, grew by exploiting its inorganic electrochemical capabilities to produce, based on chlorine, the following: bleaches, chloroform, carbon tetrachloride, insecticides, and fungicides. Union Carbide, a 1917 merger, used its learned skills based on carbides to produce carbon electrodes and metal alloys, and then moved to the production of organic products derived from waste gas of oil refineries. American Cyanamid at its Niagara Falls plant was the first American firm to produce a synthetic fertilizer. Allied Chemical, created in a 1920 merger, concentrated more on products based on coal tar and coke-oven gas – byproducts from iron and steel making. Monsanto grew rapidly by producing saccharine and then caffeine, vanilla, and other fine chemicals based on German intermediates and plant equipment. It was able to grow more rapidly than it had before the war by producing its own intermediates and obtaining equipment from U.S. suppliers. The exploitation of the economies of scope in this knowledge-based industry that permitted the development of new lines of products laid the groundwork for the polymer/petrochemical technologies whose impact on American production after World War II was second only to that of the new electronic technologies.

For the pharmaceutical industry the pattern was much the same. Growth of the leading U.S. producers came with the exploitation of German-developed coal-tar pharmaceutical technologies that produced aspirin and other barbiturates, serums for diphtheria, cholera, and other deadly diseases, and novocaine and other pain killers. The capabilities learned in developing these products through systematic research and development helped to lay the base for the antibiotic technologies that transformed the U.S. pharmaceutical industry during and after World War II.

During the 1930s the economic growth propelled by the coming of the internal-combustion engine, particularly the motor vehicle, came to an end. Although the science-based industries continued to commercialize new products and processes, the collapse of the automobile market and with it the demand for steel, glass, petroleum, and rubber was a significant factor in bringing on the Great Depression and with it the sharpest drop in gross national product to occur in the twentieth century. Nevertheless, during those interwar years, the capital accumulation and learning base were laid for the commercializing of new technologies that would drive economic growth after World War II. For, unlike the two earlier periods, the years after World War II would see the commercializing of basic new technologies not by newly formed companies but by established enterprises that used their learned capabilities to bring the resulting new industries on stream.

THE KNOWLEDGE-BASED INDUSTRIES AFTER
WORLD WAR II

The military demands of the two-front global war jump-started the American economy. It quickly brought full employment and a high level of capital utilization. Even more important in terms of long-term growth, the demands of the high-tech war provided the necessary large-scale investment and the "learning by doing" essential to commercialize new technologies that drove technical progress in the postwar years. The demands for military planes created the modern aviation industry. In 1939, only 5,865 planes were built in the United States, but in 1943 there were 85,433, and in 1944 there were 95,272. This expansion brought basic innovations in the design of aircraft bodies and engines, including jet engine propulsion, and in the processes of production. Crash programs in the development and production of high-octane gasoline and synthetic rubber helped to reshape the chemical industry on the basis of the new polymer/petrochemical technologies. The government-sponsored development of penicillin and sulpha drugs led to the therapeutic revolution that so transformed the pharmaceutical industry. Finally, the large-scale production of radio, radar, sonar, fire control equipment, and other electronic devices created new technologies that were central to the postwar information revolution.

The leaders in these transformed high-tech industries quickly replaced those of older industries on the list of the largest 200 U.S. industrial firms. Between 1948 and 1988 the large majority of new entries to that list came in chemicals (SIC 28) and electrical equipment (SIC 36). The number in chemicals rose from 23 in 1948 to 28 in 1973 then to 40 in 1988. Pharmaceuticals (SIC 283) added the most, going from 3 in 1948 to 7 in 1973 and to 12 in 1988. Of the 40 chemical firms on the list in 1988, all but one, a 1980s Wall Street concoction, had prewar roots. Most had been established before 1920. In electrical equipment the count in the top 200 went from 7 in 1948 to 16 in 1973, and then to 21 in 1988, and 4 more were ranked between 200 and 213. However, it was only in electrical equipment that postwar start-up firms began to be listed among the nation's biggest industrial firms. By 1973 two of them had made the top 200, and by 1983 eight more were found among the top 215. Of these ten firms, all but one (Xerox) was based on the new integrated circuit technologies. During these years the number of transportation equipment (SIC 37) firms remained about the same, but several of the leaders in the motor vehicle and related industries were replaced by aircraft and aero-space firms.

In 1987 the 200 largest industrial companies accounted for 43 percent of all value-added in U.S. manufacturing and 47 percent of new capital expenditures. Of the 200 in 1988, 86 were in high-tech categories – SIC 28, 36, 37, and 38 (scientific instruments). Except for the electronics firms, all these companies had been established before 1941 and a sizable number before 1914, a testimony to the significance of the large industrial firm as an instrument for capital accumulation and the acquisition of new product-specific knowledge.

Because of space limitation, I say little about aircraft and aerospace and instead concentrate on the contributions the leading firms in chemicals and electronics made to economic growth through technical progress. As to aircraft, I need only to point out that the first movers continued to maintain their competitive strength. Boeing had built the first all-metal airliner in 1933 and the first over-the-water commercial plane, the Clipper, in 1935. It became the largest producer of bombers during the war and was the first to build a commercial jet, the Boeing 707. Douglas, which merged with an aerospace firm, McDonnell, in 1967, produced the DC-3 in 1935. Its postgenerations of DCs remain Boeing's major competitor. Pratt & Whitney (now part of United Technologies) and General Electric, the first firms to commercialize the jet engine (in the 1940s), still dominate global markets for aircraft engines.

Polymer/petrochemical revolution

The polymer/petrochemical revolution that so reshaped the chemical industry reflected a simultaneous and dramatic shift in sources of supply and product markets. On the supply side crude oil and natural gas replaced coal as a cheaper and more versatile raw material. The U.S. chemical companies completed the shift by the mid-1950s. On the demand side, polymers – long-chain molecules usually having a carbon backbone – became the basis for a cornucopia of new products, opening up huge new markets. As a result, by 1970 the chemical industry's fixed assets per production worker, though well behind oil, was substantially higher than that of any other two-digit SIC category. It had the largest annual new capital expenditures, $3,111 million, of any of the two-digit groups.

The petrochemical and polymer revolution had prewar roots. Oil and chemical companies had begun to move into oil-based chemicals in the 1930s. Four oil companies – Jersey Standard (Exxon), Standard of California, Shell, and Phillips – had followed Union Carbide into the small-scale production of solvents and a few other products from petrochemicals. But it was the long-established chemical companies that pioneered in the development of the new basic polymer intermediates and the initial polymer end products. During the 1930s Union Carbide led the way in commercializing polyvinyl chloride (PVC). At the same time Dow's research on styrene pioneered in the development of a basic monomer, liquid styrene, and then a polymer, polystyrene (PS), and an end product, Styrofoam. The same company developed another oil-based chemical, vinylidene chloride, with Saran as an end product having many uses. The wartime programs in high-octane gasoline and synthetic rubber created an unprecedented demand for both PVC and PS as well as such oil-based feedstocks as styrene, ethylene, and chlorine. During the war, in 1943, Du Pont began the production of polyethylene, a polymer discovered at Imperial Chemical Industries (ICI) which Du Pont received through its Patent and Process Agreement with its long-time British ally. By the mid-1950s two more versatile polymers had been commercialized, high-density polyethylene (HDPE) and polypropylene (PP).

The commercialization of finished products such as Styrofoam and Saran from these intermediates began shortly before World War II. Du Pont in 1939 started producing nylon, an artificial silk, the first fiber that was wholly chemically made; and neoprene, a substitute for rubber. After the war came a stream of other polymer-based fibers (at Du Pont these included Dacron, Orlon, and Lycra spandex) that replaced natural fibers or blended well with them, as did acrylic-based fibers produced by Monsanto and Rohm and Haas. By 1985 man-made fibers pouring out of these and other chemical companies accounted by one estimate for 71.6 percent of the total fibers produced in the United States.

As one type of polymers was replacing natural fibers, another type, the so-called engineering plastics, was replacing metals, glass, paper, and other substances. These included strong impact-resisting materials that were more easily shaped and more cheaply fabricated than metals; also materials with unprecedented insulating, adhesive, and mechanical properties; certain packaging and wrapping materials; improved coatings and finishes; and lighter and stronger substitutes for glass, such as plexiglass and Lucite. By the 1980s the production of plastics had become a major American industry, taking markets from the producers of both primary and fabricated metals. For example, the plastic usage in an automobile rose from 12 pounds in 1950 to roughly 200 pounds by the 1970s.

For agricultural markets came new fertilizers, herbicides, pesticides, growth regulating and other crop-control products. New biological chemicals brought new medicines for humans and animals. Moreover, all of these new end products required, and often were the result of, reshaping existing intermediates and developing new ones. The production of such intermediate chemicals became a major industry of its own. All these new product markets expanded rapidly during the 1950s and well into the 1960s and in some cases beyond. Between 1950 and 1970 the overall chemical market grew at annual rates of about 2.5 times the growth rate of the gross national product.

The huge growth of markets and the availability of cheap, low-cost raw materials intensified the need for technological innovation to increase minimum-efficient scale of chemical plants. At first, throughput of existing plants was expanded on the basis of existing technology by adding another set or "train" of production processes. But merely enlarging the capacity of plants by building parallel units reduced unit costs only slightly. By means of the knowledge acquired in increasing the production of gasoline before and during the war, facilities were reshaped into "single train" plants. The construction and further improvements of such facilities, carried out by independent engineering firms, soon became a niche global industry in its own right.

During these years of growth some leaders, such as Du Pont, Monsanto, and Rohm and Haas, concentrated on the production of end products. Others, including Dow, Union Carbide, and Hercules, focused on expanding the high-volume commodity production of polymer intermediates. All continued to produce nonpolymer products that they had commercialized earlier in the century. Those concentrating on commodity polymers integrated backward to take control of refineries and even oil fields. The same concern for assured supplies caused those companies that focused more on specialty end products to maintain their production of the intermediates needed in their production processes.

As the new "single train" works came on stream and capacity soared, competition became intense. Overcapacity ruled, because minimum-efficient scale had become so much higher. So unit costs rose as the new plants operated at well below that scale. Then came the global oil crises. In 1973 the price of a standard Arabian crude rose to $11.65 a barrel (it had been $1.80 in 1970), and in 1979 it was a staggering $34.

Fierce competition, higher production unit costs, and the sharp rise in raw material costs led to one of the most significant restructuring of companies and industries that occurred in the United States during the 1970s and 1980s. Many chemical companies, whose organizational capabilities had been shaped by commercializing new products and processes, sold off their commodity polymer businesses, while oil companies, whose capabilities had always been in the exploitation of scale economies inherent in massive continuous-process production, expanded their investment in commodity polymers.

In reshaping their product lines these companies not only retained a heavy R&D commitment to the most technologically advanced products, but also focused on maintaining other lines where their long-established organizational capabilities gave them competitive strength. Thus Du Pont purchased Exxon's carbon fiber business and Hercules' Olefin Fiber Carpets Division while trading its acrylic fiber business to ICI for the latter's nylon operations. It also acquired Shell's Agricultural Chemical Division and Ford's North American Automotive Paint Division. Such product-portfolio-realigning transactions carried out by major chemical companies ran into billions of dollars.

This reconstruction strengthened the chemical industry's competitive position in international markets. By the late 1980s the industry had a surplus of exports over imports of $15.4 billion and was second only to aircraft and aerospace in that respect. Of more importance in terms of revenue earned, by 1990 a number of the leaders were reporting that 30 to 50 percent of their sales were made in foreign markets, largely from their foreign subsidiaries. In international markets the primary competitors of the U.S. chemical industry were comparable long-established German, British, and Swiss firms with roots in the nineteenth century. By then the Japanese were only beginning to enter European and American markets.

By the late 1980s the chemical companies, often using the funds received from divestitures, were expanding their output of specialty polymers and other intermediates and of such end products as additives for gasoline and food, industrial coatings, enzymes, electronic chemicals, new fibers, fiber and metal composites, new engineering plastics, ceramics, imaging equipment, electronic materials, pharmaceuticals, and medical equipment. By 1986, petroleum refining (SIC 291) still had the nation's highest fixed assets and new capital expenditures per worker. Nevertheless, total capital expenditures of the three largest three-digit SIC industries, industrial organic chemicals (SIC 286), plastics materials and synthetics (SIC 282), and inorganic chemicals (SIC 281) totaled twice the capital expenditures of petroleum refining. In value-added in manufacturing, organic chemicals with $14.7 billion and plastics with $14.1 billion were even greater than petroleum refining with $13.7 billion.

The therapeutic revolution

The development of antibiotics during World War II led the way in transforming the United States drug industry. In 1940 the first sulpha drugs had only begun to be produced commercially and penicillin had just been discovered in Britain. In the United States a government crash program was instituted to produce both. In 1942 Merck brought out the first industrially made penicillin. Pfizer, Squibb, and other established drug firms quickly followed. By the end of the war both sulpha and penicillin were produced in volume. After the war, these drug companies developed a broad range of antibiotics (such as Aureomycin and Terramycin), antihistamines, steroids, and other pharmaceuticals.

Before the war, American drug companies had carried on three businesses. They produced drugs in bulk, which were sold to pharmacists to be retailed or to be mixed into doctors' prescriptions. They made, packaged, and sold "ethical" or prescription drugs. Their third business included pills, powders and liquid patented (therefore "proprietary") medicines sold over the counter without prescriptions, as well as cosmetics, toiletries, and health care products sold over the same retail counters. With the coming of antibiotics and other related products, prescription drugs became their primary business. Production became a complex chemical process rather than a simple mixing or bottling one. Marketing shifted from selling in bulk or over the counter to contacting the doctors who wrote the prescriptions and the hospitals where they were used. Research became far more science-based and much more costly.

Those companies that made the transformation successfully in the late 1940s and 1950s are still the industry's leaders in the 1990s. By 1988, for eight of the twelve drug companies listed among the top 200 U.S. industrials, prescription drugs accounted for more than half their revenues, and for most more than two-thirds. Although income from exports was small, the revenue from foreign subsidiaries ranged from 30 to 50 percent for several of the leaders. As in chemicals, the competitors were European companies with comparable roots in the nineteenth and early twentieth centuries. Again, Japanese firms have made very few inroads into international markets.

These same 70- to 100-year-old U.S. leaders played a critical role in commercializing a most significant post–World War II technological paradigm, that based on recombinant DNA. The companies began investing in the new technology in the late 1970s, expanding their commitments in the following years. They also supported entrepreneurial start-ups, essentially research enterprises established by geneticists and biologists. The established firms provided these new research enterprises with essential production facilities and marketing outlets, as well as funding their continuing research and costly clinical trials. The new biotech concerns first licensed their products and then formed alliances with the large pharmaceutical companies that permitted them to develop their own production and, most important of all, the marketing organizations and capabilities essential to becoming full-line pharmaceutical competitors. In turn, such alliances permitted the established companies to develop their capabilities in the new technology more quickly than if they had begun the initial research in their own laboratories. The major beneficiaries of this symbiotic relationship have been the long-established enterprises. In 1994, only four of the twenty-five leading U.S. biopharmaceutical companies posted a profit – Amgen, Genetech, Chiron, and Genzyme. Two of these, Genetech and Chiron, were controlled by full-line century old pharmaceutical firms.

The electronics revolution

The foregoing review of the transformation of the chemical and pharmaceutical industries documents the central role that large enterprises have played in the technological progress of the knowledge-intensive industries of the late twentieth century. With few exceptions the new technologies were exploited by long-established large firms whose learned R&D capabilities gave them a powerful advantage over start-ups, or firms whose capabilities rested on the commercializing of less closely related technologies. The history of the electronics sector documents this point from a different perspective, for the technological innovations that drove growth in that industry came after World War II. The new semiconductor or "chip" technologies based on the transistor patented in 1948 and the integrated circuit patented in 1959, required the creation of a new set of capabilities and so provided more opportunities for start-ups and younger firms than existed in chemicals and pharmaceuticals. Nevertheless, an even smaller number of large enterprises came to dominate global markets even more powerfully than had been the case in the commercializing of new capital-intensive, scale-intensive technologies earlier in the century.

In consumer electronics the leading U.S. firms lost out to large Japanese enterprises, in good part because they failed to move quickly into the new transistor technology. As late as the 1960s, RCA, Zenith, and others were relying more on vacuum tubes than transistors or integrated circuits to power their products. In contrast, one of Japan's first major postwar exports was the transistor radio. The critical loss of the U.S. industry, however, came in the late 1960s and early 1970s when its leader, RCA, after developing and then dominating color television, failed to maintain its distinctive learned capabilities.

First it turned to commercializing a very different new electronic product, the large general purpose digital computer. It entered the market in 1965 shortly before IBM's large multiproduct System 360 came on stream. After spending half a billion dollars and five years of research effort, RCA gave up the project in 1970. The appearance of IBM's second-generation System 370 made it clear that RCA could not catch up with the industry's first mover.

RCA then began a strategy of unrelated diversification. That growth strategy, then popular in American industry, quickly dissipated RCA's funds and managerial and technical capabilities – as it did in other U.S. companies. RCA purchased car rental, frozen food, and carpet-producing companies and others providing financial and legal services. By 1975 only 25 percent of its revenue came from electronics. In the meantime, RCA's smaller U.S. competitors were finding it impossible to compete in price and performance with the high-volume Japanese electronic companies. By the 1970s, Matsushita, Sanyo, Sony, and Sharp were rapidly conquering American and European markets. Only Holland's Philips was able to hang on.

If the history of U.S. consumer electronics provides an example of the dissipation of organizational capabilities, the history of the computer – or, more properly, the electronic data-processing industry – provides an example of the successful creation of such capabilities. Success, however, came to the long-established makers of business machinery and not to electrical equipment manufacturers. Both types of companies had pioneered in computers during the 1950s on the basis of government contracts, primarily from the Department of Defense. The business machinery makers were International Business Machines (punch cards); Remington-Rand (typewriters); National Cash Register; Burroughs (adding machines); and Honeywell (heat regulators). IBM surged ahead of the rest by a strategy of almost continuous product development. It commercialized machines for two nondefense markets, one for business and commerce that called for a variety of uses but did not demand complex computation tasks, and the other for university and engineering enterprises where computing power was more important than a broad range of applications. By 1960 IBM had produced fifteen different nonmilitary computer systems. No other company had developed more than three or four. Within seven years it had transformed itself from being the world's leader in punch cards for record-keeping to becoming the world's leader in the new electronic computing technology.

IBM's fifteen systems used different types of components, peripherals, and other auxiliaries. In 1961, however, IBM senior managers made one of the boldest strategic moves in U.S. industrial history. The company would build a new generation of computers, covering a broad range of price and performance markets, for which all the hardware and software would be compatible. IBM would make its own hardware – printers, disk drives, and other peripherals, as well as semiconductors. The latter would not be based on transistors, but on the just invented, still untested integrated circuits. As Kenneth Flamm (the industry's historian) points out, the new System 360 benefited from the economies of scale in research, development, and production – and from the economies of scope in software and also in research.

Bringing the new products on stream and integrating them at different levels of price and performance proved to be enormously costly and risky. It was also an unparalleled learning experience. The cost of developing the new SIL chips went way beyond all estimates. By 1964 more money was spent on software development than had been originally planned for the entire project. The year of crisis was 1966, when there was over $600 million in the inventory of work in process. By 1967, the multitude of products began to pour onto the market. By 1969 IBM had captured 70 percent of the world market for general purpose computers. The System 360 provides a classic example of the embodiment of human with physical capital so essential to technological advance. And no other company in the world had the resources and experience required to accomplish such a task.

While IBM was in the throes of creating a System 360, new entre-preneurial firms entered the market at its low and high end. At the low end came the makers of minicomputers – small high-powered systems for university and engineering use. The first of these companies, Digital Equipment Corporation (DEC), was formed in 1957 by Kenneth Olsen, an MIT engineer who had been involved in developing defense computers and worked for a while at IBM during the 1950s. Its first successful products, the PD6 and the PD8, both using integrated-circuit technolo-gies, appeared in 1965. Then came Data General established in 1968 by Edson de Castro, who had headed the PD8 project at DEC. In the early 1970s two Massachusetts firms, Prime Computer and Wang, had moved into the production of minicomputers, and so did Hewlett-Packard, the California instrument maker, and then IBM itself. By 1980 minicom-puters accounted for 30 percent of the total computer market. At the high end of the price-performance scale, Control Data built the first super-computer, a very fast powerful mainframe computer capable of handling highly complex problems. This was announced in 1962 but the first shipment came only in 1966. In 1972 Seymour Cray, Control Data's top designer, left to start his own supercomputer firm, Cray Research.

In 1965 General Electric as well as RCA began to compete directly with the IBM 360 in mainframe products, but in 1970, after IBM's announcement of the improved System 370, GE, like RCA, decided it could not catch up with the first mover and left the market. RCA had spent over half a billion dollars, and GE had planned to spend even more, in an attempt to compete in a technology where neither had developed the necessary learning base and the resulting organizational capabilities.

IBM's stiffest competition in the 1970s came from its own products made by other companies, some under license, but more often not. (Under a U.S. Department of Justice antitrust consent decree in 1956 IBM had agreed to license its innovations to all comers.) Control Data led the way in producing IBM-compatible equipment or clones by building a full line of peripherals, first for its own use and then for selling to other comp-anies. By retroengineering and making slight changes, it stayed abreast of IBM's products without incurring development costs. Even before the growth of a replacement market, smaller companies quickly began to make IBM System 360 disk drives, printers, add-on memories, boards, and the like.

The first to attempt to clone the 360 itself came when Gene Amdahl, one of the key engineers in its development, left IBM in 1970 to form his own company. In 1972, when Amdahl needed funds to complete his project, he turned to the leading Japanese computer maker, Fujitsu. That firm, with other Japanese companies and the government agency, MITI, was then attempting to develop competitive computer technology, and was delighted to oblige. It acquired 24 percent of Amdahl's equity in exchange for technical information. Three years later Fujitsu announced that it would make computers in Japan for Amdahl to sell in the United States. As Kenneth Flamm notes: "This was the turning point for the Japanese computer industry. At last it had acquired the ability to produce computers competitively with the latest IBM models" (p. 195).

Fujitsu, working with Hitachi, developed the "M-Series" of IBM-compatible computers and peripherals. By 1976 Fujitsu had committed an additional $54 million to Amdahl, and in 1979 it increased its controlling share of the American company to 49 percent. As Marie Anchordoguy, the historian of the Japanese computer industry noted in 1989, "The M-Series today remains the mainstay of Fujitsu's and Hitachi's offerings" (p. 115). By the mid 1980s the leading European producers were getting their mainframes from Japan to sell under their own labels. Fujitsu made those sold under the labels of Siemens and Britain's ICL; Hitachi made those sold through BASF and Olivetti, and NEC made those sold by France's Bull.

Thus no learning base existed in Europe to nurture capabilities essential for continuing product and technological development. As Flamm pointed out in 1987, "The market for large business machines in Europe is now mainly competition between IBM and other American and Japanese computers." Millions spent on research by European governments and companies remained disembodied, wasted.

The history of the IBM 360/370, besides underlining the essential need for such a learning base if a national industry is to remain viable, emphasizes the importance of new technologies as a source of capital accumulation. Worldwide revenue of the U.S. computers and their related products rose from $1.0 million in 1960 to $2.5 *billion* in 1965 to $10 billion in 1970, to $21 billion in 1971, and to $37 billion in 1979, giving a compound annual growth rate of 33.5 percent. The capital value of the general purpose systems rose from much less than a billion dollars in 1960 to $5 billion in 1965, $18 billion in 1970, $30 billion in 1975, and $50 billion in 1979. By 1971, 45 percent of computers made in the United States were sold abroad for a value of $3.5 billion. By the mid-1970s U.S. firms, largely IBM, produced most of the computers sold in France and

West Germany, and at least two-thirds of those in Britain and still close to 40 percent sold in Japan.

Finally, as the computer production soared, so too did the production of related products. In this way the few companies producing mainframes and minicomputers became the core of an increasingly global network of producers, not only of peripherals but also of semiconductors and other components, software, and a wide variety of consumer computer services. For example the revenue from services rose in the United States alone from an estimated $500–$700 million in 1965 to $1.0 billion in 1973, $3.2 billion in 1975, and $5.5 billion in 1975. Revenue from software went from $400 million in 1968 to $1.1 billion in 1976 and to $2.1 billion in 1980.

The huge increase in output of computers and computer services transformed the production of chips and software. The shift to standardized chips and packaged software had parallels to the shift to high-volume production in light machinery in the 1880s and 1890s and automobiles after 1915. The transformation in software from customized to standardized application packages soared after IBM "unbundled" its software from its hardware in 1969 under antitrust pressure. By selling it to any user, IBM saw its software quickly become the worldwide standard to which applications software makers shaped their packages. Thus in 1968, of the $400 million in the U.S. revenues in software, $300 million came from customized programming. But in 1978 when the total was $1.5 billion, $1 billion of it came from packaged software and only $500 million from customized products.

With the shift from customized to standardized, mass-produced chips, the cost of a fabricating plant soared from $2 million in the early 1970s to $80 million by the end of the decade and to $300 million by the mid-1980s – and to over a billion in the early 1990s. Semiconductors quickly became one of the country's most capital-intensive industries. These rising costs of facilities reflected the complex technology of producing chips and the increasing need for careful supervision of the coordination of the processes involved. As minimum-efficient scale and output rose, per unit costs and prices dropped dramatically.

The U.S. firms that were the hardest hit by this increasingly scale-dependent technology were the small, specialized, customized producers concentrated in California's Silicon Valley. More successful in developing the new production technologies were older enterprises – Texas Instruments (TI), formed in 1931 in Houston, Texas, and Motorola, a maker of car radios established in 1927. TI, where Jack Kilby had patented the integrated chip in 1959, quickly expanded production in the United States and built a global marketing network. By the late 1960s it had fifteen wholly owned operating plants abroad. Motorola followed the same pattern on a somewhat smaller scale. By the late 1970s TI and Motorola together, in almost equal proportions, enjoyed by one estimate 70.7 percent of the U.S. market, and were as well the largest producers worldwide. Even though new mass-production technology quadrupled Silicon Valley's technological employment, the market share of the California companies was much smaller. Among those companies, Fairchild (where Robert Noyce had also patented the integrated chip in 1959) had by the same estimate 8.3 percent of the U.S. market, National Semiconductor had 7.5, and Intel 5.9.

The most successful embodiers of the new mass-production technology, however, were the giant Japanese integrated computer and consumer electronic firms, all of which produced semiconductors for their own use as well as for the merchant market. In the late seventies, they moved in strength into the U.S. market, particularly with Dynamic Random Access Memory (DRAM) chips. By the early 1980s, except for a few specialized devices, they had driven the American firms out of the production of DRAMs. If it had not been for the microcomputer revolution, the U.S. companies might have also lost out in the far more powerful new chip, the microprocessor.

The microcomputer revolution of the 1980s transformed the electronic data-processing industry as profoundly as the System 360 had done two decades before. The transformation rested on the two highly significant developments of the 1970s. One was the above-noted worldwide proliferation in the production of semiconductors, peripherals, software packages, and other related products that assured their availability and the dramatic reduction of their costs and, therefore, their price. The other was the commercialization of the microprocessor. That "computer on a chip" sharply increased the processing power of the chip even as the large-scale production decreased its cost. By the mid-1970s amateur "hobbyists" were assembling cheap, readily available components into small inexpensive computers and selling kits from which they could be constructed.

The availability of low-cost parts led to the spontaneous beginnings of the microcomputer industry. In the single year 1977 three firms in different parts of the country introduced their initial offerings – Apple Computer in California, Radio Shack (the leading retailer of consumer electronics) in Texas, and Commodore (a maker of hand-held calculators) in Pennsylvania. Others soon followed. But the industry was still in its embryonic stage when in the spring of 1980 IBM's management decided to enter it.

With a brilliant strategy, brilliantly executed, IBM almost immediately brought the industry to young adulthood. But that very act gave life to a product that in time would destroy the worldwide dominance of the mainframe, in which IBM and its clones were the leaders. IBM's management fully realized that the availability of parts and the new processing power made for a far different challenge from that of developing the System 360. Its first decision was to form an autonomous business unit to design, produce, and market its microcomputer, the personal computer or PC. In the summer of 1980, IBM's Management Committee charged a project team with building a global enterprise within a year. The team erected a plant in Boca Raton, Florida, made contracts with outside suppliers of peripherals, components (Intel was chosen), and software (Microsoft but only as second choice) and organized a global marketing and distribution network and did so on schedule. By the fall of 1981 the Boca Raton plant was producing one machine every forty-five seconds. In 1984, the third year of full production, the revenues of IBM's PC unit were $4 billion – revenues comparable to the seventy-fifth-largest U.S. industrial company. In 1985 they levelled off at $5.5 billion!

Companies – established and start-ups – swarmed into this huge and totally unanticipated market. Cloning the IBM PC was simplicity itself, compared with cloning a mainframe; and the minimum-efficient scale of production was too low to create effective barriers to entry. In 1984 and 1985 there was a shake-out in the industry, but when demand recovered in 1986 some 200 enterprises were producing IBM PC clones. The founders of the most successful of these, Compaq, had established their company in 1983 with the express intent of laying the foundations for a large global enterprise by careful financial planning, building a worldwide marketing network, and developing strong organizational capabilities. In the words of one founder, "Above all, we want team players not individualists." By the end of the decade IBM's market share had dropped to 22.3 percent of the personal computer market worldwide. By 1992 it had 17.2 percent followed by Apple with 12.3 and Compaq with 9.2 percent. The other five U.S. firms in the list of the largest fifteen worldwide held between 4.1 percent and 1.7 percent. By then the production of microcomputers was no longer concentrated.

On the other hand, the production of semiconductors and software for the personal computer quickly became as concentrated as any in the United States. All the producers of clones used Intel (or cloned Intel) microprocessors and Microsoft operating systems. Intel's franchise from IBM gave it a powerful competitive advantage based on the economies of scale. The franchise not only permitted Intel to outpace Motorola and other American firms but also to obtain and maintain a dominance in microprocessors that the Japanese firms have had difficulty in challenging. By 1991 Intel with revenues of $4.8 billion accounted for three-fourths of the output of microprocessors by U.S. companies. By then the cost of its new plant was $1.3 billion. In this highly capital- and knowledge-intensive and scale-dependent technology, the economies of scale had created higher barriers to entry in as short a time as had ever occurred in the commercializing of earlier technologies.

At the same time, Microsoft's franchise from IBM gave it powerful competitive advantage based on the economies of scope, not only in the production of software operating systems for personal computers but also in applications software for them where it became the leader. By 1991, 51 percent of Microsoft's revenues of $1.84 billion came from applications software and 36 percent from operating systems. (The rest came from hardware, books, and miscellaneous items.) By then Microsoft was making serious inroads into the markets of the nation's leading applications software producers including Lotus, Novell, Word Perfect, and Oracle. By then Microsoft's R&D expenditures were running into the hundreds of millions of dollars. The development of one operating system, NT, cost millions and five concentrated years of work. As in the case of Intel, the Japanese producers are not yet major competitors.

The electronics story thus differs from that of the other post–World War II high-tech industries in that a much smaller number of large companies dominated major markets. Few companies dominated their industries worldwide as powerfully as RCA and IBM did at the end of the 1960s. In consumer electronics the failure of RCA to maintain the needed organizational capabilities helped to assure the loss of the United States consumer electronics industry to Japan. More than a quarter of a century later, in the middle 1990s, there seems only a faint hope that U.S. firms could again become viable competitors.

On the other hand, in the electronic data-processing industries IBM's achievement in integrating both tangible and intangible capital in the creation of the System 360 gave it unprecedented worldwide dominance. After the Japanese firms acquired this technology, largely through the services of Amdahl, they continued to improve their products and processes and to enhance their organizational capabilities so as to compete effectively in world markets with the U.S. firms. The failure of the European companies in electronics, except possibly for Philips, dramatically emphasizes the necessity for developing and, even more important, maintaining a base that permits the embodiment of intangible and tangible capital within large industrial enterprises. The fact that seven of Japan's eight largest industrial enterprises in terms of capital assets in 1987 were four electronic and three automobile firms further emphasizes this point.

As important as the internal evolution of the electronic data industry has been for technological progress, its impact on other industries and other sectors of the economy may have been even more significant. In nearly all industries the new computer-aided design (CAD) and computer-aided manufacturing (CAM) (including computer-controlled machine tools and devices for automating the processes of production) have sharply increased the ratio of capital to production workers, sped up flows through the processes of production, and increased value-added in manufacturing in both the chemically processed and the machinery industries.

The new data-processing technologies may have had an even greater impact on the service sector productivity than on manufacturing. The huge growth of software applications and computer services of the 1970s continued during the 1980s. Every category in the service sector was affected. In distribution the point-of-sales cash register and the bar code permitted mass retailers to coordinate the flows of goods into their stores by direct contact with manufacturers, thus squeezing or even eliminating the wholesaler. The new software technologies increased productivity in the operations of chains of hotels, restaurants, and food stores. They had an even greater effect on banking, insurance, and other financial services. They helped to transform the provision of services in transportation, particularly airline travel, and in health care. All aspects of the entertainment business – products, productions, and distribution – were profoundly affected. The high level of productivity in the U.S. service sector in good part reflects the massive use of the new electronic hardware and software technologies in the United States since the 1960s.

CONCLUSION

If "technical progress" is the most essential characteristic of economic growth, then as the twentieth century draws to a close, the United States would seem to be in as strong a position in maintaining continuing economic growth as it was when the century began. In the first decades of rapid economic growth before World War I, the United States led the way in commercializing many of the new capital-intensive, scale-dependent technologies. In the second half of the century as the bias of growth turned toward the more science-based, knowledge-intensive, and what might be termed scope-dependent industries, the United States still maintains powerful competitive strength. This is in good part because the new technologies were largely commercialized and continued to be dominated by enterprises that were first movers in exploiting the earlier capital-intensive, scale-intensive technologies. They had the product-specific and industry-specific organizational capabilities and the funds from retained earnings that were essential to continue to commercialize the new technologies on a global scale. As was true of the earlier capital-intensive, scale-dependent technologies, unless organizational capabilities were developed and maintained, the critical learning base often disintegrated. Once lost, it was rarely regained. This was probably even more true in the knowledge-intensive, scope-dependent industries of the second half of the century than it was for the capital-intensive and scale-dependent industries of the first period of modern economic growth.

In these postwar knowledge-based industries the United States remains the leader in chemicals, pharmaceuticals, and aerospace. In electronics the United States and Europe have lost out to Japan in radios, TVs, VCRs, and other consumer electronics as well as in bulk semiconductors and certain other components. Both the United States and Europe retain strength in telecommunications, and the United States is at the forefront in such leading-edge electronic technologies as microcomputers and software. With the United States, Japanese companies are strong in information-processing equipment and with both the U.S. and European companies in telecommunications. But they have not developed a strong global presence in higher value-added chemicals and pharmaceuticals nor in aerospace. In sum, during the postwar years the European companies have maintained their competitive strength with the Americans in the older science-based industries but missed the most dynamic of the postwar technologies – those based on the transistor and the integrated circuit.

This essay has reviewed the role of the large industrial enterprise in making the United States the leader in technological change during the twentieth century. Its firms did not necessarily so become by inventing or even pioneering in the new technologies. During the first wave most of the initial innovations came from Europe, in the interwar years from both Europe and the United States, and after World War II more from the United States. The U.S. industries became worldwide technological leaders in Maddison's terms by commercializing these innovations on a scale made possible by the size of national and global markets. It was this large-scale commercialization that created the initial learning base and then the core of a larger industrial nexus, each of which, in turn, became a dynamic element in continuing learning and growth. But, as the rise and decline of companies and even industries such as consumer electronics indicate, in these high-tech industries, and also in medium technology ones such as motor vehicles and steel, the initial advantages did not insure continued strength. Learned product-specific organizational capabilities had to be maintained and enhanced. Once capabilities disintegrated, competitive power rarely returned.

Bibliographical note

Information on the pre–World War II decades and its documentary support come mainly from my *Strategy and Structure* (Cambridge, Mass., 1962), *Giant Enterprise* (Cambridge, Mass., 1964), *The Visible Hand* (Cambridge, Mass., 1977), and *Scale and Scope* (Cambridge, Mass., 1990). That on the post–World War II petrochemical, polymer, and therapeutic revolutions is from Fred Aftalion, *A History of the International Chemical Industry* (1991), pp. 207–269; Joseph L. Bower, *When Markets Quake: The Management Challenge of Restructuring Industry* (Boston, Mass., 1986), ch. 1; Peter J. Spitz, *Petrochemicals: The Rise of an Industry* (New York, 1988); Ralph L. Landau and Nathan Rosenberg, "Successful Commercialization in the Chemical Process Industries," in Nathan Rosenberg, Ralph Landau, and David C. Mowery, eds., *Technology and the Wealth of Nations* (Stanford, California, 1992); Ralph L. Landau, "Chemical Engineering: Key to the Growth of the Chemical Process Industries," in Jaromir J. Ubrecht, ed., *Competitiveness of the U.S. Chemical Industry in International Markets*, AICHE Symposium Series, vol. 86 (1990); Peter Temin, *Take Your Medicine: Drug Regulation in the United States* (Cambridge Mass., 1980), ch. 4; Henry Redwood, *The Pharmaceutical Industry: Trends, Problems and Achievements* (Felixstowe, England, 1988); James Taggert, *The World Pharmaceutical Industry* (London, 1993); F. Malerba and L. Orsenigo, "The Dynamics and Evolution of Industries,"

Industrial and Corporate Change, 1996, pp. 51–88, *Chemical and Engineering News*, March 20, 1995, pp. 12–14.

The information on the electronics revolution is from James W. Cortada, *Historical Dictionary of Data Processing: Organization* (New York, 1987); Kenneth Flamm, *Creating the Computer: Government, Industry and High Technology* (Washington, 1988) (the statistics cited are from Cortada and Flamm); Marianne Jelinek and Claudia Bird Schoonhoven, *Innovation Marathon: Lessons from High Technology Firms* (Oxford, 1990); Charles R. Morris and Charles E. Ferguson, *Computer Wars: How Can the West Win in a Post-IBM World* (New York, 1993); Marie Anchordoguy, *Computers Inc.: Japan's Challenge to IBM* (Cambridge, Mass., 1989). For the impact of new information-processing technologies on industrial processes, Shoshana Zuboff, *In the Age of the Smart Machine: The Future of Work and Power* (1984), and on the service industries, James L. McKenney, *Waves of Change: Business Evolution through Information Technology* (Boston, 1995). For broader developments in U.S. postwar industries see the spring 1994 issue of the *Business History Review* which includes articles by Alfred D. Chandler, Jr., Kim B. Clark and Carliss Y. Baldwin, and Brownwyn H. Hall.

The general statistical data up to 1970 are from U.S. Bureau of the Census, *Historical Statistics of the United States, Colonial Times to 1970* (Washington, 1975), vol. 2, especially pp. 669–680, 685, and after 1970 from U.S. Bureau of the Census, *Annual Survey of Manufactures*, Washington, (primarily from the 1987 issue). Some of these statistics appear in Tables 2.4 through 2.7 in Chapter 2. The statistical information concerning industrial research and development can be obtained from various annual publications of National Science Foundation, particularly *Selected Data on Research and Development in Industry* and *National Patterns of R&D Resources*. A June issue of *Datamation* annually provides detailed statistics and information on the electronic data-processing industry. Recent information on individual companies is from annual editions of *Hoover's Handbook of American Business* (Austin, Texas).

4

———

Great Britain: Big business, management, and competitiveness in twentieth-century Britain

GEOFFREY JONES

INTRODUCTION

Britain holds a special place in Chandler's *Scale and Scope*. In his comparative study of the evolution of large industrial firms in the United States, Germany, and Britain before 1945, it is the latter that is cast as the failure. "The British story," in Chandler's analysis, "provides a counterpoint – an antithesis – to the American experience." "Britain is the place to study enterprises' failures to develop competitive strength."[1] This chapter begins by reviewing the Chandlerian interpretation of British business history before 1945 before turning to a fuller examination of the structure of British big business and management, and its performance, after World War II. A great deal has been written about the British economy in this period, much of it in a search for the "British disease" which explains its apparently inexorable decline.[2] This chapter seeks not to duplicate this large literature, but to offer an interpretative survey, focused on the central Chandlerian concerns of the business enterprise, organizational capability, and competitiveness.

---

[1] Alfred D. Chandler, *Scale and Scope* (Cambridge, Mass.: Harvard University Press, 1990), p. 236; and "Response to the Contributors to the Review Colloquium on *Scale and Scope*," *Business History Review*, 64 (1990), p. 751.

[2] There are surveys of the literature in Bernard W. E. Alford, *British Economic Performance, 1945–1975* (London: Macmillan, 1988); Nick F. R. Crafts and Nicholas W. C. Woodward (eds.), *The British Economy since 1945* (Oxford: Clarendon Press, 1991); Roderick Floud and Donald McCloskey (eds.), *The Economic History of Britain since 1700*, vol. 3: *1939–1992* (Cambridge: Cambridge University Press, 1994); and Michael Dintenfass, *The Decline of Industrial Britain, 1870–1980* (London: Routledge, 1992). The debate is put in perspective in Barry Supple, "Fear of Failing: Economic History and the Decline of Britain," *Economic History Review*, 47 (1994), pp. 441–458. Excellent surveys of recent business history literature on twentieth-century Britain can be found in Maurice W. Kirby and Mary B. Rose (eds.), *Business Enterprise in Modern Britain from the Eighteenth to the Twentieth Century* (London: Routledge, 1994), and John F. Wilson, *British Business History, 1720–1994* (Manchester: Manchester University Press, 1995).

PERSONAL CAPITALISM BEFORE 1945

"The general failure to develop organizational capabilities weakened British industry and with it the British economy."[3] This is the heart of the Chandlerian view of British business history from the late nineteenth century until World War II. To a great extent, British firms failed to make (or make sufficiently) the three-pronged investment in manufacturing, marketing, and management that brought success to American and German firms in the new capital-intensive industries of the late nineteenth century. In a wide range of such industries, including light and heavy machinery, automobiles, electrical equipment, electrochemicals, and organic chemicals, it was American and German firms that captured the world – and even the British – market. Having missed the opportunity to become first movers, British business faced formidable catch-up problems in subsequent decades. In the interwar years, British business did "catch up" in some industries, notably chemicals and petroleum, but many weaknesses remained to haunt the British after World War II.

The fundamental problem of British business, Chandler suggests, was that British companies failed to emulate the managerial hierarchies pioneered in the United States, and opted instead for "personal capitalism." This was partly associated with the continuing prominence of family-owned firms, but the concept is widened out by Chandler to include personal "styles" of management. The upshot was that many sectors of British industry were dominated by small, highly specialized, firms. Managerial hierarchies were thin, with very few centralized management control structures. British personal capitalism could succeed in industries where the production process was relatively straightforward and offered fewer opportunities for scale economies, such as branded and packaged consumer goods, but it constrained the British ability to compete in capital-intensive industries. Personal capitalism meant, Chandler suggests, a preference for short-term income rather than long-term growth in assets, and a bias for small-scale operations which contributed to failures to invest and modernize.

The managerial and organizational weaknesses of British firms in many of the complex capital-intensive manufacturing industries before 1945 are beyond dispute. The failure of British competitiveness in those industries is also exposed in convincing detail in *Scale and Scope*. Two questions arise, however, which merit consideration, as they will also reoccur when

---

[3] Chandler, *Scale and Scope*, p. 392.

the post-1945 period is examined. The first concerns what was happening in the British economy beyond the capital-intensive manufacturing industries. The second concerns the relationship between organizational capabilities and competitive performance.

It is useful to begin with a review of Britain's overall macroeconomic performance before 1945. Britain's failure to make the required three-pronged investment in many manufacturing industries did not result in a dramatic economic decline. In fact, although Britain had lost its position as the world's largest industrial economy to the United States by the beginning of the new century, British manufacturing industry and the British economy in general remained giants in both the European and the world economy. Britain's real GDP remained considerably larger than that of Germany or France up to World War II.[4] Even at the end of the 1930s Germany's share of world exports of manufactured goods was only a little above that of Britain. At midcentury, and after the catastrophic disruption of World War II, Britain accounted for 25 percent of world manufactured exports, compared to 27 percent for the United States, 9 percent for France, 7 percent for Germany, and 3 percent for Japan.[5]

The British problem was one of relatively slow economic growth over the long run, the product of slow labor (and capital) productivity growth. Estimates of growth rates of real output per worker employed from 1873 reveal a picture of low and falling British productivity growth before 1924, as the late Victorian economy, with its low value-added, low-skilled, highly specialized orientation, was unable to deliver the productivity growth performance of economies such as Germany and the United States which had a more "high-tech" orientation. The British productivity performance improved after the mid-1920s, but still left Britain lagging behind the United States, Germany and France.[6]

This picture, however, needs careful interpretation. Table 4.1 gives absolute productivity figures for the whole British economy, rather than

[4] Angus Maddison, "Growth and Slowdown in Advanced Capitalist Economies: Techniques of Quantitative Assessment," *Journal of Economic Literature*, 25 (1987), p. 682.
[5] Nick F. R. Crafts and Nicholas W. C. Woodward, "The British Economy since 1945: Introduction and Overview," in Crafts and Woodward, *The British Economy since 1945*, p. 12.
[6] Nick F. R. Crafts, "Economic Growth," in Crafts and Woodward, *The British Economy since 1945*, p. 261. The British growth rates were 1.2 percent 1873–1899; 0.5 percent 1899–1913; 0.3 percent 1913–1924; and 1 percent 1924–1937. The equivalent rates for the United States were 1.9 percent, 1.3 percent, 1.7 percent, and 1.4 percent; for Germany 1.5 percent, 1.5 percent; 0.9 percent, and 3 percent; and for France 1.3 percent, 1.6 percent, 0.8 percent, and 1.4 percent.

Table 4.1. *Real GDP per hour worked, 1870–1986*

	United Kingdom	United States	Germany	France
1870	100	97	50	48
1890	100	113	55	49
1913	100	135	65	60
1929	100	158	65	70
1938	100	154	73	82
1950	100	185	54	70
1973	100	156	100	105
1986	100	133	105	119

Source: Nick F. R. Crafts, "Economic Growth," in Nick F. R. Crafts and Nicholas Woodward (eds.), *The British Economy since 1945* (Oxford: Clarendon Press, 1991), p. 263.

just manufacturing, and adjusts for hours worked. It also gives comparative data for the United States, Germany, and France.

It is evident that Britain had fallen seriously behind the United States in absolute productivity by the late nineteenth century, but it was not until the 1970s that the other large European economies reached British levels. Even in manufacturing the failings of the British economy should not be exaggerated. American industry as a whole was more than twice as productive as British industry by the 1920s, but into the 1930s it seems that German industry had only a slightly higher labor productivity than the British. Moreover, there were significant variations between industries. British productivity performance in comparison with that of Germany and the United States was worse in the heavy industries and much better in the lighter industries. In the interwar years British productivity was above German levels in such light industries as food, drink, tobacco, and textiles.[7] The major period of British decline relative to the rest of Western Europe, including Germany, was in the post-1950 period.[8]

These data are important because they remind us that the experience

[7] Stephen N. Broadberry and Nick F. R. Crafts, "Explaining Anglo-American Productivity Differences in the Mid-Twentieth Century," and Stephen N. Broadberry and Rainer Fremdling, "Comparative Productivity in British and German Industry, 1907–37," *Oxford Bulletin of Economics and Statistics*, 52 (1990), pp. 375–402, 403–421.
[8] Stephen Broadberry, "The Impact of the World Wars on the Long Run Performance of the British Economy," *Oxford Review of Economic Policy*, 4 (1988), p. 256. This point was made strongly by Sidney Pollard in his review of *Scale and Scope*, "The World according to Mammon," *Times Higher Education Supplement*, 27 April 1990, p. 20.

of the British in manufacturing, and more especially in the capital-intensive industries, must not automatically be assumed to be that of British business as a whole before 1945. As Supple has observed, "manufacturing industry has never accounted for as much as 35 percent of British or American, or 40 percent of German, marketed national output."[9]

British business historians have long been aware of the rapid growth of the service sector in the late nineteenth century, a sector in which British entrepreneurs appeared better able to perceive new opportunities than in manufacturing.[10] The significance of this trend for the analysis of the growth of big business has been highlighted by Wardley's data base of the fifty largest British companies (by market value) for 1904–5, 1934–1935, and 1985. This shows that Britain had a considerable number of large companies even before World War I, most of which were engaged in the provision of services. British entrepreneurs could, Wardley suggests, construct large companies. Wardley supports the view that productivity levels were higher in services than in manufacturing, and – more controversially – suggests that if market capitalization rather than nominal capitalization is used as the basis for international comparison, even the perceived difference in size between British and American manufacturing companies is much reduced.[11]

British entrepreneurs were also able to construct large-scale enterprises to engage in international business. Chapman examined British-based "investment groups" active overseas before 1914, such as Matheson and Butterfield & Swire in the Far East, and Anthony Gibbs in South America, which undertook diversified trading and industrial activities through a variety of subsidiary enterprises. The result was large business enterprises, whose scale has been disguised by confining attention to the parent company alone.[12] These business groups, which took the form of complex

---

[9] Barry Supple, "Scale and Scope: Alfred Chandler and the Dynamics of Industrial Capitalism," *Economic History Review*, 44 (1991), p. 508.

[10] Charles Wilson, "Economy and Society in Late Victorian Britain," *Economic History Review*, 18 (1965), pp. 183–98; Peter Payne, "Entrepreneurship and British Economic Decline," in Bruce Collins and Keith Robbins (eds.), *British Culture and Economic Decline* (London: Weidenfeld and Nicolson, 1990), pp. 45–46.

[11] Peter Wardley, "The Anatomy of Big Business: Aspects of Corporate Development in the Twentieth Century," *Business History*, 33 (1991), pp. 268–296. See also Norman Gemmell and Peter Wardley, "The Contribution of Services to British Economic Growth, 1856–1913," *Explorations in Economic History*, 27 (1990), pp. 299–321, and Robert Millward, "Productivity in the UK Services Sector: Historical Trends 1865–1985 and Comparisons with the USA 1950–85," *Oxford Bulletin of Economics and Statistics*, 52 (1990), pp. 423–436.

[12] Stanley D. Chapman, "British-Based Investment Groups before 1914," *Economic History Review*, 38 (1985), pp. 230–251.

networks of companies linked by cross-shareholding and interlocking directorships, possessed considerable organizational capability, even if their management structures were different from those of the integrated managerial enterprises appearing in the United States.

This point focuses attention on the significance of British overseas business activities before 1945. As foreign direct investment became a prominent form of capital export in the late nineteenth century, British business took a leading part in its growth. Britain accounted for around 45 percent of the stock of accumulated foreign direct investment in 1914 – compared with the American 18 percent and the German 10 percent – and it remained the world's largest foreign direct investor before 1945.[13] Direct investment in foreign countries (even in overseas colonies) is a risky business strategy. Such investments are unlikely to be durable without substantial competitive advantages over local competitors and other foreign rivals.

There is evidence that this early British multinational enterprise was afflicted by managerial weaknesses. Before 1914, a considerable proportion of British foreign direct investment took the form of "free-standing" companies. Tiny London head offices (usually no more than a part-time board of directors) controlled the overseas operations of such firms. The result appeared to be a fragile managerial system which, according to Wilkins, led to the disappearance of such firms over time.[14] Case studies of the more "modern" form of manufacturing multinational enterprise have also revealed managerial weaknesses. Some at least of the large British manufacturing firms which engaged in outward investment before 1939, such as Dunlop and Cadbury, are known to have experienced just the problems identified by Chandler in his critique of personal capitalism.[15]

Nevertheless it is implausible that the enormous British multinational investment of this period could not have survived, and grown, without considerable organizational capabilities on behalf of the enterprises involved. There were more successful British multinational investments than those of Dunlop and Cadbury, as well as many examples of American and other non-British multinationals making problematic forays into foreign

---

[13] John H. Dunning, *Explaining International Production* (London: Unwin Hyman, 1988), p. 74.

[14] Mira Wilkins, "The Free-Standing Company, 1870–1914: An Important Type of British Foreign Direct Investment," *Economic History Review*, 2nd ser., 61, (1988), pp. 259–282.

[15] Geoffrey Jones (ed.), *British Multinationals: Origins, Management and Performance* (Aldershot: Gower, 1986).

markets. While German and American electrical equipment provided, in Chandler's words, "light and transportation to the world's growing cities,"[16] it was often operated by British-owned utilities in Latin America, Asia, and elsewhere. German manufactured exports to such markets were financed more by British overseas banks than by German banks.[17] Free-standing companies were stronger than they looked when embedded in wider networks of firms. British enterprises active in resource exploitation and related services in the developing world – the bulk of British direct investment before World War II – faced unpredictable and volatile business environments. The use of networks of firms and informal or socialization strategies of control based on strong corporate cultures were probably more rational and effective organizational responses than the creation of bureaucratic hierarchies.[18]

There remains much uncertainty about the relationship between organizational capabilities and competitive performance in Britain before World War II. Both the significance and the consequences of the continuing attachment to personal capitalism are debatable. It is still not clear that Britain had disproportionately more family firms than Germany or the United States. Personal capitalism has been a noticeable feature of German business throughout the twentieth century. Comparative studies of the origins and behavior of British and German entrepreneurs in the nineteenth and twentieth centuries show more similarities than dissimilarities.[19]

Nor is there a consensus about the behavioral characteristics of owner-managers. British family firms did not all prefer short-term income to long-term asset growth. In some important respects British firms acted in similar ways if they were managerial or personal enterprises. Examples can be found in both types of enterprise of hostility to radical change or, in Coleman's words, an "implicit and unacknowledged obeisance to the god of continuity."[20] Conversely, both types of enterprise were active in

---

[16] Chandler, *Scale and Scope*, p. 294.
[17] Geoffrey Jones, *British Multinational Banking, 1830–1990* (Oxford: Clarendon Press, 1993), p. 96.
[18] Geoffrey Jones, *The Evolution of International Business* (London: Routledge, 1996), pp. 35, 161–162; William G. Ouchi, "Markets, Bureaucracies, and Class," *Administrative Science Quarterly*, 25 (1980), pp. 129–141.
[19] Roy Church, "The Limitations of the Personal Capitalism Paradigm," *Business History Review*, 64 (1990), pp. 703–710; Harold James, "The German Experience and the Myth of British Cultural Exceptionalism," in Collins and Robbins, *British Culture*, pp. 115–28. Dintenfass, *Decline*, pp. 64–65.
[20] Donald Coleman, "Failings and Achievements: Some British Businesses, 1910–80," *Business History*, 29 (1987), p. 9.

industrial research and development. The view put forward by Mowery and others that the amount of British R&D before 1945 was deficient rests on uncertain empirical foundations, and is in the process of being challenged. Even if they lacked organizational capabilities, by the inter-war years the research outlay of British firms may well have compared favorably to all but a few of the larger American corporations. Producers of branded, packaged goods, often family firms, appear very active in R&D.[21] An analysis of interwar American patent statistics suggests declining British innovation in the 1920s, but a considerable increase in British-based patenting in the 1930s, which contrasted with declining technological activity in the United States, France, and Germany in that decade.[22]

There is evidence also that the adoption of U.S.-style managerial hierarchies did not *automatically* improve competitive performance. The most systematic exploration of this issue has been undertaken by Broadberry and Crafts in an investigation of the productivity gap between British and American industries in the 1930s. A series of case studies of poor-productivity British industries (tin cans, electric lamps, and blast furnaces) and better-performing ones (cement and margarine) led the authors to conclude that it was "incorrect to place a very large weight on corporate structure" to explain the differences in performance. The British tin can industry had a poor productivity performance despite the transformation in the 1930s of Metal Box, the dominant British firm, into a modern industrial enterprise.[23]

It is apparent that, however important management structures were to explaining problems in the competitive performance of some British manufacturing industries, there were other factors at work, both external and internal to the business enterprise. Among such external factors,

---

[21] David Mowery, "Industrial Research in Britain, 1900–1950," in Bernard Elbaum and William Lazonick (eds.), *The Decline of the British Economy* (Oxford: Clarendon Press, 1987), pp. 189–222, and "Finance and Corporate Evolution in Five Industrial Economies, 1900–1950," *Industrial and Corporate Change*, 1, 1 (1992), pp. 1–36. See also Chandler, *Scale and Scope*, p. 389. A more favorable interpretation is in David E. H. Edgerton, "Science and Technology in British Business History," *Business History*, 29 (1987), pp. 84–103; Edgerton and Sally M. Horrocks, "British Industrial Research and Development before 1945," *Economic History Review*, 47, 2 (1994), pp. 213–238.

[22] John Cantwell, "The Evolution of European Industrial Technology in the Interwar Period," in François Caron, Paul Erker and Wolfram Fischer (eds.), *Innovations in the European Economy between the Wars* (New York: de Gruyter, 1995), pp. 277–319.

[23] Stephen N. Broadberry and Nick F. R. Crafts, "Britain's Productivity Gap in the 1930s: Some Neglected Factors," *Journal of Economic History*, 52, 3 (1992), pp. 531–558; Chandler, *Scale and Scope*, pp. 316–320.

Broadberry and Crafts have drawn particular attention to the inadequate human capital in interwar Britain, and the problems of collusion and barriers to exit in the economy, fostered by government policy.[24] This latter point seems particularly important. Elbaum and Lazonick have criticized the interwar (and later) British governments for not acting as "visible hands" which could force the atomistic small firms in cotton textiles and other industries to merge into larger, managerial enterprises.[25] However, the greater problem may well have been the long-term preference in British governments for stability and security, together with a fear of offending vested interest groups, which constantly led British public policy to foster an uncompetitive and collusive business environment.[26]

Among the factors internal to the firm other than management structure, culture may be the most significant. Unlike Lazonick, with his emphasis on institutional constraints,[27] Chandler in *Scale and Scope* prefers to leave open the "exact reasons" why the British should have preferred "personal capitalism" before 1945. He finds no obvious market or technological explanations for the British failures before 1914 in chemicals, electrical equipment, or other industries, and perhaps we approach at times a "culturist" interpretation of events – the British behaved as they did because their culture was different to that of Germany or the United States. "Since economic reasons cannot effectively explain why the British pioneers failed to make investments necessary to become or compete with foreign first movers," Chandler writes, "one has to turn to broader, more cultural explanations."[28]

British economic history has a large literature on the alleged impact of British culture on British entrepreneurship, its "anti-industrial" orientation from the late nineteenth century, and the wide divergence between British and German cultures in this respect. Much of this discussion has been simplistic and misleading, especially in regard to Anglo-German comparisons.[29] Nevertheless a far more substantial literature exists in

[24] Broadberry and Crafts, "Britain's Productivity Gap."
[25] Elbaum and Lazonick, *The Decline of the British Economy.*
[26] Geoffrey Jones and Maurice Kirby, "Competitiveness and the State in International Perspective," in Geoffrey Jones and Maurice Kirby (eds.), *Competitiveness and the State* (Manchester: Manchester University Press, 1991), pp. 4–6. The evolution of British competition policy is examined in Helen Mercer, *Constructing a Competitive Order* (Cambridge: Cambridge University Press, 1995).
[27] Elbaum and Lazonick, *The Decline of the British Economy;* William Lazonick, *Competitive Advantage on the Shop Floor* (Cambridge, Mass.: Harvard University Press, 1990).
[28] Chandler, "Response," p. 746.
[29] James, "The German Experience."

organization theory and sociology which has yielded considerable empirical evidence on how organizational structures and – perhaps especially –
managerial behavior may be influenced by cross-cultural differences, along
with many other factors. For example, Hofstede's contention that Germans are less "individualistic" and manifest stronger "uncertainty avoidance" than the British might well provide one element of an explanation
why German firms were better able to construct larger and more centralized business enterprises in the new capital-intensive industries of the late
nineteenth century. The low uncertainty avoidance of British culture would
incline Britishers more than Germans to risky, entrepreneurial activities.[30]

Also of relevance is the work of Casson on the impact of culture on
transactions costs. "High trust" societies, he argues, are able to economize
on transactions costs because fewer resources need to be used to monitor
behavior. It follows that there will be differences in governance structures
and patterns of interfirm interaction between countries according to their
"trust" levels. A particular national culture may, as Casson suggests,
yield competitive advantages, but it is not really sensible to say that entrepreneurs failed to adopt organizational structures inappropriate to their
culture.[31]

This is not the place to rehearse the numerous methodological problems faced by research into the impact of national cultures and business
organizations.[32] It may simply be observed that any movement toward
the Hofstede hypothesis that "organisations are culture bound"[33] puts in
doubt the view that organizational forms developed in one country can
be transferred to another with the same effectiveness. British-style management cannot necessarily be judged a failure simply because it did not
develop on American lines. However, culture may also explain the problem
raised by Chandler: it still remains a puzzle, even after all other explanations are taken into consideration, why British businessmen in a range
of manufacturing industries continued to prefer not to adopt the latest
machinery, or adopt more formal training for their staff, or change other

[30] Geert Hofstede, *Culture's Consequences* (London: Sage, 1984). Cautious support for
this hypothesis for the contemporary period is given by Andreas Budde, John Child,
Arthur Francis, and Alfred Kieser, "Corporate Goals, Managerial Objectives, and Organizational Structures in British and West German Companies," *Organization Studies*,
3 (1982), pp. 1–32.
[31] Mark Casson, *The Economics of Business Culture* (Oxford: Clarendon Press, 1991).
[32] See the "Conclusion," in Steven Tolliday and Jonathan Zeitlin (eds.), *The Power to
Manage? Employers and Industrial Relations in Comparative-Industrial Perspective*
(London: Routledge, 1991), pp. 273–324.
[33] Hofstede, *Cultures Consequences*, p. 252.

traditional practices, even when such ideas and innovations "enabled foreign enterprises to win customers in markets around the globe and in Britain too."[34] One speculative answer is that British managerial decision making drew on a personal value system which favored financial, entrepreneurial, and trading business activities (such as many services), and was unfavorable to the kind of skills and mental outlook needed to succeed in activities involving complex tasks and long-time horizons (such as the new capital-intensive industries).

To summarize, British economic decline before 1945 needs careful definition. The real problem was the productivity gap between Britain and the United States, which was particularly great in certain industries. Personal capitalism handicapped British enterprise in the capital-intensive industries, but the British created more effective business organizations in some services, and when they invested abroad. The problems of defective management structures within manufacturing firms were made worse by an uncompetitive and collusive environment, caused in part by defective public policy. Managerial performance in the complex capital-intensive industries may also have been handicapped by personal value systems inherent in British culture.

BRITISH BUSINESS AFTER 1945: PERFORMANCE AND STRUCTURE

There are various paradoxes about the performance of British business and the British economy after World War II. In terms of its own past history, this was perhaps the most successful period ever for the British economy, yet in an international perspective the half century after the end of the war witnessed a worse "failure" than anything seen before 1939. The period saw the decline and fall of a range of British industries, from shipbuilding to motor cars. Yet there were some sectors with strong international competitiveness, such as chemicals and – more latterly – pharmaceuticals.

During the 1950s and 1960s British productivity grew at a much faster rate than for decades, but it grew much faster still in most of Western Europe and in Japan. Britain missed the "economic miracle" era of fast growth between the 1950s and 1973, when most of Western Europe and Japan narrowed the large technological gap which had existed between

[34] Dintenfass, *Decline*, p. 71.

Table 4.2. *Output per person-hour in manufacturing, 1951–1988*

	United Kingdom	United States	Germany	France
1951	100	270	68	71
1964	100	268	117	90
1973	100	234	133	101
1979	100	243	163	129
1988	100	224	138	122

Source: Nick F. R. Crafts, "Economic Growth," in Nick F. R. Crafts and Nicholas Woodward (eds.), *The British Economy since 1945* (Oxford: Clarendon Press, 1991), p. 262.

themselves and the United States in 1950. Britain closed this gap much more slowly.[35]

The declining competitiveness of British manufacturing industry lay at the heart of the poor British performance. As Table 4.1 shows, the productivity of the British economy as a whole was not too bad in its European context even in the 1980s. This helps to explain why British income levels remained around the Western European average through the 1990s. However, the performance of British productivity in manufacturing was weak. Table 4.2 gives estimates of absolute levels of productivity in manufacturing at various benchmark dates.

Throughout the period from 1951 to 1979 German and French productivity growth in manufacturing steadily exceeded that of the British, with obvious consequences for the latter.

The problems of the manufacturing sector were reflected in Britain's external trade. Although Britain still accounted for 25 percent of world exports of manufacturers in 1950, by 1975 the proportion was 9 percent.[36] Conversely, there was a sharp rise in import penetration. In 1951 manufactured goods comprised 20 percent of imports. Forty years later they were over 60 percent. In 1983, for the first time since the Industrial Revolution, Britain imported more manufactured goods in value than it exported. Such import penetration was typical of advanced industrial economies. In the 1980s Germany, for example, had a higher level of import penetration of manufactured goods than Britain. The British problem

---

[35] Nick Crafts, "The Assessment: British Economic Growth over the Long Run," *Oxford Review of Economic Policy*, 4 (1982), p. viii.

[36] Alford, *British Economic Performance*, p. 15.

was its poor export competitiveness. The British share of world exports of manufacturing fell to almost 7 percent in the mid-1980s, before recovering to 9 percent in the early 1990s.

In some industries the extent of import penetration was striking. The old British staple industries finally succumbed. The cotton textiles industry lost most of its export markets and, from the 1960s, faced large-scale import penetration. In 1950 Britain accounted for over a third of world shipbuilding output, but thirty years later British shipbuilding was a marginal force in the world industry.[37] The British automobile industry showed the same trend. In the immediate post–World War II period, with the German car industry in ruins, Britain was a major car exporter. In 1950 the country was the world's greatest car exporter, exporting three times as many cars as the United States. But over the next decade export markets were steadily lost, and this was followed by growing import penetration. In 1965 only 5 percent of British demand for vehicles was met by imports. Ten years later the figure was 33 percent and in 1990 it was over 60 percent.

The process of continuous relative economic decline was interrupted in the 1980s. The discovery of North Sea oil played some role in sustaining British income levels. Britain became self-sufficient in oil in 1980 and then a substantial net oil exporter, and for a time this removed the persistent British balance-of-payments problem. There was also a revival in British labor productivity growth, as Table 4.2 indicates. Uncharacteristically for Britain, the productivity growth was concentrated in the manufacturing sector. In some industries, the improvement was almost miraculous. British aerospace companies, for example, improved their labor productivity by over 60 percent on average between 1980 and 1989. The data generated by O'Mahony in a study of productivity levels in British and German manufacturing industry suggest that the British performance sharply deteriorated against Germany in the 1970s, but considerably improved in the 1980s. She estimates that, by 1987, German output per person-hour in manufacturing was about 22 percent higher than British – still significant, but much less than earlier estimates reflected in Table 4.2. There continued to be marked differences between industries, however. British productivity (per person-hour) was higher than Germany in 1987 in

[37] Clive H. Lee, *The British Economy since 1700: A Macroeconomic Perspective* (Cambridge: Cambridge University Press, 1986), pp. 204–212; Elbaum and Lazonick (eds.), *The Decline of the British Economy*, especially the chapters on shipbuilding and motor vehicles. Alford, *British Economic Performance*, p. 15.

chemicals and textiles, very similar in food, drink, and tobacco and electrical engineering, and very much lower in vehicles, instrument engineering, and timber and furniture.[38] Van Ark has also suggested a more considerable narrowing of the productivity gap between British and American manufacturing between 1968 and 1989 than that indicated in Table 4.2. The van Ark data shows quite a marked British catch-up – even though the American overall productivity leadership remains strong – with a particularly strong British performance in textiles, chemicals, and basic metals.[39]

The interpretation of the productivity trends of the 1980s is difficult. It was associated with a sharp fall in employment rather than an expansion of the British manufacturing base. As O'Mahony notes in her Anglo-German comparative study, between 1968 and 1987 German manufacturing increased its output by 40 percent and decreased its employment by 7 percent, or 600,000 workers. Over the same period British manufacturing output increased by 10 percent while employment fell 37 percent, or 3 million workers. Improved British productivity was largely the result of shedding labor, mostly in the 1980s, when manufacturing fell by 2.1 million between 1979 and 1989.[40] The deep recession of the early 1980s, which virtually all accounts correlate with the subsequent productivity performance, resulted in a major depletion of Britain's capital stock. The shrinking manufacturing output led to a sharp shift in the structure of the British economy. In 1979 manufacturing accounted for 28 percent of GNP and services 55 percent; by 1990 the proportions were 22 and 64 percent respectively.[41] Even the British productivity performance looked comparatively impressive mainly because of a slowdown in productivity growth rates elsewhere.[42]

The improved British performance in manufacturing was in part associated with the growing role of foreign multinationals in the British economy. Britain had a long history as a host economy for foreign – and

---

[38] Mary O'Mahony, "Productivity Levels in British and German Manufacturing Industry," *National Institute Economic Review* no. 139 (February 1992), pp. 46–63. Comparisons with Germany may be misleading because that country has an abnormally high percentage of its work force in manufacturing.
[39] Bart van Ark, "Comparative Productivity in British and American Manufacturing," *National Institute Economic Review*, 142 (1992), pp. 63–73.
[40] Ibid., p. 55.
[41] E. Davis, S. Flanders, and J. Star, "British Industry in the 1980s," *Business Strategy Review*, 3 (1992), pp. 45–69.
[42] Howard Vane, "The Thatcher Years: Macroeconomic Policy and Performance of the UK Economy, 1979–1988," *National Westminster Bank Quarterly Review* (May, 1992), pp. 26–43; "Legacy of the Curate's Egg," *Financial Times*, 13 March 1992, p. 8.

especially American – multinationals, which had achieved prominent positions in certain British manufacturing industries by World War II. They were particularly clustered in parts of electrical and mechanical engineering, metal goods, motor vehicles, chemicals, and some food products, such as breakfast cereals and canned soup. The significance of foreign-owned companies expanded rapidly from the 1950s.[43] In 1967 inward direct investment represented 7.2 percent of British GDP. By 1990 the ratio was 21.2 percent. The average for all developed market economies in 1990 was 8.1 percent (the German percentage was 8.9, the American 7.3, and the Japanese 0.3).[44] Most of the British motor industry, electronics, and other technologically advanced sectors came to be owned by foreign companies. Between 1986 and 1993 the share of manufacturing output accounted for by foreign-owned companies rose from 18 percent to 25 percent, while over the same period the number of foreign-owned companies among the 100 largest manufacturers increased from 18 to 35. In some sectors foreign-owned companies were quite dominant. By the mid-1990s almost three-quarters of all computers manufactured in Britain were made by foreign-owned companies.

The productivity increases since the 1980s were particularly strong in the foreign-owned sector, whose productivity level was far above the average for the United Kingdom. In 1987 foreign-owned enterprises accounted for 17.9 percent of gross value-added in British manufacturing, but only 12.8 percent of employment. If productivity is defined as gross value-added per person employed, foreign-owned firms had a 48.6 percent "productivity advantage" over domestically owned firms. The size of this "advantage" increased during the 1980s, and although some of it was explained by the pattern of industry distribution, more efficient management appeared to be indicated.[45] Foreign multinationals promised the reindustrialization of the British economy, which reemerged in the late 1980s as, for example, a large exporter of electronics products such as color televisions.

The transformation of the British automobile industry by foreign

[43] Frances Bostock and Geoffrey Jones, "Foreign Multinationals in British Manufacturing, 1850–1962," *Business History*, 36 (1994), pp. 89–126; Geoffrey Jones and Frances Bostock, "U.S. Multinationals in British Manufacturing before 1962," *Business History Review*, 71 (1996), pp. 67–116; John H. Dunning, *American Investment in British Manufacturing Industry* (London: Allen & Unwin, 1958).

[44] John H. Dunning, *The Globalisation of Business* (London: Routledge, 1993), p. 290.

[45] Stephen W. Davies and Bruce Lyons, "Characterising Relative Performance: The Productivity Advantage of Foreign Owned Firms in the UK," *University of East Anglia, Economics Research Centre*, Discussion Paper no. 9106 (1991).

multinationals was remarkable. The loss of export markets followed by growing import penetration led to a precipitate fall in British automobile production from 1.9 million to 880,000 passenger cars between 1972 and 1982. Thereafter a renaissance occurred as the British lost control over the industry and new foreign companies – outstandingly the Japanese – invested in the country. A licensing agreement between British Leyland and Honda in 1978 began a process whereby Britain's largest car maker was revitalized first by Japanese technology, and later by German ownership. During the 1980s Nissan and Toyota built huge greenfield factories in Sunderland and Derbyshire. The favorable consequences of their transfer of Japanese-style lean production methods into Britain encouraged Ford and General Motors to revitalize their long-established British manufacturing operations. By the mid-1990s U.S., Japanese, German, and French multinationals completely owned the British automobile industry, except for a handful of specialist producers such as Vickers-owned Rolls-Royce, while the majority of Britain's largest component makers were also foreign-owned, again with a few exceptions such as GKN and T&N. The resulting improvements in productivity and quality under foreign ownership made the United Kingdom once again a large automobile manufacturing country. By 1994 British production had recovered to 1.4 million passenger cars, and while in 1984 only 20 percent of British output was exported, ten years later the figure was over 40 percent.[46]

Meanwhile, the degree to which British-owned firms, and even the British economy as a whole, have undergone a renaissance since the 1980s remains much in dispute. Matters look best if profitability or productivity performance are emphasized. British companies usually featured disproportionately in listings of Europe's most profitable businesses. There was strong evidence that overall productivity had improved, but this measure – and others – indicated that while Britain possessed some firms whose performances were equal to the best international levels, it also possessed a considerable tail of far less efficient firms.[47] Studies which focused on international market share typically emphasized the continued deterioration in British competitive performance.[48]

---

[46] "Clapped-out Wreck Is Transformed," *Financial Times*, 31 August 1995, p. 12; "Japanese Style Sparked Revival of Car Industry," *Financial Times*, 1 September 1995, p. 10.

[47] Peter E. Hart, "Corporate Governance in Britain and Germany," *National Institute of Economic and Social Research*, Discussion Paper no. 31 (1992), p. 3. Phil Hanson, Chris Voss, Kate Blackmon, and Bryan Oak, *Made in Europe: A Four Nations Best Practice Study* (Warwick: IBM Consulting Group, November 1994).

[48] Michael E. Porter, *The Competitive Advantage of Nations* (London: Macmillan, 1990).

Table 4.3. *The share (%) of the 100 largest enterprises in manufacturing net output, 1935–1970*

	1935	1949	1958	1970
United Kingdom	24	22	32	41
United States	26	23	30	33

Source: Barry Supple (ed.), *The Rise of Big Business* (Aldershot: Edward Elgar, 1992), introduction, p. xi.

In the postwar world the structure of British business changed radically. Family firms and family directors progressively disappeared off the corporate scene. By 1970 it would make little sense to talk of British personal capitalism. If British manufacturing industry was characterized by too many small units before World War II, this was certainly not the case subsequently. Concentration increased at a rapid pace in the 1950s and 1960s. There was a major merger wave in the 1960s, associated with the new acceptability of contested takeover bids, which led to the restructuring of large sections of British industry and a very substantial increase in the size of British corporations.[49] Britain emerged, as shown in Table 4.3, with a higher level of concentration than the United States. In the postwar world, it became the classic big-business economy.

Merger activity continued at a high level in the 1970s,[50] although the effect on the concentration level was modest, with the average level of concentration increasing only slightly between 1975 and 1979.[51] In the 1980s the apparent inexorable rise in industrial concentration finally ended, and there would appear to have been a substantial fall over the course of the decade, despite a continuing high level of merger activity. Some of the sharpest falls in concentration were in the high technology electrical and instrument engineering sectors.[52] Despite this important new trend, however, large corporations remained a more prominent feature

---

[49] Leslie Hannah, *The Rise of the Corporate Economy* (London: Methuen, 1983), chapter 10.

[50] George A. Luffman and Richard Reed, *The Strategy and Performance of British Industry, 1970–80* (London: Macmillan, 1987), p. 163.

[51] Peter E. Hart, "Recent Trends in Concentration in British Industry," *National Institute for Economic and Social Research*, Discussion Paper no. 82 (1985).

[52] Unpublished research. For the extensive merger activity in this period, see "Takeover Activity in the 1980s," *Bank of England Quarterly Bulletin*, 29 (1989), pp. 78–85.

Table 4.4. *Distribution of Europe's 500 largest companies by country (companies ranked according to sales), 1989*

Country per million inhabitants	Total number of companies among the 500	(Thereof: manufacturing companies)	Number
United Kingdom	130	(41)	2.28
Germany	103	(42)	1.68
France	72	(27)	1.29
Italy	24	(9)	0.42

Source: *Growth and Integration in a Nordic Perspective* (Helsinki, 1990), p. 56.

of the contemporary British economy than that of the other large European economies, as shown in Table 4.4.

Postwar large British companies gave more attention to their organizational structures than had their predecessors. They generally moved to adopt American structures, quite frequently as a result of employing the services of management consultants, notably McKinsey's.[53] Many British firms knew they had competitiveness problems and looked toward the American model to solve them. Channon's much-cited study traced the evolution of the M-form of organization for a sample of the ninety-two largest British companies from 1950 to 1970 (and ninety-six companies for the period 1960–1970). In 1950 he found only twelve companies in his sample had adopted a multidivisional structure, of which eight were foreign-owned and a further one was the Anglo-Dutch group Unilever. By the end of the 1950s some 30 percent of the firms in the sample had such a structure, and by 1970 the M-form was the dominant organizational form, with sixty-eight of the ninety-six sample large British corporations adopting it. The spread of the M-form signaled the rapid expansion of product diversification in large British companies. The number of single-product companies fell from 34 percent in 1950 to 6 percent in 1970. By 1970 the M-form was almost as widespread in Britain as in the United States and, given that this organizational form only became common among American corporations in the 1940s and 1950s, the scale of the

[53] Terence R. Gourvish, "British Business and the Transition to a Corporate Economy: Entrepreneurship and Management Structures," *Business History*, 29 (1987), p. 35; Tolliday and Zeitlin, "Conclusion."

British "lag" was modest. The M-form had been more widely adopted in Britain than in any other large European economy by 1970.[54]

The new British concern with improved management structures was found even – or rather especially – in the nationalized industries. During the late 1940s a considerable slice of British nonmanufacturing industry, including coal, gas, electricity, and railways, had been taken into public ownership, most of which had had a dismal performance under private ownership. After a difficult period of reorganization and rationalization in the 1950s, the coal, railways, and electricity industries in particular underwent a veritable "managerial revolution," often pioneering the introduction of improved management methods such as investment appraisal techniques and corporate planning.[55] The productivity performance of the British publicly owned sector compared favorably both to British privately owned manufacturing, and to equivalent American industries, in the period between the 1950s and the 1970s. However, most of the state-owned sector was privatized by the post-1979 Conservative governments.[56]

In the 1970s British business continued to evolve along the trends identified by Channon. A study of the top 1,000 British firms in that decade established that product diversification progressed further, if at a slower rate. Diversification, however, only exceptionally led to British firms changing their industry completely, and typically it was based on existing market or technological skills.[57]

There were also radical changes in another area of British management – its education. British companies before 1945 showed none of the American enthusiasm for employing university graduates as managers, and no enthusiasm whatsoever for any form of management education, and these sentiments continued for a time after the end of World War II. When graduates were recruited as future senior managers, the best educational background in the 1950s remained an arts degree from Oxford

[54] Derek F. Channon, *The Strategy and Structure of British Enterprise* (London: Macmillan, 1973), chapter 3; Hannah, *Rise*, chapter 10; Hannah, "Strategy and Structure in the Manufacturing Sector," in Leslie Hannah (ed.), *Management Strategy and Business Development* (London: Macmillan, 1976), pp. 184–202.

[55] Gourvish, "British Business," pp. 35–39; William Ashworth, *The History of the British Coal Industry*, vol. 5, *1946–82* (Oxford: Oxford University Press, 1986); Leslie Hannah, *Engineers, Managers and Politicians* (London: Macmillan, 1982).

[56] James Foreman-Peck and Robert Millward, *Public and Private Ownership of British Industry, 1820–1990* (Oxford: Clarendon Press, 1994), pp. 300–339.

[57] Luffman and Reed, *Strategy and Performance*, chapter 4; Michael A. Utton, "Large Firms Diversification in GB Manufacturing Industry," *Economic Journal*, 87 (1977), pp. 96–113.

or Cambridge, preferably combined with attendance at a public school. British universities also showed little interest in management education, but as firms would not employ any graduates from such programs, or offer any financial support, this was not very surprising.[58] An additional problem was that a career in British industry generally carried low esteem, with the result that graduates with good degrees rarely considered an industrial career.

In the 1960s this situation also began to change. Graduate recruitment to management began on a large scale. In the 1960s Britain's first two business schools were established, offering MBA programs closely modeled on the American pattern. In the 1980s there was an enormous expansion of the number of MBA courses. The number of British students graduating with MBAs from British business schools rose from 1,100 in 1980 to 4,500 in 1991, by which date around sixty-five different schools in Britain offered MBA programs. The same period also saw an enormous proliferation of other management training schemes.[59]

Given the British historical legacy, it is unsurprising that British managers continued to be shown in any comparative study as exceptionally undereducated. A 1987 survey showed that only 24 percent of top British management had a degree, a low level compared with management in France or Germany. When British managers had degrees, it was still rarely in engineering and often in arts subjects. "It remains true to say," Lane concluded in a comparative study of British, French, and German management in 1989, "that the promotion to top level posts of 'gifted amateurs' remains a uniquely British phenomenon."[60] Comparisons between British and Japanese managers were even more striking. At the end of the 1980s a paired study of middle and senior managers in similar British and Japanese engineering companies, banks, retailers, and newly privatized utilities established that almost all of the Japanese managers (94 percent) had either undergraduate or postgraduate tertiary qualifications, compared with less than half (42 percent) of their British

[58] Chandler, *Scale and Scope*, pp. 291–294; Channon, *Strategy and Structure*, pp. 43–45; Shirley Keeble, *The Ability to Manage* (Manchester: Manchester University Press, 1992); Howard Gospel and Reiko Okayama, "Industrial Training in Britain and Japan: An Overview," in Howard Gospel (ed.), *Industrial Training and Technological Innovation* (London: Routledge, 1991), pp. 26–8.
[59] Charles Handy, *Making Managers* (London: Pitman, 1988); Saxton Bampflyde International, *The MBA Question: Perspectives and Reality in the UK* (London: Saxton Bampflyde, 1990).
[60] Christel Lane, *Management and Labour in Europe* (Aldershot: Edward Elgar, 1989), pp. 91–92.

counterparts.[61] Nor was there any sign that the MBA would assume the status of a senior management prerequisite that it secured in the United States. The majority of British MBAs since the 1960s have gone into the financial services, and more recently also into management consultancy, while their impact on manufacturing industry remained muted.

Thus, the international competitive performance of British business, and more particularly the manufacturing sector, was relatively weak after 1945. British manufacturing was undermined by low productivity growth. British industries lost world market share, and experienced substantial import penetration. The British productivity gap with both the United States and the rest of Western Europe began finally to narrow, at least in some sectors, in the 1970s and the 1980s. This postwar period saw the replacement of personal capitalism by American-style managerial capitalism. British industry became dominated by large corporations using an M-form of organization.

ORGANIZATIONAL CAPABILITIES AND COMPETITIVENESS AFTER 1945

As before 1945, the explanation for poor British performance in certain manufacturing industries is multicausal, but two general tendencies are observable. The first is the continuation of some of the problems associated with personal capitalism. The second is the acquisition of a new set of problems following the adoption of American-style managerial capitalism.

Much of the story of British corporate success and failure after 1945 can be written in terms of the continuing British failure to make the necessary three-pronged investment in manufacturing, marketing, and management to build successful modern industrial enterprises. The British computer industry in the 1950s and 1960s, for example, demonstrated an inability to build organizational capabilities sufficient to exploit Britain's initial pioneering role in computer technology. The disadvantages of personal capitalism formed a part of this story. The British electronics firm Ferranti built and installed the first commercial computer in 1951, but the Ferranti family "refused to commit greater resources to both production and marketing," and followed a risk-averse strategy, eventually divesting from the computer business in 1963. In the 1950s

[61] John Storey et al., "Managerial Careers and Management Development: A Comparative Analysis of Britain and Japan," *Human Resource Management Journal* (1991), pp. 33–57.

Ferranti was almost a caricature of a British family firm, with business strategy being discussed between directors over " 'high table' . . . with each (director) daily taking turns to carve the joint of meat."[62]

However, there was more to the story than simply entrepreneurial failure to become first movers, and to build organizational capabilities on the lines of an IBM. The huge American defense market gave the United States companies an enormous competitive advantage over their British counterparts. Equally important, in Hendry's analysis, was the educational environment. The growth of the early American computer industry was made possible by high mobility of engineers between firms, universities, and defense establishments. Such mobility of ideas and information was absent in Britain. Inadequate public policy was a further handicap.[63]

The problems of the British-owned motor industry also provide spectacular evidence of the continuing British difficulties in organizing large manufacturing enterprises. During the interwar years the leading British car makers Morris and Austin captured a substantial share of the British domestic market away from Ford and General Motors, whose subsidiaries had initially dominated it. But the British-owned industry developed with a substantial number of plants which handicapped the achievement of economies of scale. A series of mergers – notably that between Austin and Morris in 1952 which created the British Motor Corporation (BMC) – failed to deliver rationalization in the postwar decade. After the merger, BMC maintained sixty different plants in Britain and kept separate dealerships for Austin and Morris cars. A preference for paying dividends to shareholders resulted in the lowest level of spending on new capital equipment per worker in Europe in the 1950s. This was a classic failure of organizational capability of the kind diagnosed by Chandler for pre-1945 Britain.

During the 1960s, as the British car industry began to lose its export markets, a series of defensive mergers of smaller companies culminated in the British government's encouragement of the acquisition of BMC by Leyland, a successful truck maker, in 1967. The senior management of the new British Leyland Motor Corporation, which at the time of its creation was Britain's largest single employer, had no knowledge of volume carmaking, and remained unable to rationalize production, or to confront

---

[62] Geoffrey Tweedale, "Marketing in the Second Industrial Revolution: A Case Study of the Ferranti Group, 1949–63," *Business History*, 34 (1992), pp. 96–127.

[63] John Hendry, *Innovating for Failure: Government Policy and the Early British Computer Industry* (Cambridge, Mass.: MIT Press, 1990), especially chapter 13.

inherited inefficiencies in human resource management, especially the "piecework" method of wages. Catastrophic management failures in marketing and product design and quality led to the surge of import penetration into Britain, and finally to BL's bankruptcy and nationalization in the mid-1970s. The following fifteen years saw the dramatic shrinkage of British Leyland, and its eventual privatization as the Rover group. However, it was not privatization but foreign companies which saved the enterprise. During the 1980s Rover was revitalized by Honda, which acquired a minority shareholding and provided new technology and design, and in 1994 it was purchased in its entirety by Germany's BMW.[64] Under German ownership, Rover's British management believed they could pursue a long-term strategy without short-term pressures for dividends.[65]

A new set of problems arose as British capitalism sought salvation in the American corporate model. In essence, British companies suffered from many of the same defects that Chandler has argued undermined American industrial competitiveness from the 1960s. The diversification which was made possible by American-style managerial hierarchies led eventually to diseconomies, as top management became divorced from knowledge about the products they made. Financial criteria became the key factor in many business decisions. The numbers of mergers, hostile takeovers, and divestitures accelerated as financial institutions became the owners of industrial enterprise, and companies became commodities that were bought and sold. Managers had, perforce, to focus on short-term time horizons, the daily movements in share price, or else face acquisition by predators.[66]

The effect of such factors on the erosion of competitive capabilities in British industries after 1945 was probably magnified because the British gave distinctive glosses to the American system which they imported. They adopted, for example, a particularly decentralized form of organization, in which finance was king. The headquarters of the "typical" large British company by the 1980s was notably decentralized. Headquarters

[64] Stephen Tolliday, "Competition and the Workplace in the British Automobile Industry, 1945–88," *Business and Economic History*, 17 (1988), pp. 63–78; Karel Williams, John Williams, and Coliz Haslam, *The Breakdown of Austin Rover* (Leamington Spa: Berg, 1987).

[65] "Clapped-out Wreck Is Transformed," *Financial Times*, 31 August 1995, p. 12.

[66] Alfred D. Chandler, "Managerial Enterprises and Competitive Capabilities," *Business History*, 34 (1992), pp. 29–39; "Corporate Strategy, Structure and Control Methods in the United States during the 20th Century," *Industrial and Corporate Change* 1 (1992), pp. 263–284; and "The Competitive Performance of US Industrial Enterprises since the Second World War," *Business History Review*, 68 (1994), pp. 1–72.

were often primarily concerned with financial matters; in other matters, managers in divisions were given considerable autonomy, with most production and sales decisions delegated to subsidiaries. The fact that many British companies had grown over the previous thirty years through mergers rather than organic growth encouraged such a structure,[67] although this was an obvious continuity with the British traditional practice in this regard.

The impact of the finance-driven decentralized organizational form favored by the British is debatable, but it does appear unlikely to promote sustained innovative capacity. An extreme form of the finance-driven model of British capitalism was the diversified conglomerates which grew rapidly in the 1970s and 1980s. These enterprises – of which the largest included BTR, Hanson, Williams Holdings, and Tomkins – grew by takeovers in Britain and, later, the United States. They were able to finance acquisitions by borrowing from the financial markets and banks, and maintained a self-sustaining earnings growth by the constant accumulation of companies. The supporters of such conglomerates pointed to their role in disciplining inefficient managements, but their critics questioned both their interest in, and their ability to sustain, long-term strategies centered on innovation rather than the payment of high dividends to shareholders.

BTR, Britain's eleventh largest company by market capitalization in 1992, grew rapidly from the 1970s from a modest firm in the rubber industry to a diversified industrial conglomerate. BTR's growth was based on a series of acquisitions of once-famous names in British industry, including Thomas Tilling in 1983, Dunlop in 1985, and Hawker Siddeley in 1991. It also tried, but failed, to acquire over the same period the U.S. abrasives manufacturer Norton and the British glass manufacturer Pilkington. Acquired companies had their costs forced down, usually by large-scale redundancies, and were subjected to a highly centralized system of financial control operated from a very small head office. Each subsidiary was given an annual profit plan based on return on sales – a ratio preferred to return on net assets in order to place the highest emphasis on profits. Subsidiaries were also required to file monthly financial reports, which were closely monitored to see if annual targets were being achieved. There was also rigorous supervision of working capital controls. In contrast, the

---

[67] Lane, *Management and Labour*, chapters 4 and 5; Jacques Horovitz, *Top Management Control in Europe* (London: Macmillan).

responsibility for the overall strategic plan for each subsidiary and other managerial matters devolved away from the head office.[68]

Hanson, the ninth largest British company by market capitalization in 1992, was another variant of the finance-driven conglomerate. Hanson grew from being an insignificant company called Wiles in the 1960s – it was renamed Hanson Trust in 1969 – by buying undervalued companies, breaking up and selling parts of them, and keeping some noncapital intensive parts as cash cows. During the 1980s the company made a series of spectacular acquisitions, including the Imperial Group in Britain and SCM in the United States, which demonstrated remarkable financial acumen. The Imperial Group was bought in 1986 for £2.5 billion, of which Hanson recouped £2.4 billion in subsequent asset sales, leaving Hanson in control of Imperial's large and profitable tobacco operations. Hanson's activities, which were almost entirely in Britain and the United States, came to include tobacco products, forest products, coal mining, chemicals, and bricks and construction. Hanson's strategy was strictly focused on maximizing "shareholder value" as its primary goal, an aim which was certainly achieved through the 1980s.

During the 1990s the growth of the British conglomerates faltered. The bigger these companies became, the harder it was to find acquisitions large enough to maintain earnings growth, especially as there was a decline in the number of poorly managed targets. The conglomerates experienced falling share prices as business strategies based on focus gained ground, and as innovation and investment in new-growth areas began to be regarded as more important than improving the performance of long-established but poorly managed industrial firms. In response to these trends, in 1996 Hanson broke itself up into four separate companies focused on tobacco, chemicals, energy, and building materials. The last retained the name "Hanson," and was ranked as Britain's largest brick-maker. Meanwhile, during the same period BTR initiated a new strategy to sell off many peripheral activities and restructure itself around four principal global product groups in which the firm held an advantage, either in superior technology or low cost production.

The consequences of the Hanson strategy in the 1970s and 1980s for British industrial competitiveness are ambiguous. The battery industry serves as an example of one outcome. In 1981 Hanson acquired Berec,

[68] "A Culture Shock That Won Ardent Converts," *Financial Times*, 13 January 1987, p. 14; "'Magic Dust' Loses Glitter," *Financial Times*, 15 September 1990, p. 8; "God Father Get Control," *Financial Times*, 11 March 1992, p. 10.

better known as Ever Ready. This British company was then Europe's largest manufacturer of dry cell batteries. At the time of the acquisition it showed evidence of management failure. Its American competitor, Duracell, had developed a long-life battery which had been very success-ful, but the British firm had continued to produce cheaper shorter-life batteries. After the acquisition, Hanson closed most of Ever Ready's R&D operations and, in 1982, sold almost all of its overseas operations. The German and Italian factories were sold to Duracell, the main competitor. Under Hanson, the firm developed longer-life products, but was trapped within the small British market, and in 1992 Hanson sold Ever Ready to Ralston Purina of the United States.[69] The upshot of Hanson's policy was the elimination, in a decade, of a British-owned battery industry.

There seems little doubt that British companies suffered from many of the same problems as American ones as a result of excessive reliance on increasingly irrelevant management accounting methods.[70] However, the British carried the preoccupation with accountants even further than the Americans through their employment at all levels of the management hierarchy, which was typically preoccupied with financially related goals. "British managers think industry is about making money," Lawrence observed in 1980, "Germans that it is about making three-dimensional artefacts."[71] The finance function became extremely important within British firms. British managers, in contrast to German ones, attached relatively greater importance to profits and satisfying shareholders' inter-ests.[72] They were encouraged in this orientation by the growing practice of linking managerial compensation with financial indices of perform-ance, something which was much rarer in the rest of Europe. In the 1980s Britain had thirty times as many qualified accountants as Germany, and an accountancy training was the single most common qualification of British managers. It was the British equivalent of the American MBA or the German engineering degree.[73]

There were several reasons for British business's preoccupation with accountants. The lack of formal management education until recently made

[69] "Ever Ready: Set Fair for a Longer Life?," *Financial Times*, 19 July 1987, p. 11; "Take-over Put Spark into Battery Maker," *Financial Times*, 14 April 1992, p. 12.
[70] H. Thomas Johnson and Robert S. Kaplan, *Relevance Lost* (Boston: Harvard Business School Press, 1987).
[71] Peter Lawrence, *Managers and Management in West Germany* (London: Croom Helm, 1980), p. 142.
[72] Budde et al., "Corporate Goals," p. 13.
[73] Jean-Louis Barsoux and Peter Lawrence, *The Challenge of British Management* (London: Macmillan, 1990), pp. 60–61.

accountancy one of the few qualifications available for aspiring British managers, while the fact it was an external professional qualification was attractive in a culture with a high degree of job mobility. The importance attached to financial data and their interpretation reflected the British corporate reliance on external equity finance as opposed to debt financing or the internal financing seen in France. The unstable British macroeconomic environment after 1950 probably obliged the managers of British firms to focus on financial matters.[74] The distinctive British preoccupation with finance and an accountancy-trained managerial elite provides one explanation for the alleged "short-termism" of British industry.

The emergence of an institutionalized market for corporate control, the growth of hostile takeovers, and the phenomenon of transaction-oriented mergers and acquisitions have been identified by Chandler as some of the influences on declining American competitiveness in the 1970s and 1980s.[75] British capitalism evolved in similar directions as American in this respect, and with some similar consequences. Takeover activity was high in Britain from the 1960s, and one-quarter of takeovers of publicly listed firms in the two decades after the early 1970s were hostile. One immediate result was that a good deal of senior British management time was spent planning or resisting takeovers, but there was also an impact on the time horizons in investment and other decisions. A distinction has been made in this context between the "outsider" system of corporate control which came to prevail in the United States and Britain, where ownership was dispersed among a large number of individual and institutional investors, and the "insider" systems of Japan and continental Europe, where ownership of individual firms was concentrated in the hands of a small number of other firms, banks, or families. Both systems have different merits, but it is evident that the insider systems facilitate long-term relationships with suppliers, customers, and employees of kinds that yield competitive advantages in contemporary manufacturing processes.[76]

The British emulation after 1945 of another aspect of the American model – the creation of large corporations – failed to enhance British

---

[74] Eltis et al., "Lessons," p. 18.
[75] Chandler, "Corporate Strategy, Structure and Control."
[76] Julian Franks and Colin Mayer, "Corporate Ownership and Corporate Control: A Study of France, Germany, and the UK," *Economic Policy* (April 1990), pp. 191–231; Tim Jenkinson and Colin Mayer, "The Assessment: Corporate Governance and Corporate Control," *Oxford Review of Economic Policy* 8, 3 (1992), pp. 1–10. See also, from a different perspective, John Kay and Aubrey Silberston, "Corporate Governance," *National Institute Economic Review* (August 1995), pp. 84–97.

competitiveness as much as might have been expected. British business historians have long expressed skepticism that increased concentration or size necessarily led to improved efficiency,[77] a point of view which would be shared by conventional economists and others concerned with the costs of monopoly.[78] It became apparent, especially from the 1970s, that there were limits to the efficiency gains of large M-form firms, whose performance deteriorated with excessive product diversification.[79] Research by British industrial economists has generally concluded that British mergers since the 1960s have not contributed materially to improvements in industrial performance, and rather that there have been real welfare losses.[80] Part of the problem, as Kogut has argued, was that British companies grafted the M-form onto their preexisting decentralized holding-company structures. The British versions of the M-form failed to achieve the clear distinction between strategic and operating responsibilities seen in American corporations.[81] However, even a full adoption of the M-form was unlikely to solve all the managerial problems arising from large size. The recent American business school literature pointing to the loss of entrepreneurship within large American corporations is applicable to their British counterparts.[82] It is certainly interesting that the improvement in Britain's productivity performance in the 1980s coincided with falling concentration levels – though the link between the two factors has yet to be demonstrated.

The organizational defects of large corporations were probably made worse in the British context. A particular problem after 1945 was the uncompetitive home market of British industry. In the early 1950s between 50 and 60 percent of manufacturing output was regulated by cartels. The advent of a more assertive British competition policy led to their dismantling,

[77] Payne, "Entrepreneurship and British Economic Decline," pp. 30–31; Leslie Hannah, "Visible and Invisible Hands in Great Britain," in Alfred D. Chandler and Herman Daems (eds.), *Managerial Hierarchies* (Cambridge, Mass.: Harvard University Press, 1980), p. 71.
[78] Richard B. Duboff and Edward S. Herman, "Alfred Chandler's New Business History: A Review," *Politics and Society*, 10 (1980), reprinted in Supple, *Rise*.
[79] Mowery, "Finance and Corporate Evolution," pp. 26–27.
[80] Sigbert J. Prais, *The Evolution of Giant Firms in Britain* (Cambridge: Cambridge University Press, 1976); Keith Cowling et al., *Mergers and Economic Performance* (Cambridge: Cambridge University Press, 1980). For the United States, see Morton I. Kamien and Nancy L. Schwartz, *Market Structure and Innovation* (Cambridge: Cambridge University Press, 1982).
[81] Bruce Kogut and David Parkinson, "The Diffusion of American Organizing Principles to Europe," in Bruce Kogut (ed.), *Country Competitiveness* (New York: Oxford University Press, 1993), pp. 179–202.
[82] Elizabeth Moss Kanter, *When Giants Learn to Dance* (London: Unwin, 1990); Richard Pascale, *Managing on the Edge* (London: Viking, 1990).

only to be replaced by mergers leading to growing concentration.[83] British governments between the 1940s and the 1970s continued to encourage and support actively collusive agreements in sectors as diverse as banking and agriculture, while in the 1960s and 1970s there was a series of ad hoc attempts to create "national champions" in manufacturing industry. Only against such a background can we understand the seemingly bizarre view held by some British economists that the Thatcher government's incompetence in creating such a deep recession in the early 1980s made a positive contribution to British industrial performance. The creation at this time of an exceptionally hostile environment which bankrupted a quarter of British manufacturing industry, so this line of argument goes, acted as the spur which finally stimulated British companies – or those which survived – to improve their competitiveness.[84]

Public policy before the 1980s and the lack of strong domestic rivalry meant that barriers to exit for inefficient British firms and even industries remained high. They tended to linger rather than "die" and release resources elsewhere. This is the thrust of Singleton's analysis of the post-1950 Lancashire cotton industry which, he argues, hoarded "labour which was sorely needed elsewhere. The British economy would have benefited from a speedier rather than a more prolonged period of contraction in the cotton industry."[85]

The British also failed to gain some of the benefits from the creation of larger firms and more modern management structures because of their continued underinvestment in human capital. If managers often remained "gifted amateurs," so did their workers, for few British firms showed interest in training them. Britain, like Germany, possessed an apprenticeship system, but this declined in importance, especially in the 1980s. Technical training throughout the post-1945 period was very low compared with that in Germany. The upshot was that British manufacturing industry became distinguished by low skill levels, especially at the intermediate level of technician and foreman. The majority of foremen in British industry were recruited from manual jobs and received little or no formal training. Table 4.5 shows the striking differences in the levels of skill in the British and German manufacturing labor force in 1987.

[83] D. C. Elliot and J. D. Gribben, "The Abolition of Cartels and Structural Change in the United Kingdom," in Alexis P. Jacquemin and Henry W. de Jong (eds.), Welfare Aspects of Industrial Markets (Leiden: M. Nijhoff, 1977), pp. 345–65.

[84] Geoffrey Maynard, The Economy under Mrs. Thatcher (Oxford: Basil Blackwell, 1988).

[85] John Singleton, Lancashire on the Scrapheap (Oxford: Oxford University Press, 1991), p. 232.

Table 4.5. *Qualification proportions and relative wage rates of the British and German manufacturing work force, 1987*

	Qualification proportions		Wage rates relative to unskilled	
	United Kingdom	Germany	United Kingdom	Germany
Higher level	6.7	6.0	1.7	2.2
Upper intermediate	4.4	8.2	1.3	1.7
Lower intermediate	26.3	56.4	1.2	1.2
No qualifications	62.6	29.4	1.0	1.0

Source: Mary O'Mahony, "Productivity Levels in British and German Manufacturing Industry," Na.

Since the 1970s a series of comparative studies of matched British and German plants have shown very clearly how the low skill levels of the British work force explain much of the productivity differences. The low skill levels of British workers greatly constrained flexibility in periods of rapid technical change and acted as an obstacle to the introduction of new technology.[86] From the perspective of the 1990s, it was this low skill level which served as the greatest constraint on any sustained productivity increase.

The neglect of training by British companies had several explanations. Before World War II the small sizes and weak governance structures of British manufacturing firms in many industries may have discouraged investment in training. British firms chose to externalize the management of labor in the nineteenth century, and only slowly and painfully changed their labor management practices from the 1960s.[87] The low level of training within British business also cannot be divorced from the public policy context. British government policy over a long period was characterized

---

[86] Lane, *Management and Labour*, chapter 3; Sigbert J. Prais, *Productivity and Industrial Structure: A Statistical Study of Manufacturing Industry in Britain, Germany and the US* (Cambridge: Cambridge University Press, 1981); A. Daly, D. M. Hitchens, and K. Wagner, "Productivity, Machinery and Skills in a Sample of British and German Manufacturing Plants," *National Institute Economic Review* (February 1985), pp. 48–61; O'Mahony, "Productivity Levels"; Geoff Mason, Sigbert J. Prais, and Bart van Ark, "Vocational Education and Productivity in the Netherlands and Britain," *National Institute Economic Review* (May 1992), pp. 45–63.

[87] Howard Gospel, *Markets, Firms and the Management of Labour in Modern Britain* (Cambridge: Cambridge University Press, 1992). See also Andrew Pettigrew and Richard Whipp, *Managing Change for Competitive Success* (Oxford: Blackwell, 1991), chapter 6.

by an extreme voluntarist attitude whereby education and, especially, training were left to the voluntary action of individuals and organizations.[88] Until the mid-1960s the British government denied all responsibility for training. In 1964 a system of industrial training boards was set up with the aim of encouraging training and spreading the costs between firms, but these had only a limited effect, and were abolished by the government in the 1980s. In that decade the government largely used publicly funded training to reduce unemployment rather than to raise skills. A confused variety of schemes was introduced, but only in the context of declining state funding, a reinvigorated belief that voluntarism was the solution, and the virtual demise of traditional apprenticeships.[89]

There remains the problem that (as before 1945) general criticisms of the organizational capabilities and competitive performance of British business, especially manufacturing, have to take into account British success stories as well as failures.

The invention and exploitation by Pilkington of float glass in the 1950s – a process which completely transformed the world glass industry – stands as a warning against blanket criticisms of personal capitalism. Pilkington was a private family company until 1970. The inventor of float glass, Alastair Pilkington, was recruited to, and promoted in, the firm after World War II, because he had the family name, even though the two branches of the family had separated at least fifteen generations previously. Chandler cites the recruitment of Alastair Pilkington as a prime example of the continuing British attachment to personal capitalism which "made industrial capitalism less dynamic in Britain than in the United States and Germany."[90] However, although the incident was eccentric, it *did* have dynamic results and, moreover, it showed some of the advantages of family firms. The development of the float glass process was costly and prolonged. The historian of the company argues that it was the fact that Pilkington was a family company which was "probably an important ingredient in ultimate success," because the firm was able to pursue a long-term development strategy in secrecy and without pressure for immediate profits from shareholders.[91]

---

[88] Howard Gospel, "Industrial Training and Technological Innovation: An Introduction," in Gospel (ed.), *Industrial Training*, p. 6.
[89] Lane, *Management and Labour*, pp. 72–74; "An Urgent Need to Turn the Tide of History," *Financial Times*, 26 November 1990, p. 10.
[90] Chandler, *Scale and Scope*, pp. 591–592.
[91] Theodore C. Barker, "Business Implications of Technical Development in the Glass Industry, 1945–1965: A Case Study," in Barry Supple (ed.), *Essays in British Business History* (Oxford: Clarendon Press, 1977), p. 204.

There were major British examples of organizational learning over time, as firms in chemicals, petroleum, and pharmaceuticals "caught up" to first movers elsewhere. Britain became a strong competitor in global chemical markets after ICI, created in 1926, rationalized much of the industry.[92] In the same period the Anglo-Persian Oil Company (British Petroleum in 1955) became one of the world's largest vertically integrated oil corporations.[93] Together with Shell, jointly owned with the Netherlands, and a number of smaller companies, Britain possessed a major stake in the world oil industry. In pharmaceuticals, the British learning process was much slower. In *Scale and Scope*, pharmaceuticals is correctly identified as one of the new science-based industries of the late nineteenth century in which British entrepreneurs failed to establish enterprises which could match those of Germany or the United States.[94] The failure to gain first mover advantages had a long-term impact, and through the 1960s the British industry – which had four main firms by that date (Wellcome, Beecham, ICI, and Glaxo) – was of only modest international importance.[95]

Subsequently an internationally competitive British pharmaceutical industry developed. Glaxo was the moving force. The firm was still only just in the top-100 British firms at the end of the 1970s, but a transformation followed the invention of Zantac, the antiulcer drug launched in Britain in 1981 and the United States three years later. During the 1970s Glaxo was able to take advantage of advances in understanding the biochemistry of the human body by developing methods of reducing the time-consuming stages of drug development. Skillful marketing then led to Zantac displacing SmithKline's Tagamet, and establishing itself as the "world's best-selling drug." By 1992 Glaxo was ranked as the largest British company by market capitalization and had become Europe's largest pharmaceuticals group. Glaxo's growth was not in isolation, for a cluster of fast-growing and large British pharmaceutical enterprises developed, including SmithKline Beecham (the product of an Anglo-American merger) and Wellcome. The takeover of the latter by Glaxo in 1995 created the world's largest pharmaceuticals company.

How was Britain – of all countries – able to challenge the American, German, and Swiss first movers in a science-based industry dependent

[92] William J. Reader, *Imperial Chemical Industries: A History*, vol. 2 (London: Oxford University Press, 1975).
[93] Jim H. Bamberg, *The History of the British Petroleum Company*, vol. 2 (Cambridge: Cambridge University Press, 1994).
[94] Chandler, *Scale and Scope*, pp. 278–279, 374–375.
[95] Richard P. T. Davenport-Hines and Judy Slinn, *Glaxo: A History to 1962* (Cambridge: Cambridge University Press, 1992).

upon expensive long-term research and development? The story has to be related in part to the new opportunities caused by the antibiotic revolution and the advent of the prescription drug industry. In the United States firms such as Pfizer, Eli Lilly, Upjohn, Squibb, and Merck took advantage of the new opportunities to become first movers.[96] Glaxo was successful because of an entrepreneurial willingness to build organizational capabilities. Glaxo's finance director from 1968 and CEO during the 1980s, Paul Girolami, was an accountant by training, but highly vocal on the need for the "long-term" view in decision making. He was also Italian born. The firm made a long-term commitment to basic research, invested substantial resources in building large businesses in both the United States and Japan, divested from noncore activities such as the firm's traditional baby food business, and avoided mergers and acquisitions in favor of internally generated growth.

A number of factors favored the growth of a British pharmaceuticals industry at this time. The National Health Service provided a large home market. The presence of American pharmaceutical companies in Britain from the 1950s stimulated a research climate in the industry.[97] The existence of several competing British companies was also a stimulus. This domestic competitive rivalry was sustained by the British regulatory authorities in 1972 when they ruled against proposed mergers between Glaxo and Beecham, and Glaxo and Boots.

A further area of British business success came in the food and drink industries. For most of the twentieth century these industries had less complex and capital-intensive production processes than their more high-tech counterparts, but over the past two decades technical change and other factors have led to a considerable growth in their capital-intensity. The British had traditional strengths in branded food and drink products. In the first half of the century the family firms active in the sector performed better than those in heavy industry.[98] However, British enterprises also responded well to the new conditions prevailing toward the end of

---

[96] I owe this point to Alfred D. Chandler, Jr. in a letter to the author, 30 December 1992; see reference to the therapeutic revolution in Chapter 3.

[97] Michael Brech and Margaret Sharp, *Inward Investment, Policy Options for the United Kingdom* (London: RIIA, 1984), pp. 41–62. L. G. Thomas, III, "Implicit Industrial Policy: The Triumph of Britain and the Failure of France in Global Pharmaceuticals," *Industrial and Corporate Change*, 3 (1994), pp. 451–489.

[98] Chandler, *Scale and Scope*, pp. 366–378; Robert Fitzgerald, *Rowntree and the Marketing Revolution, 1862–1969* (Cambridge: Cambridge University Press, 1995), provides a study of the British chocolate manufacturer which developed innovative marketing strategies in the 1930s.

the century. By the 1980s the food and drink industry groups accounted for 12 percent of total net output of the British manufacturing sector, and around 10 percent of total exports. The sector included some of Britain's largest firms, including Guinness (8th largest in 1992), Allied-Lyons (24th largest), Bass (28th), and Cadbury Schweppes (38th). These British firms achieved substantial rises in labor productivity during the 1970s and 1980s, and pursued successful strategies of product differentiation and product diversification. They possessed considerable capabilities in brand management and distribution, which they employed both in extensive exporting activity and through extensive multinational investments. During the 1980s the British food companies acquired a number of large American food groups; one example was Grand Metropolitan's purchase of Pillsbury. The food and drink enterprises, together with the tobacco industry, accounted for 30 percent of the total stock of British foreign direct investment in this period.

As in the case of pharmaceuticals, the British competitive performance in food and drink contradicts the general image of British enterprise lacking organizational capability in manufacturing industry. Indeed, research by Balasubramanyam on the determinants of British foreign direct investment in food and drink specifically identifies their main advantage was "in their managerial and organizational abilities," which were superior to those of the American firms they acquired, even though the American firms had superior productive efficiency. Many of the large British corporations in food and drink also had extensive operations in food distribution chains, real estate, hotels, and leisure activities. Their competitive strengths appeared to be in highly developed management skills in financial management and marketing – rather than in production management. Balasubramanyam suggests that such entrepreneurial and trading skills may have been inherited from the family-firm tradition.[99] Alternatively the "culturist" hypothesis suggested earlier might explain the good British performance in such kinds of management skills.

The food and drink industries raise a final question about the organizational capability of British business after 1945. Even in 1995 the United

[99] V. N. Balasubramanyam, "Entrepreneurship and the Growth of the Firm: the Case of the British Food and Drink Industries in the 1980s," in Jonathan Brown and Mary B. Rose (eds.), *Entrepreneurship, Networks and Modern Business* (Manchester: Manchester University Press, 1992), pp. 144–160; Balasubramanyam and Mohammed A. Salisu, "Brands and the Alcoholic Drinks Industry," in Geoffrey Jones and Nicholas J. Morgan (eds.), *Adding Value: Brands and Marketing in Food and Drink* (London: Routledge, 1994), pp. 59–74.

Kingdom held the second largest stock of foreign direct investment in the world after the United States. Throughout the postwar period and into the 1990s the British were the largest direct investors in the United States, a position maintained by extensive acquisition activity.[100] British multinational investment must have involved considerable organizational and management skills, or else it could not have been sustained. This suggests that a distinction must be made between the competitiveness of British firms and the competitiveness of the British economy. As in the case of the United States more recently,[101] British companies have shifted production and other value-added activities offshore over quite a long period, presumably in part because of deficiencies in their domestic economic environment. The discussion of the "deindustrialization" of the British economy can mislead if it fails to take account of the continued international competitiveness of British-owned business enterprise.

Thus, British business moved much closer to American managerial capitalism after 1945, but to some degree this only resulted in acquiring a new set of weaknesses. British competitive capabilities were eroded, as in the United States, by "short-termism," financially driven mergers and acquisitions, excessive diversification, and the creation of predatory conglomerates. The large managerial firm had advantages, especially in capital-intensive industries, but it also had difficulties in sustaining innovation and entrepreneurship within its boundaries. The collusive domestic market and the general reluctance to invest in human capital magnified such problems. Nevertheless the analysis of the organizational capabilities of British companies needs to incorporate British successes in certain industries as well as the continued British preeminence as a multinational investor.

CONCLUDING REMARKS

The problem about modern British business history, like that of Japan, is the constant temptation to resort to caricature. British business performance is no more a record of sustained failure than Japanese is one of

---

[100] Jones, *Evolution of International Business*, pp. 46–47, 52–54, 194–200; Geoffrey Jones, "British Multinationals and British Business since 1850," in Kirby and Rose, *Business Enterprise in Modern Britain*, pp. 172–206; Robert E. Lipsey, "Foreign Direct Investment in the United States: Changes over Three Decades," in Kenneth A. Froot (ed.), *Foreign Direct Investment* (Chicago: University of Chicago Press, 1993), pp. 113–72.
[101] Robert E. Lipsey and Irving B. Kravis, "The Competitiveness and Comparative Advantage of U.S. Multinationals 1957–1984," *Banca Nazionale Del Lavoro Quarterly Review* 40 (1987), pp. 147–164.

unmitigated success. A number of stylized facts can be agreed. First, British performance throughout the twentieth century was weaker in manufacturing than many other business activities. The overall effect was the relative decline of the British economy in a world context, although this decline was by no means as rapid or as dramatic as a focus on manufacturing alone would suggest. Second, Britain was slower than the United States and Germany to develop most of the new capital-intensive industries of the late nineteenth century. It later "caught up" in some of them, such as chemicals. In others, such as motor cars, British-owned firms caught up only to collapse subsequently. Third, Britain was slower than the United States to develop large corporations with managerial hierarchies in manufacturing, but after 1945 became a big-business economy par excellence. Fourth, British business engaged in extensive multinational investment throughout the twentieth century.

The interpretation of these stylized facts does not lend itself to straightforward generalizations. It does seem that British companies, with notable exceptions, experienced long-run problems in maintaining competitiveness in manufacturing industries with complex production processes requiring the coordination of flows of goods, and with long time-horizons needed in investment and other decisions. This problem was evident with pre-1945 British personal capitalism, when the fragmented, family-owned firms in a range of industries lost competitiveness through their persistence with craft production and labor-intensive methods. However, British weaknesses in this direction persisted when American-style managerial capitalism was adopted after World War II. The fact that industries such as automobiles and electronics could flourish in Britain, but only under foreign ownership and control, pointed to British-style corporate capitalism – rather than (say) British workers or managers – as the major handicap in many (if not all) capital-intensive manufacturing industries. Possibly British business would have done better after 1945 if it had moved toward continental European or Japanese models of corporate governance rather than looking to the United States. The British may also have fared better if industrial concentration levels had not become so high, and if a dynamic small and medium-sized enterprise sector had coexisted with the giant corporations.

Long-term continuities in aspects of British business conduct suggest that the concept of organizational capability should incorporate not only corporate structures, but also value systems deriving from nation-specific cultures. Short time-horizons and coordination problems feature prominently in many stories of British business failure, regardless of how firms were owned or managed. In addition, in twentieth-century Britain the uncompetitive domestic environment, aided and abetted by public policy makers, was a long-term negative influence on the competitiveness. Throughout the twentieth century many British firms have sought to escape from their environment through multinational investment abroad. It is noteworthy that, despite organizational weaknesses and perhaps suboptimal value systems, they were able to sustain this strategy over the long term.

Acknowledgments

I would like to thank Mark Casson, Alfred D. Chandler, Jr., Peter E. Hart, Alan Roberts, Judy Slinn, and the participants of the Florence conference in October 1992 for their comments on earlier drafts of this chapter.

5

Germany: Competition abroad – cooperation at home, 1870–1990

ULRICH WENGENROTH

"Competition abroad – cooperation at home" was the leitmotif of German manufacturing business through most of the past century. In the years before World War I, German industry developed along liberal capitalistic principles with the important qualification of a powerful protectionism resting on the two pillars of tariffs and cartels, both of which were manifestations of a deliberate government policy to curtail competition and to engineer a socially peaceful and stable transition to an industrial society dominated by the old elites. Given the extraordinary success of industrial growth and performance in Imperial Germany, this model won wide support among German industrialists as much as among the public at large. It was a point of reference through the years of upheaval to come and only gradually gave way to the acceptance of the more free-trade, neocorporatist model of today.

The watershed in this development is to be found somewhere in the late 1950s or early 1960s when the politically enforced reorientation of German business toward the principle of open markets finally won wide acceptance among management and became the cherished ideal of most of West German industrialists, ever more so since they felt they could outcompete many of their European rivals on an equal footing.

This was not the end of cooperation to be sure, but formal cooperation, the trademark of German industry over most of its history, lost much of its legal and institutional foundations through the General Agreement on Tariffs and Trade (GATT) and the coming of the Common Market. The internationalization of both the German market as well as German industry over the past three decades helped to erode the home base of German industry, the formerly well-protected, largest European economy which was both the hothouse for cartelization as well as the launching pad for forays into the export markets. When domestic and international markets merged, old-style German corporatism lost its rationale and transformed itself into the much more subtle and less rigid corporatism of today.

Any attempt to understand the mentality and rationale of German management for most of this century has to depart from the formative years in the late nineteenth century when a united Germany under Prussian rule set off to become the dominant economic player in Europe, turning many of the advantages of its natural resources as much as the size of its domestic market to its profit. The background against which this development took place was the emergence of the American model prevailing over British practice, which had dominated the earlier phases of industrialization. As one German historian of technology, Joachim Radkan, has recently stated: "After 1870 a good part of the German history of technology can be delineated as a succession of thrusts of Americanization, but also of justification of German tendencies by American models, adaptation of American technology to German conditions and counteractions against this 'Americanization.'"

For about a century – from the 1870s until the early 1970s – American technology was the much admired and imitated example for German entrepreneurs and engineers. The American model had superseded the English, as American industry or, rather, the "American system" took the lead over the old "workshop of the world" and henceforth set the standards of industrial practice worldwide. In spite of many derogatory remarks and reservations against "Americanization" – which mostly meant a specific way to organize production processes *and* design products – American production technology kept being the largely undisputed model until the early 1970s, when a euphoria for Japan created a new focus of attention, more among German industrialists than among German engineers. The "justification of German tendencies by American models," the "adaptation of American technology to German conditions," and also the "counteractions against 'Americanization,'" however, indicate that German industry did not experience a simple imitation of American practice. On its way from the United States to Germany, American technology and business organization did change notably to become an integral part of something clearly different – the German manufacturing enterprise.

SETTING THE STAGE, 1870–1918

Late nineteenth-century German industry still bore the marks of early German industrialization, with railways having been the leading sector and their backward linkages having shaped the structure of manufacturing industry. The iron and steel industry together with heavy machine building had benefited most from the rapid completion of the large German railway network, and by the mid-1860s both were well equipped to cover virtually all domestic demand. Coal, the energy basis of both the railways and the heavy industries, and a passive giant among enterprises rather than a driving force, was in ample supply and could be mined at cheap prices in several mining districts of the newly formed empire. Reliance on abundant hard coal was to become a pillar of German industrial strength until well into the twentieth century and a linchpin of business strategies among many of the most successful firms. At the same time it became the foundation of a distinctly German company structure which had its roots in the market conditions and institutional arrangements of the empire.

Coal, iron, and steel

Most visible was this pre-1914 world in the German heavy industry's (coal, iron, steel) rapid development toward a *technological* vertical integration – a vertical integration from coal to the finished product which *physically* linked the various stages of production, notably by direct gas and heat interchanges. Like most vertical integration it was started to reduce transaction costs. The incentive to integrate backward into coal mines was particularly strong after the formation of the all embracing RWKS (Rhenish-Westphalian Coal Syndicate) in 1893.

At the other end of steel production, agreed-upon output quotas for the home market ran into conflict with the earlier strategy of increasing throughput in the works following the American model, which had led the German steel managers' efforts in the advent of mass steel production in the 1870s and early 1880s. As was to become the case in other industries as well, steel managers had to square the circle of combining American-style mass production with the limited demand of the German market. The only outlets for plants driven to capacity irrespective of cartel quotas were export markets, which soon became a kind of safety valve for an industry striving for cost-cutting process innovations to compensate for fixed price inflexibility on the factor markets at home.

Cartels and tariffs quickly changed their character from granting protection to an infant industry to becoming an aggressive means for dumping exports so plants could run to capacity in times of slackening domestic demand. Only in the export market did German companies eventually compete among each other, as much as they did with their foreign rivals.

Steel was the pioneering industry in creating this typical German strategy of market avoidance and protection at home while simultaneously engaging in massive export spurts at what were frequently "dumping prices." A stabilizing factor for this "organized capitalism" was provided by the German banks, which had both directly invested in and heavily lent to the steel industry and from time to time put pressure on "undisciplined" companies to maintain cartel arrangements. Through these occasional policing operations in the industry, the banks protected their loans as much as the investment of the majority of their industrial clients.

Defensive investment to protect cartel quotas and wide-flung internalization of the earlier stages of production to circumvent artificially high cartel prices frequently led to a poor allocation of resources. On the other hand, it gave the industry a much longer time interval to plan for the use of plant and raw material sources. Since factor markets were largely imperfect, profit squeezes were to be solved in terms of engineering. Whatever the production costs of a mine or blast furnace, its product *had* to be processed. Engineers, not purchasing agents, were called on to minimize the cost of factor inputs at every stage of production.

With sophisticated networks of by-product recovery and gas and heat exchange, the extra costs of autonomy in a cartelized market were recovered to some extent at least by engineering a constant and well-controlled flow of materials from the pit head to the industrial steel consumer. Cartel quotas in this instance guaranteed that the very delicate balance of the principle of multiples between these physically interlocking stages of production was not disturbed.

The myth of the technological superiority and outstanding productivity of the German steel industry before and after World War I stems largely from these technological manifestations of market avoidance, run by mostly autocratic leaders helped by lawyers specialized in cartel negotiations and surrounded by a middle management overwhelmingly staffed by engineers. In making cartels legally enforceable, the German judicial system helped to prevent American-style trust building and to protect employment in many suboptimal plants. It comes as no surprise, though, that socialist and eventually Communist politicians saw the German heavy industries as a privately planned model for the centrally planned economies they were set to create.

Only a few companies managed before 1914 to advance into the more diversified markets of heavy engineering and – in the single case of Krupp – shipbuilding. The dominating pattern in the heavy industries was "industrial columns," or "dukedoms" as they were also frequently called, growing out of a mountain of coal in the Ruhr district and Upper Silesia. Money did not go into horizontal mergers but was sunk into coal mines.

Chemical industries

The major chemical companies, the IG Farben forerunners (Hoechst, Bayer, BASF), with an annual coal consumption equal to a steelworks were also drawn into this pattern. To secure the supply of their most important raw material and to circumvent the all-encompassing Rhenish-Westphalian coal cartel, they acquired mines of their own. The outstanding international success of the German chemical industry, however, was much more a result of its ability to turn academic research quickly into marketable products and establish an early lead in expanding fields such as dyestuffs and pharmaceuticals, where the value-added was conspicuously higher than in the old chemical processes for the production of soda, calcium chloride, and sulphuric acid, all of which had been developed and dominated by British works earlier in the century.

In the chemical industry more and earlier than in any other, the exceptionally well established German system of higher technical and scientific education bore fruit. Conceived as a means to catch up with Britain in the absence of a large industry which could provide for training on the job, the science faculties of the universities and the newly established Technische Hochschulen (technical universities) turned out great numbers of academically educated scientists and engineers. Although the majority of graduates went to government and local administration positions rather than to industry until well into the second half of the nineteenth century, an abundant supply of these crucial carriers of R&D was available when it was first needed by early science-based industries like organic chemistry.

In the German *Farbenindustrie* it was not the brilliant individual but a large number of highly qualified chemists who *systematically* synthesized new variations of established basic combinations along theoretically determined paths and thus established early technological leadership. According to Carl Duisberg, the director of Bayer, the laboratories in the chemical industry were a place where one would find "not a trace of a flash of genius" but numerous well-organized and rather tedious research programs for a great number of academic chemists, who had given Bayer 2,000 different dyestuffs on the eve of World War I. Admittedly there was absolutely no need for 2,000 dyestuffs, but with these Bayer together with

BASF and Hoechst, where similar numbers were achieved, had a firm grip on every conceivable composition of hydrocarbons, firmly shielded by a wall of patents and tacit knowledge. Between the turn of the century and World War I, Germany's share of the world's synthetic dyestuffs production amounted to approximately 80 percent.

If an increasingly wide variety of end products which did not directly compete with each other saved the chemical industry from much of the inflexibility suffered in steel and coal, with basic chemicals like alizarin cartels were indispensable in the eyes of management to guarantee profits. The collapse of the alizarin convention for a short time in 1883 resulted in one of the very few profit squeezes suffered before World War I.

With growing diversification, a clear demarcation of "fields of interest" became more important than cartel agreements. The individual companies would agree not to invade each others' product families and, at the same time, try to achieve a "fair" distribution of the overall market shares in advanced chemical products. The institutional outcome of this cooperation was the establishment of the *Interessengemeinschaften* (IG) (community of interests), pools where shares and profits were exchanged and production lines agreed upon. Between 1904 and 1908 a duopoly was formed, which after the war eventually merged into the IG Farben. The same path was followed in pharmaceuticals where another Interessengemeinschaft, the Pharma-IG, was created in 1905 comprising all important pharmaceutical producers, with the one exception of Schering of Berlin.

It was a lucky hit, which turned into probably one of the greatest windfall profits ever, that many pharmaceuticals happened to be closely related to artificial dyes in their chemical composition. The same research facilities and strategies could thus yield sophisticated products in two very promising markets at the same time without anything like proportional additions to cost. Entering into pharma products was research-driven and not an explicit strategy from the beginning. The enormous success of these scientific "by-products" not surprisingly helped to strengthen further the position of scientists within the industry. Much more than sales managers they were seen as the true money-makers and the most foresighted when it came to decide on policies. This heavy R&D bias was also reflected in the composition of top management, which was overwhelmingly being recruited among the companies' own academic chemists. In fact only in the 1980s was the first nonchemist appointed to the top position of one of the three major companies.

It was to be stressed, however, that the outstanding performance of the German chemical industry before World War I was largely limited to the science-based field of dyestuffs and pharmaceuticals. Only here could the abundant academic input be turned into a competitive edge, while more large-scale operations for simpler products were performed as successfully in other countries. Mass-produced research at all levels of the company rather than the mass production of staple goods was the strength and strategy of the German chemical industry.

Not surprisingly, though, it was in the interest of the German chemical companies that the backwardness of their main rivals be maintained and technology kept secret. Foreign direct investment therefore was only undertaken when trade barriers or patent regulations or both made exports difficult. In the United States, the German chemical industry set up production facilities after important patents had expired in that market, which was second in size only to China. A major incentive to embark on foreign direct investment in the American market was to compete against former employees of the German dyestuffs industry who joined the competition in the United States or set up their own companies after the turn of the century. Before that time, the major German companies were not interested in establishing their own production facilities in the United States, let alone accepting the offers of partnerships made by American firms. In 1899 Carl Duisburg refused "to sell our American patent rights and our technological experience for a mess of pottage of 10 million Marks." In successfully launching Aspirin and other brand names with the omnipresent Bayer cross, Duisberg expanded the company's marketing efforts to gain a strong position in the American market, alongside other German pharmaceutical producers like Merck.

While convincingly contributing to the technology-centered mentality among industrial management in Imperial Germany, the chemical industry was exceptional in not resorting to American models for its operations and plant layout. Enjoying all the first-mover privileges, the German dye and pharmaceuticals industry saw itself and was very much regarded abroad as the model. "Americanization" was to come here only after World War I had wiped out most of its worldwide monopolies and for the first time exposed the German industry to open competition on an equal footing.

Engineering

A less conspicuous though equally successful strategy of combining the input of academic engineering with an industrywide systems building effort was pursued by some of the major machine builders. Since engineering and machine building, unlike organic chemistry, was essentially a mature industry already in the late nineteenth century, the German companies had to make their way on the home and international markets against a well-established foreign competition. As soon as they had managed to meet domestic demand in the 1870s, they set out to take the American practice of mass production to Europe very much like the steel industry did at the same time. What Alexander Holley and Andrew Carnegie were to the steel managers, Pratt & Whitney and Brown & Sharpe became to the engineering and machine building sector.

Most helpful to the transfer of technology, both of hardware and of plant organization, was the Prussian army. In the wake of the Franco-Prussian War of 1871, it embarked into a crash program to replace its outdated rifles and for this purpose imported turnkey rifle factories from the United States, encouraging private enterprise to do the same if it was interested in large contracts. As in heavy industry, the 1870s marked a reorientation from British practice to the American model, with gun manufacture from interchangeable parts being the point of departure.

There were also attempts by private companies, like the Berlin Loewe Co., to run a copy of a Singer sewing machine factory, but demand in Germany did not yet support the numbers that had to be produced to work at a profit, and the whole plant was eventually converted to gun manufacture. Loewe, who then set up its own machine tool department, together with some Saxon machine tool builders became the pioneer of the "translation" of American metalworking practice to the more limited German markets. Two strategies were eventually designed at the turn of the century to achieve this end. The state and the war effort in World War I again played a crucial role in its widespread acceptance among manufacturing industries.

First, the standardization of parts, initiated in the United States, was no longer applied to just a single product or firm. Building mostly on the "Loewe norms" – that is, the internal standards of the Loewe firm, which emerged parallel to other factory standards as of the 1890s – the industry during the war agreed on what was to become an ever more sophisticated national system of standards. Interfirm standards were needed to allow for wartime mass production with an industry that was still dominated by medium-size firms. National norms were institutional devices to make growth and mergers of individual firms less exigent in the pursuit of cost reductions. They successfully performed some of the functions corporate management had to fulfill in other countries and allowed for a traditionally decentralized industry of medium-sized firms eventually to dominate large sectors of the international market.

The success of this system of standards (Deutsche Industrienorm [DIN] and the norms for electrotechnical devices by the Verband Deutscher Elektrotechniker [VDE]) made for an invaluable competitive advantage for German industry in this century, and is surely the most lasting and widespread form of German technology export so far, creating decades of path-dependence in favor of German products. It ensured a degree of interproduct compatibility unrivaled by any other system of standards at the time. This standardization of often used parts and materials created the possibility for *different* products to use a certain number of *uniform* parts, that is, making use of the advantages that large-scale production offered on a smaller scale. Again Loewe was a pioneer in this field in creating already in 1905 a new division: the "norm-factory" where multipurpose components which could be made part of many different products were manufactured.

Second, instead of a mere imitation of specialized American machines for which – despite standardization – only a limited market existed, their qualities were transferred to universal machines by using them as a carrier for all sorts of additional devices. These additional devices, through their modular design, were what eventually turned the basic tool into a specialized machine. Yet, depending on the accessories added, it became a different machine every time, so that despite higher costs for the basic tool, the amount of capital tied up in a variety of special requirements was less than would have been the case for a corresponding number of one-purpose machines. German machine tools were designed for longer depreciation periods and smaller series than their American models, while still performing the same functions. With this unique combination of flexibility and mass-production capability, they constituted both a remarkable export success for the German machine tool industry in Europe and Asia as well as the backbone of a manufacturing industry that did not yet have markets as capable of absorbing huge numbers of uniform products as in the United States. The German machine building industry thrived on midrange equipment for midrange markets, while still getting most of its ideas from the other side of the Atlantic.

Until the turn of the century American machines were meticulously and shamelessly copied. It turned out, however, that the somewhat harder European cast iron to be machined on these lathes required a redesign rather than a mere copy if the machine tools were to last. Insufficient experience with modern American machine design was now compensated for by theoretical – and especially mathematical – penetration of the machines' operational principles. It was a kind of reverse engineering that was performed on them. German industry was able to employ its greatest strength, its highly developed technical universities. Eventually this enabled the engineering and machine tool industry to more than merely catch up with technical developments abroad, as was registered with some surprise by the American *Iron Age* in 1911: "In fact, one meets with some undoubted improvement over American designs, due to characteristic Teutonic thoroughness in reducing all calculations to mathematical certainty."

Unlike the machine tool industry, heavy engineering was highly concentrated. This was largely a consequence of its roots in the German railway boom. Locomotive makers like Borsig, Schwartzkopff (BEMAG), HANOMAG, and Körting are notable examples. Together with Humboldt, DEMAG, and MAN, they formed what was the strongest national group of heavy engineering firms in Europe, covering a scope of products unrivaled anywhere else. Selling to markets all over the world these companies had elaborate networks of highly trained sales representatives, often academic engineers, who would help industrial clients in the pursuit of tailor-made solutions to location and product-specific plants. Coengineering with their customers frequently seems to be a more appropriate description of these sales representatives' activities than marketing. Theirs was not a mass market. Their comparative advantages lay with the greatest possible diversity of small-batch, high-value products where intangible assets ranked highest. They were brokers of the abundant engineering expertise in Germany and stood at the outset of what was to become the German profile in manufacturing through the twentieth century: technology-intensive investment goods based on superior craft skills and academic training. Heavy engineering was the field where the conspicuous weakness of the majority of German manufacturing enterprise – mass marketing of consumer goods – did not come into play, while its traditional strengths, such as superb technical education, could be fully turned to its advantage. If heavy engineering was impressive by international standards, it did not contribute correspondingly to the transformation of German industry toward mass production and consumerism on a scale that compared equally favorably to its neighbors.

Electricity

If there was one industry in Imperial Germany where the adoption of American technology went hand in hand with the adoption of an American way of management, it was the electric power industry. Unlike the other major industries dealt with already, it was created with a future mass market and its potential in view. It was the first large industry in Germany where solutions were sought in aggressive marketing and not in technology in the first place.

The roots for this noticeable departure from the early German model of the industrial enterprise can almost be traced back to a single outstanding personality: Emil Rathenau, founder of the AEG, and an outsider and ardent admirer of American technology and management principles at the beginning of his career. After two failures to introduce American technology to Germany, Rathenau managed to acquire the Edison-patents ahead of all competitors.

Rathenau then entered into a contract with Siemens, the largest manufacturer of electric equipment who had worldwide operations in the telegraph industry. Siemens would manufacture all the equipment other than the mass-produced light bulbs, and Rathenau would keep these and the exclusive rights to run power stations. Not surprisingly this unlikely alliance broke apart and gave rise to the AEG (Allgemeine Elektrizitäts-Gesellschaft = General Electric Company) which was controlled by Rathenau and within only three years had a greater business volume than Siemens. Under this pressure the latter also went public and was converted from a family business into a joint-stock company to follow suit on the expanding and capital hungry market for electric power.

Electricity came at a time when the financial resources of most towns were strained by the additional needs of sewerage, solid pavements, hospitals, schools, and the like for a quickly growing population. Only a few cities were rich enough to afford a power plant on top of all that. The answer to the problems of financing electrification in this situation was the *Unternehmergeschäft*. Led by the AEG, German electrical engineering companies like Siemens, Helios, Union, Lahmeyer, and the German branch of BBC created their own market by founding local and regional electrical power, tramway, and lighting companies or by taking over and "electrifying" existing ones in Germany as much as in Spain, Italy, Russia, Latin America, and elsewhere. These new companies then were obliged by stipulations in their articles of association or more subtle arrangements to buy their electrical engineering equipment exclusively from the mother firm, the *Unternehmer*, in this guaranteeing a well-protected outlet for many years to come.

The setting-up of a great number of energy-producing and -distributing companies, however, did create financial problems for the mother firms advancing all or most of the capital. They were left with a growing volume of equity capital and bonds in their portfolios against dwindling resources of liquidity. A solution to this problem was found via the creation of financial holding companies with the help and the financial backing of the great banks. These holdings took over the shares of the new public utility companies created by the electrical engineering producers; they held these titles in their portfolios during the period of construction and initial development of the electric power companies, eventually issuing bonds in order to guarantee the further inflow of long-term capital at stable interest rates.

Once the investment had "matured," yielding a profit, part of the equity capital could be mobilized and sold to the public, while the financial holdings kept only a minority share sufficient to guarantee control. In a slightly modified form this pattern was applied equally to the development of industrial users of large electric power plants, like the aluminum industry or the producers of calcium carbide. Here again the electrical engineering manufacturers triggered new activities by actively engaging in the creation of these new branches of industry which were later taken up by bona fide chemical producers.

Almost every one of the major electrical engineering companies had its own financial holding. There were separate holdings for overseas activities and of course many subholdings in the individual countries and even regions. The most spectacular of these was the AEG's 1898 creation, the Deutsch-Überseeische Elektricitäts-Gesellschaft (German Overseas Electricity Company), with a capital stock of 150 million marks and an additional 108 million marks in bonds, the largest of all German corporations operating abroad.

In spite of a very elaborate network of holdings and subholdings, however, the electrical engineering manufacturers engaging in the *Unternehmergeschäft* did take a great risk and many of them failed to protect their liquidity. The result was a major credit crisis in the industry in 1901 in Germany, as a result of which only AEG and Siemens were strengthened, having absorbed or absorbing within the next few years most of their competitors – and their respective holdings. Siemens and AEG then continued to hold their truce and respect each other's territory. More than any other new industry before, the German electrical engineering industry developed into a multinational business from the very beginning. The stability of the dominant and leading company, the AEG, seemed unassailable very much because of its firm international embeddedness. In an agreement with the American General Electric, which bore resemblances to the Treaty of Tordesillas (1494) between the kings of Spain and Portugal who decided to partition the world amongst themselves, the two largest electrical engineering manufactures of the world agreed on respective spheres of interest where they would take care of the rest of the competition. It was a worldwide Interessengemeinschaft somewhat along the institutional lines in the German dyestuffs industry.

At the last shareholders meeting before the war, Emil Rathenau was confident that "political unrest and wars in Europe" would do only little harm to the company's business since "a substantial part of our customers is spread all over the globe." Together with the big three of the chemical industry and some specialized manufactures in the then high-tech industries like Linde (refrigeration), Zeiss (optical instruments), and Bosch (electrical engineering equipment) or the Metallgesellschaft (nonferrous metals), AEG and Siemens were global players by 1914 with sufficiently extended networks and nontangible assets worldwide to even survive the havoc the disastrous war wrought on the German industry's international trading position. During the war, however, most industrialists entertained dreams of expanding the negotiated environment of the domestic market into a German dominated *Großraumwirtschaft* where private industrial planning would eventually be substituted for unpredictable competition on all relevant markets. If German industry had successfully learned to compete abroad before World War I, it had only done so out of necessity and full of contempt for the irrationality and unpredictability of the invisible hand.

THE ABORTED REFORM MOVEMENT, 1918–1933

German industry came out of World War I in a deplorable shape. Markets, patents, and direct investment had been lost abroad, together with technological leadership in many fields. In addition, the scare of socialism was haunting industrialists ever since 1918 and made them susceptible to authoritarian solutions on the labor front, as long as they would not threaten their renewed export efforts to break out of the straitjacket of import substitution abroad and the contraction of both domestic and international markets. Everyone yearned back to the golden years before World War I with a negotiated environment at home and open markets abroad. This had been the world for which the German industry was made – in terms of plant as much as in terms of organization and institutions. The few years of economic and political stabilization in the second half of the 1920s were not sufficient to put German industry back on its feet. They do show, however, the ways it would have tried to go if there had not been the upheaval of the Nazi years. And these ways, again, looked very American in many respects, while at the same time the doctrine of cooperation at home still held sway.

The 1920s saw a continued and intensified admiration of American industrial enterprise, the American way of manufacture, and large-scale operations in general. It was accepted for the first time that the ongoing protection of a great number of individual companies through cartel arrangements stood in the way of recovery and international competitiveness. The rationalization of German industry, which had already begun at the turn of the century with the move toward standardization and by-product recovery, now went beyond this predominantly technological dimension and included horizontal mergers and wide sweeping diversification.

At a time of intensified international competition and vastly inefficient use of many of its own resources, the major companies of the chemical and of the steel industries in 1925 merged into huge trusts, the IG Farben and the Vereinigte Stahlwerke (United Steel Works) respectively, the latter being explicitly framed along the model of U.S. Steel. Even industries which were dominated by medium-size firms where economies of scale were not so obvious saw ambitious schemes of large-scale production like the Vereinigte Werkzeugmaschinenfabriken (United Machine Tools Factories), a combination of four major machine tool makers. The costly parallelism of a suboptimal plant protected through cartel arrangements was no longer carried by the shrunken domestic demand. All these were mergers of desperation, however, rather than an optimistic departure for a new managerial world. Management's reflexes still opted for cartellization, both national and international, whenever possible. The numerically overblown boards of directors – IG Farben started with eighty-three, Vereinigte Stahlwerke had fifty-two – testify to the unease of these mergers as much as to the weakness of central management. There was nothing "lean" and efficient about these newly created giants.

Potent outsiders to this process of horizontal concentration tried to diversify their production and push their product line closer to the market, again continuing a prewar strategy as in the case of Krupp and the GHH, the two notable bystanders of the United Steel merger who went instead into heavy engineering, including the manufacture of trucks. The GHH in this case even left the traditional center of heavy industry in the Ruhr through its merger with the South German engineering firm MAN, the pioneer of diesel engines.

A third important path toward concentration was followed in the energy sector, where mixed enterprises for electricity and gas supply were being created. Fostered by the wartime policy to use the vast lignite deposits of West and Central Germany for electricity generation to relieve the hard coal mines of the Ruhr, new giant corporations grew out of these new power plants with the help of many city councils. The most powerful among them remained the Rheinisch-Westfälische Elektrizitätswerke (RWE), a creation of the twenty-eight-year-old Hugo Stinnes in 1898.

Stinnes, a wealthy coal merchant before the war, had been the most ambitious trust builder in the early 1920s. His enterprise, the Siemens-Rhein-Elbe-Schuckert-Union, which fell apart upon his death in 1924, comprised coal mines, steelworks, power plants, and the Siemens-Schuckert electrical engineering company, plus a great number of service sector activities from hotels to cinemas and newspapers. It was mocked that Hugo Stinnes could spend his life without resorting to outside resources. The collapse of his empire was very much welcomed by public opinion as having been built on inflationary money and megalomania, although it was not bigger than the technologically more homogeneous giants that were created a year later. In the end, its degree of diversity and the hostility of many of the takeovers were still clearly beyond what was acceptable to the German business community and the public at large. Stinnes's way of empire building was very much the kind of "Americanization" to cause counteractions and strong resentment.

The acceptable merger was one which also lent itself to technological rationalization to create a larger "organic" entity, a notion that had come out of the technocratic planning staffs of the war. Although these horizontal mergers in chemicals and steel were market-driven, they still did not signify the wholehearted acceptance of market signals as the overriding business principle, and management structure still represented production plant rather than product marketing. If there were signs that the German economy would move toward a more consumerist model, the very few years of optimism and rapid growth in the late 1920s were too short to bring about the change of mentality toward a consumer-market-oriented management.

Even in new markets like the automobile, the inability of most German manufacturers to turn their high engineering standards and the evolving system of norms to their advantage is striking. Despite a plethora of new and old car manufacturers, who produced either flimsy or overengineered models, American cars were imported in great numbers. Ford even began to assemble cars in Berlin in 1926. The only truly successful German maker in the 1920s was Opel, which had shamelessly copied a French Citroën, which again was the result of André Citroën's transfer of American ideas to France. The mass-produced Opel was the first private car to be built according to the DIN-norms. And if the mechanized assembly line in Rüsselsheim was less than fifty meters long, the Opel "Laubfrosch" (tree-frog), as it was affectionately called because it was only available in light green in the beginning, made Opel the largest manufacturer in Germany with a market share of 40 percent. Not surprisingly this was the most attractive German company for GM when it took the company over from the Opel family in 1929. Opel had already had a prewar record of American-style mass production, going from sewing machines to bicycles, of which the company was the largest German manufacturer.

All these first hesitant steps into a modern consumer society came to a halt in the wake of the Great Crash of 1929. With unemployment rapidly rising, consumer markets collapsed, pulling all other industry behind them. The inflexibility of "organic vertical integration," the pride of German engineering and management, made itself felt very painfully now and wrought havoc among the most modern plants in the chemical and steel industries. It was a lesson in the limitations of private planning and engineering rationality. In 1932 the United Steelworks were only saved from bankruptcy through tacit nationalization by the central government. Majority ownership went to the Reich for some years without its interfering in the company's policies. "Scientification" and "organic integration" on the largest scale had visibly run aground as soon as market stability and predictability could no longer be negotiated.

IG Farben was also close to bankruptcy in these years since it had sunk its money in the erection of a huge hydrogenation plant to produce oil from coal at a time when oil prices on the open market fell dramatically.

The failure to cut loose from the once all dominating coal-base of German industry proved almost fatal to the company. The technology for the refining processes had come through an R&D agreement with Standard Oil. This had been the first time for half a century that the German chemical industry had to turn to foreign help for a major new product line. It was a sign that the science-intensive strategy had its limitations when bulk production rather than product innovation was the issue. Chemical engineering, the new approach to mass-produce chemicals, like most mass-production technologies, was developed in the United States and had to be imported.

Reform of strategies and structures in both of these pillars of German industrial strength in the past – like in many other branches that were drawn to their pattern – was overdue. But instead came Nazism with its autarky policy and command economy to substitute negotiation for competition once again.

AUTARKY AND *FÜHRERPRINZIP*, 1933–1945

In Alfred D. Chandler's *Scale and Scope*, "the details of the relationships between decision-makers and local and national government bodies . . . have been left to historians of business–government relationships." This, however, is difficult to maintain in the case of German industry and it is most certainly no longer feasible when it comes to dealing with the major German companies after the Nazis' rise to power. Ever after 1933 the "internal history of the central institution of managerial capitalism" becomes a highly politicized affair with decisions on company strategies being strongly influenced or even dictated by government. Politics to a large extent became internal to the companies for the twelve years of Nazi rule and to some extent also to the twelve years of reintegration to the international markets after World War II.

The timespan 1933–1945 is a period of paramount importance in its own right, as much as the background against which the most influential managers of the transition in the postwar era saw their strategic alternatives. The often conjured "Americanization" of German industry in the 1960s was performed by men who had had their first experiences and their formative years during the Nazi dictatorship. If one is not aware of what the constraints and what the facilitations for management were in these years, it is difficult to estimate properly the scope of mental changes that this generation experienced.

With the Nazi's rise to power, trade unions and competition, being seen as the most destabilizing influences on corporate planning, were to be quelled from the very beginning. "Fair profits" were guaranteed in all government contracts, and industrywide cartels to safeguard existing companies, whatever their competitive merits, were being made compulsory. Irrespective of cost, the German economy was to be transformed for the war effort, making autarky the overriding principle. With wages frozen and labor heavily policed, the necessary savings could be enforced. Even if it is an exaggeration to claim that a clear rift ran through German industry with a pro- and anti-Nazi camp, it is still safe to maintain that there was more skepticism on the side of the export-oriented industries like chemicals and electric engineering because of the effect this policy would have on foreign trade, while the heavy industries with their continuous labor troubles looked forward to some form of tough, cost-saving rules. In addition rearmament and autarky were expected to strongly favor coal and steel.

One of the main "achievements" of the Nazis' autarky policy was in fact to block the conversion from hard coal to oil among German industry as much as the economy at large. In doing so, it petrified the technocratic mentality that had grown out of the pre-1914 cartels at a time when markets were just about to get ever more diversified. Overall thermal efficiencies and closed circles of by-product recovery and processing would continue to be guiding lines of investment rather than marketing opportunities. Ideas of an "organic economy" and forms of corporatist anticapitalism would win ever more support among management – especially middle management – itself. A most notable example of this regressive development, which cut off a modernization and internationalization of corporate structure that was already well under way, is the IG Farben, the board of which had seen the Nazi's rise to power with much apprehension since the party's first electoral successes in 1930.

Within months, however, this skepticism gave way to a deeply felt relief among a large group of management when Carl Krauch managed to sign the *Benzinvertrag* (gasoline treaty) on behalf of the IG Farben with the new regime in the fall of 1933. With prices being agreed on more than triple of what was paid on the international markets the Benzinvertrag was a first of a number of agreements that would turn IG's lingering hydrogenation plant into a guaranteed profit center and make it the cornerstone of autarky for the automobile and air war to come. Hydrogenation was firmly tied to government planning and thus gradually made independent of central board decisions. Although having been very welcome at the time, it also was one first inroad of government policies into the company's authority over its own operations.

IG Farben then was a model of a vertically and horizontally integrated combine dominating a whole industry by its own weight as much as by its more than fifty semiautonomous dependents. A most important characteristic of its management structure for the Nazi years to come was its "decentralized centralism," as it was called officially or the "Habsburg model" as it was more appropriately known to insiders. Details of production and research were left to the individual factories, which were jealous of their autonomy. Although IG's chairman Carl Bosch between 1929 and 1932 had tried to introduce a more effective organization to monitor the great number of firms' activities from the top by creating three major *Sparten* (branches), IG's directors never developed a strong interest in each other's domains. The IG remained rather polycratic with ad hoc cooperation among the units if necessary. In the late 1930s even minutes and balance sheets were not available in toto to the board's members but rather only the part that referred to their personal responsibility. Allied dukedoms rather than a commonwealth seems to be an appropriate description of the IG's internal power relations. Since the concern controlled its own general meetings through multivote preferred shares held by its subsidiaries, there was little in the way of a self-aggrandizement of the units' captains.

The outcome of this situation was an ever closer cohabitation of the Sparte 1 (hydrogenation) strongman Krauch and the Nazi government along the lines of autarky policy creating major rifts right through IG Farben. While Sparte 2 (dyes/pharmaceuticals) more or less went on like a private capitalist enterprise in a (cartelized) market environment, Sparte 1 (which also included nitrogen!) became part of a totally administered national production facility. For this part of IG Farben, the boast in the party's paper, the *Völkischer Beobachter*, in 1936 was correct: "National Socialist economic policy corresponds to the technical age. It lets capitalism run as the motor, uses its dynamic energies, but shifts the gears."

The polycratic structure of the concern allowed many plant managers to make their own deals with the military and government agencies without any authorization from the top and frequently resorting to well-engineered official "orders." This was by no means unique to the IG Farben but became a threat to the authority of many executive boards, with owners eventually being dispossessed if they did not abide by the party's strategic decisions. On the eve of World War II, the Nazi Party had acquired such a dominance over the economy that "one can scarcely speak any longer of any sort of equal relations or even of the existence of a still intact sociological unit called 'industry.'"

The way toward this all-encompassing control of industrial enterprise had already begun in the early years of the Nazi's rule with mandatory cartels all over industry that would substitute party-monitored negotiation for markets. Together with the legal enforcement of the *Führerprinzip* (principle of authoritarian leadership in industry) in bodies representing the interest of industry, it provided the command and control structures for the party to govern the allocation of resources and the material output of production. The party preferred, however, not to intervene directly in management as long as it could "convince" executives that joining the bandwagon of rearmament and autarky would be in the long-term interest of their companies. The one exception to this continued preference for the protection of private enterprise was the racist "Aryanization" policy, the expropriation of Jewish entrepreneurs for the benefit of politically loyal "Aryans." While the overall effect of this policy on the fabric of private German industry was very limited, it gave rise to a number of spectacular forced concentration processes like the absorption of the Czech-based Petschek coal empire by Friedrich Flick, the most successful and infamous parvenu in the heavy industries. On the whole, however, established industry's cooperation in this process was less than enthusiastic and the Nazi Party itself was to become the greatest devourer of industrial prey in its pursuit to acquire its own industrial basis in the economy.

The latter policy dates from the time of the four-year plan of 1936, which was meant to put German industry on a war footing within four years and brought about another intensification of autarky policies. With the German steel industry being reluctant to process poor domestic iron ore instead of rich imported ores from Sweden to the point where this came close to open sabotage, the Four-Year Plan organization began to build its own steelworks in central Germany. The plant was designed by the American engineering firm Brassert and was intended eventually to become the largest steel plant in the world, named after the party's second figure, Hermann Göring. Its construction had been given priority over all investment schemes in the private industry, in this effectively blocking their further expansion in the presence of rising demand. American-style large-scale operation was to guarantee the Hermann-Göring-Works all available economies of scale. Needless to say it was the most hated enterprise among the established companies and that it was never finished, and therefore could never dominate steel making in Germany, was felt as a great relief in the Ruhr district.

It was different with the party's second project. Close to the Hermann-Göring-Works, another huge Nazi enterprise was erected whose product no German company had been prepared to turn out. It was the Volkswagen Works and, like the steel plant, it was designed by American engineers according to the best American practice of mass production. Crucial advice was given by Ford engineers and Henry Ford in 1939 was eventually awarded the Schwarzer Adlerorden, the highest order the Nazi Party would give to foreigners. The Volkswagen works were meant to use steel from the Hermann Göring works, thus establishing a powerful industrial combine which would give the Nazi Party additional leverage to control both steel and car production in Germany.

The Volkswagen (people's car) was part of the Nazi program for mass motorization and complementary to the construction of the *Autobahnen* (highway system), although both were in the first place intended to help the war effort. Private car manufacturers had refused to build the Beetle, which they considered to be of poor design with little potential vis-à-vis foreign and domestic competition. There had been a number of alternative "Volkswagen" prototypes by makers such as Mercedes-Benz which came closer to today's design of compact cars. In the end, however, it was the outsider Ferdinand Porsche who won Hitler's personal approval. With the erection of the largest car plant on behalf of the Nazi Party, mass motorization was effectively taken out of the private sector, even if this plant turned out military vehicles exclusively during the war.

In these two schemes the Nazi Party was going to perfect what for decades had been the German engineering community's dream and, through its dominance of many companies' boards, the dream of a large group within German management as well: the American way of manufacture in a perfectly controlled environment, a technocratic economy par excellence. If this was clearly not the rule in German industry, it was a focusing point of a decades-old strategy of German industrial enterprise that saw itself very much in contrast with values held in Anglo-American business, while unconditionally admiring its superior productivity and uniformity.

In the Nazi economy of the immediate prewar years, the German industrial enterprise came closer to this ideal type than at any other period in its peacetime history. The war then saw again the by-now-familiar

concepts of *Großraumwirtschaft* from World War I which were embraced
with less unequivocal enthusiasm, however, since most of the bounty was
to go the Reichswerke Hermann Göring and its SS. Senior management
hardly put up with the straitjacket imposed on it from government as
much as from its own enthusiastic, technocratic staff. The vulnerability
of entrepreneurial autonomy in a strongly regulated environment was
one of the lasting lessons of the Nazi years and, among a substantial
group of managers, contributed to the reorientation after World War II
when once again, as in the days of Emil Rathenau, modernizers and tradi-
tionalists fought over the course of German enterprise culture.

OUT INTO THE OPEN, 1945–1990

After World War II the Western Allies under the leadership of the Americans forced West German industry to end its autarky program and dismantled the two huge concerns of IG Farben and Vereinigte Stahlwerke.
While their call for open competitive markets was received with bewilder-
ment, they met with little resistance as to the reestablishment of managerial autonomy vis-à-vis the state.

In 1945 industry was, once and for all, disillusioned with state intervention in its affairs. The state's main task in the eyes of managers, stemming the tide of socialism, was now taken over by the American military
government who soon was seen as a shield against not only communism
but against both British Labour politics and French "planification" as
well. Their antisocialist fervor made the Americans very popular, while
the anticartel and deconcentration policies at the same time were understood to be a frontal attack on the strength of German industry coming
close to a but-mildly-concealed Morgenthau plan for the deindustrialization of Germany. German industry after 1945 wanted to go back to the
golden years of the pre-1914 situation. An unregulated market was the
last thing it had hoped for. Still, this was the way economic policy under
Allied control and later under the liberalistic minister of economics, Ludwig
Erhard, was to go.

With American and European governments accommodating to the
view that a strong West German industry would be the linchpin of every
Western European security system, manufacturing enterprise quickly over-
came most of the allied postwar restrictions and could embark on an almost
unimpeded expansion from the early 1950s on. At a first glance most of
this decade looked like the reestablishment of the pre-1914 scenario with

heavy industry dominating and chemicals and engineering following suit, while other important industries like textiles remained fragmented and uninfluential. Collusive arrangements reemerged and administered prices were widespread in spite of all anticartel legislation. American technology once again was wholeheartedly embraced while propagators of consumer-oriented American business practice were met with contempt. The productivist ideal still held sway among German management – at least among those who were seen by public opinion as the protagonists of the *Wirtschaftswunder,* the "economic miracle." Unlike its competitors West German industrial management was still dominated by academically trained engineers and scientists rather than traders and economists.

Under the surface, however, the whole fabric of pre-1914 style cooperation lost its two important foundations: coal and the protected consumer market. With the end of the autarky policy, the West German economy's delayed conversion to oil eventually gathered momentum in the 1950s. At the same time the strong demand for consumer goods and the traditional subordination of German consumer goods industries encouraged efficient traders in the absence of strong protectionism to establish long-term import relations with low-wage economies. Apart from the consumers, the beneficiaries of this development were the producers of investment goods and technologically sophisticated consumer durables who could almost uninterruptedly resume their prewar position as Europe's workshop. In absorbing great quantities of consumer goods and raw materials from its neighbors machinery imports from West Germany were much easier to finance than American products, which had dominated the market in the immediate postwar years.

All "Americanization" of both consumer markets and management styles notwithstanding, the traditional prominence of producer goods industries in West Germany was therefore strengthened rather than weakened by the unfolding new pattern of competitive advantages among European manufacturing enterprise after World War II. West Germany became a consumer society along American lines without developing a correspondingly strong consumer goods industry. It paid for much of its consumption with investment goods. Since low defense commitments and allied restrictions in arms-related R&D prevented an early full-scale recovery of high-tech industries, West Germany's revealed competitive advantage for medium-technology areas had its roots in this fundamental transformation during the 1950s, which became visible only in the 1960s. It is important to stress, however, that this transformation was as politically desired and engineered by government as had been autarky in the 1930s. West Germany's integration into GATT and the EEC were powerful instruments to reverse the earlier tide of protectionism and force industry to find its place on the international markets. To whatever extent compromised in the end, the degree of laissez-faire policy chosen by the West German government was unparalleled by any other European administration and contributed substantially to the reorientation of management practices in West Germany.

In the 1960s West German industry began to adapt its structure to its reformed strategies. A wide-sweeping diversification and divisionalization movement set in. While in 1960 only about 20 percent of diversified firms had a divisional structure, in 1970 such firms were almost 70 percent. A powerful agent in this reorganization of West German industrial enterprise was American consulting firms, above all McKinsey, who helped West German management in its deliberate attempt to Americanize the structure of its enterprise. Like all earlier "Americanizations" before, however, this new wave was also shaped along German traditions of technology-centered, cooperative enterprise culture. In the same years horizontal mergers and acquisitions dominated clearly over vertical acquisitions. Thus the very important change in the West German fiscal legislation in 1968 from a tax on turnover to a value-added tax did not cause but rather confirmed and strengthened a development that was well under way. Under the old tax system vertical integration was strongly favored for tax reasons alone since it broke the cascading effect of the turnover tax which was due for every market transaction between firms. With the new value-added tax, which was already widely used in the other EEC states, this incentive for vertical integration was eventually abolished and the tax system brought in line with the now prevailing business strategies. It is important to stress, however, that it was the competitiveness of the open market, especially when tariff protection against EEC members fell in the late 1960s, rather than the fiscal legislation that brought about the reorientation toward diversification and horizontal expansion.

A potent outside agent in the eventually successful attempt to break up the closed-shop mentality among German industry was foreign companies investing in what was for many years the fastest growing market in Europe. Since foreign investors did not go into old industries, their impact was biased toward cars and chemicals rather than steel and coal and helped to produce a skewed distribution of American principles among

West German management. Simplifying the point, one could say: the more coal-based an industry was, the more hostile was its management to free-market competition, and the greater the share of FDI on a market sector, the quicker was this branch to adapt American strategies of diversification, horizontal mergers, and competitiveness. Between these two poles, a continuum spread out from the center of gravity, which moved ever further toward the American model without totally embracing it.

Coal and steel

Closest to old-style corporatism was the deconcentrated steel industry. Although there was no desire and certainly no pressure from the market to reestablish the Vereinigte Stahlwerke in a first reflex to regain managerial autonomy, most companies began to integrate backward again in the early 1950s. For a few years it looked as if the self-sustained vertical columns of the Kaiserreich were to reemerge, although the product specialization introduced by the Vereinigte Stahlwerke remained largely undisputed. With cheap imported coal and oil in the wake of the Suez crisis, however, the very foundations of this "renaissance" were quickly undermined: it did not pay any longer to own coal. For the first time in the history of German heavy industry home coal was a liability rather than a strength. In the 1960s the steel companies were eager to get rid of their coal mines as quickly as possible and incorporate them in the Ruhrkohle AG, a holding company which was subsidized and controlled by government.

The federal government's own holding of mining interests inherited from the dissolved Prussian state, the VEBA, had by then already moved away from coal and into oil refining, strengthening its position on the energy market rather than integrating forward. Having been owners of a large hydrogenation plant in the Nazi years, the prerunners of VEBA had all the necessary expertise in oil processing. With the end of autarky, they eventually had to wind up one side of their activities anyway, and in the event they did opt for oil. VEBA which also comprised the Prussian state-owned electric power network was eventually privatized in two steps in the 1960s and 1980s and is today Germany's largest energy concern with a strong engagement in petrochemicals as well.

Having completely redirected their strategies, the major steel makers during the same years tried to grow horizontally or – even better – to diversify their activities to the extent that these companies today make less than half their turnover in steel and continue to reduce this share.

Important fields of diversification were trading, heavy machine building, and, since the late 1970s, electronics. A more intensive merger movement, however, only set in at the end of the 1960s when the burden of coal had been successfully shifted to the shoulders of the Ruhrkohle AG.

With their steel operations, however, these companies' investment policies and – since the outbreak of the protracted steel crisis after 1974 – prices are under control of the ECSC (European Coal and Steel Community), which created European cartels during the 1970s and thus became one of the few reminders of the pre-1914 traditions, with the important qualification, however, that the ECSC is monitoring the decline rather than the growth of this industry. To some extent nationalization and protectionism in neighboring countries more than the West German steel managers themselves contributed to the revitalization of old-style corporatism in European steel. After ailing coal mining, which was dramatically reduced by government in all European countries, steel continued to be the most politicized of all industries. Given this degree of political control of steel making, it comes as no surprise that foreign direct investment in steel was virtually absent after World War II.

Chemical industry

Much quicker to shed their coal past were the IG Farben successors. Already in the 1950s these companies began the conversion of their technology toward oil-based plants. This was the end of vertical integration backward into coal as well as the end of isolation from the international raw material markets. Beginning with the early 1953 contract between Shell Oil and BASF joint petrochemical ventures were established in West Germany from the 1960s which helped to foster a closer cooperation between the IG Farben successors and major Western corporations. The presence of mostly American foreign direct investment further contributed to the unequivocal break with the industry's protectionist traditions.

Access to the world markets and international operations were the linchpin of the IG Farben successors' strategies. The price to be paid was dependence on British and American oil companies for supplies. This, however, compared very favorably with the strangling hydrogenation liaison with the Nazi Party and – as a side effect – saved the West German chemical industry from any serious attempt of supranational control through a body like the ECSC. Dependence on foreign markets for both raw material supplies as well as markets was to become the characteristic of the West German chemical industry. The end of autarky was like getting rid of a millstone around the neck and paved the way back to entrepreneurial autonomy, which was ever so much more promising through the stunning increase of demand for chemical products in the years to come. The growing integration of the major West German chemical producers into the capitalist world economy was more than justified in the eyes of its managers by production and profit records in many successive years.

All the successes in a free-market environment notwithstanding, the IG Farben successors were reluctant to engage in outright competition among each other. Not unlike the steel industry they developed areas of product specialization which were also respected during the horizontal merger movements. Bayer dominated in synthetic rubber and, more recently, polyurethane, pharmaceuticals, and speciality chemicals. BASF has emphasized basic petrochemicals, fertilizers, and data tape (video, audio, and some computer activities). Hoechst has its strongholds in synthetic fibers and dyestuffs. This collusive action or rather nonaction does not, however, go so far as to reactivate cartel traditions. Seeing themselves as global rather than European players, the IG Farben successors have fended off any attempt to solve the problems of excess capacities in Europe through "crisis cartels" like those in steel. They rather continue to rely on their strength in research. More than 22 percent of all research expenditure in West German industry in 1988 was undertaken by the chemical industry, which devoted more than 6 percent of its turnover to this end. Since the West German university system continued to turn out great numbers of academic scientists and engineers, and since the great numbers of refugees from East Germany had above-average qualifications, supply of R&D personnel was always abundant compared with that of neighboring countries.

Automobile industry

The positive impact of FDI on the competitiveness of West German industry was even more striking in the case of electronics and the automobile industry, both of which had a very important foreign-controlled percentage, which made a fallback on cartel arrangements and the like virtually impossible.

The automobile industry which was gravitating around the state-owned Volkswagenwerk in the 1950s eventually became the showpiece of free-market managerial enterprise in West Germany. At the same time it was the industry with the strongest competition from American subsidiaries, the GM-Opel and the Ford companies, which between them always held a quarter to a third of the West German market.

The Volkswagenwerk was left with the state after the British military government had failed to find a commercial buyer for it. Like the German car industry before the war no one in the trade believed that the idiosyncratic Beetle had any market prospects. Eventually, however, this odd vehicle turned out to perform very much what Hitler had in mind, achieving the mass motorization of Germany. Relying on the relatively large domestic market, the plant's potential for achieving outstanding economies of scale as had been envisaged by the Ford planners in the 1930s could be turned to its advantage. The Beetle became West Germany's Ford Model T and one of the country's greatest export successes, making good for its odd appearance by superb engineering and low price, both of which were largely owed to the rigidity of its Fordist roots.

Very much in line with the new doctrine of private enterprise, the federal government already in the 1950s made preparations to privatize the company. In 1960 60 percent of the shares were sold to the public in small allotments. The withdrawal of the state was definitive. No government support was made available for Volkswagen when the company faltered in 1974 after the Beetle's success had run out and the oil-crisis hit most car makers. At the time Volkswagen was in the middle of a costly transformation process from a one-product company to a multidivisional as well as multinational car manufacturer with a wide range of models from minicars to light commercial vehicles. Through this process Volkswagen absorbed a number of less successful makers in West Germany before it embarked on its European expansion in the late 1980s with the acquisition of SEAT of Spain and Škoda of Czechoslovakia. Together with a number of overseas subsidiaries from South America to China, this eventually made Volkswagen the most transnational of all European car manufactures with more than 30 percent of its operations located abroad. Volkswagen today is the largest European car manufacturer and ranks fourth worldwide.

In the West German car industry only two other makers survived the concentration process of the 1960s and 1970s: BMW and Daimler (Mercedes)-Benz both of which are operating in the niche of up-market, high-tech cars and are selling them very successfully worldwide. In 1989 they ranked fourteenth and fifteenth in the world automobile league table as to numbers of cars produced. In financial terms, however, they would undoubtedly rank much higher. In fact, Daimler-Benz is by now Germany's leading taxpayer and, with a turnover of close to 100 billion marks, the country's largest corporation. It is equally Europe's largest manufacturing company only surpassed by the Royal Dutch Shell (Oil) and the Italian financial holding IRI.

Like Volkswagen before it, Daimler-Benz embarked on a massive diversification program in the 1980s. While Volkswagen was very unfortunate in its acquisition of Adler-Triumph, a producer of office equipment, and eventually backed out, Daimler-Benz seems determined to continue on its way toward a widely diversified "technology-concern," as it labels itself. Through mergers Daimler-Benz has become Germany's dominating aeronautics manufacturer and its number two in electrical engineering equipment by absorbing the AEG or, rather, what was left of it after a disastrous failure in the early 1980s. To defend its car exports to the American market, Daimler-Benz is about to erect an assembly plant in the United States. Volkswagen closed its American plant years ago and now supplies the American market from Mexico.

BMW also has a U.S. car plant under construction and with the recent acquisition of Rover achieved a remarkable diversification and internationalization of its production range. Unlike Daimler-Benz, BMW continues to rely much more on car manufacturing in its expansion. Still, it has also begun to diversify since the 1980s in a similar fashion in going into jet engine production, where a joint company with Rolls Royce has been created. This again puts BMW in direct competition to Daimler-Benz, recalling both companies' pasts as foremost aircraft engine producers during World War II.

The stunning success of BMW, which was close to extinction in the 1960s, is often quoted as one of the strongest arguments in favor of a continued technology-bias among German industry at large and car manufacturers in particular. In pursuing a single-minded strategy of high-tech car design, BMW managed to climb to rank twenty-eight among European industrial enterprises leaving old war-horses like Krupp, MAN or Metallgesellschaft behind.

In fact, all three German car manufacturers rely first of all on their engineering reputation and much less on competitive pricing or innovative marketing, in this reflecting a century-old tradition among German industrial enterprises that has mellowed but not subsided. The difference in the market approach of the two American subsidiaries in Germany continues to be conspicuous. Nevertheless GM-Opel and Ford have been as successful in warding off Japanese competition in the absence of any trade restrictions on the West German market.

A noticeable shift toward a more aggressive marketing behavior among the three West German makers occurred only in the 1980s when they started to invade the once well-respected market segments of each other, with BMW offering luxury cars in the Mercedes class and both Mercedes and Volkswagen extending their fleets into the BMW stronghold of high powered compact limousines. In this they moved further away from the traditional domestic policy of German industry than, for example, the equally internationalized chemical companies. As to their international position, this competition on the domestic market seems to have strengthened rather than weakened them.

Electrical engineering and electronics

A very different story at the same time was the electronics industry, where especially in the subgroup of consumer electronics West German manufacturers failed miserably to hold their own. A thriving domestic industry still in the 1960s, with new tycoons like Max Grundig and well-established brand-names like AEG's Telefunken, was almost completely in foreign hands at the end of the 1980s. The only major German producer today is Blaupunkt, a subsidiary of Bosch which has its strength in automobile components. One of the most important products of Blaupunkt, in fact, is car radios. Grundig has been taken over by Philips; Telefunken, Saba, and Nordmende went to the French Thomson; Wega is now part of Sony; SEL was acquired by Nokia of Finland. This great number of now foreign subsidiaries still leaves Germany with the biggest consumer electronics industry of Europe, underlining the inability of German management to deal profitably with this mass market. The development of consumer electronics is indicative of the peculiar strengths and weaknesses of German management culture: as soon as color television became an ordinary bulk product with no exciting technological potential, German-style management lost its grip over it. Since West Germany was still turning out about one million color TV sets annually in the late 1980s, much more than any other West European country, the problem lay clearly on the side of management and not of labor and location.

Almost totally absent from the market of consumer electronics is Siemens, Germany's most successful electric manufacturer and currently sixth among European industrial enterprises in terms of turnover and first in terms of employment. Siemens until very recently was a model of the pre-1914 constellation with a large protected home market taking about half of its output and giving it the strength for impressive export successes in technology-intensive investment goods. Siemens's almost symbiotic relation with the state-owned telecommunications sector guaranteed the company long-term stability and a basis from which new technologies and their potential on the international markets could be explored. An early hope was nuclear power plants, for the production of which Siemens had joined forces with its only serious domestic competitor, the AEG. Their joint Kraftwerk Union was meant to export West German nuclear power plant technology, which was developed with enormous state subsidies for the West German market in the first place. With the nuclear technologies market collapsing and AEG being wound up, Siemens again concentrated on its traditional stronghold, the telecommunications systems, where it was very successful in developing a digital exchange that helped the company to defend its share of about 10 percent of the world telecommunications market. At the same time Siemens sought the cooperation of Philips and IBM to enter the microchip market, which it eventually did on a larger scale in the late 1980s.

Earlier attempts by federal government to develop a microchip industry through massive subsidies, much of which was given to the unfortunate AEG, had failed. Unlike Siemens AEG had lost a large part of its operative units behind the iron curtain and never recovered from this blow. In its attempt to catch up with Siemens, the company overstretched its resources and finally collapsed in the early 1980s. Siemens on the other hand always followed a very careful policy in finding promising new fields in which to invest its enormous revenues. With billions in liquid assets, it was a running joke in the German trade press for many years that Siemens in reality was a bank which ran an electrical engineering enterprise. With deregulation in German telecommunications well on its way and foreign competitors queuing up to take their share in this rich market, Siemens is now making every effort to globalize its operations further and catch up with the major microchip producers. Having won a virtual monopoly in postwar West Germany, it is now forced back into open competition in all of its markets.

Germany's second independent electrical equipment manufacturer and currently twenty-fifth among European industrial enterprises, Bosch, never enjoyed the protection of a regulated domestic market and therefore was much earlier to meet international competition with a highly diversified production program. Struggling out of its dependence on Volkswagen in the 1950s, Bosch managed to transfer its skills from electrical car components to a wide range of sophisticated electromechanical products and a large series of precision engineering products like fuel injection for diesel engines. In its expansion Bosch, unlike AEG, always avoided "Siemens territory," ending up with a production program in electrical equipment that is complementary to Siemens's. So a Bosch subsidiary is, for example, producing TV cameras and studio equipment while Siemens is taking care of the telecommunication side of TV. Its high competence in electronics notwithstanding, Bosch never seriously entertained the idea of entering the market for semiconductors, leaving this field undisputed for Siemens.

Engineering

While it remains to be seen whether Siemens manages to bring profitable, large-scale microchip production to Germany, the actual application of microelectronics was a source of continued export successes of the West German machine-building industry, putting it on par with the car producers and ahead of all other branches. Like the car industry machine building is a highly competitive and export-oriented sector with no protection of the domestic market other than EEC regulations. But in contrast to the car industry it is one of the least concentrated sectors among German industry. Even if there are some large companies like Klöckner-Humboldt-Deutz (KHD) and the diversified steel makers Krupp, GHH, and Mannesmann, all of which have their emphasis on engineering rather than steel today, machine building continues to be dominated by specialized medium-size companies. Even the larger companies like the previously mentioned ones to a certain extent fit into this pattern, as they do not turn out large series of uniform product but specialize in very heavy machinery like rolling mills, mining machinery, drying plants, steel ovens and the like.

In sidestepping Japanese competition in high-volume production of standardized equipment and concentrating on craft-skill intensive, small-batch production of tailor-made solutions, the West German machine-building industry could build on its long-standing tradition of flexible specialization. The modular design of machine tools having been a stronghold of German machine building since the turn of the century came back strengthened with computerized numeric control. Although ever more of the basic numeric control (NC) components were imported from Japan since the 1970s, they were adapted to a great variety of individual tasks and ended up in small-series batches, which made for two-thirds of West German machinery output.

While Japanese manufacturers excelled in bringing down the costs of a given machine design, the West German producers typically would do better in meeting their industrial customers' very specific requirements making a high-price product a profitable investment in the end. Since this demand pattern persisted on the markets for investment goods, the West German machine-building industry, cyclical fluctuations notwithstanding, managed to thrive during the Japanese rise to the top during the 1970s and 1980s. It adds to the by-now-familiar picture of sophisticated technology that does not lend itself so well to mass production being to the competitive advantage of German industrial enterprise. With heterogenous products, craft skills, and product innovations continuing to dominate a substantial share of the world market, the machinery industry could prosper without protection and without the concentration experienced in car manufacturing and electrical equipment. Engineering, more than the other branches of manufacturing industry, contributes to the German economy's appearance as having a position of unrivaled breadth on the export markets. It is a huge variety of different sophisticated products rather than a few market strongholds, such as the notable exception of automobiles, that characterizes the most export-oriented industry among the major economies to date.

A PROFILE LOST IN INTERNATIONAL UNIFORMITY?: GERMAN ENTERPRISE CULTURE IN THE 1990s

With its strength in cars, machines, and chemicals and its emphasis on craft skills and product rather than process innovation, the German industry was entering the 1990s in which the rules of the game were newly defined with the integration of the bankrupt East German industrial structure and the removal of the last trade barriers in the EEC. Never were there as many new horizons and as many foreign competitors to German industry at the same time. With markets in Europe, both West and East, again vastly extended and regulation everywhere on the retreat, old-style German corporatism is about to lose the last remnants of its once cherished pre-1914 fabric. With the convergence of market size and the degree of deregulation between America and Europe, industrial structure and

management values on both sides of the Atlantic seemed to have con-
verged beyond distinction as well. German top management, which was
a stronghold of engineers and scientists for more than a century is being
taken over by economists. The balance of the three-pronged investment
is eventually being tipped toward the traditionally underdeveloped marketing side to come in line with the demands of an open consumer society.

All the outlined developments toward an American-style industry structure notwithstanding, the business culture of German managers until the
present continued to bear traits of cooperatism. This was not only true
for their conflict-evading way of handling labor-relations with the trade
unions, but also among themselves. Aggressive competition and hostile
takeovers went largely counter to their values. Even if the visions of an
"organic economy" were left far behind, most German managers continued to see more than just the book value in a company. With long in-
house careers and a great part of top management having been trained as
academic engineers or scientists, organic and technocratic views of manufacturing enterprise were always being kept alive. On the level of the
executive board this attitude was reflected in a collegial management
tradition which did not lend itself to competition among board members.
The performance-related share of German managers' compensation is
typically much smaller than in American firms and not necessarily tied to
his division's performance exclusively, in this again strengthening collegial
management as well as a feeling of responsibility for the long-term stability of the whole firm.

Powerful agents for stability after World War II as much as before
World War I were the great banks. Their policy was not one of conflict
but rather of consensus with and among industry, establishing what has
been referred to as "Rhenish capitalism," the prosperity of large enterprises under the protection and sometimes even tutelage of the big banks
on both sides of the Rhine. Not only did the German universal banks
provide long-term capital for industry but they took a strong interest
in industrial enterprise itself through extended ownership of capital and
their acting on behalf of a great number of private shareholders. German
company law permits the representation of share-capital by the bank
where it is deposited, an option taken by the majority of petty shareholders. This gives the major banks virtual control over a large number
of companies and makes them the natural clearinghouses for conflicting
interests in industry, as well as giving them frequently the decisive vote in
appointing senior management or forging new alliances or mergers. Tacit

cooperation between banks and industry with the banks frequently effectively insulating troubled industry from the state and acting as an agent of
concentration has become a linchpin of stability in German industry and
a viable alternative to the kind of government intervention pervasive
among Germany's neighbors.

If a clear convergence toward the structure of American enterprise
could always be observed over the past century, differences did persist in
the field of management culture and institutions until the present. Whether
they will survive the current rough tides of intensified competition on the
larger European market and exposure to overseas competitors, however,
remains to be seen.

Acknowledgments

I am particularly grateful to Volker Berghahn, Charles Feinstein, Patrick
Fridenson, Avner Offer, and Gianni Toniolo, who made very valuable
comments on earlier versions of this chapter and saved me from one
blunder or another.

Bibliographical essay

For readers without a knowledge of German the most effective approach
to the literature and the main issues of the history of German manufacturing enterprise would be via these two publications: Alfred D. Chandler,
Jr., *Scale and Scope: The Dynamics of Industrial Capitalism*, Cambridge,
MA: Belknap, 1990; Gareth P. Dyas and Heinz T. Thannheiser, *The
Emerging European Enterprise: Strategy and Structure in French and
German Industry*, Boulder, CO: Westview Press, 1976. While Chandler
is covering the years up to 1930, Dyas and Thannheiser present German enterprise after World War II. For an embracing view of twentieth-
century big business which includes the most important Nazi years and
allows for a wider discussion of the political dimensions of German
industry, see the most up-to-date collection by Volker Berghahn (ed.),
German Big Business and Europe: 1914–1993, Oxford: Berg, 1994. A
very useful brief account of the history of Germany's innovation system
since the nineteenth century is Otto Keck, "The National System for
Technical Innovation in Germany," in Richard R. Nelson (ed.), *National
Innovation Systems: A Comparative Analysis*, New York: Oxford University Press, 1993, pp. 115–157.

A number of very interesting studies are devoted to shorter time spans. An impressive account of the aborted reform movement of the 1920s is Mary Nolan, *Visions of Modernity: American Business and the Modernization of Germany*, New York: Oxford University Press, 1994. On the Nazi approach to advanced technology, see Jeffrey Herf, *Reactionary Modernism: Technology, Culture, and Politics in Weimar and the Third Reich*, Cambridge: Cambridge University Press 1984. Still unsurpassed on "Americanization" is Volker R. Berghahn, *The Americanization of West German Industry, 1945–1973*, Leamington Spa: Berg, 1986 (New York, 1987). On German industry's competitive advantages after World War II, see Gernot Klepper and Frank D. Weiss, "Protection and International Competitiveness: A View from West Germany," in Bert G. Hickman (ed.), *International Productivity and Competitiveness*, New York: Oxford University Press, 1992, pp. 362–391.

Studies of the major German industries are very unequally represented in English. We do have very good coverage of the chemical industry until the early 1960s, which is hardly bettered in German: L. F. Haber, *The Chemical Industry during the Nineteenth Century: A Study of the Economic Aspects of Applied Chemistry in Europe and North America*, Oxford: Clarendon Press, 1958; L. F. Haber, *The Chemical Industry, 1900–1930, International Growth and Technological Change*, Oxford: Clarendon Press, 1971; Peter Hayes, *Industry and Ideology: IG Farben in the Nazi Era*, Cambridge: Cambridge University Press, 1987; Raymond G. Stokes, *Divide and Prosper: The Heirs of IG Farben under Allied Authority, 1945–1951*, Berkeley: University of California Press, 1988; Raymond G. Stokes, *Opting for Oil: The Politics of Technological Choice in the German Chemical Industry, 1945–1961*, Cambridge: Cambridge University Press, 1994.

The business history of the steel industry is less well represented in recent years. For the earlier period we have, in English, Ulrich Wengenroth, *Enterprise and Technology: The German and British Steel Industries, 1865–1895*, Cambridge: Cambridge University Press, 1994; to be chronologically followed by the more politically oriented Gerald D. Feldman, *Iron and Steel in the German Inflation, 1916–1923*, Princeton: Princeton University Press, 1977. A good overview for the recent years of the industry's European integration is Thomas Grunert, "Decision-Making Processes in the Steel Crisis Policy of the EEC: Neocorporatist or Integrationist Tendencies?" in Yves Meny and Vincent Wright (eds.), *The Politics of Steel: Western Europe and the Steel Industry in the Crisis Years (1974–1984)*,

Berlin: de Gruyter, 1987, pp. 222–307. For the interwar years there is no up-to-date alternative to the more recent German literature. In view of its explicit discussion of Alfred Chandler's presentation of the German steel industry in *Scale and Scope*, one article merits particular attention: Christian Kleinschmidt and Thomas Welskopp, "Zu viel 'Scale' zu wenig 'Scope.' Eine Auseinandersetzung mit Alfred D. Chandler's Analyse der deutschen Eisen- und Stahlindustrie in der Zwischenkriegszeit," *Jahrbuch für Wirtschaftsgeschichte* (1993), pp. 251–297.

The recent English language literature on other important industries like engineering and electronics is scattered at best and readers are referred to the more general literature cited here, which will deal with these industries. The early history of electricity generation is admirably dealt with by Thomas P. Hughes, *Networks of Power, Electrification in Western Society, 1880–1930*, Baltimore: Johns Hopkins University Press, 1983. A very stimulating account of engineering after World War II are chapters 5–7 of Gary B. Herigel, *Industrial Constructions. The Sources of German Industrial Power* (Cambridge: Cambridge University Press, 1995).

6

Small European nations: Cooperative capitalism
in the twentieth century

HARM G. SCHRÖTER

INTRODUCTION

In this chapter it is asked to what extent industry in small and developed
European nations showed patterns similar to those worked out by Alfred
D. Chandler in his volume *Scale and Scope* for the United States, the
United Kingdom, and Germany.[1] The period of investigation starts at the
turn of the century and covers the time up to the 1980s. The focus is on
Belgium, Denmark, Finland, Luxemburg, the Netherlands, Norway, Sweden, and Switzerland. The special problems of the war economies are not
presented here. However, during both world wars enterprises situated in
one of the neutral but developed states had a special potential for growth,
which a number of firms exploited well. Of this special potential for
growth, Belgian firms were excluded, since the country was occupied by
German troops in both wars. During World War II only Switzerland and
Sweden were not directly involved and could enjoy a certain potential of
special growth.

The following section presents a short recapitulation of Chandler's
three types of capitalism with emphasis on those characteristics which are
dealt with in this chapter. It is followed by a discussion on the extent to
which the Chandlerian approach can be made useful in the case of small
developed nations and their large enterprises.

In the third section the three different types of doing business are
applied to the firms of the small states. For the American competitive
type internal and external growth is looked into, while for the British
one, the role of holding companies and personal leadership of enterprises

---

[1] Alfred D. Chandler, Jr., *Scale and Scope: The Dynamics of Industrial Capitalism*, Cambridge, Mass., 1990.

is focused on. Similarities with the German cooperative approach are considered, mainly by discussing the issue of cartelization. In consequence, traces of a fourth possible type of capitalism, based on the limitations of national markets of small developed nations, are searched for.

Since no clear response to the question of types of capitalism can yet be given, the general business climate of the small states is put on the agenda. In the results the proximity of the small states to the three types of capitalism and the development of a distinct small-state type on this level is discussed.

In the last section we investigate the structural continuity of the way of doing business throughout the whole period here under question, and compare it with the development in large states. It is our thesis that the development shows a steady decline of cooperative capitalism from the 1950s onward.

COMPETITIVE, PERSONAL, AND COOPERATIVE CAPITALISM AND SMALL DEVELOPED NATIONS

We take here the types of competitive, personal, and cooperative capitalism as they have been worked out by Alfred Chandler, despite some criticism,[2] because they serve us very well as models or prototypes. However, because of the small number of firms involved, we have to amend considerations about the national business climate in order to allocate the small states to the three types of capitalism. Furthermore, it is to be stressed that all three types never existed in a totally pure form. U.S. and German firms showed traces of personal capitalism, German and British enterprises competed on various levels. American and British firms took part in international cartelization – which we use as an indicator for cooperative capitalism.[3] Therefore we cannot expect pure types to have been developed in the small states, but rather mixtures, in which a certain type is more worked out than the others. The question is, Which feature is most representative of the respective types of economies in the small states under consideration? Methodologically we follow Alfred Chandler in concluding from information on large firms as to the character of the type of capitalism.

---

[2] Important criticism was brought forward for the American case by Thomas Hughes and, even more challenging, by Roy Church for the British case. See Roy Church, "The Limitations of the Personal Capitalism," in Steven Tolliday (ed.), *Scale and Scope: A Review Colloquium, Business History Review*, 64, Winter 1990, pp. 703–710; Thomas, Hughes, "Managerial Capitalism beyond the Firm," in ibid., pp. 698–703.

[3] Alfred Chandler, too, took this as a major indicator. He pointed to other indicators such as industrial relations, but he has made little use of them throughout *Scale and Scope* (p. 395).

According to Alfred Chandler, the common features of the three types of capitalism, developed in the United States, in the United Kingdom, and in Germany represent the greatest impact on the development of industrial capitalism in all countries – and perhaps beyond: "For the past century large managerial enterprises have been engines of economic growth and transformation in modern economies,"[4] or "These industries, in turn, were the pace setters of the industrial sector of their economies."[5] Common characteristics of such enterprises are the three-pronged investments in production, distribution, and management. Such firms used hierarchies in their internal organizations, competed on oligopolistic or in some cases even monopolistic markets, and showed multiunit structures. Decisive for their growth was integration, forward into distribution and backward into raw materials or intermediates. This opened up the possibility for a large throughput to exploit the economies of scale, as has been shown with the example of Standard Oil and others. An alternative road to growth was the massive extension of core competitive advantages of the respective firms into a wide range of products. For this, the German chemical firms provided examples. Of course, strategies of scale could be complemented by such of scope and vice versa. While there were different routes to long-term economic success, there was a common destination: "At the core of this dynamic were the organizational capabilities of the enterprise as a unified whole."[6] The creation of large hierarchical organizations in enterprises has turned out to be of central importance for the development of modern industries.[7]

On the one hand this development is a common feature for all large enterprises regardless of their home basis. But, on the other hand, for all the issues mentioned, market size is an important factor[8] – which raises the question to what extent other developed but small states could reach one of the three types of capitalism, established in the economically most powerful and biggest nations of that period, the United States, the United Kingdom, and Germany, whose GNPs were at least ten times larger than that of the small nations.

The question of small nations has been touched on before. According to Herman Daems, reviewing the rise of managerial capitalism in small

---

[4] Alfred D. Chandler, "Managerial Enterprise and Competitive Capabilities," *Business History*, 34, no. 1, 1992, p. 11.
[5] Chandler, *Scale and Scope*, p. 593.   [6] Ibid., p. 594.   [7] Ibid., p. 596, 604.
[8] Alfred D. Chandler, *The Visible Hand: The Managerial Revolution in American Business*, Cambridge, Mass. 1977.

nations, "the size of the country is not a significant factor for the comparative position of large enterprises in Europe."[9] However, commentators have expressed some doubts to these strong words: "I cannot help feeling that large scale domestic markets and also large scale throughput are still decisive for the development of managerial capitalism."[10] However, in the end of his contribution, Herman Daems, too, stressed the specialty of conditions for the development of hierarchical enterprises in small nations.[11] Groups of other scholars have approached the issue of small nations as one of its own, which implies that there are differences between large and small economies.[12]

Throughput is, according to Chandler, an important condition of growth. However, it can be reached not only by serving the market of one single country but, by the means of exports, by serving several markets combined. Furthermore, markets can sometimes be served even better by means of direct investment.[13] In any case, the number of large firms is vital for our question.[14] However, in addition to considering the number of large industrial firms needed to develop hierarchies, the size of such firms should be taken into account as well. A few very large enterprises can have the same effect on the number of persons involved in such hierarchies as a variety of moderately large firms. In this context Royal Dutch Shell, Unilever, Nestlé, Swedish Match (up to 1932), and Volvo (after World War II) are to be mentioned.

In his contribution on the development of managerial capitalism in small countries, Herman Daems chose a cutoff point of 10,000 employees in the definition of a "large" firm. He himself pointed out that he made his choice "somewhat arbitrarily,"[15] but he wanted to be sure to include

[9] Herman Daems, "Large Firms in Small Countries: Reflections on the Rise of Managerial Capitalism," in Kesaji Kobayashi and Hidemasa Morikawa (eds.), *The Development of the Managerial Enterprise*, Tokyo 1986, pp. 261–276.
[10] Reiko Okayama, Comment [on Herman Daems contribution], in ibid., p. 279.
[11] "Enterprises in small countries had to use their technological capabilities to produce quality differentiated products for specialized markets" (Daems, "Large Firms," p. 275).
[12] Jaakko Honko, *Entwicklung von Innovationen in Kleinen Industrieländern* (Akademie der Wissenschaften zu Berlin), Berlin 1990; Charles P. Kindleberger, and Tamir Agmon (eds.), *Multinationals from Small Countries*, Cambridge, Mass. 1977; Harm Schröter, *Aufstieg der Kleinen, Multinationale Unternehmen aus fünf kleinen Staaten vor 1914*, Berlin 1993.
[13] Alfred D. Chandler, "Technological and Organizational Underpinnings of Modern Industrial Enterprise: The Dynamics of Competitive Advantage," in Alice Teichova, Maurice Lévy-leboyer, and Helga Nussbaum (eds.), *Multinational Enterprise in Historical Perspective*, Cambridge 1986, pp. 30–54.
[14] E.g., Daems calculated the number of large firms within the small developed nations of Europe ("Large Firms," p. 262).
[15] Ibid.

not only just large but multiunit enterprises. In contrast, Alfred Chandler used a cutoff point of 20,000-plus employees in one of his contributions.[16] Their contributions are concentrated on a relatively short period. In contrast to this, ours cover more than eighty years. During this time there has been much development, of course. Therefore, we cannot use one static definition to identify a "large" firm, since what was "large" in 1900 was rather medium-sized in the 1980s. The best would have been an adopted definition such as *Fortune*'s top 500 firms worldwide. But this is not available for the whole of our period. The growth of firms belonging to our set was more hesitant than expected. A closer look into the company histories reveals that a spurt in the development of the size of the enterprises involved took place especially from the 1960s onward.[17] Therefore we take into account firms which were, first, multiunit, second, showed a hierarchical organization, and, third, commanded a large work force. For the label "large" we defined about 5,000 employees worldwide for the time up to 1960, while from the 1960s onward 10,000 employees are needed.

The categories of about 5,000/10,000 employees plus multiunit, hierarchical organizations divide our group of small nations clearly into two parts. Whereas Belgium, the Netherlands, Sweden, and Switzerland were home to a number of large enterprises – between six and twenty-three – Denmark, Finland, and Norway presented only one or two. (As Luxemburg was in an economic union with Belgium from 1918 onward, these two states are not separated throughout this study.)

The enterprises which have been looked into amount to fifty-eight. Their names were subject to change and abbreviation over time; however, all are to be identified. They include:

> Belgium and Luxemburg: Arbed (of Luxemburg), Cockerill, Espérance-Longdoz (later merged with Cockerill),[18] Fabrique Nationale d'Armes de Guerre (FN), Gaevert (later merged with Agfa), Hadir (Haut Fourneaux et Aciéries de Differdange–St. Ingbert-Rumelange) (later merged with Cockerill), Ougrée-Marihaye (later merged with Cockerill), Petro-

---

[16] Alfred D. Chandler, "The Place of the Modern Industrial Enterprise in Three Economies," in Alice Teichova and Philip L. Cottrell (eds.), *International Business and Central Europe, 1918–1939*, Leicester 1983, p. 8.

[17] We checked the firms against the available *Fortune* lists. Most of them, but not all, were to be found in the top world 500, but were all covered by the *Fortune* lists of top international 500 (which excludes U.S. firms).

[18] Here and in all following cases "later" means during the period of our survey – up to the 1980s.

fina, La Providence (later merged with Cockerill), Solvay, Tubize, Vieille
Montagne (VM)
Denmark: Carlsberg
Finland: Neste, Outokumpu
The Netherlands: AKU (Algemene Kunstzijde Unie, later merged into Akzo),
DSM, Hoogovens, Philips, Royal Dutch Shell, Unilever
Norway: Norsk Hydro, Statoil
Sweden: AGA, Alfa Laval (later merged with Tetra Pak), Asea (later merged
with BBC into ABB), Electrolux, Gränges (later merged into Electrolux),
LME (L. M. Ericsson), Saab-Scania, SCA (Svenska Cellulosa AB), SKF,
Stora, Svenska Taendsticks AB (STAB or Swedish Match), Volvo
Switzerland: AGUT (Aktiengesellschaft für Unternehmungen der Texti-
lindustrie), AIAG (Aluminium Industrie Aktien Gesellschaft, later
Alusuisse, merged with Lonza), Bally, BBC (later merged with Asea),
Ciba (later merged with Geigy), Escher-Wyss (later merged with Sulzer),
Geigy (later merged with Ciba), Holderbank, G. Fischer, Landis &
Gyr, Lenzburg, Lonza (later merged with Alusuisse), Maggi (later
merged with Nestlé), Nestlé, Oerlikon-Bührle, Roche, Sandoz, Sastig
(Schweizerisch-Amerikanische Stickerei-Industrie-Gesellschaft), Schindler,
SIS (Industriegesellschaft für Schappe), Stehli, Suchard, and Sulzer

If arranged according to sectors of industry, as it was done in *Scale and
Scope*, the picture is the following:[19]

Group 10 (mining): Gränges, Outokumpu
Group 20 (food): Carlsberg, Lenzburg, Maggi, Nestlé, Suchard, Unilever
Group 22 (textiles): AGUT, Sastig, SIS, Stehli
Group 26 (paper): SCA
Group 28 (chemicals): AKU, Ciba, DSM, Gaevert, Geigy, Norsk Hydro,
Roche, Sandoz, Solvay, STAB, Tubize
Group 29 (petroleum and coal): Neste, Petrofina, Royal Dutch Shell, Statoil
Group 31 (leather): Bally
Group 32 (stone etc.): Holderbank
Group 33 (primary metals): AIAG, Arbed, Cockerill, Espérance-Longdoz,
Hadir, Hoogovens, La Providence, Lonza, Ougrée-Marihaye, Stora, VM
Group 34 (fabricated metals): G. Fischer, SKF
Group 35 (machinery): AGA, Alpha Laval, Escher-Wyss, FN, Oerlikon-
Bührle, Schindler, Sulzer
Group 36 (electrical): Asea, BBC, Electrolux, Landis & Gyr, LME, Philips
Group 37 (transportation equipment): Saab-Scania, Volvo

---

[19] Like the lists in Chandler, *Scale and Scope*, pp. 632–732, ours is arranged according to
the U.S. Standard Industrial Classification.

Table 6.1. *The number of large firms*

Year	1913	1938	1980
Number of companies	25	32	40
Total number of exits		9	10
Exits through mergers with firms listed above		4	6

As we expect, the total number of large firms was rising during the period of investigation (see Table 6.1). However, most large firms stayed large over time. The number exiting the list is only nineteen, about one-third the total. For a period of ninety years, with all its changes in technology, management, marketing, political framework, and the like, this is a surprisingly small amount. Furthermore, one-half of these exits was due to mergers with other firms listed here (takeovers by others were not counted).[20] Furthermore, only five of the large firms active in 1980 had been established after the 1920s.

The majority of firms was concentrated in the new industries, which underlines the impact of technological change. In this context it is worthwhile mentioning that all of the textile enterprises were reduced heavily in size during the 1930s. After 1945, the firms of this group could no longer be labeled as large. In consequence, the number of industrial groups presented here is limited, from one in the cases of Denmark and Finland to nine in Switzerland, while in the total of all of our small states the sum is thirteen.[21]

Corresponding numbers of industrial groups for the three large states were, of course, greater. In the United States and the United Kingdom, this number was the same before and after World War I, amounting in the former to nineteen, and in the latter to eighteen; for Germany it was eighteen in 1929 and sixteen in 1953.[22] While the numbers of industrial groups in the three large states correspond, there is quite a gap between the number of such groups in a small state and even the combined number

---

[20] Two more exits were caused by takeovers from other firms: Gaevert first merged with the German Agfa, a subsidiary of Bayer. Shortly after the majority of Caevert's shares were acquired by Bayer. During the 1980s, Suchard was bought by Jacobs, a German coffee firm. Some years later Jacobs-Suchard was taken over by Philip Morris.
[21] The corresponding number of groups represented are four in Belgium; five in the Netherlands; and eight in Sweden.
[22] For the United States and for the United Kingdom (Chandler, *Scale and Scope*, pp. 644–686).

of all of them. Here is a discrepancy because the combined population of the small states (around 40 million inhabitants) was not so much lower than that of the United Kingdom (about 50 million inhabitants). The industrial groups not represented in the small states are exactly those in which in the large countries, too, only a small number of firms was on the list, such as tobacco (no. 21), apparel (23), lumber (24), furniture (25), printing (27), rubber (30), instruments (38), and miscellaneous (39). In contrast, textiles (22) seems to be an exceptional group. This is surprising as textiles traditionally represented major sectors in the economies of Belgium and Switzerland. The Scandinavian tradition in shipping did not stimulate a large shipbuilding industry.[23] The exceptionally heavy investment of Belgian firms in foreign transport facilities, especially tramways, could not be counted as an industrial one, because they were free-standing firms[24] in the service sector, which had chosen the form of holding companies, doing little business at home. These enterprises, though large in capital, needed no substantial hierarchical organizations at home.[25]

In spite of an uneven distribution of large firms among the small nations, oligopolistic competition was at hand in all of our states. In case it was not carried out by large firms, it was done by other means of concentration, especially through cartelization. We therefore suggest not excluding altogether those nations which failed to produce a number of large firms until the end of the 1950s, such as Denmark and Finland.

Nearly all of our firms reacted to the limitation of their home markets by becoming multinationals even before World War I.[26] Only a handful, such as Gaevert or Carlsberg, had restricted themselves to the home market or to exports. By maintaining several plants abroad, the enterprises became more and more hierarchical. During the buildup of organizational capabilities, Belgian and Swiss firms revealed more difficulties

---

[23] There had been a substantial shipbuilding industry in Norway. However, it did not invest in production (it did not adapt to iron and to steam) and therefore declined.

[24] See Mira Wilkins, "The Free-Standing Company, 1870–1914," *Economic History Review*, 2nd ser., 41, 1988, pp. 259–282; Harm Schröter and Mira Wilkins (eds.), *The Nature of the Free-Standing Company Investigations into a Specific Form of Multinational Enterprise*, Oxford 1997 (forthcoming).

[25] The free-standing companies look very much like the prototypes of British personal capitalism.

[26] However, in this process they followed patterns which were different from the American ones as they kept in mind the limitation of their home market from the beginning (see Schröter, *Aufstieg*).

than the Scandinavian and Dutch ones.[27] While distribution networks and plants were set up abroad, facilities for R&D stayed concentrated at home. Some exceptions of this pattern emerged as late as the 1970s. Leading personnel, too, were of the home nationality. All firms showed backward or forward integration, but only a few of them developed several product lines.

The financial institutions of our states differed. While Belgium, the Netherlands, and Switzerland traditionally acted as important foreign investors, the Scandinavian countries changed from debtors to lenders. Especially in Norway foreign capital was decisive. The amount of concentration in the banking sector was considerable in Scandinavia. For instance in Sweden one bank (Skandinaviska Enskilda Banken), a bank of the type of the Société Generale in Belgium, became decisive for the growth of large industrial firms. Even the Norwegian Norsk Hydro relied on it.

U.S.-STYLE OF COMPETITION BETWEEN LARGE FIRMS

Large managerial firms, grown through expansion, merger, and acquisition, taking little part in cartelization, represent the American type of competitive capitalism. Such firms were to be found within the small nations as well. Interestingly they were clustered in a few groups of the economy: in oil, food, and, to a certain extent, in machine building.

Large enterprises in the oil sector were Royal Dutch Shell in the Netherlands, Neste in Finland, Statoil in Norway, and Petrofina in Belgium. While Royal Dutch Shell is quite well known as one of the largest firms in the world, Petrofina's case is different. Petrofina was founded in 1920 in order to take over the majority of shares of what had been before World War I German investment into the Rumanian oil fields.[28] Petrofina grew quickly as it invested downstream in refining, transport, and distribution. In 1939 it was active in nine European states and in three of their African colonies.[29] World War II caused heavy losses. However, at the end

---

[27] Several Belgian firms had lost administrative grip on their foreign direct investments in Russia before 1914. The process of how Swiss chemical firms gathered their organizational and managerial capabilities for conducting production abroad has been discussed in Harm Schröter, "Unternehmensleitung und Auslandsproduktion: Entscheidungsprozesse, Probleme und Konsequenzen in der schweizerischen Chemieindustrie vor 1914," *Schweizerische Zeitschrift für Geschichte*, 44, 1994, pp. 14–53.

[28] In 1920 such shares were held by a Swiss financial group.

[29] Crude production amounted to 1.2 million tons, while refining capacity was at 2.2 million tons (*Petrofina, 1920–1960*, n.d. [1960], n.p.).

of the 1950s, Petrofina had not only recovered, but it had invested heavily into production, refining, transportation, and distribution. It had diversified and was active in thirteen European states (colonies included), two African ones, and in the United States and Canada. Though Petrofina represented a large hierarchical enterprise, it had made only some cautious steps toward a divisional structure.[30] Any participation in cartels or any attempts of cooperation are unknown. In contrast, the coal group[31] of our large enterprises was tightly involved in national and international cartelization up to 1939. Statoil was founded comparatively late, after oil was discovered in the North Sea in the 1960s. Neste, too, grew significantly from the 1960s onward by becoming Finland's main national oil company.

In the food sector, too, competitive capitalism was widespread. Interestingly the history of the large firms involved is very similar: all of them had become multinationals before World War I and all had at least one main rival at home with whom competition was vigorous. In the Netherlands Anton Jurgens had its rival in van den Bergh, in Switzerland Nestlé had its rival in Anglo-Swiss Condensed Milk, while in the canned goods industry there were Lenzburg and Saxon. In this branch of industry the firms grew large by mergers and acquisitions rather than by internal growth. In 1920 A. Jurgens and v.d. Bergh, already in cooperation, exchanged shares with Schicht and Centra, both important companies in the former Austro-Hungarian Empire.[32] Seven years later, the Dutch firms merged into Margarine-Unie, which in its turn together with Lever Co. became Unilever in 1930. Nestlé and Anglo-Swiss merged into Nestlé in 1905.[33] The three Swiss chocolate producers Peter, Kohler, and Cailler merged into Soc. Générale Suisse des Chocolats in 1904, which in its turn was merged with Nestlé in 1929. Acquisitions were the other side of the coin. Nestlé took over Maggi (1947), while Lenzburg bought its main rivals Saxon and Seethal in 1926. A certain exception in this group, which showed the American type of competitive capitalism, is the Danish brewery Carlsberg, which on one hand took over its main national competitor, Tuborg, and on the other organized beer cartels on a national scale.

An expansion policy focusing on competition was to be found especially in the Swedish machine-building and car industry. Companies such

---

[30] See graph on the organizational structure in 1960, in ibid.
[31] Nearly all of the Belgian iron and steel firms owned coal mines.
[32] Alice Teichova, *An Economic Background to Munich*, Cambridge 1974, pp. 299–312.
[33] Its original name then was Nestlé and Anglo-Swiss Condensed Milk Co.

as AGA (machines/gas) and Alpha-Laval (separators) had only a limited amount of rivals. Such oligopolistic competition would have made it easier to cooperate, but the companies showed little intention. Volvo (cars, trucks) and Saab-Scania (aircraft, trucks, cars) too, traditionally competed. SKF (ball bearings) from Sweden, Fabrique Nationale (fire-arms) from Belgium and the Swiss firms Sulzer and Escher-Wyss (both mixed) cooperated in the field of technics, especially patents, with other enterprises. But this cannot be counted as a widespread cartelization. All these activities had little in common with cooperation but much with competition.

Interestingly, most of those firms which entered our list after World War II, such as Volvo, Neste, Saab-Scania, or Outokumpu, are not known for their cooperation, but for their policy of competition. This suggests, that competition was the better way to growth after 1945.

THE BRITISH TYPE OF PERSONAL CAPITALISM

It had been maintained by Roy Church, that personal capitalism was to be found to a great extent in the United States and in Germany as well; there was no archetype. However, our question here is to what extent such personal capitalism can be traced in the small developed states. Common characteristics of personal capitalism are, above all, that the organization of enterprises is designed around leading persons without taking resort to large bureaucratic hierarchies. In criticizing Chandler, Roy Church has substantiated Chandler's model by pointing to additional reasons why British firms saw no need in building hierarchies. British firms had no need to create special organizational steps, unavoidable by mergers or cartelization. It "enabled large British firms to become part of 'global oligopolies,' thereby inhibiting corporate expansion."[34] Thus firms of the personal capitalism type either were managed by individuals, some-times with the help of a few associates, or they were holding companies, which represented another species of this type.[35] Furthermore, there existed a substantial variety of clusters or groups of enterprises, held together by interlocking ownership or management.[36] What this British

[34] Church, "Limitations," p. 705.
[35] Chandler, Scale and Scope, p. 235.
[36] Stanley Chapman, "British Based Investment Groups before 1914," Economic History Review, 2nd ser., 38, 1985.

type lacked, was large organizations comprehending "the enterprise as a unified whole."[37]

Especially in Sweden and the Netherlands, large firms were led by managers. As has been shown in the discussion on the managerial enterprise, this does not exclude the existence of dominating persons, such as Henry Deterding of Royal Dutch Shell, or Ivar Kreuger of STAB (Swedish Match). However, the impact of these exceptional men cannot push the whole nature of their country's way of doing business toward the British personal capitalism. Furthermore, such persons passed their zenith of influence during the 1920s and early 1930s, for all large enterprise had to build large hierarchical organizations.

In Switzerland, too, management capitalism had spread its wings. But to a considerable extent personal relationships were important. For example, in Basel, seat of the famous chemical industry, little was to be obtained against the so-called Daig (Swiss: dough, paste), by which a network of old established families was addressed. AGUT, in 1914 the second largest firm by capitalization, with foreign direct investment in the United States, France, Germany, and Italy, was the leader in the interwar period in an entirely patriarchic way.[38] The son of the owner of AGUT, Mr. Schwarzenbach sen., provides another example. During World War II and the following decades he was a member of nearly all the important boards of directors of Swiss industry. He was a decisive person in the important takeovers and mergers,[39] and Swiss trade treaty negotiations during that period. But still all these issues could be traced in other states as well,[40] without placing them into the sphere of personal capitalism.

Traces of such personal capitalism were to be found in all states, but especially in Belgium. There many economic activities were connected with each other by holding companies or by financial groups of solid influence, in most cases clustered around a family. The widespread existence of holding companies and financial groups has been described as a

[37] Ibid., p. 594. Hidemasa Morikawa has put this forward as the most important point (Hidemasa Morikawa, "The View from Japan," in Tolliday, *Scale and Scope: A Review*, p. 716).

[38] Interview by the author with Dr. Schwarzenbach sen., 10 August 1986.

[39] Such as Nestlé/Maggi or the "Basle marriage," the merger of Ciba and Geigy.

[40] Jürgen Kocka, "Großunternehmen und der Aufstieg des Manager-Kapitalismus im späten 19. und frühen 20. Jahrhundert: Deutschland im internationalen Vergleich," *Historische Zeitschrift*, no. 232, 1981, pp. 39–60; Herman Daems and Herman van der Wee (eds.), *The Rise of Managerial Capitalism*, Leuven 1974; Alfred D. Chandler and Herman Daems, (eds.), *Managerial Hierarchies: Comparative Perspectives on the Rise of the Modern Industrial Enterprise*, Cambridge, Mass. 1980.

specialty of Belgium.[41] The deep structural change in the financial system
in 1935, provoked by the world economic crisis, even strengthened the
holding company as a system. Furthermore, many transactions did not
evolve out of the industrial sector, but were stimulated from outside,
either by universal banks or by holding companies.[42] This structure was
not changed until well into the 1970s.[43] The dominant position of traditional sectors was not changed either during this period.[44] In this context
it is not by chance that an idea of parallels may emerge, not only of British
and Belgian relative decline after World War I, but the role of person capitalism in the decline. Examination of such parallels, however, must await
more detailed investigation.

The concentration of heavy industry provides a good example. Cockerill
itself was organized as a holding company. Step by step it took over
nearly the entire iron and steel industry of Belgium. In 1960 Cockerill had
taken over, among others, the other three large enterprises of its group
in Belgium, La Providence, Espérance-Longdoz, and Ougrée-Marihaye.
The driving force behind these mergers and acquisitions was not so much
Cockerill itself, however, but banks and the government, in their desire
to reallocate the resources of the heavy industry in order to make it more
competitive. In spite of such aims, the enterprise of Cockerill did not grow
as much as one might have expected. This failure can be explained only
to a certain extent by the structural difficulties in the iron and steel sector,
since during the war and the 1950s there was an exceptional high demand
for such products. One of the reasons why Cockerill grew only modestly
is worked out in Chandler's approach: Cockerill was reluctant in investing in organization and in distribution. It consequently failed to rationalize the facilities of the companies under control so as to achieve economies
of scale. It contented itself more or less in acting as an industrial holding
company, which, again according to Chandler, showed not the same drive
for expansion as other organizations did. The counterexample was Arbed.
This Luxemburg-based steel mill expanded in the same way as most

[41] Herman Daems, *The Holding Company and Corporate Control*, Leiden 1978; Marc de
    Geyndt, "The 100 Largest Belgian Industrial Firms, 1892–1930: Analysis of Structure
    and Growth," unpublished manuscript Hugo Veulemans, "Gemengde Banken en Hold-
    ings in België Tidens de 19e en Begin 20e Eeuw," Leuven 1974, unpublished manuscript
    (both manuscripts were kindly sent to me by Prof. van der Wee).
[42] Veulemans, "Gemengde Banken," p. 53.
[43] Daems, "Holding Company," pp. 12–13.
[44] Herman van der Wee, "Large Firms in Belgium, 1892–1974: An Analysis of Their Struc-
    ture and Growth," in D. C. Coleman, and Peter Mathias (eds.), *Enterprise and History*,
    Cambridge 1984, p. 204.

American and German firms did, by internal and external growth, but without taking resort to a whole construction of holding companies as Cockerill did. Following this strategy, Arbed had outgrown Cockerill already in the mid-1920s.

THE GERMAN TYPE OF COOPERATIVE CAPITALISM

Because a large extent of cartelization is a strong indicator for the German type of cooperative capitalism, we will concentrate on this issue.[45] National cartelization and, building up from this foundation, international cartelization were most widespread in the chemical industry. It is not to be denied that Germany played an important role in this process, as this country headed the dyestuff, the nitrogen, and potash cartel, as well as many others. However, the German leadership was founded on quantity, or more precisely on large quotas within the various cartels, but not on a different approach to the question of economic cooperation.

The Swiss firms of Ciba, Geigy, and Sandoz formed their first cartel during World War I in anticipation of strong international competition after the cease fire. This Swiss national cartel signed the first international agreement in 1926, thus laying the foundation on which three years later the whole building of the international dyestuff cartel was erected.[46] The large firms of the Swiss chemical industry were convinced that only international cartelization could guarantee their survival and growth on the world market. In consequence, all discussions and disputes were focused in the end to obtain substantial quotas within the cartel, but not on competition outside the agreement. Participation in a cartel was just the common thing; to stay outside was so unrealistic that this possibility was hardly considered. The way of thinking was based on cooperation – which, of course, did not exclude competition, but limited it to certain areas, such as research and development, where the Swiss industry had great advantages. A certain exception was Roche, which took part in cartelization only to a certain extent, because the specialties offered by the

[45] Chandler, *Scale and Scope*, p. 395.
[46] Harm G. Schröter, "The International Dyestuffs Cartel, 1927–39, with Special Reference to the Developing Areas of Europe and Japan," in Terushi Hara and Akira Kudo (eds.), *International Cartels in Business History*, Tokyo 1992, p. 36; and "Cartels As a Form of Concentration in Industry: The Example of the International Dyestuffs Cartel from 1927 to 1939," in Hans Pohl (ed.), *German Yearbook on Business History 1988*, Berlin, pp. 113–144.

firm were not directly comparable with other products and, hence, were difficult to cartelize.

Special examples of cooperation include the work of the Dutch AKU and the Belgian Solvay. In their cooperative movements both did not need any German center of gravity to lean on. Since its foundation, Solvay cooperated with the British chemical industry, while it carried out direct investments in foreign states. After having obtained an important share of the global market, Solvay acted as a center and administrator of cartels covering a variety of alkalies and related products such as chlorine and salt.[47] The forerunner of AKU, ENKA, was founded in 1911 to produce artificial fibers. It invested abroad and, as a major step, took over the German Vereinigte Glanzstoff Fabriken (VGF) concern in 1929. In 1939 AKU's production represented 16 percent of the world's output, generated in thirty-one plants.[48] In 1960 AKU consisted of seventeen registered enterprises, VGF included, which were situated in eight countries. After taking over other firms, AKU was renamed into Akzo in 1969. Up to 1939 AKU together with Courtaulds was at the center of several international cartels for artificial fibers. Since Tubize was taken over by Solvay, this company, too, was a member in the cartel.

The largest enterprises in Scandinavia, also, took part in cartelization. Norsk Hydro played its role in the core group, the so-called DEN or Deutsch-Englisch-Norwegische Gruppe of the international nitrogen cartel. Svenska Tändsticks AB (Swedish Match) did not only cooperate with foreign governments in order to obtain match monopolies, but, as an important producer of chlorate for its matches, it took part in the international chlorate cartel, where it obtained the lion's share. In Belgium, Gaevert, a producer of photographic films, took part in international cartels from 1924 onward.[49]

The electrotechnical industry is well known for its many cartels, so it is not necessary here to go into detail. All enterprises of the group took part in this cartelization, except Electrolux, a case in which its participation

[47] On Solvay's relation to ICI see: W. J. Reader, *Imperial Chemical Industries: A History*, 2 vols., London 1970, 1975.

[48] *50 Jahre A.K.U./ENKA 1911–1961, Vergangenheit und Zahlen, Wissenswertes und Zukunftspläne*, n.d. [1961], p. 9; M. Dendermonde, *Nieuwe tijden, nieuwe schakels: de eerste fiiftig jaren van de A.K.U.*, Arnhem 1961; Wolfgang E. Wicht, *Glanzstoff. Zur Geschichte der Chemiefaser, eines Unternehmens und seiner Arbeiterschaft*, Neustadt 1992.

[49] Greta Devos, "Agfa-Gaevert and Belgian Multinational Enterprise," in Geoffrey Jones and Harm Schröter (eds.), *The Rise of Multinationals in Continental Europe*, Aldershot 1993, p. 73.

in international cartelization is not entirely clear.[50] About Landis & Gyr's attitude toward cartels little is known, since the firm concentrated on niche products. However, its extent and eagerness to take part in such cartelization were different. For the Dutch Philips its "willingness to come to an understanding with competitors" was the basis of its business philosophy.[51] Philips was a prominent member of the incandescent lamp cartel Phoebus.[52] BBC and Asea had secured their home markets by formal and informal understandings. Additionally they both took part in the major international cartels.[53] LM Ericsson in the telephone sector was one of the three major players in the world. Gentlemen's agreements, honored though unwritten, existed between the three leading firms IT&T, Siemens & Halske, and LME during the 1920s and, after the telephone fight was over, during the 1930s.[54] Besides that, several written contracts existed for matters such as patents and technical standards.

The heavy industry, represented in our group by Arbed of Luxemburg and five Belgian enterprises, too, was at the forefront of national and international cartelization.[55]

AIAG, Lonza, and VM stand in our context for the nonferrous metal sector. The oldest of these firms, the Belgian VM, embarked from its earliest beginnings in 1837 on a policy of cartelization, and it directed the international zinc cartels.[56] AIAG was different only in its age and its product. It acted as a leader of the aluminum cartel from 1901 onward, though its quota was reduced in the course of time. The cartel was suspended in 1936 because of heavy demand at the background of rearmament. Lonza took part in other cartels focused on goods made by electrochemical processes.

[50] Hexner gave a hint of Swedish firms taking part in the International Association of Household Appliances (Ervin Hexner, *International Cartels*, Chapel Hill, N. C. (146, p. 370). He did not mention any specific names, but Electrolux was the only electrotechnical firm in Sweden worth mentioning to produce such things.

[51] Ben Gales and Keetie Sluyterman, "Outward Bound: The Rise of the Dutch Multinationals," in Jones and Schröter, *Rise*, p. 204.

[52] For the international situation in the cartelization of electrical industry during the interwar period see H. Schröter, "A Typical Factor of German International Market Strategy: Agreements between the U.S. and German Electrotechnical Industries up to 1939," in Teichova et al., *Multinational Enterprise*, pp. 160–170.

[53] For Asea, see Jan Glete, *Asea under hundrar år*, Västerås 1982. For BBC see various company books, published without scientific claim.

[54] For L. M. Ericsson, see Artur Attman, Jan Kuuse, and Ulf, Olsson, *L. M. Ericsson 100 år*, vols. 1 and 2, Örebro 1976.

[55] See John Gillingham, *Coal, Steel and the Rebirth of Europe, 1945–1955*, Cambridge 1991.

[56] Greta Devos, "International Cartel Agreements in the Zinc Industry: The Belgian Case," in Dominique Barjot (ed.), *International Cartels Revisited*, Caen, n.d. [1994]

G. Fischer of Switzerland, a producer of fittings for tubes, and SCA from Sweden, one of the leading pulp and papermakers in Europe, too, took part in cartelization. In SCA's case, the paper cartel Scankraft was said to be one of the most solid cartels anywhere.[57]

All these industries preferred cooperation to open competition; some of the firms mentioned, such as Philips, AIAG, and VM, even relied on it. It seems that, for the question of cooperation or cartelization, the sector of industry to which a firm belonged was more important than the home country it was based in.

ECONOMIC COOPERATION AND THE GENERAL BUSINESS CLIMATE

In nearly all of our small states we find some sectors and firms heavily involved in cartelization, while others were not. Thus far we have seen that Sweden, Switzerland, and Belgium showed a heavy commitment to cartelization; the Netherlands, with Royal Dutch Shell and Unilever, however, shed a different light. Furthermore, in Sweden the important sector of machine building was not so much cartelized, as was the case of the food group in Switzerland. But in response to our main question on the extent to which the small developed countries were biased toward one of our three types of capitalism, our review has not yet revealed a clear picture, nor has it offered a contour of a fourth type of capitalism, special to the small developed states.

Therefore, it is worthwhile to take one more step and look into the business climate, in which economic transactions had to take place. This clearly is an amendment to Chandler's approach. However, the concept of business climate reflects the framework Alfred Chandler has pointed out in his *Scale and Scope*.[58] It also reflects some of the criticism brought forward against his approach.[59] In each nation there developed a *manière de voir*, or what can be defined as a mentality as to the proper way of doing business, and a social consensus on how to proceed in economic matters. Such *manière de voir* very much included a role for the state, for, as scholars have pointed out, in small nations "private and public sectors have had to find ways to collaborate" even more intensively than in a case

---

[57] Hexner, *International Cartels*, p. 376.
[58] Chandler, *Scale and Scope*, pp. 9, 393–395.   [59] Church, "Limitations," p. 710.

of larger nations.[60] Such collaboration encouraged economic concentration and cartelization.[61]

In the interwar period general acceptance of cartels was very high; such views were shared throughout the world, except the United States.[62] Many enterprises from small nations had experience with cartels before World War I and had found them useful. After the war, the slump in the world market in the early 1920s deeply affected the small states. Public discussions on competition and cooperation soon were strongly in favor of the latter, stressing the positive results of rationalization, allocation, and private regulation. In such discussions, again and again, the point of view of the national economy in contrast to and in competition with other national economies has been underlined. In this light national cartelization was understood as a means to strengthen the specific country's stand in the international context. In most of the debates the positive views on cartelization were not challenged, only the right of governments to intervene in such private contracts.[63] Trade unions and social democrats, too, had nothing against concentration and cartelization. It was their idea to curb the economic threat of private enterprises by the construction of large cooperative firms of their own.[64]

The case of Norway provides a good example for the general *manière de voir* in our small nations. Norway was one of the few European states which had passed during the 1920s legislation on economic concentration. By the laws of 1922 and 1926 an institution was founded which had to control and formally to approve all such movements. Wilhelm

---

[60] Karl-Erik Michelsen and Markku Kuisma, "Nationalism and Industrial Development in Finland," *Business and Economic History*, 22, 1992, p. 343.

[61] According to Peter Burke, mentality, which shapes the *manière de voir*, is structured by collective convictions – in contrast to individual ones, and by the nonwritten and nonreflected everyday approach in doing one's business (Peter Burke, "Stärken und Schwächen der Mentalitätsgeschichte," in Ulrich Raulff [ed.], *Mentalitätsgeschichte*, Berlin 1987, p. 127).

[62] Harm Schröter, "Kartellierung und Dekartellierung 1890–1990," *Vierteljahrschrift für Sozial- und Wirtschaftsgeschichte*, 81, 1994, pp. 457–93.

[63] See the debate on Swedish legislation: "Den förslagna lagstiftning angående kontroll över truster och karteller," protocol of the society for national economy of its meeting on March 16, 1922, in *Nationalekonomiska Föreningens Förhandlingar*, 1922, pp. 23–44; for Finland: Ferdinand Alfthan, *Finländska karteller: Ekonomiska Samfundets Tidskrift 1920–1921*, Helsinki 1921, pp. 278–331; in Switzerland the central government did not react to suggestions to consider this question (Motion Grimm of June 6, 1924), but it formed a commission to monitor retail prices (Preisbildungskommission des Eidgenössischen Volkswirtschaftsdepartements [PbK]) in 1926.

[64] Torsten Odhe, *Det moderna trust- och kartellväsendet*, Stockholm 1929; Hartmut Bechtold, *Die Kartellierung der deutschen Volkswirtschaft und die sozialdemokrastische Theorie-Diskussion vor 1933*, Frankfurt am Main 1986.

Thagaard, who become president of this control council, after he had succeeded in setting it up, was strongly in favor of economic cooperation, because in it he saw positive forces active for the accumulation of national wealth.[65]

His views had important repercussions, as the following example shows. It was laid down by law that cartels should be limited to one year, after which they had to be approved anew by Thagaard's council. In 1929 the Norwegian canned food industry applied for an exception to this, as it felt more comfortable to have a long-run cartel. The council not only approved this, but in its justification explained, that "in its scrutiny the usefulness [of the extended cartel] had been revealed, which by merger and cooperation and by strict planning, the economic security in production and export of canned food was sought after."[66] A general approval of cartelization cannot be expressed better than by Thagaard, the Norwegian "watchdog" on economic cooperation during that period.

The 1930s were a decade of severe economic difficulties in the Benelux states and in Switzerland, and to a lesser extent in Scandinavia, where economic growth was quite substantial. In spite of different economic preconditions, the respective policy toward economic cooperation was similar.

The Danish legislation on cartels, enacted in 1931, gave the government in Copenhagen the right to "reconsider" such agreements in which prices were covered. In 1934 the Dutch parliament passed a law which enabled the government to force those outside cartels into the respective convention.[67] Though that right never was applied up to 1939, it had a massive impact on the behavior of cartel members and outsiders by curbing competition. The same legislation was made in Belgium one year later, in 1935.[68]

In Switzerland a special commission called PbK (Preisbildungskommission) started a long-term investigation on the extent of cooperation (cartels and cartel-like understandings) from 1936 onward. The PbK relied entirely on voluntary cooperation of the firms; it had no right to question

[65] Fritz Hodne, *The Norwegian Economy 1920–1980*, Beckenham 1983, pp. 80–81; Helge W. Nordvik, "From Wilhelm Thagaard to Egil Bakke: Price Control, Cartels and Norwegian Competition Policy after World War II," unpublished manuscript.

[66] Kristen Andersen, "Die Aufsicht über Trusts und Kartelle in Norwegen," in *Kartell-Rundschau*, vol. 37, 1933, p. 81.

[67] Verrijn G. M. Stuart, *Die Industriepolitik der niederländischen Regierung*, Jena 1936, pp. 20–21.

[68] Paul Lüthi, *Der Staat und die Kartelle in der Schweiz*, Biel 1947, p. 46.

anybody. However, in a cooperative society the PbK felt no difficulties in finding cooperative firms.[69] Several branches of industry were scrutinized before World War II interrupted its proceedings.[70] The overview revealed an intensively cartelized economy covering a variety of issues from butcher's prices (purchases and sales) and a syndicate for prams up to cartels for cement, bricks, and glass. However, similar cartels were to be found, for example, in the famous Belgian brick and glass industry and in the Danish and the Swedish cement industry. Cartels in construction material were by no means a Swiss specialty.

In any case, Switzerland surely belonged to the set of most cartelized states in Europe. In 1939 about 500 cartels were active in Switzerland.[71] However, this cartelization was not perceived as a threat, but on the contrary as comfort to the national economy. In 1936 the government in its reply to a question on the floor of parliament explained its policy: any possible aims in this context are not focused on "an interdiction or a fight against cartelization, but merely at the control of cartels, especially the introduction of a duty for publication and at the fight against abuses and excesses."[72] Following this line of conviction, the Swiss PbK embarked on a policy to withhold all judgments as to value. Instead it pointed out that any steps in this context should be taken into the theoretical dimension by science, and into the practical one by policy.[73] In spite of these words, the PbK indicated in the introduction of its first publication that Swiss monopoly prices were not too high, but enabled the weaker firms in the cartel to exist.[74] However, legislation by which government was to be authorized to fight abuses of cooperation was in process when it was interrupted by the start of World War II.

In Sweden, too, cooperation was seen in a positive light. The right of government intervention was limited like in Switzerland, except that the Swedish firms had to answer questions in case of direct interrogation. But the government had no right to keep a register on cartels as in Norway,

---

[69] Preisbildungskommision des Eidgenössischen Volkswirtschaftsdepartemente, *Kartelle und kartellartige Abmachungen in der schweizerischen Wirtschaft*, vol. 1, Bern 1937, p. 5.

[70] The overviews were on building material, timber, glass, paper (ibid.), food, clothings and apparel, leather, coverings of the floor (ibid., vol. 2, Bern 1938), ferrous and nonferrous metals (ibid., vol. 3, Bern 1939).

[71] Preisbildungskommission des Eidgenössischen Volkswirtschaftsdepartements (ed.), *Kartell und Wettbewerb in der Schweiz*, Bern 1957, p. 52; Frit Marbachz *Über das Kartell und die Kartellierung in der Schweiz*, Bern, 1937.

[72] Quotation from Lüthi, *Der Staat*, p. 66.   [73] *Preisbildungskommission*, vol. 2, p. 2.

[74] Ibid., p. 7. For the problem of forced cartelization, see Hanspeter Brunner, *Zwangskartelle. Rechtsverhältnisse von Zwangskartellen in der Schweiz und in Deutschland*, Zurich 1937.

Poland, and Czechoslovakia, nor was it enabled to dissolve any private understanding.[75]

The Dutch government embarked on a more and more interventionist policy after 1930. Economic cooperation became a central issue. In 1932 the Economic Council was founded, which acted as if it were an official body.[76] This construction resembled the British PEP group (Political and Economic Planning) serving as an expert for the government. In contrast to the United Kingdom, in the Netherlands this was only the first step. In 1934 the previously mentioned law, by which outsiders could be forced into the respective cartel was passed, and in 1937 another legislation was passed, by which newly founded firms had to be approved. The aim was to protect existing enterprises against what was thought to be too much competition.[77]

There is little information for Finland and for Denmark. However, the enterprises of these countries behaved not very differently from their Scandinavian counterparts in Sweden and Norway.[78] Such similarities were revealed by the cartel examinations after World War II. Elsewhere it had been argued that in interwar Scandinavia cartelization was so widespread that this area should be classified as near the German type of cooperative capitalism.[79]

THE DECLINE OF COOPERATIVE CAPITALISM
AFTER 1945

It has been shown that the basis for cooperation within the national economies of the small states was laid before and after World War I. During the 1930s both cartelization within the economy and cooperation between government and firms or their institutions increased. In other words, cooperative capitalism mushroomed during the interwar period.

---

[75] The law was passed in 1925; see Odhe, *Det moderna trust-och Kartellväsendet*; Friedrich Neumeyer, "Kartellverhältnisse in Schweden," in *Kartell-Rundschau*, vol. 34, 1936, pp. 225–9.

[76] Marita Estor, *Der Sozial-ökonomische Rat der niederländischen Wirtschaft. Institution und Funktion eines zentralen Wirtschaftsrates als Problem der Organisation der Wirtschaftspolitik*, Berlin 1965.

[77] Erwin Zimmermann, *Neokorporatistische Politikformen in den Niederlanden. Industriepolitik, kollektive Arbeitsbeziehungen und hegemoniale Strukturen seit 1918*, Frankfurt am Main 1986.

[78] Schröter, "Wirtschaftlicher Wettbewerb."

[79] Harm Schröter, "Wirtschaftlicher Wettbewerb und Kartellierung als 'Arbeitsweise der praktischen Vernunft' in Skandinavien 1919–1939," in Michael North (ed.), *Nordwesteuropa in der Weltwirtschaft, 1750–1950*, Stuttgart 1993, pp. 95–127.

After Germany lost World War II, the type of capitalism it stood for was in question, too. As Alfred Chandler pointed out, "After the Allied victory in 1945 brought a strong commitment to competition in Europe, German managers accepted the American ways of competition but continued to cooperate more than their American counterparts."[80] A general shift to more competition took place gradually in the Western world.

For the case of Germany this topic was considered by Volker Berghahn.[81] According to him, an "Americanization" of managers took place in Germany. It meant a fundamental change in the paradigm of how to pursue economic aims on both levels, the microeconomic and the macroeconomic one. Surely the boom economy of the 1950s and 1960s provided an exceptionally good condition for Americanization, as sustained economic growth made direction by cartels more and more obsolete. Liberal economic policy was on its way to triumph during this period.[82]

In Germany cartelization was prohibited by the Allies from 1947 onward. The verdict stayed in power until it was taken over by German legislation in 1957. But it went through not without contradiction. The Federation of German Industry (BDI) lobbied for a law designed after the British Restrictive Trade Practices Act passed in 1956. By that act detrimental influences on agreements of "public interest" were interdicted, but not cartelization and monopolies as such. In spite of this, what looked to be a lukewarm anticoncentration move turned out, in the course of time, to be a strong weapon, when the law was applied in British courts. However, whereas the BDI failed in its desire, the new German law was constructed the other way round: cartelization was forbidden, and any exceptions had to be decided upon by the federal cartel agency (Bundeskartellamt). Any cartels not registered there and not explicitly approved of were invalid, legislation which is still in effect today (1994). In the German society the *manière de voir* concerning economic cooperation had begun to turn and to shift into the direction of the American way.

[80] Chandler, *Scale and Scope*, p. 592.
[81] Volker Berghahn, *The Americanization of West German Industry, 1945–1973*, New York 1986; *Unternehmer und Politik in der Bundesrepublik*, Frankfurt am Main 1985; and "Technology and the Export of Industrial Culture: Problems of the German-American Relationship, 1900–1960," in Peter Mathias and John A. Davis (eds.), *Innovation and Technology in Europe: From the Eighteenth Century to the Present Day*, Cambridge, Mass. 1991, pp. 142–161, and references to Americanization in Chapter 5.
[82] Gerold Ambrosius and Hartmut Kaelble, "Einleitung: Gesellschaftliche und wirtschaftliche Folgen des Booms der 1950er und 1960er Jahre," in Hartmut Kaelble, (ed.), *Der Boom 1948–1973, Gesellschaftliche und wirtschaftliche Folgen in der Bundesrepublik Deutschland und in Europa*, Opladen 1992, p. 17.

Was there a similar shift in economic paradigms, a decline of cooperative capitalism and an Americanization in the small nations – and when? Again there is little research on this topic.[83]

In Finland cartelization came under pressure right after World War II. The Economic Planning Commission (Talousneuvosto) comprising representatives from the employers' organizations, the trade unions, and senior government officials drew up a survey on national cartels in 1945 – without any political result. However, public discussion went on and in 1948 the government felt the necessity to form a new committee (Kartellikomitea), whose task it was to make proposals for legislation on cartels. After four years, in 1952, the committee denied the need of any change, as it was convinced cartelization to be of economic advantage for the country.[84] In spite of this, legislation was worked out on the basis of the British cartel act, prohibiting only the excesses of cartelization. The draft was handed over to parliament in 1954, where it rested for several years, before it finally was passed. As in the other small states the content and the speed of proceedings reflect the dispute between partisans of the competitive and the cooperative type of capitalism.

In Sweden, too, the winds had changed after World War II. For example, Arthur Montgomery, one of the country's leading economists, emphasized vehemently the role of open competition for the welfare of the country.[85] Since 1946 all cartels had to be registered. A government committee was set up to investigate the extent of cartelization in the country, which published several reports at the beginning of the 1950s.[86] In 1953 an act was passed prohibiting any abuse connected with cartelization. Three years later it was renewed by passing stricter definitions to come into force beginning in January 1957. These activities put Sweden at the front of small states concerning decartelization. During the years following the war, a general slump was expected worldwide like the one after World War I. The Swedish government was prepared for heavy state intervention, a situation which was by no means detrimental to cooperation. But since the economy boomed, it soon became aware that a different

---

[83] For a preliminary outline, see Schröter, "Kartellierung und Dekartellierung."

[84] For the evidence on the part of Finnish decartelization, I am indebted to information provided by Markku Kuisma; see *Kartellikomitean mietintö 1953:33*. Eduskunnan Kirjasto, Helsinki 1952.

[85] Arthur Montgomery, "Der schwedische Export in der Zwischenkriegszeit," *Außenwirtschaft*, 1, 1947, p. 11.

[86] See Leif Levin, *Planhushållningsdebatten*, Uppsala 1962; Alf Carling, "Industrins struktur och konkurrensförhållanden," in SOU (Statens Offentliga Utredningar) (ed.), *Koncentrationsutredningen* III, Stockholm 1968.

policy was needed, which was much more open to the positive side of competition.[87]

The situation in Norway was different. Norway was not exempt from the anticartel movement. But as shown earlier, it already had an official register and the government in Oslo disposed of the right to dissolve cartels. Additionally, in 1953 an act was passed by which the right of government was extended. Penalties which threatened enterprises, even their existence, could be imposed. However, Wilhelm Thagaard had not only survived but strengthened his influence. He managed to stay in power well into the 1960s. He saw that possible sanctions were not applied; in fact, there was little change until Thagaard retired. Norway provides an example of how the influence of a single person slowed down the process of decartelization and Americanization to a considerable extent.[88]

In Denmark prices of such branches of industry where concentration had taken place had to be monitored, beginning in 1949. Furthermore, a committee on monopolization (Trustkommissionen) was founded to evaluate the extent of cooperation. It published several volumes from 1952 onward.[89] On this basis legislation was passed, which focused on the economic abuse of cooperation. In contrast to Sweden and Norway, firms had the right to challenge verdicts of the monitoring institutions at court.

In the Netherlands compulsory registration of cartels was introduced during the German occupation in 1941. Although up to World War II the Dutch government had strongly favored cooperation, the tide turned after it. In 1951 an "act on the suspension of economic regulation" was passed, which in contrast to Norway was applied more and more in the course of time. However, it took several years until legislation, which prohibited the abuse of cooperation, was passed.

Belgium was extremely slow in its decartelization. The first bill, handed over to parliament as late as 1954, was not dealt with before 1957. However, the European Coal and Steel Community, in force after 1952, regulated the heavy industry sector, which was most important for Belgium. As in the case of the Netherlands, supranational legislation came

---

[87] Bo Stråth, "Der Nachkriegsboom in Schweden: Zur Frage von Kontinuität und Bruch im Gesellschaftswandel," in Kaelble, *Der Boom*, p. 181.

[88] Nordvik, "From Wilhelm Thagaard to Egil Bakke"; Harald Espeli, *Fra Thagaard til Egil Bakke. Hovedlinjer i norsk konkurransepolitikk 1954–1990*, SNF-Report nr. 39/1993, Bergen 1993.

[89] *Betænkningen af Trustkommissionen*, Copenhagen 1952–1958.

into power together with the EEC in 1958. The respective acts were not oriented at the British standard of preventing the abuse of cooperation, but at the American type of general interdiction of it.[90]

In Switzerland legislation on the abuses of cooperation, held up by World War II, was passed in 1947. But the debate on cartelization continued on a broad scale on a political as well as on a scientific level.[91] Several authors stated that it was mainly the impact of the American policy of anticartelization and the change of paradigm in Germany concerning this question which fostered a similar movement in Switzerland.[92] The prewar instrument for investigation, Pbk, was instructed to present its findings in a comprehensive volume in 1951 – an amount of work which took six(!) years, as the outflow of thirty years of monitoring was condensed into a few hundred pages.[93] It was not published before a plebiscite against cartelization called for in 1955 had put pressure on the Swiss government, a development which reminds us very much of the Finnish case. The volume was presented with the purpose to provide "the needed impartial platform"[94] for a broader discussion. However, the report showed a considerable bias in favor of cooperation.[95] It reported that in the United States annually about a quarter of all industrial output was wasted, because of an exaggerated variety of products, which was seen as an unwanted outflow of competition.[96] The specialty of the Swiss case was stressed, where, in contrast to, for example, Germany, cartels acted "as a school for consideration of the big ones towards the small."[97] Partisans of cooperative capitalism succeeded in considerably delaying all procedures. Legislation was not passed until 1962. Even then only the abuse was forbidden, but not economic cooperation in general. Because of that, the Swiss economy remained thoroughly cartelized. The Americanization showed little impact on Switzerland. Such a shift of paradigm took place as late as the early 1980s, while the old legislation still was

[90] Laid down in articles 85 to 90 of the EEC treaty.
[91] E.g., Paul Lüthi published his thesis in 1947 (Lüthi, *Der Staat*); Hugo Sieber, "Über das Ziel der staatlichen Monopol-, Kartell- und Trustpolitik," *Schweizerische Zeitschrift für Volkswirtschaft und Statistik*, 88, 1952, pp. 132ff.
[92] Sieber, "Über das Ziel," p. 132; *Preisbildungskommission*, 1957, p. 12.
[93] *Preisbildungskommission*, 1957.
[94] Ibid., p. 12.
[95] "So it could be no wonder, that the by wild competition exhausted ones (firms) first in this then in that branch of industry started to talk to each other" (in order to form a cartel which would reduce competition) (ibid., p. 29).
[96] Ibid., p. 30.   [97] Ibid., p. 34.

valid up to that time. Therefore the Swiss were called "the unmatched world champions of cartels."[98]

Thus the questioning and decline of cooperative capitalism occurred in all of the small states; but the speed in this process was very different, reflecting the political and the economic power of partisans of cooperative and competitive capitalism. While Sweden took the lead in decartelization, most of our small states showed little haste. During the period under consideration up to the 1960s, none of them approached the problem in a radical way. All states, Sweden included, if they passed legislation, enabled cooperation to go on and curbed only abuse. The process of decartelization proceeded more quickly in Germany than in the small states, where it took considerable time to succeed. Switzerland proved to be most untouched by the change of economic paradigm. In this sense, after World War II, Germany handed over its function of acting as a prototype of cooperative capitalism to Switzerland.

We can presume that the reasons for the relative slowness in decartelization lay in the tradition of how business was run in the respective countries. Even in Germany, where the war had ended both the legal possibility and the unchallenged trust in economic cooperation, the change of paradigm in favor of competition needed considerable time to be implemented. In fact, it occurred not before a new generation of managers took over, as Berghahn has shown. In contrast, the managers in our small states had no such reason for feeling defeated in the way they used to run their enterprises. Furthermore, economic and financial difficulties during the late 1940s and early 1950s called for economic regulation and cooperation. Therefore experienced managers had reasons to go on with their way of decision making as they used to do. It took time to realize that the *manière de voir* of the interwar period and the 1940s was to be changed not only in certain parts but profoundly. And in the small states, too, it was but the next generation which acted on the basis of a different business paradigm.

As long as there are no specific studies on the subject, we cannot decide if and to what extent the relative slowness of decartelization in the small nations affected their economic performance in the international markets. We can but presume that a business approach based on competition and

---

[98] Fredy Hämmerli, "Absprachen am Alpenrand. Ein teures Vergnügen: Die Schweizer sind der unangefochtene Kartellweltmeister," *Die Zeit*, no. 25, 1992, p. 44.

expansion was more suitable for a booming international economy than thinking in terms of caution, cooperation, and restriction. Furthermore, it is to be observed that phases of decartelization went parallel with phases of growth. In Germany the highest rates of growth fell into the 1950s, in contrast to all of the small nations, where the 1960s showed the peak.[99]

THE RESULTS

This contribution was focused on two objectives: first, to investigate the performance of large industrial firms from small nations according to growth and stability for more than eighty years; second, to explore the possibility of one more type of capitalism, based on small nations, similar to the Chandlerian types of competitive, personal, and cooperative capitalism.

Interestingly, the general picture of enterprises and branches of industry remained quite stable over time. For 1983 the following firms have been listed in the world's top 500: Royal Dutch/Shell (2), Unilever (16), Philips (24), Nestlé (40), Volvo (43), Petrofina (72), Ciba-Geigy (92), DSM (95), Akzo (137), BBC (142), Neste (178), Electrolux (182), Norsk Hydro (184), Asea (190), Solvay (195), Statoil (213), Roche (216), ALUSUISSE (228), LME (233), Sandoz (254), Cockerill (260), Saab-Scania (294), Suchard (364), SKF (373), Hoogovens (374), Sulzer (396), Oerlikon-Bührle (410).[100] Most of these firms include those that were on our initial list (see Table 6.1) and all the new entrants (except for Norway's state-owned oil company) had been in operation for decades. The longevity of the large firms in small countries and the small amount of turnover at the top except for mergers of exiting companies indicate that the way to stay large is to begin large.

Furthermore, except for oil and automotives, this growth took place in those clusters of competitiveness which were already their respective nation's traditional ones.[101] On the other hand, firms which exited were

---

[99] Annual growth of GNP 1950–1960/1960–1970 Germany: 7.8 percent/4.8 percent, Belgium: 2.9 percent/4.9 percent, Denmark: 3.3 percent/4.8 percent, Finland: 5.0 percent/5.1 percent, the Netherlands 4.7 percent/5.1 percent, Norway: 3.2 percent/5.0 percent, Sweden: 3.4 percent/4.6 percent, Switzerland: 4.4 percent/4.5 percent (Herman van der Wee, "Der gebremste Wohlstand. Wiederaufbau, Wachstum, Strukturwandel 1945–1980," in Wolfram Fischer (ed.), *Geschichte der Weltwirtschaft*, 6, Munich 1984, table 3, p. 43).

[100] John Dunning and Robert Pearce, *The World's Largest Industrial Enterprises, 1962–1983*, New York, 1985, pp. 171–180.

[101] Michael Porter, *Competitive Advantage of Nations*, London 1990; Silvio Borner, Michael Porter, Rolf Weder and Michael Enright, *Internationale Wettbewerbsvorteile: Ein strategisches Konzept für die Schweiz*, Frankfurt 1991.

concentrated in the branches of industry with a low rate of growth, namely textiles, leather, and iron and steel. In contrast, the firms that remained on the list clustered in the same capital-intensive industries as did those of the large enterprises in large nations. As in those nations, they played much the same roles in terms of providing continuing investment and employment, in becoming learning bases for industry-specific organizational skills and the core of a network of related enterprises. As these firms often purchased machines, tools, and other capital equipment and raw materials and supplies from neighboring nations, particularly Germany, and built up local marketing and distributions networks, their impact was felt beyond their borders.

However, firms from small countries had to meet different demands and could exploit different opportunities than their large country competitors. They relied to a much larger extent than others on operations in open markets; from the start they had to compete globally. For scale production they could not enjoy the well-known two-step strategy: first, growth on a protected national market and, then, with such a backing, worldwide expansion. They had to export from the beginning and most of them became multinational very early. A second issue, different from firms of large states, involved the opportunities during both world wars. Of these only Belgium was excluded, as the country was occupied twice. In contrast, Sweden and Switzerland were able to make use of these special conditions of development during both wars. The rise of firms such as Saab-Scania, SKF, or Volvo is not to be understood without the opportunities and necessities of the years from 1940 to 1945.

A third distinction is that the firms were more concentrated in increasingly knowledge-intensive industries such as specialized machinery, electrical equipment, chemicals, and pharmaceuticals. The decline in the number of textiles, iron and steel, and food was somewhat more than in the case of large nations.

But in general the results are well in line with the findings in other chapters in this book. No traces have been found of a special type of capitalism typical of small economically developed states. In consequence the limitation of the national market was not a factor. It did not bring capitalism that might be considered as being different from the three prototypes.

Instead there was something of all three. Each state developed a *manière de voir* of its own. In Belgium the business climate and social consensus had a bias toward the British type of personal capitalism, while Denmark,

Finland, the Netherlands, Norway, Sweden, and Switzerland were closer to the German type of cooperative capitalism. Luxembourg probably should be attached to Belgium. But except in a small number of industries, the business climate and consensus turned away from the American style of competitive capitalism. In these states the cooperative type of capitalism reached its peak of development during the 1930s. After World War II, however, it lost its influence steadily, turning more and more to the American type. Surely this process was facilitated by the booming economy, which made cooperation more and more obsolete. Nevertheless, the fundamental shift in *manière de voir*, the conviction that competition offered more advantages than cooperation, needed many years to mature. This shift began to take place mainly during the late 1950s and the early 1960s. However, in Switzerland cooperative capitalism has been preserved until today.

Acknowledgments

I want to thank all who made suggestions and criticized earlier versions of this chapter, the participants of our preconference in Florence in 1992, especially Franco Amatori, Alfred Chandler, Leslie Hannah, and Takashi Hikino.

Group 2

Followers in Western Europe

7

France: The relatively slow development of
big business in the twentieth century

PATRICK FRIDENSON

Initially the second industrial nation, France is still, some two centuries
later, the fourth industrial nation. However, it is not covered in Michael
Porter's *Competitive Advantage of Nations*, and among French or American business historians of France, nobody ever dared to write a general
business history of France. This can be explained in two ways. Despite
recent progress, many of the detailed researches necessary for such a
synthesis are still missing. On the other hand, earlier literature focused on
the performance of the French economy in the twentieth century and was
more concerned to give a positive assessment of French business and
management than to analyze the dynamics of the French large industrial
enterprise.[1] So, it is not an easy task to compare France and its firms with
those of the three nations surveyed in Chandler's *Scale and Scope*, and
then to review the post–World War II industries. Therefore, this essay
cannot aim at exhaustiveness and, given the conflicting views on French
business which have persisted among specialists for forty years, it has to
be quite personal, maybe even subjective.

The French corporate enterprise since the end of the nineteenth century
will be studied here in a Chandlerian perspective, emphasizing that the

---

[1] Among the literature available in English, see James M. Laux, "Managerial structures in
France," in Harold F. Williamson, ed., *Evolution of international management structures*,
Newark, University of Delaware Press, 1975 (a pioneering survey); Claude Fohlen, "Entrepreneurship and management in France in the nineteenth century," in Peter Mathias
and M. M. Postan, eds., *The Cambridge economic history of Europe*, vol. 7, Cambridge,
Cambridge University Press, 1978; François Caron, *An economic history of modern France*,
New York, Columbia University Press, 1979; Maurice Lévy-Leboyer, "The large corporation in modern France," in Alfred D. Chandler, Jr., and Herman Daems, eds., *Managerial
hierarchies: Comparative perspectives on the rise of the modern industrial enterprises*,
Cambridge, MA, Harvard University Press, 1980 (in later works, the last two authors
have considerably modified their views).

role of large industrial firms in the creation of wealth has been, first, to provide opportunities for investment of capital and employment of labor; second, to become the learning base for the technological developments and the managerial skills in specific industries; and, third, to become the core of a nexus of small and middle-sized related and ancillary firms.[2] But in doing so, we have to take account of two peculiarities of the French economy: the continuously high proportion of small enterprises (and the low proportion of middle-sized firms), and the active role of the French state in the economic life, which kept growing till the mid-1980s. This is why I chose to use the recent hypotheses expressed by two Japanese business historians, although the difference between Japanese firms, to which they directly apply, and French ones is obviously enormous. Yoshitaka Suzuki has contended that "the internalized allocation of human resources or the formation of an internal capital market rather than the internalized coordination of the flow of goods through vertical integration might have been a more characteristic feature in the emergence and development of modern firms elsewhere [than the United States]."[3] Tsunehiko Yui (relayed in 1992 by the American business historian W. Mark Fruin) has cast emphasis on what he calls the enterprise system. This combines organizational structures within individual enterprises, vertical enterprise groups, trade associations, and governments.[4] Thus we should fully assess factors external to the firm, including "the organizational arrangements between economic units that govern the ways in which they compete and cooperate" (Fruin).

In line with this perspective, this essay will first detail the slow emergence of big business in France during the Second Industrial Revolution, and suggest some explanations for it. Then it will link its specificity to a peculiar type of management of human resources, and also to the conditions of competition on the French market. Finally it will assess the pattern of modern industrial enterprise in France since World War II. This approach should enable us to answer the basic questions underlying the French case in a comparative analysis: how was the relatively slow devel-

---

[2] Chapter 2 of this volume.
[3] Yoshitaka Suzuki, *Japanese management structures, 1920–80*, London, Macmillan, 1991.
[4] Tsunehiko Yui, "The enterprise system in Japan: Preliminary considerations on internal and external structural relations," in *Japanese Yearbook on Business History*, 1991 (Tokyo: Japan Business History Institute). W. Mark Fruin, *The Japanese enterprise system*, Oxford, Clarendon Press, 1992.

opment of large-scale enterprises compatible with a favorable growth rate during most of the years under survey? Did the existence and activities of a state stronger than its other European counterparts (except in Germany) hinder the potential of French large corporations, or did it (like in Germany) contribute to their renewal and expansion?

THE EMERGENCE AND GROWTH OF LARGE INDUSTRIAL ENTERPRISES IN FRANCE

Before proceeding to a review of the development of large corporations, we must face an obstacle, which is itself a result of history: in most sectors (the only two exceptions being stone, clay, and glass and electrical equipment) a significant number of the largest firms were nonpublic, at least till the 1950s. This means it is particularly difficult to get data comparable with those of *Scale and Scope*. Earlier studies, by French scholars, chose therefore to concentrate on the 100 largest publicly held firms (Houssiaux) or even the 30 largest (Lévy-Leboyer).[5] Recent American research tries to overcome the difficulty. Michael S. Smith has collected data on the 200 largest publicly held firms in France in 1913, and examined among them the 100 largest manufacturing, plus the private firms of "comparable size." Bruce Kogut has done the same for selected years up to the present, for which the business press is also quite thorough.[6]

In France large corporations appeared in the manufacturing sector in two stages: at the end of the nineteenth century, and in the 1920s. The first movers before 1914 came in steel, glass, cement, electrical equipment, food processing, automobiles, and rubber.

In steel the two leaders were Forges et Aciéries de Marine et d'Homécourt and Schneider et Cie. Marine-Homécourt was an early example of managerial capitalism. Producing both steel and military applications, it relied on vertical integration through a merger and on a strategy of development of new products.[7] Schneider was, on the contrary, a family

---

[5] Jacques Houssiaux, *Le pouvoir de monopole*, Paris, Sirey, 1958. Maurice Lévy-Leboyer, "Le patronat français, 1912–1973," in M. Lévy-Leboyer, ed., *Le patronat de la seconde industrialisation*, Paris, Editions Ouvrières, 1979, pp. 137–185.
[6] Michael S. Smith, "The beginnings of big business in France, 1880–1920: A Chandlerian perspective," *Essays in economic and business history*, 9, 1993, pp. 1–24. Bruce Kogut, work in progress.
[7] Jean-Marie Moine, *Les barons du fer*, Nancy, Presses Universitaires de Nancy, 1989.

firm, a strong case of entrepreneurial capitalism. Like Marine-Homécourt, it combined vertical integration and product diversification – here into heavy industry and armament.[8] Both had thus their own managerial hierarchies, but they could also rely on cooperative arrangements, the earliest of which was the steel sales consortium of the Lorraine region, created in 1876.[9]

In glass, the French international position was at its best, with Saint-Gobain. Founded in 1665, it was "continental Europe's leading maker of flat glass" (according to Michael Smith) and had already diversified into inorganic chemicals. During World War I and the 1920s, it diversified into other chemicals. Before 1914 Saint-Gobain had become a highly efficient managerial bureaucracy with organizational capabilities in research, production, distribution, and management.[10] In the same group of industries, a mention should also be made of the French strength in building materials. The leaders were a managerial firm, the Société Anonyme des Ciments Français, and an entrepreneurial firm, the Ciments Lafarge. Lafarge had its own research laboratory since 1887, created with the help of the famous professor of chemistry Henry Le Châtelier, and it was a major tool for its diversification from lime production into cement manufacturing.[11]

In a new industry, electrical equipment, dominated by American and German companies, two French companies were nevertheless able to reach the stage of the modern industrial enterprise. We have here once more two different strategies. The Compagnie Française Thomson-Houston was born in 1893 as a joint venture between General Electric (40 percent of the shares) and a French company (60 percent). But as early as 1902 GE's percentage had fallen to 6.5. Initially, the firm had two activities: it

[8] Claude Beaud, "La stratégie de l'investissement dans la société Schneider et Cie," in François Caron, ed., *Entrepreneurs et entreprises XIXe–XX siècles*, Paris, Presses de Paris-Sorbonne, 1983, pp. 118–131. Daijiro Fujimura, "Schneider et Cie et son plan d'organisation administrative de 1913: analyse et interprétation," *Histoire, Economic et Société*, April–June 1991, pp. 269–276.
[9] Carl Strikwerda, "The troubled origins of European economic integration: International iron and steel and labor migrations," *American Historical Review*, October 1993.
[10] Jean-Pierre Daviet, *Un destin international. La Compagnie de Saint-Gobain de 1830 à 1939*, Paris, Editions des Archives Contemporaines, 1988. Maurice Lévy-Leboyer, "Hierarchical structures, rewards and incentives in a large corporation: The early management experience of Saint-Gobain, 1872–1912," in Norbert Horn and Jürgen Kocka, eds., *Law and the formation of big enterprises*, Göttingen, Vandenhoeck und Ruprecht, 1979, pp. 451–74.
[11] Léon Dubois, *Lafarge-Coppée, 150 ans d'industrie*, Paris, Belfond, 1988. Bertrand Collomb, "L'industrie européenne du ciment au XXè siècle," *Entreprises et Histoire*, May 1993, p. 100.

was a financial holding company in electrical equipment, and it produced tramways under American licenses and with much material imported from the United States. Although it kept relying on foreign patents (mostly American), it later developed organizational capabilities in manufacturing and embarked on a policy of diversification by turning out many sorts of electrical equipment. By 1913 this managerial enterprise was the second largest of France's publicly held industrial firms.[12] On the contrary, the Compagnie Générale d'Electricité was a purely European company: mostly French, with some Swiss capital. Its focus was on electrical lighting. Founded in 1898, also as a managerial enterprise, it diversified into electrical manufacturing after 1910. Despite an impressive performance, its attempts to become a multinational before World War I were failures.[13]

"In the food category, the two largest sugar refiners (Société Générale de Sucreries and Raffineries et Sucreries Say) were two to three times the size of Germany's largest. . . . The largest French brewery (Brasseries Quilmès) was comparable in assets to Germany's largest. . . . However, the other food companies that made France's top 100 in 1913 were smaller than comparable German companies," as Michael Smith has shown. At least Say practiced managerial capitalism.[14]

In automobiles, the French industry dominated Europe. The two leading companies, Peugeot and Renault, were family firms. The first mover's (Peugeot) performance was soon matched by the challenger, Renault. Both developed aggressive multinational enterprises. But they would be overtaken from 1919 onward by a late challenger, André Citroën, who personally managed an entrepreneurial firm.[15]

Rubber benefited from the boom of the French bicycle and automobile industries. Michelin competed with the British company Dunlop and the

[12] Pierre Lanthier, "Les constructions électriques en France: financement et stratégies de six groupes industriels internationaux, 1880–1940," thèse de doctorat d'Etat, University of Paris X-Nanterre, 1988; and "L'industrie de la construction électrique en France," in François Caron and Fabienne Cardot, eds., *Histoire générale de l'électricité en France*, vol. 1, Paris, Fayard, 1991, pp. 671–727.
[13] Jules Rapp, "L'histoire d'une entreprise d'électricité: la Compagnie Générale d'Electricité," Ph.D. thesis, University Paris X-Nanterre, 1985. Albert Broder and Félix Torres, *Alcatel Alsthom. Histoire de la Compagnie Générale d'Electricité*, Paris, Larousse, 1992.
[14] Smith, "The beginnings," pp. 5 and 12, to which one should add Jacques Fiérain, *Les raffineries de sucre des ports en France (XIXè-début XXè siècles)*, Paris, Champion, 1976, and Céline Girard de Mourgues, "Analyse des affiches publicitaires de bière de 1880 à 1940," DEA thesis, Ecole des Hautes Etudes en Sciences Sociales, 1992, pp. 8–22.
[15] James M. Laux, *In first gear: The French automobile industry to 1914*, Liverpool, Liverpool University Press, 1976. Patrick Fridenson, *Histoire des usines Renault*, vol. 1, Paris, Editions du Seuil, 1972. Sylvie Schweitzer, *André Citroën*, Paris, Fayard, 1992.

German Continental. A family firm, it quickly became a multinational. Its diversification in road maps and travel guides was successful. A non-related diversification in aviation during World War I was a failure and was abandoned.[16]

In two industries, however, modern industrial enterprises were formed only in the 1920s. In aluminum some organizational capabilities came before size. One French company had enjoyed a world monopoly of production (though on a small scale) till 1886. When technological innovation broke that monopoly, four challengers came to birth so as to dislodge the first mover. But their hopes were disappointed. Concentration occurred in two stages. In 1911 the five manufacturers built a sales consortium, l'Aluminium Français. It was so powerful that in 1912, with the help of a German firm, it "began to build a major aluminum complex" in North Carolina, which it had to sell to Alcoa in 1915. Then, between 1914 and 1921, the first mover, which would later be called Pechiney, absorbed three of the four challengers. Now a major firm in aluminum at the world level, it kept as its second core business inorganic chemical products.[17]

In chemicals, size had become a major issue after World War I. In 1926, fascinated by the creation of IG Farben in Germany (1925), the Kuhlmann company suggested a French Chemical Union – that is, the formation of a holding company by all the French chemical firms. Kuhlmann was "a venerable . . . producer of inorganic chemicals," to which World War I offered the opportunity to diversify into the production of dyes. The other chemical firms – including Saint-Gobain – finally refused Kuhlmann's proposal, because on one side they did not want to merge into a conglomerate and on the other their views about the role of the French state differed too much (Kuhlmann was said to be too close to the government and to the large Paris banks, Saint-Gobain was steeped in nineteenth-century liberalism).[18] Only in the neighboring industry of pharmaceuticals, where France had then a gap in relation to Germany and Britain, did a major merger take place, as the two leading firms gave birth to Rhône-Poulenc in 1928: this was an obvious consequence of the

---

[16] André Gueslin, ed., *Michelin, les hommes du pneu*, Paris, Editions de l'Atelier, 1993.
[17] Florence Hachez, "Le cartel international de l'aluminium du point de vue des sociétés françaises 1901–1940," in Dominique Barjot, ed., *International cartels revisited*, Caen, Editions-Diffusion du Lys, 1994 pp. 153–157. Mira Wilkins, *The history of foreign investment in the United States to 1914*, Cambridge, MA, Harvard University Press, 1989, pp. 282–284, 778–780. Ivan Grinberg, *Pechiney: repères historiques*, Paris, Institut pour l'histoire de l'aluminium, 1992, pp. 4–8.
[18] Daviet, *Un destin*, pp. 571–572. Jean-Etienne Léger, *Une grande entreprise dans la chimie française: Kuhlmann, 1825–1982*, Paris, Debresse, 1988.

creation not only of IG Farben, but also of ICI in Britain (1926). After 1928 Rhône-Poulenc was the largest producer of organic chemicals (except for dyes but including pharmaceuticals) in France.[19]

Thus, all the evidence available confirms Michael Smith's balanced assessment of French industrial capitalism by 1914. First, "France's largest industries clustered in the same industries that gave rise to big business elsewhere, but they were neither as large nor as numerous as the giant enterprises of the United States, Germany, or Great Britain." Second, whereas "most French industrialists continued to practice personal capitalism, . . . a number of firms managed by their founders (Renault, Michelin, Air Liquide) or by the founding families (Wendel, Schneider, Peugeot [the forerunner of Pechiney], Lafarge) were . . . beginning the transition to managerial capitalism." Only a few firms, Saint-Gobain, Thomson-Houston, the Compagnie Générale d'Electricité, and in older sectors "some of the steel companies" (at least Marine-Homécourt and Schneider) and the Raffineries et Sucreries Say had really moved into managerial capitalism.[20]

During the course of the twentieth century, as in other countries, most of the first movers stayed among the nation's largest industrial firms by enlarging and renewing their organizational capabilities, with the one major exception of steel, where all firms had to merge into one in 1986. Conversely, few of the challengers gained a lasting access to top positions, the most striking success being BSN in food and kindred products.

It is worth assessing closely the distribution of modern industrial enterprises in France in comparison with the situations in America and Germany. The United States, thanks to economies of scale, developed large corporations first in railroads, then in consumer products (which were sold packed and branded by the millions) and in mechanical engineering. As an alternative, Germany welcomed large corporations first in production goods branches, and only later did they grow in consumer goods branches. This can be ascribed to a domestic market which was certainly smaller and less homogeneous than the U.S. market.[21]

France stands in between. Large corporations were concentrated as

[19] Pierre Cayez, *Rhône-Poulenc 1895–1975*, Paris, A. Colin and Masson, 1988. Michael Robson, "The pharmaceutical industry in Britain and France, 1919–1939," Ph.D., thesis London School of Economics, 1993. Ludwig F. Haber, *The chemical industry, 1900–1930*, Oxford, Clarendon Press, 1971, p. 305.
[20] Smith, "The beginnings," pp. 5 and 13–14 (though with a few changes).
[21] Alfred D. Chandler, Jr., *Scale and Scope*, Cambridge, MA, Harvard University Press, 1990.

elsewhere in food, chemicals, metals, mechanical engineering and electrical equipment. But there were not as many large firms in 1913 in France as in Germany. First, it results from the existence of a dense commercial network in France prior to the growth of large-scale business. This did not motivate entrepreneurs to integrate production and marketing. Second, French firms focusing on consumer goods did not benefit from a wide ranging immigration which in the United States was a strong incentive for the creation of new industries and for installment sales. Although important, immigration into France was easily channeled through existing commercial facilities and small-scale credit, and its expenses mostly fueled the growth of the textile industry (where 250 companies had more than 500 employees in 1914).[22] Third, for producers' goods, the number and variety of industrial customers were generally not yet big enough. Fourth, French industry had a strategy of niches, aiming at quality products rather than cheap products and partly reflecting the heterogeneity of the national market. The fact that a number of innovations were devised by individual inventors (photo, automobile, aviation, cinema, radio) also accounts for the French emphasis on quality products.[23] All in all, except in two areas – machine-tool production (in steady decline from the 1880s to the present day) and organic chemicals – the distribution of French large firms was not very different from the other major industrial nations in 1914. In the interwar period France caught up, as we have seen, in organic chemicals. So did it in petroleum.[24]

However, in order to characterize modern industrial enterprises, size is not enough. Chandler has demonstrated that, especially in capital-intensive branches, organizational capabilities are required. How did French large manufacturing firms behave in that respect? We do not yet have all the historical evidence needed to give a full answer. From what we already know, it seems that French large corporations focused on production capabilities and reached competitiveness there, as evidenced by the various productivity growth figures available.[25]

[22] Yves Lequin ed., *La mosaïque France*, Paris, Larousse, 1988. Michèle Tribalat, ed., *Cent ans d'immigration*, Paris, PUF, 1991. Gérard Noiriel, *Population, immigration et identité nationale en France XIXè–XXè siècle*, Paris, Hachette, 1992.
[23] Laux, *In first gear*. Emmanuel Chadeau, *L'industrie aéronautique en France 1900–1950. De Blériot à Dassault*, Paris, Fayard, 1987.
[24] Takashi Hotta, "L'industrie du pétrole en France des origines à 1934," Ph.D. thesis, University Paris X, 1990. Cayez, *Rhône-Poulenc*. Daviet, *Un destin*.
[25] Maurice Lévy-Leboyer, "La grande entreprise: un modèle français?," in Maurice Lévy-Leboyer and Jean-Claude Casanova, eds., *Entre l'Etat et le marché. L'économie française des années 1880 à nos jours*, Paris, Gallimard, 1991.

The construction of organizational capabilities in marketing, management, and research was comparatively slower. Suffice it to say that before World War I, industrial research capabilities had already been formed outside of large corporations, as in silver jewelry, and in leading firms of aluminum, rubber, cement, automobiles, glass, and inorganic chemicals.[26] As for human resources, it is worth noting that as early as 1906 the Schneider company had a full personnel department (in the United States, the first one had appeared at NCR in 1901).[27] A number of large industrial enterprises had already developed sales departments: in metallurgy (Pont à Mousson), glass (Saint-Gobain), and in new industries such as automobiles, tires, or electrical equipment.[28] We also mentioned earlier multinational activities.

The very idea of organizational capabilities was present in French public discussion from the early 1900s; for example, in the metals industry, the salaried entrepreneur Henri Fayol kept lecturing on such matters. In 1916–1920 these lectures were turned into a book. Fayol advocated the necessity of strategic planning and long-term views as specific functions of top management. He called for functional structures. He would make up for strict managerial and accountancy control by allowing some autonomy to middle managers.[29] However, although well publicized, even after his death in 1925, and although relayed by the growth of management consultancy in the interwar years, Fayol's views were slow to spread into industry.[30] Some recent historians even argued that his impact abroad (notably at the Harvard Business School) was greater than in France.[31]

This leads us to conclude that the adoption of formal managerial structures in large corporations before 1914 proceeded slowly. The pioneers

[26] Marc de Ferrière, *Christofle, deux/siècles d' aventure industrielle 1793–1993*, Paris, Le Monde Editions, 1995. Muriel Le Roux *L'entrepise et la recherche: un siècle de recherche industrielle à Pechiney*, Paris, Rive droite, 1996. François Caron, "La capacité d'innovation technique de l'industrie française. Les enseignements de l'histoire," *Le débat*, September–November 1987. Gueslin, *Michelin*.
[27] Fujimura, "Schneider et Cie."
[28] Marc Meuleau, "De la distribution au marketing (1880–1939). Une réponse à l'évolution du marché," *Entreprises et Histoire*, May 1993, pp. 61–62.
[29] Tsuneo Sasaki, *Henri Fayol*, Tokyo, Bunshindo, 1984. Donald Reid, "Fayol: from experience to theory," *Journal of Management History*, 1, 1995, pp. 21–36, and "Fayol: excès d'honneur ou excès d'indignité?," *Revue Française de Gestion*, September–October, 1988, pp. 151–159.
[30] Aimée Moutet, 1995, *Les logiques de l'entreprise. L'effort de rationalisation dans l'industrie Française 1919–1939*, Paris Éditions de l'École des Hautes Études en Sciences Sociales, 1997.
[31] Robert R. Locke, *The end of the practical man: Entrepreneurship and higher education in Germany, France and Great Britain, 1880–1940*, Greenwich, CT, JAI Press, 1984.

were certainly, as one could have expected, the railways. But their structures were partly influenced by those of the state administration (which, as Jürgen Kocka observed long ago, was also felt in German industrial business).[32] Beyond the railways, we know only of three detailed cases, all typical of the U-form: the Saint-Gobain company in glass and chemicals, Fayol's Commentry-Fourchambault-Decazeville company in metallurgy and mining, the Schneider company in steel and armament.[33] The three of them had already impressive managerial hierarchies.

The first evidences of a large company adopting organizational structures resembling the American M-form were in 1930–1932 at Alsthom (electric equipment), a company which had close relations with General Electric and whose top managers had been to the United States; in the 1930s at the French subsidiary of Standard Oil, the Standard Française des Pétroles; and in 1936 at Saint-Gobain, as a new CEO took office and tried to reorganize management structures to cope better with the strategy of diversification and to increase economies of scope. It is worth remembering that the new CEO was an alumnus of the Harvard Business School and had been in contact with colleagues and followers of Fayol. In 1937–1938, the Renault company, in the car industry, decentralized its departments, but did not go further in the direction of U.S.-style managerial structures.[34]

The spread of the M-form, after reaching Pechiney in 1947, really waited for the 1950s, and moreover the 1960s (as a consequence of the merger wave) and even the 1970s.[35] Several remarks should be made here. As in Britain, management consultants, a number of them members of American firms, were influential in convincing French firms (for instance Pechiney in aluminum, Rhône-Poulenc in chemicals and pharmaceuticals)

---

[32] Georges Ribeill, *La révolution ferroviaire, La formation des compagnies de chemins de fer en France (1823–1870)*, Paris, Belin, 1993. François Caron, *Histoire de l'exploitation d'un grand réseau: la Compagnie du chemin de fer du Nord 1846–1937*, Paris, Mouton, 1973.

[33] Daviet, *Un destin*. Donald Reid, *The miners of Decazeville*, Cambridge, MA, Harvard University Press, 1985. Fujimura, "Schneider et Cie."

[34] Richard F. Kuisel, *Ernest Mercier: French technocrat*, Berkeley, University of California Press, 1967. Marc Meuleau, *Les HEC et l'évolution du management en France (1881–années 1980)*, thèse de doctorat d'Etat, University Paris X, 1992, pp. 781–784. Lévy-Leboyer, "La grande entreprise," p. 408. Jean-Pierre Daviet, "Stratégie et structure chez Saint-Gobain: un modèle français dans les années 1930?," *Entreprises et Histoire*, April 1992, pp. 42–60. Fridenson, *Histoire des usines Renault*.

[35] Gareth P. Dyas and Heinz T. Thanheiser, *The emerging European enterprise: Strategy and structure in French and German industry*, London, Macmillan, 1976.

to turn to a multidivisional structure.[36] But there were also genuine French attempts, as in the electronics industry of the 1960s, where both Thomson and CSF created French equivalents of the M-form, derived both from an intense product diversification strategy and from long-lasting contacts with American partners such as General Electric.[37] However by the mid-1970s it is believed that the adoption of the M-form in France was less complete than in Britain.[38] We may point to two reasons. In some cases, like at Pechiney, the shift to the second stage of the M-form in the late 1960s was halfhearted and managers achieved a structure which bore marked differences with McKinsey's design.[39] In a few other cases, like at Renault (1976–1984), the M-form failed, mostly because, in a little-diversified firm, it duplicated levels of decision and control, and was hastily abandoned in the wake of a major managerial and financial crisis in 1985.[40]

THE SPECIFICITY OF HUMAN RESOURCES

More specific of France is the management of human resources at the top level, as it forges a small managerial elite. Here the general tendency of French big business is different both from Great Britain and Germany. French managers cannot be shown as "exceptionally under-educated," as the British have been.[41] But the employment of *grandes écoles* graduates and university graduates, although it grew considerably during the century, always remained at a lower level than graduate recruitment in Germany. If one does not consider only large manufacturing firms, but the entire French industry, highly skilled engineers represented 0.5 percent of the industrial working population in 1913, and 7 percent in 1980.[42]

We have to look first at how French entrepreneurs of large corporations

[36] Cayez, *Rhône-Poulenc*. Martine Muller and Félix Torres, *L'identité d'un groupe: Lafarge-Coppée 1947–1989*, Paris, Lafarge-Coppée, 1991.
[37] Patrick Fridenson, "De la diversification au recentrage: le groupe Thomson (1976–1989)," *Entreprises et Histoire*, April 1992, p. 33.
[38] Geoffrey Jones, "Great Britain: Big business, management, and competitiveness in the twentieth century," Chapter 4, in this volume.
[39] Elie Cohen et al., "Les structures de Pechiney," unpublished report, Paris, Ecole des Mines, 1971.
[40] From research in progress by the author. A similar reversal happened at Hitachi, in Japan in the 1970s.
[41] Jones, "Great Britain."
[42] Jean-Pierre Daviet, "L'industrie et les défis de l'entreprise," *Les Cahiers Français*, March–April 1992, p. 75.

are trained, then at which career pattern brings them to top positions. Both are quite different from developments in Germany, as the following statistics show. In 1990 top managers at work in the 200 largest firms had entered an enterprise for the first time at the age of twenty-five in Germany and of thirty-two in France, a difference of 24 percent.[43] These differences could also be found for earlier dates in the twentieth century. These numbers show that in France, contrary to Germany, a majority of large corporations leave to the state the task of selecting their future leaders. In 1990, 45 percent of the CEOs of the 200 largest French corporations had been detected inside the French state. There are two types of exit from civil service to business. Since the 1880s and moreover the 1900s, a fraction of the most brilliant alumni of the schools which train state engineers leave immediately for a corporation. The most frequent adepts of this strategy are the top-ranking alumni of the Ecole Polytechnique, particularly the engineers of the Corps des Mines, and, since 1945, the alumni of the National School of Administration (ENA). The other exit is that of high-ranking civil servants who at a further stage of their career make a similar decision.[44]

This majority selection pattern has four implications. First, these schools bring to their students a very general education. Before World War II, the share devoted to economics was minuscule and business administration was ignored. Roger Martin, the CEO of Saint-Gobain between 1970 and 1980, testifies with regret: "In my two years at the Ecole Polytechnique and my other two years at the Ecole des Mines, I believe I never heard the words enterprise and market."[45] Since the end of World War II, this gap was finally corrected. Yet the training given by these schools, even the supposedly technical *grandes écoles*, remains rather polyvalent, a feature of consequence for both management and mobility.

Second, this education is widely divorced from research as these schools

[43] Michel Bauer and Bénédicte Bertin-Mourot, "L'Etat, le capital et l'entreprise au sommet des grandes entreprises. Les 200 en France et en Allemagne," *Revue de l'IRES*, Fall 1992, pp. 31–70.

[44] Christophe Charle, "Le pantouflage en France (vers 1880–vers 1980)," *Annales ESC*, September–October 1987, pp. 1115–1137. Hervé Joly, "L'appartenance aux grands corps administratifs comme filière d'accès au sommet des grandes entreprises dans la France de l'après-guerre (1945–1989)," DEA thesis, Ecole Normale Supérieure, 1989. Michel Bauer and Elie Cohen, *Les 200*, Paris, Editions du Seuil, 1987. Also Carroll D. Smith, "The longest run: Public engineers and planning in France," *American Historical Review*, June 1990, pp. 657–692, and Bruno Belhoste et al., eds., *La France des X*, Paris, Economica, 1995; Jacques Lesourne, ed., *Les Polytechniciens dans le siècle 1894–1994*, Paris, Dunod, 1994.

[45] Roger Martin, "Editorial," *Entreprises et Histoire*, April 1992, p. 3.

are located outside universities. This brings about another major difference with Germany, where in 1990 more than 50 percent of the top 200
CEOs held a Ph.D. Training for research began to appear in the curricula
of the French schools only in the 1960s.[46]

Third, the base for recruiting top CEOs in twentieth-century France
is small. To be sure, the number of the students in these schools since
the late nineteenth century has increased, especially since the 1970s, but
even thus the schools yield a number of applicants for top management
positions which remains smaller than the base supplied by the cadres of
German business.[47]

Fourth, the career profiles of top French CEOs directly derive from
this process of training and selection. Most are generalist managers. They
are distinguished for their strategic vision, their organizational abilities,
and their networks (including old-boy networks). They may work at such
positions successively in very different sectors. Two specific state bodies
excel in supplying these generalist top managers: the Finance Inspection
and the Mine Corps.[48] Paradoxically, the spreading of the M-form after
World War II – which I analyzed earlier – reinforced this profile of generalist
manager. Specializing top managers in strategy, planning, and control did
not necessarily require, as interpreted in France, people with a direct
experience of one core business of the industrial enterprise.

This predominance of generalist managers makes it possible for them
(contrary to German top managers) to enjoy a rather high mobility from one
company to another and from one branch to another – even in unrelated
sectors. It thus looks as if French large corporations value adaptability and
networks more than technical competence as the key feature for most CEOs.

This very distinctive pattern of selection, career, and mobility for top
managers is a source of great hierarchical distance with both the other
managers and the labor force. Most managers know that they will never
be able to reach top positions if they had not attended one of the few state
schools I already alluded to. Hence periodic outbursts of discontent by
cadres who complain that they are not associated to the key moves of their
company.[49] Most French top managers have no direct experience of shared

[46] Hervé Joly, *Patrons d' Allemagne*, Paris, Presses de Sciences P., 1996. On the slow
    introduction of research in French *grandes écoles*, cf. for instance Claude Quivoron,
    "Evolution de la formation des ingénieurs chimistes et rôle de la recherche," *Culture
    technique*, June 1991, pp. 127–179.
[47] Joly, "*Patrons III*." Bauer and Cohen, *Les 200.*
[48] Emmanuel Chadeau, *L'économie du risque*, Paris, Olivier Orban, 1988.
[49] Muller and Torres, *L'identité.*

work with either other managers or workers. Even some of the nonstate *grandes écoles* gradually modified their curricula to make them less specialized, more general, in order to increase the career potential of their graduates. Such a change happened at the major French business school, HEC, between 1953 and 1960.[50]

This two-tiered structure of the majority of French large corporations – generalists at the top, specialists below – has been recently discussed by historians and sociologists in two directions: does it prevent French big firms from being modern? does it make them less efficient than major foreign competitors?

To the first of these two questions the answer is a qualified no. As the training of a majority of French CEOs is that of an engineer, even if it is a state engineer, they are quite often able to combine the general approach which is in the tradition of their schools with an interest for the "modern" values of technological competence and productive efficiency as desired characteristics of industrial organizations.

To the second question the answer is more delicate. Most scholars suggest that there is no clear correlation between business performance and the importance of academic knowledge brought into the firm. Even in physics and mechanics (although perhaps not in electronics), it is not certain that research is the main engine for innovation. Some experts even argue that the reverse is true: innovation, born from market demand and from the imagination of feverish tinkerers, might well be the source of inspiration for research.[51] As for training, its main input might be to test characters and to bestow legitimacy to the graduates rather than to acquire specialized knowledge.[52] If one followed these theories, the French dual structure of management could not be considered as so much of a handicap.

Let us look now at the rest of the labor force. The picture that emerges is not successful. By 1914, at most 3 percent of the workers had received a vocational training.[53] In the following years, apprenticeship was not developed to the same extent as in Germany. French industrialists kept hiring massively rural labor and foreign workers. This labor policy in the long run had three major consequences. It probably slowed down automation, as it did not make the substitution of capital for labor so urgent.

[50] Meuleau, "Les HEC et l'évolution."
[51] Thierry Gaudin, *L'écoute des silences*, Paris, UGE, 1979, pp. 22ff.
[52] Claude Riveline, "A quoi sert le savoir en gestion?," *Gérer et comprendre*, March 1993, pp. 86–87.
[53] Jean-Pierre Daviet, "La France était-elle en retard en 1914?," *Les Cahiers Français*, March–April 1992, p. 9.

It increased the already striking hierarchical distance, as employers thought of authoritarian and centralized discipline as the "one best way" to control this unskilled and semiskilled labor force. It proved a disadvantage in terms of flexibility and quality from the 1970s onward. Only a minority of firms were keen on developing a corporate patriotism or a more skilled labor structure. This is of course rational, with the predominance of generalist top managers. It is also in keeping with the slow emergence of personnel departments. A real policy caring for human resources started at best in the 1950s, at worst in the 1980s, and continuity in such an effort was not always the case.[54]

Let us now consider the foreman, who is the cornerstone of the modern factory, say in the United States or Japan. In France, he does not play a central role. His education is limited, all the more as an attempt by the state to increase it had to be abandoned in 1906. Managerial hierarchies often dispossess him of his know-how. So he is left to the supervision of men and shop floor work units. It is only gradually that companies offer him further training and theoretical education. And the possibilities of promotion are restricted.[55] More flexibility came from self-taught engineers and cadres. They would account up to the 1970s for as much as 30 percent of the white-collar workers with the relevant status. Their influence was ambivalent. They could make up for the lack of specialized knowledge which characterized top managers and the insufficient flow of graduates from the *grandes écoles*. But they felt even more than the technical graduates the distance to top management.[56] And, like the vast unskilled and semiskilled work force, this was a factor behind the prolonged existence of the U-form structure in a number of large corporations after World War II.

The main conclusion of this section is that the diffusion of the large corporation in France did not change the dual pattern of recruitment till at least the mid-1970s. Till then universities produced graduates mostly for the civil service and a few extra diplomas for graduates holding already the title of alumnus of a *grande école*.

[54] Tristan de la Broise, *Pont-à-Mousson*, Paris, Inter Editions, 1988, pp. 220–224. Meuleau, "Les HEC."

[55] Philippe d'Iribarne, *La logique de l'honneur. Gestion des entreprises et traditions nationales*, Paris, Editions du Seuil, 1989, pp. 21–55, 114–122. Sylvie Vandecasteele, "Comment peut-on être contremaître?," in Yves Lequin and Sylvie Vandecasteele, eds., *L'usine et le bureau*, Lyon, PUL, 1990, pp. 93–108.

[56] Luc Boltanski, "Les ingénieurs autodidactes," in André Thepot, ed., *L'ingénieur dans la société française*, Paris, Editions Ouvrières, 1985.

THE ORGANIZATION OF INTERFIRM MARKETS

The growth and competitive success of the French larger industrial firms naturally depended on their adjustment to the behavior of the other economic institutions present on the national market. The relationships of French modern industrial enterprises to other industrial firms, to the service sector, and to government have indeed been organized during the twentieth century in ways which are partly specific to the French nation.

This is already true of the relations between industrial firms themselves. They take into account, as historians and economists have shown, two French peculiarities: the weight of large corporations in the economy is a bit lighter than in the other leading industrial nations, and simultaneously there is a relative lack of middle-sized firms. France has not yet been able to deliver satisfactory statistics on concentration during the twentieth century, so we can only estimate that the first 100 industrial enterprises contributed to 12 percent of industrial production in 1913, 16 in 1929, 27 in 1955, and 50 in 1975.[57] This significant, but still moderate growth reflects in part the smaller number of merger waves than in the United States (or in Britain) during this century. The works by Naomi Lamoreaux and Alfred Chandler stress the importance of the three merger waves (the 1900s, the 1920s, the 1960s) in shaping the configuration of corporate enterprise in America.[58] France had only two comparable merger waves: in the 1920s and in the 1960s. It is well worth noting that the mergers of the 1960s developed not only under the influence of increased international competition (due to the coming of the Common Market), but also under the pressure of the French state, which was advocating a policy of "national champions" to face foreign corporate giants. The absence of any merger wave before the 1920s could never be entirely caught up by France.[59]

All these elements may be ascribed to the smaller size of the French capital market, to which we shall later return in detail, and to the relatively limited number of new investors. By 1913, the largest French corporation, the Compagnie de Saint-Gobain, operating in both glass and chemicals,

[57] Daviet, "La France," p. 5; and "L'industrie," pp. 75–76.
[58] Chandler, Jr., *Scale and scope*. Naomi Lamoreaux, *The great merger movement in American business, 1895–1904*, Cambridge, Cambridge University Press, 1988.
[59] The most comprehensive survey remains Fernand Braudel and Ernest Labrousse, eds., *Histoire économique et sociale de la France*, section IV, vol. 1, 2, 3, Paris, PUF, 1979–1982. On mergers, see also Lévy-Leboyer, "La grande entreprise," pp. 373–374.

would have only 1,926 shareholders.[60] French savers came to buy shares massively in the 1920s, partly in the context of the merger wave. Thus they had very little experience of stock fluctuations, and were greatly shocked by the impact of the Depression of the 1930s. The frustrations they expressed then discouraged for many years new people to enter this group. The shareholders themselves aired distrust at business leaders of the large corporations, which in turn led part of them to accept the nationalizations because they felt that business leaders were cheating and despising them.[61] The further growth of the number of the shareholders would happen only from the late 1950s onward, and even more from the mid-1980s onward. The social basis necessary to sustain the capital requirements of large corporations was thus slow to assert itself and the second phase of its growth was delayed in comparison to other major industrial nations.

But this development of big business cannot yet rely on a sufficient number of performing mid-sized firms, contrary to Germany where numerous medium-scale enterprises are a key resource for competitiveness, both as generating wealth in their own right and as suppliers or subcontractors. In 1991 the ratio of the number of German mid-sized firms to the French (i.e., companies between 100 and 2,000 wage earners) was on average 1.62; even more preoccupying was the ratio for companies only between 1,000 and 2,000 wage earners: 2.18. Part of this lag depends on problems of control and transmission of capital, and on the impact of the French tax system on them.[62] Also, only a minority of post–World War II creations of medium-sized firms have been in traded activities.[63]

The success story of SAGEM, a French electronic equipment manufacturer, in the 1970s and in the 1980s is a case in point. A mid-sized firm, SAGEM was a first mover in electronic telexes where it successfully competed with the German company Siemens. Then, using economies of scope, it diversified into the production of minitels (phone network terminals) and of TV decoding boxes, then into car electronics. With 15,000 employees

---

[60] Daviet, *Un destin*, p. 648. At the Parisian Gas Company in 1889 1,047 people held 81 percent of the shares: Lenard Berlanstein, *Big business and industrial conflict in nineteenth-century France*, Berkeley, University of California Press, 1991, p. 29.

[61] Lévy-Leboyer, "La grande entreprise." Daviet, *Un destin*.

[62] Jean Gandois, ed., *France: le choix de la performance globale*, Paris, La Documentation Française, 1992, pp. 27–28. Michel Bauer, *Les patrons de PME entre le pouvoir, l'entreprise et la famille*, Paris, Inter Editions, 1993, pp. 217–237.

[63] Bertrand Dechery, *Competing for prosperity: Business strategies and industrial policies in modern France*, London, Policy Studies Institute, 1986, p. 118.

in 1992, it is obviously no longer a medium-sized firm.[64] It is but one example of those mid-sized firms which can provide critical leverage for France to remain a major industrial nation.

Given this discrepancy, how did larger firms interact with the others during this century? We shall focus on three issues: the geography of the smaller ones, the alternative between make or buy, and subcontracting. They all point to the same question: how far could larger firms become the core of a network of related activities? The geography of small and medium-sized firms gives only one – yet major – case of industrial cluster, the Paris region. There (like in the Ruhr), from the end of the nineteenth century till at least the 1950s, the growth of large-scale companies in metallurgy and in mechanical engineering created outlets for smaller firms which supplied them both in specific products and in specialized know-how. The issue of the supply and subcontracting relationship is much more complex (and historians' current knowledge much more fragmented). In several industries, clusters and nexuses have indeed existed: in the automobile industry since about 1908, in the aircraft industry and in electrical equipment since the mid-1920s, in materials building for an even longer period. In electrical equipment this nexus often took the shape of groups where firms were connected by personal links or by subtle types of control. In other sectors cooperation was purely informal, and firms exchanged information and other services.[65]

In a second stage, some larger firms turned to vertical integration, reinforced by subcontracting. The rationale was often distrust about quantities, regularity of delivery, quality, and prices – that is, transaction costs. After World War II, integration generally declined step by step, in favor of purely commercial contracts between larger firms and suppliers, on a short-term basis, which was a major source of uncertainty and dependence for the suppliers. Only during the 1980s, under the influence of the Japanese model, did such relations evolve to real partnerships, including, in mechanical engineering, allied networks of small and medium-sized firms.[66]

---

[64] Pierre Faurre et al., "La compétitivité française dans l'électronique," *Entreprises et Histoire*, May 1993. Michèle Thouverez-Brochot, "Internationalisation et compétitivité des moyennes entreprises industrielles françaises," *Entreprises et Histoire*, June 1994, pp. 9–19.

[65] Ginette Kurgan-Van Hentenryk and Emmanuel Chadeau, "Stratégie et structure de la petite et moyenne entreprise depuis la Révolution industrielle: rapport général," in Herman van der Wee and Erik Aerts, eds., *Debates and controversies in economic history*, Leuven, Leuven University Press, 1990, pp. 173, 182, 184, 187. Michel Lescure, *PME et croissance économique*, Paris, Economica, 1996.

[66] For the auto industry, see Fridenson, *Histoire des usines Renault* and Christophe Midler, *L'auto qui n'existait pas. Management des projets et transformation de l'entreprise*, Paris, Inter Editions, 1993. For mechanical engineering, Gandois, ed., *France*, p. 28.

So, we can draw three conclusions. On the whole period, network relationships did exist, but were limited chronologically and geographically. This may be one of the reasons underlying the current insufficient number of medium-sized enterprises, as dependence and sometimes antagonism were not propitious to their dynamism. The same characterization applies also to the relationship between some larger firms and some of the larger firms that were their suppliers, which became confrontational in some sectors (contrary to Germany).

When one turns to the issue of competition between firms on the same markets, the picture that emerges is much more distinctly that of quite frequent cooperation. The conditions of competition were not so different from Germany. Like other European States, France had no laws that limited or controlled the industrial and commercial cartels and ententes which proliferated after the 1870s. Only one article in the French Penal Code of 1810, article 419, made it illegal to influence prices. In 1852 it had been used by the French state as a veritable antitrust law against the largest French coal mine. But after 1870 French jurisprudence weakened its impact; a very ambitious antitrust action undertaken during World War I (about calcium carbides) led to a general acquittal, and in its aftermath the article was amended in 1926: coalition became fully lawful.[67] An elaborate network of industrial and commercial ententes, "less powerful than German cartels but probably second only to them in quantity," was patiently assembled in various branches.[68] Ententes and cartels, national or international, were particularly efficient in building sales facilities and organizations. Thus they often created some of the marketing capabilities which I have shown to be missing in a number of early large corporations in France. They were also a substitute for the relative shortage of managerial resources. For instance, the French Aluminum Cartel of 1911 and, after World War I, several trade associations created laboratories and technical departments.[69]

---

[67] Charles Freedeman, "Cartels and the law in France before 1914," *French Historical Studies*, Spring 1988, pp. 482–487. Robert O. Paxton, "The calcium carbide case and the decriminalization of industrial ententes in France, 1915–26," in Patrick Fridenson, ed., *The French home front, 1914–1918*, Providence, Berg, 1992, pp. 153–180.

[68] Paxton, "The calcium carbide case," p. 153.

[69] Jean-Pierre Daviet, "Trade associations or agreements and controlled competition in France, 1830–1939," in Hiroaki Yamazaki and Matao Miyamoto, eds., *Trade associations in business history*, Tokyo, University of Tokyo Press, 1988, pp. 269–295. Hachez, "Le cartel"; Emmanuel Chadeau, "International cartels in the interwar period: Some aspects of the French case," in Akira Kudo and Terushi Hara, eds., *International cartels in business history*, Tokyo, University of Tokyo Press, 1992, pp. 98–113. Charles E. Freedman, *The triumph of corporate capitalism in France, 1867–1914*, Rochester, University of Rochester Press, 1993, pp. 112–128.

Two qualifications should be added here. Some sectors always stayed outside cartels, most strikingly the auto industry, or could only sustain unstable trade agreements, as the chemical industry, where ententes were numerous, but specific and sometimes short-lived. Some cartel agreements produced a good outcome as in the aircraft industry, some others, as in iron and steel industries, curtailed innovation and discontented consumer industries (contrary to Germany).

This brings us to a parallel with Germany after World War II. It took Germany twelve years (1945–1957) to pass a legislation on competition, which was only in part inspired by American rules. In 1950 the French government finally decided not to send to parliament an antitrust bill which Jean Monnet and his Planning Commission had drafted. A majority of French politicians wanted to keep as much interfirm cooperation as possible in times of hardening international competition. In 1952 and 1953, the French government issued two decrees against restriction of competition and collusive agreements. This was a limited step.[70] Only in the 1970s and the 1980s was the protection of competition strengthened.[71]

A second major issue is the relationship between French large industrial firms and the financial sector (banks, stock exchanges, trading companies). With the banks, it is certainly a different relationship from those – each quite opposite – prevailing in Britain or Germany. To assess it, we shall take into account the revisions introduced by recent research, and distinguish between small and medium-sized businesses and large corporations. The behavior of the French banking system matters all the more as, in opposition to the nineteenth century, industrial firms resorted more and more to credit and to the stock market and less to self-financing.

Contrary to what was earlier believed, the French banking system was generally rather adequate and satisfactory in the provision of short-term credit to small and medium-sized businesses. There was only one exception, in the 1920s, where these businesses experienced a financial gap, a lack of financial facilities.[72] Long-term investment facilities became available, however, only more recently, first in the 1960s, then in the 1980s. It should be observed that before there was not simply a hesitation on the

---

[70] Matthias Kipping, "Concurrence et compétitivité. Les origines de la législation anti-trust française après 1945," *Etudes et Documents*, 6, 1994, pp. 429–55. Volker R. Berghahn, *The Americanisation of West German industry, 1945–1973*, Leamington Spa, Berg, 1986, pp. 155–181.

[71] Hervé Dumez and Alain Jeunemaitre, *La concurrence en Europe*, Paris, Editions du Seuil, 1992.

[72] Lescure, "Les petites et moyennes entreprises."

part of banks to commit themselves in such matters and an absence of relevant organizational facilities, but also a strong reluctance from small entrepreneurs to accept bankers among their board members.[73] As for the financing of the creation of small and medium-sized businesses, there is indeed a lag between France and the United States. Venture capital appeared in the United States during the 1950s. In France it really took off during the 1970s, and its second period of intense growth came in the mid-1980s.[74]

If we turn now toward large corporations, recent research suggests that between 1880 and 1914 a rapprochement between banks and industrial firms was visible in a number of sectors like steel, chemicals, electricity, and telephone, whereas other sectors preferred to rely mostly on self-financing and other banks retreated from industrial activities. As industrial investment intensified in the 1920s, a number of banks answered industrial firms' requests for advice, expertise, and investment, notably the Banque Lazard and the Banque de Paris et des Pays Bas, which were both tempted to adopt the German or Belgian model of the universal bank.[75] After World War II, with a further increase in industrial investment, self-financing was once again the usual solution, supplemented by either emissions of shares and bonds on the stock market or long-term loans from quasi governmental financial corporations. From the early 1960s to the early 1980s, the picture entirely changed, and French large corporations borrowed heavily from banks. This debt economy was mostly a short-term debt. Thus it led to a greater fragility of French large corporations (in 1980 short-term debts would represent 50 percent of Saint-Gobain's balance sheet!), most of which were clearly undercapitalized. This development of bank credit was made possible by a strict division between financial institutions: on one side lenders, on the other borrowers. However, in the 1980s large corporations gave a priority to the reduction of their debts, contrary to small and medium-sized enterprises. They increased their own resources.[76] French investment banks during

---

[73] Bernard Desjardins et al., "Les banques françaises ont-elles aidé les entreprises?," *Entreprises et Histoire*, December 1992, p. 89.

[74] Jean Lachmann, "Evolution du capital-risque en France," *Entreprise et Histoire*, December 1992, pp. 35–48.

[75] Eric Bussière, *Paribas, l'Europe et le monde 1872–1992*, Antwerp, Fonds Mercator, 1992.

[76] Jean-Pierre Daviet, *Une multinationale à la française, Saint-Gobain 1665–1989*, Paris, Fayard, 1989. André Straus, "Structures financières et performances des entreprises industrielles en France dans la seconde moitié du XXè siècle," *Entreprises et Histoire*, December 1992, pp. 19–33. Desjardins et al., "Les banques."

a third wave of investment in the industry (after those of the 1900s and 1920s) in the 1960s and early 1970s, adopted a more diversified and sometimes more cautious strategy in the 1980s.[77] Resort to foreign banks (including American private investment banking houses) increased also considerably during the course of the twentieth century.

On the whole, I would rather be tempted to argue, on the basis of available scholarship, that, although its American and German counterparts could raise large amounts of capital more quickly and often at a lower cost, the French banking system itself, although less sophisticated, was not such a major limit to industrial financing in France. On the other hand, the model of the German universal bank was never completely adopted in France. The relationships of bankers to industrialists remained alternately the supply of services and the partnership (whether forced or voluntary).

In addition, as we just hinted, the financial market was small. To a large extent, the size of French firms was long limited by the mediocre size of the French stock exchange. As late as 1985 the value of the French stock market was one fourteenth of its American counterpart, a disproportion which was much larger than the gap between the national products and incomes of the two nations.[78] This situation had significant consequences. Up to the 1940s, many firms were forced to develop holding structures in order to reach more easily for available capital. The larger ones began, largely through retained earnings, to develop their own financial capabilities in the 1920s, which they would considerably extend from the 1960s onward, as a substitute to a sufficient partnership of the financial market.[79] Therefore, the size of the market cannot be only analyzed as a limitation. It was also an incentive to new forms of firms and to new organizational capabilities in financial matters for large corporations: holding companies, more durable than most American ones, financial joint agencies, later industrial groups' banks. To be fair, a distinction should be made between the period up to 1914 and the years after. Before 1914, the French stock market, however small, opened itself to industrial firms. But most firms did not try to enter it as they were not accustomed to taking such an initiative. Only a few firms intervened

[77] Bussière, *Paribas*. Desjardins et al., "Les banques."

[78] Personal communication from Maurice Lévy-Leboyer.

[79] Patrick Fridenson, "Renault face au problème du franc et du risque devises 1957–1981," in Maurice Lévy-Leboyer, ed., *Du franc Poincaré à l'écu*, Paris, Comité pour l'histoire économique et financière de la France, 1993, pp. 583–592. Karine Ohana, *Les banques de groupe en France*, Paris, PUF, 1991.

on the market: most electrical equipment companies, and expanding firms like Schneider, Saint-Gobain, or Peugeot. After 1914 and till 1945, enterprises became more eager to move into the stock market, but the state managed to occupy a large part of the market because of its own financial needs.

In terms of services, another important issue is to know whether French large industrial firms could rely for their exports on the organizational capabilities of general trading companies (as, say, the Japanese and Koreans, but even the Germans and British). Of course, this did not matter for the industries of luxury goods. For the other sectors, preliminary research shows mixed evidence. We know at least of one general trading company since the 1880s: Louis-Dreyfus.[80] France was able to develop trading companies working in colonial Africa, in Latin America, in Asia, and in prerevolutionary Russia, but generally they were "more efficient on the import side of external trade and were even selling raw materials to third countries."[81] So, both in the domains of commodities and of finished products French manufacturers ready to export may not have had enough services of large trading companies. From the 1960s onward a few of the large corporations decided to develop their own subsidiaries in that field to try and partly overcome this weakness.[82]

Last but evidently not least comes the question of the state. We have already dealt here with several aspects of its role toward large corporations, and it is not possible to give now a full picture of the other aspects. Let us focus on three points which are relevant to our study. The state tried to protect French firms against foreign competitors and multinationals. From the 1880s till the 1960s it set protective tariffs. It kept a close control of foreign investment and started to impose quotas of French-built components.[83]

The regulation of the economy was not favorable to the improvement of competitiveness. The state strongly hampered the competitiveness of the French industry by imposing fifty years of price control, from 1936

[80] Claude Boquin, "Le pied marin en affaires," Paris, Ecole de Paris du Management, 1993.
[81] Pierre Chalmin, "International commodity trading companies in Europe," in Shin'ichi Yonekawa and Hideki Yoshihara, eds., *Business history of general trading companies*, Tokyo, University of Tokyo Press, 1987, pp. 289–291.
[82] Ohana, *Les banques de groupe*.
[83] Raymond Poidevin, "La peur de la concurrence allemande en France avant 1914," in *1914. Les psychoses de la guerre*, Rouen, Publications de l'Université de Rouen, 1985, pp. 77–84. André Gueslin, *L'Etat, l'économie et la société française XIXè–XXè siècle*, Paris, Hachette, 1992.

to 1986. The consequences on financial reserves, competition, and performance of such a policy are obvious.[84] Let us simply remark that since the early 1950s German large corporations did not endure price control. Beyond its own effects, price control was also the result of state sensitivity to the short-term concerns of peasants, small shopkeepers, or civil servants, which were often antagonistic to the long-term needs of industry.

From World War I onward, the state started to promote "national champions" in sectors deemed strategic by the military or by the politicians. It gave orders, loans, subsidies, and other facilities to existing large firms. It also set up mixed companies (as in chemicals for dyes, then for oil) or state-owned enterprises (in chemicals for nitrogen, then for potash).[85] This policy was reinforced after World War II, and was long shared by other European powers. It did provide an additional basis for the development of large corporations in France. Yet the promotion of national champions had at least two drawbacks. It often led to conglomerates, which later had great difficulties refocusing on their core businesses. In addition, the concept of competitiveness which governments defined was primitive, and often ignored the necessity of improving organizational capabilities and of weaving clusters of performing small and especially medium-size enterprises around large-scale firms. The degree of state intervention considerably increased after 1945, but this change has to be examined in detail within a review of post–World War II performance and competitiveness of French big business.

ORGANIZATION AND PERFORMANCE OF LARGE
INDUSTRIAL ENTERPRISES SINCE WORLD WAR II

Patterns of convergence

Two major challenges faced the French larger industrial enterprise during those years. There was the legacy of World War II: defeat, destructions, military occupation, and temporary loss of touch with international technological change. Then there was the reinforcement of international competition, with the European Coal and Steel Community, soon followed by

[84] Hervé Dumez and Alain Jeunemaitre, *Diriger l'économie. L'Etat et les prix en France (1936–1986)*, Paris, Editions L'Harmattan, 1989.
[85] John F. Godfrey, *Capitalism at war: Industrial policy and bureaucracy in France, 1914–1918*, Leamington Spa, Berg, 1987, pp. 157–180. Hotta, "L'industrie du pétrole." Daviet, *Un destin*, pp. 569–570.

the European Economic Community, finally evolving into a European Single Market: a move desired and actuated by French governments. The overall record of the French economy can be summarized by two brief statements. Both real GDP per hour worked and output per person-hour in manufacturing improved considerably (although there was an apparent slowdown in the 1980s). Yet the size of French industry in 1992, according to a 1993 survey by the Ministry of Industry, was half the size of its German counterpart.

Three major trends of convergence characterize the French large corporations: a greater convergence with other industrial nations, a differentiated competitiveness and organization in the key industries, and the mixed record of state intervention. All these reduced French exceptionalism.

The most obvious element of convergence was the decline of personal capitalism and the gradually smaller importance of family capitalism. Of the latter trend there are famous examples: the replacement of a family chairman by the salaried manager Roger Martin in the fabricated metal products firm Pont-à-Mousson in 1964 (and he and Pont-à-Mousson would take over Saint-Gobain in 1969) or the gradual substitution of managers for family members in the top positions of the Peugeot automobile company in the 1960s.[86] Similarly, within the steel industry, the de Wendel company was unable to maintain its branch leadership. The nationalizations of 1944–1948 (for aircraft engines and for the Renault automobile company) and of 1982 (at least for steel) brought important contributions to this process as they promoted a type of managerial capitalism. In addition, what was called in the 1950s "the French management gap" greatly diminished: the state and the chambers of commerce invested in modern business education, and most large industrial firms invested in the recruitment of managers (although certain weaknesses linger in some areas of marketing).[87]

The second area of convergence was the growth of foreign direct investment in the French economy. However, the movement was not unidirectional. Some major foreign players had to leave the field. In electrical and electronic equipment General Electric sold off its financial holdings in Thomson in 1953. In 1969 Thomson broke the "principal

---

[86] Roger Martin, *Patron de droit divin*, Paris, Gallimard, 1984. Jean-Louis Loubet, *Automobiles Peugeot. Une réussite industrielle 1945–1974*, Paris, Economica, 1990.

[87] Robert R. Locke, *Management and higher education since 1940: The influence of America and Japan on West Germany, Great Britain, and France*, Cambridge, Cambridge University Press, 1989, pp. 199–211 and 243–250.

agreement" signed in 1919 by which General Electric provided it with technical knowledge. In 1964, General Electric reentered French business when it took control of the national computer champion, Bull. But it quit Bull in 1970, as it came to the "early conclusion that the computer business was IBM's." In the automobile industry, Ford sold its subsidiary in 1954 (and came back in 1970 only on a limited scale: the production of gearboxes), Chrysler did the same in 1978, and Fiat had sold its controlling interests in 1963.[88]

The entries of foreign firms outweighed the exits. The most important case was in pharmaceuticals. In 1967, the German first mover, Hoechst, took a controlling interest in the French challenger (to Rhône-Poulenc), Roussel-Uclaf, and acquired the majority in 1974. This was a far-ranging change for both the corporate culture of the company and the entire French pharmaceutical industry.[89] In addition the Japanese began to invest in France, starting with consumer electronics. A number of foreign companies already present in France before World War II increased their commitment. The French subsidiary of IBM provides us with a remarkable example. Initially, it was devoted to sales and assembly only. After World War II, with the computer revolution, it made the three-pronged investment in production, marketing, and management, and even in research.[90]

The last area of convergence has been the intensity of French industrial investment abroad, especially after 1960. In the 1960s France was even at the third rank among OECD nations for foreign industrial investment, slipping nevertheless to the sixth position in the 1970s. Its targets were mostly other industrial nations. Conversely, it exported a high amount of goods, and ranked between third and fifth in world exports during the period.[91] French industry was indeed exploiting economies of scale and

---

[88] John Kay, *Foundations of corporate success: How business strategies add value*, Oxford, Oxford University Press, 1993, p. 10. Chantal Le Bolloc'h Puges, *La politique industrielle française dans l'électronique*, Paris, Editions L'Harmattan, 1991, p. 45. James M. Laux, *The European automobile industry*, New York, Twayne Publishers, 1992. Mira Wilkins, *The maturing of multinational enterprise: American business abroad from 1914 to 1970*, Cambridge, MA, Harvard University Press, 1974.

[89] Richard F. Kuisel, *Seducing the French: The dilemma of Americanization*, Berkeley, University of California Press, 1993. Jacques Robin, "La culture d'entreprise dans l'industrie pharmaceutique française de Clin-Midy à Roussel-Uclaf," in Jean Gatty et al., eds., *Identité et culture d'entreprise*, Paris, ADITECH, 1989, p. 87.

[90] Jacques Vernay, *Chroniques de la Compagnie IBM France 1914–1987*, Paris, IBM France, 1988.

[91] Charles-Albert Michalet, "Panorama général de l'industrie française dans l'économie mondiale: 1950–1975," in [Christian Stoffaes, ed.], *L'industrie française face à l'ouverture internationale*, Paris, Economica, 1991, pp. 11–16. Gérard Lafay, "Evolution de la spécialisation de l'industrie française dans les échanges internationaux," ibid., pp. 17–19.

scope. But this export and multinationalization drive incurred some problems. A number of large companies had not sufficient organizational capabilities or lacked competitive vigor, and, a little like the Japanese auto companies at their beginnings in the United States, had disastrous experiences. More generally, this international expansion became a major incentive for organizational learning in the French corporations, and prompted them to improve their organizational capabilities. During this drive joint ventures became much more frequent. They were "especially fragile" on the U.S. market, but more solid elsewhere, as we shall see for the aerospace industry.[92]

However, two characteristics still differentiated the French experience form other nations: the close relationships between government and business fostered by the *grandes écoles* education and an acceptance, even a willingness, to nationalize or to found national enterprises. They were reflected in the government's policy of creating national champions in the capital-intensive, technologically advanced industries which had become dominated by global oligopolies. Members of the elite policy-making group did so by merging and reshuffling an industry's national leaders. Then, if such reshuffling failed to improve performance, the government took over the enterprise and further restructured it.

The reshaping of product portfolios

In France, as in the United States, Britain, and Germany and its smaller neighbors, nearly all the enterprises that dominated major industries – chemicals, pharmaceuticals, glass, electrical/electronic equipment, metals, motor vehicles, rubber, and oil – became the learning bases for industry-specific organizational capabilities, well before World War II. The leaders, particularly in the high-tech industries, not only maintained the capabilities in their existing product lines but expanded into closely related industries where their learned capabilities gave them a competitive advantage.

After World War II such growth through diversification became increasingly carried out by mergers and acquisitions rather than internal investment and product development. Often, as in the case of American firms, enterprises entered businesses where their learned core capabilities gave them little competitive strength. In the 1970s and 1980s they

---

[92] Mira Wilkins, "French Multinationals in the United States: An historical perspective," *Enterprises et Histoire*, May 1993, pp. 14–29.

reshaped their product lines so as to focus on those whose production and distribution rested on such competencies. This restructuring was carried out through selling, buying, and swapping operating divisions. A comparable reshaping of product portfolios occurred in the United States (as discussed in Chapter 3); but there the government played no role. In France the government's role was critical and was shaped by its policy of promoting national champions.

In chemicals an early move toward such product realignment came as early as 1960 when the CEO of the aluminum giant Pechiney suggested that the four companies other than the market leader, Rhône-Poulenc, (i.e., Pechiney, Saint-Gobain, Ugine, Kuhlmann) should merge their chemical divisions. This did not succeed. Only a joint venture between Pechiney and Saint-Gobain (which would have preferred Kuhlmann as partner) was achieved. That joint venture rationalized and modernized its capabilities, but this was not enough. In 1969 Pechiney sold its share of that chemical unit to Rhône-Poulenc. In 1971, the glass giant Saint-Gobain also turned its share in the joint venture over to Rhône-Poulenc, receiving payment in a significant block of Rhône-Poulenc's securities. Rhône-Poulenc's CEO then suggested a merger between his company and Saint-Gobain Pont-à-Mousson. The size "would be a little bigger than Britain's ICI." The project, which met hostility from several top executives within Rhône-Poulenc, was vetoed by the president of the republic, Pompidou.

But Rhône-Poulenc's increased strength in chemicals was more apparent than real. Moreover, although it had successfully made the postwar move into antibiotics, antihistamines, and silicones, it had to rely on licenses from American patents for the most strategic products and on the continued production of products dating from the beginning of the century. Also there was a discrepancy between the growth of the market and conversely the diversification of products and its managerial capabilities. Top management was weak and became dominated more by former high-ranking civil servants than by industrialists. Moreover, the firm had kept the corporate culture of a medium-sized company and it was insufficiently structured. This had two consequences: an enormous development in artificial textiles thanks to technology transfer (the licenses of Du Pont's Nylon and ICI's Tergal), which was very profitable but which made the whole group vulnerable to any downturn in textile prices and accentuated its fragmented character, and a cosmetic adaptation of its strategy and organization structure to world competition. Heavy losses came between 1979 and 1982. The nationalization of 1982 brought about a refocusing on chemicals, a much better top management, and an aggressive international policy, exploiting economies of scope and including the purchase of divisions of three major U.S. chemical companies. The group now has five core businesses: organic and mineral intermediaries; chemical specialties; fibers and polymers; agrochemicals; and pharmaceuticals, the last-named being the most profitable.[93]

In these same few years Pechiney had also expanded and contracted. In 1971 the national champion policy led to the merger of Ugine, Kuhlmann, and Pechiney. The new firm was thus the sole producer of aluminum in France, entirely controlling its production and fabricating. But the merger had made it more of a conglomerate with seven different industrial divisions. The nationalization of 1982 was followed by portfolio restructuring through the divestiture of its activities in steel, dyes, and other chemical products. Shorn of these activities, the group focused effectively on aluminum products. After purchasing two U.S. companies in the 1980s, it became the world's third largest aluminum producer behind Alcoa and Alcan. The high level of debts which was partly a consequence of the expansion led to further divestitures in 1995, as the company revised its definition of its core business.[94]

In electrical equipment and electronics, we find again two first movers of the pre–World War I years: Thomson and Compagnie Générale d'Electricité, both expanding through diversification before having to refocus on their core businesses. Thomson combined internal growth and a bold strategy of acquisitions. It developed its electrical equipment business and its other specialties: consumer appliances, electronics, and telecommunications. It also enlarged its size by mergers, particularly with Brandt (mostly consumer appliances: 1966) and with CSF (electronics and telecommunications: 1967–1968). These two mergers considerably increased Thomson's research and marketing capabilities. Thomson's top management was replaced by the executives of the smaller company, Brandt. In 1969 the new management initiated the negotiation with the Compagnie Générale d'Electricité of what has been called the Yalta of French electronics. By this deal Thomson exchanged its electrical equipment business (organized in a joint venture since 1928, named Alsthom) for CGE's consumer appliances and data-processing division.

Although the intention of this swap was to have each company refocus

[93] Cayez, *Rhône-Poulenc*. François Quarré, *Rhône-Poulenc, ma vie*, Paris, Economica, 1988.
[94] Dechery, *Competing*, pp. 87–91. Georges-Henri Soutou and Alain Beltran, eds., *Pierre Guillaumat, la passion des grands projets industriels*, Paris, Rive droite, 1995.

on core capabilities, Thomson was soon expanding both through becoming multinational in 1974 and moving in 1975 into telecommunications. But the heavy losses resulting from the telephone business and the excessive growth of its top management, combined with lack of planning and budget control, brought it into crisis. Again as in chemicals, nationalization in 1982 brought the appointment of new top management, considerably improved the managerial capabilities and induced a refocusing on the company's major businesses: industrial electronics and consumer electronics. This strategy led to numerous divestitures in minor sectors, and to a second swap with Compagnie Générale d'Electricité in 1983 in which Thomson traded its ailing telephone business for CGE's military and consumer electronics divisions. Then followed a policy of acquisitions, particularly in consumer electronics (Germany's Telefunken in 1983, Britain's EMI, and America's RCA-GE in 1987). The U.S. government vetoed Thomson's attempt to buy LTV in defense electronics. Thus Thomson reached world size: it is the world's second largest maker of defense electronics, and the fourth largest of consumer electronics. However, these two markets decelerated in the late 1980s, as the cold war wound down and as the Japanese all but completed their conquest of global consumer electronic markets. Thomson may be overcoming its precarious position by improving its managerial capabilities in consumer electronics and by developing joint ventures in defense electronics. But the market prospects obviously call for major initiatives, and very difficult ones.[95]

The Compagnie Générale d'Electricité has had, on the whole, a better performance. This may be due to financial resources supplied by the nationalization of electricity plants in 1946, the specificity and profitability of its successive core businesses inside electrical equipment and electronics, a very decentralized structure, and an earlier professionalization of its top management. After nationalization in 1982, it not only obtained Thomson's telephone business, but at the same time also divested itself of its construction and public works which represented 20 percent of its turnover. It then acquired in 1986–1987 the European business of ITT after the liberal French government of 1986 had vetoed an agreement between CGE and AT&T for the U.S. market. The intense difficulty met in integrating Thomson's telecommunication division after 1983 prepared

[95] Sébastien Clerc, "La religion de la taille critique: Thomson de 1944 à 1974," *Revue Française de Gestion*, September–October 1988. Fridenson, "De la diversification."

management for a much more successful takeover of ITT's subsidiary: integration was carried out more quickly, but more cautiously, and American bureaucratic corporate culture was replaced by CGE's polycentric style of responsibilities for unit managers. Thus CGE reached the second rank among world telecommunication makers. In its other core business, power and transport systems (which includes nuclear power), the company formed a joint venture with Britain's GEC, GEC-Alsthom, which has become a major world player comparable with Siemens and Mitsubishi. In 1986 the company became again a private enterprise. In 1991, the firm changed its name to Alcatel Alsthom, a symbol of its regained industrial identity with respect to its two core businesses.[96]

From the industries reviewed, we may divide the history of the national champions' policy in two successive stages, where the state played two successive and opposite roles. As a French consultant put it, "Concentration into diversified conglomerates in the 1960s [was] largely a result of a government-inspired approach, implemented by the financial-technocratic establishment. Divestment and new specialization in the 1980s were in part made possible by the new role of the state as a shareholder. Management however played a much more significant role." France's large corporations then had "much more homogeneous business portfolios."[97]

In two other high-tech industries, aerospace and computers, which government both considered as strategic for defense and even independence, government intervention had simply to tackle the issue of French decline and finally resorted to international cooperation.

In computers, the market was large, rapidly growing, and very profitable. Nevertheless Bull, a business machine company founded in 1931 that became the French first mover in the 1950s, lost ground after 1960, when it was the world's third-largest firm behind IBM and Britain's ICL. This decline may be ascribed to four causes. Its technical capabilities soon reached their limits, as the successors of the highly competitive Gamma 60 range failed to live up to their reputation. Then the company fell prey

---

[96] Broder and Torres, *Alcatel Alsthom*, pp. 202–467. Pierre Le Roux, "Histoires de fusions," unpublished seminar paper, Ecole Polytechnique, May 17, 1991. Laurent Citti, "Un grand groupe industriel et l'innovation: Alcatel Alsthom," in Philippe-Jean Bernard and Jean-Pierre Daviet, eds., *Culture d'entreprise et innovation*, Paris, Presses du CNRS, 1992, pp. 137–145.

[97] Le Roux-Calas, "L'entreprise." Léger, *Une grande entreprise*. Grinberg, *Pechiney*, pp. 10–18. Jean-Yves Quenouille, "1995: comment définir le Pechiney de demain?," *Direct News*, November 28, 1994, pp. 1–2.

to successive owners (four in eighteen years), which broke its identity. The first of these takeovers (by GE) infuriated so much the French president, General de Gaulle, that the French government itself set up a challenger, which not only failed and had to merge with Bull, but in the interval made Bull's domestic market position more vulnerable. Finally, between the mid-1960s and the early 1980s, the company followed a defensive strategy, based on the occupation of captive markets. The management which the ultimate owner, the French state, appointed in 1983 fared no better. It followed a global "wish-driven" strategy for which it "simply lacked capabilities." It therefore had to accept the entry of the Japanese firm NEC into its capital and a last resort agreement with IBM. On the whole, Bull's performance and its organizational capabilities from 1960 to the early 1990s were not satisfactory. This was a fate common to the domestic computer manufacturers of the principal European powers. But this observation does not exonerate the French state and Bull's top management from their own responsibilities in this trend.[98]

For the aerospace industry, the postwar story is quite different. The situation in 1945 was absolutely disastrous, despite nationalizations (with mergers) in 1937 and 1945: almost no markets outside the French army and the French airlines, no up-to-date technology, no finance. The path to resurrection was long and marred by significant failures (such as the Franco-British supersonic Concorde). But its two major directions (product specialization, and international cooperation) were ratified by the markets and allowed the development of organizational capabilities. It is true that the state both helped it and hampered it (for instance, by mistaken pressures on the then private aircraft maker Dassault). But after painful years of learning technology, products, and markets, the three remaining players, for aircraft Aérospatiale and Dassault (the latter with a quickly diminishing competitiveness) and for engines SNECMA, have moved from sheer dependence to active interdependence, that, in turn, led to a line of commercial jets produced by Airbus, now the only world competitor to the two American leading producers. Its market success relies on three types of international cooperation: the aircraft is produced by a joint venture between the French state-owned company and a German firm, later an English firm; the engine results from a partnership between SNECMA and America's General Electric; the whole production process is geared toward cluster relationships between manufacturers and suppliers

---

[98] Dechery, *Competing*, pp. 132–43.

or subcontractors. The price paid for this reentry on world markets and its durability are still to be assessed.[99]

In the space business, the French position seems paradoxically better. The French government initiated another European consortium, Arianespace, in 1973, in order to launch commercial satellites. Initially based on French scientific capabilities, it has proven successful. A private firm, created in the 1960s, Matra, started producing guided missiles. Highly successful, it made a major unrelated diversification into media, acquiring the oldest and largest French publisher, Hachette, after having taken the management of a major commercial radio network. It is now the twenty-seventh largest French firm. A further diversification into a TV network was a total failure. So, space remains one of its core businesses, and, as in aircraft, the French source of competitiveness resides in research (in public institutes and in firms) and in specialization.[100]

In addition to the government's critical role in high-tech industries, the French government played a leading part in the reshaping of two other major industries, oil and steel. In oil, the new state-owned group Elf, which Gaullist governments created (as they did in computers) as a challenger to the national first mover (Compagnie Française des Pétroles) between 1962 and 1966, prospered. It became in the 1980s the largest French firm by assets and the world's seventh largest oil company.[101]

The decline of the steel industry has been a worldwide phenomenon. As in Germany, the European Coal and Steel Community after 1974 took control of prices and investments. As decline continued, the liberal government of 1978, confronted by the risk of the industry's collapse, decided on a quasi nationalization of the companies. The nationalization itself was achieved by the left in 1982 and led gradually to a general

[99] In a vast literature I have selected Francis Lorentz, "De la volonté d'être une entreprise: Bull," in Gatty et al. *Identité*, pp. 108–112; Jocelyne Barreau and Abdelaziz Mouline, *L'industrie électronique francaise: 29 ans de relations Etat-groupes industriels (1958–1986)*, Paris, LGDJ, 1987; Kay, *Foundations*, pp. 3, 10, 11, 13, 332. Pierre Mounier-Kuhn, "Bull, a worldwide company born in Europe," *Annals of the History of Computing*, 41, 1989, pp. 279–298. Raymond-Alain Thiétart, "Les actionnaires face aux gestionnaires: le cas d'une grande entreprise," *Revue Française de Gestion*, January–February 1992, pp. 75–83. Jean-Pierre Brulé, *L'informatique malade de l'État*, Paris, Les Belles Lettres, 1993.
[100] Emmanuel Chadeau, "L'industrie aéronautique," in [Stoffaes], *L'industrie francaise*, pp. 117–128. Emmanuel Chadeau, "Contraintes technologiques et stratégies internationales: le moteur d'aviation, 1920–1970," *Entreprises et Histoire*, April 1992, pp. 61–78.
[101] Ohana, *Les banques de groupe*, pp. 115–121. Emmanuel Chadeau, ed., *L'ambition technologique: naissance d'Ariane (1969–1975)*, Paris, Rive droite, 1995. On the first mover, see Emmanuel Catta, *Victor de Metz*, Paris, Total, 1990.

merger. Its result, Usinor Sacilor, tapped on better organizational capabilities, was much more innovative and competitive than its predecessors, but had to face hard times.[102]

In the other major industries, the large French firms were generally able to maintain their competitiveness by themselves, and government played a lesser role. This was obviously the case of the automobile industry. Between 1945 and the early 1960s the two first movers pursued with success opposite policies: Renault (now state-owned), a volume strategy targeted at the lower end of the market; Peugeot, a niche strategy. From the early 1960s onward they felt strong enough to carry a full range of products. Their challengers, Citroën and Simca and, in trucks, Berliet could not survive. In 1983–1985 both companies barely escaped bankruptcy, as their organizational capabilities had deteriorated, leading to an aging of the range, a decline of the quality, and an overcapacity both in dealers and in workers. Yet both were able to recover, to improve their capabilities substantially, to move toward "lean production," and to become highly profitable. Beyond this return to organizational learning which made both firms creative organizations, two other features may be emphasized. Since the early 1960s, competition between the French car makers has coexisted with cooperation (for advanced research or for the making of major components by joint subsidiaries). Mergers, which were achieved in the 1970s, were major sources of destabilization of both companies.[103]

In rubber, the Michelin company vigorously improved its competitive position: at world level it was seventh in 1960, third in 1974, second in 1978, and first in 1989, even before taking over the Uniroyal Goodrich Tire Company in 1990. It pursued a single-minded strategy: innovative products based on technological research and economies of scale. But American and Japanese competition forced it to resort to massive lay offs, which was the price it had to pay for growing with an organization substantially unchanged since the 1960s.[104] Michelin remains, like Peugeot, a stronghold of family capitalism.

Undisputed success came in three traditional sectors which have been

[102] Philippe Mioche, "La sidérurgie et l'Etat en France des années 1940 aux années 1960," Ph.D. thesis, University Paris IV, 1992, and *Jacques Ferry et la sidérurgie française depuis la seconde guerre mondiale*, Aix, Publications de l'Université de Provence, 1993. Jean-Gustave Padioleau, *Quand la France s'enferre*, Paris, PUF, 1981. Eric Godelier, "De la stratégie locale à la stratégie globale: la formation d'une identité de groupe chez Usinor (1948–1986)," Ph.D. thesis, Ecole des Hautes Etudes en Sciences Sociales, 1995.
[103] Laux, *The European automobile industry*. Midler, *L'auto*.
[104] Alain Jemain, *Michelin. Un siècle de secrets*, Paris, Calmann-Lévy, 1982, pp. 13–23.

undergoing extensive technical change in the past three decades: glass, food and drink, and materials building. In glass, Saint-Gobain's growth did not prevent the appearance of a major technological gap vis-à-vis its British competitor Pilkington, which invented and produced the revolutionary float glass (sold from 1957 onward). The gap had two initial origins: Saint-Gobain's research department had concentrated on incremental innovation rather than on the finding of another technical system; Saint-Gobain's technical experts were skeptical about the potential of the British invention when it became known. This episode revealed two weaknesses in the company's organizational capabilities: fundamental research had been neglected in favor of applied research, and market surveys (and market research) had been underdeveloped. In the recent words of one top executive, "We produced well, but we researched and sold badly."

So, Saint-Gobain had to adapt its entire industrial strength to float glass. This immense effort was fruitful and enabled it to conquer new markets. But in the short run it made the company vulnerable. This was one of the foundations for BSN's attempt at a hostile takeover in 1968–1969, after which Saint-Gobain had to merge with the large producer of pig iron tubes, Pont-à-Mousson. The company after the merger increased its investments in research, marketing, and management and has become a rare case of a successful merger in largely unrelated businesses. The only question open to debate was whether the extent of its further diversification should be reduced.[105] During the brief period of nationalization (1982–1986), government imposed the selling of its acquisitions in computers and semiconductors. It is still an open issue.

In food and drink, except for the volume production of bulk sugar, few large companies had appeared in France. One brand new player succeeded in dominating the industry and reaching world size: BSN, now the ninth largest French industrial enterprise. It was initially a glass company, born from a merger in 1966, and immediately a challenger to the first mover Saint-Gobain. Though ten times smaller, it undertook at the end of 1968 a hostile takeover of Saint-Gobain. When this bold move failed (in February 1969), BSN embarked on an entirely opposite policy: product diversification. It decided to fill its glass bottles with mass consumption goods, the contents of which would be in its possession. This was achieved by external growth. BSN acquired successively mineral water

---

[105] Jean-Pierre Daviet, *Une multinationale.* "Intervention of Mr. Bailly," in [Stoffaes], *L'industrie*, pp. 188–189.

businesses, yogurt, pasta, sweets, mustard, champagne, biscuits, and sauces, not only in France, but also in Germany, Italy, Spain, Britain, the United States, and Japan. Its current size is now one-fourth of Nabisco and Philip Morris. In glass, its strongest organizational capabilities had been in production and finance. For its diversification into food, BSN developed its marketing resources. It adopted the divisional structure. The large sums it had to devote to research were the major reason for its aggressive multinational strategy, in order to reap the highest economies of scale possible. The larger sums needed for both research and external growth prompted in 1980–1981 the divestment of one of its early core businesses, flat glass.[106]

Cement provides an example of new technologies bringing new opportunities to be exploited by large enterprises. For the world structure of the industry radically changed in the 1960s and 1970s. The introduction of do-it-yourself concrete in the 1960s provoked a market explosion, which led to an electronic automation of the production process. Economies of scale, based on the same technical and commercial culture, led to the multinationalization of firms. These two breakthroughs enabled European enterprises to take the world leadership. There were, however, two strategies among the Europeans. The French and the Belgians practiced downstream integration (do-it-yourself concrete, prefabrication, distribution), while the British, Italians, and Germans rejected integration and focused on cement. The French leader, Lafarge, became second in the world industry, just behind a Swiss company. Other factors behind its performance were vigorous external growth, systematic closing of uncompetitive production sites, creation of an "industrial holding" at the top of its structure, and a sophisticated management of its human resources.[107] Its diversification in biotechnology did not prove successful enough and was divested.

On the whole, it seems that wherever it used or stimulated the learned organizational capabilities of large firms, the French government played a broader and more innovative role in its relationships with big business than did the German government and was more successful than those of Britain, Italy, and other European countries.

---

[106] Francis Gautier, "B₃N," in [Stoffaes], L'industrie, pp. 178–185. In 1994 BSN was renamed Danone.

[107] Léon Dubois, Lafarge-Coppée. Martine Muller and Félix Torres, L'identité. Olivier Lecerf, Au risque de gagner. Le métier de dirigeant, Paris, de Fallois, 1991. Collomb, "L'industrie européenne."

At a more general level, industrial policy has been a mixed blessing. There have been good results: reconstruction and modernization after World War II (with American financial help), the building of a nuclear energy industry (but without including the costs of decommissioning), the growth of a space industry, the catching up of French telephone and telecommunications since 1974.[108] Yet there have been characterized failures where government promoted a product or tried to reduce a French gap for purely political reasons.[109] Also the recurrent practices of subsidies to the ailing branches of the First Industrial Revolution or to their reconversion were for a long time contradictory and sometimes counterproductive.[110] Clearly, industrial policies which compensate for weaknesses do not often succeed, whereas those which stress the exploitation of distinctive capabilities may have long-term effects.[111]

The two waves of privatizations (one in 1986 involving CGE, Saint-Gobain, Matra, and the second starting in 1993 with Rhône-Poulenc and Elf) may signal the end of the postwar era where industry managers and government officials conceived of competition as a *Kriegspiel* which they might play together. They leave unchanged two major issues which appeared in this survey: the difficulties often occasioned by mergers and acquisitions, and the quasi-cyclical variations of organizational strength.[112]

CONCLUSIONS

We have stressed a number of features which account for the relatively good performance (except in the 1930s and probably most of the 1980s) of the French industry in the twentieth century: the growing number of large corporations; their larger size; the protracted but significant development of organizational capabilities, first in production and later, to a

---

[108] Pascal Griset, "Le développement du téléphone en France depuis les années 1950. Politique de recherche et recherche d'une politique," *Vingtième Siècle*, October–December 1989, pp. 41–53. Jean Bouvier and François Bloch-Lainé, *La France restaurée, 1944–1956*, Paris, Fayard, 1986. Kuisel, *Seducing the French*.

[109] Elie Cohen, *Le colbertisme high tech*, Paris, Hachette, 1992. Patrick Fridenson, "Selling the innovation: French and German color TV devices in the 1960s," *Business and Economic History*, 1991, pp. 62–68. Le Bolloc'h-Puges, *La politique industrielle*. Pierre Mounier-Kuhn, "Le Plan Calcul, Bull et l'industrie des composants: les contradictions d'une stratégie," *Revue Historique*, July–September 1994, pp. 123–153.

[110] Elie Cohen, *L'Etat brancardier*, Paris, Calmann-Lévy, 1989.

[111] Kay, *Foundations*, pp. 332–335.

[112] Jocelyne Barreau (ed.), *L'Etat entrepreneur. Nationalisation, gestion du secteur public concurrentiel, construction européenne (1982–1993)*, Paris, Editions L'Harmattan, 1990. Hervé Dumez and Alain Jeunemaitre, "Privatization in France: 1983–1993," in Vincent Wright, ed., *Privatization in Western Europe*, London, Pinter, 1994, pp. 83–104.

lesser extent, in research, marketing, and management; a specific recruitment and use of human resources; and the progress made in the direction
of an environment more favorable to industry. We have not masked,
though, the weaknesses that persist: the insufficient growth of medium-
sized enterprises, the contradictions, limitations, or excessive interventions
of government, the distribution of skills among the labor force, the long
shortage of general trading companies or of trading capabilities within
industrial firms.

Simultaneously, this chapter pleads for the recognition of the specificity
of the French response to technological change. The replacement of personal capitalism and of family firms by the managerial firm was slower
than in Germany, but most French historians would agree that this was
not a real obstacle to growth.[113] The role of government was probably
broader than in Germany, and in different directions: more government
ownership (at least from the late 1940s) and more scientific research in
state institutions (but often with insufficient synergy with industry), but
there was after 1950 a parallel commitment to the European Economic
Community. Indeed these features and others point to the persistence
of what recent business administration scholars called a French way of
working together, framed in the eighteenth century: a society cemented by
a logic of honor and differentiating strongly noble tasks and vile ones,
legitimate or nonlegitimate methods of command, the pivotal place of
the state in a society of ranks, the modest place of contractual links.[114]
The post–World War II business history of France shows that the corporations which succeeded – as in most other countries, a majority of first
movers – mixed a sense for innovation with an adaptation of French
work-related values. *Tabula rasa* was either impossible or failed.[115] Yet
most French top enterprises did not stick passively to traditional learning
bases. They were able to chose between its variants, to set aside some of
its aspects, to strengthen the potentially vital elements of their corporate

[113] Maurice Lévy-Leboyer, "The family firm in French manufacturing industry," in Akio
Okochi and Shigeaki Yasuoka, eds., *Family business in the era of industrial growth*,
Tokyo, University of Tokyo Press, 1984, and "Le patronat français, 1912–1973,"
pp. 137–188. François Caron, "L'entreprise," in Pierre Nora ed., *Les lieux de mémoire*,
3rd series: *Les France*, vol. 3, Paris, Gallimard, 1993, pp. 323–375. Emmanuel Chadeau,
"The large family firm in twentieth-century France," *Business History*, 35, October
1993.
[114] d'Iribarne, *La logique*, pp. 35–55. Philippe Jean Bernard and Jean-Pierre Daviet (eds.),
Culture d'entreprise.
[115] See the case of the Calor house appliances company, in Maurice Hamon and Félix Torres
(eds.), *Mémoires d'avenir*, Paris, Belfond, 1987.

culture, to multiply joint ventures or technological cooperation with foreign companies. Also in a number of industries – though not all – relations with suppliers shifted from a strict transaction cost pattern to a growing recognition of interdependency.[116]

Still the gap with major German firms remains high in two significant sectors: machinery and chemicals, and in the most dynamic of twentieth-century industries managerial elites have yet to complete their emancipation from the nation's government. Perhaps the recent changes in ownership – 30 percent of capital now belongs to American and British investors – and the privatizations, combined with closer European integration, will affect not only corporate governance, but also the process whereby the senior elite circulates and reproduces, or even brings into question, the "home-grown, interventionist and original" French model.[117]

Acknowledgments

My thanks to Alfred D. Chandler, Jr., Leslie Hannah, Matthias Kipping, Bruce Kogut, Alan Kramer, and Maurice Lévy-Leboyer for their comments on the first draft of this paper.

[116] Edward H. Lorenz, "Neither friends nor strangers: Informal networks of subcontracting in French industry," in Diego Gambetta (ed.), *Trust: Making and breaking cooperative relations*, Oxford, Basil Blackwell, 1988.

[117] Jonathan Charkham, *Keeping good company: A study of corporate governance in five countries*, Oxford, Oxford University Press, 1995. Hervé Dumez and Alain Jeune Maitre, "Privatizations," pp. 102–103. Denis Woronoff, *Histoire de l'industrie en France*, Paris, Le Seuil, 1994.

8

Italy: The tormented rise of organizational
capabilities between government and families

FRANCO AMATORI

THE ADVANCE OF INDUSTRIALIZATION

Italy was the first country in southern Europe to have reached a stable
stage of industrialization, a remarkable outcome given the false leaps and
the failures of other Mediterranean nations.[1] Italy started to go further
than what a historian defined as "a first coat of industrial paint" in the
1880s.[2] In that decade, in addition to the traditional industries such as
food and textiles, others such as metallurgy and chemical and mechanical
productions become "visible." Alexander Gerschenkron has calculated that
by 1887, starting from a base of 100 in 1881, the production of the textile
sector is equal to 136, food equal to 106, metallurgy is 414, mechanics
equals 185, and chemicals have reached 267.[3]

But for Italy we can really only talk of an "industrial revolution" when
we reach the period that goes from 1896 through 1914, with the period
from 1896 until 1908 having particular relevance. Again, Alexander
Gerschenkron calculates for those years an annual rate of increase in industrial production of 6.7 percent but another reliable economic historian,
Stefano Fenoaltea, writes of a 7.6 percent increase for those same years.[4]

This phase is characterized by the following elements:

A change in the industrial structure so that heavy sectors (metallurgy,
mechanics, mining) – which counted for 19.8 percent of the value of
industrial production in 1895 – have reached 30.6 percent by 1914

---

[1] See the classic study of J. Nadal, *El fracaso de la revolución industrial en España, 1814–
1913*, Ariel, Barcelona, 1975.
[2] L. Cafagna, "Profilo della storia industriale italiana", in L. Cafagna, *Dualismo e sviluppo
nella storia d'Italia*, Marsilio, Venice, 1989, p. 293.
[3] Quoted from R. Romeo, *Breve storia della grande industria in Italia*, Mondadori, Milan,
1988, p. 38.
[4] V. Zamagni, *Dalla periferia al centro*, Il Mulino, Bologna, 1990, p. 106.

A change in the structure of foreign trade with an increase of imports of
raw materials while exports of finished products grow

An original solution to the problem of energy sources, given the lack of
coal – the application of so-called white coal, hydroelectric energy

Another original solution to another serious problem created by the first
intense industrialization, the disequilibrium in the balance of payments,
given the need for imports – a solution this time found in the financial
flow provoked by the remittances of millions of Italian emigrants

Even in this phase it is not possible to speak of a "big spurt," especially
if we compare Italy with other "latecomers" such as Russia or Japan. In
this respect, it is interesting to consider the fact that in Italy in 1914 the
simple production of raw silk was almost equal to the value of all steel
products and that in the Italian industrial apparatus there were serious
absences such as the electromechanical and the organic chemical sectors.
The industrial development was very much characterized by territories. A
real industrialization took place in the northwest area of the country, the
so-called "industrial triangle" (Milan-Turin-Genoa), while there was an
industrialization more superficial in the northeast and central regions and
even weaker in the South.[5]

It is with World War I that industrialization appears to be on a road
with no return (as can be seen in Table 8.1). Thanks to orders from the
Ministry of Arms and Munitions for the "industrial mobilization," we see
a boom. At the end of the conflict, if we take a series of products considered of fundamental importance at the time (such as steel, cement,
electrical energy, automobiles, sulfuric acid, superphosphates, and artificial textile fibers), Italy can be considered the eighth most important producer in the world.[6] The war also reconfirmed the gap between North and
South.

When the inevitable postwar crisis ends in the 1920s, industrial growth
is rather substantive, with an annual average increase of 6.6 percent in the
years between 1921 and 1929, which actually reached 9.5 percent in the
period between 1921 and 1926.[7]

The tremendous world crisis of the 1930s did not sweep away much
of the solid foundation of Italian industry. On the contrary, the rebuilding
of a military apparatus in the years preceding World War II emphasized

---

[5] L. Cafagna, "Profilo", pp. 297–303, and Romeo, *Breve storia*, pp. 51–54, 67–74.
[6] V. Castronovo, *L'industria italiana dall'Ottocento ad oggi*, Mondadori, Milan, 1980,
p. 150.
[7] Ibid., p. 167.

Table 8.1. *GNP disaggregation for activity sectors 1861–1981
(constant prices 1938)*

	1861	1913	1938	1963	1981
Agriculture	46.1	37.6	26.6	16.5	6.1
Industry	18.4	24.9	30.3	49.5	37.1
Services	30.4	32.0	31.7	26.0	44.8
Public administration	5.1	5.5	11.4	8.0	12.0
Total	100%	100%	100%	100%	100%

Source: V. Zamagni, *Dalla periferia al centro*, Il Mulino, Bologna, 1990.

again the role of heavy industry. In the same period, the government's policy of "autarky" and the fragmentation of world markets did little to help Italian attempts to catch up with countries in the forefront: between 1929 and the beginning of World War II, Italian industrial production had an increase of 15 percent, for the first time since 1900, a rate which was inferior to the other nations of Western Europe.[8]

But a real takeoff happens after 1950. In the succeeding twenty years, GNP grows at a rate of almost 6 percent (5.8 in the 1950s, 5.7 in the following decade).[9] The industrial structure becomes much stronger in basic sectors such as oil and steel, and the production of durable consumer goods starts to solidify, while "light" sectors such as apparel, shoe manufacturing, and household furnishings move from their roots as "craftsmen" to true industries.

Italy enjoys a golden period in the years following the birth of the European Economic Community (1958–1962). In 1961 GNP's rate of growth reaches a record 8.6 percent. It continues on a similar path, at least during the first part of the 1960s. Italy accrues its industrial production, of which exports are an important part, and in this way the country can cover the costs of necessary imports. Notwithstanding this impressive industrial development, debt with foreign countries does not grow because of the low salaries paid. These, in addition to rendering Italian products more competitive in international markets, limit (given low consumption levels) the necessity for imports.

Even Italy was forced to suffer during the turbulent 1970s with the end of international monetary stability and the two oil shocks, a difficult

[8] Romeo, *Breve storia*, p. 152.   [9] Zamagni, *Dalla periferia*, pp. 423–424.

situation made more serious for Italy by strong social and trade union conflicts. In 1975 the country experienced negative economic growth. Nevertheless, between 1973 and 1980 the average annual rate of growth of GNP was 3.7 percent, superior to that of other European nations and the United States and equal to Japan's. Following three years of stagnation in the early 1980s, GNP proceeded to grow at an annual rate of approximately 3 percent for the remainder of the decade, among the highest in an international comparison.[10] Italy was by now a member of the "G-7", the club of the most industrialized Western nations whose policies affect the entire world economy. Nevertheless, even with such prestigious standing, the economic problems of Italy are far from being resolved. The South is still lagging far behind, serious gaps remain in the country's industrial apparatus – for instance the chemical and electronic sectors – and public spending which exceeds 50 percent of the GNP is a serious brake for general economic development.[11]

THE ACTORS

The student of Italian industry is immediately impressed by the permanent importance in the system of small businesses. In 1981 59 percent of the total labor force is employed in factories with less than 100 workers. As indicated in Table 8.2, this percentage is similar to that of Japan in approximately the same period while the same value for the United States was 23 percent, for the United Kingdom it was 25 percent, for France it was 29 percent, and for Germany it was 30 percent.[12] On the other hand, recent research on all the Italian industrial corporations in existence between 1907 and 1940 emphasized the scarce concentration of Italian industry when considered as a whole,[13] although by the 1970s the significance of the largest industrial enterprises reached an internationally comparable level (see Table 8.3).

The small dimension characterized Italian industrial structure even in

---

[10] Ibid., p. 425.

[11] For a "critique" of the Italian economy's performance in the past century, see N. Rossi and G. Toniolo, "Un secolo di sviluppo economico", in P. L. Ciocca, ed., *Il progresso economico dell'Italia*, Il Mulino, Bologna, 1994.

[12] Zamagni, *Dalla periferia*, p. 438.

[13] R. Giannetti, G. Federico, and P. A. Toninelli, "Size and Strategies of Italian Industrial Enterprises (1907–1940): Empirical Evidence and Some Conjectures", *Industrial and Corporate Change*, no. 2, 1994.

Table 8.2. *Features of the productive system for some countries*
(benchmark years)

Year and country	Firm's average dimension (number of workers)	% of workers in firms with less than 100 employees
1961		
Italy	8.4	55.3
Germany	17.3	36.8
Great Britain	85.3	18.8
Japan	16.9	n.a.
1971		
Italy	10.0	52.3
Germany	22.8	33.5
Great Britain	60.7	24.7
Japan	16.8	53.6
1981		
Italy	9.3	59.3
Germany	28.4	29.9
Great Britain	56.8	24.6
Japan	14.9	50.0

Source: F. Onida (ed.), *L'industria italiana nella competizione internazionale*, INCE, Milan, 1988.

Table 8.3. *Big business in Italy (percentage of sales held by the top 100 companies)*

Year	Sales/total manufacturing (current prices; percentiles)
1971	43.3
1976	38.6
1981	49.2
1986	38.9
1991	40.1

Sources: Mediobanca, *Le principali società italiane*, Milan, various years; Centro Studi Confindustria, *Economia in cifre*, SIPI, Rome, 1985, 1986.

the golden years of the "economic miracle" between the 1950s and 1960s.[14] But the real moment of glory for small enterprise in Italy took place in the stormy 1970s when it appeared as a last resort for the nation's economy.[15] It was then that the country appeared to rediscover a form of industrial organization theorized by Alfred Marshall – the district, oriented toward the production of one single product, a goal often obtained through a division of labor (a deverticalization) among small companies.[16] To the researchers it was clear that small business and districts had a centennial history, a long learning process, and a slow strengthening with the passage from craftsmanship to industry.[17] The small Italian enterprise became a model of "flexible capitalism" at an international level.[18]

This glorification of small firms in Italy is anything but new. We had a glamorous example in this respect immediately after World War II in the debate of the Economic Committee during the Constitutional Assembly. Here prominent business leaders, among them the president of Confindustria (the Italian Confederation of Industry), insisted that Italy should carefully avoid the threat of big business. The most eloquent declaration during the debate came from the managing director of the automobile company Alfa Romeo, Pasquale Gallo, who proposed that the only viable strategy for the entire Italian automobile industry was that of "organized craftsmanship" based on the Swiss model. He is quoted as having said "we think of having with Fiat a 'large' corporation; instead Fiat is a small American enterprise. . . . Alfa Romeo has a classic, exceptional product. . . . Americans are not interested in small companies but in large ones. Alfa Romeo can be rescued."[19]

But Pasquale Gallo and the other industrialists who agreed with his vision of the economic future of Italy were wrong. Instead, the person

[14] In 1961, the average dimension of Italian works, in terms of employment, was 8.40 workers. See F. Onida, ed., *L'industria italiana nella competizione internazionale*, Istituto Nazionale Commercio Estero, Milan, 1988.

[15] See, for instance, N. Colajanni, *L'economia italiana dal dopoguerra ad oggi*, Sperling e Kupfer, Milan, 1990, pp. 230–233.

[16] See G. Beccatini, ed., *Mercato e forze locali: il distretto industriale*, Il Mulino, Bologna, 1987, and G. Fuà and C. Zacchia, eds., *Industrializzazione senza fratture*, Il Mulino, Bologna, 1983.

[17] See, e.g., F. Amatori, "Per un dizionario biografico degli imprenditori marchigiani," in S. Anselmi, ed., *Le Marche*, Einaudi, Turin, 1987.

[18] See M. J. Piore and C. F. Sabel, *The Second Industrial Divide*, Basic Books, New York, 1984, and M. E. Porter, *The Competitive Advantage of Nations*, Free Press, New York, 1990, pp. 421–453.

[19] Quoted from G. Sapelli, "L'organizzazione del lavoro all'Alfa Romeo, 1930–1951. Contraddizioni e superamento del 'modello svizzero,'" *Storia in Lombardia*, no. 2, 1987, p. 111.

who better foresaw the future was Fiat's president, Vittorio Valletta, who strongly believed in mass production.[20] In fact, Italy as a nation wishing to catch up with the center of world capitalism could not avoid the impact of the Second Industrial Revolution and of its logics in economic and organizational terms.[21] Steel, heavy machinery, transportation equipment, electric and chemical industries (and we can also add mass distribution) – that is, the core sectors – were as concentrated in Italy as in the world's leading nations. In addition, first movers, even if through changes provoked during the decades by the process of mergers and acquisitions, permanently dominated their sectors. The companies which are today considered to be the most important Italian corporations were all founded between the end of the nineteenth and the beginning of this century. As happened everywhere in the industrialized world, the first big businesses were the railway corporations (e.g., the Società Italiana per le Strade Ferrate Meridionali).[22] By 1905 the railways were nationalized and the indemnities to the companies were utilized, in a good-sized portion, to finance the growing electric industry. Not surprisingly, the electric companies from that time to the early 1960s, when in its turn the electric industry is nationalized, are the core of Italian economic power. Already in the 1920s, the electric industry had attained a nominal share of capital equal to 20 percent of the entire capital of Italian corporations and Edison, the largest electric company, controlled 56 of the 200 companies operating in the industry sector.[23] Eventually Edison gradually changed into a conglomerate and after World War II directed its investments toward the chemical industry. In fact, following the nationalization of the electric sectors between 1964 and 1966, of the two major electric enterprises, first SADE and then Edison itself merged with the most important Italian chemical company, Montecatini. In the end it appears to have become a sort of continuous chain: from railways to the electric industry and then to the chemical industry, even if the final passage proved to be rather unsuccessful, given the poor performance of Montedison, as the new giant in the chemical sector was named.

Montecatini had been founded in 1888 as a mining company.[24] As producer of pyrites, on the eve of World War I the company embarked on

---

[20] V. Castronovo, *L'industria italiana*, p. 280.

[21] In this case the compulsory reference is to the work of Alfred D. Chandler, Jr.

[22] See M. Merger, "Origini e sviluppo del management ferroviario italiano," *Annali di Storia dell'Impresa*, no. 8, 1992.

[23] On Edison, see B. Bezza, ed., *Energia e sviluppo*, Einaudi, Turin, 1986.

[24] On Montecatini, see F. Amatori and B. Bezza, eds., *Montecatini. Capitoli di storia di una grande impresa*, Il Mulino, Bologna, 1990.

a strategy of vertical integration to produce sulfuric acid. In 1920, thanks to the profits garnered during the war and to the support of Italy's major banks, Montecatini absorbed the two most important producers of fertilizers, Unione Concimi and Colla e Concimi. In the course of the 1920s the company acquired an unquestionable supremacy within the Italian chemical industry, thanks to the production of nitrogen fertilizers through the original Fauser electrolytic process.

The other important chemical company Snia Viscosa,[25] dominant in the field of rayon, attained momentum in the 1920s when it was one of the world leaders for this same product. Snia was the creation of a Piedmontese empire builder, Riccardo Gualino, who eventually succeeded in involving the company in his financial troubles. By 1930, control of Snia had passed to the British Courtaulds while management remained in Italian hands with Franco Marinotti leading the company. In recent years Snia, through complicated vicissitudes, has moved from being under the control of Montedison to that of Fiat.

The modern steel industry in Italy was started in 1884 with the birth of Terni,[26] the first Italian company to use the Martin-Siemens process. Terni failed to build an integrated steel cycle. In 1899 Elba, a producer of cast iron from blast furnaces, was founded. Shortly thereafter Terni and Elba were united together in the so-called steel trust, while in 1910 the Roman financier Max Bondi was able to build up the first integral cycle steelworks in the Tuscan town of Piombino. Bondi succeeded in doing something more. During World War I, in 1918, thanks to a series of financial alliances, he reached his goal of unifying under one corporation, Ilva, all the integrated cycle Italian steel plants. Three years later Bondi went bankrupt due to an unwise policy of diversification which revealed him to be more of a speculator than an industrial builder. Nevertheless, his enterprises became the core of what later would become under government control the Italian sector of large steel plants. Another player in the steel industry was Falck, a successful family-run company in the Milan area which produced steel from scrap iron and has permanently held since the 1920s a share of 10 to 15 percent of the Italian market.[27]

[25] For the SNIA case, see Romeo, *Breve storia*, and N. Colajanni, *Il capitalismo senza capitale*, Sperling e Kupfer, Milan, 1991, pp. 26, 166–168.

[26] For Terni, see F. Bonelli, *Lo sviluppo di una grande impresa in Italia*, Einaudi, Turin, 1975.

[27] On the Italian steel sector, AA. VV., *La siderurgia italiana dall'Unità ad oggi*, CLUSF, Florence, 1978; F. Bonelli, ed., *Acciaio per l'industrializzazione*, Einaudi, Turin, 1982; M. Balconi, *La siderurgia italiana 1945–1990*, Il Mulino, Bologna, 1991.

The panorama of Italian big business cannot be considered complete without a few more names. First, Fiat,[28] the automobile manufacturer founded in 1899 in Turin. By the 1920s Fiat controlled almost 90 percent of the Italian automobile production and today the company is the center of the most important private industrial concern of the nation. Another company which must be mentioned is Pirelli,[29] the first producer of rubber in Italy. Founded in 1872, by the beginning of the new century the company progressively moved away from telegraph and submarine cables to tires. Olivetti,[30] founded in the Piedmont town of Ivrea at the beginning of the 1900s, acquired in a short time a clear predominance in the field of office machinery. Ansaldo[31] in Genoa and Breda[32] in Milan have become over the years leaders in the heavy machinery industry; Bocconi emerges as the first and most important department store in the country, a family enterprise which in 1917 was taken over by a group of businessmen from Lombardy and Piedmont who eventually changed the company's name to La Rinascente. At the beginning of the 1930s, a group of managers from within the company gave birth to another important mass retailer, Standa.[33]

By the eve of World War II, the scenario of big industry in Italy, that is the one that via mergers and acquisitions will bring us to the contemporary period, is almost complete. The only major player absent is Ente Nazionale Idrocarburi (ENI),[34] the petrochemical group founded at the beginning of the 1950s by the state-owned company entrepreneur, Enrico Mattei.

A "POLITICAL CAPITALISM"

In the end, the morphogenesis of Italy's industrial system does not appear to be very different from that of other advanced nations. As in the central

---

[28] On Fiat, see V. Castronovo, *Agnelli*, UTET, Turin, 1971; P. Bairati, *Valletta*, UTET, Turin, 1983; Progetto Archivio Storico Fiat, *I primi quindici anni della Fiat*, 2 vols., Angeli, Milan, 1987; *Fiat 1915–1930. Verbali dei consigli di amministrazione*, 2 vols., Fabbri, Milan, 1991; and *Fiat 1899–1930. Storia e documenti*, Fabbri, Milan, 1991.

[29] For more on Pirelli, AA. VV., *Dalla prima guerra mondiale all'autunno caldo*, Angeli, Milan, 1985, vol. 1, and P. Bolchini, *Il gruppo Pirelli-Dunlop: gli anni più lunghi*, Angeli, Milan, 1985, vol. 2; B. Bezza, "L'attività multinazionale della Pirelli," *Società e Storia*, no. 35, 1987.

[30] On Olivetti, see B. Caizzi, *Camillo e Adriano Olivetti*, UTET, Turin, 1962.

[31] On Ansaldo, see M. Doria, *Ansaldo. L'impresa e lo stato*, Angeli, Milan, 1989.

[32] On Breda, see AA. VV., *Dalla Società italiana Ernesto Breda alla finanziaria Ernesto Breda, 1886–1986*, Pizzi, Milan, 1986.

[33] On Bocconi, Rinascente e Standa, F. Amatori, *Proprietà e direzione. La Rinascente 1917–1969*, Angeli, Milan, 1989.

[34] On ENI, M. Colitti, *Energia e sviluppo in Italia. La vicenda di Enrico Mattei*, De Donato, Bari, 1979, and G. Sapelli and F. Carnevali, *Uno sviluppo tra politica e strategia. ENI (1953–1985)*, Angeli, Milan, 1992.

nations of modern capitalism, there are core sectors and others which are considered peripheral, even if the latter often have more significance in Italy. What is different for Italy is the group of actors and their strategies. Given the timing of Italy's entry onto the scene of industrialization and its endowment of resources, the country appears an ideal ground for testing the theory of Alexander Gerschenkron who, in order to explain the development of latecomer countries, considers "substitutive factors" as compared with "entrepreneurs," the main characters of the classic British case.[35]

Gerschenkron's theory that "Bank" and "State" are protagonists for latecomers seems rather convincing for Italy if we can put emphasis on the role of the state. It is true that the so-called German model of the "mixed bank" was decisive between the beginning of the century and the great crisis of the 1930s in promoting and sustaining the most important industrial initiatives of the country. But it is also equally correct to state that the bank always had the economic policy of the government as its bottom line and, above all, the bank often saw its industrial initiatives rescued by the government.

The student of modern Italy's economic history who defined the Italian model as a "precocious State capitalism" was right.[36] De facto the government became the most important economic actor in the country immediately after Unification because of fiscal drag, the construction (in this way fiscal drag was utilized) of fundamental infrastructures such as railways, and the support of business through orders. In the 1880s it was the government which fostered a real infraction of the mechanisms of market economy so as to channel the country toward the industrialization process. Up to that point the Italian economy had been based on agriculture and its exports. Both were dramatically challenged during the 1880s by the flood of agricultural products from overseas made possible by the revolution in transportation. The substantial drop in the prices of agricultural products rendered obsolete a model of economic development which had been valid in Italy since the beginning of the eighteenth century. It was now possible to respond to the emerging challenge with consistent political choices intended to direct the country toward industrialization.

In this period the word "industrialization" was synonymous with the

---

[35] A. Gerschenkron, *Economic Backwardness in Historical Perspective*, Harvard University Press, Cambridge, MA, 1962.

[36] F. Bonelli, "Il capitalismo italiano. Linee generali di interpretazione," in AA. VV. *Storia d'Italia. Annali I. Dal feudalismo al capitalismo*, Einaudi, Turin, 1978, p. 1204.

word "steel" meaning that decisions had to be (1) protective tariffs in favor
of cast iron and steel products; (2) convincing efforts so that national railways and shipyards would buy Italian made steel; and (3) privileges for
Italian steel companies in the use of local iron ore. The government did
this and something more. In 1884 it promoted the birth of an enterprise,
Terni (taking its name from the town near Rome where it was located),
to become Italy's largest steel producer. The government largely financed
the purchase of the machinery and, as was mentioned previously, set up
tariffs intended to discourage steel imports, and guaranteed orders from
shipyards and railroads. The entrepreneur entrusted with the project was
Vincenzo Stefano Breda (not by chance a businessman involved in major
public works projects financed by the government), who envisioned an
audacious plan to build up an integrated cycle steel production process,
the only mass-producer of steel in Italy.

Breda, however, underestimated the technical, financial, and organizational complexity of his project. In addition, the entire affair was not
lacking in speculative aspects. Thus the firm, unable to respect contracts
signed with the navy for the supply of battleship armor, found itself on
the brink of bankruptcy in 1887, only three years after its founding. The
government, however, was committed to a policy aimed at self-sufficiency
in steel production and, therefore, intervened and rescued the company.
The navy paid in advance for 2,500 tons of battleship armor and the Banca
Nazionale, through the distribution of new paper money, granted additional loans. This episode, not an isolated event, is critical to understanding the country as it demonstrated that in Italy a company considered
strategic for the industrial national apparatus could enjoy a financial
protective network.

In the decades between the beginning of the century and World War
II, the government supported big business through orders. Excluding the
obvious, such as the periods of the two wars, it is enough to remember
that two enterprises such as Ansaldo and Breda (Ernesto Breda, not to
be confused with Vincenzo Stefano, the founder of Terni) in the early
years of the century owe their fortunes to the orders of the army and the
nationalized railways.[37] In addition, the government created special institutions to finance the electric and chemical industries.[38] But the most
typical Italian characteristic of government intervention was the use of

[37] D. Bigazzi, "Grandi imprese e concentrazioni finanziarie," in AA. VV., *Storia della società italiana. L'Italia di Giolitti*, vol. 20, Teti, Milan, 1981, pp. 102–103.
[38] Bonelli, "Il capitalismo italiano," pp. 1232, 1234.

"rescues." If in 1887 the State had arranged the rescue of a large corporation, by 1911, under the aegis of the Banca d'Italia (central bank), the entire
steel sector (whose crisis risked ruining the major banks of the country)
was the recipient of the same cure.[39] In 1922 it was the turn of the industrial firms controlled by a big bank, Banca Italiana di Sconto.[40] Among
these firms was Ansaldo which had become with World War I the first
industrial concern of the nation. A historically significant date in this long
practice of rescuing can be considered June 24, 1937, when IRI (Istituto
di Ricostruzione Industriale) was declared a permanent institution.

IRI was a public holding company formed four years earlier in order
to free the Italian banking system from its close ties with the big industry,
which threatened to sweep it away and to create economic chaos in the
country. IRI had two major tasks: to grant long-term loans to the companies which had been affected by the Depression and to take over the
industrial securities held by the country's three major banks (Banca
Commerciale Italiana, Credito Italiano, and Banco di Roma) and eventually sell them to private buyers. It soon became apparent that it would
be impossible to achieve the latter goal as there were not, in Italy, economic forces (with the exception of the government) which could not only
purchase the banks' shareholdings in sectors such as steel, shipyards, and
public utilities but could also finance the continual investments required
by the same. Therefore, IRI had to be more than a temporary owner. It
was forced, instead, to provide a unified management of a consistent
segment of the national economy. On the eve of World War II, IRI controlled 80 percent of the production in shipbuilding, 45 percent in steel,
39 percent in the electrical mechanical industry, and 23 percent in the
mechanical industry.[41]

But the importance of the government's economic behavior goes beyond
its quantitative weight. It deeply influenced entrepreneurial choices and
actions. While in the Chandlerian model regarding the most advanced
countries a firm grows primarily for economic reasons (i.e., to cut costs
per unit), in the Italian experience we often encounter firms which grew
for strategic reasons (i.e., to find themselves in a better position to bargain
with the political powers). At the beginning of the century the leaders of
the steel trust (which included Terni and Elba) and Max Bondi knew

---

[39] F. Bonelli, *La crisi del 1907*, Fondazione Einaudi, Turin, 1971, and Bigazzi, "Grandi
imprese," pp. 98–99.
[40] E. Cianci, *Nascita dello Stato Imprenditore in Italia*, Mursia, Milan, 1977, pp. 43–58.
[41] Romeo, *Breve storia*, p. 135.

perfectly well that their intention of enlarging production capacity was economically irrational but they also realized that greater growth would guarantee preferable treatment from the government for their own companies.[42] Pio and Mario Perrone, leaders of Ansaldo, wanted to create (both before as well as after World War I) a giant vertically integrated enterprise that could serve the country in times of war as well as peace and which would be able "to produce and to sell the finished products of a powerful industrial nation: electric systems from telephones to streetcars and electrified railways; vehicles from automobiles to trucks and airplanes; ships of every dimension and category for the high seas."[43] Since the government was its principal customer, and Ansaldo embodied a lasting national interest, the Perrones and their technocrats considered it acceptable to make long-range plans that the state would then be obliged to protect from eventual market fluctuations.

In the 1920s Terni pursued a strategy of diversification, becoming the most important producer of electric power in central Italy and also expanding its activities into the electrochemical sector. Even then the link with the government remained essential for the company's welfare. There was a sort of negotiation: Terni would continue to sustain the burden of military steel production, even in very difficult times, but the government was forced to promise profitable conditions for the development of Terni's new activities, setting up a favorable regulation for the use of public waters and assigning to Terni an adequate position in the national chemical cartels. Montecatini had to undertake huge investments (hydroelectric plants) in the 1920s to develop the Fauser method in order to produce nitrogen fertilizers. To justify the investment, Montecatini had to have the full domain of the domestic market. Also in this case there was a *do ut des*: the fascist government issued a strong protective tariff in 1931 but at the same time, shortly after, "invited" the company to rescue numerous chemical and mining firms with consequences for Montecatini that in the new climate of the 1950s would be fatal. In the end, if American capitalism can be defined as "managerial," the British version as "personal," and German as "cooperative," it does not seem excessive to term Italian capitalism as "political."[44] Incidentally it is interesting to note that the

---

[42] Bigazzi, "Grandi imprese," pp. 87–98.
[43] R. Webster, "La tecnocrazia italiana e i sistemi industriali verticali: il caso dell'Ansaldo (1914–1921)," *Storia Contemporanea*, no. 2, 1978, p. 227.
[44] A. D. Chandler, Jr., with T. Hikino, *Scale and Scope: The Dynamics of Industrial Capitalism*, Harvard University Press, Cambridge, MA, 1990.

Italian interventionist government forgot some tasks that should belong to it: no form of antitrust regulation whatsoever and very little fostering of research for industry.[45]

GOVERNMENT INTERVENTION: SUCCESSES

The birth of the "state entrepreneur" was probably inevitable since Italy had to resolve a crucial point as it was the only industrialized European nation where, from the beginning of its economic development, the industrial investments far exceeded private savings power as reflected in the issuing of securities. This lag had to be filled in some way. Private capitalism was unquestionably a fundamental component of the national economy, but it also proved to be unable to bear by itself the cost of sectors considered essential for an industrial nation. Furthermore, the worldwide economic depression of the 1930s was unable to make up for the lack of private initiative with the intervention of international capital. No other alternative remained but the direct action of the government.

But if state intervention was a necessity, it was also possible to say that, especially in the period after World War II, in some circumstances there were good results. Intervention was not limited to the administration of what already existed, but it was also deeply innovative. The two most significant cases in this respect were the steel and petrochemicals sectors. In the first half of the century, steel was probably Italy's most serious industrial problem. After Terni's failure to build up its integrated cycle plant that was intended to be Italy's only mass-producer, there was a proliferation of steelworks absolutely disproportionate to the limited domestic market. The crisis of the sector, especially for Ilva, its most important player, was particularly apparent in the 1930s. At the beginning of this period in Sofindit (the holding company which oversaw the industrial shareholdings of the Banca Commerciale Italiana, the bank which controlled Ilva), there was a group of managers firmly intent on creating a modern steel industry in Italy. Their leader, Oscar Sinigaglia, conceived a plan based on three points: (1) the creation of a new, large, complete-cycle plant in Genoa able to supply the most industrialized area of the country, (2) rigorous productive specializations of all the other factories and modernization of techniques and organization, and (3) a shut down of the

---

[45] In this respect, see as an example, V. Zamagni, "L'industria chimica in Italia dalle origini agli anni '50," in Amatori and Bezza, *Montecatini*.

old and inefficient plants and dismissal of unnecessary personnel. Sinigaglia
anticipated that the workers laid off would be absorbed by the growing
machinery industry, which at that point enjoyed the supply of cheaper
steel. His central idea was that a large steel sector in Italy could justify its
existence only by being competitive at the international level. Sinigaglia
tried to rationalize the sector in 1933 when he was named president of
Ilva. But he was soon forced to resign due to a conflict with the old company's management which strongly believed in protectionism, cartels, and
orders from the government. Sinigaglia's struggle was taken over by his
pupil, Agostino Rocca, who in 1937 was elected chief executive officer
of Finsider, IRI's steel holding company. In fact, after serious battles with
the old management and with some of the private steel companies such
as Falck and Fiat, Rocca was able to build a complete-cycle plant at
Cornegliano near Genoa. Nevertheless, the project had some technical
flaws and perished in 1943 when the German army completely dismantled the works. Sinigaglia returned at the end of the war as the president
of Finsider, intent on materializing his own plan (notwithstanding strong
opposition by the leftist parties and unions) which would utilize ERP
funds. In 1953, the year of Sinigaglia's death, the Cornigliano plant was
fully operative. Italy, which had never exceeded an output of 3 million
tons of steel, reached by 1960 an annual output of 8.2 million tons,
moving from ninth to the sixth position in the world. Especially important was that under Sinigaglia a cohesive, competent, agressive managerial
team (which was also familiar with American industrial practices) emerged.
Cornigliano's inner organization was designed by the American consultancy, Booz-Allen and Hamilton, and hundreds of workers and engineers
received their training at ARMCO's plant in Middletown, Ohio.[46]

The oil problem is a more recent issue for Italy, when compared
with the steel industry. In 1926 the government founded AGIP (Azienda
Generale Italiana Petroli), a company intended to research, process, and
sell oil. AGIP had the merit of forming a group of highly specialized technicians but business-wise it was not a great success. By the end of World
War II the government decided to liquidate the company as a residue of
the fascist regime. But the decision was completely overthrown by Enrico
Mattei, the executive in charge of closing down the company. From the

[46] See F. Amatori, "Cicli produttivi, tecnologie, organizzazione del lavoro. La siderurgia a
ciclo integrale dal piano autarchico alla creazione dell'Italsider (1937–1961)," *Ricerche
Storiche*, no. 3, 1980, and the more recent G. L. Osti with R. Ranieri, *L'industria di Stato
dall'ascesa al degrado*, Il Mulino, Bologna, 1993, chs. 2 and 4.

experiences Mattei had acquired prior to entering public life, he held the strong conviction that there was a need for an active role of the government in the economy. Mattei had experienced the life of the emigrant when the 1929 Depression compelled him to move from a small town in central Italy (where he had become the general manager of its largest factory, a tannery, by his early twenties) to Milan. In the Lombard metropolis he soon developed a successful chemical firm which was nevertheless affected by the difficulties (typical of other Italian companies in the field) of its supplies of raw materials, controlled by multinationals. Thus, he was attracted by the theories of economic nationalism but, at the same time, adverse to the fascist use of nationalistic concepts aimed more toward achieving a superficial grandeur than at creating consistent national prosperity. Familiarity with the progressive Lombard Catholicism formed his cultural and political ideas based on social justice, ideals that were strengthened by his struggle during the Resistance as a leader of the Christian Democrat partisans.

From these influences and experiences, Mattei drew a conception of the government undertaking broad economic action to overcome Italy's historical backwardness, that is, its inferiority in comparison with the big industrialized countries and the poor living conditions of a large segment of the population. Such an action had to be free from any bureaucratic burdens. It would utilize the most advanced techniques, the finest managerial skills, and, above all, the most talented entrepreneurs available. To this it was necessary to assure the required flexibility: the economic risks and even the aggressive lobby toward political power inevitably connected with the entrepreneurial activity were justified in Mattei's mind by the interest of the majority of the people and the consent of a wide range of political forces.

It is not feasible in the limits of this chapter to follow the complicated story of Enrico Mattei from his appointment as "commissary" at AGIP in 1945 to his death in a plane crash in 1962 at the peak of his career. I will, rather, deal with some of the crucial aspects of Mattei's strategy. After having greatly increased AGIP's capacity in mining research and distribution of natural gas in the Po Valley, following a tough political battle, Mattei obtained from the government the monopoly on these activities. Consistent with his concept of public interest, Mattei did not take advantage of this situation by raising prices but was still able to guarantee financial independence to the company. Starting from this basis, when AGIP became part of the larger holding ENI, he attempted to build up a vertically integrated oil company. ENI already owned an oil distribution network which drew its supply from American and British multinationals. Mattei looked for new suppliers and started new ventures with the producing nations for oil mining in order to overcome the initially inferior position and reach a backward integration. The limits of the Italian oil market and the political issue of increasing employment in southern Italy pushed ENI into the chemical sector. Here, starting from the basis of natural gas, Mattei attained a major success by building up a petrochemical plant in Ravenna to an adequate scale dimension which, de facto, was able to put an end to the quasi monopoly previously enjoyed by Montecatini in the field of nitrogen fertilizers. Mattei, however, was not interested in pursuing diversification beyond a certain point, recognizing that it could become a serious source of weakness for his creation. By the beginning of the 1960s the image of ENI was that of a pivotal element of the "Italian economic miracle," a company run in the best interest of the nation.

GOVERNMENT INTERVENTION: FAILURES

The positive results of government intervention cannot be denied and they form an integral part of the very successful performance of the Italian economy in the 1950s and 1960s. It is also clear that we have often seen good results which are due to the "private initiatives" of "public entrepreneurs." There was not much coordination within the system of state-owned enterprises. For example, at the end of an intense decade, Mattei's goal was to integrate within one corporation the nation's public energy policy, including electric and nuclear energy. Such an ambitious project was defeated on the one side by the opposition of leftist parties which feared an excessive concentration of power and, on the other side, by the lobby of the electric industry which fought to avoid expropriation. It is interesting to consider the fact that the latter group also included IRI's electric holding company. Discussing the Italian government's policy of intervention, the scholar Franco Bonelli rightfully talked of "capitalisms of state,"[47] while to express the same concept Giuliano Amato (a former Italian prime minister but also an excellent academic interested in relations between business and government) used the expression "liberal protectionism," meaning that government intervention in Italy's economy was hardly coordinated and harmonized in a plan of economic development for the country.[48]

---

[47] Bonelli, "Il capitalismo italiano," p. 1251.
[48] G. Amato, ed., *Il governo dell'industria in Italia*, Il Mulino, Bologna, 1972, pp. 15–17.

In any event, the government was not an absent shareholder. It is true that Alberto Beneduce, the economic advisor of Mussolini who designed IRI's structure, had no desire of nationalizing the entire economy but was intent on creating a system of enterprises able to survive successfully in a competitive environment. Nevertheless, there was a chain of command and the politicians were on top. After World War II, with the end of fascism, IRI was on the verge of being dismantled. But since its existence was solidly rooted in Italian economic history, it was preserved and, with the arrival of Mattei's ENI, in 1956 the Ministry of State Shareholdings was created. The ministry fully controlled public holdings such as IRI and ENI and in the following years added others including EFIM (primarily heavy machinery) and EGAM (mining). In turn, the public holdings controlled partially (but always for more than 50 percent) their sector holdings, which in turn controlled the operating companies, all of whom eventually referred to the holding's management and the ministry in the final analysis. This pyramidlike system reconfirmed the role of command of the politicians – something especially dangerous in a political system such as Italy's, in which an American-style change in the "spoil system" was impossible since the leading opposition force (the Communist Party) was permanently excluded from the government. At a point in the mid-1950s, the secretary-general of the Christian Democrats, the leading political party, even theorized the necessity for his party to glean resources from state-owned enterprises so that it could be independent from the support of private business.[49] The commands of political power – for example, a famous legislative bill in 1957 which obliged state-owned companies to set up 40 percent of their new investments in the southern part of the country – provoked the so-called "improper financial burdens" for which the parliament had to compensate with an endowment fund (i.e., government financing outside the normal channels of the financial market). In spite of the existence of this additional funding, it was very difficult for management to operate in a situation dominated by external constraints, and in the end it proved impossible to distinguish management inefficiency from objective difficulties.[50]

In this way, even what seemed a consolidated success turned into a failure. After the excellent results of the "Sinigaglia plan," the leading group of Finsider, instead of reinforcing and modernizing its existing

---

[49] N. Kogan, *L'Italia del dopoguerra*, Laterza, Bari, 1969, pp. 166–167.
[50] See P. Saraceno, *Il sistema delle imprese a partecipazione statale nell'esperienza italiana*, Giuffrè, Milan, 1975, pp. 58–70.

plants (which would have been the most logical choice in economic terms), chose at the beginning of the 1960s to build up a new complete cycle plant in the southern city of Taranto which would become the largest Italian steel plant. The reasoning behind the choice to expand production capacities is found in the research of political consensus, which, in its turn, is bound to an increase in employment levels. To reach this goal, Taranto expanded essentially cheap mass production, when the international situation of the steel sector in the 1970s and 1980s would have required a contraction in production capacities and the production of specialized steel characterized by high added value. In her study of the Italian steel industry between 1945 and 1990, Margherita Balconi writes of an "occult" and "superior" board of directors at Finsider composed of the representatives of political parties.[51] This "hidden" board of directors in the second half of the 1960s found a link to the management with a group led by Alberto Capanna who defeated the old group formed by Sinigaglia. The outcome was a disaster. By the mid-1970s, under the pressure of unions and political parties, Finsider even accepted the prospect of initiating construction of another complete-cycle plant in Gioia Tauro, near Reggio Calabria. Reality was stronger than politics and the plant was never finished and never produced even a pound of steel but the waste of monies was substantial. In 1988 Finsider was de facto bankrupt and IRI's steel activities had been put under the old name of Ilva. Today for the Italian steel sector there is a new key decision maker – the European Economic Community – which imposes precise limits to national production capacities.

The story of the past thirty years of ENI has many similarities with that of Finsider. Because ENI was more involved in the chemical sector and also in this field there was a disproportion between production capacities and market necessities in the 1960s, ENI decided to take control of the "sick giant" of the chemical industry, Montedison, in 1968. The government soon intervened and put a halt to the operation because the common political judgment was that in this way the balance between public and private capitalism would have been altered. It was decided to create a syndicate for the control of Montedison but a good part of ENI's shareholdings were kept out of the syndicate. In this way the rationalization of the sector was impossible. At the end of the 1970s another political

<hr>

[51] Balconi, *La siderurgia italiana*, p. 17. The most important pages on this topic can be found in G. L. Osti, *L'industria di Stato*, chs. 5 and 7.

command imposed that ENI take over all the "smoking ruins" of the Italian chemical industry, the result of the failure of companies such as Societá Italiana Resine (SIR), Liquigas, and parts of Montedison itself: in their strategies of expanding plants, the behavior of these companies was quite similar to that of the steel tycoons at the beginning of the century.[52] But the government did not impose on ENI only the chemical "ruins." In 1962 ENI was forced to take over an old textile company, Lanerossi, for "social" reasons. Lanerossi was, in its turn, the leader of another group of inefficient companies. As the industry was completely unrelated to ENI's traditional interests, Mattei's creation had become more a "public holding for economic development" than a true corporation.[53]

Nowadays, the crisis "formula" of government intervention begun in the early 1930s has an element of common sense. The Ministry of State Shareholdings has been dismantled, public holdings such as EGAM and EFIM have been liquidated, a process of privatizing IRI's companies has been initiated (an example is Alfa Romeo, bought out by Fiat), and the same IRI and ENI have been transformed into common corporations eventually open to private shareholders. The government has abolished the executive committees of the boards of directors of ENI and IRI which had been filled with representatives of the various political parties. Decisions such as these have been welcomed by commentators and public opinion in general. But no one can deny that it will be difficult to find private shareholders interested in debt-ridden corporations such as IRI and ENI. It will be equally difficult, after years of a less than correct relationship between politics and management, to render the latter competitive in an unprotected market.[54]

PRIVATE BIG BUSINESS AND ITS LIMITS

It would be misleading to think that the entire system of Italian big business is strictly dependent on the government. Certainly public policy is important for any large enterprise that will always search out protective tariffs, orders, and public financing. Nevertheless, a good portion of large

---

[52] See G. F. Lepore Dubois and C. Sonzogno, *L'impero della chimica*, Newton Compton, Rome, 1990, and A. Marchi and R. Marchionatti, *Montedison (1966–1989)*, Angeli, Milan, 1992.

[53] F. Carnevali, "Il gruppo ENI dalle origini al 1985," in Sapelli and Carnevali, *Uno sviluppo tra politica e strategia. ENI (1953–1985)*, p. 100.

[54] See as an example the article of B. Visentini, "L'oscuro futuro degli enti di stato," *La Repubblica*, August 12, 1992, p. 1.

Table 8.4. *Distribution of the top 100 companies by industry sectors,*
1966–1990 (percentage)

	1966	1970	1975	1980	1984	1990
Trade	7	13	13	15	4	9
Foods	11	9	10	9	7	7
Chemicals, rubber, pharmaceuticals	11	12	13	10	17	15
Mechanicals, machinery, vehicles	21	13	13	13	18	18
Metals	9	8	7	10	8	7
Oil	15	14	13	12	17	15
Textiles	5	5	3	3	—	1
Electrical machinery, electronics, & similar	—	10	11	10	9	10
Others	21	16	17	18	20	18
Total	100	100	100	100	100	100

Source: Mediobanca, *Le principali società italiane*, Milan, various years.

Italian firms – and many of those large enterprises are concentrated in capital-intensive industries as is the case in many other industrialized nations (see Table 8.4) – owes its existence to the continuous engagement in the three-pronged investments in production, in the integration of production and distribution, and in the enrollment and promotion of good management. In the final analysis, this is what is behind the capacity to cope with the challenges of the market.

In this respect, the most significant case is that of Fiat, today Italy's largest private corporation (see Table 8.5). When the company was founded in 1899, it was well endowed with capital and also supported by the finest members of Turin's aristocracy and business community, but it was not superior to firms such as Itala, SPA, and Isotta Fraschini, which, like Fiat, were eager to assume supremacy in the Italian automobile industry. The key to Fiat's success was the ability of its management group and, especially, its central figure, Giovanni Agnelli, to understand the significance of the urgent necessity to integrate vertically both in range of production (from foundries to chassis manufacturing) as well as that of production with distribution and also the investment of managerial resources in technical, financial, and commercial areas. It is the higher degree of integration,

Table 8.5. *Italian big business in an international perspective*
(ranking of the major Italian corporations vis-à-vis the world's
200 largest corporations) (benchmark years)

Year and companies	Sales (in US$ 000s)	Ranking
1959		
Fiat	700,800	74
Montecatini	471,513	133
Pirelli	411,200	173
1969		
Montedison	2,483,200	42
Fiat	2,280,002	50
ENI	1,616,800	92
Pirelli	1,067,100	165
Italsider	972,160	185
1979		
ENI	18,984,960	14
Fiat	18,300,000	16
Montedison	8,199,258	62
Pirelli-Dunlop	5,982,611	105
Italsider	3,743,941	187
1989		
IRI	49,077,200	11
Fiat	36,740,800	15
ENI	27,119,300	28
Ferfin[a]	12,046,900	85
Enimont[b]	11,191,500	100
Pirelli	7,541,500	170
Olivetti	6,585,800	196

[a] The holding which controlled Montedison.
[b] A joint venture between ENI and Montedison.
Source: *Fortune* magazine's listing of the corporate 200.

as compared with other companies, that explains a good deal why Fiat
counted for 50 percent of the Italian auto market by the eve of World War
I. But integration is especially useful in explaining the dramatic growth
which Fiat had during the war when producing trucks, airplane engines,
arms, and munitions moved it from the position of thirtieth to that of

third in the hierarchy of Italian corporations. One of the greatest moments
of Giovanni Agnelli's career, at this point Fiat's owner, was to have avoided
the conglomerate dispersion phenomenon. A good part of the war's profits
was reinvested in the construction of the new, most up-to-date vertical
plant of Lingotto in Turin. In any case, in Italy even the most modern
enterprises must face the hard reality of the poor domestic market. In
1921, if Italian GNP per capita is equal to 1, the French enjoy a 1.7, the
British a 1.9, the Netherlands a 2, and the United States a full 3.6.[55] It is
true that at the same time the system for selling Italian corporations'
products abroad was fully operative. In 1922, 70 percent of the country's
automobile production was sent abroad. But exports are always risky. When
in the second part of 1926 Mussolini decided to pursue a strong deflation-
ary policy to respond to the needs of his domestic constituency as well as
those of his American creditors, Italian car exports dropped dramatically.
If to monetary policy we add the consequences of the Great Depression,
we can easily understand why the number of automobiles exported fell
from 34,141 units in 1926 to 11,940 cars five years later.[56] In the end, for
the entire period between the two world wars there is a big gap between
Italy and the other advanced nations. In 1939 there were 25 million
vehicles circulating on the roads in the United States, 2 million in Great
Britain and just slightly less in France, 1.3 million in Germany, and less
than 300,000 in Italy. In 1938 there were only 7 vehicles for every 1,000
inhabitants in Italy, while Germany was able to boast 18, France 43,
Great Britain 44, and the United States a full 114 vehicles for every 1,000
inhabitants.[57] When Fiat's engineers went to study Ford's Detroit plant in
1926 they wrote home in a report that the comparison between American
and Italian assembly processes is like comparing a mountain torrent with
a stagnant rivulet in the plains.[58] The maximum of Fordism which Fiat
could ask for is the proposal in the 1930s by managing director Vittorio
Valletta recommending that Fiat workers group themselves into partnerships of four to purchase a Balilla (then the cheapest car manufactured by
Fiat) to use for going to work each day and which each of the partners
could enjoy for one Sunday every month![59]

[55] G. Fuà, *Lavoro e reddito*, Angeli, Milan, 1981, p. 245.
[56] F. Amatori, "Impresa e mercato. Lancia 1906–1969," in AA. VV., *Storia della Lancia.
Impresa, tecnologie, mercati*, Fabbri, Milan, 1992, p. 14.
[57] Ibid., pp. 41–42.
[58] D. Bigazzi, "Gli operai della catena di montaggio: la Fiat 1922–1943," in AA. VV., *La
classe operaia durante il fascismo*, Feltrinelli, Milan, 1980, p. 918.
[59] Bairati, *Valletta*, p. 69.

This is the same Italy in which the mass retailer, La Rinascente, had good success with "five and ten" shops rather than department stores and where the major chemical company's major business comes from the agricultural market. In this kind of economic environment, the ownership of large private companies does not need extended managerial hierarchies. In Italy, in fact, in the 1920s and 1930s there was a good knowledge of what happened in the United States and Germany in the organizational field at both the workshop level and that of the general organizational design of a corporation.[60] The problem was that there was not enough pressure to apply this knowledge, as the example of Montecatini demonstrates.

No one can deny that at the end of the 1930s Montecatini was the giant of the Italian economy. It had 60,000 employees, consumed one-tenth of Italian electric power, and its shares were considered equal to government bonds. But in an international comparison, all of Montecatini's weaknesses appeared. It was far behind in the production of industrial chemistry and its organizational design was rather primitive. Until 1920 the enterprise was controlled by the Donegani family of Leghorn, which had a history of maritime activities and trade. Following the previously mentioned acquisitions of 1920, the company was taken over by the large banks. Gradually, the shareholders became more and more scattered so that by the 1930s the major shareholder was IRI with 8 percent of the company's stock. But between 1910 and 1945 Montecatini's control and management was strictly in the hands of one person, Guido Donegani, so, notwithstanding the structure of the property, Montecatini can very well be defined as an "entrepreneurial company." From the mid-1920s the firm followed a strategy of diversification, starting from the production of sulfuric acid and nitrogen. The instrument to organize this kind of policy was to create subsidiary companies all closely watched by Donegani and a few personal collaborators. In the years between the two wars, there is no trace at Montecatini of an organizational debate such as that at IG Farben or ICI.[61] Only in 1962, when Montecatini was on the verge of a catastrophe, did the top management propose to adopt a multidivisional structure. This history matches perfectly with the image of a "limited suffrage" capitalism. At the end of the 1930s, Ettore Conti, a leading figure of the Italian electric industry, wrote in his journal "In this period in which we say daily that we want to go toward the people, in reality a financial oligarchy has

[60] G. Sapelli, *Organizzazione, lavoro, e innovazione industriale in Italia fra le due guerre*, Rosemberg e Sellier, Turin, 1978.
[61] Chandler, *Scale and Scope*, pp. 358–366, 564–584.

been formed which resembles in the industrial field the old feudalism. The production is greatly controlled by a few groups who in turn are controlled by a single man. Agnelli, Cini, Volpi, Pirelli, Donegani, Falck, and a few others literally dominate the various branches of industry."[62]

A NEGATIVE PORTRAIT AT THE END OF THE 1960S

The idea that a company is a personal or family domain seems to materialize as a persistent culture. It survives even when the evolution of the socioeconomic environment puts an end to the constraints to growth caused by scarcity. Family enterprise appears to be dominant in a systematic research undertaken by the American scholar Robert J. Pavan on the 100 major Italian firms (by sales revenue) between 1950 and 1970.[63] Pavan observes that for the entire period consistently almost half of these companies were family-controlled (forty-eight in 1950, forty-nine ten years later, and forty-four in 1970). Their dimensions are various and, at the time, rather different: there is a spectrum that goes in 1970 from Martini and Rossi, a family business ranked last in the hierarchy of 100, to the second-place Fiat, which is also a family concern. Pavan finds a clear correlation between family control, scarce diversification, limited expansion abroad, and a kind of fear of multidivisional structures. "These companies" he writes "have seldom adopted multidivisional structures even if they are the first to experience it. This is the proof that family control and divisional structures do not exclude each other but rather that a delay in the introduction of this kind of organizational design can be attributed to ignorance, fear of losing control or privacy, or to weak external pressure to act according to economic principles. Families have always been helped in taking care of their priorities by managers and divisionalization is nothing more than the use of managers engaged in complex problems that exceed the knowledge and the capacities of the family."[64] A corollary to this quotation is the rarity of advanced systems of planning and control and the nonexistence of a system of rewards and penalties for managers related to performance. But clearly in Pavan's book the dominance of familism creates a national climate. Montedison in 1970 is the number one Italian corporation and its control appears to be managerial. In addition, it is essentially a diversified chemical firm. Still, at the top control is in

[62] Quoted from Romeo, *Breve storia*, p. 152.
[63] R. Pavan, *Strutture e strategie delle imprese italiane*, Il Mulino, Bologna, 1976.
[64] Ibid., p. 100.

the hands of a few – a president assisted by a secretary-general and by "services" for the functions of finance, sales, and production. Pavan does not seem to be very surprised by this organizational structure in the most important Italian firm. In fact, Montedison is the merger of two companies, Montecatini and Edison, that, according to Pavan, combines the worse of certain elements. In fact the two merge into a new corporation that is structured as a holding company with a small headquarters staff which leads the complex by guidelines that combine the worse aspects of an autonomy at the peripheral stage, similar to anarchy, with autocratic decisions by the central layers, taken without adequate knowledge of the problems.

FAMILY VERSUS MANAGEMENT

The negative influence of the "families" outlined in Pavan's portrait seems confirmed by an examination of four important cases.

1. The story of La Rinascente can be in large part identified with that of two families – Brustio and Borletti. The two were relatives but also had two distinct roles in the company, the first representing management (and in control of a small amount of the shares) and the second acting as owners. In forty years (1920–1960) of management the Brustio family created one of the best managerial groups in the world in the retailing industry, as was recognized by a 1967 report of the American consulting firm, Cresap, McCormick and Paget. The relationship between the Brustios and the Borlettis was good during the first generation when ownership guaranteed freedom and safety for the management. The troubles started with the second generation when Borletti, in addition to being president of the firm, wanted to be part of the management without having the necessary skills. In this way La Rinascente, which up to that point had been by far the leading company of mass retailing in Italy, lost its supremacy in the field. The struggle between management and ownerships became uncontrollable up to the point that the company, weakened by internal fighting, was taken over in 1969 by IFI, the financial holdings of the Agnelli family. IFI gave control to a new CEO with no experience in retailing. The result was that in 1975 the company suffered a loss as had never before been experienced, and the situation improved only when a management team formed during the Brustio years was brought back to manage the company.

2. At the end of the 1950s, Olivetti was at the peak of its success. Predominance in the Italian market of office machinery was absolute but the company was also very effective on the international scene; in 1959, it bought out the old, prestigious American firm, Underwood. Also noticeable was the fact that in those years Olivetti created an electronic division with a very advanced laboratory for research connected with the University of Pisa, and started a joint venture with the Italian corporation Telettra and with the American Fairchild Semiconductor to produce semiconductors.

All of Olivetti's problems arose with the death of its leader, Adriano Olivetti. He had been an extraordinary entrepreneur, as talented in business as he was sensible to the problems of the relationship between the company and the surrounding social environment. Adriano's only fault was his centralized style of leadership. With his death harsh fighting started within the Olivetti family, as it tried to find a new leader but with no results. This happened when the competitive environment, especially in electronics with the presence of IBM, had become very tough. Olivetti was in serious financial problems in 1964 when it was taken over by a group of banks and industrial companies, among which was Fiat. The new leadership immediately decided to liquidate the electronic division, selling it to General Electric. In this case the government did not intervene to rescue a precious investment.[65] Olivetti went back into electronics in the 1970s but in very different conditions, which compelled it to start partnerships with American giants such as AT&T and Digital. Claudio Ciborra, who has studied the first of these agreements, rightly defines it as reflecting "asymmetric affinities."[66]

3. At the end of the 1970s, in the middle of the crisis of state shareholdings, ENI retreated from Montedison, which was subsequently taken over by a financial block, Gemina, controlled by some of the finest names of the Italian capitalist establishment, including Agnelli, Pirelli, Orlando, and Bonomi. This group handed over leadership of the company to an experienced manager, Mario Schimberni, who worked out a strategy to make Montedison finally into a profitable company, namely, by abandoning mass production and specializing in fine chemicals and pharmaceuticals. To get the necessary financial resources, Schimberni, who was surrounded by a competent and aggressive cohort of managers, took over a holding company, BI-Invest, and an insurance company, Fondiaria, respectively controlled by two members of the new "ownership" of Gemina

[65] See L. Soria, *Informatica: un'occasione perduta*, Einaudi, Turin, 1979.
[66] C. Ciborra, *Le affinità asimmetriche*, Angeli, Milan, 1986.

– Carlo Bonomi and the powerful Mediobanca, an investment bank. These actions put Schimberni in sharp conflict with Gemina, which eventually withdrew from Montedison. Schimberni wanted to make Montedison a public company. De facto, Montedison was taken over in 1986 by the Ferruzzi family, which had accumulated an outstanding fortune in the trade of grain. Schimberni went straight on his way to forming a public company and in 1987 proposed a substantial increase of capital that the American investment bank, Wertheim Schroeder, agreed to finance. But the Ferruzzis, aware of the strength of their majority shares, opposed this operation and Schimberni was dismissed. His industrial strategy was continued even if new struggles with ENI and fighting within the Ferruzzi family made its full success uncertain. Perhaps the most glamorous episode of the battles between the Montedison controlled by the Ferruzzi family and ENI is illustrated in the 1988 creation of a joint venture between the two – ENIMONT. Its stated goal was to rationalize the basic productions of the Italian chemical industry but it soon became apparent that the Ferruzzis' intentions were strictly speculative and the joint venture broke up two years later.[67]

4. Even at Fiat, notwithstanding the long industrial experience of the Agnelli family, everything has proceeded less than smoothly. After the death of the senior Giovanni Agnelli in 1945, and with his grandson Gianni too young at the time (Giovanni's son, and Gianni's father, Edoardo, had died ten years earlier), control of the firm was handed over to long-time collaborator Vittorio Valletta. This great manager, governing Fiat as a vicar of the "family," brought the company to a level of success never previously attained (it is with Valletta that the lag between the number of automobiles in Italy and that in other countries disappeared). At the beginning of the 1970s – Valletta had retired in 1966 – the old management knew a phase of stagnation that, coupled with the difficult times created by the oil shock, put Fiat into a crisis. To revitalize the company, in 1976 the Agnellis (Gianni and his brother Umberto), now full leaders, nominated a young, combative manager by the name of Carlo De Benedetti for the position of chief executive. De Benedetti lasted only 100 days as he soon started fighting with the family regarding Fiat's strategy. The Agnellis believed that the automobile was a mature product to be progressively abandoned while De Benedetti held the opposite view and asked for massive new investments in the corporation's core sector. In fact, the

[67] M. Borsa with L. De Biase, *Capitani di sventura*, Mondadori, Milan, 1992, pp. 137–145, 151–161.

following years confirmed De Benedetti's ideas and under the able guidance of two managers, Cesare Romiti and Vittorio Ghidella, Fiat found
itself in the 1980s fighting for first position in the European market against
Volkswagen. Once again, however, in 1988 the head of Fiat Auto (the
core company of the group), Vittorio Ghidella, was forced to leave the
company for advancing a conflicting strategy, a situation that greatly
resembled that experienced by De Benedetti more than a decade earlier.
In the mid-1980s Ghidella supported the idea of merging Fiat and Ford
Europe to create a very competitive giant, which would also have effectively weakened the Agnelli family's ownership position.[68]

CONCLUSIONS

Looking back at Italian economic development in the past century, we
can say that it would probably have been impossible for Italy to acquire
a modern industrial apparatus without a strong government intervention.
But Italy is not the only nation where government, in order to overcome
an initial backwardness, is very active. There is clearly a Far East–Asiatic
model of public intervention (as shown with Japan and South Korea)
where the government does not own businesses but, instead, compels
the enterprises which it supports to be competitive on a global basis.
In Italy the state wanted to be owner and so ended up pursuing a kind
of "command economy" which more closely resembled that of socialist
Eastern Europe or Franco's Spain. It is very important to note that the
most significant decisions on public intervention in the economy (during
the entire course of the period considered) were undertaken at the *maximum* political level: by Giovanni Giolitti at the beginning of the century, by
Benito Mussolini in the interwar years, and by the leaders of the Christian
Democratic party in the 1950s. But there is a difference between the years
preceding 1950 and those which followed. In the first part of the century, these decisions were implemented by professional civil servants and
experienced managers, while after World War II the presure of politicians
on management was much stronger. The goal of obtaining political consensus clearly prevailed on the market result.

Government action of course affected that of private big business. For
instance, in the 1980s when a policy of "privatization" of state-owned
enterprises was begun, the policy materialized more on the basis of the

---

[68] G. Turani, "Gli immortali di Torino," *Uomini e Business*, May 1989.

weight of the various lobbies (or according to political – i.e., discretionary – criteria) than according to the objective interests of the national industrial apparatus. Much more influential on private big business was the enormous expansion of public debt in order to finance the welfare system and a disproportionate public administration, from the second half of the 1970s onwards. Interest rates on government bonds and securities were so high as to discourage a diffuse investment in industrial securities and hence the full coming of a modern public company. It is true that the government tried to balance this heavy disadvantage for firms with orders, tax breaks, and social "shock absorbers" (the "cassa integrazione" unemployment program), but all these are old tools that often favored inefficiency and corruption. Government was not too concerned in creating the legal framework where modern business could develop and prosper. Only very recently has there been the creation of an antitrust authority, the signing of a bill outlawing insider trading, and moves toward the creation of industrial investments favored by mutual and pension funds.

All this (in addition to a national culture which at every level privileges familism rather than universalistic relationships) favored the permanence of a "limited suffrage" form of capitalism. To explain the end of the 1980s, we can paraphrase Ettore Conti's earlier quoted remark by adding the names of De Benedetti (who now controls Olivetti), Gardini (leader of the Ferruzzi Group), and Berlusconi (a tycoon in the broadcasting industry) to those of Agnelli and Pirelli.

The evolution of the banking system after the 1936 bill which inhibited banks from owning industrial shares certainly did not contribute to reducing the power of the "families." It has been impossible in Italy to have a strong investor similar to the German model, while the high level of debt made possible by bank loans facilitated the control by very few hands of the major Italian private corporations. In 1946 the state created a merchant bank, Mediobanca, to support the rebirth of industry. But its aged and prestigious leader, Enrico Cuccia, strongly believed in the role of families, thinking that only those who own can stay adequately on top of management. In favor of the families, Cuccia tended to "freeze" large quotas of a company's shares and organized syndicates of control.[69]

[69] See Colajanni, *Il Capitalismo senza capitale*, and F. Tamburini, *Un siciliano a Milano*, Longanesi, Milan, 1992.
  The importance of family control in large Italian firms has recently been reaffirmed in research promoted by the Bank of Italy. See F. Barca et al., *Assetti proprietari e mercato delle imprese*, vols. 1–3, Mulino, Bologna, 1994.

In an age of global competition and interdependence in which it is necessary to mobilize the maximum amount of resources, Cuccia's philosophy does not appear very appealing. Schimberni's idea of creating public companies free of the control of government or families and governed by salaried, competent managers, even if momentarily defeated, seems much more convincing. In any event, in all the sectors where technology permits the full use of economies of scale and scope the evidence suggests that also for Italy the wealth of a nation cannot avoid big business. The unsatisfactory performances of La Rinascente and its competitor Standa effectively mean that, with the creation of the Single Market of 1993, other European mass retailers can freely open their stores (leaving the sector here at risk). The defeats of Montedison, ENI, and Olivetti strongly contribute to the negative commercial balance in chemicals and electronics.[70] This statistic can hardly be compensated by the success of small businesses in labor-intensive sectors if Italy wishes to remain inside the core of modern world capitalism.

[70] Confindustria, *Evoluzione dei settori industriali nel 1993*, SIPI, Roma, 1994, pp. 72–80 and 146–152.

9

Spain: Big manufacturing firms between
state and market, 1917–1990

ALBERT CARRERAS AND XAVIER TAFUNELL

INTRODUCTION[1]

At the end of the nineteenth century, the Spanish economy was still largely
agrarian. Its exports, mainly oriented toward Western European countries, were primary products – mainly agricultural and mineral. Since the
1850s it attracted much foreign investment in railway building and mineral development. Railway and telegraph networks, the essential base for
large-scale industrial enterprise, although not very large, were completed.
With a population of about 17 million inhabitants, and a low density for
European standards, it constituted a medium-sized market.

By 1890 the government was a constitutional monarchy with a bicam-
eral legislature. Universal suffrage for males only was approved this year.
A stable political system was in place with Conservatives and Liberals
alternating in office. The Spanish policy was basically liberal and favorable
to business development. Government itself played a minimal direct role
in the economy, operating the postal and telegraph systems. As many other
European countries, Spain switched to higher tariffs in 1891 because of
the impact of the agrarian depression. Textile and steel producers took
advantage of the new protectionist mood.

The victory of the United States over Spain in 1898 and the resulting
loss of its once global empire brought a *regeneracionismo* movement in
politics, with a strong bias for economic development and industrial
growth. The succeeding years were marked by a wave of new investments
(increasingly by Spaniards as well as foreigners) in urban transportation

---

[1] We pay more attention to the factors underlying the performance of big Spanish firms
in the longer version of this chapter (same authors and title). Economics Working Paper
no. 93, Universitat Pompeu Fabra, Barcelona, 1994, pp. 6–14.

and utilities, shipping, sugar refining, the growth of universal banking enterprises and stock exchanges and more public investments in port development, roads, irrigation schemes, and the like. These investments brought a dramatic increase in investment–output ratios. Furthermore, the government managed to achieve budget surpluses after a long century of chronic indebtedness. At the same time, the government increased the subsidy to public education and formed new technical schools. These schools, concentrated largely on civil and mining engineers, became the primary sources for industrial managers in Spain.

In these ways, Spain participated, though somewhat belatedly, in the prosperity and economic growth that Europe enjoyed during the two decades before the outbreak of World War I. The war itself was a period of economic euphoria for the nonbelligerent Spain. After the war the country experienced a continued period of economic expansion under the dictatorship of general Primo de Rivera. There was an upsurge in industrial output, a rise in urbanization, and large internal migration movements and new heights were reached in capital formation ratios. The economic depression of the 1930s reached Spain very mildly. The fall of Primo de Rivera, the exile of the King Alfonso XIII in 1931, and the new Second Republic opened an era of continuing political conflict and labor unrest. The political and social reformism of the new Republican regime was unable to win over the traditional ruling classes (the upper bourgeoisie, the aristocracy, the military, and the Catholic Church), which supported, jointly with the Castilian small landowners, the Franco uprising of July 1936. The resulting civil war lasted until March 1939.

After 1939, Franco, as chief of state, carried out a policy of economic autarky, or self-sufficiency, cutting back foreign trade and investment, nationalizing (usually foreign) private enterprises in major sectors, and creating new industrial firms through the newly created INI (Industrial National Agency – an imitation of Mussolini's IRI). Franco's policies eventually closed the country to foreign investment and trade, except for the previous commitments with the Axis powers. As a result, even though Franco's Spain did not become a combatant in World War II, it did not take part in the postwar reconstruction and transformation that began to bring rapid economic growth and prosperity to other European countries and Japan in the 1950s.

Only by 1960, after the dismantling of the more extreme autarkic regulations, the devaluation of the nation's currency (too much overvalued, as in Salazar's Portugal, because of the nation's "prestige"), and the entrance in the network of international organizations, did government policies begin to change. So from the early 1960s to the mid-1970s, Spain did enjoy what would be the "golden years" for most of the major Western economies: this was the period of the Spanish "economic miracle" (over 7 percent GDP and over 10 percent industrial output growth rates from 1960 to 1975). Then after 1975, Spain, like the other European countries and the United States, with the leveling off of demand, inflation, and increasing global competition, faced the industrial and banking crisis, complicated in Spain by political change. Franco died in 1975 and the first democratic elections were held in 1977. It took some time to attract the attention of politicians to economic problems. They did it in the early 1980s, first, by devoting huge resources to the refloating of large industrial firms and banks; and, second, by bringing Spain into the EEC in 1986 and opening the country to the world economy.

THE HISTORICAL DEVELOPMENT OF SPANISH BIG BUSINESS

Given the state of business history in Spain, we have acutely felt the need for a preliminary approach to big business in general before addressing the development of manufacturing firms. We have constituted a data base with the 200 top firms measured by their assets.[2]

Big business and the wealth of the nation

Altogether, the first 200 firms have evolved in the way illustrated in Table 9.1. Big business increased quite strongly between 1917 and 1930. The depression of the 1930s, the civil war, and the autarkic period partly destroyed the assets of the big firms during the period up to 1948. Big business grew again in the 1950s but the 1960 level is really not much higher than in 1930. The only real change came in 1974.

What do these figures mean compared with the national balance sheet?

[2] The paper we submitted to the preconference (A. Carreras & X. Tafunell, *National Enterprise. Spanish Big Business, 1867–1990*, Florence, European University Institute, 1992) contained a detailed appendix with the methods and sources used to establish these lists of 200 top firms, and the lists themselves. Limitations of space have obliged us to exclude the bulk of this information from this new version. An improved series of tables with the data for 1917 to 1974 can be found in A. Carreras & X. Tafunell, "La gran empresa en España, 1917–1974. Una primera aproximación," *Revista de Historia Industrial*, 3 (1993), pp. 127–175.

Table 9.1. *Total assets of the 200 largest Spanish firms, 1917–1974*
(in million pesetas)

	Current pesetas	1917 pesetas
1917	12,426	12,426
1930	27,175	22,029
1948	70,079	16,436
1960	383,146	27,813
1974	4,080,615	112,013
1990	28,469,824	126,548

Note: Current prices have been transformed in real terms through a GDP deflator.
Sources: 1917–1974: A. Carreras & X. Tafunell, "La gran empresa en España, 1917–1974. Una primera aproximación," *Revista de Historia Industrial*, 3 (1993), pp. 127–175. 1990: *Anuario El País, 1992*, Madrid, Ediciones El País, 1992, *El País* (Negocion) (1990), December, 30, pp. 21–26, and *Expansión* (1990), December, 29, pp. 16–22 following the same criteria presented in A. Carreras & X. Tafunell, ibid. For the GDP deflator, Leandro Prados, *Spain's Gross Domestic Product, 1850–1993: Quantitative Conjectures*, Madrid, Universidad Carlos III, mimeograph copy, 1995, table D.3.

It is too hard to say because of lack of adequate figures.[3] An alternative macro measure of the changing importance of the top 200 firms may be given comparing their total assets with the GDP, in current terms. We reach the results shown in Table 9.2. The ratio fluctuates between 53 and 87 percent of GDP. There are four periods. The first one, from 1917 to 1930, suggests an increase in the weight of the top firms. We may assume that the trend was in motion even before 1917. The second one, 1930 to 1948, corresponds to a very depressed period, mainly consisting in the long and slow recovery after the 1936–1939 civil war. The third, from 1948 to 1974, covers the most expansive era of the century. By 1974 the ratio reaches its maximum value. The last period, since 1974 to 1990, is

[3] There are some estimates of the Spanish capital stock for some benchmark years, but they suffer from inconsistency among them. See A. Carreras, "Renta y Riqueza," in A. Carreras (ed.), *Estadísticas históricas de España (siglos XIX y XX)*, Madrid, Fundación Banco Exterior, 1989, pp. 533–588; A. Corrales & D. Taguas, "Series macroeconómicas para el período 1954–1989: un intento de homogeneización," in C. Molinas, M. Sebastián, & A. Zabalza (eds.), *La economía española. Una perspectiva macroeconómica*, Barcelona, Antoni Bosch/I. E. F., 1991, pp. 583–646; and André A. Hofman, "The Capital Stock of Spain in the 20th Century," paper presented to the European Historical Economics Society Workshop on *Long-Run Economic Growth in the European Periphery*, La Coruña, 1993.

Table 9.2. *Proportion of the total assets of the 200 largest Spanish firms to the Spanish GDP*

1917	69%
1930	83%
1948	53%
1960	65%
1974	87%
1990	63%

Notes: The assets and the GDP have been valued at current pesetas.
Sources: Assets in current prices, see Table 9.1; GDP in current pesetas: Leandro Prados, *Spain's Gross Domestic Product, 1850–1993: Quantitative Conjectures*, Madrid, Universidad Carlos III, mimeograph copy, 1995, table D.1.

a substantive reduction of the relative size of the Spanish big firms. The industrial and banking crisis has produced its biggest harm to these firms.

Sectoral change in big business

What is the sectoral content of Spanish Big Business? Table 9.3 answers this question. There is a dramatic change through the period under review (in what follows we will pay more attention to the assets than to the number of firms). In 1917 railway companies were completely dominant with almost half of the assets of the 200 main firms. The transport firms in question were mainly railways, but also shipping companies. Four other sectors were on an almost equal footing – manufacturing, mining, utilities, and finance – and had the same aggregate weight as the transport firms.

In 1930 the hegemony of railways and shipping companies was still there, but in clear decline. Other sectors seemed more dynamic, with utilities showing clear and quick progress, manufacturing gaining a few percentage points, finance showing slight progress, but mining declining more quickly than transports.

Basically the same situation appeared in 1948. The weight of the transport sector increased slightly, in spite of the nationalization of the main railway companies. Below transport two sectors emerged to achieve a strong position: manufacturing and utilities. Finance made no progress,

Table 9.3. *Sectoral composition of the 200 largest firms, 1917–1990*

Sector	1917	1930	1948	1960	1974	1990
A. *Number of firms*						
Mining	47	15	8	7	7	3
Manufacturing	45	61	76	110	82	89
Utilities	26	41	41	31	23	22
Construction & public works	2	5	22	9	10	15
Transports	58	37	20	14	14	7
Finance	18	31	25	22	57	53
Others	4	10	8	7	7	11
Total	200	200	200	200	200	200
B. *Assets (in percentage)*						
Mining	11.9	7.3	2.4	2.4	2.2	0.8
Manufacturing	14.3	20.1	23.6	44.7	27.1	26.7
Utilities	12.5	27.0	23.4	25.5	29.8	38.6
Construction & public works	0.2	0.6	3.4	1.5	2.7	7.2
Transports	49.3	31.8	34.9	18.7	9.1	4.8
Finance	10.7	11.8	11.3	6.2	28.0	18.5
Others	1.0	1.3	1.0	1.0	1.0	3.3
Total	99.9	99.9	100.0	100.0	99.9	100.0

Notes: Utilities includes electricity, gas, water, and telephone. Construction includes the societies devoted to housing development.
Sources: 1917–1974: A. Carreras & X. Tafunell, "La gran empresa en España, 1917–1974. Una primera aproximación," *Revista de Historia Industrial*, 3 (1993), pp. 127–175. 1990: *Anuario El País, 1992*, Madrid, Ediciones El País, 1992, *El País* (Negocios) (1990), December, 30, pp. 21–26, and *Expansión* (1990), December, 29, pp. 16–22 following the same criteria presented in A. Carreras & X. Tafunell, ibid.

mining almost vanished, and construction (especially housing development) expanded.

The 1960 benchmark showed a radically different situation. Manufacturing had almost half of the assets. We will see in the next section how important has been the role of publicly owned industrial firms. The utilities remained at a very high level, railway transport declined, and the weight of finance – mainly banking – was reduced.

In 1974 the situation was again strongly modified. Utilities attained a first position. Finance was at an almost equal level. Its increase was more than fourfold compared with 1960 – a jump that was well observed in contemporary literature. Manufacturing firms accounted for more than a quarter of the total assets but were very far from their 1960 success. Intriguingly enough, the fall of manufacturing happened when all the indicators pointed to a complete success of Spanish industrialization, much more than in the previous period. A careful look at the top firms could clarify the situation.

The 1990 pattern is quite different to the previous benchmark. The financial sector suffers the effects of an important banking crisis. Utility companies attain an outstanding leading position. Construction and "others" (retail, communications, and so on) grow, too. Manufacturing manages to keep its portion despite the devastating crisis of the late 1970s and early 1980s.

Compared with the situation in 1917, the proportions have been completely overturned. Instead of railways, shipping, and mines, we have utilities and manufacturing and banks.

The top firms

For a closer look at Spanish big business, it may prove useful to focus attention on the top firms. We have selected the top twenty, that is, the first decile, which historically represented 50 to 60 percent of the total assets of the 200 companies.

The list of the top twenty, presented in Table 9.4, requires a few comments, since we will now consider the changing sectoral structure just described as it is perceived through the top twenty.

The first two benchmarks are dominated by the two main railway societies – Norte and M-Z-A – accompanied by a few other giants like Andaluces, Tánger-Fez or Madrid-Cáceres-P(ortugal) and Medina C.(-Zamora-Orense-Vigo), later absorbed by Oeste (de España). After 1941 they were absorbed by RENFE and disappeared.

The mining companies appeared among the top twenty in 1917 (Rio Tinto, Tharsis, and the mining parts of S.M.M. Peñarroya and Duro Felguera). Rio Tinto, R.C. Asturiana, and S.M.M. Peñarroya survived in 1930 only to vanish from the top positions in 1948.[4]

There were four utilities in 1917 among the first twenty. The main one, in the seventh place, was a gas company that was entering into the

---

[4] Because of lack of data for the R.C. Asturiana in 1917, it missed the top positions that it likely deserved by then.

Table 9.4. *The twenty largest firms, 1917–1990*

	1917	1930	1948	1960	1974	1990
1	Norte (T)	C. Ferroc. M-Z-A (T)	RENFE (T)	RENFE (T)	Cía. Telefónica (U)	Cía. Telefónica (U)
2	C. Ferroc. M-Z-A (T)	Norte (T)	Cía. Telefónica (U)	ENSIDESA (Ma)	Banco Central (F)	Hidrola (U)
3	Banco España (F)	CHADE (U)	CHADE (U)	Cía. Telefónica (U)	Iberduero (U)	Iberduero (U)
4	Rio Tinto (Mi)	Barcelona Traction (U)	Riegos y Fuerzas E. (U)	E.N. Calvo Sotelo (Ma)	Hidrola (U)	RENFE (T)
5	Ferroc. Andaluces (T)	Banco España (F)	Iberduero (U)	Hidrola (U)	RENFE (T)	Unión Eléctrica Fenosa (U)
6	S.G. Azucarera (Ma)	Riegos y Fuerzas E. (U)	CAMPSA (O)	Iberduero (U)	ENSIDESA (Ma)	ENDESA (U)
7	Catalana de Gas (U)	R.C. Asturiana (Mi)	Banco Hispano A. (F)	CAMPSA (O)	Banesto (F)	FECSA (U)
8	Madrid-Caceres-P. (T)	S.M.M. Peñarroya (Ma)	S.E. Const. Naval (T)	E.N. Bazán (Ma)	Banco Bilbao (F)	C. Sevillana Electr. (U)
9	Riegos y Fuerzas E. (U)	Cía. Telefónica (U)	Banesto (F)	Altos Hornos V. (Ma)	FECSA (U)	Banco Bilbao Vizcaya (F)
10	Ferroc. Zafra-Huelva (T)	Ferroc. Tánger-Fez (T)	Banco Bilbao (F)	ENDESA (U)	Unión Eléctrica (U)	Banco Santander (F)
11	Energía Eléctrica C. (U)	Ferroc. Andaluces (T)	Banco Vizcaya (F)	C. Sevillana Electr. (U)	Banco Hispano (F)	Banco Central (F)
12	S.M.M. Peñarroya (Ma)	S.E. Const. Naval (T)	Unión Eléctrica M. (U)	ENHER (U)	FENOSA (U)	REPSOL (Ma)
13	Ferroc. Medina C. (T)	Catalana de Gas (U)	C. Sevillana Electr. (U)	CEPSA (Ma)	EMPETROL (Ma)	CAMPSA (O)
14	Tharsis Sulphur C. (Mi)	Rio Tinto (Mi)	Banco España (F)	FECSA (U)	C. Sevillana Electr. (U)	El Corte Inglés (O)
15	Barc. Electricidad (U)	Cía. A. Tabacos (Ma)	Altos Hornos V. (Ma)	FENOSA (U)	Banco Santander (F)	Iberia (T)
16	Duro-Felguera (Ma)	C. Trasatlántica (T)	E.N. Bazán (Ma)	Saltos del Sil (U)	Banco Vizcaya (F)	ENSIDESA (Ma)
17	Cía. A. Tabacos (Ma)	CAMPSA (O)	U.E. Explosivos (Ma)	Banesto (F)	Iberia (T)	Banesto (F)
18	S.E. Const. Naval (Ma)	C.N. Ferroc. Oeste (T)	E.N. Calvo Sotelo (Ma)	Unión Eléctrica M. (U)	ENDESA (U)	Grupo Torras (O)
19	Cía. Transmediterr. (T)	S.G. Azucarera (Ma)	Tabacalera (Ma)	U.E. Explosivos (Ma)	U.E. Rio Tinto (Ma)	CEPSA (Ma)
20	Banco Hispano A. (F)	Banco Bilbao (F)	Hidrola (U)	S.E. Constr. Naval (Ma)	Astilleros Esp. (Ma)	Banco Hispano A. (F)

Notes: (Mi): Mining company; (Ma): Manufacturing; (U): Utilities; (T): Transport; (F): Finance; (O): Others.

Sources: 1917–1974: A. Carreras & X. Tafunell, "La gran empresa en España, 1917–1974. Una primera aproximación," *Revista de Historia Industrial*, 3 (1993), pp. 127–175. 1990: *Anuario El País, 1992*, Madrid, Ediciones El País, 1992, *El País* (Negocios) (1990), December, 30, pp. 21–26, and *Expansión* (1990), December, 29, pp. 16–22 following the same criteria presented in A. Carreras & X. Tafunell, ibid.

electricity business. All four were developing their activities around the Barcelona area. The situation changed in 1930. The third, fifth, and sixth societies were utilities, as were the eleventh and thirteenth. In 1948 the first four after RENFE were utilities, and a total of seven entered the list. The very top were less utility-intensive in 1960 but the overall performance was still better than in 1948, with ten companies among the first twenty. In 1974 there were still eight and in 1990, six but in the first eight positions.

The emergence of the manufacturing sector is more difficult to document mainly because of the lower size of the mean firm: five in 1917, the same number in 1930 but in a lower position, six in 1948, seven in 1960 with a better ranking, and only four in 1974 and three in 1990. The best moment was achieved in 1960 with the second biggest corporate firm (ENSIDESA) belonging to the manufacturing sector.

The finance firms were banks. Before the civil war the main private bank was the Banco de España (the central bank), much larger than any of the others. After 1939 its size diminished to the advantage of the other banks. So the two banks present in 1917 and 1930 became five in 1948, six in 1974 and five in 1990. The banks reached their highest importance in 1974 with the second record and five other firms among the first 20.

The rise of public "national" firms

All in all here we have a first map of Spanish capitalism. The sectoral content changes and so do the names of the firms. But we get the impression that the turnover at the top is perhaps too high. Do the old 1917 big firms survive in top positions by 1990? Not at all! Among the 1917 top twenty, there is only one – Banco Hispano, in twentieth place – that survives in 1990 in the top situation (but it was absent in 1930 and 1960!). If we accept a continuity between Riegos y Fuerzas (del) E(bro) and FECSA, we can add a second candidate.

A summary may be provided through a table of survivors remaining among the top twenty, Table 9.5. The major discontinuities were perceivable since 1948. At that particular moment, only five out of the top twenty could be traced back to the same group in 1917, while ten out of the top twenty in 1948 survived until 1990.

What changes occurred among the top Spanish firms? They may be classified into two groups: those flowing from normal market evolution (absorptions and mergers, slow growth, and even bankruptcies) and those stemming from state intervention. Here we will focus on the latter.

Table 9.5. *Survivors from one year to the other among the twenty largest firms, 1917–1990*

1917–1930: 11				
1917–1948: 5	1930–1948: 9			
1917–1960: 2	1930–1960: 5	1948–1960: 13		
1917–1974: 2	1930–1974: 2	1948–1974: 10	1960–1974: 12	
1917–1990: 1	1930–1990: 2	1948–1990: 10	1960–1990: 12	1974–1990: 16

Sources: 1917–1974: A. Carreras & X. Tafunell, "La gran empresa en España, 1917–1974. Una primera aproximación," *Revista de Historia Industrial*, 3 (1993), pp. 127–175. 1990: *Anuario El País, 1992*, Madrid, Ediciones El País, 1992, *El País* (Negocios) (1990), December, 30, pp. 21–26, and *Expansión* (1990), December, 29, pp. 16–22 following the same criteria presented in A. Carreras & X. Tafunell, ibid.

At the very beginning, in 1917 – just as through the nineteenth century – Spanish capitalism was a private business. The state was completely absent. From 1917 to 1930 the normal operation of the market explains the novelties, including two foreign ventures as Franco-Española de Ferrocarriles de Tánger a Fez (Morocco) and the Compañía Hispano-Americana de Electricidad, on CHADE (Argentina). There are a few and quite significant exceptions, mainly the enforcement of two monopolistic firms through the state intervention: Compañía Telefónica and CAMPSA. In both there was a mixture of private and public. The private and foreign was hegemonic in the telephone company, while it was the public in command in CAMPSA because of its fiscal significance (the capital was mainly private and native).

The monopolistic state-tutored arrangement was dramatically increased in 1948 through RENFE. A real nationalization was made that gave the whole monopoly of railway operation, except for narrow gauge railways, to this state agency. The national-public content was increased in Cía. Telefónica, nationalized in 1944. RENFE and Cía. Telefónica were the two top firms. They were accompanied by CAMPSA, which was sixth. The state, through the INI (Instituto Nacional de Industria) decided to intervene actively in the economic life creating new firms. Two of them were quite considerable by 1948: E. N. Bazán (shipbuilding) and E.N. Calvo Sotelo (petroleum distillation and refining), sixteenth and eighteenth, respectively.

In 1960 the four top Spanish firms were public: RENFE, ENSIDESA (steelworks), Cía. Telefónica and E.N. Calvo Sotelo. The seventh and the eighth were public, too. And the tenth, twelfth, and fourteenth. Nine out of fifteen! They were unmistakably public: the letters E.N. stay for "Empresa Nacional" (i.e., National Enterprise). Where they seemed to be absent, it is always possible to find them: RENFE stands for Red *Nacional* de Ferrocarriles Españoles, and Telefónica stands for Compañía Telefónica *Nacional* de España. Out of the nine public firms, most were created from scratch by the state (ENSIDESA, E.N. Calvo Sotelo, E.N. Bazán, ENDESA, ENHER). Some (RENFE, Cía. Telefónica, CAMPSA, ENASA) were created through the (paid) nationalization of previous firms. The state activism constitutes the main event of these years.

Interestingly enough, the top public firms in 1960 featured very low profits – if any.[5] Our following benchmark (1974) shows a slowly declining role for the state firms. There are still six among the first twenty (Cía. Telefónica, RENFE, ENSIDESA, EMPETROL (the merger of the old E.N. Calvo Sotelo with two other publicly owned refining companies), Iberia, and ENDESA), and they still occupy very high positions: first, fifth, sixth, thirteenth, seventeenth, and eighteenth. The public sector also had a large portion of Astilleros E(spañoles) – a merger of S.E. Const(rucción) Naval, E.N. Bazán, and Euskalduna. By 1990, the situation is very similar to 1974: six public firms (Cía. Telefónica, RENFE, ENDESA, REPSOL, Iberia, and ENSIDESA).

The rise of the public enterprise – but a very particular kind of it, usually named "national enterprise" – constitutes the main discontinuity in one century of Spanish big business. Spanish "national enterprises" were created to address national problems and not to expand through the world. They fixed a political ceiling to their sectoral and territorial expansion. They were just the opposite of a "global enterprise." Indeed, they were created with autarkic goals and without parliamentary consent.[6] They were quite different from the other Western European public firms. Some

---

[5] We have measured the profitability as: profits/net assets (source: *Anuario Financiero y de Sociedades Anónimas de España*, Madrid, Revista Financiera, 1918–1975). We divide the twenty top firms in 1960 according to their character – private or public. The mean profitability for the (eleven) private firms is 5.1 percent. The remaining firms are to be divided in two groups: (1) the monopolies (telephone [public] and petroleum [private]), with a profitability of 5.0 percent; and (2) the public firms not legally monopolistic (six), with a mean profitability of 1.9 percent. This last group has two electric companies with "high" profits (3.6 percent) and four manufacturing firms with low profits (1.0 percent). We do not have data for RENFE, which used to be run with huge losses.

[6] P. Martín Aceña & F. Comín, *El INI: cincuenta años de industrialización en España*, Madrid, Espasa-Calpe, 1991.

of their features were "Western," while others were "Eastern." It is this amazing mixture that makes the Spanish experience so interesting, and close to some Eastern Europe, Latin America, and Third World cases.

THE HISTORICAL DEVELOPMENT OF
BIG MANUFACTURING FIRMS

Our data base on big Spanish firms yields a limited amount of manufacturing firms, properly speaking. We have built a data set of the fifty top manufacturers for each benchmark year, ranked by their assets.[7] The international and historical comparisons of leading Spanish firms are only possible within this framework.

Industrial distribution of large enterprises

As for the patterns of industrial apportionment, a first look at the Spanish experience will be informative. In order to ease the comparison with the United States, the United Kingdom, and Germany we use the SIC American sectoral breakdown in Table 9.6. Spanish manufacturing shows one sector of continuing, though slightly declining, strength – basic metal industries – and another of increasing weight, transport equipment. The former was the larger during the first part of the century, the latter from 1960 to 1990. Chemical industries were more fluctuating but used to represent more than 10 percent. Food products were the major declining field while petroleum the main growing one. If we add food, tobacco, and textiles – mainly final-demand-oriented – we can wonder about the reasons of their abrupt decline, from 38 to 8 percent. The 1990 benchmark introduces a sharp contrast: the boom of electrical machinery and electronic equipment up to 20 percent.

A comparison with the three other major economies (the United States, the United Kingdom, and Germany for 1917, 1930, 1948, and 1974)[8] reveals some points quite clearly: an initial strength (1917) in a few areas – food and tobacco and metal, transport and chemistry. By the end of the period the car, oil, and metal system is dominating. Through the century

---

[7] For 1917 to 1974, see A. Carreras & X. Tafunell, "La gran empresa en España, 1917–1974. Una primera aproximación," *Revista de Historia Industrial*, 3 (1993), pp. 127–175. The data for 1990 come from *Anuario El País, 1992*, Madrid, Ediciones El País, 1992.

[8] Alfred D. Chandler, Jr., *Scale and Scope: The Dynamics of Industrial Capitalism*, Cambridge, Mass., Belknap Press, 1990, chap. 1, tables 6, 7, 8.

Table 9.6. *Distribution of the fifty largest manufacturing enterprises, by industry*

Group	Industry	1917	1930	1948	1960	1974	1990
20	Food	11	9	7	5	2	3
21	Tobacco	2	2	3	2	1	1
22	Textiles	6	4	1	1	1	0
23	Apparel	0	0	0	0	0	0
24	Lumber	1	0	0	0	0	0
25	Furniture	0	0	0	0	0	0
26	Paper	1	1	2	0	4	3
27	Printing and publishing	1	2	0	0	0	1
28	Chemicals	7	4	9	10	9	5
29	Petroleum	0	1	2	3	5	5
30	Rubber	0	0	0	0	2	0
31	Leather	0	0	0	1	0	0
32	Stone, clay, and glass	2	2	1	0	4	4
33	Primary metals	10	11	10	10	6	4
34	Fabricated metals	1	1	0	1	0	1
35	Machinery	0	0	0	0	3	1
36	Electrical machinery	1	3	4	4	1	10
37	Transportation equipment	7	7	10	13	12	11
38	Instruments	0	0	0	0	0	0
39	Miscellaneous	0	3	1	0	0	0
—	Conglomerate	0	0	0	0	0	1
	Total	50	50	50	50	50	50

Sources: 1917–1974: A. Carreras & X. Tafunell, "La gran empresa en España, 1917–1974. Una primera aproximación," *Revista de Historia Industrial*, 3 (1993), pp. 127–175. 1990: *Anuario El País, 1992*, Madrid, Ediciones El País, 1992.

Spain is much more concentrated than the others in transport equipment,[9] while remaining much weaker in machinery (electrical and nonelectrical). Generally speaking, it is more the U.K. pattern than the American or German.

The cost advantages derived of market considerations – proximity of raw materials, transport and energy costs, labor, capital, entrepreneurs – were at work up to the civil war. They tended to be forgotten during the autarky (1939–1959), when the state intervention assigned the resources in a quite arbitrary way. Consequently, the market pattern of specialization became weaker and weaker. The figures mobilized in Table 9.6 suggest, mainly for 1917 and 1930, a particular pattern, with food and tobacco industries, textiles, cork, some chemicals, basic metals, and transport equipment at the core and of the system. Our hypothesis is that the industrializing policy of the Francoist regime, with its strong autarkic content, pushed in noncompetitive directions, with notorious failures, and countered those firms and sectors with natural growing potential. The harvest was many, small, noncompetitive manufacturing firms.

The top manufacturing firms[10]

A first look at the top ten may be useful. Table 9.7 provides the list of the ten top manufacturing firms between 1917 and 1990.[11] A quick glance at the table is enough to realize that some sectors are well represented while others are absent – or almost, if we consider their weight in the industrial

---

[9] This seems an intriguing feature. Some explanations can be developed. First, we may recall the very high social saving estimate reached by Antonio Gómez Mendoza, *Ferrocarriles y cambio económico en España, 1855–1913*, Madrid, Alianza, 1982. As the business was relatively better than in other countries, it is not surprising to find a higher proportion of big business devoted to the building of railway equipment – once the frontiers have been closed to the imports. Second, the relative size of the Spanish fleet has also been reassessed. Jesús Mª Valdaliso has convincingly argued about the Spanish relative specialization on shipbuilding as the outcome of a high intensity of maritime transportation in the Spanish economy. Indeed, shipbuilding is one of Spain's leading sectors throughout the twentieth century until its recent crisis. Jesús Mª Valdaliso, *Los navieros vascos y la marina mercante en España, 1860–1935. Una historia económica*, Bilbao, Instituto Vasco de Administración Pública, 1991.

[10] We pay much more attention to the building and maintenance of industrial leadership in the longer version of this chapter (same authors and title). Economics Working Paper no. 93, Universitat Pompeu Fabra, Barcelona, 1994, pp. 34–48.

[11] We consider manufacturing firms only those that, as their main activity, produce manufactured goods. The firms that are also involved in mining or distributing activities have been included only when most (i.e., more than 50 percent) of the value of their assets is employed in manufacturing activities. Because of this criterion being used, we have excluded very big firms with an important manufacturing component, such as Rio Tinto, Tharsis Sulphur and Copper, Royale Compagnie Asturienne des Mines, or CAMPSA.

Table 9.7. The ten largest manufacturing firms, 1917–1990

	1917	1930	1948	1960	1974	1990
1	S.G. Azucarera (20)	S.M.M. Peñarroya (33)	S.E. Constr. Naval (37)	ENSIDESA (33)	ENSIDESA (33)	REPSOL (29)
2	Duro Felguera (33)	S.E. Constr. Naval (37)	Altos Hornos V. (33)	E.N. Calvo Sotelo (29)	EMPETROL (29)	ENSIDESA (33)
3	Cía. A. Tabacos (21)	Cía. A. Tabacos (21)	E.N. Bazán (37)	E.N. Bazán (37)	U.E. Rio Tinto (28)	Grupo Torras (—)
4	S.E. Constr. Naval (37)	S.G. Azucarera (20)	U.E. Explosivos (28)	Altos Hornos V. (33)	Astilleros Esp. (37)	CEPSA (29)
5	Papelera Española (26)	Cía G. Corcho (39)	E.N. Calvo Sotelo (29)	CEPSA (29)	CEPSA (29)	SEAT (37)
6	H. Fabra & Coats (22)	Altos Hornos V. (33)	Tabacalera (21)	U.E. Explosivos (28)	SEAT (37)	FASA-Renault (37)
7	Altos Hornos V. (33)	Sider.Mediterráneo (33)	Cros, S.A. (28)	S.E. Constr. Naval (37)	Altos Hornos V. (33)	General Motors (37)
8	Tabacos Filipinas (21)	U.E. Explosivos (28)	ENASA (37)	REPESA (29)	Ford España (37)	Altos Hornos V. (33)
9	Astilleros Nervión (37)	Cros, S.A. (28)	S.G. Azucarera (20)	S.M.M. Peñarroya (33)	E.N. Bazán (37)	CASA (37)
10	S.E. Constr. Mecánic. (34)	Duro Felguera (33)	La Maquinista (37)	Tabacalera (21)	Tabacalera (21)	IBM España (36)

Notes: SIC classification in brackets (see table 6 for the content of the two-digit classification).

Sources: 1917–1974: A. Carreras & X. Tafunell, "La gran empresa en España, 1917–1974. Una primera aproximación," *Revista de Historia Industrial*, 3 (1993), pp. 127–175. 1990: *Anuario El País, 1992*, Madrid, Ediciones El País, 1992.

value-added. In fact, out of the thirty-three firms that have been in the top-ten positions during any of those years, eleven belong to the transportation equipment sector, six to the primary and fabricated metal industries (a branch closely related to the transportation equipment sector), five to oil refining and petrochemicals, four to the food and tobacco, two to the chemicals, and four to other manufacturing (paper, textiles, cork, and electronics) – but only for one benchmark each.[12] If we pay attention to the continuity, the best performers are the steel firms, the transportation equipment firms, and the food-processing ones, followed by the chemicals. The industry has developed much later but also much faster, reaching the top ten in the last benchmarks. The same should be said of the car-making industry. Just the reverse is true for the consumption-goods-producing industries. They were present, though not outstanding, during the first third of the century, but vanished later on. Intermediate- and capital-goods-producing industries dominate our rankings – but not all their subsectors. There are very significant exceptions such as the machinery building and the electrical and electronic equipment (but for IBM España). These weaknesses reveal the main features of Spanish big manufacturing firms sectoral composition – quite different from that of economically more advanced countries, as has been discussed already.

The foundation of big manufacturing firms hasn't been time neutral, as Table 9.8 indicates. Let's focus our attention on the incorporation dates for the top ten in any of the 1917–1990 benchmarks. The big manufacturing firm was born in Spain in the 1880s. Afterward we have to wait until the early years of the century to find new incorporations: from 1900 to 1904 six more came to life. During the remaining years of the first decade there was only one addition, just as for the whole of the second decade. By the end of the third (1929) two more came into being, but none during the fourth. After this long drought, the first years of the Franco regime were very productive: nine new (big but for IBM-España) incorporations from 1941 to 1951. But the next one had to wait for eighteen years! From then (1969) to 1990 seven more were created, distributed unevenly but without any clear timing.

Is there any rationale behind this peculiar temporal pattern? Of course, there is. The first great wave (1896–1904) was a merger wave. Five out of the seven big incorporations were mergers that attempted to form gigantic firms with monopolistic power within their sectors. It is

---

[12] The remaining firm (Grupo Torras, an industrial conglomerate) was too diversified to be classified under a sectoral heading. Nevertheless, it is to be said that it included the largest chemical firm (i.e., ERCROS).

Table 9.8. *The ten largest manufacturing firms, classified by incorporation date*

1855	La Maquinista (A)	1941	IBM España (B)
1881	S.M.M. Peñarroya (B)	1942	E.N. Calvo Sotelo (C)
1881	Cía. A. Filipinas (A)	1945	Tabacalera (C)
1887	Cía. A. Tabacos (A)	1946	ENASA (C)
1888	Astilleros Nervión (A)	1947	E.N. Bazán (C)
1896	U.E. Explosivos (A)	1949	REPESA (C+A)
1900	Duro Felguera (A)	1950	ENSIDESA (C)
1901	Papelera Española (A)	1950	SEAT (C+A+B)
1902	Altos Hornos V. (A)	1951	FASA-Renault (B)
1903	H. Fabra & Coats (B+A)	1969	Astilleros Esp. (C+A)
1903	S.G. Azucarera (A)	1970	U.E. Rio Tinto (A)
1904	Cros, S.A. (A)	1974	EMPETROL (C)
1908	S.E. Const. Naval (A+B)	1974	Ford España (B)
1917	Sider. Mediterráneo (A)	1979	General Motors (B)
1923	CASA (A)	1984	Grupo Torras (B)
1929	Cía. G. Corcho (A+B)	1987	REPSOL (C)
1929	CEPSA (A)		

Notes: (A): Spanish private-owned; (B): Foreign private-owned; (C): Spanish public-owned.
Sources: 1917–1974: A. Carreras & X. Tafunell, "La gran empresa en España, 1917–1974. Una primera aproximación," *Revista de Historia Industrial*, 3 (1993), pp. 127–175. 1990: *Anuario El País, 1992*, Madrid, Ediciones El País, 1992.

clearly the case of Papelera Española, S.G. Azucarera, Altos Hornos de V(izcaya), and, of course, U.E. Explosivos, a legal monopoly (like the Cía. A. Tabacos).[13] The same merger origin can be traced for the S.E. Const(rucción) Naval (incorporated in 1909) and for the Cía. G. Corcho (1929), but not for the other big firms founded during the first four decades of the twentieth century.[14]

[13] Gabriel Tortella, "La implantación del monopolio de explosivos en España," *Hacienda Pública Española*, 108–109 (1987), pp. 393–410.
[14] CASA, Duro Felguera, and Cros can't be related to this strategy because of their very limited market power when they were incorporated. H. Fabra & Coats, a firm linked to the First World textile producer (J&P Coats) but operating in a very fragmented and competitive market, failed to enter into the merger, monopoly-oriented pattern. The emergence of Siderúrgica del Mediterráneo was, much to the contrary, a challenge to the hegemonic position of Altos Hornos de Vizcaya. See Manuel Girona, *Minería y siderurgia. Sagunto (1900–1936)*, Valencia, Institució Valenciana d'Estudis i Investigació, 1989, and Eupenis Torres Villanveva, *Ramón de la Sota: historia económica de un empresario*

While the first wave of manufacturing giant firms was led by market developments, the second was almost entirely carried out by state intervention. But for IBM-España and Fasa-Renault, all the new big manufacturing firms were publicly owned. The state had full responsibility in the new incorporations and in the radical change with the previous trend in big firms creation.

The incorporations of the past two decades are mainly the combined outcome-of both forces: market development and state intervention. The latter would be responsible for the founding of EMPETROL and REPSOL, whereas the former would be accountable for the U.E. Rio Tinto merger. Astilleros Esp(añoles) was a combination of both. The real innovation was the appearance of quite a number of multinational branches: Ford España and General Motors España have renewed the top positions of big manufacturing firms.[15]

How big were manufacturing firms in Spain?

To answer this question, we have relied heavily on the three appendixes of *Scale and Scope*. We have assumed that the data were comparable, although some precaution has to be kept in mind. Our first move has been to assess the size (in Spanish currency) of the 200th firm in the United States, the United Kingdom, and Germany for each of the three relevant years. Afterward we compare the size of these firms (the 200th) with the Spanish ranking of manufacturing firms.

Table 9.9 shows the result. The comparison immediately reveals a pattern of stability of the size of Spain's big industrial firms from 1917 to 1930, followed by a sharp reduction from 1930 to 1948. By 1948 the size of the 200th U.S. industrial firm (measured by the assets) was impossible to reach for the first Spanish firm. The same held true for the British. Though we lack the relevant data, we have the impression that the declining trend continued at least until 1960. It was clearly reversed by 1974, and even more by 1990.

Some Spanish firms reached a quite impressive size in international terms. In 1917 this was the case of the S.G. Azucarera (sugar producer and refiner), tenth among the British manufacturing firms and seventh

(1857–1936), Madrid, Universided Complitense, 1989. CEPSA was created not to become a monopolist (there was a legal monopolist at that time – CAMPSA) but to take advantage of the limited space of free action allowed by CAMPSA.
[15] The Grupo Torras was a very peculiar case: a holding of Spanish (mainly manufacturing) firms controlled by an investment trust (KIO – Kuwait Investment Office) owned by the Kuwaiti government. By 1993 the Grupo Torras went bankrupt.

Table 9.9. *Position of the 200th manufacturing firm of the United States, Great Britain, and Germany within the Spanish ranking of manufacturing firms, 1917–1974*

	United States	United Kingdom	Germany
ca. 1917[a]	4th	26th	21th
ca. 1930[b]	4th	26th	39th
ca. 1948[c]	1st	8th	42nd
1974	7th	—	—
1990	12th	—	—

[a] 1917, 1919, and 1913, respectively.
[b] 1930, 1930, and 1929.
[c] 1948, 1948, and 1953.
Sources: A. Carreras & X. Tafunell, "La gran empresa en España, 1917–1974. Réplica a una nota crítica," *Revista de Historia Industrial*, 6 (1994), pp. 165–172, and *Fortune* (1975), May, pp. 210–229, and August, pp. 156–161; *Fortune* (1991), 22 April, pp. 122–141, and 29 July, pp. 70–103.

among the Germans, and second among the British food manufacturers and first among the Germans. The Azucarera was an outstanding case. The three following firms (Duro Felguera, Cía. A. Tabacos, and S.E. Const(rucción) Naval) had a similar size – around $25 million. They were small among the big American firms, but substantive among the British (around the 30th) and the German (around the 35th). Still in 1930 the first Spanish manufacturing firm, S.M.M. Peñarroya, was to be placed 13th among the British and 4th in the German ranking. But in 1948 not even the largest Spanish industrial firms were able to enter among the first U.S. 200; the first was only 100th among the British and 50th among the German. Checking the *Fortune* 500 world list for 1990 (1991) the situation is as follows: REPSOL, the Spanish manufacturing giant, is 102nd by assets; the second Spanish industrial concern, CEPSA, is 379th – and both are petroleum refiners. The high level reached by the public holding INI (24th) is not reflected in our data because we have considered each of the INI firms separately and because *Fortune* includes the assets of the electrical firms owned by the INI, so the estimate becomes inconsistent. By its assets REPSOL is the 31st U.S. industrial corporation, the 8th U.K., and the 11th German. It may represent a catching-up. Unfortunately for Spanish pride in big business, the second firm – CEPSA, a petroleum refiner, too – is substantively smaller (three times).

Assessed by sales and not by assets Spanish firms were absent by 1962 and 1967.[16] They only appeared in 1972 (SEAT). The following bench-mark – 1978 – is one of clear success: 7 firms (EMPETROL, U.E. Rio Tinto, CEPSA, Tabacalera, ENSIDESA, SEAT, Altos Hornos V(izcaya)) enter among the top 497. The industrial crisis reduced the Spanish pres-ence by 1982 to 3 (EMPETROL, CEPSA, and Tabacalera). By 1990, and according to *Fortune*,[17] the situation was not very different: 4 firms (INI, REPSOL, CEPSA, and Tabacalera). The trend of the first Spanish firm in the ranking is continuously increasing: 452th in 1972, 215th in 1978, 167th in 1982, and 62nd in 1990.

In short, Spanish big business has become comparatively smaller through a good deal of the twentieth century. It probably reached its minimum international size around 1960. Afterward it has improved its overall position.

PRODUCTION AND MANAGEMENT

Production and technology

We have approached the investment in production and new technology through the change in assets, that is, variation in assets in real terms (pesetas of 1917). As usual, we concentrate on the first ten manufacturing firms. For the sake of the dynamics, we follow each firm on the top from the beginning to the end of the period. For the sake of simplicity, we aggregate them in six major sectors: consumer goods (20 to 27 according to Table 9.6 classification); metal products (33 and 34); transportation equipment (37), chemicals (28); petroleum products (29), and others (only 36, electric and electronic equipment).

By 1917, as is indicated in Table 9.10, we have a set of manufacturing firms with their assets concentrated in sectors like food and tobacco, iron and steel and shipbuilding. From 1917 to 1930 the individual experiences had a lot in common: all the sectors expanded. The 1920s were a very prosperous period also for Spain. The top manufacturing firms engaged in expanding their productive capacity – that is, they invested in production. New firms appeared. The previous primacy of final-demand-oriented

[16] According to *Profitability and Performance of the World's Largest Industrial Companies*, London, *Financial Times*, 1975; and J. Dunning & R. Pearce, *The World's Largest Industrial Enterprises*, Gower, Westmead, 1981, and *The World's Largest Industrial Enterprises, 1962–1983*, Gower, Aldershot, 1985, in their rankings of 497 world's largest industrial enterprises (classified by sales).
[17] *Fortune* April 22, 1991, pp. 122–141; and July 29, pp. 70–103.

Table 9.10. Changes in assets values (in million pesetas of 1917)

Sectors	1917	1917–30	1930–48	1948–60	1960–74	1974–90
Consumption goods	618.1	564.4	–516.0	342.8	818.2	3.6
Metal products	371.1	980.9	–1,097.8	3,293.2	2,767.5	–2,768.0
Transportation equipment	192.6	408.0	14.0	1,471.9	4,139.0	–422.2
Chemical industry	60.2	206.2	–21.6	462.2	1,468.3	–1,531.3
Petroleum products	—	91.5	104.4	2,142.0	1,722.9	–1,965.4
Others	—	—	—	—	—	924.4

Sources: A. Carreras & X. Tafunell, *National Enterprise. Spanish Big Business, 1867–1990*, paper presented to the Pre-Conference on Global Enterprise, Florence, European University Institute, "La gran empresa en España, 1917–1974. Una primera aproximación," *Revista de Historia Industrial*, 3 (1993), pp. 127–175, and table 6. The deflation has been made using the GDP deflator, Leandro Prados, *Spain's Gross Domestic Product, 1850–1993: Quantitative Injectures*, Madrid, Universided Carlos III, mimeograph copy, 1995, table D.3.

products switched, although not dramatically, to intermediate sectors like primary metal products. Transportation equipment, chemicals, and petroleum products also enjoyed substantive investments in productive capacity.

The period 1930–1948 was a disastrous one. Most firms were unable to make positive net investments.[18] With a few exceptions of small caliber, the private sector was unable to invest in production. Only the newly created "national enterprises" (Calvo Sotelo, E.N. Bazán, ENASA) committed themselves to a substantive growth in production. The outcome was a sharp contraction in asset value, particularly in the previous leading sectors: consumer goods industries and metal products. The traditional foundation of Spanish big firms was severely shaken. The expansions, very modest, came from petroleum products and transportation equipment, and were strictly related to public investment.

The years 1948 to 1960 revealed a very different standing. Prosperity came back for all the firms. Some were unable to compensate for the disinvestments made in the previous period, mainly in the more final-demand-oriented firms. The huge (in historical terms – we are using 1917 pesetas) real expansion in production came again from the public sector: ENSIDESA and E.N. Calvo Sotelo made enormous investments. Other newly created public firms followed their pattern: E.N. Bazán, SEAT, and ENASA. They worked in sectors with high economies of scale, and the private firms of those sectors also expanded. The major changes, in relative terms, came in oil refining: the investment expansion was more than tenfold. Metal products, chemicals, and transportation equipment also enjoyed substantive investment policies. Altogether, the change in technological leadership was completed: new sectors emerged, new firms appeared, while the old sectors and firms declined.

The period from 1960 to 1974 was the golden era of Spanish economic miracle. It is no wonder, considering how large were the investment commitments of the top manufacturing firms. Nevertheless, the expansion of the top firms was not so dramatic compared with that in 1948–1960. Some of the old ones continued their decline. Many of the recently created and publicly owned firms lost momentum, while some private ones got their own dynamism. Transportation equipment – mostly car making, but also shipbuilding – was the leader in new investments. The chemical industry enjoyed the quickest growth. But the bet for expansion was common to all the sectors. Metal and petroleum products insisted in their

---

[18] Perhaps the assessment of their performance is worsened by the fact that they were slow in revaluing their assets according to inflation. Nevertheless, we have checked their market value and the results found fluctuate closely around the book value.

enlargement of productive capacity and a few of their firms reached dimensions that began to be noticeable in international terms.

Except for some of the car makers, the period 1974–1990 has been extremely painful. It can only be compared with 1930–1948, but with a much worse aggregate performance. The recently expanding sectors and firms have suffered a tremendous contraction: steelmaking (2,768 million 1917 pesetas), oil refining (1,965), chemicals (1,531), shipbuilding (1,720). It is shocking how similar these figures are to those of the previous expansion. The worst performing, the shipbuilding companies, has led to the closing of entire shipyards and to the abrupt decline of their hometowns. The extent of the crisis sheds a dark shadow on the assessment of the previous investment strategies. The performance is worse the more public the company is. Only the automobile industry had a less critical development. Two firms developing new technologies have reached the range of the top-ten manufacturing: CASA (an aircraft builder, publicly owned) and IBM España (with a strong commercial component).

The overall impression is one of too high discontinuity. The firms seem unable to protect their production investments, and everything done in a period can vanish in the following. This fragility may be the outcome of state hyperactivism combined with rent seeking.

Management[19]

A real managerial tradition begins in Spain only toward the early 1960s. Schools of management and a management culture with specialized journals begins then.[20] There was an engineering basis for such a tradition since the last century, with a host of specialized journals.[21] The years around World War I – notorious in our story for so many reasons – were also the period of multiplication of economic and business journals.[22]

[19] Not until after the completion of this chapter did we learn of Mauro F. Guillén, *Models of Management: Work, Authority and Organization in a Comparative Perspective*, Chicago, University of Chicago Press, 1994. A whole chapter (pp. 152–204) is devoted to Spain.
[20] W. C. Frederick & C. J. Haberstroh, *La enseñanza de dirección de empresas en España*, Madrid, Moneda y Crédito, 1969; Andrés Suárez Suárez, "Los estudios de Economía de la Empresa en la Universidad Española," *Economistas*, 2, (1983), pp. 16–24.
[21] Ramón Garrabou, *Enginyers industrials, modernització econòmica i burgesia a Catalunya (1850–inicis del segle XX)*, Barcelona, L'Avenç/Col.legi d'Enginyers Industrials, 1982.
[22] Albert Carreras, "Renta y Riqueza," in A. Carreras (ed.), *Estadísticas históricas de España (siglos XIX y XX)*, Madrid, Fundación Banco Exterior, 1989, pp. 533–88; M. V. de Diego & J. Timoteo, *La prensa económica y financiera, 1875–1949. Fuentes hemerográficas para la historia de la economía y la hacienda en España*, Madrid, Instituto de Estudios Fiscales, (monograph No. 35), 1985.

The protohistory of modern management was to be found in railway companies, but our knowledge of this is very limited.[23] The industrial firms began to modernize through the adoption of Taylorism. Taylor's "Scientific Organization of Labor" began to be known since 1914 and was first adopted in steelworks and engineering firms during the 1920s.[24] The civil war provoked some dramatic changes in the management of large firms. The managers loyal to the Republican regime lost their positions after the war. A new managerial class rose with good political connections as its main asset. Moreover, the wave of nationalizations and the creation of many new "national enterprises" opened the way to new managers. An interesting feature of Spain's postwar years is the fact that many of these came from the military and diffused their own culture in the managerial field. After the stagnating 1940s, the creation of the "Comisión Nacional de Productividad" (National Productivity Commission) in 1952 and, just afterward, the by-products of the U.S.–Spain military agreement of 1953, opened a new period. For some twelve years the activity of managerial retraining and of professional development was very much intensified. Many "productivity missions," public grants, new committees, new specialized journals, and, eventually, even new management schools built new managerial capabilities in Spain's business world.[25] The movement slowed down since 1964 when the management schools became well established and the foundations of the catching-up, too.[26] It was also the end of the most proliberal (in economic terms) stage of the Franco regime.

The main paths for the introduction of new management techniques were the consulting firms. They were of French or U.S. origin, and the first to operate were created in 1952 (TEA) and 1953 (Bedaux).[27] Still, nowadays they retain a critical role in the introduction and diffusion of the most advanced technology related to labor management – robotics.

---

[23] But the situation is beginning to change with Javier Vidal, "La estrategia internacional de las empresas ferroviarias españolas durante la segunda mitad del siglo XIX (1850–1914): una aproximación," paper presented to V Congreso de la Asociación de Historia Económica, San Sebastián, pp. 271–283.

[24] José Mª Vegara, La organización científica del trabajo. ¿Ciencia o ideología?, Barcelona, Fontanella, 1971; J. Tomás & J. Estivill, "Apuntes para una historia de la organización del trabajo en España, 1900–1936," Sociología del Trabajo, 1 (1979), pp. 17–43.

[25] José Luis Herrero, "El papel del Estado en la introducción de la OCT en la España de los años cuarenta y cincuenta," Sociología del Trabajo, 9 (1990), pp. 141–166.

[26] Social capabilities as described by Moses Abramovitz, "Catching-Up, Forging Ahead and Falling Behind," Journal of Economic History, 46, 2 (1986), pp. 385–406.

[27] Pedro Egurbide, "El 'consulting' en España," Información Comercial Española, 513, (1976), pp. 133–137.

Another hint of the modernity of management is the introduction of new technologies – calculators. According to Santiago López the first companies to install calculators were the railway companies during the 1930s.[28]

The diffusion of top management as differentiated from ownership has been present for a long time in Spanish business life. This was the case for the railway and the mine business of the nineteenth century. The existence of foreign investment induced a higher complexity in the firm organization. So early top management was foreign. A further and critical step toward the emergence of a native class of managers in the manufacturing sector was the merger wave at the end of the nineteenth century. The mergers introduced systematically a top management component. The new firms were always multiplant (not multidivisional): S.G. Azucarera, Cía. A. Tabacos, Papelera Española, U.E. Explosivos, Altos Hornos V(izcaya), and so on. The investment role of Spanish banking from World War I also allowed for the diffusion of management ownership cleavages on a more modern basis. By 1960, Linz and De Miguel observed this new pattern in a large sample of in-depth interviews with business leaders.[29] The trend was confirmed in another research conducted by Payno around 1970.[30] At that moment, the manager was much more present in business life. Nevertheless, there has never been in Spain a "managerial revolution." Managers have remained well under the control of the ownership.[31] Indeed, most of the current problems in the summit of some Spanish big firms are not due to poor monitoring of managers but to poor monitoring of the owners in charge of the management.

THE UNMAKING OF ORGANIZATIONAL CAPABILITIES BETWEEN STATE AND MARKET

A provisional conclusion that can be reached for Spain is the failure to build organizational capabilities of the kind needed to develop "global

---

[28] Santiago López, *Los orígenes de la Tercera Revolución Tecnológica en España*, unpublished manuscript.

[29] J. Linz & A. de Miguel, "Fundadores, herederos y directores en las empresas españolas," *Revista de Investigaciones Sociológicas*, 81 (1963), pp. 5–38; 82 (1963), pp. 184–216, and 85 (1964), pp. 5–28; "Nivel de estudios del empresario español," *Arbor*, 219 (1964), pp. 33–63; "Características estructurales de las empresas españolas: tecnificación y burocracia," *Racionalización*, 1 (1964), pp. 1–11; 2 (1964), pp. 97–104; 3 (1964), pp. 193–208; and 4 (1964), pp. 289–296.

[30] Juan Antonio Payno, *Los gerentes españoles*, Madrid, Moneda y Crédito, 1973.

[31] Vicente Salas, "Estructura de propiedad, profesionalización gerencial y resultados de la empresa," in J. L. García Delgado (ed.), *Economía española de la transición y la democracia*, Madrid, Centro de Investigaciones Sociológicas, 1990, pp. 421–443.

enterprises." We perceive, in a simplified approach, two main reasons. The first derives from the unrestricted working of markets. The second from the intervention of the state. Let's begin by the explanations coming from the market side.

We have mentioned the limited size of the market and the role of the commercial policy. We would like to suggest here that even when the market was growing smoothly and no reallocative policy was undertaken, nothing really significant developed in the direction of building organizational capabilities.

An interesting test is the development of trademarks. Alfred Chandler has indicated the centrality of brand names for the development of organizational capabilities. They are critical in the deployment of marketing policies, in the formation of managerial hierarchies, and in the investment in new technologies. The brand name represents the key to mass consumption. A recent article by Mira Wilkins underlines and expands these considerations.[32] As she, interestingly enough, points out, her interest in trademarks, the legal term on which brand names are based, arose with a question by Juan Linz on the absence of Spanish trademarks. The question, formulated at the beginning of the 1960s, has received a detailed and fascinating answer by Mira Wilkins, with a delay of more than a quarter of a century – quite a normal feature in the social sciences. The substance of Wilkins' response is: trademarks are related with levels of income. The richer the country (in per capita terms), the more likely it develops its own trademarks. It may be possible to introduce some delays or inertia in order to cope with some outlier observations but, generally speaking, here we have a simple and sound theory. The high standards of living in the turn-of-the-century United States was responsible for the first upsurge of well-diffused and recognized trademarks. Other European countries followed, but with significant delays. Indeed, trademarks were identified with American products for many decades. If this approach is a sound one, we may expect the rise of Spanish trademarks in the coming years. Moreover, given the previous, continuous, and spectacular growth of Spanish per capita income since the 1950s, we may wonder how is it that we are still short of Spanish trademarks – as we are.

But, is the trademark so well related to per capita income? It is difficult to test this correlation. How can we measure trademarks? A shortcut is

---

[32] Mira Wilkins, "The Neglected Intangible Asset: The Influence of the Trade Mark on the Rise of the Modern Corporation," *Business History*, 1 (1992), pp. 66–95.

multinationals or, at least, giant firms. Daems developed a test of this kind in order to realize the underlying factors to the growth of big firms.[33] He provided some puzzling facts, such as the astonishingly high level of large U.K. firms in real per capita terms among the European countries or, on the contrary, the surprisingly low level of Spanish large firms in the same terms. Just as the United Kingdom had by 1982 many more large firms than expected, Spain had less. Spain was not alone: Norway and Austria were in a similar situation. A possible, but insufficient, explanation was low R&D levels. Another line of reasoning is to check the revealed comparative advantage of a country against the set of sectors more conducive to giant firms. This is the line we would like to explore.

As Chandler has argued, you do not get modern business enterprises with managerial hierarchies, huge size, and well-known brand names in every manufacturing industry.[34] There are some where big firms do not appear. The difficulty of developing trademarks and brand names is even bigger outside the manufacturing sector. You do not get trademarks out of the agricultural or the mining sector – at the very maximum you get *dénominations d'origine*. And you fail to get trademarks with services not amenable to foreign trade.

Those countries that have a set of comparative advantages located in sectors where trademarks are unlikely to develop may grow – perhaps not so quickly – but will fail to achieve a large size for their top firms. Even when they develop big firms, they will tend not to be of the brand-name kind. Exporters of food products, minerals, raw materials, and semimanufactured goods are ideal candidates for this class. Here we find Spain, other Mediterranean countries, some Scandinavian countries (Norway, Finland until very recently), Austria, South Africa, Australia, New Zealand, the wealthiest countries of Latin America, Canada, and so on.

The testing of this hypothesis is much too demanding within the space at our disposal, but we will try to develop it in the near future. Meanwhile, we simply suggest that the peculiar comparative advantage of Spain was not conducive to the developing of trademarks, at least until 1970. Oranges and fruits, iron ore, lead, pyrites, wine, and oil were unlikely candidates for trademarks. Even the late growth of industrial exports was linked to nontrademark sectors: shoemaking and shipbuilding. During

[33] Herman Daems, "The Size of the Firm: Theoretical and Empirical Reflections on European Industrial Hierarchies," in *Piccola e grande impresa: un problema storico*, Milano, Franco Angeli, pp. 73–91.
[34] Alfred D. Chandler, Jr., *Scale and Scope*.

the past twenty years Spain has begun to show a very competitive profile in one particular sector typically trademark led: automobiles. Spain is currently a major world exporter of cars. These cars have well-recognized brand names: Ford, Opel (General Motors), Volkswagen, Renault, Nissan, and so on. Spain has entered the era of trademarks through non-Spanish multinational firms. This is what "global enterprise" also means.

CONCLUSION

The market-defined comparative advantages haven't been conducive to the growth of big Spanish firms. The factor endowment was also inimical, mainly because of income factors – too much abundant labor, limited capital, even unsatisfactory human capital, and cultural attitudes that are not business-oriented.[35]

The state was also responsible. Public intervention defined a set of priorities that destroyed the potential, though limited, for big-firm development within the Spanish economy. The autarkic policies of the 1940s and 1950s produced a painful misallocation of resources. New firms were created and attracted huge public investment in sectors and/or locations quite inconvenient in a context of an open-market economy. The rise of new "national" firms meant a major discontinuity in the history of Spain's big firms. They were too big not to disturb previously existing private firms; they were too small in the world context and too distant from the competitive edge. The slow growth of private, market-oriented firms, though modest and perhaps marginal in core technology terms, was abandoned for the new national giants. They failed to survive the exposure to the market and are still diverting huge resources to finance their deficits.

Spain has failed to develop global enterprises of national origin. It is entering in the world arena through the invitation of global enterprises to operate within Spain. It may well happen that we will see global enterprises directed by Spaniards well before we see Spanish global enterprises.[36]

---

[35] See note 1.

[36] After the completion of this chapter an alternative view has been developed in Francisco Comin & Pablo Martin Acena, *Los rasgos historicos de las empresas en España: un Panorama*, Documento de Trabajo 960s, fundalisn Empresa Pública, Programa de Historia Económica, Madrid, 1996. A summarized version has been published as "Introduction" in Francisco Comin & Pablo Mastin Aceña, eds., *La empresa en la historia de España*, Madrid, Civitas, 1996, pp. 17–33.

Group 3

Late industrializers in East Asia
and South America

10

Japan: Increasing organizational capabilities of
large industrial enterprises, 1880s–1980s

HIDEMASA MORIKAWA

THE GERM OF ORGANIZATIONAL CAPABILITIES
OF JAPANESE INDUSTRIAL ENTERPRISES

Japan, to its good fortune, avoided colonization, thanks to its quick
emergence from self-imposed isolation and mutual restraint among the
Western powers. Its continued independence was one way in which Japan
differed from Korea or China. In fact, Japan not only managed to eliminate its unequal treaties with the Western powers by about 1910 but also
turned Korea into its own colony and began working toward domination
of East Asia.

The key to Japan's building a solid economic foundation while maintaining its independence under the impact of the West was industrialization. With its limited natural resources, industrialization was the only
route to economic independence, a route Japan followed rapidly. Thanks
in part to the effects of government protection and promotion immediately after the Meiji Restoration (1868), modern industries started up in
the 1880s, and the economy began to achieve takeoff.[1] During the modern business enterprise's sudden rise to power as the principal actor in
industrialization, some of these modern business enterprises grew sufficiently large to set up a hierarchy.

Those who discuss the modern business enterprise in prewar Japan
always talk about *zaibatsu*. The zaibatsu, like the *chaebol* in contemporary Korea, was a major presence in the business history of prewar Japan.
One can define a zaibatsu briefly as a diversified enterprise group exclusively owned and controlled by a single wealthy family. In developing

---

[1] Takafusa Nakamura, *Economic Growth in Prewar Japan*, Yale University Press, 1983.

countries, there are few entrepreneurs with the ability and will to industrialize, while there are many types of industries that should be developed.
It thus is almost inevitable that a single big entrepreneur will come to
manage a variety of businesses, in the process forming a zaibatsu (or
chaebol).

That statement should, however, not be misinterpreted to imply that
all private enterprises in prewar Japan were zaibatsu-run. Many private
enterprises were joint-stock companies established by a large group of
shareholders. Conspicuous examples of such joint-stock companies were
the large cotton spinning and electric power enterprises. Moreover, zaibatsu
did not necessarily operate the banks; some zaibatsu did own banks,
but other banks were not associated with zaibatsu. What is very interesting is that the zaibatsu avoided, as much as possible, investing the non-
zaibatsu funds on deposit at their banks in their own growth. Self-financing
was the basic zaibatsu financial policy.[2]

After its long years of isolation, Japan was late in moving into foreign
markets, and the domestic market was limited, as the 1880 population of
only 36.65 million and the low standard of living indicate. But prior to
the Meiji Restoration, an Osaka-centered, sophisticated national network
of wholesalers had developed. Sail-powered shipping was the means of
transportation that made possible nationwide distribution of goods. The
existence of this national market was a part of the infrastructure advantageous to industrialization in Meiji.

From the 1880s on, population growth (reaching 69.56 million in
1936), urbanization, and rising levels of consumption combined with
the spread of railroads, steamships, and telegraph, all of which were first
introduced immediately after the Restoration, to create a swift expansion
of the national market. The *sogo-shosha* (general trading companies)
were also actively pioneering overseas markets, mainly in Asia but with
expansion to Europe and America. Their activities backed up Japan's
industrialization.

Industrialization proceeded in Japan in a broad range of fields but only
two types of industries were internationally competitive: labor-intensive
industries such as silk reeling, cotton spinning, paper making, and sugar
refining, and mining industries, including coal and copper mining. What
Japan exported to overseas markets were also labor-intensive products

---

[2] Hidemasa Morikawa, *Zaibatsu: The Rise and Fall of Family Enterprise Groups in Japan*,
University of Tokyo Press, 1992.

such as raw silk, cotton textiles, coal, and copper. Through these exports, Japan was able to import the capital-intensive products such as machinery needed for industrialization.

At last, during World War I, Japan, taking advantage of the market vacuum caused by the stoppage of exports from the European countries, saw its iron and steel, shipbuilding, machinery, chemicals, and other capital-intensive industries begin to grow. The restoration of exports from Europe after the war and the postwar recession, however, made sustaining that growth difficult.

In 1936, as the fact that Japan's cotton textiles had the greatest world market share indicates, its labor-intensive industries had achieved competitiveness on international levels. But Japan's capital-intensive industries still lacked the might to compete internationally. For example, if we compare output in steel ingots, we find that in 1936 the United States output totaled 49 million metric tons, Germany 20 million metric tons, the Soviet Union 16 million, Great Britain 12 million, France 7 million, and Japan only 5 million metric tons.[3] A comparison of automobile production for 1933 reveals an even larger gap: while the United States produced 1.92 million cars, Great Britain 286,000, France 185,000, and Germany 105,000, Japan produced only 25,000 cars. Moreover, that figure includes not only GM and Ford products built at factories in Japan but also three-wheeled motorcycles.[4]

There were obvious reasons for the relative underdevelopment of capital-intensive industries in prewar Japan. First, the domestic market was small. As mentioned earlier, in 1936 the population of Japan stood at 69.59 million, two-thirds of whom lived in farming villages. Furthermore, since the quality of output of Japan's capital-intensive industries was not sufficient to satisfy even this limited domestic market, imports retained a large market share. Under these market conditions, there was no hope for making large-scale investments to exploit economies of scale.

Second, Japan's situation was typical of a developing nation. The development of capital-intensive industry was dependent on the acquisition of technology from abroad and required time. With the exception of weapons production, which was generously funded by the military, its technologies had simply not reached international levels.

[3] Hiromi Arisawa (ed.), *Gendai Nihon Sangyo Koza* (Collected works of modern Japanese industries), Iwanami Shoten, 1959, vol. 2, appendix, p. 10.
[4] Masahisa Ozaki, *Nihon Jidoshashi* (History of the Japanese automobile industry), Jikensha, 1942, pp. 584–585.

Despite their disadvantages, however, Japan's industrial enterprises steadily gained some strengths that facilitated the building up of their own organizational capabilities in the postwar period. One fact working in their favor was that Japan and its industries as a whole were fired by a desire to catch up. The competitiveness of Japan's industrial enterprises was directed not only at rivals in the advanced countries but also at domestic competitors. A second advantage was that, early in Japan's drive to modernize, highly educated salaried managers had begun being promoted within the job hierarchy of large industrial enterprises and had come to participate in their top management. These managers showed a marked tendency to give priority to the reinforcement of corporate organizational capabilities, rather than expanding the wealth of the owners. The development of managerial enterprise was not limited to joint-stock companies alone, but was in evidence also in those symbols of family control, the zaibatsu.[5]

A third advantage was that networks of unique skills were being created before the war. One factor was the close, cooperative relationships blue-collar workers formed on the work site through the extended period permitted by the lifetime employment system. Those relationships were the underpinnings for the on-the-job training given to them. Another was the practice of hiring large numbers of highly educated engineers and assigning them to production sites, where they worked as colleagues with blue-collar workers. To make this practice work, engineers were imbued with respect for the work site during their university education, and practical training in factories or mines reinforced that respect.[6]

THE PRIVATE EQUIPMENT INVESTMENT DURING AND SHORTLY AFTER THE WAR

The germ of organizational capabilities sowed before the war did not grow smoothly into the fast-growing economy of postwar Japan. In the 1930s, Japan started a war of aggression against China and also began constructing a command economy, which was useful for concentrating

---

[5] Hidemasa Morikawa, *Prerequisites for the Development of Managerial Capitalism: Cases in Prewar Japan*, pp. 13–15 in Kesaji Kobayashi and Hidemasa Morikawa (eds.), *Development of Managerial Enterprise* (Proceedings of the 12th Fuji Conference), University of Tokyo Press, 1986.

[6] Hidemasa Morikawa, *The Education of Engineers in Modern Japan: An Historical Perspective*, pp. 143–145 in Howard F. Gospel (ed.), *Industrial Training and Technological Innovations: A Comparative and Historical Study*, Routledge, 1991.

economic resources on war, to sustain the war effort and rule Asia without being dependent on America and England, who were sympathetic to China. Economic and territorial expansion proceeded hand in hand until 1941, when Japan, insanely forcing the Allied Powers to fight it in the Pacific Theater of World War II, brought about its own ruin.

During the fifteen years of war, Japan's capital-intensive industries did indeed undergo rapid growth. The aim was, of course, to increase production of weapons needed in a war of aggression, and the military was in command. That orientation led to sacrificing the textile industry and other labor-intensive industries. In 1930, three main capital-intensive industries (metal, machinery, and chemicals) accounted for 34.6 percent of industrial output; in 1945, their share had grown to 76.8 percent. The ratio of the number of employees in those industries to total industrial employment, 23.6 percent in 1930, had soared to 60.2 percent in 1945.[7]

Those increases were the result of the military's expanding the productive capacity of capital-intensive industry companies. There was a marked increase in the number of factories, machines, engineers, and workers in capital-intensive industry companies. American bombing inflicted much damage, but the industry was not completely destroyed. Thus, the productive capacity of Japan's capital-intensive industries, which had undergone such expansion during those fifteen years, should have been a valuable legacy, very useful to the growth of the economy in postwar Japan.

Simply adding demand where plants, machinery, and workers exist will not, however, start an economy growing on its own. Restructuring was necessary, and a consensus needed to be reached to make the changes possible. First, the economic system, organized on a war footing, had to be reorganized into a peacetime market system. To do so, industrial enterprises, which had been enjoying guaranteed profits, with orders for military production and infusions of inflated currency, had to rebuild managerial skills to reduce costs and improve competitiveness. Second, industrial enterprises had to catch up technologically, through introducing the newest techniques and facilities from the advanced countries, since the cessation of the flow of technological information during the war had put them substantially behind.

Since such restructuring required pouring enormous investments into

---

[7] Nihon Tokei Kenkyusho (ed.), *Nihon Keizai Tokei-shu* (Collected statistical data the Japanese economy), Nihon Hyoron Shinsha, 1958, pp. 56, 296.

industrial enterprises, consensus on their importance, among people in general and among those holding stakes in the corporations, was essential to this effort. Without restructuring and the consensus to make it possible, the large-scale productive capacity Japan built up during the war would be no more than an inherited white elephant.

After the defeat, however, that consensus was lost for a time. The people were stunned by the hardships of war, the defeat, and the occupation (a first-time experience for the Japanese). Rather than working steadily to build up output, people resorted to labor disputes to raise wages or threw themselves into speculative transactions to earn money by taking advantage of shortages and inflation.

Labor disputes were frequent immediately after the war. That change was due in part to the success of the Communist message and organization, but also to a reaction to stripping away of workers' rights during the war. The number of such disputes increased from 94 in 1945 to 810 in 1946, 683 in 1947, and 913 in 1948. The number of disputes as well as the number of participating workers (26,054) peaked in 1948.[8]

The situation gradually began to change in mid-1948. The Japanese had begun to hope industry would recover its vitality, to improve their own lives. The workers had discovered the distortions behind the labor conflicts the Communists had led them through. In addition, the occupation authorities had dropped several of their policies, including the dismantling of the zaibatsu, the purging of owners and managers who had contributed to the war effort, and the ban on compensation for the enormous corporate losses incurred in the defeat. (Most losses were caused by payments outstanding for weapons the military had ordered and, after the dismantling of Japan's military, had not paid for.) These measures came as a relief to top-level industrial managers, who until then had not been able to see much of a future.

A climate of consensus inside and outside industrial enterprises sparked a trend toward rapid increase in private equipment investment. But although that consensus provided an important framework, it does not offer a sufficient explanation of the process of vitalization of equipment investment in postwar Japan's industrial enterprises. More detailed research is necessary here.

There were, first, several special factors behind the growth of private equipment investment that began around 1950.

[8] Ibid.

1. The reforms enacted by the occupation forces, including zaibatsu dissolution, the Decentralization of Excessive Economic Power Act, and the Antimonopoly Act, destroyed the prewar industrial order and touched off severe competition between industrial enterprises.

2. In 1948, the occupation authorities announced they would employ drastic policies to put a stop to worsening inflation (the Nine Principles). In March 1949 they moved to put into action the Dodge Line, a detailed plan drawn up by the president of the Bank of Detroit, Joseph Morrell Dodge. The plan included a switch from deficit spending to surplus financing, the abolition of government subsidies for industry, and linkage of the Japanese economy to the world market. One part of the plan was to peg the yen–dollar exchange rate at 360 yen to the dollar. The Dodge Line resulted in a severe recession; to ride it out, Japanese industrial enterprises were forced to fall back on rationalization and to cut costs.

3. To rationalize and decrease costs, corporations fought off extreme resistance from labor unions to cuts in personnel. At the same time, building new plants and renewing aging facilities meant that large-scale investments were necessary, but because of the recession, there were no spare funds to be had.

Then, in June 1950, war broke out in Korea, and Japan became a supply base for the UN forces fighting on the Korean Peninsula. Japan's capital-intensive industry enterprises received orders for repairing weapons and cars, as well as supplying materials for the U.S. army (so-called special procurements); with those earnings they were able to ride out the financial difficulties of the recession. One could say that after undergoing the surgery outlined in the Dodge Line, Japan received an injection of stimulants from the Korean War.

4. The 1950 to 1951 special procurement boom brought about an expansion of consumer demand. The 1930s had witnessed the first steps toward the growth of a mass market in the major cities of Japan, but the war had promptly destroyed it; now there was a trend toward revival. However, because of aging equipment, supply capacity was not sufficient to meet consumer demand. Aided by easier financial conditions, a by-product of the special procurements, equipment investment was increased to fill the gap between supply and demand.

5. The enactment of the Foreign Capital Law in 1950 enabled Japanese industry, which had been excluded since the war, to access industrial technology from the United States and Europe. Naturally, this had a stimulating effect on equipment investment.

6. Although domestic demand grew, imports increased as long as domestic supply capacity did not expand, quickly putting Japan's balance of payments in the red. This situation, known as a low ceiling on the balance of payments, hindered economic growth. To raise Japan's supply capacity and to reinforce the ability of domestic products to compete against imported goods, the Japanese government thought it necessary to promote equipment investment among industrial enterprises; several laws were established to that end, and enterprises received tax breaks.

The result was the beginning of the trend toward increasing private equipment investment, which took off around 1950.

WHY THE VIGOROUS EQUIPMENT INVESTMENT AFTER 1950 SUCCEEDED

Aided by consensus within the enterprises and in the wider society and stimulated by changes in the economic climate, Japan's industrial enterprises were committing all their resources, from about 1950 on, to restructuring through equipment investments.

Several examples will clarify this process. Toyota, for instance, made equipment investments totalling 6,100 million yen in a five-year modernization plan launched in April 1951. For a company capitalized at 418 million yen in 1951, that was a drastic step indeed. Moreover, when the five-year plan came to an end, it had a capacity of only 3,000 cars a month. Half a year later, in October 1956, its capacity topped 5,000 cars a month. While the investment paid off, it was an extremely bold move for a small-scale assembly manufacturer at a stage when motorization had hardy begun in Japan.[9]

Toshiba increased its equipment investment from 5,600 million to 29,500 million yen in the five years between 1957 and 1961, as shown in Table 10.1. Since Toshiba was capitalized at 9,600 million yen in 1957, it too was not going halfway with equipment investments. Toshiba, like its rival Hitachi, was entering a new business, home appliances. Moreover, equipment investments were necessary to secure an advantage amid stiff competition.[10]

Kawasaki Iron & Steel carried out 18,100 million yen in equipment investments between 1950 and 1954. Much of that was spent on launching its production of pig iron, a new field, and for the construction of what was Japan's most up-to-date integrated iron and steel works in Chiba.

[9] Toyota Motor Inc., *Toyota Jodosha 30-nen Shi* (30 years of Toyota Motor), 1967.
[10] Toshiba Inc., *Toshiba 100-nen Shi* (100 years of Toshiba), 1977.

Table 10.1. *Toshiba equipment investment (million yen)*

	Total	Home appliance share
1957	5,600	700 (12.5%)
1958	9,900	1,500 (16.7%)
1959	13,400	1,400 (10.4%)
1960	21,000	3,600 (17.1%)
1961	29,500	6,200 (21.0%)

Source: Toshiba Inc., *Toshiba 100-nen Shi* (100 Years of Toshiba), 1977.

When the company announced the plan to build the Chiba works in 1950, it was capitalized at 500 million yen; equipment investments on that scale were thus highly risky for it. With two new companies resulting from the split of the government-funded Japan Iron and Steel (Nihon Seitetsu) in 1950, as a result of the Decentralization of Excessive Economic Power Act under the Occupation, Yawata Iron and Steel and Fuji Iron and Steel, in the market, Kawasaki Iron & Steel, anticipating intensified competition and a failure to maintain self-sufficiency in pig iron production, was forced to invest boldly in equipment.[11]

Bridgestone Tire (now Bridgestone) devised a five-year modernization plan for 1951–1955, in which it spent 1,000 million yen on equipment investment, including rayon tire production facilities. The company had been capitalized at 525 million at the start of the plan, and it sustained a 2,000-million-yen loss due to a collapse in rubber prices after it embarked on the plan. Nonetheless, it pushed ahead with restructuring through equipment investment needed for the climate of intense competition it expected.[12]

Examples from other companies could also be adduced here. In each case, investment in production equipment was paralleled by investments in organizing a marketing network and shaping the company's management structure. The funds to carry out what Chandler has called "three pronged investment" were, for the most part, provided by a fifty-fifty combination of self-financing (capital increases and retained earnings) and bank borrowings.

[11] Seiichiro Yonekura, "The Postwar Japanese Iron and Steel Industry: Continuity and Discontinuity," pp. 211–220, in Etsuo Abe and Yoshitaka Suzuki (eds.), *Changing Patterns of International Rivalry* (Proceedings of the 17th Fuji Conference), University of Tokyo Press, 1991.
[12] Bridgestone Inc., *Bridgestone 50-nen Shi* (50 years of Bridgestone), 1982.

The vigorous investment in equipment that Japan's industrial enterprises carried out from 1950 on was a classic example of "the enduring logic of industrial success": continuing reinvestment was the only means to securing competitive advantage and growth of the company.[13] A "strategic intent" to win not only in domestic competition but also in competition in the world markets, despite a lack of managerial resources, was at work.[14] Nonetheless, logic and intent alone could not lead to these companies' risk-taking investment behavior, much less to their success. Why did such a large number of players with that logic and intent emerge? What were the conditions they relied upon in making their vigorous investments?

Answering the first question requires a description of the overall development of the managerial enterprise in postwar Japan. As mentioned earlier, salaried managers had long made remarkable gains in the top management of prewar large-scale enterprises in Japan, but, as Table 10.2 shows, the development of the managerial enterprise was still in a transitional phase in 1930.

At first glance it appears that there is a clear trend for managerial enterprise to be predominant. But in 1930, only 42 (26.6 percent) out of 158 large-scale enterprises had filled more than half of their top management positions with salaried managers. Even if we include former high-ranking bureaucrats, the number is only 52 companies (32.9 percent). Managerial enterprises clearly were not dominant.

If we look at the reverse side of the coin, we find that the owners still carried great weight as far as the top management of large-scale enterprises was concerned. As mentioned earlier, in prewar Japan there were two kinds of large-scale enterprises, family enterprises exclusively owned and managed by a single family (most of them belonged to the zaibatsu – even though they had the form of joint-stock companies, shares were not sold on the market) and joint-stock corporations under joint ownership, the shares of which could be freely sold. On the surface it appears that the zaibatsu owners were more powerful, but at Mitsui or Sumitomo, the owner families were rulers in name only; the top management was essentially under the control of the salaried managers. At Mitsubishi the owners (the two Iwasaki families) and the salaried managers cooperated

---

[13] Alfred D. Chandler, Jr., "The Enduring Logic of Industrial Success," vol. 68, pp. 130–140, in *Harvard Business Review*, March–April 1990.

[14] Gary Hamel and C. K. Prahalad, "Strategic Intent," vol. 67, pp. 63–76, in *Harvard Business Review*, May–June 1989.

Table 10.2. *The development of managerial enterprises in Japan,*
1905–1930

No. of salaried managers in top management	No. of companies					
	1905		1913		1930	
0	47	(33)	48	(39)	15	(11)
1	22	(32)	38	(39)	27	(17)
2 or more	5	(9)	29	(37)	113	(127)
2 to half					71	(75)
More than half					42	(52)
Unknown	1	(1)	0	(0)	3	(3)
Total	75	(75)	115	(115)	158	(158)

Notes: In producing this chart, the author chose three years for comparison: 1905, 1913, and 1930. Briefly, large-scale enterprises were defined as those companies whose paid-up capital exceeded a certain amount, and they were classified according to the number of salaried managers participating in their top management. (For simplicity, the author has omitted listing these enterprises' paid-in capital, the basis used for selecting large industrial enterprises.) The numbers in brackets include the number of companies with former highly placed bureaucrats received directly into top management (a process known as *amakudari* in Japanese) as salaried managers. Japanese students of management are divided on the question of whether it is proper to include *amakudari* among salaried managers, which is why I have prepared two sets of numbers.
Sources: Shogyo Koshinsho, *Nihon Zenkoku Shokaisha Yakuinroku* (Japanese Directory of Company Directors), published yearly.

in top management. Such zaibatsu were developing into managerial enterprises.

Nonetheless, there were zaibatsu, such as those of the Yasuda and Asano families, for example, in which family members held the majority of the top management positions. In the Asano zaibatsu, the owner family monopolized all positions in top management. Some zaibatsu families clearly held tight control. Moreover, while the Mitsui or Sumitomo de facto top management was in the hands of salaried managers, decisions about hiring or firing top managers or approving policies were made, de jure, by the owner families. We must not overestimate the development of managerial enterprises in the zaibatsu of prewar Japan.

The managerial enterprise was also developing in the more open joint-stock companies, which were jointly founded and owned by several entrepreneurs. The influence of the owners of these companies, however, remained even more conspicuously powerful than in the zaibatsu. Because all shares of the zaibatsu companies were in the possession of the owner families or their holding companies, many wealthy people who were not able to buy these shares bought up shares in non-zaibatsu companies, thus becoming major shareholders. In fact, such persons were major share-holders and part-time directors of several companies concurrently. In some companies, large shareholders formed factions and competed over the posi-tion of company president. Using their authority as directors, they also pressured the companies to pay large dividends to shareholders. Major shareholders also used information obtained from the company to acquire large profits in their own businesses. Most of them were interested neither in the long-term growth of the company in which they were large share-holders nor in strengthening its organizational capabilities. They were only interested in earning massive short-term profits.

But after 1930, the tide was turning toward managerial enterprises; in particular, during the war, salaried managers greatly increased their influ-ence over industrial enterprises. In order to build up systems for weapons production, the military expressed a desire to expand the role of full-time salaried managers and replace the part-time owner managers in the top management of capital-intensive industry enterprises.

Then came the dissolution of the zaibatsu, implemented by the Occu-pation after the war. The zaibatsu owner families completely withdrew from top management: they were compelled to give up their shares in the zaibatsu corporations and were no longer the owners. The zaibatsu all but disappeared, and the corporations which made up the old zaibatsu no longer had owner managers; salaried managers took their places. Although in legal terms they had been subordinates, employed by the zaibatsu families, they were already the de facto decision makers in most zaibatsu before the war. With the dissolution of the zaibatsu, they became the dominant top managers in the former zaibatsu corporations in name as well as reality.

Major shareholders in non-zaibatsu companies were not directly af-fected by the zaibatsu dissolution, but they did lose property because of the tax and land reforms enforced by the occupying authorities, including a wartime gains tax and higher property and inheritance taxes. To meet these higher taxes, they were obliged to part with a large number of shares in non-zaibatsu companies.

According to my research, of the 100 individual top income earners in Japan in 1944, not a single one was found among the top 100 in 1954. Property redistribution was implemented on such an extensive scale by the occupying forces that it brought about great changes among the shareholders of large corporations. Through this process, the zaibatsu families and major individual shareholders disappeared from among the owners of postwar large industrial enterprises, their place taken by corporate and minor individual shareholders. Of course, those who ceased to be owners also vanished from the top management of these large industrial enterprises. Their places were taken by salaried managers, who had been progressing conspicuously toward top management in the prewar period and had reinforced their influence during the war. With the company within their control, the salaried managers put priority on long-term profits, not the short-term gains that shareholders in general aim for. Moreover, the majority of Japan's salaried managers were promoted from inside and were strongly attached to the enterprise in which they had spent years honing their skills. They were committed to building up their enterprise's organizational capabilities. In addition, unlike the intrusive major shareholders of the prewar period, the new shareholders of the postwar period (corporate and minor individual shareholders) did not block policies based on the long-term views of the salaried managers, interfere with the financial soundness of the company by demanding high dividends, manipulate stock prices, or sell their shares when it would profit them. The reasons why an increasingly large proportion of shares in major companies were owned by corporate shareholders will be discussed later.

The salaried managers themselves were subject to one large change as a result of occupation policies. Because of the purges, many top managers of large corporations, salaried managers included, were judged to have cooperated with the war effort and were ousted. The first step came in October 1945, when the top managers in the zaibatsu head offices were forced to resign and forbidden to set foot in the office. Then in January 1947, those who had held the offices of president, vice-president, chairman, vice-chairman, senior executive director, executive director and full-time auditor in major corporations prior to September 1945 met the same fate. ("Major corporations" were defined by Occupation policies as corporations with capital exceeding 100 million yen and with a high degree of concentration.) In January 1948, all those who were in the top management of designated subsidiaries of the zaibatsu prior to November

1945 were forced to resign. The number of managers who were forced to resign due to these measures, excluding duplications, reached approximately 5,000.

The purges had widespread impact on the business world. One effect was a rejuvenation of the top management in major corporations. The average age of top managers was sixty in 1945, but dropped to fifty after the purges; control had shifted to a generation of remarkable stamina and vitality. A second effect was that many top managers who assumed office after the purges had graduated from university in the post–World War I period known as Taisho Democracy and cherished liberal ideals that they had pursued throughout their business lives. Third, the majority had no experience serving in top management but had been promoted from the middle ranks after a purge of their superiors. Some were even promoted to top management from production and distribution operating units, and many had an understanding of the needs and feelings of blue-collar workers.[15]

These shifts in the characteristics of top managers and shareholders strengthened the logic of industrial success and strategic intent. Salaried managers, however, were not the only innovators in the postwar period. Among those who had made use of the business opportunities available after 1930 to found new industries, there were many founders. They were also owner managers, but they were dedicated to reinforcing organizational capabilities; unlike the old owners, they did not insist on increasing their personal wealth. These included Toyoda (Toyota), Matsushita (National-Panasonic), Ishibashi (Bridgestone), Honda, Torii (Suntory), to name only a few. They, like the new salaried top managers, played an indispensable role in postwar industrial growth in Japan.

After the death or retirement of these founders, skillful salaried managers either cooperated with the founding families or the families put them in charge of top management. Today Japan's large-scale industrial enterprises are, with very few exceptions, run by salaried managers. If we add the drop in the percentage of shares owned by individual shareholders, we find that Japan has almost entirely entered the age of the managerial enterprise.

Our second question was, what were those who had the logic and

[15] Hideaki Miyajima, *Zaikai Tsuiho to Shin Keieisha no Tojo* (The purge in the business world and the appearance of the new top executives), pp. 8–28, in Hidemasa Morikawa (ed.), *Sengo Keieishi Nyumon* (Postwar business history of Japanese companies), Nihon Keizai Shimbunsha, 1992.

intent to decide on the vigorous investment in equipment that began in 1950 relying on in their risk-taking behavior? The top-level decision makers in large postwar industrial enterprises were salaried managers promoted from inside and founders. Both led their enterprises to vigorous investment in equipment from about 1950 on. What these two types of managers had in common was extensive experience with the unique internal skills network that had been built up within Japanese industrial enterprises from an early period, well before the war. The salaried managers, of course, had themselves been trained within that network and worked their way up from the ranks to reach top management positions. The founders also deliberately created skills networks themselves. Both these home-grown salaried managers and founders were aware of information concerning the engineers and workers who formed the skills network and were in turn respected by them.

When the top management of Japan's large industrial enterprises in roughly 1950 decided to embark on large-scale equipment investments far out of proportion to their limited managerial resources, they were motivated by more than the logic of industrial success and strategic intent. These top managers were certain that the managers, engineers, and workers they themselves had trained would, in a competitive environment, improve their product-specific and company-specific skills, form a tightly knit network, and readily accept the new equipment and technology they were introducing. The result would be the formation of stronger organizational capabilities. It was that confidence that led to their daring investment programs.

In this sense, the younger salaried top managers who had been promoted from within the company and the founders who had emerged in the 1930s and 1940s were well suited to guide the growth of the Japanese economy in the new postwar environment. (The functions of skills networks in Japanese industrial enterprises are discussed later in this chapter.)

THE SKILLS NETWORK IN JAPANESE INDUSTRIAL ENTERPRISES

Increasing private equipment investment took off in about 1950, whereupon a virtuous cycle kicked in. Increasing equipment investment led to marked expansion, which generated new business opportunities, stimulated competition for market share, and then encouraged further equipment investment. In fact, from the 1950s on, these were followed by the

Table 10.3. *Growth rates and changes in real private equipment investment, 1955–1989*

Period	Investment (billion 1985 yen)	Change
1955–1959 average	3,470.4	
1960–1964 average	9,170.3	+164.2%
1965–1969 average	16,897.9	+84.3%
1970–1974 average	31,003.5	+83.5%
1975–1979 average	31,784.4	+2.5%
1980–1984 average	41,395.2	+30.2%
1985–1989 average	61,233.4	+47.9%

Source: Economic Planning Agency statistics.

trend to export expansion; along with both private equipment investment and individual consumption, exports played a role in raising the rate of economic growth, but the leading role was played by private equipment investment. In the late 1950s, the phrase "investment calls forth further investment" came into use.[16]

Behind this process, the "enduring logic" was consistently at work: ceaseless reinvestment strengthened organizational capabilities, to secure competitive advantages.

The growth rate of private equipment investment was remarkably high (Table 10.3). An international comparison of the ratio of private equipment investment to GNP (in real terms) reveals Japan's high level of private equipment investment. Japan poured more of its GNP into private equipment investment than other countries (Table 10.4).

But an industrial enterprise's organizational capabilities consist of both physical facilities and human skills. Lively private equipment investment in Japanese industrial enterprises from the 1950s put the requisite physical facilities in place. What about human skills?

[16] If we, for example, look at how the *Keizai Hakusho*, 1970 edition, an economic information publication issued by the government of Japan, subdivides contribution by final demand for the production increases in mining and manufacturing between 1958 and 1961, we find that the figure for private equipment investment is highest at 41.4 percent, followed by personal consumption at 22.6 percent, inventory investment at 13.8 percent, and exports at 11.0 percent. Ten years later exports had reached the same level as personal consumption, while private equipment investment remained in the lead with approximately 40 percent.

Table 10.4. *Ratio of GNP for real equipment investment in the manufacturing industries (%)*

Year	Japan	United States	West Germany
1967	6.8%	4.0%	4.7%
1969	8.5	3.8	5.9
1971	7.4	3.4	5.6
1973	6.8	3.5	4.3
1975	5.5	3.6	3.6
1977	4.7	3.6	3.7
1979	4.7	3.9	3.8
1981	5.5	4.2	3.8
1983	5.4	3.6	3.5
1985	6.6	4.4	3.7
1987	6.0	3.9	—

Note: The figures for 1967 and 1969 are based on different standards than those for 1971 on.
Source: Bank of Japan statistics.

With the achievement of consensus on restructuring Japan's economy and industrial enterprises in 1950, the rebuilding of human skills networks began, as did equipment investment. One requirement for upgrading human skills was introducing the latest technologies from the United States and Europe, to which Japan had had no access during the long gap caused by the war. The commitment to network building itself was another characteristic of the postwar period. Japanese industrial enterprises had worked to form skills networks before the war. Interviews with older engineers indicate, however, that while efforts were made in this direction before the war, they were not as well planned or integrated. Only after the war was a concerted effort made to ensure coordination between processes and a smooth flow of information. As a result, fuller, better skills networks developed.

To summarize the unique features of the skill network in Japanese industrial enterprises, one must mention several factors. One is the close, cooperative work relationships that blue-collar workers formed on the work site over the extended period of time permitted by the lifetime employment system. Another is the skills that blue-collar workers mastered through on-the-job training at the production or development site. A third factor was the relationship of cooperation between blue-collar workers and highly educated engineers on the work site, to improve technologies. Fourth, information flowed smoothly among personnel, without being restricted by existing hierarchical structures.[17]

It was the existence of such skills networks that made possible the rapid development of many different products and small-lot manufacturing of multiple products to satisfy an increasingly finely subdivided market.[18] Their most important effect, however, has been the high quality of goods produced. The result is a smaller number of defective products (including returned goods) and high yields. High yields mean that a larger output can be obtained with the same investment in plant and facilities, for larger economies of scale and cost reductions.

For instance, over the two decades between 1957 and 1976, Japan, the United States, and six European Community nations happened, coincidentally, to make the same $27 billion investment in their iron and steel industries. By 1976, they had achieved approximately the same productive capacities: 167 million tons annually in the EC countries, 159 million tons in the United States, and 151 million tons in Japan.[19] Japan's capacity, in fact, was a little lower than the others. According to Barnett and Schorsh, however, by 1980 the average output of the main processes in Japan's iron and steel industry had, in all fields other than those using electric furnaces, surpassed that of the United States.[20]

Some of that difference is doubtless owing to differences in capacity utilization related to market conditions and to the scale of iron and steel mills. Nonetheless, the difference in yields resulting from higher quality has also undoubtedly had a great impact.

The book *Made in America* provides another example. In a comparison of defects in new automobiles made in Japan and the United States, it reported the International Motor Vehicle Program at MIT "found that the number of defects reported in the first six months of use is almost twice as high for cars produced in American plants as in Japanese plants."[21]

Similar U.S.-Japan comparisons have been made for ICs and other

[17] Nikkei Sangyo Shimbun (ed.), *Nihon no Seizogijutsu Tsuyosa no Himitsu* (Secrets of the strong Japanese manufacturing technology), Nikkei Science-sha, 1992.
[18] Michael L. Dertouzos, Richard K. Lester and Robert M. Solow, *Made in America*, MIT Press, 1989, pp. 48–49.
[19] Hans Mueller and K. Kawahito, *Steel Industry Economics: A Comparative Analysis of Structure, Conduct and Performance*, New York, 1978, p. 1.
[20] Seiichiro Yonekura, *Tekko*, vol. 1, p. 268, in Shinichi Yonekawa, Koichi Shimokawa and Hiroaki Yamasaki (ed.) *Sengo Nihon Keieishi* (Postwar Japan's business history), Toyo Keizai Shimpo-sha, 1991.
[21] M. L. Dertouzas et al., *Made in America*, pp. 75–77.

semiconductor products. Among ICs (16K dynamic RAM chips) purchased by Hewlett-Packard of the United States, sampling results found the following defect rates: J_1 (Japanese manufacturer 1), J_2, and J_3 scored 0 percent; A_1 (American manufacturer 1), 0.19 percent; A_2, 0.11 percent; and A_3, 0.19 percent. In the field, J_1 products had a failure rate per 1,000 hours of 0.01 percent; J_2, 0.019 percent; and J_3, 0.012 percent. By contrast, A_1 had a 0.09 percent failure rate per 1,000 hours; A_2, a 0.059 percent rate; and A_3, a 0.267 percent rate.[22]

Data are also available for comparing U.S. and Japanese defect rates in the room air conditioning industry. Restricting the study to the median type, researchers found a 3.3 percent defect rate in parts and materials for the American product and 0.15 percent for the Japanese. Figures for defective products on the assembly line are especially compelling: an average of 63.5 defects per 100 for the American products and 0.95 per 100 for the Japanese.[23]

It is highly developed skills that bring about the dramatic effect of producing good-quality goods in the factory and raising yields. Moreover, those skills must be linked across the production process, not concentrated in a handful of people. Without a skills network that reaches across all the companies performing their separate functions – materials and processing companies, assemblers, and parts makers – higher quality and higher yields are not possible.

The skills networks in Japanese industrial enterprises have worked to overwhelmingly good effect in the machinery (automobiles, electrical equipment) and metals (steel, copper) industries. But they have not achieved noteworthy success in chemical industries, including pharmaceuticals. The same is true of the software industry. In these industries, Japanese industrial enterprises, far from winning a high world market share, have even lost ground to European and American enterprises that have entered the Japanese market. Japan's unique skills networks are systems characteristic of industries such as machinery and metallurgy that succeed through the cooperative efforts of those who have the skills, and in which skills are developed through on-the-job training and the accumulation of experience. The skills network does not work in industries that rest on the creative breakthroughs of individuals of genius, as is the case for the chemical and software industries. It is not effective in forming the skills

[22] Nihon Denshi Kikai Kogyokai, p. 30 in *Integrated Circuit IC Guidebook*, 1981 edition.
[23] David A. Garvin, *Managing Quality: The Strategic and Competitive Edge*, Free Press, Macmillan, 1988, p. 201.

of engineers who are highly imaginative and have fully digested a broad range of basic research. Thus, we should avoid blanket statements about the skills networks in Japanese industry.

JAPAN AS COMPETITIVE MANAGERIAL CAPITALISM

Alfred Chandler has provided a clear-cut categorization of the modern industrial enterprise: the American pattern is competitive managerial capitalism, the British is personal capitalism, and the German is cooperative managerial capitalism. Can the industrial enterprise system that developed in postwar Japan be subsumed under one of these categories?

My view – a view that may arouse strong criticism – is that Japan has developed competitive managerial capitalism. What about the *keiretsu*, one may ask, Japan's large enterprise groups? Don't they interfere with free competition? Considering the keiretsu and the "notorious" role of MITI, many may ask if the Japanese system can be better described as cooperative managerial capitalism. Nonetheless, the Japanese system can well be regarded as competitive managerial capitalism, because of the competitive nature of its oligopolistic firms' behavior.

We must not forget that Chandler's categorization of the modern industrial enterprise is mainly based on the competitive pattern among oligopolistic firms in each country's domestic market. Patterns in international competition and overseas trade policies are of secondary significance. Historically every country has eventually guided international competition to be more favorable to its own side, through regulation of trade and protecting industries. If we consider that behavior in assigning our categories, then we must conclude that competitive capitalism exists nowhere in the world. While I myself am strongly critical of Japan's protectionism, I regard it as a separate issue from classifying the Japanese modern large enterprise.

Here I would like to clarify two issues: the role of MITI and the structure of Japanese enterprise groups. Neither has critically altered the basic characteristics of Japan's competitive managerial capitalism.

Since 1950, the Japanese government – MITI in particular – has carried out a skillful industrial policy of broad application, to reinforce the competitiveness of Japan's capital-intensive industries and protect them from imports. MITI's protectionist role was quite understandable in a late-coming nation. It continued to play that role, however, even after Japan's capital-intensive industries had extracted themselves from their backward position and had acquired advantages in international competition. Moreover, the use of nontariff barriers that depend on restrictions not clearly spelled out in law has been criticized for its unfairness overseas, not surprisingly, and in Japan as well.

Criticizing MITI is not, however, the main theme of this essay. I would rather stress that, despite its powerful protectionist role and its influences on the industrial environment, MITI was unable to organize industrial enterprises in the same industry into one coherent body that would dance to its tune. It was unable to restrict competition between large industrial enterprises.

For instance, MITI revealed its "People's Car Plan" in 1955. Designed to enhance the competitiveness of Japanese passenger cars in the international market, it would have concentrated its protection on one company (one resembling the European "national champion") that succeeded in test production of a 350–500 cubic centimeter class high-performance subcompact car, to make cost reductions possible through mass production and sales. Opposition by the car manufacturers, however, meant that the plan was never carried out. In the mid 1960s, MITI attempted to have the nine Japanese passenger car manufacturers merge into a smaller number of companies that could develop the production and sales capacity to stand up to GM or Ford. That, too, failed, owing to opposition by the car manufacturers.[24]

Similarly, in 1967, MITI determined that the minimum capacity of ethylene plants would be 300,000 tons per year and announced that it would not permit construction of plants that did not meet that standard. This measure was intended to find a way out of the situation then prevailing: the nine ethylene manufacturers (with eleven plants) were engaged in fierce competition and were not able to reach international levels in mass-production capacity. Once again, however, MITI was unable to restrict competition between industrial enterprises. In fact, its policy had a terrible result: two more enterprises entered the field, so that eleven companies each built plants with 300,000 tons or more of annual capacity. Even now, Japan's petrochemical industry suffers from overcapacity and is in financial difficulties.[25]

As these examples indicate, no matter how much power MITI may

[24] Juro Hashimoto, *Nihon Keizai-ron* (Essays on Japan's economy), Minerva Shobo, 1991, p. 287.
[25] Sekiyu Kagaku Kogyo Kyokai, *Sekiyu Kagaku Kogyo 10 nen shi* (10 years of the petrochemical industry in Japan), Sekiyu Kagaku Kogyo Kyokai, 1971, pp. 197–201.

wield, it cannot control Japanese industrial enterprises. While criticizing MITI for its outdated protectionist role, one should not confuse that criticism with a view of MITI as having managed to organize Japan's industrial enterprises according to a single central plan and to control them.

A brief international comparison with the experiences of other nations best illustrates the basic characteristics of Japanese business–government relations. In developing and regulating modern industry, the Japanese government, particularly MITI, could theoretically utilize the various policy means that have been articulated in other chapters, especially those on latecomers. Government-owned enterprises, for instance, could, in theory, have been one of the means, as was primarily the case of Italy, Spain, and Argentina. Japan, however, made little use of such enterprises, particularly after World War II. So its economy did not suffer from a common trouble: that public enterprises choke out the dynamic development of private firms. Nor then did Japan have to utilize the Italian way of rescuing troubled enterprises, by extensively committing public financial resources. In contrast to Argentina, furthermore, the Japanese government did not rely on foreign multinational enterprises for the country's industrial modernization. By systematically regulating the inflow of foreign direct investment, while encouraging and directing incoming technological transfer, the government tried to develop the competences of large domestic firms.

Japan's government policies mostly aimed at promoting the investment of resources in human, technological, and financial capabilities on the part of the private sector. Within the economic environment thus formulated the oligopolistic enterprises in appropriate industries competed against each other, as has also been the case of Korea. Whenever the government's policies became too restrictive, as just described, Japanese large companies, individually or collectively, possessed enough leverage against the government, political as well as financial, to reject the policies. Competitive managerial capitalism in Japan has thus flourished *alongside* the extensive government intervention with dynamic competitive forces.[26]

Japanese enterprise groups are of two types: brethren and parent–child. Neither type of group hinders oligopolistic competition. On the contrary, they both promote it.

Brethren-type enterprise groups are formed by corporations with inter-

[26] Chalmers Johnson, *MITI and the Japanese Miracle*, Stanford University Press, 1982, pp. 311–312.

locking shareholdings. In this type of group, each member has completely independent decision-making powers. When necessary, the member corporations' presidents will coordinate plans, but the presidents' meeting never makes the group act in terms of a single unified strategy.

A parent–child enterprise group comes about when a corporation, pursuing vertical integration or a diversification strategy, spins off business units as subsidiaries rather than retaining them as divisions within itself. In that case, the parent corporation functions as a holding company as well as an operating company. Its top management has considerable say in the decision making of the subsidiaries.

Brethren-type enterprise groups were first formed in the latter half of the 1950s by large corporations formerly part of the Mitsubishi, Sumitomo, and Mitsui zaibatsu. The zaibatsu dissolution program had stripped their owner families and holding companies (which had been the head corporations in the zaibatsu structure) of their shareholdings in the zaibatsu companies. The holding companies themselves were dissolved, and, as a provision of the Antimonopoly Act, pure holding companies were forbidden.

To the extent that shareholders who had acquired zaibatsu company shares when they were on the market interfered with decision making, the top salaried managers at these former zaibatsu companies were hindered from managing efficiently based on a long-range perspective. Thus, these companies used assistance from their former zaibatsu bank to buy up outstanding shares in group member companies on the market or new shares when the member companies increased their capitalization. Because Japanese corporations have, since before the war, been prohibited from holding their own shares, these zaibatsu group members bought and held each others' shares. The goal was to provide stable shareholders for fellow former zaibatsu companies and to facilitate the exercise of authority by their top salaried managers.

As stated earlier, Japan entered the managerial enterprise era during its postwar period of rapid economic growth. The existence of cross shareholdings within brethren-type groups was a condition favoring the dominance of the managerial enterprise. In addition, the close personal ties among enterprises that had belonged to the same zaibatsu before the war also aided efficient formation of brethren-type enterprise groups. A group of corporations that knew each others' management well, had long-standing business dealings, and shared information and resources were able to work together to move into new fields (petrochemicals or nuclear energy, for instance). Such moves were an effective use of the brethren-type corporate enterprise group.[27]

In the early 1960s, three leading banks – Fuji, Sanwa, and Dai-ichi – brought together major enterprises with which they had close ties through lendings to form their own brethren-type groups modeled on the Mitsubishi, Sumitomo, and Mitsui groups. These had the same functions and purposes as the groups formed of former zaibatsu companies. Today, therefore, there are six major brethren-type enterprise groups in Japan.[28]

The purpose of the parent–child enterprise groups was to promote the growth of the parent's subsidiaries, not retain control. Had control been the goal, the parent company would not have spun the operating units off as legally independent subsidiary companies (in Japanese, *bunshaka* or splitting off companies) but would have retained them as divisions within it. Making the units legally independent companies meant creating posts for corporate officers, motivating them, forcing them to experience risk, and building up managerial skills. If, as a result, the subsidiaries grew, then the parent corporation and the keiretsu as a whole would gain deeper financial resources and acquire more posts for middle-level and top management, while also being able to respond to changes in the product life cycle. There is, of course, need for care, to prevent subsidiaries that had gained stature from leaving the group.

These subsidiaries include not only former operating units of the parent company but also firms that, having formed a long-term business relationship with the parent company, permitted it to buy their shares and participate in their management, and were added to the *keiretsu*. Examples of long-term business relationships include supplying parts to the parent company or producing goods from materials the parent company produces. But the relationship is not simply a matter of dealing in goods; the role of the technological guidance the keiretsu member receives from the parent company and of their relationship of technological cooperation to upgrade skills must not be overlooked.

The simplest place to see the structure of a parent–child group is in the relationships between assemblers and parts manufacturers in the automobile industry. Japan is not unique in that assemblers and parts manufacturers have long-standing business relationships. The issue is, however, a distinctive characteristic of the vertical relationship between assemblers

---

[27] Takeo Kikkawa, *Kigyo Shudan no Seiritsu to Sono Kino* (Emergence and function of Japanese enterprise groups), pp. 69–74, in Morikawa, *Sengo Keieishi Nyumon*.
[28] Ibid.

and parts manufacturers in Japan's auto industry. That characteristic is not found in the closed nature of their business dealings. As will be shown, a parts manufacturer does not supply parts only within one group. Nor do assemblers purchase parts only from within the same group. In this respect, the situation is as in other countries.

What, then, is distinctive about these relationships? One characteristic is the large number of parts manufacturers. That is owing to the low percentage of in-house parts procurement among Japanese auto manufacturers: only 20 to 30 percent, far lower than the roughly 60 percent seen at GM or Ford. A second distinctive feature derives from the first: there is a hierarchy of parts manufacturers. The first tier of parts manufacturers supplies parts to the assembler (the auto manufacturer), the second tier supplies parts to the first tier, and the third tier supplies parts to the second tier. The auto manufacturer owns shares in the first-tier parts manufacturers, and controls their management. The second and third tier of parts manufacturers are smaller, and their shares are usually closely held. They do not need to develop cross-shareholding relationships with the first-tier manufacturers.

A third distinctive feature is that the relationships between the auto manufacturer and first-tier parts manufacturers or between the higher and lower tiers of parts manufacturers go beyond cross-shareholdings, control, and the buying and selling of parts. There is a relationship of close guidance to improve efficiency and quality. The auto manufacturers do make strict demands of the parts manufacturers in terms of cost, quality, and delivery schedules and do supervise them closely, but they also act as guardians and teachers, providing technical guidance or guaranteeing bank loans. That also holds true for the relationship between higher- and lower-tier parts manufacturers.[29]

Gauging the size of a parent–child group by its number of subsidiaries, Table 10.5 gives the top twenty of these groups and their total assets as of June 1991.

Both the member companies in brethren-type groups and the head company in parent–child groups are, in almost all cases, large managerial enterprises with full-time salaried managers promoted from within the company carrying out top-level decision making. The top management of each of these large enterprises carries out decision making independently,

---

[29] Kazuo Wada, *The Development of Tiered Inter-firm Relationships in the Automobile Industry: A Case Study of the Toyota Motor Corporation*, vol. 8, pp. 27–36, in Business History Society of Japan (ed.), *Japanese Yearbook on Business History*, 1991.

Table 10.5. *The big twenty parent–child enterprise groups in Japan*

Group	No. of subsidiaries	Total assets ($million)	Brethren-type group (nominal)	Industry
Mitsui & Co.	739	58,845	Mitsui	Trading
Mitsubishi Corp.	671	65,662	Mitsubishi	Trading
Matsushita Electrical Ind.	385	28,914		Electrical machinery
Honda	295	10,848		Automobile
Nissan	274	25,733	(Fuji Bank)	Automobile
Toshiba	255	24,935	Mitsui	Electrical machinery
Hitachi	242	28,247	(Fuji Bank)	Electrical machinery
NYK	235	5,964	Mitsubishi	Shipping
NEC	198	21,001	Sumitomo	Electrical machinery
FACOM	196	20,334	First Bank	Electrical machinery
Nippon Steel	195	24,840		Iron and steel
Toyota	193	45,051	(Mitsui)	Automobile
Mitsubishi Heavy Ind.	182	24,289	Mitsubishi	Engineering
Asahi Glass	180	6,952	Mitsubishi	Glass
Asahi Chemical Industry	176	7,719		Chemical
Sumitomo Metal Industries	157	14,601	Sumitomo	Iron and steel
Sekisui Chemical	152	4,772	(Sanwa Bank)	Chemical
NTT	152	80,955		Communications
NKK	138	16,588	Fuji Bank	Iron and steel
Kobe Steel	134	14,456		Iron and steel

Source: '92 Kigyo Keiretsu Soran ('92 Survey on Corporate Groups), Toyo Keizai Shimpo-sha, 1992.

but the head company in a parent–child group has more autonomy. That is, the top management of brethren-type enterprise groups is absolutely not required to follow all the same ideas and policies, but they do tend to avoid actions that will discommode other members of the group or will be criticized by other managers. The top management of the head company in a parent–child group is in this respect freer, though not absolutely free. Apart from government regulation, they must pay heed to the advice of the banks that have provided their enterprises with funds.

As Table 10.5 indicates, almost all major corporations that are part of brethren-type groups have also formed parent–child groups, which they head. But it is not the case that all corporations at the head of parent–child groups also belong to brethren groups. For instance, Nippon Steel, Matsushita, and Sony are not members of any brethren group. In addition, some companies are only nominally members of brethren groups: they participate more or less ceremonially, as the result of business or financial ties in the past. In such cases, the company does not have close ties with the brethren group; its role as the leader of an independent parent–child group is more important. Examples include Toyota in the Mitsui group and Hitachi or Nissan in the Fuji Bank group.

What should be noted is that neither the brethren-type nor the parent–child groups were formed so that companies that originally were competitors in the same industry could collude in setting prices and production levels. Since the groups support their member corporations' engaging in ferocious competition for market share with other corporations in other groups, far from restricting competition, they intensify it.

Some group members do depend on their group's support, neglecting to enhance their organizational capabilities and avoiding tackling their competitors, but such examples appear only rarely, among companies in declining industries. In fact, the group's raison d'etre is to put member corporations in an advantageous competitive position; that is in itself evidence of the groups' value in promoting competition.

Recent criticism in America and Europe of these groups functioning to restrict competition have addressed a different aspect of these groups' role. When member companies, of either brethren or parent–child groups, do business with each other (in raw materials, parts, finished products, credit, services of trading companies, or construction), companies outside the group, whether they are Japanese or foreign, cannot participate. Thus, the criticism is that nonmembers are being excluded from these transactions.

Indeed, Japanese corporations do tend to prefer dealing with members of their enterprise groups rather than outsiders in everything from purchasing to sales. Looking at one example, automobile manufacturers, and the ratio of products parts manufacturers sell to the assembler in the same parent–child group, we find that forty-five of the fifty-one parts manufacturers sell 50 percent or more of their output to the assembler, the parent company of their group. Moreover, thirty-two of those parts manufacturers sell 70 percent or more of their output to the parent company, and thirteen, or one-fourth, sell 90 percent or more of their output to it.[30]

These figures do seem to indicate that the group's nature is to restrict participation of outside companies. But the reasons why the group members deal more often with each other than with outside companies must be understood. They have a long experience of doing business with other members of the same group, they feel personally close to managers in the other enterprises in the same group, and they have considerable information about those enterprises' operations and confidence in their skills and product quality. Those advantages do not operate in dealing with companies in other groups, with which they have less experience. Since to achieve the same level of knowledge and trust in a nongroup company would require acquiring information about that company over a considerable period of time, it would generate excess transaction costs. In general, transactions within the group will unquestionably be more advantageous. But that generalization does not cover all cases.

If a transaction outside the group can guarantee a supply of good-quality products at a price so low that it cancels the advantage of the lower transaction cost of intragroup transactions, then member enterprises would seek such transaction partners outside the group. The group has no power to restrain its members from doing so or require that they restrict their dealings to within the group if that will be disadvantageous. Let us suppose that there did exist such a group that required behavior that ignored business rationality. Then internal conflicts would soon destroy it.

Moreover, it would be unusual for an enterprise to expend its capacity for supply in intragroup transactions alone. Not being satisfied with intragroup trading, they enter the marketplace outside the group, and fierce competition occurs there.

[30] Hiroshi Fujimoto, *Jidosha Sangyo Keiretsu no Jittai to Kongo no Hoko*, p. 27 in '92 *Kigyo Keiretsu Soran*, Toyo Keizai Shimpo-sha, 1992.

For instance, among the six big brethren-type groups, intragroup sales account for only a portion of group members' total sales. In 1981, that figure was 20.4 percent for manufacturing enterprises within these groups and only 7 percent for trading companies. On the purchasing side, intragroup purchases accounted for 12.4 and 18.2 percent, respectively.[31] Whether one judges that degree of dependency on intragroup transactions to be large or small may vary with one's stance, but it is at least clear that intragroup transactions cannot provide enough business and that transactions outside the group are by no means prohibited.

These points lead me to conclude that industrial enterprises in Japan today definitely do not restrict competition, despite their membership in enterprise groups or keiretsu, a unique intermediate organization. While enterprises within each group cooperate with each other, the highly competitive relationship between groups is dominant.

[31] Sawako Yamamoto, *Keiretsu Torihiki no Kyoso Seisakujo no Mondai*, pp. 19–20. '92 *Kigyo Keiretsu Soran*, Toyo Keizai Shimpo-sha, 1992.

11

South Korea: Enterprising groups and
entrepreneurial government

ALICE H. AMSDEN

INDUSTRIALIZATION THROUGH LEARNING

At the heart of South Korea's industrial transformation has been the
family-controlled, diversified big business group, or *chaebol*. The enterprise system that is centered around the chaebol, which I call state entrepreneurial capitalism, has differed from the established classifications of
modern enterprise systems, such as the personal capitalism of Britain, the
competitive managerial capitalism of the United States, or the cooperative
managerial capitalism of Germany.[1] Korea's enterprise system most closely
resembles that of Japan's prewar *zaibatsu*, and both enterprise systems
are part of a more general "late"-industrializing paradigm.[2] But Korea's
enterprise system differs from that of Japan insofar as the chaebol were
denied their own banking affiliates by a state-owned banking system. This
accorded the government through its credit allocation far more power
over the process of industrialization and the policies of big business than
was characteristic even of Japan.

With Japan's "demonstration effect" – which showed that it was possible for a backward country to industrialize – the Korean government
staked its own survival on economic growth rather than cronyism, and
used its power to promote systematic capital accumulation through savings

---

[1] Alfred D. Chandler, Jr., *Scale and Scope: The Dynamics of Industrial Capitalism* (Cambridge, MA: Harvard University Press, 1990).

[2] For Japan see Hidemasa Morikawa, *Zaibatsu: The Rise and Fall of Family Enterprise
Groups in Japan* (Tokyo: University of Tokyo Press, 1992); for a discussion of the late-
industrializing paradigm, see Takashi Hikino and Alice H. Amsden, "Staying Behind,
Stumbling Back, Sneaking Up, Soaring Ahead: Late Industrialization in Historical Perspective," in William J. Baumol, Richard R. Nelson, and Edward N. Wolff, *Convergence
of Productivity: Cross-Country Studies and Historical Evidence* (New York: Oxford University Press, 1994).

336

and investment. It not only supported big business but also disciplined it by exacting performance standards in exchange for various subsidies, such as preferential credit and protection from foreign imports and investments. Political loyalty was a necessary but not sufficient condition for receiving lucrative incentives. If a targeted firm proved itself to be a poor performer, it ceased being subsidized – as evidenced by the high turnover among Korea's top-ten companies between 1965 and 1985.[3] In turn, Korean companies grew big enough to insist on a workable standard of honesty and efficiency on the government's part. A system of "countervailing power" arose, comparable with that described in the United States by Galbraith,[4] with two crucial differences: labor was missing from the equation, and the powerhouse in Korea in the period 1962–1989 was decisively government.

Korea's GNP in this period grew annually at a breakneck average rate of over 8 percent (Table 11.1 presents some basic macroeconomic data), transforming this populous yet resource-poor former colony of Japan into an emerging East Asian industrial power. Growth was triggered by a military government committed to economic development. In mid-1965 the government lifted restrictions on imports for export processing but strengthened protection for domestic industries and subsidies for exports, thereby precipitating an export boom in light manufactures. In the 1970s the government launched an ambitious investment plan for heavy industry. By the 1980s exports of "mid-technology" products such as steel, ships, and then automobiles and consumer electronics became Korea's leading sector.

Despite world record rates of economic growth the chaebol still managed to increase their share of GNP, which is the rough measure of their power that has most excited public ire. By 1988 the revenues of the top-ten business groups equaled about 60 percent of GNP, up from 15 percent in 1974. The revenues of the top four groups alone more than quadrupled in relation to GNP, from 10 percent to 46 percent over the same time period (see Table 11.2).[5]

[3] For instance, only three of the ten largest chaebol in 1965 remained among the top-ten companies in 1975. See Linsu Kim, "South Korea," in Richard R. Nelson (ed.), *National Innovation Systems* (New York: Oxford University Press, 1993).

[4] John K. Galbraith, *American Capitalism* (New York: Houghton Mifflin, 1952).

[5] The concentration of the chaebol is less dramatic when their share of value-added or even shipments is examined, although even some estimates of sales show less extreme concentration than the data in Table 11.2. See, for example, Kyu-Uk Lee, S. Urata, and I Choi, "Recent Developments in Industrial Organizational Issues in Korea" mimeograph copy (Washington, DC: Korea Development Institute and World Bank, 1986). Discrepancies appear to arise due to different definitions of "company," which sometimes refers to a

Table 11.1. Macroeconomic indicators, 1962–1994

| | 1969 | 1979 | 1989 | 1994[a] | Average annual change, % | | | |
					1962/1969	1970/1979	1980/1989	1990/1994[a]
Per capita GNP (US$)	210	1,644	4,968	8,824[b]	—	—	—	—
Real GNP (bil. US$)	6.6	61.4	209	297	8.9	8.9	8.3	7.5
Exports (bil. US$)	0.7	14.7	61.4	93.7	41.7	38.1	15.9	9.2
Imports (bil. US$)	1.6	19.1	56.8	96.8	27.5	29.6	13.0	10.8
Gross domestic investment[c] (% of GNP)	27.9	35.9	34.7	36.2	—	—	—	—
Gross saving[d] (% of GNP)	21.4	28.4	36.3	35.3	—	—	—	—
Inflation (CPI, %)	—	—	—	—	11.5	15.2	8.4	7.3

[a] 1994 data are preliminary.

[b] Per capita income reached $10,000 in 1995.

[c] 11.8% in 1962.

[d] 11.0% in 1962.

Source: Bank of Korea, *Economic Statistics Yearbook* (Seoul: Bank of Korea, various years).

Table 11.2. *The top-ten business groups' share of GNP, 1974–1988*
(combined sales)

Groups	1974	1978	1984	1988[a]
1	4.9	6.9	12.0	15.2
4	10.3	20.7	44.3	45.9
10	15.1	30.2	67.4	60.9

Notes: Share of GNP Figures = (Aggregate revenues of the largest one, four, and ten business groups/GNP) × 100 for each year. Data for sales are more reliable than data for value-added, but overstate the position of leading enterprises. Sales data indicate position of leading enterprises, including their consumption from suppliers.
[a] Not strictly comparable with previous years due to different source.
Sources: 1974, 1978, and 1984: Seok Ki Kim, "Business Concentration and Government Policy: A Study of the Phenomenon of Business Groups in Korea, 1945–1985," Ph.D. Dissertation, Harvard Business School, 1987; 1988: Compiled from Bankers Trust Securities Research and Korea Investors Service, Inc. *Zaebols in Korea* (Seoul: 1989).

South Korea has achieved world-record growth rates without any of its leading, large family-controlled enterprise groups enjoying the competitive advantage of pioneering technology, the hallmark of the First and Second Industrial Revolutions. Even European countries that fell behind their neighbors economically could usually exploit some original artisan technology in world markets to help them earn invaluable foreign exchange (examples are French porcelains, Czech crystal glass, Italian designs, and Spanish sherry). South Korea's industrialization has been a pure case of learning, or borrowing technology that has already been commercialized by firms from other countries. The absence of an asset in the form of original technology, modern or indigenous, is the meaning I attach to industrializing "late."[6]

By this definition Japan was the first successful late industrializer, but Japan's industrialization was facilitated by the significant market power

business group and sometimes to a business affiliate only. The data in Table 11.2 for 1974, 1978, and 1984 refer to groups and were compiled from raw sales data by Seok Ki Kim, "Business Concentration and Government Policy: A Study of the Phenomenon of Business Groups in Korea, 1945–1985," Ph. D. Dissertation, Harvard Business School, 1987.
[6] Alice H. Amsden, *Asia's Next Giant: South Korea and Late Industrialization* (Oxford: Oxford University Press, 1989). See also Alice H. Amsden, *The Rise of the Rest: Late Industrialization outside the North Atlantic Region* (in preparation).

it derived from being a colonizer. Neither Korea nor Taiwan, its principal colonies, enjoyed comparable power. In addition, Korea and Taiwan had the nontrivial task of having to compete against Japan itself. Korea, with a population of over 40 million people, twice that of Taiwan's, is possibly the first major ex-colony of a great power to reach a high level of industrial transformation and per capita income ($10,000 by the end of 1995), with neither proprietary technology nor colonial leverage over product markets and raw materials.

Two general properties of late industrialization have been the interventionist state as well as the diversified business group. Without proprietary technologies to capitalize upon, and with the risks inherent in specializing in a narrow product range whose technology is exogenously controlled, leading enterprises throughout Latin America, Asia, the Middle East, and South Africa have tended to diversify widely into technologically unrelated "mid-tech" industries.[7] The diversification pattern of the chaebol is a good example of this, and is depicted in Table 11.3. Obviously the degree of diversification and its unrelatedness diminish the smaller the business group, but considering that the top-twenty business groups in Korea have diversified widely, and together control over 300 subsidiaries, unrelated diversification in Korea is marked.

While diversified business groups tend to be ubiquitous in late-industrializing countries, they are proportionately greater and larger in Korea than elsewhere.[8] The size and resource concentration of Korea's top business groups are partly due to politics (discussed later) and partly to Korea's growth pattern, which has taken the form of a great spurt

---

[7] Amsden, *Asia's Next Giant*, and Hikino and Amsden, "Staying Behind." There are general reasons behind the rise of diversified business groups, as well as country-specific reasons which influence their absolute size, the industries in which they operate, and other particularistic characteristics. Business groups in Taiwan, for example, tend to be smaller than in Korea due to government credit allocation and industrial licensing policies (see the representative case of the Aurora Group in Bing-Eng Wu, "The Aurora Group," in N. T. Wang (ed.), *Taiwan's Enterprises in Global Perspective* (Armonk, NY: M. E. Sharpe 1992), pp. 309–25. Writing about Japan, Hidemasa Morikawa notes: "The main sources of the enormous wealth of the larger *zaibatsu* families lay in profits accumulated from government patronage [as in Korea] and mining. . . . The *zaibatsu* were thus a product of the owner families' money and their salaried managers' desire to diversify" (*Zaibatsu*, p. xxiii). Cultural and other societal influences on Korean business history in general were also undoubtedly influential, but limited space precludes giving them their rightful due. For a cultural interpretation of Korean big business, see Roger L. Janelli with Dawnhee Yim, *Making Capitalism: The Social and Cultural Construction of a South Korean Conglomerate* (Stanford, CA: Stanford University Press, 1993).

[8] Alice H. Amsden and Takashi Hikino, "Project Execution Capability, Organizational Know-how, and Conglomerate Corporate Growth in Late-Industrialization," *Industrial and Corporate Change,* 3, 1 (March 1994), pp. 111–147.

Table 11.3. *The chaebol's diversification pattern, 1984*

Business group	Single	Dominant	Related	Unrelated	
		(Percent of Size Group, %)			
10 largest (213)[a]	0	10	10	80	= 100%
11–20 largest (123)[a]	0	20	30	50	= 100%
21–50 largest (206)[a]	0	30	47	23	= 100%
51–108 largest (246)[a]	21	36	33	0	= 100%
Total (788)	11	31	34	24	= 100%

[a] Total number of subsidiaries for size category.
Source: Young Ki Lee, "Conglomeration and Business Concentration in Korea," in Jene K. Kwon (ed.), *Korean Economic Development* (New York: Greenwood Press, 1990).

rather than a gradual expansion. Korea's manufacturing base at the end of the Korean War (1950–1953) was negligible compared with that of Brazil, Mexico, Argentina, and India, and Korea had to make a big push in order to catch up.[9] Hothouse growth tends to decrease the chances for firms of different size and structure to germinate, since competition for scarce resources is more intense than under evolutionary conditions. Furthermore, the prevalence of private big business groups in Korea stems from the paucity of foreign and state enterprises, a reflection of national policy. The only major state-owned manufacturing firm in Korea is the Pohang Iron and Steel Company (POSCO), and apart from industries oriented toward labor-intensive exports and some high-tech joint ventures, there is no mid-tech sector dominated by foreign firms. The output share of domestic private big business in Korea is thus extraordinarily high partly because the alternatives are missing. Gereffi found that, out of a country's ten largest companies in 1987, state and foreign companies accounted for nine in Brazil, eight in Mexico, four in Taiwan (all four state enterprises), and only one in Korea (POSCO).[10] Korea, therefore,

---

[9] The ratio of manufacturing to agricultural net product in 1955 was only 0.20 for Korea compared with 1.32 for Argentina, 0.72 for Brazil, 1.00 for Mexico, and 0.30 for India (which was low due to India's vast agricultural sector rather than the underdevelopment of its industry).
   See Alfred Maizels, *Industrial Growth and World Trade* (Cambridge: Cambridge University Press, 1963).
[10] Gary Gereffi, "Big Business and the State: East Asia and Latin America Compared," *Asian Perspective*, 14, 1 (Spring–Summer 1990), pp. 5–29.

provides an excellent laboratory to study big, private, indigenous business in late industrialization (although from a short historical perspective).

This chapter addresses three questions. First, why was it the chaebol, rather than another type of business organization, that developed Korea's forces of production? This question is formulated to emphasize the importance of entrepreneurship, which is necessary for the forces of production to be thoroughly transformed. Korea's big business groups have been as objectionable politically and socially as the robber barons of the United States or the zaibatsu of Japan. They may also have been inefficient in their formative years in not scrupulously maximizing output per unit of input at the margin.[11] But beyond any doubt they have been enterprising learners – absorbing foreign technology, diversifying production, and pumping out exports.

Given that the chaebol have dominated the Korean economy, and given that the Korean economy has diversified and grown exceptionally fast, the chaebol's effectiveness as industrializers is taken for granted. The second question addressed, therefore, is, What accounts for the chaebol's competitive success?

The third question relates to the role of the state. If, as defined by Schumpeter, entrepreneurship involves the conception of new economic opportunities and the coordination of the resources necessary to exploit

---

[11] Theoretically, one would *not* expect to find high estimates of total factor productivity growth for late-industrializing countries because such countries grew by borrowing new technology rather than by innovating their own new products and processes. Therefore, improvements in their productivity should be incorporated in capital stock and labor inputs, in which new technology is embodied, rather than in a shift in a production function, which is what the residual in econometric estimates of total factor productivity allegedly captures. Assuming perfect capital and product markets, total factor productivity growth for technology borrowers should be zero plus a small margin for what could be called "mini-innovation," or whatever firm-level learning is necessary to make borrowed technology work. The empirical evidence for total factor productivity for South Korea and other late-industrializing countries tends to be contradictory and based on unreliable data for capital. For high estimates of total factor productivity growth in South Korea, see World Bank, *The East Asian Miracle: Economic Growth and Public Policy* (Washington, DC: World Bank, 1993). For low estimates, see Jene K. Kwon and Kyhyang Yuhn, "*Analysis of Factor Substitution and Productivity Growth in Korean Manufacturing, 1961–1981,*" in Jene K. Kwon (ed.), *Korean Economic Development* (New York: Greenwood Press, 1990), pp. 145–66; and Jene K. Kwon, "The East Asian Challenge to Neoclassical Orthodoxy," *World Development*, 22, 4 (April 1994), pp. 635–44. An inkling that data on total factor productivity are unreliable may be found in the results of Alwyn Young, as cited by Paul Krugman, "Myth of East Asia's Miracle," *Foreign Affairs* (November–December 1994), pp. 62–78. Young's data measure total factor productivity growth for 1970–1985 for sixty-six countries. Counterintuitively, Egypt, Pakistan, Botswana, Congo, and Malta rank at the top while Switzerland ranks at the bottom. See Alwyn Young, "Lessons from the East Asian NICS: A contraction view," *European Economic Review*, 38 (1994), 964–973.

them, then the state has been Korea's greatest entrepreneur. Without original technologies to underscore competitiveness and shape the economy's direction of change, the state's role in all late-industrializing countries has been far more active than even Alexander Gerschenkron entertained.[12] Because big business–focused growth and proactive state intervention have gone-hand in hand in Korea, and because both business and government have been entrepreneurial, and both have relied heavily on hierarchies of managers to execute their plans, I have called Korea's enterprise system state entrepreneurial capitalism (which is not to be confused with Franco Amatori's characterization in Chapter 8 of Italy's enterprise system as political managerial capitalism).

Both state entrepreneurial capitalism and the chaebol's excesses have elicited prolific and passionate criticism from numerous Korean scholars, particularly those educated in the United States.[13] If, however, one infers from the fact of Korea's rapid growth that big business has done a respectable job in developing the productive forces, then, given the government's ubiquity in the economy, one must also concede that the government has done a respectable job. One cannot argue simply on the basis of theory that Korea might have grown even faster with smaller firms and less government intervention because there is no evidence for this, not even from a country roughly comparable with Korea. While the excesses of big business and the state cannot be denied, what is important is to draw inferences from the fact that Korea was one of the world's poorest countries in the early 1960s but one of the richest late-industrializing countries by the early 1990s. A critical question addressed in this chapter, therefore, is, To what does the state owe its effectiveness?

SPECIALISTS VERSUS GENERALISTS

On the eve of Korea's big spurt in the mid-1960s two types of business organizations existed side by side. Each had the potential to develop the

---

[12] Alexander Gerschenkron, *Economic Backwardness in Historical Perspective* (Cambridge, MA: Harvard University Press, 1962).

[13] For two typical criticisms see Young Ki Lee, "Conglomeration and Business Concentration in Korea," and E. Han Kim, "Financing Korean Corporations: Evidence and Theory," both in Kwon, *Korean Economic Development*, pp. 325–58. Korea has many more American-trained economists (at the Ph.D. level) than Japan, with three-times Korea's population: between 1970 and 1990 American-trained Korean economists numbered 801 whereas American-trained Japanese economists numbered only 305. See Alice H. Amsden, "The Specter of Anglo-Saxonization is Haunting South Korea," in Lee-Jay Cho and Yoon Hyung Kim (eds.), *Korea's Political Economy: An Institutional Perspective* (Boulder, CO: Westview Press, 1994), pp. 87–126.

productive forces, which then meant investing in infrastructure (ports and highways) and simple import-substitution industries, such as sugar refining, fertilizers, and cement. The capital intensity of these investments necessitated rather large-scale undertakings, but the two types of business organizations already in existence in Korea were both relatively large (in terms of employment and capital assets). One type of business was specialized, dedicated to cotton spinning and weaving, the major manufacturing activity since the colonial period. Another type – the progenitor of the chaebol – involved entrepreneurs who had entered a particular business line as a consequence of acquiring Japanese confiscated properties or American-aid related "loans" and foreign exchange, both of which were highly politicized and irregular processes (and a later cause of popular resentment against the big business groups). These entrepreneurs were quick to make money in whatever industry the opportunity arose. Hence, they may be described as generalists.

It is a mystery why, despite its early prominence, Korea's cotton-spinning and weaving industry never became the crucible for diversification into other industries. With possibly one exception (the Sunkyong group), no major chaebol arose with cotton spinning and weaving as its core activity.[14] Political favoritism alone provides no clue because many textile magnates themselves arose by acquiring confiscated Japanese property, and the textile industry in the 1950s and 1960s also received a large share of official government subsidies. The textile industry was by no means slighted politically.

An important part of the answer concerning industrial leadership has to do with the fact, discussed later, that unlike the generalists, textile companies never invested in the "organizational capabilities" that Alfred Chandler has pointed out are necessary for expansion, and without which diversification and management of capital-intensive investment projects cannot occur.[15]

In theory, diversification into capital-intensive industries could have been undertaken by entirely new firms. Given, however, Korea's hothouse growth trajectory, and the problem – without any organizational foundations – of putting together the large investments necessary for early import substitution projects, that pattern was decidedly not the one Korea followed. As pioneering study on Korean business observed, "A high

[14] As discussed later, a few chaebol did have as their original activity woolen textiles or synthetic fibers.
[15] Chandler, *Scale and Scope*, and Chapter 3 in this book.

percent of the expansion of industrial output has come from existing rather than new firms. . . . What has to be explained is not how new entrepreneurs were found but how old firms grew."[16]

The cotton textile industry

After the Korean War textile manufacturing engaged the largest and most modern companies in the country.[17] According to an industrial census taken in 1967, a total of only 150 manufacturing establishments employed more than 500 workers, and 29 percent of these were in the textiles sector, which represented a larger percentage than the textile sector's share in manufacturing value-added, 14 percent, or share in exports, 21 percent.[18] Textiles not only remained Korea's single most important export through the 1980s but also an industry with a significant share of all large firms. Table 11.4 compares data on the distribution of approximately 200 of the largest manufacturing firms in Korea, Japan, Germany, and the United States. In 1983 the textile industry (defined broadly to include the manufacture of synthetic fibers) still accounted for as much as 13 percent of big Korean enterprise, compared with only 5.5 in Japan, 2.0 in Germany, and 1.7 in the United States.

Firm size per se, therefore, is not the critical variable in predicting which type of firm will successfully diversify. Instead, what matters is whether firms invest in the professional management and other organizational capabilities that are necessary to grow. In this respect the textile industry was backward. Table 11.5 presents a breakdown for 1983 of managerial resources by industry, where the ratio of administrative employees to operatives serves as a surrogate for managerial resources. As can be seen from the table, the textile industry had the third lowest ratio of administrators to operatives among twenty industries.

[16] Leroy P. Jones and Il Sakong, *Government, Business, and Entrepreneurship in Economic Development: The Korean Case* (Cambridge, MA: Harvard University Press for the Council on East Asian Studies, Harvard University, 1980), pp. xxxii, 179.

[17] One study states: "In the pre-liberation period, when most of the modern industries were transplanted from Japan, the textile industry utilized the most contemporary production and management methods. In the 1950s, the textile industry was instrumental in the recovery and modernization of production facilities." See Yung Bong Kim, "The Growth and Structural Change of Textile Industry," in Chong Kee Park (ed.), *Macroeconomic and Industrial Development in Korea, Essays on the Korean Economy*, vol. 3 (Seoul, Korea: Development Institute, 1980), p. 190.

[18] Economic Planning Board, *Report on Mining and Manufacturing Survey* (Seoul: Government of Korea, 1968).

Table 11.4. *Percent distribution of 200 largest manufacturing firms
in Korea, Japan, Germany, and United States, by industry*[a]

Industry, standard industrial classification	Korea[b] (1983)	Japan (1973)	Germany[c] (1973)	United States[d] (1973)
20. Food	14.5	9.0	6.0	12.1
21. Tobacco	4.1	0.0	3.0	1.7
22. Textiles	12.8	5.5	2.0	1.7
23. Apparel	1.7	0.0	0.0	0.0
24. Lumber	0.6	0.5	0.0	2.2
25. Furniture	0.0	0.0	0.0	0.0
26. Paper	1.7	5.0	1.0	5.0
27. Printing	0.6	1.0	3.0	0.5
28. Chemicals	16.3	17.0	15.1	14.9
29. Petroleum	2.9	6.5	4.0	12.1
30. Rubber	4.1	2.5	1.5	2.8
31. Leather	0.6	0.0	0.5	0.0
32. Stone, clay, glass	4.1	7.0	7.5	3.9
33. Primary metal	11.6	13.5	9.5	10.5
34. Fabricated metal	1.2	2.5	7.0	2.8
35. General machinery	2.9	8.0	14.6	9.4
36. Electrical machinery	10.5	9.0	10.5	7.2
37. Transport equipment	9.8	10.0	7.1	10.5
38. Instruments	0.0	2.5	1.0	2.2
39. Miscellaneous	0.0	0.5	0.5	10.5
Total	100.0	100.0	100.0	100.0

Column header: Percent Distribution

[a] Ranked by sales.
[b] 172 firms, which include units of business groups.
[c] 199 firms.
[d] 181 firms.
Sources: Korea: Compiled from Economic Planning Board, *Report on Industrial Census*, vol. 1, 1983 (Seoul: 1985); Japan, Germany, and the United States: Adapted from Alfred D. Chandler, Jr., *Scale and Scope: The Dynamics of Industrial Capitalism* (Cambridge, MA: Harvard University Press, 1990).

Table 11.5. *Managerial resources by industry, 1983*

Industry, standard industrial classification	Administrative employees/ 100 operatives[a]	Family workers/ 100 administrative employees[a]
Food	30.0	11.0[b]
Tobacco	17.0	0.0[c]
Textiles[d]	9.3	16.8[e]
Apparel[d]	8.7	20.4
Lumber	14.2	32.1
Furniture	12.2	37.5
Paper	20.8	12.0
Printing	34.0	14.5
Chemicals	44.0	3.7
Petroleum	46.1	2.6
Rubber	7.3	6.2
Leather	12.1	18.8
Stone, clay, glass	18.5	13.6
Primary metal	23.0	4.4
Fabricated metal	19.3	14.3
Machinery	22.6	12.2
Electrical machinery	17.7	4.5
Transport equipment	31.1	2.9
Instruments	15.6	9.3
Miscellaneous	10.9	17.9

[a] Figures for administrative and family workers refer to males only to avoid inflating the administrative and family categories with female clerical workers. See discussion in text.

[b] Average of food and beverages.

[c] A government monopoly exists in the tobacco industry.

[d] Adjusted for the fact that many female administrative employees in these industries are front-line supervisors. Adjustment takes the form of inflating the number of male administrators in these industries by the ratio of males to total administrators in the all-manufacturing average.

[e] Excludes shoes.

Source: Compiled from Economic Planning Board *Report on Industrial Census*, vol. 1, 1983 (Seoul: 1985).

The industries with the lowest ratios of administrative employees to operatives in Table 11.4 are relatively labor-intensive. Because they generally expand by means of "capital widening," they have less need for organizational resources than capital-intensive industries. That is, they usually expand by replicating the existing ratio of capital to labor, an example being expansion in the apparel industry by means of another seamstress and sewing machine. By contrast, in capital-intensive industries subject to "capital deepening," expansion usually takes the form of an increase in the amount of capital employed per labor unit.[19] Generally deepening requires greater technological capability and more scientific knowledge because technical parameters do not change linearly. Greater capabilities are required in capital-deepening industries with respect to buying nonstandardized technology that tends to be science-based, starting-up more specialized pieces of equipment, maintaining such equipment, and troubleshooting. The switchover from a labor-intensive to a capital-intensive operation also changes the whole way a firm must be managed, with capacity utilization and age of equipment becoming more strategic. Therefore, capital-intensive industries tend to require more organizational resources than labor-intensive ones.[20]

The "flagship" industry (initial activity) of most chaebol in Korea has been capital-intensive, including such industries as sugar refining, soap, construction, steel, and metallurgy. Where "textiles" represented a group's starting point, as in the Hyosung, Kohap, and Kolon groups, they usually involved the manufacture of synthetic fiber, not the spinning and weaving of cotton. The former embodies a chemical process which uses more capital and administrative employees per worker than the latter. The Samsung and Hanil chaebol invested in woolen textiles in their early growth phase, but even woolen textiles demand more managerial resources than cotton textiles insofar as their quality requirements are higher. That some chaebol diversified on the basis of synthetic textiles or even worsteds, but not cotton spinning and weaving, therefore, is an example that supports the overall point about the importance for diversification of a strong administrative base. Despite the fact that cotton textiles were Korea's leading sector in the 1960s, none of the top-ten chaebol that consolidated their power originated as cotton textile producers.

---

[19] Ralph G. Hawtrey, *Capital and Employment* (London: Longmans, 1937).
[20] Amsden, *Asia's Next Giant*.

Developing versus deriving organizational capabilities

Immediately after seizing power in 1961 President Park Chung Hee accused leading enterprises in a wide range of industries of engaging in more corruption than typical during the corrupt enough foreign-aid era of the 1950s. The cited industries included textiles, paper, coal mining, fertilizers, flour, alcohol, glass, pottery, livestock, real estate, construction, warehousing, and trade.[21] Other than textiles these are the capital-intensive industries in which the chaebol sunk their roots. Nevertheless, the list's nonmanufacturing activities – real estate, construction, trade – do not require much in the way of organizational capabilities. Yet three chaebol (Samsung, Hyundai, and Daewoo) out of "The Big Four" had their origins in such service industries (the fourth, Lucky-Goldstar – now the LG group – got its start in chemicals and electronics assembly). A foundation in construction (Hyundai) or import–export trade (Samsung) provided the leading chaebol with a commercial bridge to other activities. Samsung, for example, made its fortune importing sugar (a state-granted monopoly when foreign exchange was very scarce), which then helped it vertically integrate backward to found its first manufacturing operation, a sugar refinery. A service base, however, does not necessarily provide an organizational and/or technological bridge to manufacturing.

The nonmanufacturing origins of the two leading chaebol suggest that organization-building is not strictly determined by industry of origin.[22] It is possible to become a good manufacturer and build organizational capabilities from a nontechnically related base. Today's most successful chaebol made the necessary investments proactively, whereas the conservative textile firms did not.

[21] See his autobiography *The Country, the Revolution, and I*, trans. by L. Sinder (Seoul: no publisher, 1963).
[22] The textile industry, under other conditions and in the presence of different alternatives has, in fact, been the springboard for diversification. For example, a leading Korean-owned company founded in 1919 was the Kyongsong Spinning and Weaving Company (now Kyongbang Ltd.). It actively supported national causes, diversified into publishing by establishing what is now Korea's largest daily, the Dong-a Ilbo, and was one of the first companies to go public. See Carter J. Eckert, *Offspring of Empire: The Koch'ang Kims and the Colonial Origins of Korean Capitalism, 1876–1945* (Seattle: University of Washington Press, 1991). Thus, in a period in Korean history when few large-scale enterprises existed other than textile companies, the latter did demonstrate expansionary leadership. Moreover, the textile industry has been in the forefront of expansion in other countries, such as the Alpargata group in Argentina and the Romero and Brescia groups in Peru, although the latter are not diversified very much out of textiles. See Eduardo Enrique Vasquez Huaman, "State and Business Groups in Peru: 1968–1989," Master's thesis, St. Anne's College, Oxford University, 1991.

In the case of Hyundai Construction, it petitioned the government in the mid-1960s to own its own cement-making facility. Despite the vertical linkage with construction, cement-making never became one of Hyundai's major activities, and the mill it established was uncharacteristically small. Instead, Hyundai treated its cement investment as a pilot operation or learning experience, with respect to how to construct an industrial plant and how to manage one. Insofar as the cement plant was Hyundai's first venture into the field of manufacturing (as opposed to construction), Hyundai unpackaged its technology transfer. It bought technology from one cement plant process specialist (Allis Chalmers) and technical consulting services for general engineering advice and know-how from another (George Fuller). Hyundai's success at technology assimilation is suggested by the fact that in each sequential expansion of its cement plant it bought fewer technical functions from outside.[23] Instead, it built its own technical staff in-house step by step. Some of the staff which had acquired generic knowledge were then used to undertake intragroup diversification into new areas. Diversification itself became an economy of scope for Hyundai, which soon excelled at mobilizing a task force to buy foreign technology, erect a plant, and start operating it. Experience in diversifying allowed Hyundai to move into new industries rapidly and at relatively low cost.

As for building the capabilities necessary to manage new *manufacturing* affiliates on a day-to-day basis, Hyundai used its cement plant as a laboratory to train its construction managers before assigning them to new affiliates in other manufacturing industries. Trainees gained experience in inventory management, quality and process control, capacity planning, and so forth, thus spreading basic middle and lower managerial skills throughout the Hyundai organization. The first president of Hyundai Motors, for example, was a former president of Hyundai Cement.[24]

In the case of the Samsung group, it was one of the first chaebol to build a groupwide training system soon after establishing its first manufacturing affiliate in 1953. All new managers were recruited and trained at the group level. They were then dispatched, at the company's discretion, to affiliates. Interaffiliate communication was facilitated by the closeness of graduates of the same training class. Samsung began to attract the top

---

[23] The successful assimilation of imported technology is apparent in the manufacturing affiliates of other chaebol as well. For the case of the Samsung group's Chonju Paper Company affiliate, see Alice H. Amsden, "The Rise of Salaried Management," in Kwon, *Korean Economic Development*, pp. 359–370.

[24] See Amsden, *Asia's Next Giant*.

university graduates for its middle management posts, and professional management diffused to all parts of the company.

THE THREE-PRONGED INVESTMENT

According to Chandler, for big business to succeed in the age of industrial capitalism it must make a three-pronged investment.[25] It must invest in plants large enough to realize economies of scale. Once these plants are established it must invest in the distribution networks necessary to secure inputs and dispose of outputs. Finally, it must invest in management, both at the top of the organization and in the middle rung of each operating unit. The Korean big business groups generally did all three. The plants they invested in were large possibly to a fault, but most business groups also emphasized human resource development of middle and lower managers at the plant level, which was the appropriate level to stress given that it was at this level that foreign technology had to be infused, adapted, and improved to become a competitive weapon.

Large-scale plants

Big business in Korea invested a lot generally. Both aggregate domestic savings and gross capital formation shot up over time, the latter rising as a share of GNP in roughly twenty-five years from 0.12 in 1962 to 0.36 in 1989 (see Table 11.1).

In particular, Korea invested a lot in machinery and equipment. Professor Morikawa compares Japan's investments in real equipment favorably with those of the United States and West Germany for the period 1967–1987.[26] If we add Korea to Mr. Morikawa's comparison (see Table 11.6), then Korea outshines Japan, exceeding its coefficient for almost all years beginning in the mid-1970s (assuming we are measuring the same phenomenon). Of course, Japan's investments may have been higher earlier in its own development, but Korea's investments in capital stock in the early stage of its industrial transformation are impressive in absolute terms.

Finally, without question Korean big businesses invested enough to realize plant-level economies of scale. Indeed, critics of the chaebol argue that they overdid it. In "Texasian" fashion, Korea boasts the world's

---

[25] Chandler, *Scale and Scope.*

[26] Hidemasa Morikawa, "Increasing Organizational Capabilities of Japanese Industrial Enterprises – Focusing on the Postwar Period," mimeograph copy, Keio University, 1992. See also Chapter 10, this volume.

Table 11.6. *Investments in machinery and equipment, Korea, Japan,*
United States, Germany, 1967–1987 (% of GNP)

Year	Korea	Japan	United States	West Germany
1967	5.3	6.8[a]	4.0	4.7
1969	5.7	8.5[a]	3.8	5.9
1971	6.5	7.4	3.4	5.6
1973	8.1	6.8	3.5	4.3
1975	7.8	5.5	3.6	3.6
1977	10.8	4.7	3.6	3.7
1979	13.5	4.7	3.9	3.8
1981	10.2	5.5	4.2	3.8
1983	9.6	5.4	3.6	3.5
1985	9.7	6.6	4.4	3.7
1987	11.8	6.0	3.9	—

[a] Different source from data beginning 1971.
Sources: Japan, United States, and West Germany: Bank of Japan as cited
in Morikawa, Chapter 10 in this volume; Korea: compiled from Economic
Planning Board, *Major Statistics of Korean Economy* (Seoul: various dates).

largest shipyard, the world's largest cement plant, the Third World's largest steel mill, and so forth.[27]

Whatever the political motivation of the Korean government in targeting the same, small subset of business groups to undertake major new investment projects, its choice also had a sensible, practical logic: the smaller the number, the easier the monitoring. Moreover, business groups selected to undertake major capital investments tended to have experience in successfully establishing and/or running large-scale operations in other industries. Thus, in selecting a business group in 1971 to diversify into what soon became the world's largest shipyard, the government was more impressed with experience in large-scale project management than with industry-specific experience in small-craft shipbuilding. The government bypassed seven small shipyards as potential project executors and instead chose Hyundai Construction for the task. In addition to Hyundai Construction's experience in large-scale project execution at home and in Vietnam, the civil engineering of the construction business and the naval engineering of shipbuilding shared key technological elements in common.

[27] Information in the next three paragraphs is from Amsden, *Asia's Next Giant.*

In the case of the world's largest cement mill, it began small, as part of a Korean cement company in the 1970s that went bankrupt during the severe price competition that followed the 1973 energy crisis. The mill was then sold by the government (the country's banker) to the Ssangyong group, founded by a party elder and crony of Park Chung Hee, with experience only in a small soap factory and textile plant (which, in an uncharacteristic move for a chaebol, was sold to finance entry into cement making). Without much experience in large-scale projects, Ssangyong enlarged its newly acquired plant step by step, relying first on a semi-computerized process-monitoring system before moving to an automatic one, and gradually building up a first-class total quality control system.

In the case of the state-owned Pohang Iron and Steel Company (POSCO), it was ranked in 1986 as the world's sixth-largest steel producer, with an annual output of 11.3 million tons.[28] One of the alleged reasons for its public ownership related to scale. The World Bank and other official lenders in 1967 wanted Korea to invest in a smaller mill (by a tenfold order of magnitude) than what the Korean government wanted. To raise the finance for a larger operation the government tapped official financial channels in Japan (including war reparations). A former military man became chairman of POSCO, and with technical assistance from Shin Nippon Seitetsu (Nippon Steel), Japan's own former state-owned steel producer, built POSCO in stages into what by the late 1980s had become Korea's most profitable enterprise.

Trade and distribution channels

A stunning fact about Korean big business is not just its rapid growth and diversification but also its export orientation. On average the Korean economy exports as much as 35 percent of its GNP (Japan in the 1960s and 1970s exported only around 10 to 20 percent), and the chaebol have been among the economy's leading exporters.[29] Given the importance of

[28] United Nations Industrial Development Organization, *Industry and Development Global Report 1988/89* (Vienna, 1988).

[29] According to a survey of 3,000 selected enterprises by the Bank of Korea, Korea's "Big Four" chaebol in 1994 (Hyundai, Samsung, LG, and Daewoo) accounted for 57 percent of exports, as mentioned in "A Survey of South Korea," *The Economist*, June 3, 1995, p. 12. By way of indirect evidence one can examine the exports of general trading companies – nine in total, all owned by leading chaebol. The GTCs' share of total exports was 13.3 percent in their founding year, 1975, then rose to 48 percent in 1983, and then declined to about 38 percent in 1989 (which was still much higher than the 10 percent share of Japanese GTCs in Japan's total exports). Sung-Hwan Jo, "Promotion Measures

exporting, the sales and distribution function with respect to overseas trade has been key.

The demands for investments in overseas marketing have varied by industry, and in the early postwar phase of industrial development Korean manufacturers of labor-intensive exports could generally rely for their distribution on either foreign buyers (who frequently bought made-to-order products on an "OEM" basis),[30] or foreign traders (especially Japanese general trading companies). Nevertheless, by the 1990s many Korean enterprises (unlike their smaller Taiwanese counterparts) began to eschew OEM contracts and to develop (or at least try to develop) their own designs and brand names.

The marketing function possibly represented a proportionately smaller investment for Korean big business than for American or European big business in an earlier era because the Koreans could piggyback in overseas markets on the well-established distribution networks of American and European companies operating in the same business lines. In the case of automobiles, for example, once dealerships in the United States no longer became exclusive (owing to antitrust considerations), and once they agreed to distribute Hyundai's cars, the investments required for Hyundai to enter the U.S. market dramatically diminished.

The overseas marketing function of Korean big business evolved in the context of group structure and government assistance. First, it was handled in times of crisis by reliance on the total capabilities of the business group in question, with the help of the government. Both were used by Hyundai Heavy Industries (HHI), for example, the Hyundai group's shipbuilding affiliate, during a sharp economic downturn in the days when ships still represented a highly differentiated export product for Korea. In such a depressed market, and only months after HHI began operations (with its completions still behind schedule), several ship buyers refused delivery. HHI responded by vertically integrating forward and founding the

for General Trading Companies (1975)," in Lee-Jae Cho and Yoon-Hyung Kim (eds.), *Economic Development in the Republic of Korea: A Policy Perspective* (Honolulu: East–West Center, University of Hawaii, 1991), and Kwang-Suk Kim, "Trade and Industrialization Policies in Korea: An Overview," mimeograph copy, Kyung Hee University, Seoul, 1991, pp. 511–526.

[30] OEM is the abbreviation for original equipment manufacturer. For an account of the importance of foreign buyers in Korea's early labor-intensive export success, see Larry Westphal, Kim Linsu and Carl J. Dahtman, "Reflections on the Republic of Korea's Acquisition of Technological Capability," in N. Rosenberg and C. Frischtak (eds.), *International Technology Transfer: Concepts, Measures, and Comparisons* (New York: Praeger, 1985), pp. 167–221.

Hyundai Merchant Marine Company. This sister company then absorbed HHI's undelivered vessels. The government, as owner (at the time) of one of Korea's major refineries, cooperated by decreeing that all crude oil deliveries to Korea be carried in Korean-owned ships.[31]

Second, the government encouraged the chaebol's formation of general trading companies (GTCs). Such companies received special fiscal incentives and subsidized credit beginning in 1975 as part of a national drive to reduce dependence on Japanese *sogo-shosha*.[32] By the mid-1980s every major chaebol had its own GTC (there were a total of nine), although a decade later they still did not offer the diversified services their Japanese counterparts offered; their trading activities were mostly restricted to serving their own group's needs, with more than two-thirds of their revenue coming from export business.

Differences in domestic distribution patterns in Korea and Japan reflect historical differences in the timing of the emergence of general trading companies. Japanese zaibatsu established GTCs before they themselves grew large whereas the Korean chaebol grew large before they established GTCs, which were principally planned and initiated by the government to promote exports. GTCs in Korea thus accounted for a much smaller share of domestic trade than did their Japanese counterparts (the sogo-shosha were estimated to account for about one-third of Japan's total domestic wholesale trade).

Numerous small retail stores, particularly those offering modern industrial products, have been organized and controlled by large manufacturers through various trade restraints such as exclusive dealerships and resale price maintenance. In 1991, for instance, Samsung, LG, and Daewoo, owners of the three major electronics firms, sold their products through their own exclusive distribution networks of around 4,000 stores, each with less than four employees on average.[33] The only stores in which consumers can make comparison shopping are department stores, which are often owned by chaebol. In the case of automobiles, Hyundai sold its cars domestically through two channels. One was owned and operated by Hyundai Motors (similar to the pattern followed by Daewoo Motors), and the other was owned by a Hyundai unit that specialized in selling

---

[31] Amsden, *Asia's Next Giant.*

[32] Dong-Sung Cho, *The General Trading Company: Concept and Strategy* (Lexington, MA: Lexington Books, 1987).

[33] Jie-Ae Sohn, "Feeling the Heat: Korean Distributors Fear Competition," *Business Korea,* 9, 3 (September 1991), pp. 18–22.

service warrantees. Neither Daewoo nor Hyundai used its GTC to sell cars at home.

Thus, by the early 1990s the "retailing revolution" had not arrived in Korea in the form of the emergence of large-scale discount outlets. Nevertheless, foreign (particularly Japanese and American) manufacturers and retailers began to try to alter the retailing industry by pressuring the Korean government to liberalize retail markets and by slowly establishing large-scale stores.

Plant-level human resources

Until the late 1980s the chaebol never diversified into any industry in which the supply of foreign technology was unavailable, but technology acquisition was only the first step along the road to gaining global competitiveness. Because technology is tacit, implicit, and never fully codified, as pointed out by Nelson,[34] it invariably has to be adapted and modified in order to work. This requires engineering competence and a shop-floor focus, because the requisite capabilities of workers and managers to make borrowed technology work can be developed only on the shop floor.

One reason why the chaebol (and zaibatsu) were successful in developing the forces of production is that they built organizations conducive to technology assimilation and, ultimately, to the generation of the incremental improvements in productivity and quality that became their competitive weapon. First, the professional middle managers they hired tended to have technical backgrounds. This is evident from Table 11.7, which shows the growth in managerial resources in Korea between 1960 and 1980. Whereas the number of general managers rose over this period by a factor of 2:2, the number of engineers skyrocketed by a factor of 10:2. Moreover, management generally kept in close contact with the ranks. As expected, larger enterprises have a much greater number of departments and sections than do smaller enterprises. Their management is more extensive. Nevertheless, they have only marginally more managerial layers. In fact, enterprises with 200 to 300 workers have been found to have more levels of hierarchy than enterprises with over 5,000.[35] These findings

---

[34] Richard R. Nelson, "Innovation and Economic Development: Theoretical Retrospect and Prospect," in Jorge M. Katz (ed.), *Technology Generation in Latin American Manufacturing Industries* (London: Macmillan, 1987), pp. 78–93.

[35] Seoul National University, College of Business Administration, *Current Situation and Tasks to Be Done by Korean Firms* (Seoul: College of Business Administration, Seoul National University, 1985) [in Korean].

Table 11.7. *Growth in managerial resources in the manufacturing sector, 1960–1980*

Employment category	1960	1980	Increase (1980/1960)
Engineers	4,425	44,999	10.2
Managers	31,350	69,585	2.2
Service, clerical, sales	36,015	474,600	13.2
Production	404,735	2,206,851	5.4
Total	479,975	2,797,030	5.8
Administrative/production[a]	0.13	0.10	
Administrative and clerical/production	0.18	0.27	

Note: Manufacturing sector includes transportation and communication workers.
[a] Administrative includes engineers, managers, sales, and service workers (clerical workers excluded).
Source: Adapted from Alice H. Amsden, *Asia's Next Giant: South Korea and Late Industrialization* (New York: Oxford University Press), p. 171.

suggest the relative compactness of management in big Korean firms, which facilitated their shop-floor orientation.

In the case of POSCO, its best managers were initially assigned to line rather than staff jobs. Even shift supervisors were experienced engineers with college degrees. Additionally, POSCO emphasized on-the-job operations training for all its technical managers. Newly recruited engineers with university backgrounds were required to work on all three shifts in order to become familiar with every operation. The staff of the quality control department had to work in the plant for three months.[36]

FAMILY OWNERSHIP AND TOP MANAGEMENT

Partly because the chaebol are still quite young and remain family owned and managed, Korea's enterprise system resembles the personal capitalism of Great Britain. Among the top 50 chaebol in existence in 1984 only

[36] Amsden, *Asia's Next Giant*.

Table 11.8. *Family management of the chaebol, 1984*
(background of chairpersons of top fifty chaebol)

	1–10	11–20	21–30	31–40	41–50	Total
	\multicolumn{6}{Group ranking by sales}	
Founders	5	4	4	6	8	27
Founder's kin	5	5	6	3	2	21
Professional managers	0	1[a]	0	1[b]	0	2
Total	10	10	10	10	10	50

[a] Kia Group: the group experienced severe financial trouble in the early 1980s, which, under pressure from the Korean government, resulted in the entire removal of the founding family from its ownership and management. The group was reorganized by professional management and became associated with Ford and Mazda.

[b] Samyang Group: The group's CEO was Kim Sang Hong, a long-time right-hand man of the founder. Because three sons of the founder were active in the management of the group, Kim's tenure was regarded as a transitional situation.

Sources: Minho Kuk, "The Governmental Role in the Making of *Chaebol* in the Industrial Development of South Korea," *Asian Perspective*, 12, 1 (Spring–Summer 1988); and *Business Korea*, various issues.

5 had been established before World War II.[37] Among 149 listed industrial corporations, 75 percent had less than 30 years experience in 1983.[38] The top managers of only two groups (KIA and Samyang) were professionals unrelated directly to the founding family (see Table 11.8).[39] Nevertheless, unlike the case of British personal capitalism, Korean big businesses have been characterized by significant managerial hierarchies with capable salaried managers. By the 1980s all the major chaebol had a functionally departmentalized planning and coordination office (*kijosil* or *hoejangsil*) whose size was substantially larger and more balanced than its counterparts

[37] Minho Kuk, "The Governmental Role in the Making of *Chaebol* in the Industrial Development of South Korea," *Asian Perspective*, 12, 1 (Spring–Summer 1988).
[38] Ungki Lim, "Ownership and Control Structure of Korean Firms: With Application of Agency Cost Theory," in Dong-Ki Kim and Linsu Kim (eds.), *Management behind Industrialization: Readings in Korean Business* (Seoul: University Press, 1989), pp. 110–132.
[39] KIA's main activity is manufacturing vans and more recently, motor vehicles (in collaboration with Ford). The Samyang group was established in 1924 as part of the same founding family that formed Kyongsong Spinning. It consists of three major business arms: food, textiles (silk and polyester), and chemicals.

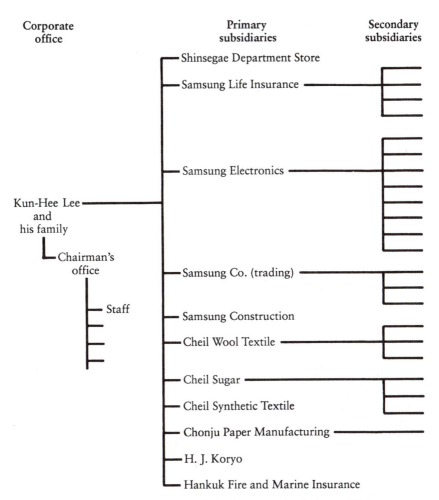

Figure 11.1. Organization of the Samsung chaebol, ca. 1988.
Source: Compiled from company information.

in American conglomerates or British family enterprises.[40] Most impressive of the corporate offices is that of the Samsung group depicted in Figure 11.1, in which a senior salaried manager administers the chairman's office composed of ten departments, each with some 250 professionals responsible for various industries and functions.[41] Therefore, Korean big

[40] Amsden and Hikino, "Project Execution Capability."
[41] Young Ki Lee, "Conglomeration and Business Concentration in Korea," in Kwon, *Korean Economic Development*, pp. 325–340.

businesses are more of the Chandlerian "entrepreneurial" rather than "personal" variety.

As illustrated in Figure 11.1, at the top of a typical business group in Korea was the founding family or family holding company, which was usually not incorporated. These families, through substantial if not majority shareholding, controlled all the operating units, which were legally independent but mostly privately held. Some of the large, significant subsidiaries, such as Hyundai Motors, Samsung Electronics, Goldstar (Electronics), and Daewoo Heavy Industries, had their shares publicly traded. Nevertheless, even the publicly held companies were in fact controlled by the family through its own holdings and intragroup mutual share holdings. At most, some groups were more open to nongroup ownership than others. For instance, in the Samsung group, out of eleven significant operating units nine were publicly held whereas in the Hyundai group, out of twenty-one significant operating units only five had been converted into publicly held corporations.

Each major operating unit or subsidiary, in turn, controlled many smaller subsidiaries. This subordinate level of subsidiaries was usually privately held and majority-controlled within the group. Often there was one more layer of subsidiaries and associated companies which were privately held and minority controlled within the group. Concerning equity holding, this three-layer tight hierarchy was common, even though the group or individual operating units may have had regular transactions with other companies or "outside" companies, as noted earlier.

By the 1990s there was some conflicting evidence that family ownership and management practices in Korea were weakening. Even an earlier reputable survey undertaken of 107 enterprises in 1983 showed that 20.9 percent of nonfamilial company presidents had been selected from within the company and 29.0 percent came from outside.[42] Nevertheless, with the exception of KIA, which by 1988 had become one of Korea's top-ten business groups, all the other leading chaebol remained family-owned and -managed.

---

[42] Jung Nyun Kim, "Growth of Enterprise and Management Capability," *Monthly Chosun* (in Korean), February 1984, as cited by Dong-Ki Kim, "The Impact of Traditional Korean Values on Korean Patterns of Management," in Kim and Kim, *Management behind Industrialization*, pp. 133–160.

STATE ENTREPRENEURIAL CAPITALISM AND
THE DISCIPLINE OF BUSINESS

Prewar Japan and postwar Korea share in common family-owned and/or family-controlled enterprise groups. These groups have operated in many technologically unrelated industries, have employed extensive hierarchies of middle managers, and have occupied key positions in both countries' economic development. Nevertheless, unlike the prewar zaibatsu, the chaebol have not had their own banks. The banking and corporate finance functions are carried out by the Ministry of Finance. To a far greater extent than in Japan, therefore, the Korean state subsidized business as well as disciplined it.

The big business groups in Korea (and in Japan) have been self-disciplined to the extent that they have competed fiercely with one another, despite the fact that group affiliates are expected to buy from each other if no better product is available from "outside" firms.[43] (This intense intergroup market competition is what has persuaded Morikawa that Japan's enterprise system resembles the American system of competitive managerial capitalism.)[44] Nevertheless, after 1975 intergroup competition in Korea was enhanced immeasurably by the government: each chaebol tried to qualify to establish a general trading company – which held out large profit-making opportunities – by meeting tough government performance standards regarding minimum export volume and number of export products.[45] Only in the early 1990s, at government's instigation, did groups even begin to cooperate in technology sharing.[46]

Under Japanese colonialism all banks in Korea (and Taiwan) were state-owned. After a brief interlude in the 1950s when, at the insistence of American aid advisers, state commercial banks were divested to private

---

[43] Market concentration peaked in the late 1970s but has generally decreased over time as markets have deepened. In 1970, 1977, and 1987 the share of oligopolies in shipments went from 35.1 percent to 48.6 percent to 40.2 percent, while the share of competitive market structures went from 39.9 percent to 26.1 percent to 44.3 percent. See Kyu-Uk Lee, S. Urata, and I Choi, "Recent Developments in Industrial Organizational Issues in Korea," mimeograph copy (Washington, DC: Korea Development Institute and World Bank, 1986), and Kyu-Uk Lee and Jai-Hyong Lee, *Business Groups and Economic Concentration* [in Korean] (Seoul: Korea Development Institute, 1990).

[44] Morikawa, Chapter 10 in this volume.

[45] Cho, *The General Trading Company*.

[46] "Technology Flows," *Business Korea*, 10, 2 (August 1992), p. 53. For a general discussion of competition policy in Japan and Korea, see Alice H. Amsden and Ajit Singh, "The Optimal Degree of Competition and Dynamic Efficiency in Japan and Korea," *European Economic Review*, 38 (1994), pp. 941–951.

owners (better described as speculators), they were swiftly renationalized by the military government of Park Chung Hee (banks in Taiwan in this period never succumbed even temporarily to privatization). With nonbank financial institutions still relatively weak, the Ministry of Finance has maintained tight control over all forms of credit, which gives the government even today enormous leverage over the private sector.[47] For instance, by regulating the financial portfolios and size of nonbank financial institutions, and by retaining power to investigate their financial irregularities, the government can still effectively determine the price of credit.

In addition, the Ministry of Finance and Economic Planning Board (now merged into the Ministry of Finance and Economy) have disciplined companies by means of price controls, in the name of curbing monopolistic abuses and dampening inflation. As late as 1986 the prices of 110 commodities were under government guidance, including flour, sugar, coffee, red pepper, electricity, gas, steel, chemicals, synthetic fibers, paper, drugs, nylon stockings, automobiles, and televisions. While such surveillance formally ended with liberalization after 1987, key oligopolies are still subject to government price surveillance. In the case of automobiles, for example, for thirty years no foreign cars were to be seen on Korean roads and no Korean cars were to be seen on foreign roads. All the same, the industry's leader, the 90 percent locally owned Hyundai Motor Company, became the first late-industrializing automobile maker to export to Europe and the United States. The industry was induced to cut costs and thereby raise profits because automobile prices were, and continue to be, supervised by the government. Typically Korean automobile companies have been allowed to set the price of a new model above world prices, which has helped them recoup fixed investment, but then are pressured to keep prices down, which has induced them to improve productivity and quality. Between 1974 and 1991 average prices of Korean automobiles in real won *fell* for small, medium, and large models.[48]

The Korean government's five-year plans have targeted specific industries for special support, and specific businesses within these industries

[47] Alice H. Amsden and Yoon-Dae Euh, "South Korea's 1980s Financial Reforms: Goodbye Financial Repression (Maybe), Hello New Institutional Restraints," *World Development*, 21, 3 (1993), pp. 379–390. Until recently Korean companies could not persuade foreign banks to lend to them without a guarantee from the Korean government. This dependence gave the government control over the allocation of foreign credit as well as domestic credit.
[48] Alice H. Amsden and Kang Jong-yeol, "Up-Scaling in the Korean Automobile Industry," paper prepared for the International Motor Vehicle Program, MIT, Cambridge, MA, 1995.

have been targeted for incentives to carry out government plans. If in Japan the relations between business and government have been "cooperative," in Korea (and a fortiori in Taiwan) they have been hierarchical, with government on the top. A positive result relates to Korea's subsidy allocation system. Given the absence of proprietary technology and the inadequacy of low wages as a competitive weapon in all but the most labor-intensive industries, protection from foreign competition and subsidization of credit have been commonplace in late industrialization (even the Korean cotton textile industry had to be subsidized in the 1920s and then again in the 1950s and 1960s because it could not compete at market-determined production costs against the more efficient textile industry of Japan).[49] Subsidization, however, is an open invitation to low quality and high costs, as manifest in many industries in Eastern Europe, India, and Latin America. Korea and Taiwan have generally avoided such inefficiency because their subsidies have been allocated according to a distinct principle. In slower-growing, late-industrializing countries, subsidies have tended to be allocated according to the principle of "giveaway." In Korea and Taiwan, subsidies have been allocated according to the principle of "reciprocity," in exchange for concrete performance standards that are monitored by fairly competent state officials.[50]

The most important performance standard has pertained to exports. The government protected Korean industry from foreign competition but at the same time forced it to meet export targets determined jointly by business and government, thereby bridging the dichotomy between export-led growth and import substitution.[51] Targeted firms and industries were given subsidized credit and access to foreign exchange, but at the same time they were prevented from engaging in capital flight – legislation passed in Korea in the 1960s stipulated that any illegal overseas transfer of $1 million or more was punishable with a minimum sentence of ten years' imprisonment and a maximum sentence of death! Companies were allowed to import foreign technology but they were pressured to build their own technological capabilities, being constrained by the Ministry

[49] Amsden, *Asia's Next Giant*.

[50] Alice H. Amsden, "The Diffusion of Development: The Late-Industrializing Model and Greater East Asia," *American Economic Review*, 81, 2 (May, 1991), pp. 282–286; Alice H. Amsden, "A Theory of Government Intervention in Late Industrialization," in L. Putterman and D. Rueschemeyer (eds.), *The State and the Market in Development* (Boulder, CO: Lynne Rienner, 1992), pp. 53–84.

[51] Y. W. Rhee, B. Ross-Larson, and G. Pursell, *Korea's Competitive Edge: Managing the Entry into World Markets* (Baltimore: Johns Hopkins University Press, 1984).

of Science and Technology to import the same technology only once and at the lowest possible cost.[52] Firms were permitted to exploit their labor, and working hours were among the longest in the world. But they had to invest in labor training (or pay a tax to finance government training programs). Local firms were always given the advantage over foreign firms, but the government used the threat of foreign entry to elicit good performance.

Most of all, firms were disciplined informally, in the form of bureau chiefs in the Ministry of Finance, Ministry of Commerce and Industry, and Economic Planning Board telephoning company CEOs or top managers and lecturing them on appropriate behavior ranging from buying locally made inputs, introducing specific foreign technologies, investing (or not) in new capacity (all capacity expansions required government approval), diversifying export markets, and improving product quality. Such arm-twisting was facilitated in Korea by the fact that the same small set of companies operated in multiple industries – the government had to deal with a relatively small number of groups (in Japan, by contrast, the number of leading enterprises was larger: the automobile and electronics industries, for example, were dominated by different companies). The group form of business, moreover, facilitated discipline because the performance of a single conglomerate could be judged on multiple counts – only if a group succeeded in one industry would it be rewarded by the government with a license and credit to enter yet another industry.

Thus, discipline of business by government took various forms, both direct and indirect, including stimuli to competition associated with the formation of general trading companies, price controls, credit allocation conditionality, performance standards attached to subsidies, and informal "administrative guidance."

The importance of state discipline over big business was appreciated by Korean President Park Chung Hee, along with his keen appreciation (some would say to a fault) of the central role of big business in catching up. He writes in his book, *Our Nation's Path*:

One of the essential characteristics of a modern economy is its strong tendency towards centralization. Mammoth enterprise – considered indispensable, at the moment, to our country – plays not only a decisive role in the economic development and elevation of living standards, but further, brings about changes in the structure of society and the economy. . . . Therefore, the key problems facing

---

[52] Linsu Kim, "South Korea."

a free economic policy are coordination and supervisory guidance, by the state, of mammoth economic strength.[53]

The ability of the government to discipline subsidy recipients meant that a long-term approach to profit maximization could be adopted. Oligopolistic sectors were supported for lengthy periods but ultimately became competitive internationally.

The Korean state officials who monitored subsidies were recruited from the same elitist universities that provided the salaried managers employed by the big business groups. Middle management in the bureaucracies of government and business was one and the same. The "golden parachute" system that existed for government officials in Japan existed for them in Korea. According to Hattori,[54] the background of as many as one-third of Korea's top salaried corporate managers was in government service (including public enterprise).

"NEW INDUSTRIAL POLICY" IN THE 1990S

By the 1990s the enterprise system of state entrepreneurial capitalism in Korea was facing new challenges. Demands for democracy erupted in 1989 and finally triumphed in the demise of the military rule which had earlier conditioned business–government relations. At the same time Korean enterprises were trying to adjust themselves to the complexities of diversifying into more demanding technology areas. Government support of business was still necessary at the margin, protecting infant high-tech sectors from foreign competition and providing them with cheap credit for R&D. Yet the old formula of allocating such support reciprocally, in exchange for monitorable performance standards, was under siege. *Any* support for business was opposed by Washington and the Korean general public. Big business was not adverse to subsidies, but had become powerful enough to resist (or at least rail against) "conditionality."

The debate surrounding the government's "new industrial policy" focused on the persistence of the chaebol's family ownership and exclusive control, which, in people's perceptions, symbolized the old undemo-

---

[53] Park Chung Hee, *Our Nation's Path: Ideology for Social Reconstruction* (Seoul: Dong-A, 1962), pp. 228–229.

[54] Tamio Hattori, "The Relationship between *Zaibatsu* and Family Structure: The Korean Case," in Akio Okochi and Shigeaki Yasuoka (eds.), *Family Business in the Era of Industrial Growth: Its Ownership and Management*, International Conference on Business History, Proceedings of the Fuji Conference (Tokyo: University of Tokyo Press, 1984), pp. 111–141.

cratic regime. Particularly controversial was the hierarchical structure of the groups and the enormous power the families exercised over them. The top decision-making function was still almost completely vested in the private family circle, and, therefore, to the dismay of the public (and business historians), little information was available on the way decisions, especially related to finance, were made.

Korea's international competitive environment had also changed. Korean wages were no longer low by world standards, new product development (or improvement) was more urgent, and government support to business was being reduced. The chaebol were being pressured by the government to abandon their generalist approach and specialize in fewer business areas in order to achieve scale economies, to expand marketing networks, and to recruit managers who understood market research, product development, brand promotion, and so forth. Chandlerian three-pronged investment was becoming even more critical as the chaebol's need to upgrade increased.

Yet certain fundamentals of the Korean system of industrial development remained intact in the mid-1990s, thirty years after the start of rapid industrial growth. The rhetoric was one of liberalization (in keeping with a new General Agreement on Tariffs and Trade) but the reality was otherwise.[55] For instance, the private sector accounted for roughly 80 percent of Korea's R&D expenditures (compared to only 20 percent of Taiwan's R&D), but the most important mechanism for funding corporate R&D was preferential state credit. Government scaled down its direct support to capital-intensive industries but strengthened its patronage of technology-intensive industries. After thirty years of government favoritism toward big business, small and medium-sized enterprises were given more weight, but support to them did not take a free-market form. Instead, the Ministry of Finance and Economy instructed the banking system to apportion smaller enterprises a specified share of total credit. Trade was free except in the one case that mattered for Korea's long-term competitiveness: there was a ban on selected imports (such as automobiles and consumer electronics) from Japan and from Japanese-owned factories in third countries if, in the latter case, the domestic content of

---

[55] For a general discussion of the persistence of support to business after the Uruguay Round and the formation of a new World Trade Organization in 1995, and the costs of forcing such support to take covert rather than overt forms, see Alice H. Amsden, "Post-Industrial Policy in East Asia," 1995, Council on Foreign Relations, Asia Project Working Paper, 58 East 68 Street, New York, NY, 10021.

these imports was under 60 percent. These barriers were justified by the fact that Korea ran a chronic and large trade deficit with Japan and had to diversify its source of imports. In fact, restrictions on Japanese-made imports afforded Korean high-technology industries effective protection from their toughest competitors.

Thus, Korea's big businesses and enterprise system were changing in conjunction with global developments and endogenous industrial maturation. But history seemed to matter. Korea's lack of proprietary technologies to industrialize, and its long and continuing struggle to catch up with the world technological frontier, created institutions, such as the chaebol, which were emblematic of a latecomer. By the 1990s these institutions had begun to evolve toward something new, but not necessarily toward something similar to what characterized the industrial leaders of the North Atlantic region, whose rise to riches was inseparable from innovation of major new technology.

12

═══════════════════════════════════════

Argentina: Industrial growth and enterprise organization, 1880s–1980s

MARÍA INÉS BARBERO

INTRODUCTION

The aim of this chapter is to examine the main forms which enterprise organization showed through the industrialization process in Argentina, from the nineteenth century to the present. This process started early in comparison with the majority of developing countries, but it had certain aspects and complex rhythms which clearly distinguished it from the path followed by most developed nations. This is why it is difficult to establish the impact of the Second Industrial Revolution on the local industry precisely, because it took place gradually and presented specific characteristics, which in turn affected the way in which enterprise organization developed.

A lineal evolution toward the predominance of capital-intensive industries did not occur in the Argentine case, and during the 1930s growth was led by a labor-intensive sector, the textile industry, which had started to develop in the 1920s. In other industrial sectors classified by Alfred Chandler as increasingly capital-intensive, such as metalworking and electrical appliances, small family-owned firms and workshops predominated until the 1950s. In some cases, such as railroad machinery, only repair workshops existed until the end of World War II. Other capital-intensive sectors, as food production or petroleum refining, were quick to develop, and, in the case of the car industry, assembling plants were installed by multinational companies in the 1920s.

What can be found since the beginning of this century, more than an evolution toward the predominance of large managerial firms is the coexistence of different types of enterprises: small family-owned firms, large enterprises domestically-owned, affiliates of multinational companies, and

368

Table 12.1. *Population*

Year	Inhabitants (millions)
1869	1.7
1895	3.9
1914	7.9
1947	15.9
1960	20.0
1970	23.7

Source: National Censuses.

state-owned firms. From the 1930s to the 1950s a process of dispersion took place, but from 1960 onward industries tended to concentrate again.

The evolution of enterprise organizations was conditioned by the industrial structure, public policies, and the size of the market. Public policies varied, and throughout the past century the state favored the development of diverse types of enterprises, from large foreign companies to small domestic firms and state-owned enterprises at different moments. In the market, from the 1920s onward manufacturing production was destined mainly to internal consumption, which caused difficulties in the scale economies, as local demand was very limited due to the reduced population (Table 12.1).

This chapter examines the salient features of enterprise organization in the industrial sector. In order to analyze these features, we have defined various stages based on the relative weight of different organizational models during the past century.

Case studies are scarce, so empirical evidence is not enough to establish a typology based on comparative data. Therefore, information obtained from companies' history is combined here with that provided by other approaches, such as the analysis of industrial structure, the relationship between the development of certain industrial activities and the expansion possibilities of big firms, as well as the influence of government policies and market conditions.

ENTERPRISES IN THE ORIGINS OF ARGENTINE INDUSTRIALIZATION (1880–1920)

As can be seen in the figures corresponding to the sectorial participation in the GDP (Table 12.2), the Argentine industrial sector experienced

Table 12.2. *Long-term changes in shares of major sectors in total output (%; constant prices of 1970)*

Year	Agriculture	Mining and manufacturing	Construction	Electricity, gas, and water	Transportation and communication	Servi
1900	30.2	16.3	5.5	0.1	4.6	43.
1920	28.9	17.4	2.3	0.4	7.8	43.
1940	23.1	23.7	3.9	0.6	9.0	39.
1960	15.4	27.6	4.8	1.1	10.7	40.
1980	12.5	27.1	6.5	3.5	10.6	39.
1990	16.8	23.5	1.8	5.4	12.1	40.

Sources: CEPAL, *Series históricas del crecimiento para América Latina*, Santiago de Chile, 1978 (data for 1910 to 1970); Banco Central de la República Argentina, *Oferta y demanda global al cuarto trimestre de 1990*, Buenos Aires, agosto 1991 (data for 1980 and 1990).

Table 12.3. *Growth rates of the GNP and of the GDP per capita*
(constant prices of 1970)

Period	Growth rates of the GNP (%)	Growth rates of the GDP per capita (%)
1901–1910	86.0	31.5
1911–1920	15.7	−9.4
1921–1930	53.8	17.5
1931–1940	28.2	10.1
1941–1950	33.0	33.0
1951–1960	29.0	10.4
1961–1970	42.5	25.6
1971–1980	22.4	4.6
1981–1990	−3.0	—

Sources: CEPAL, *Series históricas del crecimiento para América Latina*,
Santiago de Chile, 1978; Banco Central de la República Argentina, *Oferta y
demanda global al cuarto trimestre de 1990*, Buenos Aires, Agosto 1991.
Banco Central de la República Argentina, *Cuentas Nacionales. Series
Históricas*, Buenos Aires, 1976.

gradual growth since the end of the nineteenth century, which was favored
by the country's entry into the world market as producer of foodstuffs
and agricultural raw materials. To a great extent, as a result of different
kinds of linkages, the development of primary export activities produced
effects which were transmitted to the global economy.[1]

The process of economic expansion generated by the growth of
exports was accompanied, at the beginning, by an accelerated modernization of the system of transportation and public utilities, led by the
development of railroads (Table 12.3). The construction and management of railroads was in the hands of large enterprises of foreign capital,
dominated mainly by those of British origin.

Even though the railroad companies occupied a central place in the
Argentine economy, the impact of railroads on local industry was much
more indirect than in Western Europe or the United States. In Argentina,
for different reasons, railroads did not originate the development of the

---

[1] Roberto Cortés Conde and Shane Hunt (eds.), *The Latin American Economies*, New
York, Holmes & Meyer, 1985, p. 5; Lucio Geller, *El crecimiento industrial argentino
hasta 1914 y la teoría del bien primario exportable*, in Marcos Giménez Zapiola (comp.),
El régimen oligárquico, Buenos Aires, Amorrortu, 1975, pp. 156–200.

metal and metalworking industries through backward linkages, since the European companies that built them imported rails and equipment from their countries of origin. This was caused in part by legislation allowing the free import of railroad material, but also by the scarcity of mineral resources, both of which were obstacles to the development of primary metals, machinery, and transportation industries. Local manufacturing of railroad equipment started only after World War II, when railroads were nationalized.

Whether railroads contributed to the formation of human resources from the point of view of management and the training of workers and technicians is more difficult to answer. Railroads gave birth to workshops where the machinery was repaired and wagons were built. The railroad workshops were among the biggest metalworking establishments, and many engineers and technicians who later worked for industrial firms were trained there. It is more complex to draw a parallel with the pioneer function of manager formation and modern enterprise organization studied by Chandler for the United States.[2] The difficulty stems from the fact that the higher levels of the management of the Argentine railroad companies were in the hands of foreigners and most of the strategic decisions were taken abroad. Nevertheless, it can be assumed that a learning process was possible for the local human resources at middle-management levels.

The manufacturing industry grew gradually since the end of the nineteenth century, reaching 17.4 percent of the GDP in 1920 (Table 12.2). The structure of the industrial sector, according to the data provided by the industrial census of 1914 revealed a strong predominance of the food industry (53 percent of the value of production), followed by construction, apparel, and light metallurgy (Table 12.4).

To a great extent the industrialization process took place thanks to the supply of external resources: capital, entrepreneurs, and labor. Even though the investment of foreign capital in the manufacturing industry was very limited and mostly concentrated in the production of frozen and chilled beef, the role of the workers and entrepreneurs who remained in the country as immigrants became essential. Considering the whole country, foreign-born entrepreneurs accounted for 64.3 percent in 1914, and that proportion was much higher in the main coastal cities.

The high proportion of foreign owners in the industry can be explained

---

[2] Alfred Chandler, Jr., *The Visible Hand: The Managerial Revolution in American Business*, Cambridge, Mass., Belknap Press of Harvard University Press, 1977.

Table 12.4. *Share of the different sectors in the industrial production*

Sector	Number of firms (%)	Production (%)
1914		
Food	39.1	53.3
Apparel	14.6	8.6
Building materials	17.6	12.5
Furniture, vehicles	9.1	4.6
Artistics, ornament	2.0	0.8
Metallurgy and kindred products	6.7	5.0
Chemicals	1.1	3.0
Printing	2.9	2.1
Textiles	5.0	2.1
Miscellaneous	1.9	8.0
Total	100.0	100.0
1935		
Food and tobacco	28.7	37.0
Textiles	11.7	15.6
Lumber	9.8	3.0
Paper	0.5	0.9
Printing and publishing	5.5	4.0
Chemicals	2.2	3.9
Petroleum, coal products	0.1	3.9
Rubber	0.1	0.7
Leather	2.6	2.6
Stone, clay, glass	5.5	1.8
Primary metal and fabricated metal products	9.3	5.7
Machinery, vehicles	12.5	6.7
Electricity	2.2	5.6
Construction	3.8	3.6
Mining	0.4	2.2
Miscellaneous	5.1	2.8
Total	100.0	100.0
1946		
Food and kindred products	22.4	32.7
Tobacco	0.1	2.4
Textiles	2.5	13.5
Apparel	13.1	8.1
Lumber	12.7	5.1

Table 12.4. (cont.)

Sector	Number of firms (%)	Production (%)
Printing, publishing	3.7	2.9
Chemicals	2.5	7.4
Petroleum and coal products	—	3.1
Rubber	0.1	0.9
Stone, clay, glass	7.6	3.6
Primary metals and fabricated metal products	11.5	7.6
Vehicles and machinery	15.3	5.6
Machinery and electrical appliances	2.2	1.3
Miscellaneous	5.2	1.9
Electricity and gas	1.1	3.9
Total	100.0	100.0
1974		
Food and tobacco	21.8	27.8
Textiles, apparel	14.5	13.5
Lumber	15.6	2.1
Paper and printing	4.3	4.0
Chemicals, petroleum and coal products, rubber, plastics	4.9	16.7
Nonmetallic mineral products	11.3	3.1
Primary metals	1.1	8.6
Metal working	24.2	23.9
Others	2.3	0.3
Total	100.0	100.0

Sources: República Argentina, *Tercer Censo Nacional*, vol. 7, *Censo de las industrias*, Buenos Aires, 1917. República Argentina, *Censo Industrial de 1935*, Buenos Aires, 1938. República Argentina, *Censo Industrial de 1946*, Buenos Aires, 1952. República Argentina, *Censo Nacional Económico de 1974*, Buenos Aires, n.d.

in part by the number of foreigners within the economically active population,[3] but it should be pointed out that, in a majority of the cases which have been studied, the immigrant entrepreneurs of this period had a

[3] Roberto Cortés Conde, "El crecimiento de la economía, de las industrias y la inmigración italiana," in Francis Korn (comp.), *Los italianos en la Argentina*, Buenos Aires, Fundación Giovanni Agnelli, 1983, p. 34.

certain technical skill in the activities they had chosen.[4] This can be linked to the fact that emigration could be an option to avoid the proletarization of artisans in their native countries, as has been observed in the Italian case.[5] Another factor is that immigrants coming from rural areas where the putting-out system was extended started off with certain industrial experience. Finally, the studies on family strategies in the emigration processes reveal that in most cases immigration can be seen as part of an entrepreneurial strategy developed by the family group, in which the emigration of some family members contributed to the maintenance of those who stayed at home. For the Argentine case, it has been pointed out that even immigrants coming from the less industrialized areas of Europe had certain attitudes on work and saving which favored their insertion into the more modern economic sectors.[6]

The small family-owned firm founded by immigrants – developed by slowly substituting the import of industrial goods – was widespread in the first stage of Argentine industrialization. This was evident in most of textiles and apparel, building materials, light metallurgy, printing and food industries, and in general in all the sectors of low capital concentration.

Besides the small firms of immigrant origin, larger enterprises were already operating in some sectors by the end of the nineteenth century. The higher degrees of concentration were to be found in some branches of the food industry – beef, sugar, flour, beer, in a lower degree in wine and cookies – in match and paper industries and to a lesser extent in the metallurgical industry. There were also some big firms in the textile and glass sectors.

There were different traits among large enterprises. The sector with the largest-size industry and the most modern in technology and organization was the frozen meat industry, where big British and American firms operated. The most important innovations, repeating those in their mother companies, had been introduced by American companies, like Swift and Armour, which had settled in the country at the beginning of the century. They produced mainly for foreign markets, but part of their production

[4] Manuel Chueco, *Los pioneers de la industria nacional*, Buenos Aires, Imprenta de la Nación, 1886; Jorge Sergi, *Historia de los italianos en la Argentina*, Buenos Aires, Editora Italo Argentina, 1940; Dionisio Petriella and Sara Sosa Miatello, *Diccionario Biográfico Italo-Argentino*, Buenos Aires, Asociación Dante Alighieri, 1976.
[5] Ercole Sori, *L'emigrazione italiana dall'Unità alla Seconda Guerra Mondiale*, Bologna, Il Mulino, 1979, pp. 92–93.
[6] Gino Germani, *Política y sociedad en una época de transición*, Buenos Aires, Paidós, 1965, p. 201.

was for local consumption – before World War I, 14 percent of their total production was sent to big urban centers.[7]

Most large enterprises in other industrial sectors were owned by domestic capitalists or by immigrants or foreign entrepreneurs who had settled in Argentina. The growth of the market had favored concentration in the production of some goods for mass consumption, such as flour and sugar. In the first case, since the end of the nineteenth century a substitution process of small mills took place, and big firms developed in urban areas thanks to the agricultural expansion and to the modernization of the transport system. One of the biggest enterprises, Molinos Rio de la Plata, was created in 1902 by a large cereal export company, Bunge y Born.[8] The sugar industry was highly integrated right from the beginning, because firms were simultaneously producers of raw materials, and most of them belonged to local landowners. According to the census figures, in 1914, 60 percent of the firms in that sector were joint-stock companies, and 51 percent of the mills were run by salaried managers.[9]

One of the most remarkable aspects of enterprise organization in this period is the existence of economic groups with greatly diversified investments, and which were active in the manufacturing sector since the last decades of the nineteenth century. Although different in origin, they had in common an important availability of capital provided by other economic activities, mainly commerce and finance, and by their control of banking institutions. In the context of an economy with difficult access to long-term credit, this meant a strong advantage and allowed them to invest in different industrial activities, taking over smaller firms in many cases.

The conformation of groups with an extensive investment diversification implied an expansion of the large enterprise quite different from the kind of organization studied by Alfred Chandler for the United States, and similar to other Latin American cases in this period,[10] and maybe

[7] Ernesto Lahitte, *Frigoríficos*, in República Argentina, *Tercer Censo Nacional*, vol. 7, *Censo de las industrias*, Buenos Aires, Talleres Gráficos de L. J. Rosso, 1917, p. 518; Mirta Lobato, *El taylorismo en la gran industria exportadora argentina (1907–1945)*, Buenos Aires, Centro Editor de América Latina, 1988; Peter Smith, *Carne y Política en la Argentina*, Buenos Aires, Paidós, 1968, pp. 41–54.
[8] Ernesto Lahitte, *La industria harinera*, in República Argentina, *Tercer Censo Nacional*, pp. 497–499; Jorge Schvarzer, *Bunge y Born. Crecimiento y diversificación de un grupo económico*, Buenos Aires, Grupo Editor Latinoamericano, 1989, p. 27.
[9] Ernesto Lahitte, *Consideraciones sobre el censo de la industria azucarera*, in República Argentina, *Tercer Censo Nacional*, p. 566.
[10] Mario Cerutti and Menno Vellinga, *Burguesías industriales en América Latina y Europa Meridional*, Madrid, Alianza Editorial, 1989; Enrique Florescano (coord.), *Orígenes y*

closer to the Japanese *zaibatsu* or the Korean *chaebol*. In these groups
the incorporation of new companies cannot be explained by the principles
of integration. Rather, it is related to an aggregate of various activities not
always interrelated, as can be seen from the following examples.

Each of these groups presented, in turn, traits of its own. The Banco
de Italia y Rio de la Plata group was formed by successful Italian immigrants who started accumulating capital through commerce and real-estate
operations, and had began to invest in industry after the bank was created
in the 1870s. The leading industrial firm of this group toward the end of
the nineteenth century was the Compañía General de Fósforos, which
undertook a process of vertical integration from the 1910s to the 1920s,
producing cotton, chemicals, paper, cardboard, and printing materials.[11]
The Tornquist group had also originated in the activity of an immigrant's
son of German origin, who had started acting in commerce and had established a financing company in 1874 in association with businessmen
from Antwerp. By the late 1910s the group controlled over fourteen industrial companies, comprising beer, sugar, meat, metallurgy, machinery, furniture, tobacco, glass, candles, and soap.[12] Another great group was Bunge
y Born, a branch of a commercial Belgian firm, established in Argentina
in 1884 and whose first activity was the export of grain, extended later
to other goods. In the industrial field it developed at first the flour industry
and, in the 1920s, also the textile, chemical, and tin-container industries.[13]

By the first decade of this century, the bigger companies were already
organized as joint-stock companies and had already undergone the process of separation of ownership and management. For the Banco de Italia
y Rio de la Plata group, it was usual to hire managers who had some
working experience in Italy for their industrial companies, whereas the
Tornquist group tended to hire German managers.[14]

desarrollo de la burguesía en América Latina (1700–1955), Mexico, Nueva Imagen,
1985.

[11] María Inés Barbero, "Il profilo degli industriali italiani e il loro contributo allo sviluppo
economico argentino (1914–1940)," in *Affari Sociali Internazionali*, 15, no. 2, 1987,
pp. 199–200.

[12] Ernesto Tornquist y Cia, *The Economic Development of the Argentine Republic in the
Last Fifty Years*, Buenos Aires, Ernesto Tornquist & Co., 1919, pp. 201–203; Fernando
Madero, *Ernesto Madero*, in Gustavo Ferrari and Ezequiel Gallo (comps.), *La Argentina
del Ochenta al Centenario*, Buenos Aires, Sudamericana, 1980, pp. 628–629.

[13] Raúl Green and Catherine Laurent, *El poder de Bunge y Born*, Buenos Aires, Legasa,
1989, pp. 26–28 and 91–96; Schvarzer, *Bunge y Born*.

[14] María Inés Barbero, *Empresas y empresarios italianos en la Argentina. 1900–1920*, in
Maria Rosaria Ostuni (a cura di), *Studi sull'emigrazione. Un'analisi comparata*, Milano,
Electa, 1991, pp. 306–310.

INDUSTRIAL ENTERPRISES BETWEEN WARS (1920–1940)

At the beginning of the 1920s some significant changes started taking place in the structure of Argentine industry, which were also apparent in enterprise organization.

A first aspect of these transformations was the accelerated growth of the textile industry, which lasted until the 1940s, and which was sustained by the supply of local raw material. Some large enterprises were established, but the characteristics of this sector favored the development of small and medium-size firms and the putting-out system. According to the 1935 industrial census, there were almost 33,000 textile laborers who worked at home, accounting for 30 percent of the labor force in this sector.[15]

Another striking characteristic of this stage was the direct foreign investment in the manufacturing sector, led by American firms. The installation of affiliates of multinational companies coincided with a general process of expansion of those firms and with favorable conditions in the local market. The depressed record of growth of the 1910s, reflecting the dislocation of exports, imports, immigration and investment created by World War I and its immediate aftermath, was followed in the 1920s by a period of high rates of growth for the Argentine economy (Table 12.3) and as well for the industrial investment and the import of capital goods.[16] Increased tariffs on manufactured goods favored *in loco* production, and there were no restrictions to the installation of foreign companies, which were also favored by the patents laws.

Foreign companies chose new fields of industrial activity, such as chemicals (Duperial), the pharmaceutical industry (Parke Davis, Bayer, Colgate-Palmolive), rubber (Pirelli), electrical appliances (Otis, IBM), and also new branches of the foodstuff industry. In certain sectors, such as the automobile industry, foreign companies (Ford, Chrysler, General Motors, Fiat) did not actually manufacture but only assembled automobiles with imported parts, thus lowering the cost compared to the import of the final finished product.[17]

The increase of direct foreign investment in industry had great impact among the big firms, with the affiliates of multinational companies

[15] República Argentina, *Censo Industrial de 1935*, Buenos Aires, Casa J. Peuser Ltda., 1938, p. 25.
[16] Javier Villanueva, "El origen de la industrialización argentina" in *Desarrollo Económico*, 12, no. 47, October–December 1972, p. 458.
[17] Eduardo Jorge, *Industria y concentración económica*, Buenos Aires, Siglo XXI, 1971, pp. 98–102 and 142–143.

increasing their share of total output. They introduced technological and organizational innovations, as well as management and labor. Anyway, the factories they established in the 1920s were not of a big size, as the 1929 ranking of the largest industrial firms shows. With the exception of General Motors, the meat-packing and the petroleum-refining companies (Standard Oil, Diadema), the multinational companies are absent there (Appendix 12.A.1).

The crash of 1929 and the Depression in the 1930s deeply affected Argentine industrialization, since the reduction in imports speeded up the substitution process and the diversification in local production. The coefficient of manufactured imports, which had reached 51 percent of final demand in 1925–1929, dropped to 19.5 percent in 1940–1944.[18]

During the 1930s the installation of affiliates of multinational companies continued. These firms operated in metallurgy and machinery (Argentrac, Armco, Pechiney), electrical appliances (Philco, Philips), chemicals and pharmaceuticals (Union Carbide, Johnson, Upjohn, Abbott), rubber (Firestone, Good Year), textiles (Sudamtex, Ducilo), and the food industry (Fleischmann, Quaker, Adams). The leading role still remained in the American firms. Many of them had established themselves as importers and dealers in the 1920s and started assembling and manufacturing in the following decade.[19] In other cases, multinational firms that had started production in the 1920s and that combined imports with local manufacturing had to increase production and substitute for some of the products they used to import.[20]

The economic groups which had established themselves early in Argentina, of domestic or foreign capital, diversified their investments in order to substitute for imported goods. The new conditions also provided a framework for the expansion of national, middle-sized enterprises.

WORLD WAR II, PERONISM, AND THE TRANSFORMATIONS OF INDUSTRIAL ENTERPRISES (1940–1952)

In all these cases there was a certain continuity during the 1930s with the processes that had started in the previous decade, but it should be

---

[18] CEPAL, *Análisis y Proyecciones del desarrollo económico. El desarrollo económico en la Argentina*, Mexico, 1959, vol. 2, p. 160.

[19] Jorge, *Industria*.

[20] María Inés Barbero, *Itinerario de una empresa italiana en la Argentina. Pirelli entre 1910–1945*, mimeo, p. 83.

also underscored that at the end of 1930s deep transformations which would be characteristic of the Argentine industry until the 1950s became apparent.

The conditions derived from import constraints favored the rise of small and medium-sized firms of national capital. A research study based on industrial censuses indicates that between 1935 and 1954 a process of dispersion in the Argentine industry occurred, especially in the expanding sectors, such as textiles, metallurgy, machinery, and electrical appliances.[21] Industrial censuses' data also show a diminishing share for stock companies: in 1935 they accounted for 5.6 percent of all firms, but they controlled 53.8 percent of total production; in 1947 their share decreased to 3.3 percent of all firms and to 45.2 percent of total production.[22]

This dispersion accelerated during the 1940s, favored mainly by two factors. The first was the outbreak of World War II and the severe import difficulties of Argentina's economy. The second factor was the setting up of government policies fostering small and medium-sized firms – especially since 1946, when the Peronist government took office – which included highly protective tariffs and public loans.

In this period a large number of small enterprises was born, mainly in highly labor-intensive sectors, such as the textile and metalworking industries, where repair workshops multiplied and then switched to production. On the other hand, foreign investment was deterred by the authorities, and this added up to the difficulties that foreign companies found during the war, mainly due to supply problems.

On the basis of case studies among the metalworking industry, an Argentine scholar has established a series of idiosyncratic traits of enterprises created in this period, representing, to a large extent, the characteristic features of domestic firms born during the first period of import substitution. First, they used backward technology, mainly because they had obsolete equipment or imitated older designs obtained by dismantling machinery in use. Second, they produced, with a few exceptions, for the internal market, which limited the possibilities of an expanded demand. Factories were small and their production scale amounted to 10 to 20 percent of their European or American counterparts. Firms also showed

---

[21] Arturo Goetz, "Concentración y desconcentración en la industria argentina desde la década de 1930 a la de 1960," in *Desarrollo Económico*, 15, no. 60, January–March 1976, pp. 510–511.

[22] República Argentina, *Censo industrial de 1935*, p. 23; República Argentina, *Censo industrial de 1946*, Buenos Aires, 1952, p. 52.

a high degree of integration due to the lack of a good network of suppliers for parts and components; further, they tended to broaden their production mix as the domestic market gradually became saturated. All this hampered the possibilities of obtaining scale and specialization economies and limited the competitiveness of enterprises. To a large extent these characteristics remained still valid in more recent times.[23]

Another major change that occurred in the 1930s, which was more visible in the 1940s, was the increasing participation of the state in industrial production, in the first place in the chemical and steel industries, and later also in airplane and automobile production. This participation took place mainly through military-dependent enterprises, and was related to the prevailing opinion among the military that industrialization was a requisite for economic autarky and territorial defense.[24] State participation increased at the end of the war, when nationalizations took place, a policy that included railroads and most public utilities.

An increasing diversification and complexity in the industrial structure resulted from the process of import substitution accentuated by the depression of the 1930s and much more so by the war. This showed up in the relative decrease of the food industry and in the advance of slowly developing sectors as textiles, metalworking, and chemicals. As has been pointed out, local steel production also began in the mid-1930s, reaching its peak in the 1940s, when along with state participation the presence of the private sector started to grow.

Although the industrial growth rate was high during the 1940s (Table 12.3) this model of import substitution (which has been called an "easy stage of import substitution") generated important disturbances in the balance of payments, which in turn had an effect on the global economy. Two main factors contributed to that effect. First, industrial production was almost exclusively destined for the internal market and therefore it did not generate a flow of foreign currency into the country. Second, the industrial sector was not sufficiently integrated and depended on imported raw materials, intermediate goods, and machinery, with the consequent demand for foreign currency. Although this problem was structural, it became more apparent in the early 1950s, when a critical conjuncture

---

[23] Jorge Katz et al., *Desarrollo y crisis de la capacidad tecnológica latinoamericana. El caso de la industria metalmecánica*, Buenos Aires, 1986, pp. 9–11.

[24] Marta Panaia and Ricardo Lesser, *Las estrategias militares frente al proceso de industrialización*, in Marta Panaia, Ricardo Lesser, and Pedro Skupch, *Estudios sobre los orígenes del peronismo/2*, Buenos Aires, Siglo XXI, 1973, pp. 101–111.

combined a decrease in exports with a reduction in the state reserves, which curtailed the capacity to import and checked the growth of industry.

THE SECOND STAGE OF IMPORT SUBSTITUTION
(1952–1976)

Industrial growth from the early 1950s onward was strongly conditioned by public policies destined to combat the limitations of the "easy import substitution," through the promotion of the development of several industrial sectors which were expected to generate a manufacturing sector more integrated and less dependent on external supplies. The sectors pushed up were mainly steel, chemicals, machinery, vehicles, and equipment.

One of the pillars of those policies was to attract foreign investments through promotion laws granting easy terms for the installation of industrial plants, warranting the free import of capital goods and a high level of protection.[25] This originated in turn the installation of a large number of companies and manifestly increased the participation of foreign capital in industrial activities, as can be seen in the ranking of the fifty largest industrial companies in 1975 (Appendix 12.A.2). According to the 1963 economic census, a quarter of total industrial production came from foreign enterprises, and almost 50 percent was contributed by firms that had started operations around 1958.[26] In 1973 they produced 50 percent of total value-added by the largest enterprises.[27]

Among foreign enterprises American companies prevailed once more, whereas there was a smaller participation of European investments. Multinational companies were active on highly capital-intensive sectors with a high degree of concentration. The leading sector in this stage, siphoning a significant portion of foreign investment, was the automobile industry. It experienced a quick expansion, also thanks to the unsatisfied internal demand.

The strong presence of foreign companies in industrial activity produced

[25] Oscar Altimir, Horacio Santamaria, and Juan Sourrouille, "Los mecanismos de promoción industrial en la posguerra", in *Desarrollo Económico*, 6, no. 21, April–June 1966, pp. 119–124.
[26] Jorge Katz and Bernardo Kosacoff, *El proceso de industrialización en la Argentina: evolución, retroceso y prospectiva*, Buenos Aires, Centro Editor de América Latina, 1989, p. 52; Juan Sourrouille, Bernardo Kosacoff, and Jorge Lucangeli, *Transnacionalización y política económica en la Argentina*, Buenos Aires, Centro Editor de América Latina, 1985, p. 27.
[27] Daniel Azpiazu, Miguel Khavisse, and Eduardo Basualdo, *El nuevo poder económico*, Buenos Aires, Hyspamérica, 1988, pp. 59–61, 81.

important transformations in enterprise organization, since their features differed largely from those of domestic firms, which was characteristic of the first stage of import substitution process. Multinational companies were technologically more modern even though they did not always use the latest technology available in their country of origin, and on average they had doubled the productivity levels of the domestic firms.[28] It is not irrelevant to point out that affiliates of multinational firms can reproduce in local markets the organizational structures developed by their parent companies, and not only in relation to production, but also as far as administration and management are concerned, applying the principles of multifunctional enterprise. Later we will analyze how local market conditions could influence and modify some of the original aspects of these firms.

Another characteristic feature of the second substitution stage was the process of expansion of state-owned enterprises in the production of basic inputs, particularly in the steel field, where there was no participation of multinational companies and where a single state company, SOMISA, accounted for half of the total local production from the 1960s onward.[29] Finally, the large national firms continued operating and diversifying their production, although they were left behind, as already mentioned, by the multinational companies.

The share of the different types of companies among the fifty main industrial firms can be observed in Appendix 12.A.2, which provides information on the situation in 1975.

The first salient element is that the food industry, in almost all the first places in 1929, had been displaced by the petroleum, steel, and automobile industries.

In 1975 over a global number of fifty companies, twenty-three were multinational affiliates, whereas there only were twelve in 1929, five of which were meat-packing firms. By 1975 the leading sectors, regarding multinational companies, were basically the automobile, petroleum, and chemical industries. The frozen meat-packing plants have been nationalized and displaced to a lower position in the ranking.

In the 1975 ranking state-owned companies had become very important. There are eight of them, two of which – a petroleum and a steel company – occupy the first positions.

Regarding private domestic enterprises, some of the larger ones are

---

[28] Sourrouille et al., *Transnacionalización*, p. 35.
[29] Adolfo Dorfman, *Cincuenta años de industrialización en la Argentina (1930–1980)*, Buenos Aires, Solar-Hachette, 1983, p. 168.

part of big economic groups. For example, Molinos Rio de la Plata, Grafa, and Compañía Química belong to the Bunge y Born group. Others, such as the private steel companies (Acindar, Propulsora Siderúrgica, Dalmine), were created in the 1940s onward.

CHANGES IN THE INDUSTRIAL LEADERSHIP SINCE 1976

The period starting in 1976, when a new military government took over, brought great changes in the industrial sector and in entrepreneurial leadership. At that time a stage of decrease in manufacturing activity began, lasting to the end of the 1980s, a phenomenon characterized as the "disindustrialization" of the Argentine economy. The industrial output fell more than 20 percent between 1975 and 1982, reaching similar levels to those of fifteen years before, the share of manufacturing in the GDP diminished from 28 to 22 percent, and 20 percent of the biggest industrial plants closed.[30]

This was due to multiple reasons. On the one hand, the industrial development had been sustained since the war by a highly protective model, oriented to the internal market and scarcely competitive at international levels, a model which seems to have found its limits at the beginning of the 1970s. At the same time, the macroeconomic conditions and the public policies of the military government had a negative effect on the manufacturing sector, actively contributing to the reduction of industrial activity. In the early 1980s a situation of great instability was generated by the acceleration of the inflationary process, by the increase of external debt, and by fiscal disturbances.

The new economic conditions did not affect the different industrial sectors in the same way. On the one hand, the textile, apparel, shoemaking, and lumber industries and part of the metalworking industry were the more vulnerable to external competition and suffered more damage than other industries. On the other hand, the sectors benefiting most were those with state-granted promotion mechanisms (aluminium, paper, steel mills, cement, and petrochemicals) and those supplying state-owned companies (telephone equipment, petroleum, energy, heavy building, nuclear, and some metalworking industries).[31]

---

[30] Daniel Azpiazu and Bernardo Kosacoff, *La industria argentina. Desarrollo y cambios estructurales*, Buenos Aires, Centro Editor de América Latina, 1989, p. 20.
[31] Jorge Schvarzer, "Cambios en el liderazgo industrial en el período de Martínez de Hoz," in *Desarrollo Económico* 23, no. 91, October–December 1983, pp. 395–417.

From the point of view of entrepreneurial leadership, a great advance of local economic groups took place at the same time that the share of multinational companies decreased. Among the private domestic capital groups whose position got stronger in this last stage, we find two sectors. On the one hand, groups organized at the end of the nineteenth century have maintained a high position since then. On the other, groups formed around firms organized in later stages, which decided to extend their activities to new fields and new geographical regions, operating in some of the areas protected by the state.

This last stage implied a new increase in economic concentration and fundamental changes in the relative weight of the different industrial sectors. Some of them, like metalworking, electromechanical, and capital goods sectors lost strength, while the commodity-producing sectors, like steel mills, chemical, and aluminium, and the regional industries associated with new promotional regimes affirmed themselves.[32]

SOME REFLECTIONS ON INDUSTRIAL ENTERPRISES IN ARGENTINA

On the basis of what has been said here, some reflections can be drawn as to the characteristics of industrial enterprises and, in particular, the conditions in which the large enterprise developed in Argentina.

The first set of questions which can be asked concerns whether big business, according to the Chandlerian model, did exist. What were the characteristics expansion assumed, and can a positive correlation be proved between large managerial enterprise development and the wealth of the nation?

As Chandler has stressed, the birth and development of big business are favored by two kinds of factors: the size of the market (and the possibilities for mass production and distribution) and the nature of technology, because they are closely linked to the development of capital-intensive industries.[33]

In Argentina, the size of the domestic market limited the possibilities for the expansion of a large enterprise with a big production and distribution scale. One of the typical traits of Argentina is its relatively scarce

---

[32] Katz and Kosacoff, *El proceso de industrialización*, p. 60.
[33] Alfred D. Chandler, Jr., with the assistance of Takashi Hikino, *Scale and Scope: The Dynamics of Industrial Capitalism*, Cambridge, Mass., Belknap Press of Harvard University Press, 1990, pp. 21–31.

Table 12.5. *Relative size of Argentine industrial firms, 1935–1947*

No. of workers	Firms (%)		Workers (%)	
	1935	1947	1935	1947
0	27.9	17.1	—	—
1 to 10	57.1	67.6	17.9	19.5
11 to 25	8.3	8.4	12.4	11.6
26 to 50	3.3	3.2	10.8	9.9
51 to 100	1.8	1.9	11.9	11.6
101 to 200	0.9	1.0	11.6	12.3
201 to 500	0.5	0.6	12.7	13.8
501 to 1000	0.1	0.1	8.2	8.4
More than 1000	0.1	0.1	14.5	12.9

Source: See Tables 4.2 and 4.3.

population: in 1947 there were 16 million inhabitants, and 20.6 million in 1960, a figure equivalent to one-third of the German population at the beginning of the twentieth century, or to a quarter of that of the United States at that time. Local production for the domestic market restricted, to a great extent, the development of big business. Many foreign enterprises which set up affiliate companies did so not because of the market size but because of import restrictions, such as those from the 1930s.[34] The relative size of Argentine industrial firms can be seen in Tables 12.5 and 12.6.

Since the 1950s the development of capital-intensive sectors favored the installation of large firms. Nevertheless, the size and characteristics of the market altered the operation of some multinational enterprises. Automobile plants, for instance, did not reproduce the operation scale and work organization they have in more developed countries, reproducing, in turn, some features of national companies: much smaller scale, discontinous technologies, and a greater integration, due to the limited network of part suppliers, which resulted in lower productivity than that of automobile plants in more mature countries.[35]

Although in the 1960s nontraditional industrial goods significantly increased their share of total exports (from 3 percent in 1960 to 24 percent

[34] Vernon L. Phelps, *El crecimiento de las inversiones extranjeras en la Argentina, 1910–1934*, in Marcos Giménez Zapiola (comp.), *El régimen oligárquico*, p. 344.
[35] Juan Sourrouille, *El complejo automotor en la Argentina*, Mexico, Nueva Imagen, 1980, p. 22.

Table 12.6. *Relative size of Argentine industrial firms, 1974*

No. of workers	Firms (%)	Production value (%)
0	0.1	—
1 to 10	85.5	8.8
11 to 25	7.9	7.0
26 to 50	3.0	7.5
51 to 100	1.6	10.0
101 to 200	0.9	12.6
201 to 300	0.3	8.0
301 to 500	0.2	8.5
501 to 1000	0.1	10.5
More than 1000	0.1	26.6

Source: See Table 4.4.

in 1975), the bulk of industrial production was still destined for the domestic market.

A second problem to be stressed is that many of those industrial sectors traditionally associated with big business expansion developed late in Argentina; for example, basic metals production and some sectors of the chemical and transportation equipment industries started their production only in the 1940s.

A key factor for the possibilities of development of the large firms since the 1940s was state policies, which regulated industrial credit and established priorities through industrial promotion regimes. In this sense, it should be pointed out that these policies favored during the first stage – the 1940s and the beginning of the 1950s – the development of the small and medium-sized enterprises of native capital, and also the state participation in some key sectors of the economy, such as steel mills, railroads, and public utilities. This trend started changing at the beginning of the 1950s, and state measures favored in turn multinational companies, mainly from the end of the 1950s and throughout the 1960s. Afterward, especially since 1976, state policies favored great domestic economic groups.

The strong weight of state action created without doubt very different conditions from the ones considered by Alfred Chandler. The situation seems nearer to that described by Jürgen Kocka for the beginnings of German industrialization (which he compares with that of developing countries), in which the economic success of various enterprises appeared closely linked to the political ability of entrepreneurs.[36] There also appears to be a strong contrast with the Korean case, since a policy of aims on the side of the state, with prizes and punishments for the entrepreneurs, did not exist.

In general, throughout the period studied we can point out the coexistence of three kinds of large enterprises: the great domestic firms (in many cases made up of diversified economic groups), the multinational affiliates, and the state-owned companies.

The phenomenon of the structure of the different kinds of big firms is still to be studied in detail. We may assume that the most innovative enterprises were the multinational affiliate companies, designed according to the experience of their parent firms and having high productivity rates. We have already made some remarks on the subject, as, for instance, the scale limitations due to the size of internal demand or the use of technologies that were obsolete in the country of origin. It must also be taken into account that some specific conditions of the Argentine market, such as powerful trade unions since the 1940s, generated some changes in the organizational systems originally foreseen. Finally, we must point out that multinational companies operated since the 1950s in a context of strong governmental protection through tariffs and with close supervision of the installation of new firms.

And at this stage we should ask ourselves to what extent the more modern firms were affected by local conditions, dedicating so much energy to lobbying as to increase efficiency. The situation became worse after 1976, when, as a consequence of the financial policy and later of increasing inflation, speculation became the most profitable activity, so that financial managers started playing a key role in the management of the companies.

The development of large enterprises of native capital was strongly linked to access to credit and technology. This meant a great advantage for the companies belonging to the strong economic groups we have mentioned but also, in this case, to big firms enjoying considerable state protection.

Although there seems to be few cases where small and medium-sized enterprises achieved a satisfactory expansion, it is rather usual to find a big enterprise which was large at birth, or a medium-sized firm, taken

---

[36] Jurgen Kocka, "*Los empresarios y administradores de negocios en la industrialización de Alemania,*" in Peter Mathias and Michael Postan (eds.), *Historia Económica de Europa. Universidad de Cambridge*, vol. 7, Madrid, EDERSA, 1982, vol. 1, pp. 718–719.

over by a bigger one. In the cases where small and medium-sized companies achieved expansion, the innovative capacity of the entrepreneurs and their ability to gain certain market niches seem to have played a key role. In some of the studied cases, there is a correlation between expansion and production for foreign markets, including direct investment abroad.

The study of big state-owned enterprises as they relate to organization, efficiency, and productivity is still to be done. Such a study will have to consider different stages in the development of state-owned firms. It seems their performance decreased when investments began to be difficult because of the fiscal imbalances. But these enterprises have also some structural problems linked to the influence of political factors on management, aggravated by political instability. Another issue to be stressed is that some of the industrial state-owned companies were private firms with economic difficulties or in failure when they were absorbed by the state, such as the meat-packing plants and sugar-producing companies. This explains the rankings of Conasa, Swift, and CAP in 1975.

The industrial development of Argentina has no doubt been difficult and incomplete. Determining the extent to which entrepreneurs and firms are responsible for the difficulties of industrial development, while operating in a framework of unstable economic conditions and strong state protection, might be, in the Argentine case, a more appropriate concern than considering the contribution of big business to the wealth of the nation.

Acknowledgments

I would like to thank participants at the Florence Conference and my Argentine colleagues Samuel Amaral, Alicia Bernasconi, Roberto Cortés Conde, Jorge Schvarzer, and Jorge Walter for their comments on the preliminary paper.

APPENDIX

The following tables rank the fifty largest industrial enterprises for two years: 1929 and 1975. The 1929 firms are ranked by assets; the 1975 firms by sales. Tables include information about the origin of capital owners: national private firms (N) (including immigrant-owned companies), state-owned firms (S), and foreign companies (F). In order to make the data comparable with the cases analyzed by Chandler in *Scale and Scope*, we have classified firms according to the United States Standard Industrial Classification. The sources used are, for 1929, "Prensa Económica," Buenos Aires, September 1981, and, for 1975, "Prensa Económica," Buenos Aires, May 1977.

Table 12.A.1. *The 50 largest industrial enterprises in Argentina, ranked by assets, 1929*

Rank	Firm	Assets (pesos millions)[a]	Major product line (SIC code)	Origin of capital
Group 20: Food and kindred products				
1	Frigorífico Armour	96.9	201	F
3	Swift de La Plata	73.4	201	F
4	Azucarera Tucumana	53.3	2062	N
5	Frigorífico La Blanca	50.4	201	F
6	Ledesma	46.5	2062	N
10	Cia. Sansinena	41.5	201	N
13	Cervecería Quilmes	33.8	2082	N
16	Azucarera Concepción	29.4	2062	N
17	Azucarera Bella Vista	27.6	2062	N
19	Simón Mattaldi	16.2	2085	N
20	Frigorífico Wilson	22.2	201	F
21	Refinería Arg. de Azúcar	21.7	2062	N
26	Bodegas y Viñedos Tomba	20.0	208	F
28	Giol	18.3	208	N
29	Azucarera Padilla	17.4	2062	N
31	Saint	16.0	2065	N
32	Anglo Argentino	15.5	201	F
34	Magnasco	14.6	202	N
35	San Pablo	13.9	2062	N
39	Cinzano y Cia	12.5	208	F
40	Mate Larangeira	11.8	209	N
44	Noel	9.8	2065	N
48	Bagley	8.8	205	N
49	Fco. Uriburu	8.2	208	N
50	Schlau	7.2	2082	N
Group 21: Tobacco manufactures				
3	Manuf. Tabaco Piccardo	65.1	211	N
19	Cia. Nac. de Tabacos	26.1	211	N

Table 12.A.1. (*cont.*)

Rank	Firm	Assets (pesos millions)[a]	Major product line (SIC code)	Origin of capital
Group 22: Textile mill products				
8	Campomar y Soulas	44.4	223	N
12	Soulas	34.4	223	N
25	Fab.Arg.Alpargatas	20.0	221	N
38	Oertl y Vedetta	12.3	221	N
43	E.Dell'Acqua	10.4	221	N
46	Masllorens	9.0	221	N
Group 24: Lumber and wood products				
45	Quebrachales Fusionados	9.4	241–242	F
Group 26: Paper and allied products				
14	Fabril Financiera	31.7	262	N
23	La Papelera Argentina	21.3	262	N
Group 27: Printing and publishing				
37	La Nación	13.2	271	N
47	Peuser	8.8	273	N
Group 28: Chemicals and allied products				
27	Drog. La Estrella	19.1	283	N
Group 29: Petroleum and coal products				
7	Standard Oil	44.4	291	F
9	Diadema Argentina	42.2	291	F
15	Astra	29.8	291	N
19	Cia. Nac. de Petróleo	27.1	291	N
Group 31: Leather and leather products				
36	Franco-Arg. Curtiembre	13.8	311	N
Group 32: Stone, clay, and glass products				
22	Cia. Arg. Cemento Portland	21.7	324	F
42	Cristalerías Rigolleau	10.7	312–322	N
Group 33: Primary metals industries				
36	South Mining American	11.0	333	F
Group 34: Fabricated metal products				
24	Tamet	20.1	346–349 [332]	N
Group 37: Transportation equipment				
11	General Motors	38.2	371	F

[a] 2.39 pesos = 1 dollar.

Table 12.A.2. *The 50 largest industrial enterprises in Argentina,*
ranked by sales, 1975

Rank	Firm	Sales (pesos millions)[a]	Major product line (SIC code)	Origin of capital
Group 20: Food and kindred products				
12	Molinos Rio de la Plata	48.5	204	N
14	Sancor	45.0	202	N
17	Conasa	40.3	2062	S
23	Ledesma	33.7	2062	N
24	Swift	33.4	201	S
27	Sasetru	30.8	207	N
34	Nestle	26.5	209	F
43	CAP	21.3	201	S
49	Azucarera Concepción	17.5	2062	N
Group 21: Tobacco manufactures				
7	Nobleza	60.9	211	F
28	Massalin y Celasco	29.9	211	F
41	Piccardo	21.6	211	F
Group 22: Textile mill products				
11	Alpargatas	50.8	221	N
35	Sudamtex	26.4	221	F
36	Grafa	25.2	221	N
Group 26: Paper and allied products				
9	Celulosa	55.2	262	N
Group 28: Chemicals and allied products				
25	Duperial	32.8	281	F
29	Ducilo	29.7	281	F
44	Cia. Química	20.1	281	N
Group 29: Petroleum and coal products				
1	YPF	554.7	291	S
6	ESSO	61.9	291	F
22	Amoco	35.7	291	F
32	Shell	27.7	291	F
Group 30: Rubber and miscellaneous plastic products				
33	Fate	27.6	301	N
39	Good Year	24.0	301	F

Table 12.A.2. (*cont.*)

Rank	Firm	Sales (pesos millions)[a]	Major product line (SIC code)	Origin of capital
Group 32: Stone, clay, and glass products				
30	Loma Negra	29.1	324	N
Group 33: Primary metals industry				
2	SOMISA	199.2	331	S
4	Acindar	96.4	331	N
10	Propulsora Siderúrgica	52.7	331	N
18	Santa Rosa	39.6	332	N
19	Fabricaciones Militares	39.6	331 [281,289]	S
20	Dalmine	38.9	331	N
21	Gurmendi	38.5	332	N
47	Tamet	19.0	332	N
Group 35: Machinery, except electrical				
40	IBM	22.8	357	F
42	Olivetti	21.4	357	F
48	M. Ferguson	18.9	352	F
Group 36: Electric and electronic equipment				
31	Pirelli	28.2	364 [301–306]	F
45	Siam	19.8	363	S
46	Philips	19.8	365	F
Group 37: Transportation equipment				
3	Fiat	128.6	371	F
5	Ford	69.4	371	F
8	Renault	58.9	371	F
13	Chrysler	47.9	371	F
15	Mercedes Benz	43.4	371	F
16	General Motors	40.9	371	F
26	Safrar-Peugeot	31.3	371	F
37	IME	24.9	371	S

Note: figures for foreign-owned petroleum companies are very low because in 1975 YPF monopolized gasoline sales.

[a] 2.73 pesos = 1 dollar.

Group 4

Centrally planned economies in Eastern Europe

13

USSR: Large enterprises in the USSR –
the functional disorder

ANDREI YU. YUDANOV

One could say that the history of the USSR economy, with all its virtues
and vices, is mostly a history of large enterprise. Indeed, in hardly any
other country was the buildup of large enterprises given such top priority,
as it was in the USSR. For all that, their history has yet to be written:
we find no basic, seminal works setting forth the pertinent facts and
figures in a systematic way. The author of this chapter is not a historian
but an economist, laying no claim to tackling such an ambitious task. The
purpose of this chapter is a somewhat different one.

The socialist economy was a highly specific type of market economy,
but for all the official denials, it was, in fact, a market economy: Soviet
large enterprises made the greatest contribution to the wealth of the
nation when they operated in the spirit of the marketplace, and proved
to be ponderously inefficient, when made to function otherwise. That is
the causal nexus examined here.

BRIEF REVIEW OF HISTORY OF LARGE ENTERPRISES IN THE USSR

Large enterprises first emerged in Russia in the prerevolutionary period.
While Russian industry lagged behind that of the leading European countries and the United States, it still had a high degree of concentration: in
1910, large plants employing over 500 persons accounted for 53.4 percent of the country's labor force (as compared with 33.0 percent in the
United States). The especially high level of concentration was achieved in
shipbuilding, rubber industry, nonferrous metal production, electric and
transportation equipment production (see Table 13.A.1). Large enterprises
were predominantly structured as syndicates operating as joint-stock

companies engaged in marketing on a commission basis. The syndicates
Prodamet (sales of metals), Produgol (sales of coal), Prodvagon (sales of
railway cars), and Med (copper) controlled 60 to 75 percent of the trade
in their line of commodities, and together with the weaker syndicates in
the food and light industries, were in fact typical oligopolies. Had these
Russian syndicates continued their natural development, they would have,
most likely, gradually taken the shape of industrial and trade groups,
much like those, say, which later emerged in Japan (*zaibatsu*) or in South
Korea (*chaebol*). At any rate, an attempt (not allowed by the government) to transform the major syndicate Prodamet into a trust and to
supplement its marketing functions with producer functions was, in fact,
made in 1900.[1]

But history took a different turn: after the October 1917 Revolution,
large-scale industry was nationalized: in the course of the civil war that
followed, nationalization acquired a total character. In November 1920,
all enterprises employing over five to ten persons passed into the ownership of the state. Normal economic activity of enterprises was virtually
ruled out by the military situation (at some critical points in time, the
Soviet government controlled no more than 10 percent of the country's
territory) and the early Marxist dogmas (such as the abolition of money
and trade in the socialist society). Plants were supplied with raw materials
and foodstuffs for their workers free of charge, and similarly handed over
to the state the finished product they turned out as ordered. The results
for large-scale industry in that period were disastrous: by 1920, output
was down to one-seventh of the 1913 level.[2]

The New Economic Policy (NEP) period marked the start of industrial
rehabilitation and the beginnings of the history of large Soviet enterprises
as autonomous subjects of the socialist economy. Lenin's NEP was, historically, the first attempt to transform socialism toward enhancing market
and private-enterprise elements, and it subsequently served as a model for
numerous reforms in various countries, ranging from the Prague Spring
to the present-day reforms in China.

The NEP is certainly one of the most successful periods in the development of the Soviet economy. Within a short period of time – from 1921
to 1925/1926 – the prewar level of industrial output was restored, as

[1] Чунтулов В. Т. и др. Экономическая история СССР. – М.: Высшая школа, 1987,
с.118.
[2] Союз Советских Социалистических Республик.// большая советская энциклопедия, т.
50.–БСЗ, 1957, с.284.

highly rapid growth rates (over 40 percent a year) went hand in hand with relatively high, balanced development. It is not surprising that living memory still tends to regard the NEP as "the time when there was everything" – that is, as a period when the marketplace brimmed with goods. It helped to bring down unemployment to very low levels, and for all practical purposes, inflation was halted. Those were the only years in which the Soviet ruble was convertible.

State trusts were the protagonists of economic rehabilitation. From 1921 to 1924, the bulk of nationalized factories were in a sad state, with incomplete equipment, and suffering from a shortage of skilled labor and heavy underloading of capacities. They were divided into three categories: one was closed down, sold off, or leased to private persons; another was put in mothballs; while the third, the most viable plants, were allowed to take over equipment and personnel from the closed factories and to run all the production. These plants were then amalgamated into trusts, on the technological and territorial principle.

In 1922 and 1923, trusts were formed in something like 90 percent of state industry, a total of 421 units; 140 of these employed over 1,000 persons (see Table 13.A.2), and accounted for about 90 percent of employment by state trusts.[3] The trusts were, consequently, amalgamations of the best plants of the former Russian Empire, with a potential surpassing that of all the other enterprises in the war-ravaged country. In 1924/ 1925, trusts accounted for almost 80 percent of gross industrial output.

In the NEP period, the trusts operated on the principles of market economies, their purpose being the making of profit, with high profit margins a key task facing trust management. Trusts were free to price their products, except for the part covered by direct government orders, and it was also up to them to secure the best level of wages they could bargain out of the trade unions under collective agreements.

Meanwhile, the role of the trusts was sharply curtailed in investment: only 20 percent of their profits were retained in the form of so-called reserve capital designed to cover losses and expand production; 80 percent of their profits were remitted into the state budget. Accordingly, the investment activity of the trusts was confined to small current outlays, and production was mainly based on old plants and equipment. It was up to the state to finance the start-up of new large-scale production units

---

[3] История социалистической экономики СССР / Под ред. Виноградова В. А. и др., т.2. – М.: Наука, 1976, с.79–80.

(in that period, primarily giant electric power plants). Marketing was carried on through syndicates, which in the NEP period were all-Union associations of trusts funded by the trusts involved. The syndicates, in effect, came to monopolize the wholesale trade (see Table 13.A.3).

We find, therefore, that whereas in the West it was the firms that developed into large modern enterprises and "made the three interrelated sets of investment in production, distribution, and management required to achieve the competitive advantage of scale, scope or both,"[4] things were quite different in the Soviet economy, even in the most market-oriented period of its development.

Large Soviet enterprises, like their Western counterparts, had a large volume of output and a ramified marketing network, which made it possible to use the advantages of scale and scope, and it is not surprising that in the running of these producer and marketing capacities, the trusts made use of an organizational structure that was very similar to that of the classic American multiunit enterprises.

The large trust Yugostal (Southern Steel), for instance, consisted of fourteen metallurgical mills, seven plants for the making of metal goods, three coal pits, with coke and by-products, and three limestone and dolomite works. Each of these units was run by its own manager, while staff activities catering for the trust as a whole were concentrated at headquarters.

Consequently, one could well apply to trusts the definition of the modern industrial firm as "a collection of operating units, each with its own specific facilities and personnel, whose combined resources and activities are coordinated, monitored, and allocated by a hierarchy of middle and top managers." The concluding part of this definition is even more applicable to trusts: "It is the existence of this hierarchy that makes the activities and operations of the whole enterprise more than the sum of operating units."[5] Indeed, it is coordination of plant operations and establishment of ties between these as a result of the organizing activity of trust management that made it possible, virtually without investments, to restore and then to surpass the prewar level of production.

The cardinal distinction between the trusts and Western firms, however, is that the large-scale production of the former did not result from their own investment activity: in a sense, they inherited the plants from the enterprises which had earlier put in the money to build them up.

This peculiar role of user, but not creator, of core producer capacities

---

[4] Alfred D. Chandler, *Scale and Scope: The Dynamics of Industrial Capitalism*, Cambridge, Mass., Belknap Press, 1990, p. 35.
[5] Ibid., p. 15.

is characteristic of large Soviet enterprises not only in the first post-revolution years, but throughout the entire period of socialist economic development, the sole difference being that the trusts of the NEP period got their plants as a result of the distribution of nationalized property, while the latter-day large enterprises were based on new state start-ups.

It is an interesting fact that during the economic reform of the mid-1960s, the shift of the center of gravity in investment activity to the level of the individual enterprise came to be regarded as an important political objective, but even then it was the state that made all the capital investments with a recoupment period of over five years (i.e., virtually all the major projects considering the long periods of construction in the USSR). Earlier on, however, a substantial part even of current investment was financed gratuitously for the enterprises out of the state budget.

Consequently, large enterprises in the USSR never had a say in deciding on the strategic parameters of their production or their movement in time. The producer capacities at each enterprise were almost a fixed magnitude, so that they could increase output only by altering their use-coefficient, or by making limited investments of capital. Indeed, any radical expansion of production lay beyond their terms of reference, and required intervention by the state organs of administration (see Table 13.1).

Nevertheless, the trusts were not all that hampered in their practical activity in the NEP period: after all, what they had to do was to resume the functioning of existing capacities, instead of building up new ones.

Another peculiarity of Soviet large enterprises which became manifest at the early stages in the development of the socialist economy was their detachment from the marketing network. The syndicates of the NEP period were, of course, formally under the trusts which set them up, but the individual trust did not have much real say with the syndicate marketing the products of all the large enterprises in the industry. The syndicates soon developed into heavily bureaucratized marketing management agencies. But what was even more important is that the agency of the syndicates gradually deprived the trusts of direct connections with the market. All the products of the most important branches of industry were sold through the syndicates. Thus, whereas in the early 1920s, the trusts carried on vigorous advertising drives (one could recall, for instance, the series of placards designating 1923 for Rezinotrest (rubber trust) by A. Rodchenko, a leader of the Russian artistic avante-garde), by the end of the NEP period, advertising had lost its functional significance: in the 1930s, advertising became an element of street and shopfront decoration, and virtually disappeared in the following decades.

Table 13.1. *The role of centralized state investments in the USSR*

	Centralized Investments as % of Total Investments	Centralized Investments as % of Investments by State and Co-operative Enterprises
1918–1928	45.5	100.0
1928–1932	86.3	95.0
1933–1937	85.4	93.9
1938–1941	82.5	95.5
1941–1945	81.2	97.7
1946–1950	80.9	96.0
1951–1955	81.6	95.5
1956–1960	73.0	87.5
1961–1965	77.3	88.1
1966–1970	71.7	81.3
1971–1975	71.2	80.2

Source: Народное хозяйство СССР в 1975 г. – М.: Статистика, 1976, с.502, 505.

All of that inevitably put a heavy damper on the activity of trust management. The basic function of the headquarters of large Western enterprises is to coordinate and monitor the flow of goods through the processes of production and distribution, and to allocate resources for future production and distribution. By contrast, ensuring current production was the central task of the management of Soviet large enterprises.

Therefore, from the early stages in the development of socialism, Soviet large enterprises, in contrast to Western enterprises, were not a self-contained but an open-ended system: some of the decisions most crucial for the development of the enterprise, those taken inside the large Western corporation, lay outside the brief of the large Soviet enterprise.

Moreover, this feature in the activity of the large Soviet enterprises became most pronounced in the post-NEP period, with the ever more intense centralization of the Soviet economy under the Stalin dictatorship. Year after year, the enterprises were gradually stripped of their competence, as many of their old functions were increasingly concentrated on the industry (ministry) or central-state level.

Many of the subsequently chronic defects of the Soviet economy –

superbureaucratization, wastefulness, shortages of goods, and the like – have their roots in that very period, but our repudiation of dictatorship should not serve as ground for any one-sided, negative assessment of the development of the economy as a whole from the 1930s to the 1950s, a period in which it was patently dynamic (double-digit rates of growth). The country went through industrialization, leading to the emergence of a powerful, self-sustaining complex of basic industries. The USSR's economic strength likewise made itself known by the victory in World War II.

The massive spread of large-scale production provided the basis for positive advances; the government was well aware of the technical side of the economies of scale and scope; many of the plants built in that period (the Moscow and Gorky Motor Works, the Stalingrad Tractor Works, the Urals Heavy Engineering Works, among others) were deliberately designed as the largest in the world or in Europe, with the use of the then most efficient technologies. Mass supplies of machine tools, presses, trucks, and the like from these plants helped to transform the up-to-then technically lagging country. The Urals Heavy Engineering Works, for instance, was dubbed, for a very good reason, the "the plant-making plant." And if one finds disproportions simultaneously building up in the USSR economy, one of the main causes lay in violation of the economic principles on which large enterprises must function.

Under a government decision taken in 1929, trusts were no longer required to concentrate on the making of profit, but on fulfillment of the production plan. This was one of the results of the drastic change of economic policy manifested in the adoption of the first five-year plan, following Stalin's acquisition of power the year before. Under the plan, which determined the volume and range of production, enterprises were to conclude contracts, with expressly designated suppliers attached to each user of the product. The trusts were simultaneously deprived of their pricing rights: prices were henceforth to be fixed by state agencies as the sum of costs and average profit. Somewhat later, in 1936 and 1937, the connection between the price of the product and the activity of the producer-enterprise was totally severed. In order to level the playing field for users forcibly attached to different suppliers, price was fixed as an average for the industry as a whole, regardless of the costs of a given producer. Besides, in 1931 and 1932, there came the basic rate reform which laid down a single set of basic pay rates for similar posts and positions throughout the national economy, which were binding for enterprises throughout the country. Enterprises were not allowed to increase wages and salaries over and above the established basic rate even for their most valuable executives and operators, and any manager found to be in breach of the rule was faced with criminal prosecution.

Consequently, the Soviet large enterprise was not allowed (or was allowed within limits) to determine, at its own discretion, scope of production; range of production; prices; investments; wages and salaries; and suppliers and purchasers.

On the governmental level there was a parallel formation, with a gradually ever more clear-cut structure, of agencies vested with corresponding functions on the scale of the whole country. Gosplan and the sectoral ministries set up in the early 1930s monitored total output and the main lines of investment. Gossnab and Gostekhnika, set up in 1947, handled supply of enterprises and realization of the finished product, and also the introduction of new hardware and technology. A special Gosplan department was engaged in fixing the prices of goods (only in 1965 was it set apart as a ministry known as Goskomtsen). Other departments were responsible for working conditions and remuneration of labor (the corresponding ministry later came to be known as Goskomtrud), and for quality and standardization (later Gosstandard).

The remaining powers vested in the management of large enterprise in the USSR – despite the large scale of production – did not, therefore, exceed those which in the modern American or European M-form corporation are usually exercised by the operating unit, and were much narrower than those of the subsidiary management, to say nothing of the corporate head office. One could put this in yet another way: in some respects, large Soviet industrial enterprises could be regarded not as independent entities, but as operating units within the framework of the countrywide superstructure.

This sheds some light on yet another key aspect of the large Soviet enterprise, namely its fluid makeup. Because all the enterprises were entirely in state ownership, any changes caused no more difficulties than does the start-up or wind up of a new division within a private corporation. Even under the NEP, trusts were repeatedly reorganized, as several trusts were integrated into one or disintegrated into independent parts.

Centralized management of production was so intensified from the 1930s to the 1950s, that in some periods it is very hard to decide at which structural level of industry the enterprise was to be regarded as something like an independent one. Thus, from 1929, the trusts ceased to take care of current producer activity, their functions then being concentrated on technical steering, rationalization of production, and reconstruction of plants. The trusts of that period cannot be regarded as enterprises; they were transformed into specialized organs of state administration. In that period, individual plants and factories which had earlier been a part of the trust makeup became the basic unit in industry: they were given the status of legal person, and made responsible for state-plan fulfillment. But they remained only production units. To this day, "enterprise" in the Russian language is still synonymous with "plant" and not with "firm," while "multiunit enterprise" is designated by *obyedineniye* (association) or by the American term "corporation."

The windup of trusts and the takeover of their functions by Moscow-based sectoral ministries was paralleled by the formation of territorial-production administrations, known as the *glavk*, or *glavnoye proizvodstvennoye upravleniye*. These brought together technologically or territorially allied groups of plants in each industry. The glavks were vested with producer functions (responsibility for plan fulfillment by a group of plants), marketing functions, and supply functions, and had to operate on what was known as the "self-support" principle (or financial self-sufficiency in current operations). What is more, plants within the glavks were not sufficiently autonomous. Thus, the sale of products at average-industry prices gave a high profit margin to low-cost plants, while losses were in store for high-cost plants. The glavks restored the balance by taking money away from the former and handing it over to the latter, an operation which seems to be similar to the intrafirm transfer of capital within the framework of the large corporation. It seems that from the 1930s to the 1950s, it was the glavks that exercised most of the function of large enterprises, and so could be regarded as quasi enterprises, or almost enterprises, despite the fact that they were legally part of the ministerial apparatus.

Comparing the lists of the largest corporations of United States, England, and even Germany (in spite of the tremendous political upheavals), one can see that large enterprise in the West, once it has taken up leading positions in the industry, is then capable of maintaining these for a very long time. One student of this matter put it very aptly when he said that "there appears to be a widespread presumption amongst economists that it is the fate of dominant firms to decline." However, "the empirical evidence indicates that the presumption of decline is based on extremely weak foundations. Dominant firms do decline, but the notion that there is anything quick, systematic or inevitable about it is doubtful."[6]

Large enterprises in the USSR did not enjoy this kind of stability of position, and the implication is that there were no natural consequences of stable leadership either, such as long-term development strategy, reliable business reputation, in-house traditions, or long-term learning and transfer of expertise and experience. The big plants did not, of course, physically disappear with each new reorganization, and many of the industrial giants built in the period of industrialization still turn out the bulk of goods in their line. But large enterprises, as collections of operating units, were periodically subjected to destruction, and not just in terms of changes in top-level management (say, substitution of glavks for trusts). Within the framework of the new organization, new cooperation ties were established between incoming plants, while there was a loss of old ties with plants moving into an "alien" glavk or trust. A new enterprise (or quasi enterprise), in effect, came into being.

A striking example of such changes comes from 1957, when, after Stalin's death, an attempt to reduce centralization of the management of the economy, as a part of Khruschev's rise to power, was made by dismantling the sectoral ministries. They were replaced by territorial organs of administration of industry (sovnarkhozy). The outcome was a sharp spurt in autarkic trends in some parts of the country, a decline in countrywide specialization, and the onset of hard times for plants depending on supplies from other regions. One could say that there was a disintegration of some quasi enterprises (sectoral glavks) and the formation of others (territorial sovnarkhozy), with the new entities bringing together plants which were less allied with each other. No wonder the abrupt and comprehensive, and in many cases technologically unwarranted, perestroika, generated some painful phenomena in the economy. Within a few years, the sectoral ministries had to be reconstituted.

The next reorganization of industry along other lines proved to be more successful than the unhappy experiment of the territorial sovnarkhozy. In the late 1950s and early 1960s, there came on the scene enterprises initially called "Soviet firms," and later "production associations." The first few of these were founded in Lvov Region (Ukraine), followed by several others in Leningrad; a great many appeared in the 1970s, when the next set of economic reforms came in 1965 after Khruschev was ousted

[6] Peter A. Geroski, "Do Dominant Firms Decline?," in *The Economics of Market Dominance*, ed. D. Hay and J. Vickers, Oxford: Blackwell, 1987, p. 143. See also Alice P. White, *The Dominant Firm*, Ann Arbor: UMI Research Press, 1983, pp. 20–21.

Table 13.2. *Production and science-production associations in USSR industry*

		Percent in:	
	Number of Associations	Industrial Output	Employment in Industry
1964	380	—	3.0
1970	608	6.7	
1972	1,101	—	—
1975	2,314	—	—
1980	4,083	48.2	50.1
1985	4,378	53.3	52.7
1987	4,367	51.0	56.2

Source: Народное хозяйство СССР в 1972 г., – М.: Статистика, 1973, с.159; 1987, с.82; Крук Д. М. Структура промышленного предприятия и пути ее совершенствования. – М.: Экономика, 1965, с.214.

and Brezhnev became party secretary and Kosygin became premier. And in the 1980s the production associations became the prevalent type of enterprise (see Table 13.2).

Associations were created mainly for economies of scale through the merger of several plants into more closely knit production and technological entities than it had been possible to achieve in the glavks and other quasi enterprises. The then soviet prime minister Aleksei Kosygin wrote in 1970: "Standing alone, the plant finds it hard to identify demand, arrange supply and marketing, improve specialization and cooperation, centralize auxiliary operations, etc. These functions must be vested in the associations" (Table 13.2).

Indeed, the first Soviet firm, called Progress (Lvov), was created through a merger of five once independent footwear factories, each initially with the full cycle of production. With the formation of Progress, the head factory concentrated on the making of uppers for all the others, which confined themselves to putting the shoes together, each factory specializing in one product line. The head factory also started a large laboratory, pilot production, and auxiliary services catering for the firm as a whole. All of this, taken together, made for a marked growth of productivity and reduced costs.[7]

[7] Крук Д. М. Структура промышленного предприятия и пути ее совершенствования. – М.: Экономика, 1965, с.213.

Developments ran a similar course at one of the best-known high-technology associations in the USSR, LOMO (Leningradskoye Optiko-mekhanicheskoye Obyedineniye). It was set up on the basis of several instrument-making and optical plants in Leningrad, with a very wide range of production (almost 500 products), 45 to 50 percent of which was turned out in single units or in small batches. With the formation of LOMO, production was concentrated and specialized: one plant, instead of two, began to make microscopes; foundries were operated at only two of the plants; a single large-scale repair shop and instrument-making shop were set up. Components were standardized and unified, and research, finance, and managerial services were merged, and all of this likewise yielded a considerable effect.

M. P. Panfilov, LOMO's director general, estimated cost savings in the first year to have totaled 2.2 million rubles, a vast amount in the early 1960s; 47 percent of the economies came from concentration and specialization of production; 29 percent from standardization and unification; and 16 percent, from greater efficiency in research, finance, and managerial services.[8]

The first few associations founded in the USSR recorded average productivity growth of 20 to 25 percent.[9] However, later on these figures markedly declined because associations were being set up for political instead of economic reasons.

Production associations (and also research–production associations, usually formed on the basis of some large research institute), like the NEP-period trusts, were given some economic autonomy, but this was heavily curtailed as compared with the trusts (to say nothing of Western corporations). One could say that "partially" is the adverb that best describes the powers of the associations: they were able partially to influence payroll levels and the living conditions of their employees, and partially to make their own investments, but the funds at their disposal for these purposes (and also for developing the real potentialities of the enterprises) were small, ranging from 14 to 21 percent of profits in the 1970–1987 period.[10]

The structure of the production association, as the fairly typical LOMO shows (see Figure 13.1), is in general terms highly similar to the structure

---

[8] Панфилов М. П. Советская фирма действует. Из опыта работы ленинградского оптико–механического объединения. – Л.: Лениздат, 1964, с.133–134.

[9] Крук Д. М. Указ. соч., с.212.

[10] Народное хозяйство СССР в 1987 г. – М.: Статистика, 1988, с.580.

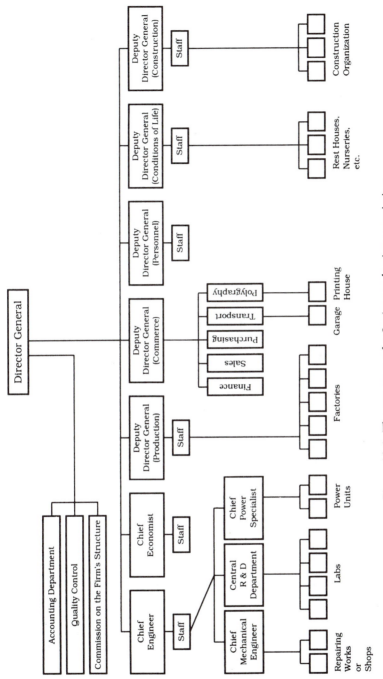

Figure 13.1. The structure of a Soviet production association.

of the U-form multiunit, multifunctional enterprise, with the corporate office, functional departments, and operating units, and the corresponding top, middle, and lower levels of management quite clearly identifiable. A closer look, however, reveals at least three essential peculiarities.

First, the top level of management at the Soviet enterprise is clearly simplified, there being no supervisory board, which one finds in many Western countries; the board of directors is not institutionally identified: the heads of the production, finance, and other basic services are not members of the board, but are deputies of the director-general; there are no senior officers in charge of law, public relations, or real-estate services.

It stands to reason that this peculiarity of the structure of the Soviet association is directly connected with the limited nature of its powers in making strategic decisions. A situation in which decisions on basic development matters were not taken at the enterprise proper, but at higher tiers of the state power did not require such a complex organization of top management, as that of the private firms in market economies.

In other words, the fundamental activities carried out by top management in large capitalist industrial firms, that of strategic planning and allocation of funds and personnel necessary to carry out that strategy, was determined by a single government agency, Gosplan. Still more striking, even after the 1965 reforms top and middle managers in associations and enterprises had very little discretionary authority in setting wages, hiring and firing, and determining and allocating bonuses.

Second, major departments in capitalist industrial enterprises were departments for distribution and marketing, purchasing, and finance, as well as for production. In the production association depicted in Figure 13.1, most of non-production functions were carried out by small offices under the director of commerce – offices whose status was comparable with the transportation and polygraphy offices. Instead the major departments were, in addition to commerce, those for engineering, economics, personnel, conditions of life, and construction. In the U-form enterprise comparable units would be listed as corporate staff departments. In other words, the production association depicted in Figure 13.1 is little more than a production unit writ large; it is not a multifunctional enterprise in the terms used in describing industrial enterprises in market economics.

These structural differences emphasize the role of the other powerful central government agency, Gossnab, the central materials planning and allocation office that carried out another critical activity of top and middle management in the capitalist U-form structure, that of coordinating the flow of materials through the processes of production and distribution – a function Alfred Chandler refers to as "the visible hand." Gossnab not only hampered the coordination of the flow of goods, but also the coordination of knowledge between different functional activities so essential to maintaining and improving the quality of products and processes. This latter situation was exacerbated by the fact that major R&D was done under auspices of Gosplan and Gostekhnika sectoral research institutes which had little contact with the R&D departments of the associations that carried out only limited routine R&D activities.

Third, this structure also reflects the marked tendency of the Soviet enterprise towards autarky, or self-sufficiency. One will, of course, find enterprises among European or American firms (and more often among South Korean ones) with their own building divisions, repair works, printing works, nursery schools, and health-care facilities, but that is hardly typical, while it is the general rule for Soviet associations to have such services. It is, moreover, common practice to have farm divisions to supply workers with foodstuffs, and in the 1980s associations frequently set up railway-car repair shops to expedite the forwarding of the finished product.

The production associations proved, historically, to be the final type enterprise to evolve in the Soviet planned economy, and they can be credited with the formation in the USSR in the 1960s and 1970s of the mass consumer society, when consumer durables first came within the reach of the people at large on anything like a sizable scale. But it was their low efficiency, as compared with the large Western firms, that was one of the causes behind the crisis of the Soviet system. Nowadays, production associations are trying to adapt – painfully and not all that successfully, for the time being – to the conditions of the economic marketplace, while remaining the core of the country's industry in the post-USSR era.

Consequently, large enterprises in the USSR had many common features with large Western firms, relying on a roughly similar technological base: large-scale technological complexes adapted to the mass output of standardized products. The structure of Soviet enterprises, especially in the NEP period and over the past thirty years, has been similar to that of classic U-form multiunit and multifunctional firms, while the basic distinctions (limited powers in strategic decision making; in-and-out movement of operating units; simplified top-level management; and even – as will be shown – a tendency toward autarky) are grouped around the main features of large industrial enterprises in the USSR, namely, their functioning as an integral part of the countrywide superstructure.

Could that be the main cause of lower efficiency of Soviet enterprises as compared with Western firms? In the past, under rigid ideological pressures, Soviet economists always assessed any peculiarity of socialism as an advantage. We should not like to swing to the other extreme and brand as a defect any difference Soviet enterprises may have from Western enterprises. The real state of affairs is much more complicated. The fact that Soviet firms were part of the countrywide superstructure did lower their efficiency, but not as a hard-and-fast rule; it only did so when it made them violate the objective rules on which large enterprises operate.

CAUSES OF INEFFICIENCY: DESTROYED COMMUNITY OF FIRMS AND LACK OF STRATEGIC INDEPENDENCE

In medical practice, the causes for which various organs of the human body do not function are usually classified as morphological and functional. The former originate when the organ has been injured or underdeveloped, and so cannot function normally; in the latter case, the organ is itself sound, and does not function because of the conditions in which it is expected to function. It is this latter situation, we feel, that applies to large enterprises in the USSR. Their powerful producer and managerial potential was unable to function at full stretch because these enterprises were compelled to perform functions inappropriate to them. At the same time, Soviet enterprises lacked the opportunity (and full incentive as well) to improve their performance in the sphere of their core activity – in mass, standard production.

In the Soviet Union, there was a lack of the natural community of companies adhering to different competitive strategies, something that will be found in any market economy, and large enterprises were forced to adopt functions performed by other types of firms in conventional conditions.

At this point, a short theoretical digression is in order. The notion that the economy is a natural community of firms is not generally accepted. Over the past decades, M. Porter, H. Friesewinkel, and H. Hinterhuber made a great contribution, in their pioneering works, to identifying various types of competitive strategies.[11] The thrust of their studies, however, is on the individual firm, and its quest for optimal behavior in the market-place, depending on its potentialities. But the problem of interaction between all types of firms, and of economic development as a result of this spontaneous and self-regulating process, is a problem that has not been studied.

But the point is that from the angle of the economist in this country (and probably in other socialist countries), habituated, as we have been, to being constantly faced with the effects of lack of such interaction and division of labor between various types of firms, it is the functioning of the Western economy as a coherent community of companies that appears to be the most essential factor of efficient firm activity.[12] After all, each firm does its own business!

One could identify at least four basic types of strategy:

1. Volume strategy consists in concentrating production on output of mass, standard products. The basic source of strength of a company doing so lies in the fact that such production can usually be arranged more effi-ciently and with lower costs than the making of small batches of widely differing goods. The volume strategy-firms rely on this advantage in their efforts to dominate a vast market, to oust competitors from it, and to attract the mass consumer with their relatively low-price and standard-quality products.

2. Niche strategy consists in specialization on production of special, pecu-liar goods for a small but lucrative portion of the market. The niche-companies gain their market strength due to the fact that their goods become indispensable for a certain group of consumers. Such a company tries not to get scattered and captures the maximum portion of a small market segment.

3. Customized strategy implies small-scale unspecialized production for immediate satisfaction of any (often local) market demand. The strength

[11] See Hans H. Hinterhuber, *Wettbewerbsstrategie*, Berlin: de Gruyter, 1982; Michael E. Porter, *Competitive Strategy: Techniques for Analyzing Industries and Competitors*, New York: Free Press, 1980; Michael E. Porter, *Competitive Advantage: Creating and Sustaining Superior Performance*, New York: Free Press, 1985; Harald Friesewinkel, *Gutachten zum Thema: Qualitative und quantitative Charakterisierung deutscher Pharma Unternehmen*, Zurich, 1988.

[12] This concept of a coherent community is extensively used in the theoretical biology. It was forwarded by two scholars. Russia has a sad record of priority in this sphere. The theory of natural community of living subjects adhering to different competitive strate-gies was first proposed by L. G. Ramensky in 1935 and was totally neglected here. But forty years later it was rediscovered independently by the Englishman J. P. Grime.

of these firms, lies in the fact that their products and services are most customized. Such companies are in constant quest of higher margins in any field within their reach: they are prepared to reorient their drive, to expand or reduce its scale, thereby displaying the spirit of free enterprise in its purest and most consummate form.

4. Innovative (pioneering) strategy consists of concentrating on exploration and discovery, with the main factor being introduction of basic innovations on the market ahead of the pack. Such companies open themselves to great risk by pinning their hopes on unpredictable breakthrough innovations, so seeking to create a new market and to benefit from being there first and alone.

The compensation principle is crucial to the market interaction of various types of firms: as a company develops one set of features, it usually sheds others, and as it becomes more efficient in one area, it has to pay the price of being less efficient in others.

Thus, far from all these ways are open to large firms: they are certainly efficient in their own (and only in their own) place, as makers of mass, standard products. Indeed, their size is more of a constraint than an advantage in areas where success depends on individual approach to clients (customized strategy). Nor do they find attractive the narrow segments of the market (niche strategy) which calls for much specialized expertise, and where the giants find themselves hemmed in. The pioneering strategy is, likewise, not suitable for the large companies. The record shows that they have had modest successes as pathfinders, and it is nowadays a textbook case[13] that while the largest corporations "spend far more proportionately on research and development than do small firms, and are responsible for the majority of minor innovative changes, it is the small firms who introduce the bulk of major innovative changes."

The trouble with the Soviet economy was that the community of companies which took shape in the USSR, in effect, consisted of firms of a single type, namely, large volume-producers, or of enterprises which had other objects and proportions, but which, in practice, had to abide by the same rules of behavior as the large enterprises.

Let us look upon the situation of the firms adhering to customized strategy. First, the Soviet Union just did not have enough such small enterprises that could pursue it. The analysis of size distribution of industrial establishments (see Table 13.3) shows that the share of small plants (with number of employed less than 100 persons) in the Soviet industry in 1960

[13] Graham Donnelly, *The Firm in Society*, London: Pittman, 1987, p. 68.

Table 13.3. *Size distribution of industrial plants according to persons employed in the USSR and in Germany (1960)*

Size class in no. of workers	No. of enterprises (%)			No. of workers (%)		
	FRG*	USSR**	(3)=(2):(1)	FRG*	USSR**	(6)=(5):(4)
	(1)	(2)	(3)	(4)	(5)	(6)
1–100	85.5	43.6	0.51	19.0	5.6	0.29
101–200	6.7	20.0	2.99	10.7	7.9	0.74
201–500	5.9	20.7	4.22	17.3	17.4	1.01
501–1000	1.6	8.6	5.38	12.9	15.8	1.22
over 1000	1.3	7.1	5.46	40.1	53.3	1.33
Total	100	100	1	100	100	1

* Size distribution of plants. ** Size distribution of enterprises. 1960 in USSR existed no associations. That is why figures show distribution of single-plant-enterprises, which makes them generally comparable with German figures. *Source*: IDW Zahlen zur wirtschaftlichen Entwicklung der BRD. Ausgabe 1987. – Koeln, Instituts-Verlag, 1987, Tab. 69; Народное хозяйство СССР в 1972 г. – М.: Статистика, 1973, с.192.

was two to three times less (depending on the mode of measurement) than in Germany. (In 1960 before the coming of associations, a plant was an enterprise.) Accordingly the share of large enterprises in the USSR was considerably overstated in comparison with Germany. The same peculiarity of size distribution of enterprises in the socialist economy (caused, as we see it, by the centralized manner of creating of new enterprises) can be seen in Czechoslovakia (see A. Teichova, Chapter 14, this volume).

Second, contrary to the nature of small business, even the smallest enterprises in the USSR had to operate under a long-term annual or even five-year plan of production. Range of products, suppliers, and purchasers were dictated to the small enterprises; they had the prices of their products set in accordance with the countrywide price lists; they had to conform to fixed staff establishments, pay rates, and so forth. What is more, small plants had to copy even the management structure of large enterprises, running, say, the same number of departments as the latter, despite the much smaller volume of work of each operating unit. "As a result, at the small plant, a shop with superintendent, deputy superintendent, and shop bureau [the typical organs of lower-level of management in operating units] had the same number of workers as a division at a large plant run by a single foreman."[14] Small Soviet enterprises were functionally not small in any sense, but were large enterprises in miniature, if one could put it that way.

It is perfectly clear that, in such a state of things, small enterprises in the USSR, in contrast to small firms really adhering to customized strategy did not look to any flexible satisfaction of consumer demand. On the contrary, they strove to turn out standard products, doing so, moreover, on a small scale and, for that reason, inefficiently. This had an extremely negative effect on the quality and upgrading of the finished product. Throughout the world, improvement of the finished product leads to tougher requirements on parts and components. In the USSR, by contrast, any new design was usually modified (worsened) in such a way that the semifinished goods already being turned out by suppliers could still be used. That is why even current renewal of models was such an extremely trying exercise at Soviet plants.

The consumer found himself in an even tighter spot when the making of parts and components for a specific product was assigned to a large enterprise, which found it unprofitable to turn out small batches and was not afraid of any penalties for nonfulfillment of planned assignments of minor importance. That is why failure to meet delivery deadlines was rather the rule than the exception.

It is a curious fact that such problems are not specific to the socialist economy. Many Western firms face similar worries when trying to get large enterprises to perform uncharacteristic functions. "When McDonald's wanted exclusive products, it found too many large processors unwilling to provide anything but the standard products they sold everyone else," says fast-food corporation historiographer J. Love.[15] Thus, the giant Kraft failed to heed the company's demand for a sharper cheddar flavor. The basic distinction between that situation and the very similar cases regularly faced by Soviet enterprises is that there is, in the United States, a natural community of companies pursuing different competitive strategies, something that offers the possibility of choice. Thus, in the preceding case, McDonald's coped with its difficulties by switching to the small firm Schreiber (Wisconsin), which was eager to meet all the special requirements.

[14] Крук Д. М. Указ. соч., с.186.
[15] John F. Love, *McDonald's: Behind the Arches*, Toronto: Bantam Books, 1988, p. 325.

By contrast, large Soviet enterprises kept coming up against chronic and intractable problems with their suppliers. No statistical data were ever published on this score, for obvious political reasons, and it is the view of the observer of the scene that erratic supply of parts and components and their low quality were Worry Number One for the management of large enterprises. At any rate, in the questionnaire, answered in 1970 by 241 directors of enterprises, reference to poor suppliers was given most often (48 percent of questioned) as the excuse for unsatisfactory enterprise operations.[16] Almost every technically complex line of production in the USSR was run under a constant threat of stoppage for lack of some minor part or widget.

Incidentally, this source of difficulties was still existing in the first stages of incomplete transition to a market economy. A poll taken in January 1992 at the constituent congress of the Union of Industrialists and Entrepreneurs of Russia concerning the causes of possible production cutbacks at the various enterprises yielded the following figures:

Lack of raw and other materials,	70 percent
Disruption of traditional cooperation ties,	40 percent
Political instability,	15 percent
Lack of orders for enterprise products,	12 percent
Lack of funds,	3–5 percent

(I am thankful to Dr. J. Boyeva for letting me have these unpublished returns.)[17]

Large Soviet enterprises usually strove to get rid of dependence on suppliers by setting up their own production of parts and components, with the underlying trend toward autarky, or self-sufficiency.

But that was not an ideal way out either. The mass of small ancillary production units which Soviet large enterprises used to "sprout" were decidedly unproductive and unmanageable. At the expense of core production, they absorbed vast resources. In the early 1960s, ancillary operations in USSR industry employed 50 percent of the work force, as compared with only 30 percent in the United States.[18]

A close analogy to this phenomenon can be found in other countries, for example, in Argentina, where lack of a good network of suppliers also

---

[16] Аганбегян А. Г. Управление социалистическим предприятием. – М.: Экономика, 1972, с.286, 287.

[17] боева И., Долгопятова Т., Широнин В. Кризис экономической системы и поведение предприятий (итоги анкетного опроса). – М.: неопубликовано, янв. 1992.

[18] Крук Д. М. Указ. соч., с.195.

caused overintegration and lower productivity of large enterprises (see Chapter 12, in this volume).

There was a marked restraint of technical progress at large enterprises because of the absence in the Soviet economy of another type of company, innovative companies. Throughout the postwar period, the results of research were hardly commercialized, and this continued to be one of the most acute problems facing the country. While Soviet science was a world leader in some fields, the transfer of these achievements to the economy was excruciatingly slow.

Here are only two of the most egregious examples. The "dry" technology of cement production was first developed in the USSR, and worked something like a miraculous change in the structural materials industry by making it possible to reduce costs in this energy-intensive production down to a fraction of the old figure. By 1987, this technology was used in the FRG to turn out 90 percent of all cement; in Japan, 78 percent; in the United States, 58 percent; and in the USSR itself, only 18 percent. One finds a carbon-copy case with the continuous pouring of steel, a basic technology for metallurgy. In 1987 continuous pouring of steel in the USSR accounted for 16 percent of the total, whereas in most of the developed countries, the figure ranged from 60 to 95 percent. What is more, imported equipment was prominently installed at Soviet plants, despite the country's generally recognized priority in its development.[19]

Retrograde bureaucrats were most often cast as the villains of the technical-slowdown piece. There is hardly any doubt that the proliferation of bureaucratic practices in the USSR was a heavy brake on development, but the root causes of the phenomenon probably lie much deeper: after all, the official at the ministry denying support to yet another innovator was, in effect, acting in the interests of the large enterprises.

It was noted in the analysis of various types of competitive strategies that large enterprises throughout the world take a cautious attitude to radical innovations, and act as their initiators on relatively rare occasions, a fairly rational line of behavior, because the price of error (including R&D error) is too high with the vast scale dictated by mass production. Preference is, therefore, given not to uncertain pioneering, but to current, highly predictable technical progress.

Here is the view of these matters taken by Akio Morita, head of Sony, one of the most innovative Japanese firms.[20] "We have heard several

[19] Народное хозяйство СССР в 1987 г. – М.: Статистика, 1988, с. 18–21.
[20] Морита А. Сделано в Японии. История фирмы СОНИ. – М.: Прогресс, 1990, с.332.

reports on remarkable discoveries, but have still decided that they were not fit for commerce and stopped working on them. This is much better than allowing work to proceed on an unfeasible project, something that will take up even more funds. Knowing when to stop, and when to go on working is to hold the key to success."

In this respect, the situation at large Soviet enterprises was absolutely similar to that in the West. At Soviet plants, the innovator or inventor (especially someone from outside) was *persona non grata*, and that was for a very good reason. Everyone has heard of the numerous cases in which enterprises found themselves in a tight fix when trying to fulfill government decisions on applying new technology. The project often looked good, but was in fact impracticable. The point is, however, that the losses in this case were not met by the visionary inventor or by the bureaucrat who succumbed to arm-twisting, but by the enterprise to whose lot fulfillment of the project had fallen. There the analogy ends. Pioneering projects rejected by large enterprises in the USSR were shelved. In the United States and (to a lesser degree) in Europe this risky business is handled by development firms. Venture capitalists (like the well-known Alpha Partners Investment Model) have developed various ways of dividing risk (risk sharing) which enables them to finance such firms without unduly jeopardizing their own position. Sooner or later, commercial success comes to this or that pioneer, and then comes the time of takeover of the new product market by the large corporation. The mass production of a well-established novelty is, by definition, best tackled by the large corporation.

The message is that in the West pioneers prepare a commercially viable product for subsequent multiplication by volume-strategy firms. Large enterprises in the USSR have no one to rely on, and they have actively resisted radical technical progress. "The main cause [of the USSR's technical lag] lies in the extreme disbenefits of applying new hardware and technology at maker plants," according to N. Blinov, a leading designer of hardware for X-ray medicine in the USSR.[21]

A basically similar situation has also taken shape with the fourth type of company, the specialized firms. Soviet industry has virtually had no experience in forming specialized enterprises in the course of product differentiation, when the firm invests its product with the special qualities that make it so distinct from all the other similar products, thereby expanding the range of supply on the market.

---

[21] Наука и жизнь, №12, 1990, с.77.

By contrast, the prevalence of large enterprises over all the other types of firms led to the impoverishment of the Soviet product market, for it was the large enterprises which were in the habit of shedding small-batch production from their programs. There was a powerful trend toward unification of all the products made in the country, and the diversity both of consumer and of investment goods was extremely limited.

As a result, goods were often used for other than their designated purpose, and so fell short of meeting requirements. Universal machine tools were used for jobs where higher productivity could be got out of specialized machine tools; enterprises in need of small delivery trucks were forced to buy heavy-duty trucks; chemical labs were unable to purchase many highly pure reagents and so had to make their own out of standard chemicals. Consumers, for their part, got used to stores offering one version of sewing machines and household air conditioners, and to finding that most color TV sets differed only in name, even when they were turned out by different plants.

Let us emphasize once again that this less-than-attractive picture cannot all be blamed on large Soviet enterprises or be regarded as a sign of their weakness. The trend to limit the range of production of the most popular types of goods is characteristic not only of Soviet enterprises but of any large corporations, because it helps to make better use of economies of scale. "A high volume, limited product line producer cannot also be a low volume varied products producer. . . . Variety costs money,"[22] says H. Mather, a specialist on competition in U.S. industry. The real source of this kind of difficulties in the Soviet economy was the absence of firms whose commercial prosperity would directly depend on product differentiation.

So, without flexible and reliable suppliers, laboring under shortages of specialized equipment, and being deprived of the possibility of relying on the experience of pioneering firms in commercializing technical innovations, Soviet large enterprises inevitably – simply in virtue of the environment – had to lose out in efficiency to their Western counterparts. Another fact to bear in mind is that the USSR economy was largely closed to the rest of the world, and this prevented Soviet industrial giants from making use of achievements in other countries.

But what were, after all, the results of their core activity – in mass, standard production? We feel that here the picture was very much a mixed

[22] Hal. Mather, *Competitive Manufacturing*, Englewood Cliffs, NJ: Prentice-Hall, 1988, pp. 55, 169.

one: along with the prevalent features of inadequate efficiency, there were also instances of considerable success.

Among the latter, one could list, in particular, the great positive contribution made by large enterprises to the development of the nation in the course of:

1. Industrialization of the USSR in the 1920s and 1930s
2. Shaping of the defense economy during World War II
3. Development of a world-class defense industry (aircraft, missiles, nuclear weapons) in the postwar period
4. Creation of a mass consumer society in the USSR in the 1960s and 1970s

The USSR was industrialized in a very short time (of the developed countries, Japan alone had such a fast pace in industrialization). And while industrialization was financed by blatantly barbarous methods (plunder of the peasantry), the organizational and technical backup of the process in which the vast country was transformed exclusively through the efforts of the large enterprises was, per se, an outstanding achievement.

The same applies to the activity of Soviet large enterprises in the military field. At the outset, the Soviet defense industry had a very much smaller potential than that of Germany – quite apart from losing almost one-half of it in the early stages of World War II but by the end of the war it surpassed the enemy both in quantity and quality of the hardware it turned out. A complicated situation took shape after the war as well. The overall superiority of the U.S. economy did not prevent the USSR from maintaining a general parity in the defense field, and even from forging ahead along some lines. Whatever our attitude to the "cold war" as such, in purely economic terms, the successes of Soviet enterprises were impressive.

The achievements of Soviet large-scale industry in creating a mass consumer society are less well known (and may appear to be more controversial). Output of consumer goods in the USSR has, in effect, never risen to the Western level, but the breakthrough in market saturation in the 1960s and 1970s still appears to be substantive. Thus, in 1960, TV sets were owned by 8 percent of Soviet families, and in 1975, by 74 percent; refrigerators, respectively, 4 and 61 percent; washing machines, 4 and 65 percent; vacuum cleaners, 3 and 18 percent; sewing machines, 39 and 61 percent; cars, 0.6 and 8 percent.[23]

---

[23] Народное хозяйство СССР в 1987 г. – М.: Статистика, 1988, с.426.

There are two common features to all the above situations. First, the activity of large enterprises was geared to tackling priority countrywide tasks with powerful state support. The superstructure covering the entire economy throbbed as a single complex, creating a most-favored regime for the enterprises concerned. The per hour [*sic!*] timetable for output of key armaments throughout the vast country during the war, or green fields investments which at one stroke created several new industries in implementing the aerospace program, give an idea of the scale of the state's economic and extraeconomic efforts.

Second, the very gist of the tasks being tackled accorded with the nature of large-scale production. The mass output of standard goods (standard types of equipment in the industrialization period, of weapons in the war period, and of basic types of consumer goods in the 1960s and 1970s) made it possible to realize economies of scale and scope. Let us recall that the results turned out to be negligible when vast investments were poured into agriculture, where large-scale production does not have any crucial advantages.

Massive state support, given in the right direction, therefore is the formula of success of large Soviet enterprises. It is, perhaps, no accident that these achievements usually appeared at critical moments of historical development (war, industrialization, new industries), when national efforts were naturally concentrated on one narrow area. But weaknesses inexorably surfaced in a normal environment, when enterprises were no longer central to national priorities. Compared with Western enterprises, most large Soviet enterprises turned out low-grade, outdated products and, besides, had a lower level of productivity.

Inadequacy of strategic independence was the basic cause behind these weaknesses, as it was already said in a brief survey of the history of Soviet large enterprises, and what now needs to be done is to explain the concrete mechanism of the negative impact of that circumstance.

Standard goods have the chief – and perhaps sole – merit of lending themselves to effectively organized production. All things considered, standard products can hardly appeal to the consumer: developed to meet some averaged-out wants, standard products can satisfy the need of the concrete consumer no more than in general terms.

Meanwhile, it is imperative for the maker of standard goods to attract consumers, and that on a massive scale: no one has a greater fear of capacity underloading than does the large volume-producer. The tremendous burden of fixed costs confronts the firm with the prospect of serious losses in the event of any decided drop in production. Chandler has aptly called it the "throughput problem" of the large enterprise.

The way out is to "bribe" the consumer by making him conscious of its virtues and oblivious of its vices, and that is where the previously mentioned effectiveness of production comes in. For one thing, the large enterprise can offer attractive prices because of its low costs.

Let us recall Henry Ford's provocative maxim about the customer being free to choose a car of any color, so long as it was black. Ford's sardonic humor must have been lost on those who preferred to have their car come in colors of red, yellow, or blue. But it is a matter of record that Ford's famous Model T was available in only one color and enjoyed unprecedented demand. It is perfectly obvious that customers were not attracted by the monotony of color: it was accepted and tolerated because of the sensational cheapness and the proverbial reliability of the early Ford cars.

Pricing policy is, however, only one strand of the matter. The money put by the large enterprise into lowering the price of a product may be used to provide higher quality or better service at the old price. In practice, an optimal proportion is found to determine which combination of price, quality, and other elements can exert the strongest attraction on the most massive customer strata.

The strategic cycle of the volume-producer's market behavior, therefore, consists in the following: to sell many of its products, they must be offered at a relatively low price (i.e., in proportion to quality, service level, etc.); and if the products are to be low-priced, they must be turned out en masse (reduction in average fixed costs).

Both these main instruments – prices and scale of production – were obviously beyond the reach of the large Soviet enterprise. Prices were fixed at one and the same level for all the makers (just as was quality, which had to conform to national standards). Because of the minimum investment resources at the disposal of the large enterprise, it was unable to exercise strategic management of output volume. In effect, the Soviet volume-producers were unable to make money in the way money was made by its Western counterparts, namely, by boosting output of generally accessible products.

A major manifestation of such "frigidity" of large Soviet enterprises can be seen in the peculiar development of manufacturing technology within enterprises. Research and engineering departments, which existed within their framework, proved their worth only in sustaining current production. However, this task also was not that easy, taking into account the previously mentioned difficulties in getting supplies of half-finished products and spare parts. However, they were extremely reluctant to develop new products and know-how, since there was no need in them.

Alice Amsden described the economic growth of South Korea as "industrialization-through-learning." By analogy the innovation processes within Soviet enterprises can be described as "stop-go-learning." The enterprises themselves played the role of a "stop" factor – their behavior was determined by their urge to continue ad infinitum the manufacturing of products, which had been put into production in former times. The innovation process could be upheld only due to a very powerful pressure from outside, for which purpose a bulky system of "branch" (i.e., fulfilling tasks set by branch ministry) institutes, engaged in research and development work, has been established. In 1990 1,054,000 people were employed in these institutes, while at the enterprise level the same work was done by 127,000 people.[24]

The "forced upon" and outward, in relation to enterprises, mechanism of scientific and technological process was not, of course, effective in any way. In those spheres, where the USSR got ahead of other countries, the "frigidity" of enterprises did not allow it to use first-mover advantages and, thus, the leading positions were lost. And in the most odious cases (like that of motor cars) scientific and technological process degenerated into a repeatedly ongoing process of copying outdated Western know-how of a previous generation. Moreover, every newly repeated know-how was not subjected to improvements and, for that reason, in due course copying had to be resorted to again.

Centralization of key decision making and concentration of the bulk of the vast country's resources put into the hands of the socialist state in the USSR an instrument of power unmatched in any other period of history. This power was used to solve a number of major economic problems, and it was the large enterprises, the type of firm which best lent itself to centralized management, that had the chief role to play in all the transformations over the seventy years of the socialist era. But the price paid for it was the rundown of the natural mechanism by which companies function in the economy, and this price proved to be much too high. For this, the large enterprises were penalized with a declining efficiency.

---

[24] Народное хозяйство СССР в 1990 г. – М.: Статистика, 1991, c.30.

PERSPECTIVE

The massive changes that began with the coming of Gorbachev's perestroika, led in June 1987 to the abolishment of the countrywide economic superstructure. The elimination of Gosplan (and to a much greater extent, the process of privatization begun in 1993–1994) meant that the senior managers of production associations would have to develop managerial capabilities comparable with those created long ago in the capitalist economies.

This process is developing with difficulty, taking sometimes rather absurd forms. Thus in 1992–1993 the most widespread form of the adjustment of top managers to the hardships of market economy was the policy aimed at disintegration of their own enterprises. In a large number of small independent enterprises, even technologically indivisible complexes were destroyed. There were two mechanisms of destruction: first, the most profitable parts separated from the enterprises for the reason that the management of the large enterprise had no financial possibility to privatize the whole association; and, second, there were organized so-called associated small enterprises to produce consumer goods. In such cases new entrepreneurs paid bribes to managers of large enterprises. The worst thing about both ways is that they hindered the normal work of the rest of the large enterprise and often caused its complete disintegration and loss of know-how.

By the time this chapter was completed (December 1994), the state of affairs in large enterprises in Russia remained very difficult. Deprived of the state support and incapable of getting adjusted to independent market activities, they experienced a grave crisis. In the most of them the rate of capacity utilization is not more than 30 to 40 percent. For example, the largest computer factory "Kvant" (nominal capacity is 1 million computers per year) utilizes only 5 percent of its capacity.

However the process of transformation of large enterprises gradually makes them look more like enterprises of developed market economies. From this point of view it might be very important to notice how they have been building up of late their own distribution network which previously they didn't possess.

Right after elimination of Gosnab and Gosplan, private commodity exchanges began to carry out the function of countrywide distribution of goods. The first commodity exchanges were formed in the USSR in the spring of 1990. Out of this first generation two exchanges have become the largest in Russia – Moscow commodity exchange and Russian commodity and raw material exchange. The number of commodity exchanges which had in Russia the legal status of profit organizations grew up very quickly and in 1991 there existed more than 1,000 commodity exchanges. This exceeded the total number of exchanges in the rest of the world. And this proved to be the golden age of commodity exchanges. Many analysts considered the exceptional role they played in the economy as a main feature of the "Russian path to capitalism." However, this flourishing didn't last long – starting from the second half of 1992 (active market reforms began in Russia in January 1992), the commodity exchanges started to experience financial troubles. Their number reduced. In the beginning of 1994 there existed already 130 exchanges. In September 1994 only 47 of them decided to stay in business and applied for the new registration. The explanation of this phenomenon of rapid growth and disastrous fall of commodity exchanges in Russia is rather simple. They turned out to be "market Gosnab" – the market replica of the previous centralized system of distribution. They were not firm-oriented or in other words not interested in the marketing of each separate firm's produce. That is why in spite of all predictions the exchanges in the long run didn't become the symbol of "the Russian model of capitalism." In accordance with Chandlerian theory, large enterprises have taken the place of commodity exchanges as organizers of countrywide distribution networks.

Thus, starting approximately from the second half of 1993 many Russian large enterprises started to build up their own distribution networks (of them the most advanced are VAZ (Lada cars), LOMO (optical equipment), KAMAZ (trucks, refrigerators, washing machines), Novomoskovsk chemical plant (in cooperation with Procter & Gamble). Developing distribution networks is also the main direction of business activities of foreign multinationals in Russia.

Moreover, even now, while the market in Russia is not developed yet, the absence of distribution networks is considered as one of the most serious factors of competitive weakness. For example, the head of state agency for bankrupt enterprises Sergei Belyaev said in his interview to Kommersant weekly (no. 33, 6 September, 1994) that the largest vodka-producing plant Crystal (this enterprise is also the quality leader of the branch) was included in the list of potentially bankrupt enterprises because of poor financial performance caused by the lack of distribution networks.

[In our opinion the most recent Russian experience testifies to the correctness of the modern theories of large enterprise.]

APPENDIX

Table 13.A.1. *The top-five corporations' share of the total stockholders' equity in some industry groups of the Russian Empire (1911–1913)*

Industry group	Total stockholders' equity, rbl. mill.	Concentrations ratio (%)
1. Shipbuilding	19.3	98.5
2. Production of matches	9.9	93.9
3. Rubber products	45.8	92.8
4. Nonferrous metals extraction	15.0	90.7
5. Production of explosives	5.8	87.9
6. Nonferrous metals industries	23.2	87.1
7. Electric equipment	61.6	81.5
8. Transportation equipment	65.0	79.2
9. Electric energy	86.4	77.5
10. Gold extraction	84.7	74.7
11. Farm equipment	42.6	73.9
12. General machinery	113.8	73.4
13. Production of salt	7.9	67.0
14. Tobacco manufactures	35.7	60.2
15. Mechanical machinery	73.2	59.8
16. Lumber and wood products	14.3	58.7
17. Leather products	32.4	54.1
18. Production of alcohol and wine-making	12.8	48.4
19. Cement industry	55.8	42.8
20. Ferrous metals	255.8	40.4
21. Cotton industry	378.2	15.4

Source: Лившин Я. И. Монополии в экономике России. – М.: Соцэкгиз, 1961, с.13.

Table 13.A.2. *The largest trusts of the USSR after the civil war (with over 5,000 workers on 1 January 1922)*

Rank SIC		No. of workers	No. of plants
1.	35 GOMZA	39,454	12
2.	22 Orekhovo-Zujevski h/b trusts	36,141	8
3.	33 Yugostal	35,000	3
4.	22 Ivanovo-Voznesenskoje h/b i Lnjanoe objedinenije	29,496	28
5.	33 Yugno-uralski trust	23,070	21
6.	22 Lnopravlenije	20,195	18
7.	22 Bogorodsko-Tsholkovskoje h/b objedinenije	19,240	10
8.	33; 35 Maltsevskoje objedinenie	19,235	16
9.	22 Presnenski h/b trust	17,855	6
10.	20 Sakhorotrest	16,090	214
11.	22 Tverskoi h/b trust	14,177	7
12.	35 Permski trust	14,084	12
13.	22 Serpukhovskoi h/b trust	12,121	5
14.	23 Mosshvej	12,096	28
15.	33 Bogoslovski trust	11,962	3
16.	22 Mossukno	11,688	23
17.	30 Rezinotrest	10,487	7
18.	32 Zentralni steklofarforovi	10,097	17
19.	26 Zentrobumtrest	10,000	7
20.	22 Vjaznikovskoe Lnjanoe objed.	9,855	18
21.	33 Visogorski trust	9,752	12
22.	33 Gormet	8,992	21
23.	22 Moskovski h/b trust	8,809	7
24.	33, 35 Gospromzvetmetall	7,408	4
25.	22 Tombovskoje sherstjanoe obied.	7,275	7
26.	21 Petrotabtrest	7,272	16
27.	24 Severoles	7,271	42
28.	22 Petrotekstil	7,155	20
29.	22 Kovrovski h/b trust	7,087	9
30.	22 Yaroslavskoje Lnjanoe objed.	6,492	9
31.	35 Moskovski mashinostroitelni	6,456	12
32.	Lensoloto[a]	6,000	7
33.	36 Elektrotekhnicheski trust	5,676	10
34.	Bassol[b]	5,630	5
35.	23 Petroodeshda	5,539	13
36.	373 Yugni sudostroitelni trust	5,220	3
37.	35 Petrogosmashtrest	5,212	13

[a] Extraction (gold).
[b] Extraction (salt).
Source: Список трестов и объединений обрабатывающей и добывающей промышленности, состоящих в ведении ВСНХ и подчиненных ему органов. – М.: ВСНХ, 1922, разл. с.

Table 13.A.3. *The syndicates' share of the total industries' shipments value in the USSR (1923–1929, %)*

Industry branch	1923/ 1924	1925/ 1926	1927/ 1928	1928/ 1929[a]
1. Textile	34.6	64.6	90.7	95.6
2. Metals and machinery	20.5	33.7	46.2	n.a.
a. Ferrous metals	n.a.	n.a.	100.0	100.0
b. Machinery and equipment	n.a.	n.a.	35.0	55.0
3. Petroleum	98.2	99.0	98.0	98.3
4. Leather and leather products	49.8	54.4	90.5	96.4
5. Silicious products	33.8	42.4	68.3	93.5
6. Fish products	—[b]	74.0	91.0	96.0
7. Salt	68.0	92.4	96.4	97.0
8. Fats, oils, soap	11.0	40.0	44.7	56.0
9. Matches	—	11.9	91.0	98.2
10. Tobacco	13.2	37.0	73.0	97.5
11. Starch and sugar	—	81.0	98.5	100.0
12. Canned food	—	—	93.0	100.0
13. Lumber and wood products	—	—	68.0	96.0
14. Chemicals	—	—	64.0	97.3
15. Building materials	—	—	30.0	85.0
16. Paper	—	—	65.5	84.6
Total Industry	n.a.	n.a.	82.2	90.6

[a] Plan figures. 1929 – official end of the NEP-period.

[b] — no syndicates; n.a. = not available.

Source: Синдикаты СССР в цифрах и диаграммах за пять лет 1923/1924–1927/1928. – М.: ВСС, 1928, с.3; Синдикатная система СССР. – М.: ВСС, 1929, с.7.

Table 13.A.4. *The turnovers of syndicates in the USSR*
(1927/1928, rbl. mill.)

Syndicate	Trade specialization	Turnover
1. VTS	Textiles	2,712.8
2. Sakhorotrest	Sugar	714.0
3. VMS	Metal	644.5
4. VKS	Leather	600.2
5. Neftesyndicate	Petroleum	472.7
6. Textiltorg	Textile	313.2
7. Maslojirtrest	Fats, oils, soap	174.8
8. Rezinotrest	Rubber	170.7
9. Gosribsyndicate	Fish	132.0
10. Prodasylikat	Siliceous products	126.7
11. Khimsyndicate	Chemicals	110.2
12. Bumsyndicate	Paper	96.9
13. Metallosklad	Metals	88.1
14. Lesosyndicate	Lumber, wood products	86.4
15. VMTS	Machinery, equipment	73.4
16. Makhorsyndicate	Tobacco	64.3
17. Spitchsyndicate	Matches	52.6
18. Stromsyndicate	Building materials	34.6
19. Solesyndicate	Salt	27.0
20. Krakhmalpatsyndicate	Starch, sugar products	18.9
21. Konservsyndicate	Canned food	14.3

Source: Синдикатная система СССР. – М.: ВСС, 1929, с.74.

Table 13.A.5. *Size distribution of industrial enterprises according to persons employed in the Russian Empire and in the USSR (1901–1925)*

Size class in no. of workers	No. of enterprises (%)			No. of workers (%)		
	1901	1911	1925	1901	1911	1925
1–50	68.7	64.2	50.5	12.7	10.6	5.2
51–500	27.1	30.3	40.3	35.3	33.4	26.0
Over 500	4.2	5.5	9.2	52.0	56.0	68.8
Over 1,000	n.a.	3.9[a]	3.4[b]		43.7[a]	54.5[b]
Total %	100	100	100	100	100	100
No.	20,895	18,302	7,375	2,270	2,542	1,764

[a] 1913: not strictly comparable with others.
[b] 1924/1925: figures due to different sources.
Source: Струмилин С. Г. Избранные произведения., т.2 – М.: АН СССР, 1963, с.169.; История социалистической экономики СССР / Под ред. Виноградова В.А. и др., т.2 – М.: Наука, 1976, с.248; Народное хозяйство СССР в 1958 г. – М.: Статистика, с.1.

Table 13.A.6. Size distribution of industrial enterprises according to persons employed in the USSR (1930–1987)

Size class in no. of workers	No. of enterprises (%)				No. of workers (%)			
	1930	1960	1975	1987	1930	1960	1975	1987
1–100	50.0	43.6	28.7	27.2	5.9	5.6	2.2	1.7
101–200	18.3	20.0	20.3	19.5	6.3	7.9	4.2	3.5
201–500	15.9	20.7	24.0	23.8	12.0	17.4	11.1	9.7
501–1,000	7.8	8.6	12.5	13.1	13.1	15.8	12.5	11.7
1,001–3,000	5.9	5.5			25.1	24.2		
		12.1	13.8			35.6	36.2	
3,001–5,000	1.1	n.a.	n.a.	n.a.	11.2	n.a.	n.a.	n.a.
5,001–10,000	n.a.	1.4	2.4	2.6	n.a.	18.9	34.4	37.2
Over 5,000	1.1	n.a.			26.4	n.a.		
Over 10,000	n.a.	0.2	0.8	0.9	n.a.	10.2	19.0	21.6
Total (%)	100	100	100	100	100	100	100	100
No.	9,662	n.a.	46,793	46,840	3,605	22,620	34,054	38,139

Source: Народное хозяйство СССР. Статистический справочник 1932 г. – М.-Л.: Союзгиз, 1932, с.430; Народное хозяйство СССР в 1972 г. – М.: Статистика, 1973, с.192, 193; . . . в 1984 г, с.159; . . . . в 1987 г, с.197.

14

Czechoslovakia: The halting pace to scope and scale

ALICE TEICHOVA

INTRODUCTION

In contrast to most other countries of Central and Southeast Europe, Czechoslovakia has enjoyed an advanced level of industrialization from a relatively early period. This together with its tradition of democracy has had a profound effect on its economic, social, and cultural development. The Czechoslovak independent state began to exist in 1918 when it arose out of the ruins of the Habsburg Empire, it was destroyed by National Socialist German occupation between 1939 and 1945, it was restored after 1945 in a frustrated attempt to reconstruct a democratic republic with a "specific way to socialism," and is at present splitting up its society and economy into two separate states: the Czech Republic and the Slovak Republic.

In this contribution attention will be focused on industrial development from the establishment in 1918 to the pending demise in 1990 of the Czechoslovak economy, dealing first with structural change, second with concentration and large industrial enterprise, and last with an examination of scope and scale of production in the Czechoslovak market economy from 1918 to 1948 and in the Czechoslovak planned economy from 1949 to 1988/1989.

STRUCTURAL CHANGE, 1921–1988/1989

The place of the industrial sector in the economy

According to the first census carried out in the newly founded Republic of Czechoslovakia (ČSR) in 1921, the state had a population of 13,612,424 and covered an area of 140,519 square kilometers. As the economically

Table 14.1. *Occupational distribution according to sectors of the Czechoslovak economy, 1921–1980 (in %)*

Year	Total	Agriculture & forestry	Industry & trades	Other branches services
ČSR				
1921	100	39.6	33.8	26.6
1930	100	34.7	34.9	30.4
ČSSR				
1950	100	30.9	36.3	32.8
1961	100	24.4	47.4	28.2
1970	100	16.4	48.0	35.0
1980	100	13.1	48.8	38.1

Sources: Vývoj společnosti v číslech, p. 90; *Statistická ročenka ČSR* (Prague, 1937); *Statistická ročenka ČSSR* (Prague, 1981); *Statistická příručka ČSR* (Prague, 1932); *Historická statistická ročenka ČSSR* (Prague, 1985), p. 66.

relatively most advanced successor state, it contained more than half of Austria-Hungary's industrial potential and just under half of the workers who had been employed in the empire's industry, while only encompassing a fifth of its total area and a quarter of its inhabitants.

During the interwar years the importance of the secondary sector for Czechoslovakia's economy increased constantly. Already in 1921 33.8 percent of the working population were employed in industrial occupations. This figure rose to 34.9 percent in 1930 (see Table 14.1). Until 1929 the increase in industrial production was greater than in the majority of European countries.

This fast economic growth was the direct consequence of increased capital investment and the resulting creation of industrial capacity. According to League of Nations statistics of the world's industrial economies in 1930 Czechoslovakia belonged to the ten most industrialized economies and to the seven largest armament producers. Because of this historical reality, it is unrewarding to rank and to compare the Czechoslovak economy with relatively economically backward countries or with latecomer economies. Unlike the European latecomers, Czechoslovakia's big business developed on the basis of both domestic and foreign capital investment rather than on government-supported industrial growth. In order to have some relevance, comparisons of economic indicators given in this chapter will be made with advanced economies. For the interwar period Czechoslovakia's economy bears comparison with the small industrially advanced European countries discussed by Harm Schröter in Chapter 6, while for the period from 1948 to 1980 with that of the Soviet Union analyzed by Andrei Yudanov in Chapter 13 in this volume.

In terms of industrial output for Czechoslovakia as a whole, the period of rapid economic growth experienced mainly from 1924 to 1929 was halted as a result of the economic crisis of the early 1930s at the same time as the negative effect of the West–East gradient of industrial production stymied recovery. This is shown by the low average annual rate of growth (1.5 percent) of total industrial output between 1913 and 1937. In principle, it was not possible to overcome the crisis of the 1930s due to inadequate modernization and the failure to implement the necessary restructuring measures before the dismemberment of the state on the eve of World War II. During World War II the Nazi-occupied "Protectorate of Bohemia and Moravia" became an important center of armament production within the German war economy. This added to the weight of the producer goods industries when the independent state of Czechoslovakia was restored in 1945.

Within less than a decade after 1945 the introduction of economic planning – the initial two-year plan followed by five-year plans – led not only to profound economic change, but also to the most radical social restructuring in Czechoslovak history. With regards to structural change Table 14.1 illustrates the considerable shifts in the occupational distribution of the population according to economic sectors between 1950 and 1980. Its share rose from 36.3 to 48.8 percent in the industrial sector and fell from 30.9 to 13.1 percent in agriculture, while there was a small rise of employment in the tertiary sector, mainly taken up by the growing bureaucracy. Employment in this sector stagnated in comparison with that in the service industries in the advanced Western capitalist economies.

With each new five-year plan, increasing numbers of persons from all social groups were sucked into paid employment in the totally nationalized industries. A large number came from the formerly excessive agricultural population and from the dissolution of commercial enterprises as well as financial institutions. Women contributed most to the expansion of the number of employed persons: between 1950 and 1972, of the total increase of 1,602,000 workers, 1,258,000 or 78.5 percent were women. A contradictory situation arose: on the one hand, the planners strove to employ an ever increasing number of workers in production; on the other hand, acting against the demands of the economy for more workers were the low retirement age, conscription, the swelling bureaucratic apparatus, the large number of young people in higher education, and the social measures taken to boost the birth rate. Because the reserves of labor had been largely exhausted, any future increase in output sought by the planners during the 1980s could only have been achieved by a general increase in productivity.

It should, however, be noted that in the years from 1945 to 1988, when the industrialization of Slovakia was pushed ahead at high speed by each successive five-year plan, the steepness of the West–East gradient of the pre-Munich republic was mitigated to a large extent so that the gap between Slovakia and the Czech Lands had, in the course of forty years, been substantially reduced.

Branch structure of industry, 1920s–1980s

Czechoslovakia was the only country in Central and Southeast Europe where industrial development resembled that of Western Europe, with producer goods industries being strengthened in relation to consumer goods industries. Although the share of the iron and steel, mechanical engineering, and chemical industries in Czechoslovak industrial production lagged behind that of the West European countries, the rate of growth of the producer goods industries in Czechoslovakia was higher than that of the country's overall industrial production – that is, the share of mining and metallurgy and engineering in the total number of workers employed and in the total consumption of mechanical energy increased in the 1930s because between 1929 and 1937 a shift from consumer to producer goods industries took place within the economy, which was caused to a significant extent by preparations for defense. The output of Czechoslovakia's producer goods industries (above all mining, electricity, metallurgy, engineering, and chemicals) overtook between 1923 and 1937 that of consumer goods industries, and, for the first time in the country's industrial history, textile production was in relative decline.

In historical perspective, the process of structural change which had started in the pre-1938 Czechoslovak economy was continued at a faster, planned rate after 1945 and especially accelerated after 1948. However, in order to comprehend the fundamental structural changes which took place in Czechoslovak society, it is necessary to explain them in conjunction with the revolutionary interventions in property relationships between

1945 and 1953. In this short period of time, the basis of the capitalist social order was destroyed. The economic foundation of this transition consisted of the nationalization of all means of production so that finally only personal possessions remained in private hands.

Compared with the interwar years, there was a significant increase in the rate of overall economic growth in Czechoslovakia during the years from 1948 to 1980. National income had increased sixfold by 1980, so had industrial production. The size of the labor force increased by 27 percent between 1948 and 1980. Also Czechoslovak exports rose over five times during the same period. Hence, when considering aggregate rates of growth in this period, the economic performance of Czechoslovakia superficially seems to be comparable with that of similarly structured Western industrial nations. This would deserve more thorough analysis which would exceed the scope of this chapter. Two points, however, should be made: whereas structural change according to sectors displays similar characteristics to that taking place in the post-1945 period in the Western industrial countries, particularly in the reduction of the primary sector, it differs in the relationship of growth between the secondary and the tertiary sector – that is, the service industries (which were ranked as nonproductive) lagged far behind the industrial and building sectors. A further, often neglected, but important difference is the fact that in the leading Western industrial economies the rate of growth of exports exceeded in the period discussed here the rate of industrial production. This provided incentives for technological advance, specialization, and growth of productivity of labor.

In the period of central planning in Czechoslovakia the distribution of gross capital investment played a decisive role in the structural changes taking place between both the sectors of the economy and the branches of industry. Thus, in Czechoslovakia, the decision-making process for the distribution of gross capital investments took place in the administrative system according to primary political directives from the planning body. Since the 1950s producer goods industries had regularly received preferential treatment so that the index of investments in the so-called productive sector had climbed from 100 in 1948 to 1,459 by 1980, of which industry rose to 1,092. Developments in the individual branches of industry are shown in Table 14.2 for the years 1948 to 1975. The priority accorded to industrial production is very noticeable. On average the productive sector accounted for 70 percent while industry to circa 40 percent of total investments. This confirms that the constant expansion of

Table 14.2. *Distributive shares of gross capital investment in the Czechoslovak economy 1948–1975 (in %)*

Sector	1948–1955[a]	1956–1960[a]	1961–1965[b]	1966–1975[b]
Productive sector	70.0	73.0	74.4	71.8
Industry	42.3	40.3	42.9	37.7
Building	2.1	3.0	2.6	3.8
Agriculture & forestry	10.4	16.3	15.0	11.6
Transport & communication	12.9	10.1	10.4	11.7
Trade	1.2	2.1	2.0	3.2
Others	1.1	1.2	1.5	3.8
Unproductive sector	30.0	27.0	25.6	28.2
Science & research	0.6	0.9	1.0	1.3
Housing	18.0	15.7	15.2	15.7
Health & social security	2.0	1.4	1.5	1.6
Schools, culture, & sport	3.0	4.1	4.1	4.8
Communal services & administration	6.4	4.9	3.8	4.8
Total	100.0	100.0	100.0	100.0

[a] In 1964 prices.
[b] In 1967 prices.
Sources: F. L. Altmann and J. Sláma, *Strukturentwicklung der tschechoslowakischen Wirtschaft und ihre Rückwirkung auf den Aussenhandel* (Osteuropa-Institut, Munich, December 1979), p. 5 (calculated from *Statistická ročenka* 1966, 1972, 1976).

investments and the increase in accumulation, especially in the growth of fixed assets, retained a central position in the priorities of the planned economy during the entire period of its existence. For an understanding of the basic trends of economic growth or stagnation in Czechoslovakia between 1948 and 1980, this perception is of fundamental importance. With the exception of the brief but historically significant reform movement between 1966 and 1968, the priorities of the central planners remained economic growth based on continuous increases in investment, as well as greater output of producer goods. Defense expenditure was generally high but fluctuated according to changes in the intensity of the cold war. This in turn led to frequent changes in the composition, organization, and targets of economic plans. In the next section the administratively directed process of centralization and concentration in industrial production is discussed.

Therefore, problems repeated themselves with varying degrees of intensity. The fundamentally erroneous assumption made by the planners that a continuous increase in gross capital investment and in the output of producer goods is consummate with an efficient economy became apparent as early as 1953–1955, when two one-year plans had to be inserted into the five-year plan pattern. But its full impact was felt during 1961–1965 as it became impossible to meet even the initial demands of the third five-year plan. It had to be rescheduled after the first year and the rest of the planning period was improvised with successive one-year plans. It became increasingly obvious that the centrally administered planned economy was not capable of coordinating the processes of economic life.

CONCENTRATION AND LARGE INDUSTRIAL ENTERPRISE

The size and structure of industrial enterprises in the Czechoslovak market economy, 1918–1938

The initial rapid rise in industrial production was accompanied by moves to introduce labor-saving devices in the production process, to reduce costs of production, and to improve profit margins which thus gave new impetus to the trend to rationalization and concentration in Czechoslovak industry. This process of concentration had differing effects on the individual branches of industry, ranging from an effective oligopolistic structure in iron and steel, mechanical and electrical engineering, chemicals, and shoe production, to widespread dispersion in the food, textile, and clothing industries.

Due to the lack of long series of comparable statistics for the interwar period, it is not possible to quantify continuous lines of development. A survey of larger industrial enterprises was conducted by the Czechoslovak Statistical Office in 1926 but the criteria it was based on make comparisons with later more comprehensive censuses difficult and only fragments of information for 1926 can be used. For example, some of the size classes of enterprises do emerge and form at least a useful insight into the development in 1926 of a few but significant large enterprises in the textile, engineering, and leather (shoe) industries. The census of 1930 does provide a basis for comparing the pre-1938 and the post-1948 structural developments. (See Table 14.3, which ranks the largest 3, 20, and 50 enterprises by industry.)

On census day, 27 May 1930, a total of 378,015 mining and industrial enterprises were counted. The overwhelming majority – 336,577 undertakings employing between one and five people – consisted of handicraft workshops or small specialist establishments. The small operations with up to five employees represented 89 percent of all enterprises but used only 10.5 percent of total motive power. On the other hand, 41,438 units with six or more employees, that is 11 percent of all industrial enterprises, consumed 89.5 percent of all motive power consumed by Czechoslovak industry.

The overwhelming majority of Czechoslovak workers was employed in medium-sized to large-scale undertakings. A tendency toward concentration is clearly visible from the opposing direction taken by the number of enterprises and the employment figures. The dynamism of this process between 1930 and 1990 can be demonstrated by the growth of large industrials between 1926 and 1990. Comparisons of consecutive censuses of industrial enterprises (calculated from censuses cited in the sources to Table 14.3) show that in 1930 the 124 largest enterprises with 1,001+ workers, which made up 0.3 percent of their total number accounted for 16.1 percent of the total number of workers, while by 1990 the 501 largest enterprises with 1,001+ workers accounted for 35.6 percent of their total number which employed 80.1 percent of the total number of workers. A further indication of the growth of large enterprise is shown in Table 14.4 which, based on the industrial census of 1930, presents the concentration ratio for the largest 3, 8, and 20 enterprises by SIC groups (for comparability both U.S. and UN Standard Industrial Classifications are given in Table 14.4). The results show great similarities with contemporary Western European economies as concentration, measured by employment (unfortunately no other measure is available) was substantial in a few often interrelated industry groups, listed here in descending order: engineering (motor cars, railway carriages, wagons), primary metals (furnaces, rolling mills), chemicals (fats, oil, cosmetics), and leather (shoe industry); in textiles only the marginally important spinning and weaving of jute showed a high concentration radio. The largest firms in pre-1938 Czechoslovakia were clustered in approximately the same industry groups as in the Western economies analyzed by Alfred Chandler,

Table 14.3. *Distribution of largest industrial enterprises in Czechoslovakia by industry, 1926–1971 (ranked by numbers employed)*

SIC group	Industry	1926[a]			1930[b]			1971[c]		
		3	14	107	3	20	50	3	20	50
10	Mining of coal & lignite			32			8		2	2
13	Mining of magnezit									1
14	Stone, sand, & clay						3			1
15	Food & beverages			18[d]						3
17	Textiles		4	22		1	9		4	7
19	Leather/shoes			2		1	4		2	2
20	Wood products			1						3
21	Paper			1			1			1
22	Printing									1
24	Chemicals			2		2	3		2	3
25	Rubber & plastics									1
26	Glass & ceramics			6						2
27	Basic metal products	2	6	12			1	1	1	6
29	Engineering (machinery, equipment, armaments)	1	4	11	1	11	19		6	11
31	Electrical engineering				1	1			1	1
32	Communications (radio, television, electronics)							1	1	1
34	Motor vehicles				1	1		1	1	1
32	Aeroplanes									1
40	Electricity, gas, gaseous fuels								1	1
45	Building/Construction					2	3			1

[a] 3 = enterprises with more than 6,800 workers (6,801+); 20 = enterprises with more than 2,500 workers (2,501+); 107 = enterprises with more than 1,000 workers (1,001+).

[b] 3 = enterprises with more than 12,750 workers (12,751+); 20 = enterprises with more than 2,300 workers (2,301+); 50 = enterprises with more than 1,550 workers (1,551+).

[c] 3 = enterprises with more than 82,000 workers (82,001+); 20 = enterprises with more than 36,600 workers (36,601+); 50 = enterprises with more than 17,200 workers (17,201+).

[d] 17 sugar refineries and 1 beer brewery.

Sources: Calculated from *Zprávy Státního úřadu statistického Republiky Československé*, 11 (1930), pp. 58–67, 486, 499–500; *Československá statistika*, Sčítání živnostenských závodů Republiky Československé, 27. května 1930 (Census of industrial enterprises of the Czechoslovak Republic, 27 May 1930), part 4, vol. 120 (Prague, 1936), pp. 88–89; *Kalendář pro ekonomy*, Federatívní statistický úřad (Prague, 1972), pp. 198–205.

Table 14.4. *The largest industrial enterprises by industry groups from 1930 census (concentration ratio based on employment figures)*

SIC group		Product group in high-concentrated industries	Concentration ratio			No. of Enterprises	No. of Employees
U.S.	UN		3	8	20		
22	17	*Textiles* Spinning & weaving mills (jute)	31.8	66.1	94.7	55	10,743
28	24	*Chemicals* Fats & oils, cosmetics	47.0	56.1	66.5	184	7,537
		Heavy chemicals	35.7	56.0	84.7	99	14,591
31	19	*Leather* Shoe industry	44.4	52.3	61.0	785	36,586
33	27	*Primary metals* Furnaces & rolling mills	65.7	87.7	99.4	26	49,637
		Iron & steel foundries	36.4	65.4	84.4	52	4,866
34	28	*Fabricated metals* Production of other metals	39.8	61.7	84.6	84	4,982
		Wire & wire products	43.0	72.7	86.0	65	6,968
35	29	*Engineering/machinery* Textile machinery	36.8	73.9	95.8	32	3,697
		Railway carriages & wagons	95.4			5	6,632
		Motor cars	96.2			7	6,435
36	31	*Electrical wires and cables*	68.3	88.4		18	2,689

Source: Alice Teichova and P. L. Cottrell, "Industrial structures in West and East Central Europe during the inter–war period," in Alice Teichova and P. L. Cottrell (eds.), *International Business & Central Europe, 1918–1939* (Leicester, 1983), table 2.2, p. 38.

Table 14.5. *Sectoral pattern of top fifty Czechoslovak firms (VHJs), 1971*

SIC group	Industrial sector	No. of Firms	No. of Employees
10	Mining of coal & lignite	2	118,435
13	Mining of nonferrous metal	1	31,763
14	Quarrying (stone & earth)	1	24,085
15	Food and beverages	3	54,303
17	Textiles	7	277,052
19	Leather products	2	63,932
20	Wood products	3	85,529
21	Paper	1	29,600
22	Printing	1	18,420
24	Chemicals	3	115,885
25	Rubber & plastics	1	24,816
26	Glass	2	43,463
27	Metallurgy (basic metals)	6	290,394
29	Engineering (mechanical)	11	421,226
31	Engineering (electrical)	1	58,998
32	Radio, TV, communication	1	82,055
34	Automobile production	1	137,240
35	Aircraft production	1	26,485
40	Electricity, gas, steam, & gaseous fuels	1	40,228
45	Building & construction	1	18,977
	Total	50	2,331,886

Source: See Appendix, Tables 6, 14.A.1.

"The Place of Modern Industrial Enterprise in Three Economies" and Alice Teichova and Philip Cottrell, "Industrial Structures in West and East Central Europe during the Inter-war Period" [in A. Teichova and P. L. Conttrell (eds.), *International Business and Central Europe, 1918–1938* (Leicester, 1983), pp. 31–55]. Significantly this also emerges in comparing the Chandler figures for 1973 in *Scale and Scope: The Dynamics of Industrial Capitalism* (Cambridge, Mass., 1990), (table 5, p. 19) with those of the Czechoslovak large enterprises for 1971 which will be referred to later (see Table 14.5).

The category of largest enterprises rose dramatically after nationalization in 1948 and the reorganization of industry into giant enterprises.

Based on the industrial censuses of 1926, 1930, and 1971, Table 14.3 lists the three, twenty, and fifty largest enterprises by groups according to the UN Standard Industrial Classification. These results show again great similarities with industrially advanced Western economies.

As part of the process of concentration, companies developed a pyramid corporate structure which created opportunities for wide-ranging connections within the Czechoslovak economy itself, as well as favorable conditions for further capital expansion in Southeast Europe, via subsidiary companies of Czechoslovak banks and industrial concerns. This formed a significant incentive for foreign investors and was further reinforced by the comparatively low cost of well-qualified labor, the relatively stable political conditions of a bourgeois democratic system, as well as the strategic and geographical position of the ČSR. Thus the interwar economy of Czechoslovakia was integrated into the spreading network of multinational (international) enterprise not only through foreign trade, which absorbed over 30 percent of total output, but above all through capital ties and international cartels. These I traced in fairly great detail in my book *An Economic Background to Munich International Business and Czechoslovakia* (Cambridge, 1974).

Concentrated industries and leading enterprises

The Czechoslovak metallurgy industry was the most highly concentrated industry not only within the framework of the national economy but also on an international plane. The extraordinary tendency in the Czechoslovak metallurgy industry toward concentration was based on the growth of the three largest concerns, or "The Big Three" – the Vítkovice Mining and Foundry Works (founded 1843), the Mining and Metallurgic Company (founded 1905), and the Prague Iron Company (founded 1863) – in which British and French capital played a decisive and German capital a not insignificant role. These companies dominated a well-organized and effective national cartel, the Selling Agency of the United Czechoslovak Ironworks, which was probably at that time the most comprehensive and tightest monopoly structure within the International Steel Cartel. From a 65 percent share of domestic steel production when the cartel was formed in 1921, the "Big Three" came to hold 90 percent after it had been in existence for fifteen years. As one of the main branches of industry with a relatively modern plant and equipment, the metallurgy industry formed the basis of a technically advanced mechanical and electrical engineering industry. In common with developments in other industrially advanced West European countries (see Schröter's Chapter 6 in this volume), there was a trend to amalgamation between the supplier and user industries. As a rule, the metallurgy industry took on the leading role in this process of vertical concentration, either through buying up majority holdings in the foundries, cable, chain, nail, locomotive, and bridge-construction factories, as well as in mechanical and electrical engineering, or through incorporation into cartels controlled by the metallurgy companies or through both methods.

The Czechoslovak mechanical engineering industry was relatively diversified. At one end of the spectrum there was a large number of medium-sized and small factories and workshops. At the other end of the scale, there was a high degree of concentration. As in other branches of industry, foreign capital also participated in the strongest and most highly concentrated companies of the mechanical and electrical engineering industry. The most important foreign investment in this sector was the decisive holding of the French iron and steel concern, Schneider Creusot, in the Škoda Works (founded 1856), Czechoslovakia's leading mechanical and electrical engineering and armaments concern. The Škoda Works not only held first place in the Czechoslovak engineering industry but their significance in East Central and Southeast Europe can be compared with Vickers in Britain, Schneider in France, and Krupp in Germany. The expansion of the Škoda Works into one concern, which basically controlled the whole of the engineering industry, was primarily pursued through the purchase of companies or majority holdings in companies at home and abroad between 1921 and 1938. The high point of these endeavors was reached in 1935 when, after a long and strenuous competitive struggle, an agreement was reached with the Škoda Works' biggest competitor in the domestic market, the Czech-Moravian Kolben Daněk Company (ČKD, founded 1871). This agreement covered all major Czechoslovak manufacturers – including the very important armament works of Zbrojovka Brno, the home of the bren gun, as well as other large engineering factories in Brno – and, in practice, rounded off the process of concentration in the mechanical engineering and armaments industry before World War II.

Like the mechanical engineering industry, the Czechoslovak chemical industry was dominated by one concern, the Spolek pro chemickou a hutní výrobu (Association for Chemical and Metallurgical Production, founded 1858), the largest chemical company in Central and Southeast Europe after Germany's IG Farben–Industrie AG and which, through investments and patents, was closely linked to the Belgian Solvay Company. Their joint subsidiary companies were spread through all countries of Southeast Europe. In the case of Czechoslovakia, the chemical industry held an almost symbolic position in the economic structure of the country. Whereas the leading concerns were linked with Belgian, British, and French capital, 60 percent of all cartel agreements made by the Czechoslovak chemical industry with foreign partners was concluded with its greatest competitor, the German chemical industry.

The petroleum and vegetable oil industries were closely connected with the chemical industry. All major manufacturers in this sector in Czechoslovakia were completely controlled by foreign capital which acquired no less than 97 percent of the total nominal share capital of this industry. This exceptionally large proportion of foreign investments was due to the almost complete dependence of Czechoslovak production on imports of raw materials and semimanufactured products for further processing. The most marked concentration arose in the production of goods from vegetable oils and fats when, in a series of fusions between 1919 and 1938, the biggest company, Schicht Brothers from Ústí nad Labem (founded 1882), was taken over step by step by the Anglo-Dutch trust of Lever Brothers. The Schicht Works controlled the production as well as the market for soap and vegetable fat products in Czechoslovakia and Southeast Europe. In the course of the 1930s they became the Central and Southeast European arm of the multinational trust of Lever Brothers and then Unilever.

Of all other branches of industry – the bulk of which belonged to the consumer goods industry – only the shoe industry, in which foreign capital played no important role, exhibited a similar degree of concentration. In 1937, the company Bat'a in Zlín (founded 1894) manufactured approximately 47.8 million pairs representing six-sevenths of the entire Czechoslovak shoe production. In its Czechoslovak combine the company employed 41,814 persons. The Bat'a Works also held a monopoly position among Czechoslovak shoe exporters. With the exception of 1930, between 1928 and 1938, Czechoslovakia held first place among the world's leading shoe exporters after overtaking Britain and the United States. In the reconstituted Czechoslovak Republic in 1945 the Bat'a concern owned 26 companies, including mines, transport, building, publishing, and insurance enterprises, while a further 107 Bat'a companies abroad were spread over forty countries.

The process of concentration gradually came to encompass almost all other branches of industry in Czechoslovakia – for example, textiles, glass, porcelain, ceramics, paper, food processing, wood, leather. However, the process of concentration in these historical and – due to the nature of the production methods – scattered industries developed in other ways. Basically, there are two lines of development in the Czechoslovak case which gave rise to increasing concentration and centralization. One line of development led via the principal banks which, commercially and financially, controlled a whole range of dependent companies producing a variety of different commodities. The other line of development moved in the direction of cartelization through agreements between manufacturers and, later, through legislation: by the 1930s almost 70 percent of Czechoslovak industry was linked to cartels (see detailed analysis of international cartels in Teichova, *An Economic Background*, and Schröter's emphasis on the significance of cartels in Chapter 6 in this volume).

All the economic forces which reinforced the existing trend toward industrial concentration were given additional impetus by the extraordinarily long duration of the economic crisis in Czechoslovakia. An even faster pace of concentration was forced on Czech industry when its greatest enterprises were taken over by Nazi Germany and integrated into Germany's war production. Thus the reconstituted Czechoslovakia entered the post-1945 period with a distorted industrial structure because the extreme demands of arms production under German occupation overstrained and exhausted the capacities of mining and heavy industry, while other branches of industry had shrunken and were technically neglected.

THE CENTRALLY PLANNED ECONOMY, NATIONALIZED INDUSTRY, AND LARGE ENTERPRISE

Czechoslovakia became the first country after the Soviet Union to nationalize completely big business, banks, and insurance companies. In several nationalization waves starting from 1945, first key industries and big enterprises with more than 500 employees, after February 1948 private companies employing more than 50 people, and finally to 1953 all small businesses of the nonagrarian sector were affected. As a result the social groups of artisans, tradesmen, and capitalist entrepreneurs as well as peasant smallholders were decimated after 1948.

Economic planning took its initial steps with the start of a two-year plan (1947–1948) and this was followed by a series of five-year plans – interrupted in 1954 and 1955 by two one-year plans – according to the Soviet model. In connection with the diverse range of opinions among

Czechoslovak economists and politicians about economic planning, there ensued a struggle to gain control of the reins of power which the Communists won in February 1948. Accordingly, their concept of giving priority to a restructuring of production with the emphasis on heavy industry and rapid industrialization in Slovakia was passed by the Czechoslovak parliament on 28 October 1948 with the law introducing the first five-year plan. By February 1949 all initiatives in the direction of economic democracy – including the pluralistic Central Planing Commission with its economic experts, representatives of all political parties, and trade unions – had been suppressed.

As the supreme planning body, the State Planning Office, holding ministerial rank, was established. It was subordinated to the Czechoslovak government, which after 1969 became the Federal Government of the Czechoslovak Socialist Republic. Putting into practice the federal principle, it created two governments, that of the Czech Republic and that of the Slovak Republic. The State Planning Office was responsible to the governments of the republics and in the last instance to the federal government. It stood at the top of a hierarchy with four main levels: immediately subordinate to the State Planning Office were the ministers for the individual branches of industry who, in turn, were in charge of twenty-four main administrative bodies. Right at the bottom were the enterprises. This pyramid formed the basis of the centrally planned economy in which organization, management, and control of industry were in the hands of the Communist state. (Compare to the Soviet structure headed by Gosplan described by Yudanov in Chapter 13 of this volume.)

Figures 14.1 and 14.2 show the organizational line of state management from the top level of government to the basic level of national industrial enterprises. Although this chapter is concerned primarily with the largest industrial enterprises, which were centrally administered by state organs, for completeness Figure 14.1 also charts the line of management from local authorities to the small and medium-sized regional, district, and communal enterprises as well as enterprises of producer cooperatives, whose former importance excepting agricultural organizations had been greatly diminished after 1948. In the course of frequent reorganizations, branches of industry were several times combined or subdivided and levels of responsibility and decision making shifted. Figure 14.2 illustrates the most far-reaching changes in the organizational structure of large-scale industry from 1959, which ended in even larger production units and tighter concentration in 1985.

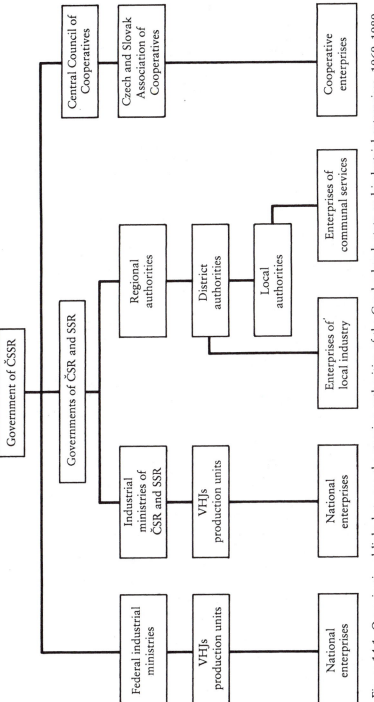

Figure 14.1. Organizational links between the steering authorities of the Czechoslovak state and industrial enterprises, 1969–1989.
Abbreviations: ČSSR' = Czechoslovak Socialist Republic; ČSR' = Czech Socialist Republic; SSR = Slovak Socialist Republic.
Source: Václav Průcha, *Úvod do národohospodářského plánování* (introduction to national economic planning), (Prague, 1988), p. 14.

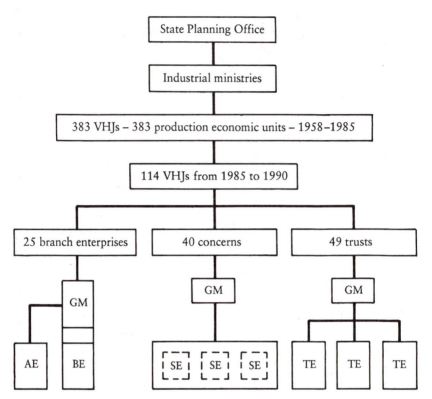

LEGEND:

☐ Legally independent units

[⌐ ⌐] Legally dependent units

Figure 14.2. Organizational structure of industry during economic planning
in Czechoslovakia, 1959–1990.
Abbreviations: VHJ = production economic units; GM = general management;
BE = branch enterprises; AE = associated enterprises; SE = subsidiary
enterprises; TE = trust enterprises.
Note: Before 1958, there were twenty-four main administrative bodies
responsible to ministers; after 1958, 383. VHJs were reduced to 114 by
31 December 1985 ≃ their organizational forms were: branch enterprises,
concerns, and trusts.
Source: As figure 14.1.

Apart from the State Planning Office, whose name kept changing, the ministries, and the leading functionaries of enterprises, the decision-making process on all levels of the economy was powerfully influenced by the Communist Party hierarchy: not only through the Central Committee of the Communist Party but also through its regional, district, and local party offices. They could determine the appointment or dismissal of managers of industrial enterprises and could impose their views on questions concerning changes in production, employment, financing, and sales. Indeed, the fate of leading industrial personnel was to a greater extent in the hands of the Communist Party apparatus than managed by the state bureaucracy. While responsibility was formally and legally vested in the state, party organs could and did interfere for better or worse in all economic spheres. Undoubtedly, this resulted in uncertainty and inefficiency. The question of responsibility was never settled in the period described now as "Party–Government."

In adopting an imitation of the Soviet system no account was taken of the substantial differences in social and economic traditions and conditions. The maximization of economic growth through the greatest possible increase in production, above all of producer goods industries, became the official basis of all economic theory and practice.

As the most industrially advanced Comecon country, next to the German Democratic Republic, Czechoslovakia's industry was allocated oversized tasks: on the one hand, it made a major contribution to the industrialization of the other relatively backward member economies and, on the other, it had to expand its armament production significantly. Forced acceleration of growth accompanied by dramatic changes in the organization and targets of the first five-year plan was in a wider sense also a reaction to the trade embargo imposed by the West as part of a further wave of the cold war, exacerbated by the outbreak of "hot war" in Korea. Carried out hastily under the guidance of Soviet experts, the huge increase in planned targets considered politically necessary had a long-term impact on the structure of the economy of the postwar republic. Accordingly, Czechoslovakia became the machine shop of Eastern Europe, at the same time as high-pressure armaments production strained the economy to breaking point.

During the first years of the first five-year plan an unparalleled rate of growth occurred (from 1948 to 1953 total industrial production rose by 14.1 percent and producer goods by 18.5 percent). Soon the consequences of *maximum* instead of *optimum* growth manifested themselves when barriers to growth began to appear. This led to a tentative move in 1958 toward improving but not changing the centrally controlled system: a third level was introduced into the hierarchical planning pyramid by creating 383 Production Economic Units (Výrobní hospodářská jednotka = VHJ), comparable in many ways to the Production Associations that a little later replaced the glavaks in the USSR (see Chapter 13 by Yudanov in this volume), and by abolishing the 24 main administrative bodies which, like the glavks, had been responsible to the ministries. From the early 1950s to the end of the 1980s there were many twists and turns in the organizational pattern of industrial enterprises as difficulties in the economy mounted. The planners tried to overcome them by periodically reorganizing the structure of production and, in conformity with often contradictory political decisions, either to tighten the economic command regime or to allow timidly some space for limited market forces to assert themselves.

Industrial enterprises continued to be organized according to branches of industry with VHJs (Production Economic Units) superficially comparable with Western corporations heading subsidiary enterprises (see Appendix Table 14.A.1, "The fifty largest industrial firms, 1971"), with each unit managing its own budget independently of the ministries. Of the planned decentralization, however, only this organizational aspect of the 1958/1959 survived because the financial reins were immediately tightened again by the central planning authority and the imbalances in the Czechoslovak economy worsened. Indeed, at the last change in industrial structure in 1985 – before the demise of the Communist state – the number of VHJs was reduced from 383 to 114 and thus concentration was emphasized (see Figure 14.2).

Concentration and monopolization in industry had developed since the turn of the century. However, this process increased rapidly both during the period of the capitalist market economy (1918–1945) and at a greatly accelerated pace during the socialist planning system. In this connection it is imperative to point out the substantial difference between the process of concentration in market economies of the capitalist system and planned economies of the formerly existing socialist system. The latter did not know insolvencies and bankruptcies or competitive takeovers, fusions, or mergers based on technology, marketing, and, above all, criteria of profitability. Sizes of enterprises in the planning system increased organizationally by government decrees or ministerial orders, dividing and merging enterprises according to criteria and targets imposed by the economic plan rather than according to market forces or production-technological requirements. A large part of this process of concentration consisted of organizationally amalgamating enterprises of the same branch of industry, such as mining, metallurgy, engineering, building, textiles, leather, and food, and putting them under the control of the appropriate industry ministry, frequently irrespective of their former place in production linkages.

In the course of planning, beginning with the early 1950s, many of the vertically concentrated combines of interwar Czechoslovak big business were disaggregated – among them large enterprises founded in the nineteenth century such as Bat'a, the Vítkovické horní těžířstvo (Vítkovice Mining and Foundry Works), the Škoda Works, and the Czechmoravian Kolben- Daněk Co. This interrupted the technical chain of production in their multiunit organizational structure. Overriding technical considerations, planners allocated the individual enterprises to centrally managed organizations, such as the VHJs, which – as mentioned earlier – were arranged according to branches of industry. New firms were thus created and often their production programs changed. However, in important cases the interruption of chains of production was not possible. Thus some of the vertical rather than horizontal monopolistic organizations, founded in the mid-nineteenth century survived.

In order to give a picture of the composition of output of the here described tightly concentrated industrial sector, it should be noted that the overwhelming share of total Czechoslovak industrial output (91 percent in 1985) was produced by national enterprises. Based on UN International Standard Industrial Classification (SIC), the volume of production of industrial national enterprises was divided thus: 3.6 percent in mining, 91.7 percent in manufacturing, and 4.7 percent in production of electricity, gas, water, and steam (*Statistická ročenka*, Prague 1986, p. 347).

The largest enterprises and management structure

Any comparable judgment has to be made – as stated earlier – by taking recourse to employment statistics which obviously are less satisfactory than more sophisticated indicators. In addition comparability of the size classes of enterprises is seriously impaired by the fundamental difference between the socioeconomic framework of the Western market economy and the East European planned economy, as has been pointed out already. In spite of these qualifications statistical evidence has been examined to show at least the trends in the development of the largest enterprises, both in the long term in one country (Czechoslovakia) and in a cross-country comparison. The results are described here and are statistically presented in the following tables.

On every count the enormous weight of engineering, which includes armament production, stands out conspicuously, as the rank order of industries presented in Tables 14.3, 14.5, and 14.6 confirms. Table 14.3 ranks them by numbers employed in three categories (three, twenty, and fifty largest industrials) in three bench years (1926, 1930, and 1971). In all categories and bench years the engineering industry held first place, while the second and third places were taken up by basic metal products in 1926, by automobile production and electrical engineering in 1930, and by basic and fabricated metal products and communications (radio, TV, and electronics) in 1971.

Table 14.5 arranges the largest fifty industrials by industries, which gives a comparable picture with the rank order of industrial branches of other West European economies. This also strikingly emerges from Table 14.6, which presents a comparison of the largest Czechoslovak industrial enterprises with more than 20,000 employees in 1971 with the same size category of enterprises in the Unites States, Britain, West Germany, and France in 1973. These enterprises numbered 40 in Czechoslovakia, 50 in Britain, 29 in Germany, 24 in France, and not surprisingly 211 in the United States. They are ranked by industry and country as in table 5, p. 19, of Chandler's *Scale and Scope*. Thus, at the beginning of the 1970s in the planned economy of Czechoslovakia, giant enterprises in this comparatively small country (15 million inhabitants) were found in similar industrial branches as with the leaders in machinery production, including armaments and motor cars, electrical machinery, primary and fabricated metals, as well as large production units in textiles and shoes. The Appendix contains the individual listing of the fifty largest Czechoslovak firms (VHJs – Economic Production Units) which, as in large corporations, stood at the head of centralized combines. Their sectoral pattern is illustrated in Table 14.5, which again confirms the rank order of industries described earlier. The largest and most concentrated industries of the planned economy of the Czechoslovak Communist state trace their origins in most cases to the second half of the nineteenth century, for example, in iron and steel, mechanical engineering, chemicals, textiles, shoes, as the dates of founding the leading enterprises show. Already in the capitalist market economy, industry became the most important sector

Table 14.6. *Distribution of world's largest industrial enterprises with more than 20,000 employees, by industry and country*

SIC group U.S.	UN	Industry	United States	Great Britain	West Germany	France	Czechoslovakia
20	15	Food	22	13	0	1	0
21	16	Tobacco	3	3	1	0	0
22	17	Textiles	7	3	0	1	7
23	172	Apparel	6	0	0	0	0
24	20	Wood products	4	0	0	0	2
25		Furniture	0	0	0	0	1
26	21	Paper	7	3	0	0	1
27	22	Printing & publishing	0	0	0	0	0
28	24	Chemicals	24	4	5	6	3
29	11	Petroleum	14	2	0	2	0
30	25	Rubber & plastics	5	1	1	1	1
31	19	Leather products	2	0	0	0	2
32	14	Stone, clay, &					
	26	Glass	7	3	0	3	2[a]
33	27	Primary metals	13	2	9	4	6
34	28	Fabricated metals	8	5	1	0	0
35	29	Machinery [of this:	22	2	3	0	12
	34	Motor cars (ČSSR/1)					
	35	Aeroplanes (ČSSR/1)]					
36	31	Electrical machinery	20	4	5	2	1
	32	Electronics, radio, TV	0	0	0	0	1
37		Transport equipment	22	3	3	4	0
38		Instruments	4	0	0	0	0
39		Miscellaneous	2	0	0	0	0
	40	Electricity, gas, & gaseous fuels	0	0	0	0	1
		Conglomerate	19	2	1	0	0
		Total	211	50	29	24	40

[a] 1 enterprise in group: stone & clay, and 1 enterprise in group: glass.
Sources: For United States, Great Britain, West Germany, and France (data from 1973), see Alfred D. Chandler, Jr., *Scale and Scope: The Dynamics of Industrial Capitalism* (Cambridge, Mass., London, 1990), table 5, p. 19, for Czechoslovakia, see *Kalendář pro ekonomy* (Calendar for economists), FSÚ (Federal Statistical Office), (Prague, 1972), pp. 198–205.

and this position was enormously strengthened, especially due to the overemphasis on producer goods industries, from 1948 to 1989 during the implementation of successive five-year plans.

Economic historians have as yet not paid attention to the study of management in the concentrated industry of the planned economy of Czechoslovakia. An idea of the management structure can be given here which was put into effect between 1959 and 1990 (see overall organizational structure in Figure 14.2). This has been described in the text. The management structure of national industrial enterprises is charted in Figure 14.3. A comparison of Figure 14.3 to that of the Soviet production associations, Figure 13.1, emphasizes the close similarity between enterprise organizational structure in the two planned economies. The centralized organizational structure is conspicuous. Criticism has been directed at the time-consuming, cumbersome, rigid, and uninventive methods and forms of management in the oversized, monopolistic, and bureaucratically administered national enterprises. In this respect the question of why this form and structure of management failed to produce efficient economic results is only now being seriously investigated. But in the centrally planned economy of Czechoslovakia, as in that of the USSR, managerial discretion was severely constrained, for as Yudanov stresses, "decisions most critical for the development of the enterprise, those taken *inside* the large Western corporation, lay *outside* the brief of the large Soviet enterprise" (Chapter 13, this volume).

CONCLUSION

I am aware that at the risk of oversimplification I am broaching a complex problem in this concluding section. However, in the context of this contribution the fundamental difference between the economic criteria for industrial production in a capitalist free-market economy and a centrally administered and controlled planned economy of the Communist system which existed between 1948 and 1989 in Czechoslovakia has to be pointed out, which renders comparisons extremely difficult. In the last analysis the measure of economic success in the capitalist free-market economy is profitability, while the measure of achievement in the planned economies was the fulfillment of the prescribed targets of the economic plan. In the planned economies of the Czechoslovak socialist state, managers had no responsibility to shareholders but they had to answer for their decisions and actions to a hierarchical set of planning authorities

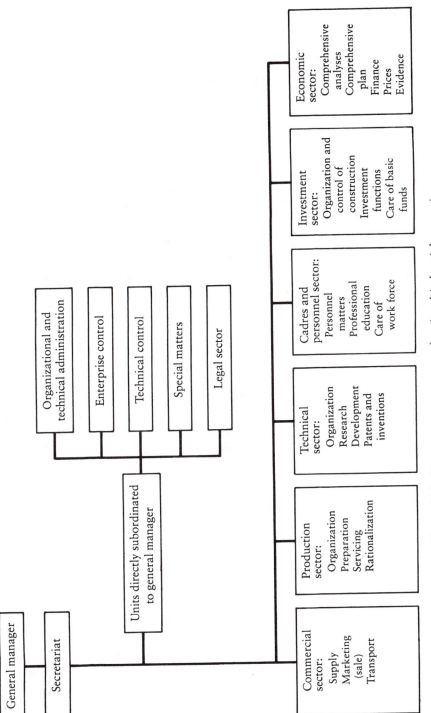

Figure 14.3. Management structure of national industrial enterprises.
Source: As figure 14.1.

headed by the State Planning Offices. The market mechanism had – except for limited areas mainly connected with foreign trade – been replaced by planned targets. Because cost–benefit analyses had been abandoned, production costs, income, profits, and prices could neither form the basis of entrepreneurial decisions nor measure the efficiency of economic units. For the management of enterprises it was a matter of indifference: whether their products were finding buyers or simply keeping the shelves of the warehouses full, whether they were making profits or losses, or whether their investments were used rationally. The sole measure of success was the fulfillment of the planned targets which from the head office to the individual works were laid down mechanically and in detail, prescribing the actual physical quantities each individual economic unit was to produce. Because fulfilling the plan also determined the distribution of materials and financial resources, managements tended to exaggerate and falsify their reports of success, to inflate demands on investment funds and labor and wage funds, as well as unnecessarily hoard and hold excessively large stocks. In this way, distorted information influenced the decision-making process from the lowest level of the enterprises right to the top of the State Planning Office. Thus management "for better or worse" was engaged in the all-pervading exercise of fulfilling the successive five-year plans, in the course of which bureaucratization, party-political interference in the decision-making process, and increasing malpractices distorted the basic aim of "socialist economic planning" which can be found in the preamble to the first five-year plan: namely, that socialist planning would continuously increase the standard of living of the population.

Acknowledgments

The author wishes to express her gratitude to the following institutions for their assistance during her research: the Wiener Institut für Internationale Wirtschaftswergleiche, especially to Mrs. Hana Rusek, and the library and archive of the Federální statistický úřad / Český statistický úřad / Slovenský úřad in Bratislava. She also should like to thank Dr. Eduard Kubů for his help in gathering statistical material. She is particularly grateful to Professor Josef Faltus for his helpful comments to her first draft. For any errors and omissions she is, of course, responsible herself. The author is deeply grateful to the funding bodies which generously furthered her research during the 1980s and 1990s, above all, the British Economic and Social Research Council and the Austrian Federal Ministry of Science and Research.

Bibliographical note

There is a hiatus in historical research and writing on changes in structure, organization, and management of industrial enterprises in the Czechoslovak economy. The author gathered the required information for this contribution from the censuses conducted by the State Statistical Office of the Czechoslovak Republic during the interwar period and from published as well as unpublished statistical surveys of the Federal Statistical Office of the Czechoslovak Socialist Republic for the period after World War II (see sources to figures 14.1–3, tables 14.1–6, and Appendix). For documentary evidence, economic and historical interpretations and assessments the author has largely drawn on her publications: *An Economic Background to Munich International Business and Czechoslovakia, 1918–1938* (Cambridge, 1974); *The Czechoslovak Economy, 1918–1980* (London, 1988); *Kleinstaaten im Spannungsfeld der Großmächte Wirtschaft und Politik in Mittel- und Südosteuropa in der Zwischenkriegszeit* (Vienna, 1988), and "East-central and South-east Europe, 1919–1939," in Peter Mathias and Sidney Pollard (eds.), *The Cambridge Economic History of Europe* (Cambridge, 1989), vol. 8, pp. 887–983. Further important material was gained from two completed research projects supported by the Economic and Social Research Council (United Kingdom). In the first project on "Economic History of Eastern Europe," I participated in a research team directed by Michael C. Kaser, which resulted in the publication of M. C. Kaser and E. A. Raolice (eds.), *The Economic History of Eastern Europe, 1919–1975*, 3 vols. (Oxford 1985, 1986), to which I contributed chapter 5, "Industry," vol. I, pp. 222–322. The second research project on "Multinational Companies in Interwar Eastern Europe," which I directed, resulted in the publication of Alice Teichova and Philip L. Cottrell (eds.), *International Business and Central Europe, 1919–1939* (Leicester, 1983). From the latter volume, chapter 2, "Industrial Structures in West and East Central Europe during the Interwar Period," by Alice Teichova and P. L. Cottrell, pp. 31–55, is particularly relevant. All the cited publications contain lists of sources and bibliographies.

APPENDIX

Table 14.A.1. *The fifty largest industrial firms, 1971 ranked by number of employed (from 10,000+)*

Name and place of firm	Group	No. employed
1 Hutnictví železa (metallurgy), Prague	271	166,480
2 Československé automobilové závody, (Czechoslovak automobile works), Prague	341	137,240
3 Tesla, Prague	32	82,055
4 Ostravsko-karvinské doly (Ostrava-Karvina mines), Ostrava	10	81,516
5 Bavlnářský průmysl (cotton industry), Hradec Králové	17	72,434
6 Továrny strojírenské techniky, Prague (engineering-technology factories)	292	59,643
7 Závody silnoproudé elektrotechniky (electrotechnical engineering works), Prague	31	58,998
8 Závody těžkého strojárstva (works for the production of heavy machinery), Martin	291	48,367
9 Vlnářský průmysl (wool industry), Brno	17	45,581
10 Slovchema, chemická výroba (Slovchema, chemical production), Bratislava	241	44,795
11 ČKD, Prague	29	44,580
12 Škoda, Plzeň	29	44,480
13 Závody všeobecného strojírenství (general engineering works), Brno	291	43,373
14 Český obuvnický průmysl (Czech shoe industry), Gottwaldov	19	41,971
15 České energetické závody (Czech power works), Prague	40	40,228
16 Zbrojovka (Armaments), Brno	292	40,203
17 Pletařský průmysl (knitting industry), Písek	172	39,821
18 Chemopetrol, Prague	241	38,688
19 SHD – Severočeské hnědouhelné doly (North Bohemian lignite mines), Most	10	36,919
20 Podniky oděvního průmyslu (clothing factories), Prostějov	172	36,613
21 Slovakotex-slovenské textilné podniky (Slovak textile factories), Trenčín	17	36,158
22 Chepos (machines for chemical industry), Brno	29	33,934
23 Prago-Union (household goods), Prague	29	33,530
24 Závody přístrojů a automatizace (works for machine tools and automation), Prague	29	33,172
25 Závody průmyslové chemie (industrial chemical works), Pardubice	24	32,402

Table 14.A.1. (*cont.*)

	Name and place of firm	Group	No. employed
26	Dřevařský průmysl (wood industry), Prague	20	32,379
27	Drevoúnia (wood union), Žilina	20	32,199
28	Rudné bane a magnezitové závody (ore mines and magnezit works), Bratislava	132	31,763
29	Průmysl papíru a celulózy (paper and cellulose industry), Prague	21	29,600
30	Omnia (machines and arms production), Bratislava	29	28,472
31	ZVL (machinery and armaments works), Považská Bystrica	29	26,617
32	Aero, Prague	353	26,485
33	Průmysl Jablonecké bižutérie (Gablonz jewelry industry), Jablonec nad Nisou	261	25,687
34	České závody gumárenské plastikářské (Czech rubber and plastics factories), Gottwaldov, now Zlin	25	24,816
35	Československé cihlářské závody (Czechoslovak brickworks), Brno	141	24,085
36	Ivtas, Chrudim	27	23,737
37	Lnářský průmysl (linen industry), Trutnov	171	23,484
38	Hutní druhovýroba (metallurgical secondary products), Prague	271	23,354
39	Slovakotex-Slovenské odevné podniky (Slovak clothing factories), Trenčín	172	22,961
40	Sigma (pumps), Olomouc	29	22,729
41	Ogako (leather), Partizánske	19	21,961
42	Nábytkářský průmysl (furniture industry), Brno	202	21,951
43	Kovohutě (nonferrous metallurgy), Prague	272	20,160
44	Pivovary a sladovny (beer breweries and malthouses), Prague	155	19,311
45	Prefabrikácia, Bratislava	452	18,977
46	Elitex (textile machinery), Liberec	292	18,789
47	Polygrafický průmysl (printing industry), Prague	22	18,420
48	Průmysl technického skla (technical glass industry), Prague	261	17,776
49	Masný průmysl (meat industry), Prague	151	17,738
50	Mlékárenský průmysl (dairy industry), Prague	154	17,254

Note: Business groups in this list are arranged according to UN International Standard Industrial Classification of all economic activities. Firms consisted of 383 production economic units – Výrobní hospodářská jednotka (VHJ) – between 1959 and 1985, 68 of which employed more than 10,000 persons.
Source: *Kalendář pro ekonomy*, Federatívní Statistický Úřad (Prague, 1972), pp. 198–205.

Part III

Economic and institutional environment
of big business

15

Organizational competences, firm size, and the
wealth of nations: Some comments from a
comparative perspective

GIOVANNI DOSI

The richness of the contributions on which I am asked to comment – let
alone the pioneering work of Alfred Chandler, which inspires most of
them – makes the task of a general discussant very difficult and certainly
prevents a thorough examination of the multiple lines of inquiry pursued
in each chapter. More modestly, what I shall attempt to do in the following is to flag a few questions, conjectures, results, and puzzles that emerge
from a comparative reading of the chapters concerning national experiences. Some of my observations are motivated by theoretical concerns
while others have mainly an empirical nature: the link among all of them
is the effort – common to all chapters – to disentangle the complex relationships between organizational change and the differential ability of
nations to produce and accumulate wealth. Let me start from the basics.

SOME CHANDLERIAN HYPOTHESES REVISITED

As a sort of introduction, it might be useful to summarize my own interpretation of the Chandlerian analysis. As I see it, the most general propositions (which, indeed, I fully share) are the following.

1. Over the past century, organizational learning and organization-embodied
   technical change have increased their importance as sources of growth.
   This basically paraphrases Chandler's own statement at the beginning
   of his chapter in this book emphasizing the importance of "how streams
   of capital and efforts of the working force were organized and how
   technologies of production have been created or improved" and of "the
   ability of industrial entreprises to adopt and develop these technologies
   and to devise essential administrative structures to coordinate the flow of
   materials."

465

2. The nature of organizational structures is not neutral vis-à-vis the ability to accumulate coordinating and technological competences, so that particular forms of corporate organizations entail a higher learning potential than others.
3. Organizational and technological knowledge is not uniformly distributed and uniformly accessible across countries.
4. Differential competences in organizational coordination and technological innovation determine differential possibilities of growth *not only of individual firms but of the entire countries where firms originated.*

These are, in my view, the *core* propositions, which are supplemented by other, more phenomenological hypotheses which might also be much more contingent on particular industries, countries, historical periods.

5. There are size thresholds for the ability of firms to internalize the capability of mastering the activities of innovation, production, and marketing in complex products, so that, other things being equal, "bigness" confers a differential advantage.
6. A typical pattern of evolution of many technologically dynamic activities is toward rather concentrated oligopolistic structures (both nationally and on the world markets), whereby an "oligopolistic core" interacts with a variegated galaxy of smaller producers, suppliers, customers, and so on.
7. Members of the oligopolistic core tend to be "first-movers."
8. The potential for organizational and technological learning is correlated with the degrees of mechanization of production, as proxied by capital–labor ratios.

In my view, the general Chandlerian vision stands or falls on the former four fundamental hypotheses: to repeat, I strongly think it stands, while I also consider unfortunate the inclination of many readers and scholars to use the "special" or phenomenological generalizations to validate the general model. I shall come back to the fallacies associated with such approaches. First, however, I want to briefly comment on the core features of the interpretation.

ORGANIZATIONAL CAPABILITIES AND GROWTH

A first major thing that Alfred Chandler has taught us is to appreciate the importance of the epochal change associated with the emergence of the modern corporation: an organization which for the first time internalizes many activities previously undertaken by more impersonal and decentralized market interactions, and – even more important – systematically develops and reproduces special internal knowledge for coordination, production management, and innovation. In terms of economic theory, this easily links with an "evolutionary" *competence-based* theory of the firm.[1] The focus here is on the ways knowledge is generated, stored, augmented (and, also, possibly destroyed) within organizations, rather than on the availability and distributions of resources per se.

A fundamental consequence for the economist is indeed that anyone subscribing to this view ought to become immediately skeptical of writing "production functions" – except, maybe, for purely accounting purposes. Since a good deal of the explanation of the levels and changes in output rests on the ways production and innovative research is organized, the very notion of some invariant relationship between inputs and outputs (and, worse still, under an assumption of competitive markets and equilibrium) is either tautological or plainly wrong. Reformulated, the central proposition is that it is primarily organizational competences which determine the ability of efficiently producing and augmenting income. Note that in order to make this a *macro* proposition on the determinants of growth differentials across countries – that is, on the "dynamics of wealth of nations" – one must add also two further qualifications, namely, that these organizational competences are not randomly distributed across countries, and that there are some systematic factors which make this asymmetric distribution relatively persistent over time.

Well, a good deal of work has recently gone into the study of the international distribution of technological competences as revealed by their outcomes, for example, innovations or patents. And, in fact, asymmetric distributions and their persistence come out strongly corroborated

---

[1] A. D. Chandler, "Organizational Capabilities and the Economic History of the Industrial Enterprise," *Journal of Economic Perspective*, 6, 1992, pp. 79–100; D. Teece, G. Pisano, and A. Schuen, *Dynamic Capabilities and Strategic Management*, CRM, Graduate Business School, University of California, Berkeley, CCC Working Paper, 1992; G. Dosi, D. Teece, and S. Winter, "Toward a Theory of Corporate Coherence," in G. Dosi, R. Giannetti, and P. A. Toninelli (eds.), *Technology and Entreprise in a Historical Perspective*, Oxford, Clarendon Press of Oxford University Press, 1992; D. Teece, "The Dynamic of Industrial Capitalism: Perspectives on Alfred Chandler's 'Scale and Scope,'" *Journal of Economic Literature*, 31, 1993, pp. 199–225; G. Dosi and L. Marengo, "Some elements of an Evolutionary Theory of Corporate Competences," in R. W. England (ed.), *Evolutionary Concepts in Contemporary Economics*, Ann Arbor, University of Michigan Press, 1994; B. Coriat and G. Dosi, "Learning How to Govern and Learning How to Solve Problems: On the Co-evolution of Competences, Conflicts and Organizational Routines," paper presented at the Prince Bertil Symposium, Stockholm School of Economics, June 1994, IIASA, Laxemburg, Austria, Working Paper.

by the evidence. Moreover, they appear to be powerful determinants of export flows and aggregate income growth.[2]

However, the highly complementary (and even more ambitious) Chandlerian route to establish the same proposition is by tracking the degrees of development and diffusion across countries of the modern managerial corporation as a proxy for the "competence-embodying" organization either in its "American" archetype or other variants – such as the "German" cooperative-managerial firm. In this respect, I find Chandler's original reconstruction of the intertwined relationships between the development of the *American*, multiproduct, innovative corporation and *American* growth patterns powerfully convincing.[3] Another, trickier task is to develop a theory of growth *differentials* (and/or income differentials) based on cross-country variations in organizational forms. It is the enterprise that Chandler himself has pioneered in his *Scale and Scope* and this book follows on. As fascinating as the endeavor is, it faces some formidable challenges.

A first one concerns the very nature of the hypothesis to be tested. One naive version is that the American organizational archetype is (or has been) the "one best way" for competence building and, thus, after normalizing for other relevant factors, one should expect a positive correlation between "Americanization" of the domestic industrial structure and growth.

A more sophisticated version would claim that there are multiple organizational forms yielding roughly equivalent coordinating efficiency and learning potentials, even if in a finite and small number. Hence, the analysis would involve a sort of "combinatorial exercise," attempting to identify the competence characteristics of different combinations of

---

[2] See K. Pavitt and L. Soete, "International Differences in Economic Growth and the International Location of Innovation," in H. Giersch (ed.), *Emerging Technologies: Consequences for Economic Growth*, Tubingen, JCB Mohr, 1981; G. Dosi, K. Pavitt and L. Soete, *The Economics of Technological Change and International Trade*, Brighton, Wheatsheaf/Harvester, and New York, New York University Press, 1990; I. Fagerberg, "A Technology Gap Approach to Why Growth Rates Differ," *Research Policy*, 16, pp. 87–99 1987; I. Fagerberg, "Why Growth Rates Differ," in G. Dosi et al. (eds.), *Technical Change and Economic Theory*, London, Francis Pinter, and New York, Columbia University Press, 1988; G. Dosi, C. Freeman, and S. Fabiani, "The Process of Economic Development: Introducing Some Stylized Facts and Theories on Technologies, Firms and Institutions," *Industrial and Corporate Change*, vol. 3, pp. 1–26 1994; P. Patel and K. Pavitt, "*Technological Competences in the World's Largest Firms: Characteristics, Constraints and Scope for Managerial Choice*," SPRU, University of Sussex, Working Paper, 1994.

[3] A. D. Chandler, *Strategy and Structure*, Cambridge, MA, MIT Press, 1962; A. D. Chandler, *The Visible Hand*, Cambridge, MA, Belknap Press of Harvard University Press, 1977.

traits and "map" them into different countries. As I understand it, this is indeed the spirit of *Scale and Scope*, as well as of other investigations on the comparative properties of organizational structures.[4] On the contrary, the "naive version" of the hypothesis does not seem prima facie to find much empirical corroboration. Counterexamples easily come to mind: for example, Italy, the fastest growing country in the postwar period after Japan, is probably also the single major economy that remained most distant from the "American" model; the UK, as Jones discusses in his chapter, through the adoption of the divisionalized organizational form often appears to have combined the weaknesses of the latter with preexisting specifically British ones; Denmark and Sweden have been growing at a comparable pace, but Sweden has developed big managerialized companies, while Denmark has relied on a network of small and medium-sized firms; the proportionally fattest tail of small, plausibly nonmanagerialized, firms is found precisely in the two fastest growing countries of OECD, namely Japan and Italy.

Another major challenge to this endeavor regards the precise identification of the linkages between "big business" and the rest of the national economy: how is the former nested in the "national community of firms," to use Yudanov's expression? How do the rates and directions of competence accumulation in big firms affect the overall national patterns?

One has some evidence collected by Keith Pavitt, Pari Patel, and colleagues at SPRU, University of Sussex, with regards to patenting, confirming that big national companies shape to a significant extent the patterns of technological specialization of each country. And recent work has gone into the anatomy and feedbacks characterizing "national systems of innovation."[5]

However, a lot of work has still to be done in order to link the modal or "archetypical" nature of national organizations with the differential dynamics of the wealth of nations.

[4] Just to name a few, in different perspectives, see for Britain versus the United States, W. Lazonick, *Competitive Advantage on the Shopfloor*, Cambridge, MA, Harvard University Press, 1990; on Japan versus the United States, M. Aoki, *Information, Incentives and Bargaining Structure in the Japanese Economy*, Cambridge, Cambridge University Press, 1988; on Japan versus the classic "Fordist model," B. Coriat, *Penser à l'envers*, Paris, Bourgois, 1991.

[5] See R. Nelson (ed.), *National Innovation Systems*, Oxford, Oxford University Press, 1993; B. A. Lundvall, (ed.), *National Systems of Innovation*, London, Francis Pinter, 1992. See also the broad fresco provided by *Made in America* and other comparable national studies such as *Made in France*: see M. L. Dertouzos, R. K. Lester, and R. M. Solow, *Made in America*, Cambridge, MA, MIT Press, 1989; D. Taddei and B. Coriat, *Made in France*, Paris, Hachette, 1993.

WHAT KIND OF ORGANIZATIONAL CAPABILITIES?

I have emphasized so far that, in my view, the crucial intermediate step between organizational forms and macroeconomic growth rests in the distinctive capabilities associated with the former. But, in turn, capabilities are likely to have many dimensions. A first one certainly concerns *technological* capabilities, that is the elements of firm-specific knowledge apt to generate and quickly to acquire technological innovation. Capabilities that might be quite different concern the ability to *coordinate* complex processes of production and distribution. Moreover, these capabilities might reside in the strategic abilities of the top management; or alternatively they might be a collective property of the whole set of *organizational routines* that the firm embodies. I mention these distinctions because I suspect that only a finer identification of the nature of competences of various organizational forms might foster progress in our understanding of their dynamic performances. For example, Kogut has argued that the major distinctive source of "superiority" of the American modern corporation did not rest so much in scale or R&D intensity but in its routines for the control and rationalization of labor processes. An argument similar in spirit has been made with respect to the Japanese organizational form and its ability to coordinate "horizontal" information flows. And a symmetric argument has been made to explain British sluggish performance in productivity and innovation.[6] If this is true, however, it should also influence where to look for competence differences across organizational forms, away from an almost exclusive focus on formal structures and strategic management attributes, and toward the fine properties of organizational behaviors and routines, concerning, for example, the management of throughputs, the control of labor processes, the distribution of knowledge among the various actors within the organization, and the relationships between R&D, production, and marketing.

[6] See B. Kogut, "National Organizing Principles and the Erstwhile Dominance of the American Multinational Corporation," *Industrial and Corporate Change*, 1, 1992, pp. 285–317. For some recent international comparisons, see also B. Kogut (ed.), *Country Competitiveness*, Oxford, Oxford University Press, 1993. For Japan, see K. B. Clark and T. Fujimoto, "Product Development and Competitiveness," paper presented at the Conference on Science, Technology and Growth, Paris, OECD, 1989; T. Fujimoto, "Reinterpreting the Resource-Capability View of the Firm: A Case of Development Production System of the Japanese Auto Industry," paper presented at the Prince Bertil Symposium, Stockholm School of Economics, June 1994. For Britain, see E. Lorenz, "Economic Decline in Twentieth Century Britain: The Cotton, Shipbuilding and Car Industries," *Industrial and Corporate Change*, 3, pp. 379–404 1994; Lazonick, *Competitive Advantage on the Shopfloor*.

Moreover, interesting trade-offs might emerge between different types of competences. For example, Pavitt has argued that the archetypical M-form corporation while solving a complex coordination problem makes intrinsically more difficult the accumulation of cross-divisional competences for technological innovation.[7] Conversely, one may find examples of organizations extremely good in developing technological competences but unable to master coordination and "three-pronged" investments (in the history of semiconductors, Fairchild is a case in point). These dilemmas and trade-offs might emerge also at the level of whole national systems. For example, I would be prepared to argue that the relatively decentralized Italian system might have been quite good at accumulating coordination competences, through "networking," as many have argued, but it has been much less conducive to technological innovation, especially in complex products requiring internalization of formal R&D activities.

ORGANIZATIONAL FORMS AND INSTITUTIONAL EMBEDDEDNESS

How far can one go in the interpretation of the links among organizational forms, competences, and collective economic performances without bringing into the picture the broader institutional structures defining each "political economy"? In fact, there are two sides to the question. One is, so to speak, a "functional" issue: that is, to what extent, by observing a "naked" organizational form, can one approximately predict its capabilities and performances independently from the institutional context in which it is placed? Or, putting it in other terms, holding the organizational forms constant, what percentage in the variances in performances are accounted for by, for example, British labor practices; linkages between German banks and firms, stock-market induced short-termism in the United Kingdom and United States, and French or Japanese government policies etc.?

The other side of the question is explicitly dynamic, namely, to what extent does a national institutional setup shape and constrain both the viable organizational forms that can emerge and their subsequent behaviors?

Here, I put under the heading of "institutions" the formal and

---

[7] K. Pavitt, "Technology, Innovation and Strategic Management," in J. McGee and H. Thomas (eds.), *Strategic Management Research: A European Perspective*, New York, Wiley, 1986.

customary forms of governance of the markets for labor, finance, and products, and the relationship between the state and the firms.

The "embeddedness hypothesis" of Mark Granovetter, of course, implies a corollary of limited transferability of organizational forms across national economies and a powerful effect of national institutions upon the "set of opportunities and constraints facing individual actors," irrespective of the organizational form, as Zysman has recently forcefully argued.[8] In fact, many of the chapters in this volume – and especially those on France, Germany, Italy, Spain, Argentina, and Korea, as well as Czechoslovakia and the USSR – tell various embedded stories to explain the genesis of the observed industrial structures. But it is still not clear to what extent "embeddedness" accounts for performances (as it emerges sharply in Amsden's analysis of Korea) or, conversely, whether it primarily affected the path of development to particular structures without affecting subsequent performances (some readers would take this to be the implicit messages of the Wengenroth's and Morikawa's chapters on Germany and Japan).

ORGANIZATIONAL COMPETENCES, SIZE, AND INDUSTRIAL INNOVATION

As mentioned earlier, in my reading, the relationship between the modern corporation and internalization of competences for coordination and innovation is the *general* hypothesis, while the further conjecture on some monotonic relation between competences and size (or on some size-related thresholds) might be more contingent on specific technologies and historical periods. For example, the size distribution of innovating firms appears highly dependent upon the nature of the knowledge upon which innovation draws – that is, what I call elsewhere the nature of sector-specific "technological paradigms."[9]

In fact, around a decade ago, Keith Pavitt developed a quite revealing sectoral taxonomy of the characteristics of the innovating firms.[10] According to that taxonomy there is indeed one group of sectors which fully

[8] M. Granovetter, "Coase Revisited: Business Groups in the Modern Economy," *Industrial and Corporate Change*, vol. 4, pp. 93–130 1995; J. Zysman, "How Institutions Create Historically Rooted Trajectories of Growth," *Industrial and Corporate Change*, vol. 3, pp. 243–283 1994.

[9] G. Dosi, *Technical Change and Industrial Transformation*, London, Macmillan, and New York, St. Martin's Press, 1994.

[10] Pavitt, "Technology, Innovation and Strategic Management."

conforms with a "monotonicity hypothesis" – in fact, they are called by Pavitt "scale-intensive" (including most continuous process industries, consumer durables, transport equipment). As regards "science-based" industries, he finds a bimodal distribution (with large but also small Schumpeterian firms undertaking a large percentage of innovation). Conversely, no scale-bias emerges among "specialized suppliers" of, for example, machine tools and scientific instruments. Elsewhere one has suggested an interpretation of the pattern of diversification of business forms, somewhat isomorphic to this taxonomy, as a function of the levels of technological opportunities, the degrees of cumulativeness of technological progress (i.e., the degrees to which innovative successes are serially correlated), the "convergence" among different technological trajectories, the importance of cospecialized assets (another word to mean something very similar to Chandler's "three-pronged investments") and, finally the effectiveness by which markets selected firms on the grounds of differential performances.[11]

All this to introduce sector-specific and technology-specific qualifications on the simplest version of a scale-bias hypothesis on competence accumulation. (A similar point can be made with respect to technical economies of scale in production.)

However, the other conjecture on the widespread occurrence of an international "oligopolistic core" in many industries need not rely necessarily on scale biases. What it needs is just some form of cumulativeness (as defined earlier) in competence accumulation and a market environment rewarding better-performing firms with above average growth. Hence, putting it roughly, it might not be that a firm is "good" (i.e., innovative, efficient, etc.) because it is big, but it has become big because it has been systematically good. In fact, evolutionary models of this type easily show the emergence of concentrated oligopolistic structures notwithstanding constant returns to scale.[12] Note that while cross-sectionally the two models (scale-biased performances vs. differentiated and cumulative learning) might be observationally indistinguishable, dynamically the

[11] G. Dosi, D. Teece, and S. Winter, "Toward a Theory of Corporate Coherence," in G. Dosi, R. Giannetti, and P. A. Toninelli (eds.), *Technology and Entreprise in a Historical Perspective*, Oxford, Clarendon Press of Oxford University Press, 1992.
[12] See for results of this type S. Winter, "Schumpeterian Competition under Alternative Technological Regimes," *Journal of Economic Behavior and Organization*, vol. 5, pp. 287–320 1984; G. Dosi, O. Marsili, L. Orsenigo, and R. Salvatore, "Learning, Market Selection and the Evolution of Industrial Structures," *University of California, Small Business Economies*, 7, pp. 411–436.

properties are likely to be quite different. So, for example in the "learning" model no ex-ante prediction can be made in general on the probability distribution of growth rates conditional on size. Conversely, under the "scale" model, one would expect, say, mergers to yield, in probability, higher performances and higher growth. The different implications of the two models for the dynamics of the wealth of nations are also straightforward: other things being equal, higher concentration determines higher growth in the latter but not in the former model.

In terms of empirical evidence, the simplest "scale" model does not fare too well. Mergers do not generally yield higher rates of growth – although they are possibly beneficial in terms of rationalization of production. Rates of growth appear to be either uncorrelated or negatively correlated with size. And, finally, the size distribution of business firms appears to have been roughly constant (approximately Pareto-distributed) over all the period for which one has data, if anything with some departure in favor of the smallest size cohorts in the last couple of decades.[13]

These points do not imply the irrelevance of scale, but the impact of the latter might be more subtle and indirect. First, in many sectors, one might find size-related *threshold effects* in production and innovation. Second, and at least equally important, core oligopolistic firms might be a fundamental source of innovation which partly spin off to other firms and drive the growth of the whole industry. (In fact, my diagnosis of the Italian industrial system is precisely that its weak oligopolistic core will make innovation and growth fragile in the long-term also for smaller/younger firms.)

A somewhat related question concerns the *emergence* of oligopolistic structures themselves. At a fine level of sectoral disaggregation – say automobiles, televisions, or tires – longitudinal data often (although not always) reveal some rather invariant "life cycle" properties, with a turbulent beginning, characterized by a lot of entry and exit, unstable market shares, and an emphasis on product rather than process innovations. At some point, a big shake-out in the industry is associated with a diminution of producers, higher concentration, a more stable oligopolistic core,

[13] One surveys and tries to interpret all this evidence in G. Dosi and R. Salvatore, "The Structure of Industrial Production and the Boundaries between Firms and Markets," in M. Storper and A. J. Scott (eds.), *Pathways to Industrialization and Regional Development*, London, Routledge, 1993, and Dosi et al., "Learning, Market Selection and the Evolution of Industrial Structures."

the establishment of a "dominant design" or a "dominant technological paradigm," and more emphasis on process innovation.[14]

The story clearly overlaps with the Chandlerian one. First, the members of the "core" are likely to be early entrants in the industry (it is a weaker proposition than literal first movers, but in the same spirit). Second, those that turn out to be dominant incumbents often start to invest massively in manufacturing, distribution, marketing. A third proposition, which would make the link even stronger, is that dominant incumbents are with reasonable probability diversifiers from related sectors (I have not seen any empirical test of this kind, but with the longitudinal micro data currently available, I think it could now be done).

The complementarities between an explicit evolutionary story of each industry and the identification of the organizational and strategic attributes of the firms which made it into the "core oligopoly" are even more crucial in a comparative international perspective. As such, the description of the winners alone suffers from a heavy ex-post selection bias: what accounts for the heavy participation of some countries *and in some sectors*, but not others? At one extreme one might resort to some kind of entrepreneur-driven explanation (those firms that made it were led by far-sighted entrepreneurs who did the right thing at the right time). I must confess that I am quite skeptical about it, notwithstanding the obvious importance of the quality of strategic management, because it would imply a level of randomness in the international distribution of successes not born by the evidence: compare the systematic German strength in mechanical engineering, electrical equipments, and chemicals; the American one in chemicals, agricultural and resource-related machinery, electronic and defense-related sectors. But then we are back to the issue of the *institutional embeddedness* of the processes of industrial evolution in each country. And, indeed, many of the country studies in this book begin to clarify the nature of this embeddedness, especially with respect to political factors, the nature of the educational system and the links between finance and industry. For example, the way political actions influenced industrial change is particularly clear in the Carreras-Tafunell chapter on Spain and Amsden's one on Korea; and a convincing account of the role of the educational system comes out of Friedenson's, Jones's,

---

[14] S. Klepper, "Entry, Exit, Growth and Innovation over the Product-Cycle," Carnegie-Mellon University, Working Paper, 1993.

and Wengenroth's chapters on France, the United Kingdom, and Germany. But, ideally, one would still like to see several explicitly dynamic industrial studies whereby one could see the unfolding of, small or big, microevents and, together, the impact of more systematic forces – either political decisions, the educational characteristics of the work force and management, the policies of banks, or the technological spillovers from public research agencies.

A final point regards the ability of the modern "learning" organization to survive through major technological discontinuities (and a few times also to generate them). In this respect, also the data on innovative output (e.g., patenting) confirm this pattern. And this capability of adjustment might underlie also the robust statistical evidence on the tendential "immortalization" of a subset of industrial incumbents: the probability of death, in fact, appears to *fall* with age.[15]

LEARNING, GROWTH, AND CAPITAL INTENSITIES

There is little doubt that, as Chandler suggests, the development of the modern competence-embodying corporation is not randomly distributed across sectors, but is concentrated at least initially in science-based and scale-intensive sectors. And, as shown, this pattern is also correlated with capital–labor ratios – as such, a good proxy for the degrees of mechanization/automation of production. (As a measure of "capital intensity" – that is, of the amount of income that an economy or an industry has to devote to capital investment in order to produce what it does – I would use capital–output ratios: but this would lead us astray into economists' disputes on production theory.)

I would like to simply introduce some caveats, first, on the correlation between capital–labor ratios, on the one hand, and learning potential, on the other. Certainly, a good deal of learning concerns precisely production automation and continuous flows of throughputs: hence, the ratio does capture the realization of productive learning. However, another significant aspect of learning concerns product innovations, and that learning potential might be uncorrelated, or even negatively correlated with capital–labor ratios. Compare, for example, machine tool production, drugs, and

[15] See P. Patel and K. Pavitt, "Technological Competences in the World's Largest Firms: Characteristics, Constraints and Scope for Managerial Choice," SPRU, University of Sussex, Working Paper, 1994. See, also for some discussion, Dosi et al., "Learning, Market Selection and the Evolution of Industrial Structures."

software with oil refining: certainly the former have been a major source of innovative opportunities – much greater than the latter – notwithstanding much lower degrees of automation.

Second, and relatedly, for these same reasons I would be quite careful in using capital–labor ratios as proxies for the growth potential of each sector (i.e., the other link, in addition to innovative learning, with the wealth of nations). I am not aware of disaggregated statistical studies of this sort: a priori, I would expect some positive correlation between capital–labor ratios and sectoral growth to be there, but also a large unaccounted variance.

Third, technical progress tends to affect the performance of capital goods, the efficiency by which they are used, and, thus, also capital–labor ratios. For example, elsewhere, we find, on British data, that the ratio tended to fall in a few highly dynamic sectors within electronics: this was *not* due to the fact that the degrees of automation were falling, but, on the contrary, capital-embodied technical progress was so rapid that the required amount of capital per worker, as one measures it, shrank.[16] For similar reasons, even if one were able to produce reasonably comparable figures on "real" capital stocks, I would be rather cautious in interpreting international comparisons in capital–labor ratios (or for that matter, capital–output ratios): they might reveal different degrees of automation as well as different efficiencies in exploiting similar levels of automation as well as different qualities of the capital stock.

EARLYCOMERS AND LATECOMERS: SOME DISTINCTIVE PATTERNS OF CHANGE

There are some striking differential features which emerge from the comparison between "first-coming" and "late-coming" countries – concerning the organizational structure of the leading firms, the way they emerged, and the role of the policies (and, further, one should distinguish as Amsden argues, between countries that were late but riding *new* technologies, such as Germany, and countries that arrived late *in already established technologies*).

First, most late-coming countries (but not all – cf. Denmark at the turn of the century or Taiwan nowadays) appear to be characterized by a precociously concentrated industrial structure in the leading sectors, with

[16] L. Soete and G. Dosi, *Technology and Employment in the Electronics Industry*, London, Francis Pinter 1982.

major corporate actors that, almost from the start, are highly diversified: in fact they are *more* diversified than their "frontier" counterparts.[17] There are certainly good reasons for that. Some have to do with the concentration in large business groups of novel and scarce managerial competences. Others concern the sheer size of financial resources required to overcome "entry barriers" as latecomers. Yet others relate to the generally long waiting period between upfront investments and profit flows, which only big, diversified, bank-supported and/or state-supported groups might be able to efford. In any case, quite often, relatively big size and diversification is not the outcome of being differentially good at the technological and competitive game, but rather a precondition to enter it. This applied to Japan, applied to Korea, but also to advanced countries in laggard sectors.[18]

Second, public policies in catching-up countries probably mattered much more than in frontier ones (even if one should not forget the institutional and political ingredients of the very success of frontier countries themselves, such as post–World War II United States). In a sense, it is in catching-up countries where profound trade-offs between criteria of "static efficiency" of resource allocation, as signaled by markets, and "Schumpeterian efficiency," as defined in terms of learning potentials, are most likely to emerge: hence, also the potentially beneficial role of policy measures aimed at "distorting" market signals themselves, reshaping industrial structures, and governing the mechanisms of technology transfer.[19] Notwithstanding the effort of later generations of economists to reconstruct an original virginity, this happened in early United States, Germany, France, Japan, and Italy, as well as in current newly industrializing countries

---

[17] For example, the chapters in this volume by Barbero on Argentina and Amsden on Korea and Alice Amsden, *Asia's Next Giant*, New York, Oxford University Press, 1989. For comparative discussions, see A. Amsden and T. Hikino, "Project Execution Capability, Organizational Knowhow and Conglomerate Growth in Late Industrialization," *Industrial and Corporate Change*, vol. 3, pp. 111–148, 1994; M. Cimoli and G. Dosi, "Technological Paradigms, Patterns of Learning and Development: An Introductory Roadmap," *Journal of Evolutionary Economics*, 1995; Granovetter, "Coase Revisited: Business Groups in the Modern Economy"; G. G. Hamilton and R. C. Feenstra, "Varieties of Hierarchies and Markets: An Introduction," *Industrial and Corporate Change*, vol. 4, pp. 51–92, 1995.

[18] See, for example, the European experience in semiconductors, where, unlike the United States, only major incumbents had a try. Dosi, *Technical Change and Industrial Transformation*; F. Malerba, *The Semiconductor Business*, Madison, University of Wisconsin Press, 1985.

[19] See Amsden, *Asia's Next Giant*; Dosi et al., *The Economics of Technological Change and International Trade*; C. Johnson, L. D'Andrea Tyson, and J. Zysman (eds.), *Politics and Productivity*, Cambridge, MA, Ballinger 1989.

(NICs). Some packages of policy measurement turned out to be more successful than others, but this is not the place to undertake a comparative policy assessment. For the purposes of these comments, let me just emphazise this deeply *institutionally shaped* nature of initial industrial organizations among latecomers, which set them apart from other organizational structures which resulted from more decentralized mechanisms of evolution of industries. Interestingly, these birthmarks seem to carry over their impact also up to much later stages of industrialization and also shape subsequent forms of corporate organization and competence-accumulation (Japan and Germany, as compared with Anglo-Saxon countries, are good examples).

SOME CONCLUSIONS

In these comments, I went through what I consider to be some of the major Chandlerian hypotheses on the coupled dynamics between organizational evolution and the dynamic of the wealth of nations. The focus here has been on *competence accumulation* as the crucial link between the two and, relatedly, on the different learning potentials that different organizational architectures might entail. Many of these hypotheses naturally link with somewhat parallel research efforts in the domain of economic theory aimed at establishing "evolutionary" foundations to aggregate dynamics and, admittedly, it is with these theoretical spectacles that I have tried to assess the contributions to this volume. A theory-inclined reader can certainly draw a long list of precious elements of evidence, stylized facts, puzzles from the contributions to this volume. And one is stimulated to reply with an equally long list of challenges and theory-driven questions still awaiting an answer. This is what I have tried to do in these notes. Let us just make sure that this fruitful exchange continues.

Acknowledgments

Support by the Italian National Council (CNR, "Progretto Strategico") and the International Institute of Applied Systems Analysis (IIASA), Laxemburg, Austria, is gratefully acknowledged.

16

Managerial control, capital markets,
and the wealth of nations

TAKASHI HIKINO

Alfred Chandler's theory of managerial capitalism has critically influenced all serious research on the rise and development of big business since the Second Industrial Revolution of the late nineteenth century. Originally constructed based mainly on the prime case of the United States from the 1880s to the 1950s, the Chandlerian vision of managerial capitalism emphasized the strategic primacy of discretionary decision making by senior, inside management which possesses the competitive advantages of the knowledge of markets and technology. The Chandlerian model presented a coherent analytical structure centered around the core concepts of learned and accumulated knowledge and organizational capabilities, based on which his approach can be applied to other national economies and different historical time periods. The Chandlerian framework actually has stimulated extensive comparative research on large industrial enterprises of many other nations, this particular book being one of them.

As the most influential historical theory of managerial capitalism, the Chandlerian model has faced a more than fair share of criticism from various perspectives: historical, economic, political, and sociological. From the theoretical viewpoint the most pointed criticism to date has come from an approach broadly called agency theory and corporate governance. Taking as their primary examples the mediocre financial performance and the decline in international competitiveness since the 1970s of many large U.S. enterprises, scholars mainly of finance economics and corporate law have documented many cases of managerial decision making and organizational implementation working against the economic welfare of shareholders, the firm, and the American economy. Sharply pointing out the dysfunction of internal monitoring mechanisms, these critics demanded a drastic overhaul of the corporate governance structure and suggested the enforcement of external disciplinary devices, particularly those of capital markets. The accountability of top management, which is the cornerstone of managerial capitalism, became the focus of controversy.

The purpose of this chapter is threefold: first, to clarify and elaborate the Chandlerian theory of managerial capitalism; second, to review the major arguments based on corporate governance and relate them to the Chandlerian model; and, third, to examine the findings of the national chapters in this book in the light of these two apparently opposing views.

MANAGERIAL ENTERPRISES AND LEARNED KNOWLEDGE

In the Chandlerian framework of managerial capitalism, what economists call the asymmetry of information plays a critical role in assigning strategic decision-making functions to senior inside management. In advancing the primacy of the control of long-term strategic investment decisions by full-time senior management – which consists of salaried managers usually with little equity stake who are coherently structured above divisional and functional hierarchical organizations within the modern industrial enterprise – Chandler repeatedly and persuasively emphasizes the need and necessity for a top management team possessing, among other types of information, the learned and accumulated knowledge of factor and product markets and production technology in particular industries in which their firms operate.[1]

In terms of the access to and control of critical information, inside senior management possesses a distinct advantage over stakeholders such as shareholders, debt holders, customers, employees, the community, and the government. This is primarily because full-time top management, by definition, gathers, screens, and processes the key strategic and operational information of its own firm and surrounding markets in order to make

---

[1] For the latest version of Chandler's approaches to large industrial enterprises, see Chapter 2 of this volume. Previous writings of Chandler which are particularly relevant to the issue of managerial capitalism are "Introduction: The Rise of Managerial Capitalism and Its Impact on Investment Strategy in the Western World and Japan" (with Herman Daems), in Herman Daems and Herman van der Wee, eds., *The Rise of Managerial Capitalism* (Louvain: Leuven University Press, 1974); *The Visible Hand: Managerial Revolution in American Business* (Cambridge, Mass.: Harvard University Press, 1977), particularly "Introduction: The Visible Hand"; *Scale and Scope: The Dynamics of Industrial Capitalism* (Cambridge, Mass.: Harvard University Press, 1990), particularly part I, "Introduction: Scale and Scope."

critical decisions. By contrast, outside parties, including those operating in capital markets, are usually involved in many firms simultaneously so that they do not have the time, capacity, and, in a sense, need to obtain and analyze the detailed information of one particular individual company. Chandler thus argues:

> The functional and general administrative capabilities developed by the middle and top managers of these enterprises through the years of competition and growth . . . intensified the separation between ownership and management. . . . The increase in the number of critical decisions made by managers was far more responsive for the further separation of ownership and management than was the dispersion of stock holdings. Part-time, outside directors had almost no way to obtain the detailed information or gain the broad understanding needed to make the long-term investment decisions on which the continuing health and growth of the enterprise depended. This was difficult enough for the full-time, inside directors, who had spent a lifetime in that (or related) industry.[2]

Chandlerian managerial capitalism has thus evolved as comprising knowledge-oriented senior management and supporting managerial hierarchy. In terms of historical evolution, managerial enterprises emerged after two phases of owner control of large industrial enterprises, *personal enterprise* and *entrepreneurial enterprise*, whose behavioral characteristics with respect to their goals and investment patterns are different from those of managerial enterprises.[3] Two basic factors determine the behavioral patterns of those three phases or types of large industrial enterprises: the *capabilities* of strategic decision makers in terms of learned and accumulated knowledge; and the *goals* of those decision makers in terms of their firms' growth and profitability.

Personal enterprises represent classic firms whose owners manage and whose managers own. In this type of firm, strategic management is not separated from operational administration, and a managerial hierarchy in charge of functional operations remains limited. Without an instrumental organizational device for the accumulation of information about markets and technology, however, owners can not endogenize and systematize such knowledge. Without the competitive advantage of the accumulated

---

[2] Chandler, *Scale and Scope*, p. 232.

[3] These three typologies are best expressed in Chandler and Daems, "Introduction," pp. 5–6. Those classifications should be understood as the Weberian ideal-type categories. Each large industrial enterprise in every nation does not necessarily follow the evolutionary pattern from personal enterprise to managerial enterprise. See, for example, Jan Glete, "Swedish Managerial Capitalism: Did It Ever Become Ascendant?," *Business History*, 35, no. 2, April 1993, pp. 99–110.

knowledge about markets and technology, Chandler argues, the owners of personal enterprises had to be cautious in investing their own capital in expanding their firms in new and risky markets. The major goal of the owners, therefore, remained conservative in seeking short-term profitability and stable income. According to Chandler, many of Britain's large industrial enterprises exhibited this behavioral pattern.[4] Following this line of Chandler's argument, capital markets play a critical role of coordinating investment flows into new firms and markets.

In enterpreneurial enterprises, the second phase of owner control that represents a transition from personal enterprises to managerial ones, the hierarchy of management is already established, but owners still control or critically influence the strategic investment decisions. Pre–World War II *zaibatsu* of Japan discussed in Hidemasa Morikawa's chapter and postwar Korean *chaebol* which is analyzed in Alice Amsden's chapter on South Korea both belong to this category, although those enterprise groups are different from a classic case of entrepreneurial enterprise in that product diversification preceded the establishment of managerial hierarchy.[5]

In identifying learned and accumulated knowledge as the source of and justification for managerial discretion, Chandler's theory of managerial capitalism has two distinctive characteristics. First, Chandler has constructed a *positive* theory of managerial capitalism which represents a sharp contrast to conventional theories before his. Scholars beginning with Adolf Berle and Gardiner Means had a *passive* version of managerial capitalism insofar as they identified dispersed stock ownership as the source of managerial discretionary power. Simply because no owners, individual or institutional, came to have enough of a block of voting stocks to exercise ownership control, management, almost by default, could now possess strategic decision-making power.[6]

Second, as Chandler emphasizes the learning capabilities of senior management, the ownership of the firm per se is no longer a primary

---

[4] Chandler, *Scale and Scope*, chapter 7, particularly pp. 291–294. For the criticism of this view, see Chapter 4 of this volume on Great Britain by Geoffrey Jones, and Roy Church, "The Limitations of the Personal Capitalism Paradigm," *Business History Review*, 64, no. 4, Winter 1990, pp. 703–710.

[5] For extensive analyses of those enterprise groups, see particularly Hidemasa Morikawa, *Zaibatsu: The Rise and Fall of Family Enterprise Groups in Japan* (Tokyo: University of Tokyo Press, 1992); and Alice H. Amsden, *Asia's Next Giant: South Korea and Late Industrialization* (New York: Oxford University Press, 1989).

[6] Adolf A. Berle and Gardiner C. Means, *The Modern Corporation and Private Property* (New Brunswick, N.J.: Transaction Publishers, 1991). The book was originally published in 1932.

issue. Critical to his model is the long-term commitment and capacity of senior managers, who should be organized in a coherent manner within the firm's structure to enhance their capabilities to accumulate usable knowledge concerning internal operations and external markets. Owners, as long as they are committed and competent, can then be capable managers. His positive attitudes toward recent management buyouts illustrate this perspective.

The Chandlerian learning and knowledge underpinnings of managerial enterprises are particularly significant in dynamic capital-intensive industries, which Chandler regards as the engine of industrial economic growth. As learned knowledge has increasingly played a key function for the long-term growth and viability of economic institutions, oligopolistic enterprises in capital-intensive industries exhibit competitive advantages over smaller firms in such industries, or enterprises in labor-intensive industries. This is because large enterprises in capital-intensive industries have accumulated the systematic information of markets and technology within their managerial hierarchy. Because firms in capital-intensive industries often face critical decisions of large-scale investments that are discontinuous and uncertain, they must create an organizational learning device to minimize the risk and maximize the benefits of such investments.

Once this complementarity between the physical capital investment and the internal knowledge accumulation is institutionalized, large enterprises in capital-intensive industries can theoretically continue to be a positive and influential contributor to economic growth. As many oligopolistic firms that originated in capital-intensive industries transformed themselves into the new leaders of knowledge-intensive industries, their accumulated knowledge enabled them to enter new geographical and product markets when demand for their original product lines leveled off and/or new markets related to their original product lines opened up opportunities for growth.

The recognition of the learned and accumulated knowledge within large industrial enterprises is essential for understanding the relationship between these firms and capital markets. When such knowledge is shared within an organization and thus becomes public goods in the firm, it becomes a source of positive externalities, bringing long-run efficiency and dynamic competitiveness. The internal and organic evolution of the existing firm, compared with the establishment of new firms through capital market mechanisms, is thus beneficial to the welfare of the economy as a whole. This is mostly because, given the tacit, fungible, and

nonpatentable nature of the internal organizational knowledge of technology and markets, such knowledge does not realize its full value in external
market transactions. Because new firms cannot purchase such knowledge
off-the-shelf in the market, such knowledge becomes an entry barrier for
the new firm and a source of increasing returns for the original firm.

Institutions of capital markets, in the meanwhile, have tried to enhance
their capabilities in comprehending the technical components of industrial production processes. In particular, those organizations have recently
boosted their internal technological competence by recruiting many Ph.D.s
in science and engineering. Without actual and ongoing experiences of
production processes, however, their knowledge remains mainly concep-
tual and theoretical. As has been emphasized in Chapter 2, it is empirical
and practical knowledge in product development, manufacturing operation, and marketing that is critical to the *commercial* success of new
products and processes, in which large industrial enterprises excel. Technological knowledge on the part of capital market institutions should
certainly help them to find investment or divestment opportunities and
to monitor the performance of industrial enterprises. But such knowledge
cannot substitute for the accumulated know-how of manufacturing firms.

In the critical case of product diversification, learned and accumulated
knowledge about product and technology can enhance the entry of existing enterprises into new markets, as long as such markets are reasonably
related to the original ones and thus accumulated knowledge is transferable and usable. By comparison, new firms that can be created by the
capital market mechanism suffer from the burden of transaction costs
resulting from imperfect information related to markets of inputs, products, and particularly technology.

In essence, discretionary managerial power in strategic decision making is the key ingredient in the Chandlerian framework for accumulating
the shareable knowledge and building up the "organizational capabilities" of the modern industrial enterprise. As long as large industrial enterprises administered by senior full-time management continuously evolve
by taking advantage of their transferable knowledge, the dynamic and
internal growth of individual large enterprises and the overall stability of
the membership of oligopolistic industries become a source of wealth in
modern nations. Within the microeconomic and institutional contexts
that have existed since the Second Industrial Revolution, managerial
capitalism has exhibited more dynamics than personal, family, and financial
capitalism or centrally planned economies.

MANAGERIAL AND ORGANIZATIONAL MISBEHAVIOR
AND THE AGENCY PROBLEM

The popular criticism that the Chandlerian managerial enterprise has faced mainly originated in the less-than-impressive performance since the 1970s especially of such famed U.S. large enterprises as RCA, U.S. Steel, the "Big Three" automobile manufactures, and even Xerox and IBM. Enough evidence has been accumulated of managerial misbehavior and organizational incompetence to suggest that the effectiveness of managerial enterprise was not necessarily given or automatic under conditions of rapidly changing technology and markets and intensifying international competition.

Particularly troubling was the wasteful way that many large enterprises invested their resources. In the 1970s and 1980s the top management of many U.S. large corporations regularly refused to divest resources from mature businesses and/or invested their firms' earnings into low-return ventures in order to sustain the continuous growth of their businesses and thus hold onto their prestige and lavishly paid jobs.

The resulting mediocre performance of many large enterprises meant that conventional internal *and* external monitoring mechanisms for managerial accountability did not function properly and new monitoring devices were necessary. The rapid change and enormous complexity of markets and organizations made it difficult to obtain and analyze information necessary to monitor adequately the performance of senior management.

Managerial capitalism in the United States had long enjoyed a good reputation up to the 1960s. According to Chandler, senior management of large industrial enterprises could make investment decisions without effective pressure from owners who were mostly wealthy individual shareholders. With a capital structure in which investment funds came mostly from retained earnings and debt financing played a relatively minor role, senior managers could exercise their discretionary power without much constraint. This classic managerial capitalism thus continued until the 1960s when the transient institutional investor increasingly became the major shareholder and gradually started to voice its concern about the effectiveness of managerial control.

The most theoretically coherent criticism of investment misbehavior of large corporations came from Michael Jensen, a finance economist who perceived that "Technological and other developments that began in the mid-twentieth century have culminated in the past two decades in a similar situation [to the late nineteenth century]: rapidly improving productivity, the creation of overcapacity and, consequently, the requirement for exit."[7] Jensen then criticized the failure of large American corporations to face this challenge:

[T]he infrequency with which large corporate organizations restructure or redirect themselves [into downsizing and exit] solely on the basis of the internal control mechanism in the absence of crises in the product, factor, or capital markets or the regulatory sector is strong testimony to the inadequacy of these control mechanisms.[8]

Although Jensen generally recognizes the dynamic shift of technological change and international competition since World War II, his understanding of strategic opportunities and necessities for large corporations, particularly those of the United States, to cope with the new economic reality is substantially different from that of Chandler's. Partially reflecting the different perception of the Third Industrial Revolution, Jensen focuses on the failure of many large American corporations to downsize in and exit from mature product markets. He easily found many cases of large industrial companies experiencing difficulties of exit, such as General Tire, General Motors, and Eastman Kodak, to name a few. This was because, according to Jensen, conventional ineffective governance systems cannot overcome an inherent organizational defense mechanism which results in a failure of a firm's owners to force its senior management to maximize efficiency and long-run market value.

This inability of owners to monitor and control senior management is an important case of an "agency problem" in which the top management, as the agent of shareholders and debt holders, may serve its own interest at the cost of the firm's owners. This potentially problematic aspect of managerial capitalism was recognized as early as 1932 in the classic work of Adolf Berle and Gardiner Means, *Modern Corporation and Private Property*. In articulating a consequence of the eventual separation of ownership and control, they claimed:

---

[7] Michael C. Jensen, "The Modern Industrial Revolution, Exit, and the Failure of Internal Control Systems," *Journal of Finance*, 48, no. 3, July 1993, pp. 833, 854. Other articles of Jensen's which are particularly relevant to the Chandlerian perspective are "Eclipse of the Public Corporation," *Harvard Business Review*, 67, no. 5, September–October, 1989, pp. 61–74; (with William H. Meckling) "Knowledge, Control and Organizational Structure," in Lars Werin and Hans Wijkander, eds., *Contract Economics* (Oxford: Blackwell, 1992), pp. 251–291.

[8] Jensen, "Modern Industrial Revolution," p. 854.

The position of the owner has been reduced to that of having a set of legal and factual interests in the enterprise while the group which we have called control, are in the position of having legal and factual powers over it. . . . [T]he interests of control [then] are different from and often radically opposed to those of ownership. . . . [P]ersonal profits at the expense of the corporation [thus] become practically clear gain to the persons in control and the interests of a profit-seeking control run directly counter to the interests of the owners.[9]

Later controversy over managerial capitalism questioned whether growth of some sort, rather than profitability, was the orientation of nonowner managers. Thorstein Veblen and later John Kenneth Galbraith suggested that growth becomes the primary goal of management because both the engineer manager (in the case of Veblen) or the technocrat (in the case of Galbraith) seeks to maximize technical opportunities related to the growth of the firm. Robin Marris also identified corporate growth as a target of managerial control, but he emphasized personal promotional opportunities as the driving force behind growth-oriented management. William Baumol and recently Oliver Williamson further elaborated this growth push of managerial enterprises within the neoclassical economics framework.[10]

In the sterilized textbook version of this managerial enterprise thesis, senior management aims to target the growth maximization of sales, market share, and other indices of a firm's expansion as long as the firm is achieving a conventionally acceptable level of profitability. This is because, first, nonowner salaried managers are no longer primarily concerned with maximizing profitability. They are more interested in the long-term growth of the size of their enterprises, because this tends to maximize their own income and personal as well as corporate prestige. This is also because mostly nonactive shareholders stay away from interfering in the strategic behavior of a firm as long as a reasonable rate of profitability is assured.

One point, on the other hand, should be noted about personal, owner-controlled and -managed firms. Although, by definition, they do not suffer from agency problems compared to managerial enterprises, they do not

---

[9] Berle and Means, *The Modern Corporation and Private Property*, pp. 113, 114, 115.
[10] Thorstein Veblen, *The Engineers and the Price System* (New York: Huebsch, 1921); John Kenneth Galbraith, *The New Industrial State* (Boston: Houghton Mifflin, 1967); Robin Marris, *The Economic Theory of "Managerial Capitalism"* (New York: Basic Books, 1969); William J. Baumol, *Business Behavior, Value, and Growth* (New York: Harcourt, 1959); and Oliver E. Williamson, *The Economics of Discretionary Behavior: Managerial Objectives in a Theory of the Firm* (Englewood Cliffs, N.J.: Prentice-Hall, 1967).

necessarily constitute a more efficient and viable economic organization because opportunity costs to avoid agency problems can be high. Owners in reality do not always maximize efficiency and profitability. Entrepreneurs who are instrumental in the initial phenomenal growth of such firms, for instance, often become inept leaders, whose investment decision making takes economically suboptimal directions. They sometimes pursue their own personal goals, as the famous case of Henry Ford illustrates. Or their concerns about successors may cloud their decision making, as many family enterprises experience. Owner-managed firms, by nature, usually lack internal mechanisms to police and correct these problems, which results in a wasteful use of resources. In the end, therefore, external competitive market forces have to discipline such enterprises by making their market share smaller and their financial outcome less profitable.

CHANDLERIAN MECHANISM FOR EFFICIENCY AND ACCOUNTABILITY

As the Chandlerian framework emphasizes the asymmetry of market and technology information in favor of inside senior management, it also has to recognize the hazard resulting from this imperfect and incomplete distribution of information and knowledge among senior management and various internal and external stakeholders. Given the lack or shortage of information on the part of these stakeholders, managers can and actually often do keep their own knowledge private, which results in the tolerance of suboptimal firm performance or the maximization of their own utility. The very learned and accumulated knowledge of top management that made the managerial enterprise dynamic can possibly be the source of the inefficient performance of the firm and/or the economy.

Although Chandler emphasizes the primacy of large industrial enterprises, particularly those administered by salaried management in dynamic capital-using and then knowledge-intensive industries, he has been careful on the issue of managerial effectiveness by disavowing the seemingly automatic-piloting mechanism of managerial discretionary decision making toward long-run profitability and dynamic growth. He actually acknowledges the abuse and incompetence of managerial decisions and the ineffectiveness of organizational implementation.[11] Even though he admits

---

[11] For a concise summary of Chandler's view of American corporate performance after World War II, see "The Competitive Performance of U.S. Industrial Enterprise since the Second World War," *Business History Review*, 68, no. 1, Spring 1994, pp. 1–72.

occasional abuse and incompetence, however, in the final analysis Chandler values the positive economic contribution of large industrial enterprises. Thus, his framework of managerial capitalism basically remains function-alist and efficiency-driven.

The Chandlerian model of large industrial enterprises theoretically con-tains two separate instruments to monitor the inefficiency and enhance the effectiveness of strategic investment decisions and operational imple-mentation carried out by the senior management of large industrial enter-prises. They are the knowledge accumulated within senior management and oligopolistic and international rivalry.

The critical disagreement between the Chandlerian knowledge-based growth perspective and the Jensenian restructuring position in terms of the effectiveness of large managerial enterprises in the Third Industrial Revolution at least partially reflects the different facets of drastic eco-nomic change they emphasize. For Chandler, the Third Industrial Revolu-tion is the opening of market and technological opportunities which large industrial enterprises with "organizational capabilities" can and actually did exploit for their continuing growth. For Michael Jensen, by con-trast, "The Modern Industrial Revolution" mainly means both capacity-expanding and obsolescence-creating technological changes that result in economywide excess capacity worldwide. This excess capacity must be eliminated through the effective mechanisms of internal corporate governance and/or external capital markets. In short, for Chandler the main concern of the Third Industrial Revolution has been the issue of entry, while Jensen's eyes focus on the matter of exit.

It is thus logically conceivable that the Chandlerian and Jensenian mechanisms function simultaneously to promote their separate agendas in different industry segments of the American economy. This division-of-labor thesis is supported by a study of corporate restructuring by Bronwyn Hall.[12] Her research reveals that corporate reorganizations induced by capital markets have been concentrated in low-technology areas, while high-technology industries have not been significantly affected by similar forces. Thus, as Jensen advocated, capital markets are instrumental in re-organizing those low-tech mature industries, while, as Chandler predicted,

---

[12] Bronwyn H. Hall, "The Impact of Corporate Restructuring on Industrial Research and Development," *Brookings Paper on Economic Activity: Microeconomic, 1990* (Washing-ton, D.C.: Brookings Institution, 1990); and "Corporate Restructuring and Investment Horizons in the United States, 1976–1987," *Business Histroy Review*, 68, no. 1, Spring 1994, pp. 110–143.

high-tech growing fields have often been organized by the internal growth mechanism of knowledge-enhanced existing enterprises.

In the Chandlerian model the built-in growth drive (rather than profit maximization) of managerial enterprises is justified as long as a firm's growth originated in and resulted from the application of accumulated knowledge in new markets. This model, thus, has a strong explanatory power in industries in which markets have been expanding and techno-logical changes have been endogenized within large enterprises. The chem-ical industry has been the quintessential example in which established firms from the United States and Europe have been instrumental in com-mercializing new processes and products.

Chandler's idea can also be useful in thinking about institutional instru-ments that can be utilized in emerging economies where there is a need for entry into many industries and where capital markets, which can contribute to coordinating investment in mature economies, are usually still under-developed. The emergence of the diversified business group is an example of an institution that has evolved to undertake multiindustry entry.[13]

The Jensenian perspective, by contrast, can be applied more effectively to industries where markets are mature and saturated and the transfer-ability of accumulated knowledge is limited. Examples are the steel and rubber industries in major industrial nations. Jensen's framework is also useful in understanding why restructuring processes of the same indus-tries with excess capacity have differed by country. In economies where capital markets are well functioning and active investors are present, indus-try reorganizations can be carried out quickly and extensively, whereas in countries where this financial and institutional mechanism is missing reorganizations are problematic. The limited success of the restructuring of commodity chemicals in Japan, for instance, compared with that in the United States, is a case in point.

The second Chandlerian mechanism to prevent the inefficient use of resources by large enterprises is oligopolistic rivalry. In capital-intensive industries where economies of scale are substantial, the market race be-tween large firms is essential to check managerial and organizational inefficiency. Chandler explicitly incorporates these market forces as a key part of his managerial capitalism mechanism. His model, thus, is different

---

[13] For a comparative perspective on large industrial enterprises in emerging economies, see Alice H. Amsden and Takashi Hikino, "Project Execution Capability, Organizational Know-How and Conglomerate Corporate Growth in Late Industrialization," *Industrial and Corporate Change*, 3, no. 1, 1994, pp. 111–147.

from some other approaches to economic transactions which unilaterally emphasize the supremacy of organizational administrative coordination over market mechanism.[14]

The initial investment into a plant with a minimum efficient size is a necessary condition for a company to participate in the oligopolistic rivalry game, as has been repeatedly emphasized by Chandler. Yet the large-scale factory can theoretically be prone to inefficiency unless it is open to cost competition from other large-scale producers. This is not simply sociological insofar as large and complicated organizations tend to be prone to operational slack. It is also because large-sized firms or plants, even with operational underutilization and inefficiency, can often survive better than smaller competitors on purely economic grounds – they enjoy lower long-run average costs due to substantial economies of scale. For this reason, the functional and operational as well as strategic competitions from other oligopoly members with similar cost structures are a critical condition to insure the efficiency of large industrial enterprises.

Oligopolistic competition does not necessarily come from domestic rivals within the same industry. As large industrial enterprises in conventionally capital-intensive industries accumulate usable knowledge, they enter into related industries where that knowledge is transferable. Or, particularly after World War II, as both Chandler and Jensen stress, international competition became one of the prime forces that enforces the drive to efficiency. As markets became globalized, entry by multinationals into various domestic markets was instrumental in keeping the efficiency level of an industry of those nations high.

DIVERSE EXPERIENCES OF VARIOUS ECONOMIES

Beside the case of the United States that was just examined in the context of the Chandler-Jensen controversy, a universal question of Chandlerian managerial capitalism in the broad context of many national economies is both the exercise of discretionary power in strategic decision making by senior management and the performance monitoring and control of such management by other stakeholders. Individual chapters on these economies

---

[14] The latest work in this tradition in economic and business history is William Lazonick, *Business Organization and the Myth of the Market Economy* (Cambridge: Cambridge University Press, 1991). See also Chapter 17 of this volume which is written by Lazonick and Mary O'Sullivan.

give a complicated picture of these two forces working simultaneously under various institutional arrangements.[15]

One clear case of the absence of both managerial discretionary power and effective performance monitoring is the "enterprise" of the Soviet Union and Czechoslovakia under central planning. As Yudanov and Teichova clarify, senior managers in these respective economies were not endowed with any means of strategic decision making. Working within the framework of the countrywide superstructure, the enterprise more closely resembled a product division or an operating unit of a large industrial firm in a market economy. In the Soviet Union, for instance, for each enterprise Gosplan was responsible for planning investments in physical facilities and necessary personnel. The central bureaucracy also determined an enterprise's product categories, output level, salaries and wages, and input and product prices. Managers were thus stripped of their strategic-decision opportunities over resource allocation and product portfolio and simply performed the single and limited function of fulfilling the prescribed targets of a certain product that had been assigned from the upper level of hierarchy.

Enterprises in planned economies also suffered from the absence and failure of performance monitoring devices. As discussed in detail in Yudanov's and Teichova's chapters, the managers in operating units in centrally planned systems exploited the planning bureaucracy's lack of product and process information and knowledge by *maximizing* necessary inputs for an assigned output – what Janos Kornai refers to theoretically as a "soft budget constraint."[16] Stripped of its strategic-decision opportunities, senior management exercised its remaining decision-making and discretionary power in a way that was harmful to the viability of their manufacturing organizations. Thus, as production units, enterprises in centrally planned economies failed in both allocative and technical efficiency.

[15] International comparison of corporate governance, corporate finance, and capital markets is still limited. A few useful works are: David C. Mowery, "Finance and Corporate Evolution in Five Industrial Economies, 1900–1950," *Industrial and Corporate Change*, 1, no. 1, 1992, pp. 1–36; Michael Porter, *Capital Choices: Changing the Way America Invests in Industry* (Washington, D.C.: Council on Competitiveness, 1992); Mark J. Roe, *Strong Managers, Weak Owners: The Political Roots of American Corporate Finance* (Princeton: Princeton University Press, 1994), particularly part 4; and Stephen Prowse, "Corporate Governance in an International Perspective: A Survey of Corporate Control Mechanisms among Large Firms in the U.S., U.K., Japan and Germany," *Financial Markets, Institutions and Instruments*, 4, no. 1, February 1995, pp. 1–63. For corporate finance in emerging markets, see Ajit Singh and Javed Hamid, *Corporate Financial Structure in Developing Countries* (Washington, D.C.: World Bank, 1992).

[16] Janos Kornai, *The Socialist System* (Princeton: Princeton University Press, 1986).

Strategic learning did not take place at the senior level of the enterprise because the limited scope of a firm's operation does not allow management to accumulate knowledge that is usable in other functions and areas and because management anyway was not given an opportunity to employ critical decision-making capabilities.

In government-owned enterprises in market economies, the chapters on Italy, Spain, and Argentina strongly suggest that political noise imbedded in the structure and environment of firms often prevented both the constructive exercise of managerial discretion and performance monitoring and enforcement purely based on economic grounds. Often protected as monopolies and "national champions," such enterprises did not face competitive market forces which should have functioned as effective instruments to ensure the full potential employment of these firms' resources.

At the other end of the spectrum, Amsden's chapter on South Korea illustrates an interesting combination of performance enhancing mechanisms based on market and policy forces. She argues that the Korean government successfully monitored the performance of big chaebol by setting clear and simple standards for operation and export and enforced this mechanism by subsequent rewards and punishments. These disciplinary instruments were effective in part because Korea's industrial policy targeted several chaebol groups to compete against each other in a constellation of industries. Thanks to this intergroup rivalry government could penalize a firm for its inefficiency. Because one firm's loss can be easily compensated by another firm's gain, the economy at large was not destabilized in terms of production, export, and employment.

Korea's example makes one significant theoretical point concerning monitoring entities. Performance monitoring can be done by a political organ such as a government bureaucracy as long as it acts solely out of economic motives. In the case of Korea, the government's self-empowerment and bureaucratic interference into economic issues for political reasons were repressed in part by the government's huge financial and economic stake in the chaebol's successful performance. Because a well-functioning private capital market was absent and because the rapid expansion of enterprises did not allow internal retained earnings as an adequate source of investment, the chaebol's family owners mainly had to rely on credit from the government. The government could discipline the chaebol, and the chaebol performance affected the government's legitimacy and survival.

Korean-type government monitoring was possible in part because the economy was at the stage of development when product characteristics were relatively simple and uniform and technological knowledge required to monitor performance was still within the grasp of a government bureaucracy. This system naturally faces a formidable challenge as the country moves toward a mature industrial economy and its products become more complicated, sophisticated, and technology-oriented.

Many of Korea's chaebol have reached the phase of Chandlerian entrepreneurial enterprise, which poses a significant unanswered question. According to Amsden, owners of these huge groups have constructed a substantial managerial hierarchy to administer widely diversified business activities. More and more senior salaried managers take over strategic decision-making functions. According to Morikawa, this was exactly what happened to a few prominent Japanese zaibatsu before World War II. How, under these circumstances, do owners or their family members monitor the performance of senior management? Given the size and scope of the industries in which they operate, effective control over these managers seems formidable.

A different puzzle concerns another form of group enterprise networks found in Japan after World War II and discussed in detail by Morikawa. Contrary to the entrepreneurial enterprises of zaibatsu before the war, Japan's postwar group organization is a form of managerial enterprise whereby individual enterprises within a group were each other's shareholders as in Mitsubishi, Mitsui, and Sumitomo. Regular meetings among constituent enterprises usually play more of an information-exchange and coordinating function than strategic decision-making function. Within an arrangement of "mutual ownership and mutual control" the top management of constituent enterprises basically selects outside directors and makes key long-term investment decisions itself. We still do not have a clear picture of how senior managers make strategic decisions and avoid wasteful investment when constrained by managers of allied enterprises. Morikawa's chapter leads us to speculate on two questions: what is the actual mechanism of performance monitoring and enforcement within a group, when senior managers do not possess detailed information and knowledge of products, technology, and markets of other member companies? Do commercial banks at a group's core have enough capabilities to monitor and enforce performance?

CONCLUSION

The Chandlerian thesis of managerial capitalism prizes the strategic utilization and application of learned knowledge of insider senior management. The full exploitation of accumulated knowledge is critical to the continued dynamic growth of large industrial enterprises and their positive contribution to economic development. This knowledge infrastructure is particularly critical in the present environment in which the strategic factor of growth has become information resources. Authors of the chapters in general seem to agree with the positive contribution of Chandlerian managerial knowledge.

Thanks to an ongoing controversy on corporate governance, however, we also have to examine how modern industrial enterprises in various countries at various times invent and maintain effective monitoring mechanisms. Without these mechanisms the knowledge of management can be misdirected. A few studies in this book give some solutions to these complicated puzzles, as just briefly explored. Yet problems of control and monitoring are still unanswered in most cases. In the case of Germany we need to know more about the role of universal banks, for instance. To what extent did these Grossbanken involve themselves in the strategic decision making of industrial enterprises, and how did they monitor performance? Even for the United States a significant question still remains: what caused the apparent sudden change of managerial capitalism around the 1960s and 1970s? Was it the abuse or idiosyncracy of managerial knowledge? Were capital markets instrumental in initiating the alleged short-term investment horizons of industrial enterprises? To answer these questions what is now acutely needed is more empirical and comparative investigation. This book has ably initiated such a process.

17

Big business and skill formation in the wealthiest nations: The organizational revolution in the twentieth century

WILLIAM LAZONICK AND MARY O'SULLIVAN

BIG BUSINESS AND ORGANIZATIONAL LEARNING

The authors of the national chapters in this book say very little about the role of the labor forces that big businesses have employed to create national wealth. Our contribution seeks to fill this gap by focusing on investment in the skills of millions of individuals within the managerial organizations and production processes of the dominant enterprises of the most competitive economies – those of the United States, Germany, and Japan.

How have these massive investments in skill formation been accomplished? The most successful industrial economies have relied heavily on private-sector business enterprises to plan the strategy and implement the structure that results in skill formation. Yet corporate decisions to invest in human assets almost invariably reflect the educational foundations on which enterprise training must build as well as social norms concerning the social groups, based on gender, race, and class, who are likely to be most receptive to corporate training and identify most closely with corporate goals. A system of skill formation and the organizational learning it makes possible are collective processes, and are influenced by the particular social environment in which they occur. These social influences, which typically take on a national character, are most evident in the willingness of major corporations to invest in the skills of shop-floor labor and to integrate these skills into the organizational structure of the enterprise as a whole, as well as in the evolving social relations between managers and workers.[1] The following historical summaries of the process

---

[1] See William Lazonick and Mary O'Sullivan, "The Governance of Innovation for Economic Development," report to Studies on Technology, Innovation, and Economic Policy (STEP) Group, Oslo, Norway, August 1995.

of skill formation in the United States, Germany, and Japan in the twentieth century seek to identify the social conditions in each of the nations that have imparted unique characteristics to the ways in which the skills of managers and workers are developed and utilized within the nation's major industrial enterprises. In the conclusion, we highlight some of the main implications of the different systems of skill formation for changes in international competitive advantage.

UNITED STATES

Like Germany and Japan, the United States experienced a managerial revolution in industry from the last decades of the nineteenth century.[2] The emergence of a transcontinental market, linked by a transcontinental communications system and populated by millions of independent farmers and artisans, created vast business opportunities for enterprises that planned and coordinated the processes of production and distribution. To do this planning and coordinating, entrepreneurs had to build teams of committed managers, and, particularly in the more capital-intensive industries, those enterprises that built the most committed and skilled managerial teams were able to capture huge market shares.[3]

Unlike Britain with its accumulations of skilled labor supplies in industrial districts, the interregional and interoccupational mobility of workers in the United States rendered skilled labor scarce throughout the nineteenth century.[4] The alternative opportunities for self-employment as farmers and artisans available in the United States made skilled wage labor not only expensive but also difficult to discipline. Even in the early Lowell textile industry, when U.S. industrialists wanted to engage in mass production, they had to look to skill-displacing technological change to overcome the constraints on labor supply that a highly mobile work force imposed. It was for this reason that nineteenth-century American manufacturers did not simply adopt British machine technologies that had been designed to be operated by a much more stable and abundant labor force. To ensure the development and utilization of the skill-displacing technologies, U.S.

---

[2] Alfred D. Chandler, Jr., *Scale and Scope: The Dynamics of Industrial Capitalism*, Harvard University Press, 1990; Alfred D. Chandler, Jr., Chapter 3, in this volume.

[3] Alfred D. Chandler, Jr., *The Visible Hand: The Managerial Revolution in American Business*, Harvard University Press, 1977.

[4] William Lazonick, *Competitive Advantage on the Shop Floor*, Harvard University Press, 1990.

industrialists had to invest in managerial structures. The result was the rise of the American system of manufactures by the middle of the nineteenth century.[5]

Until the last decade of the nineteenth century, a formal system of higher education was relatively unimportant for the development and utilization of technology, in part because American industry was only beginning to make the transition from the machine-based First Industrial Revolution, in which shop-floor experience remained important, to the more science-based Second Industrial Revolution, in which systematic formal education was a necessity. Hence the earlier integration of higher education into the industrial economy in Germany, where state efforts to build the nation's military strength stimulated growth in the new science-based industries as well as the scientific transformation of certain sectors of the traditional machine-based industries.

As Alfred Chandler[6] has shown, besides providing the infrastructure for the rise of national markets, the highly organized transcontinental railroad networks were important early schools for late nineteenth-century managers in other industries, such as iron and steel and machinery. Indeed, during the last half of the nineteenth century and beyond, many technical specialists and managers developed their skills, less through formal education and more by moving from one industry to a technologically related one – for example, from armaments to sewing machines or from bicycles to cars.[7] From the late nineteenth century, however, the system of higher education became central to supplying technical and managerial personnel to the burgeoning bureaucracies of America's industrial corporations.

A classical college education, modeled on Oxford and Cambridge, had in the mid-nineteenth century held sway in the United States at institutions of higher learning such as Harvard and Yale. With the rise of managerial organization, however, public institutions of higher education – the land-grant colleges – were transformed to meet the requirements of U.S. industry for line and staff specialists. From the 1890s the U.S. Department of Agriculture in effect transformed the land-grant colleges

[5] David A. Hounshell, *From the American System to Mass Production, 1800–1932*, Johns Hopkins University Press, 1984; see also William Lazonick and Thomas Brush, "The 'Horndal Effect' in Early U.S. Manufacturing," *Explorations in Economic History*, 22, January 1985, 58–96.

[6] Chandler, *The Visible Hand*.

[7] Hounshell, *From the American System*; see also Ross Thomson, *The Path to Mechanized Shoe Production in the United States*, University of North Carolina Press, 1989.

into operating divisions of a huge organizational structure that extended from the federal government laboratories to make contact with millions of farmers. In regional experimental stations attuned to improving the productivity of local crops, technical specialists, trained in the land-grant colleges, applied science to industry. Through extension services, county agents sought to diffuse the resultant technologies to the mass of farmers who, in their combined roles as "plant" managers and "shop-floor" workers, transformed purchased inputs into salable outputs.[8] Also from the 1890s, U.S. manufacturing enterprises began to take an interest in the land-grant colleges – MIT among them – as a source of supply of scientists and engineers.[9] For this was a time when, for the sake of developing new technologies, the most prominent U.S. mass-production enterprises were building in-house capabilities to apply science to industry[10] and, for the sake of utilizing these new technologies, were successfully eliminating craft control of production from the shop floor.[11]

The growing importance of the land-grant colleges in American economic life in turn put pressure on the classical colleges to make their scientific and educational activities relevant to the needs of industry. Especially after the turn of the century, when (largely through philanthropic foundations established by business fortunes) wealth accumulated in industry provided massive funding for education, industrial enterprises could make use of the entire system of U.S. higher education, whether privately or publicly funded. Industrial enterprises increasingly recruited managerial personnel from the system of higher education, and then, through in-house training and on-the-job experience, developed the productive capabilities of these employees and promoted the best of them to middle-level and upper-level managerial positions.

That there was room at the top for such career managers had been ensured by the separation of asset ownership from managerial control

[8] Louis Ferleger and William Lazonick, "The Managerial Revolution and Developmental State: The Case of U.S. Agriculture," *Business and Economic History*, 22, 2, 1993, 67–98.

[9] David Noble, *America by Design: Science, Technology, and the Rise of Corporate Capitalism*, Oxford University Press, 1977; John W. Servos, "The Industrial Relations of Science: Chemical Engineering at MIT, 1900–1939," *ISIS*, 71, 1980.

[10] Leonard Reich, *The Making of American Industrial Research: Science and Business at GE and Bell, 1876–1926*, Cambridge University Press, 1985; David A. Hounshell and John Kenly Smith, Jr., *Science and Corporate Strategy: Du Pont R&D, 1902–1980*, Cambridge University Press, 1988; David C. Mowery and Nathan Rosenberg, *Technology and the Pursuit of Economic Growth*, Cambridge University Press, 1989, part 2.

[11] David Montgomery, *The Fall of the House of Labor*, Cambridge University Press, 1987; Lazonick, *Competitive Advantage*, ch. 7.

over the utilization of these assets and the returns that they generated.[12] As late as the 1890s in the United States, ownership of industrial enterprises had been integrated with managerial control. Yet over the next generation, a separation of ownership from control occurred in the most successful and enduring U.S. industrial enterprises.

The managers now in control were salaried employees. Increasingly in the first decades of this century, the salaried employees who rose to positions of top management in U.S. science-based enterprises had been recruited to their companies as university graduates in search of careers. The education that they received, moreover, provided them with the basic cognitive capabilities to apply science to industry – capabilities which they improved primarily through in-house training and experience during the course of their careers.[13]

Besides reorganizing the process of developing new technologies, these managerial structures provided the organizational foundations for transforming the utilization of process technologies on the shop floor. During the rapid postbellum expansion of American industry, U.S. manufacturing enterprises, and particularly those that had tried to compete on growing national markets, found that they had to rely extensively on skilled labor to coordinate – and even, in many cases, plan – production activities. In contrast to Britain, however, American reliance on skilled shop-floor labor to coordinate production activities was generally short-lived, as U.S. industrialists developed technological and organizational alternatives to leaving skills, and the control of work, on the shop floor. By employing unskilled immigrants from Eastern and Southern Europe, by investing in deskilling technological change, and by elaborating their managerial structures to plan and coordinate the productive transformation, U.S. industrial capitalists attacked the craft control that workers – typically of British and German origin – had staked out during the 1870s and 1880s.[14]

The initial response of shop-floor workers to the exercise of managerial control was to form craft unions. Union membership in the United States rose from 440,000 in 1897 to 2.7 million in 1914, primarily in affiliation with the American Federation of Labor. In industries such as railroads, mining, shipbuilding, building and construction, publishing and printing, clothing, and cigars that were charactized by intense product-market

---

[12] William Lazonick, "Strategy, Structure, and Management Development in the United States and Britain," in Kesaji Kobayashi and Hidemasa Morikawa, eds., *Development of Managerial Enterprise*, University of Tokyo Press, 1986, 101–46.
[13] Ibid. [14] Montgomery, *The Fall of the House of Labor*.

competition, some unions secured the right to engage in collective bargaining for their members. But in the more oligopolistic industries such as steel, copper and other light metals, light machinery, automobiles, glass, chemicals, and electrical equipment that were central to the American rise to manufacturing dominance, workers lacked representation, thus marking the first three decades of this century as the "nonunion era" in American industrial history. When employers refused to bargain with unions, shop-floor workers turned to the restriction of output to exercise direct control over the relation between the work effort they provided and the pay they received. During the nonunion era, employers used both political and economic power to undermine workers' attempts to assert shop-floor control. They relied on repression, instigated and financed both privately and publicly, to eliminate radical elements in the American labor movement. But having deprived their workers of militant alternatives, leading industrial employers also gained the cooperation of their shop-floor workers by sharing some of the managerial surplus with them and by holding out (what during the 1920s at least appeared to be) plausible promises of employment security.[15]

The phenomenal productivity growth that U.S. manufacturing experienced in the 1920s could not have been achieved without managerial success in gaining control over work organization on the shop floor. At the same time, however, the decades-long managerial offensive against craft control, combined with the evolution of a highly stratified educational system that effectively separated out future managers from future workers even before they entered the workplace, left a deep social gulf between managers and workers within U.S. industrial enterprises. During the 1920s, even as many dominant industrial enterprises shared some of their surpluses with workers in the forms of higher wages and more employment security, U.S. managers, ever fearful of a reassertion of craft control, continued with their quest to take, and keep, skills off the shop floor.[16]

The Great Depression, with its massive layoffs of blue-collar workers even by many of the most progressive employers of the 1920s, served to deepen the social separation of management from the shop-floor labor force. In response, several unions left the American Federation of Labor (AFL) to form the Committee for Industrial Organization (CIO) with the

---

[15] See David Brody, *Workers in Industrial America*, Oxford University Press, 1980.
[16] Lazonick, *Competitive Advantage*, chs. 7–10.

goal of organizing shop-floor workers by industry rather than by craft. Within a short period from 1937 to 1940, the CIO, with governmental backing, had organized nearly all the major oligopolistic industries. In 1941 union membership stood at 10.5 million, with 5.0 million in the CIO and 4.5 million in the AFL. The labor movement was thus able to obtain a measure of economic security for workers that private enterprise had failed to provide. When, in the renewed prosperity of the 1940s, dominant mass producers once again sought to gain the cooperation of workers by offering them high wages and prospects of secure employment, these enterprises had to deal with powerful mass-production unions.

These unions did not challenge the principle of management's right to plan and coordinate the shop-floor division of labor.[17] In practice, however, the quid pro quo for union cooperation was that seniority be a prime criterion for promotion along well-defined lines, and ever more elaborate job structures, thus giving older workers preferential access to a hierarchical succession of jobs paying gradually rising hourly wage rates. In return, union leadership sought to ensure orderly collective bargaining, including the suppression of unauthorized work stoppages.

Despite the relative absence of skill formation on the shop floor in American industry, the United States emerged as the world's industrial leader in the immediate postwar decades because of its by then unparalleled systems for developing new technologies, especially in the science-based industries. These systems integrated the research of corporate research facilities with those of the government and universities. Even during the Great Depression, major corporations had expanded their research capabilities.[18] During World War II and subsequently in the context of the cold war and the expansion of the welfare state, the U.S. government, through national and university facilities, moved beyond agricultural research into the military and medical areas.[19] By the late 1950s, these intricate linkages between the government, major corporations, and institutions of higher education became known as the "military-industrial complex."

[17] Ibid., ch. 9.
[18] Alfred D. Chandler, Jr., "From Industrial Laboratories to Departments of Research and Development," in Kim B. Clark, Robert H. Hayes, and Christopher Lorenz, eds., *The Uneasy Alliance: Managing the Productivity-Technology Dilemma*, Harvard Business School Press, 1985; David C. Mowery, "Industrial Research, 1900–1950," in Bernard Elbaum and William Lazonick, eds., *The Decline of the British Economy*, Oxford University Press, 1986, 191–192.
[19] Don E. Kash, *Perpetual Innovation: The New World of Competition*, Basic Books, 1989.

Given this continuous innovation, from the 1940s to the mid-1960s, union–management cooperation in the coordination of shop-floor relations permitted high enough levels of productivity of deskilled, monotonous, and hence alienating work. By sharing with blue-collar workers some of the gains that came with international dominance, U.S. mass-producers exercised a substantial degree of control over the supply of effort on the shop floor. But, the structures of cooperative labor–management relations that prevailed in the U.S. era of economic dominance would prove problematic when more powerful modes of developing and utilizing technology came on the scene.

GERMANY

During the nineteenth century Germany put in place the world's most sophisticated system of higher education that ultimately would make the nation a leader in the science-based chemical and electrical industries. The foundation for Germany's world renown in the field of academic technical education was laid in the early part of the nineteenth century. State-building ambitions, particularly those of Prussia in the wake of its ignominious defeat by Napoleon, provided the initial incentive for the promotion of technical education. Specifically, in its attempts to foster economic growth, the Prussian bureaucracy identified a need for specialized occupational instruction to be provided outside the orbit of general education. The Berliner-Gewerbe Institute was established in 1821, followed by a number of other technical institutes (originally *polytechnische Schulen*, renamed *technische Hochschulen*) and a network of trade schools in the provinces. These technical schools played a central role in fostering the marriage between science and technology that ultimately made the Germans world industrial leaders.[20]

Engineering was not regarded as a legitimate academic field at this stage, and engineers were generally restricted from the higher ranks of the civil service. As a result, the teachers at these technical schools were accorded a lower status than university professors, a status which they endeavored to elevate by incorporating more theory into their subject and by adopting the university tradition of *Wissenschaft* (science) in their

---

[20] Kees Gispen, *New Profession, Old Order: Engineers and German Society, 1815–1914*, Cambridge University Press, 1989; Wolfgang Konig, "Technical Education and Industrial Performance in Germany: A Triumph of Heterogeneity," in Robert Fox and Anna Guagnini, eds., *Education, Technology and Industrial Performance in Europe, 1850–1939*, Cambridge University Press, 1993, 68.

research. They succeeded in creating a third science, *Technik*, a unique combination of scientific knowledge and craftsmanship. In 1900 the technische Hochschulen became the first educational institutions in the world to award engineering doctorates.[21]

Many engineers were opposed to these developments, and called for engineering education that was less academic. They contended that an overemphasis on theoretical knowledge in the education of engineers was undermining German industrial performance, particularly in industries such as light machinery in which American mass producers held the advantage.[22] In the 1890s the German government introduced a new type of nonacademic engineering education that was consciously modeled on the practical skills and shop training of American engineers (even as "shop culture" was making way for "school culture" in the United States).[23] The new schools, the *Ingenieurschule*, were designed to supplement the existing system of higher technical institutes. The setting up of mechanical laboratories at the longer established schools also allowed them to become more integrated into industrial activity.[24]

A bitter battle over professional status broke out among German engineers around the turn of the twentieth century. This conflict between an academic group and a more practice-oriented faction ultimately led to the concentration of power in the engineering profession in the hands of a third group – the managerial and entrepreneurial engineers, who had an interest in integrating theory and practice and who had the ability to cement the links between German industry and technical education.[25] These links in turn were the foundation for Germany's competitive advantage in chemicals, metals, electrical machinery, and heavy machinery.

Besides supporting industry's efforts to restructure education for technical skill formation, the German state also played a significant role in stimulating a demand for industrial skills. The establishment of the *Zollverein* in 1834 transformed a collection of diverse local markets into one integrated German market. The states' program of economic unification,

[21] Robert R. Locke, *The End of the Practical Man: Entrepreneurship and Higher Education in Germany, France, and Great Britain, 1880–1940*, Jai Press, 1984; Konig, "Technical Education."

[22] Gispen, *New Profession.*

[23] Kees Gispen, "Engineers in Wilhelmian Germany: Professionalization, Deprofessionalization, and the Development of Nonacademic Technical Education," in Geoffrey Cocks and Konrad H. Jarausch, eds., *German Professions, 1800–1950*, Oxford University Press, 1990; Monte Calvert, *The Mechanical Engineer in America, 1830–1910*, Johns Hopkins University Press, 1967.

[24] Konig, "Technical Education," 78.   [25] Gispen, *New Profession.*

and subsequently Bismarck's "blood and iron" campaign for political unification, provided important stimuli for investment in the expansion of a railroad network and in the construction of a transportation and communication infrastructure more generally.[26] The resultant physical integration of the German states created the potential for entrepreneurs to reap economies of scale and scope available in the new and transformed capital-intensive and increasingly knowledge-intensive industries – economies that these companies needed to generate returns on substantial investments in physical and human capital.[27]

The development of the German infrastructure created an unprecedented demand for technical knowledge. Engineers were recruited in droves not only by those immediately involved in infrastructural construction, such as the railroad companies and the electrical equipment manufacturers, but also by supplier industries like metals and machine building. Indeed, nearly all of the German heavy machinery enterprises initially expanded to satisfy the demands of railroads, shipbuilders, iron producers, and mining companies.[28] The German states, particularly the Prussian Imperial State as it built its vast military machine, were also important customers for sectors such as steel, chemicals, and shipbuilding.

Advances in technical knowledge sometimes created new investment opportunities, with the organic chemicals industry as the clearest example of such a phenomenon. The researchers in the laboratories of German chemical companies, universities, and technical institutes were so central to the development of the chemicals industry that it could be claimed that technical knowledge had founded an entire industry.[29]

In other cases new industrial opportunities presented themselves and brought forth advances in technological learning for their exploitation. In the electrical industry, for example, engineers focused on minimizing costs and ensuring product safety in their attempts to compete with well-established alternative energy and lighting systems in the 1860s and 1870s. They achieved these objectives through standardization that permitted the use of interchangeable parts to drive down costs, and allowed the electrical companies to maintain high standards of product quality.[30] The

[26] W. O. Henderson, *The State and the Industrial Revolution in Prussia, 1740–1870*, Liverpool University Press, 1967, 191.
[27] Chandler, *Scale and Scope*, 411.   [28] Ibid., 457.
[29] W. O. Henderson, *The Rise of German Industrial Power, 1834–1934*, University of California Press, 1975, 186.
[30] Robert A. Brady, *The Rationalization Movement in German Industry; A Study in the Evolution of Economic Planning*, University of California Press, 1933, 180.

manufacturing and design discipline that the electrical engineers developed during this process diffused through the German economy because of the electrical industry's technological linkages with many other sectors.[31]

In the German machine industry, such patterns of concentration and standardization were less prevalent. Few companies could compete in light machinery with the Americans who had built a competitive advantage using mass-production methods based on interchangeable parts and high throughput to drive down unit costs. The markets that the Germans served encouraged a different production philosophy. They focused on heavy machinery that was generally built to customer specifications, often those of the government. Their competitive advantage in serving these customers depended on their ability to acquire and develop technical skills in functional design and precision manufacturing.[32]

Despite differences across sectors, many German companies came to rely on technical knowledge to achieve quality in design and manufacturing, and to compete in markets where such emphases could form the basis for sustainable competitive advantage. In the first few years of the century, the balance of German exports shifted from textiles and consumer goods to technically based industries that relied on such knowledge.[33]

The more important scientific technology became for the activities of the business enterprise, the more likely it was that technically trained recruits would take over managerial functions.[34] By 1900 many German companies had built substantial hierarchies of salaried managers, a large number of whom were engineers. Some of these managers had even advanced to the supervisory boards of these companies to participate in strategic decision making. Managerial hierarchies were more common in Germany than in Britain at this time, but family control remained more pervasive in German enterprises than in American ones. However, in many well-known German companies, the original entrepreneurs and their family members were talented engineers in their own right.

In the course of its industrialization, the industries in which Germany acquired international competitive advantage were more dependent on a distinctive national system of managerial skill formation than shop-floor skill formation. In some of these industries, such as chemicals, shop-floor

---

[31] Ibid., 185.

[32] See Ulrich Wengenroth, Chapter 5 in this volume; see also Jurgen Kocka, "The Modern Industrial Enterprise in Germany," in Alfred D. Chandler and Herman Daems, eds., *Managerial Hierarchies: Comparative Perspectives on the Rise of the Modern Industrial Enterprise*, Harvard University Press, 1980, 104; Chandler, *Scale and Scope*, 457.

[33] Chandler, *Scale and Scope*, 410.   [34] Kocka, "Modern Industrial Enterprise," 95.

workers were required to have very few skills. In industries that did require shop-floor skills, such as the electrical and heavy machinery sectors, German employers dominated the process of skill formation for their workers.

It was only as the century unfolded that the Germans developed a unique process of shop-floor skill formation at the national level. The skills that this process developed were organizationally integrated with managerial skills after World War II to form the basis for German competitive advantage in markets where product quality was critical, such as luxury cars, precision machine tools, and optical equipment.[35]

The emergence of a distinctive German system of skill formation for shop-floor workers depended critically on the transformation of the formal educational structure, and specifically the vocational training system. The German apprenticeship system has its roots in the guild system of craft apprenticeship in the Middle Ages. By the middle of the nineteenth century, the forces of economic liberalism had severely undermined the old corporate order. Moreover, the repression by the Prussian state of journeyman organizations severely weakened these institutions. Thus, there was considerably less continuity in Germany than in Britain between the traditional craft-based organizations of the *Handwerk* sector and the trade union movement. Notwithstanding the fact that journeymen were the mainstay of the German labor movement in its early years, by the end of the nineteenth century it was more class conscious and less craft conscious than in Britain where craft organization took root in the industries of the First Industrial Revolution.[36]

In many of the new industries of the Second Industrial Revolution that formed the core of German industrial dynamism, the novelty and technical complexity of their processes meant that existing craft skills could not take root on the shopfloor with the same alacrity that they had in industries like textiles. Thus German unions, like U.S. industrial unions, relied mainly on membership recruitment and strikes rather than craft control on the shop floor to win wage concessions from individual

---

[35] Frank Vogl, *German Business after the Economic Miracle*, Macmillian Press, 1973.

[36] Jurgen Kocka, "Problems of Working-Class Formation in Germany: The Early Years, 1800–1875," in Ira Katznelson and Aristide R. Zolberg, eds., *Working Class Formation: Nineteenth-Century Patterns in Western Europe and the United States*, Princeton University Press, 1986; Mary Nolan, "Economic Crisis, State Policy, and the Working-Class Formation in Germany, 1870–1900," in Katznelson and Zolberg, *Working Class Formation*; Keith Burgess, *The Origins of British Industrial Relations: The Nineteenth Century Experience*, Croom Helm, 1975; Lazonick, *Competitive Advantage*, ch. 6.

employers.[37] In the early years of the new century the labor movement was confronted by the powerful industrialists who had emerged from the process of industrial concentration in the form of a unitary Federation of German Employers (Vereinigung der Deutschen Arbeitgeberverbande: VDA). This organization was opposed to unions, and did everything in its power to defeat organized labor.[38] The need to negotiate with the highly organized employers led the unions to adopt centralized structures themselves.[39] The unions registered some gains in the negotiation of agreements with employers at the national and regional levels. In the prewar years, however, employers controlled the workplace and dominated the process of shop-floor skill formation.[40]

The apprenticeship system in *Handwerk* supplied many workers to the burgeoning industrial sector but it was not specifically designed to serve the needs of rapidly growing knowledge-intensive and capital-intensive industries.[41] There were differences across industrial sectors in the value of traditional craft skills in industrial production. In the machinery industry, for example, the artisanal skills of locksmiths, mechanics and blacksmiths were important whereas in the steel industry the benefits of craft apprenticeship were fewer.[42] But, in general, the larger employers invested in their own facilities and programs to modify and supplement the traditional training structures. Thus, in the early decades of the twentieth century many large factories had their own apprentice school in which workers were trained.[43] Concerned that this type of vocational training would tie workers to individual companies and reduce the power of the mass labor movement, the response of the unions was to push for training systems that were standardized and regulated at the national or industrial level.[44]

The survival of the traditional apprenticeship structures depended on the economic viability of the *Mittelstand*, the medium-sized enterprises that accounted for a large share of German economic activity at the time of unification. The Bismarck government had a clear political interest in

[37] Walter Kendall, *The Labor Movement in Europe*, Penguin Books, 1975, 96; Gerard Braunthal, *Socialist Labor and Politics in Weimar Germany: The General Federation of German Trade Unions*, Archon Books, 1978, 21; Nolan, "Economic Crisis," 381.

[38] Kendall, *Labor Movement in Europe*, 97; Nolan, "Economic Crisis," 392.

[39] Braunthal, *Socialist Labor*, 21.   [40] Kendall, *Labor Movement in Europe*, 98.

[41] Arndt Sorge and Malcolm Warner, *Comparative Factory Organization: An Anglo-German Comparison of Management and Manpower in Manufacturing*, Gower Publishing, 1986, 185.

[42] Gary Herrigel, *Industrial Constructions: The Sources of German Industrial Power*, Cambridge University Press, 1996, 95.

[43] Brady, *Rationalization Movement*, 44, 187.

[44] Sorge and Warner, *Comparative Factory Organization*, 185.

bolstering the position of this group as a buffer against the rise of the socialist movement.[45] After the 1870s, however, when modern industrial companies increasingly entered the traditional markets of all artisans, the demise of traditional apprenticeship seemed imminent. The German Reich introduced new legislation in 1897, 1900, and 1908 in an attempt to secure the economic position of the *Handwerk* sector in this climate of rapid industrialization. These acts established the basis of obligatory guilds, restored their corporation rights, and introduced the "limited certificate of competence" requirement for the training of apprentices.[46]

Although the Weimar Constitution left the prewar social structure intact, working-class demands were accorded more consideration at least in the early years of the republic. The Weimar period saw the continuation of the trend in union–employer relations toward the consolidation of the power of the unions at the national and regional levels rather than at the level of the individual enterprise or plant.[47] In an attempt to ensure that their influence had as great an impact as possible, and to restrict the autonomy of individual employers, the unions attempted to formalize many elements of the employment contract.[48] In 1925 the unions introduced occupational profiles and training plans for a variety of apprenticeships. The training structures in handicraft, industry, and services, however, remained independent.[49]

That the unions were more concerned with building the political basis for their power than with preserving skills on the shop floor (as the British unions sought to do in the twentieth century[50]) became particularly apparent in the Weimar period. Since the power of labor had been institutionalized to a considerable extent in the Weimar Republic, the unions were confident of their ability to gain a fair share of the national wealth and were willing to promote measures to build the competitive strength of German industry. Thus following a period of initial indifference to scientific management, the German Free Unions accorded it their wholesale support in the 1920s.[51]

[45] Wolfgang Streeck, *Social Institutions and Economic Performance: Studies of Industrial Relations in Advanced Capitalist Economies*, Sage Publications, 1992, 112.
[46] J. Munch, *Vocational Training in the Federal Republic of Germany*, European Centre for the Development of Vocational Training (CEDEFOP), 1982; Fred McKitrick, "The Stabilization of the Mittelstand: Artisans in Germany from National Socialism to the Federal Republic, 1939–1953," Ph.D. dissertation, Columbia University, 1994, ch. 6.
[47] Braunthal, *Socialist Labor*, 87.   [48] Ibid., 153.
[49] Sorge and Warner, *Comparative Factory Organization*, 185.
[50] Lazonick, *Competitive Advantage*, ch. 6.
[51] Guillén, Mauro, *Models of Management: Work, Authority, and Organization in a Comparative Perspective*, University of Chicago Press, 1994, 109.

The introduction of collective bargaining and the increased regulation of the employment contract during the Weimar period restricted the power of the employers to a certain degree. At the shop-floor level, moreover, the establishment in 1920 of works councils (*Betriebsrate*) in plants with more than fifty employees represented an explicit attempt to give workers a voice in plant operations. The process of rationalization and concentration of industrial activity that took place during the Weimar years, however, strengthened the power of industrialists and weakened that of workers and their unions. As employers regained their prewar strength they became more resistant to the demands of the workers.[52]

During the Weimar period it became apparent that the Kaiserreich's legal protection of the Handwerk sector had not ensured its economic viability. Throughout the 1920s the Handwerk sector felt threatened by dynamic industrial enterprise on the one hand and the socialism of the working classes on the other. Some of those who lost out channeled their fears and frustrations into politics, and ultimately into support for the National Socialists. During the last half of the 1930s and the early 1940s, the Nazis mobilized and reorganized the productive capabilities of the German economy for war. As part of that process they forcibly integrated the *Handwerk* system of apprenticeship into German industry. They also standardized and regulated the training system, thus laying the foundation for the modern German system of apprenticeship.[53]

With the establishment of the Federal Republic of Germany after World War II, an institutionalized and highly regulated system of industrial relations emerged. A dual system of worker representation was set up in German industry with responsibility and authority divided between industrial trade unions and institutions of co-determination. In this system the unions exert a significant influence at the industrial and regional levels through the process of collective bargaining whereas at the level of the individual enterprise their control is only informal. At the enterprise level, however, workers' representation on supervisory boards and, to a more widespread extent, works councils gives workers a legal voice in company operations.

This dual system of representation also applies to the system of worker training. After World War II the government of the Federal Republic of Germany retained training structures in much the same way that the Nazis had shaped them. The regulation and administration of apprenticeship

---

[52] Braunthal, *Socialist Labor*, 175; Nolan, "Economic Crisis," 392.
[53] McKitrick, "Stabilization of the Mittelstand."

training changed, however, to reflect the new social order. Trade unions were included on the vocational training committees of chambers of commerce, and became involved with government ministries and employers' associations in the joint regulation that takes place in the top decision-making bodies of the overall training system. At the level of the enterprise, the works councils have the right to negotiate with the individual employer about the structure of the in-firm training program and are involved in its implementation in the workplace.

Despite criticisms of the training system, central to the postbellum success of West German industry has been the integration of the blue-collar skills that the training system has developed with the technical skills of managers.[54] The establishment of the German system of apprenticeship, with its inclusion of the unions and the government as strategic decision makers in the worker-training process, reduced the autonomy that employers had in setting a strategy and structure of worker skill formation to suit the needs of their particular enterprises. The apprenticeship system, however, allowed employers to reap the benefits of the organizational learning derived from a collective training process that is explicitly designed to accommodate the technological demands of a variety of industries. In certain industries and competitive environments, this trade-off has proven highly attractive to employers. In historically stable technology industries, high-quality worker skills have compensated for a loss in enterprise flexibility. In industries that involve high levels of innovation, and thus place a premium on enterprise flexibility, the trade-off may not have been as attractive.

Worker skills have played a pivotal role in the competitive strategies of those large West German companies that compete on the basis of product quality, and have allowed them to build competitive advantages in markets such an luxury automobiles, precision machine tools, and electrical machinery in which German industry has traditionally been heavily involved. In newly emerging, high-technology sectors such as computers, semiconductors, and telecommunications, however, Germany has been unable to put in place a skill-formation system that can yield national competitive advantage.[55]

Besides contributing to the success of large companies that have

---

[54] Munch, *Vocational Training; Financial Times*, 3, June 1991.

[55] Wengenroth, "Competition Abroad"; Peter J. Katzenstein, "Industry in a Changing West Germany," in Peter J. Katzenstein, ed., *Industry and Politics in West Germany: Toward the Third Republic*, Cornell University Press, 1989, 25.

competed on the basis of quality in product and process, the same training system has also provided the foundation for the competitive advantage of many of the small and medium-sized enterprises that constitute the German Mittelstand. Before the reunification of Germany, companies with less than 500 employees represented approximately 50 percent of West Germany's GDP and two-thirds of its work force. Mittelstand companies are responsible for the training of most of Germany's apprentices.[56] Many of these medium-sized enterprises have developed strong positions in high-quality niche markets such as precision machine tools and laser optics through the excellence in product design and production flexibility that their workers' and managers' technical skills permit.[57]

JAPAN

Over the past two decades, Japanese manufacturing has outperformed U.S. manufacturing in the mass production of consumer durables, particularly automobiles and electronic equipment. These are the industries in which U.S. industry had its greatest international competitive advantages in the first six decades of this century. Having gained competitive advantage in the consumer durable industries, Japanese manufacturing has also made great progress in vertically related capital goods industries: machine tools, electrical machinery, and semiconductors. In recent years, the Japanese have been able to combine their capabilities for developing and utilizing process technologies to achieve low unit costs with movements into higher-quality markets, such as precision machine tools and luxury automobiles, that had been dominated by specialized producers, and in particular the Germans.

The lack of prior industrial development even in the later Tokugawa period, compared with Britain, the United States, and Germany in mid-nineteenth century, meant that, after the Meiji Restoration in 1868, the Japanese state had no choice but to promote the education and enterprise that would generate a broad-based system of skill formation. Although, in the late nineteenth century, the Japanese state consciously pursued a national economic development strategy, it relied on private-sector enterprises to formulate the investment strategies and implement the organizational

[56] *The Economist Survey: West Germany*, Oct. 28, 1989.
[57] Gary B. Herrigel, "Industrial Order and the Politics of Industrial Change: Mechanical Engineering," in Katzenstein, ed., *Industry and Politics*, 191; W. R. Smyser, *The Economy of United Germany: Colossus at the Crossroads*, St. Martin's, 1992, 68.

structures that would permit the development and utilization of technology. The state did, however, make critical investments in the educational
system, so that within two decades after the Meiji Restoration, the Japanese
system of public education was virtually universal and the system of higher
education was turning out a steady supply of engineers who then acquired
specialist skills working for private-sector companies that were building
managerial structures.[58]

A characteristic organization in Japanese industry is the enterprise
group, or *keiretsu*. The original enterprise groups in modern Japan were
the family-controlled *zaibatsu* that led the development of heavy industry
– particularly machinery and shipbuilding – and built up Japan's military
strength from the late nineteenth century until World War II. Some of
the most important *zaibatsu* originated through the efforts of political
entrepreneurs, who used their connections to the Meiji government to
gain privileged access to resources and rights (such as minerals and transportation) that were crucial to Japanese development strategy. To make
good on their leading roles in Japanese economic development, the zaibatsu
families delegated substantial decision-making power to professional
managers who used this power to build formidable managerial structures.

In the aftermath of World War II, the Allied occupation forced the dissolution of the zaibatsu by implementing the widespread distribution of
equity shares, and mandating the deconcentration of the enterprise groups.
In the 1950s, however, the enterprise groups reemerged with much the
same membership as the old zaibatsu while some new groups formed, and
the Japanese business community undertook a "cross-shareholding movement" to ensure that ownership rights in constituent companies would
reside with other industrial and financial companies that would act as
"stable shareholders." These owners have sought neither high yields nor
capital gains on their equity positions. Rather, cross-shareholders hold the
shares for the sake of ensuring the development and utilization of technology, which over the long run generates more business for the companies
in the activities in which their competitive advantages lie.[59]

---

[58] See Hiroyuki Odagiri and Akira Goto, "The Japanese Sysytem of Innovation: Past,
Present, and Future," in Richard R. Nelson, ed., *National Innovation Systems*, Oxford
University Press, 1993, 76–114; Hidemasa Morikawa, Chapter 10 in this volume.

[59] Robert J. Ballon and Iwao Tomita, *The Financial Behavior of Japanese Corporations*,
Kodansha International, 1988; Michael Gerlach, *Alliance Capitalism: The Social Organ-
ization of Japanese Business*, University of California Press, 1992; Hideaki Miyajima,
"The Transformation of Zaibatsu to Postwar Corporate Groups – from Hierarchically
Integrated Groups to Horizontally Integrated Groups," *Journal of the Japanese and
International Economies*, 8, 1994.

Since World War II, former zaibatsu such as Mitsubishi, Mitsui, and Sumitomo, shorn of family control, have reemerged as horizontal keiretsu to remain powerful corporate actors in the Japanese economy, along with a few other large groups built up either by powerful banks or by industrial enterprises that have emerged as dominant in their industries. In the automobile and electronics industries, for example, Toyota, Fujitsu, and Sony have spawned vertical keiretsu through which they plan and coordinate group activities, including the creation or acquisition of vertically related enterprises as new needs for the development and utilization of technology arise. Enterprise groups permit the core companies to enjoy the advantages that the vertical integration of production and distribution creates for the borrowing of technology and the implementation of process and product innovation, without enduring the disadvantages of unmanageable bureaucracies that stifle technological and organizational change. By circumventing the intrafirm organizational structure through subcontracting arrangements with satellite firms, the core company can pursue new investment strategies that require entrepreneurial initiative and leaps in technological ability.

The growth of enterprise groups provides core companies with the opportunity for strategically locating more labor-intensive activities in smaller firms in which the technical specialists have direct proprietary interests in enterprise performance, and in which control of the terms of employment and work conditions need not be shared with the enterprise unions that have become central to labor–management relations in the dominant companies. Although as subcontractors for the core enterprises, the satellite firms can in principle act independently, in practice the very success of the innovative strategies of the dominant enterprises and their commitment to maintaining long-term relations with their subcontractors lead the smaller firms to view themselves as members of an integrated organizational structure.[60]

Over time, some of these "satellites," if technologically successful, have taken on lives of their own, as in the case of Fanuc, the company set up by Fujitsu to develop numerical control units for machine tools.[61]

---

[60] Ronald Dore, *Flexible Rigidities: Industrial Policy and Structural Adjustment in the Japanese Economy, 1970–1980*, Stanford University Press, 1986; Michael Best, *The New Competition: Institutions of Industrial Restructuring*, Harvard University Press, 1990, ch. 5; Michael Smitka, *Invisible Handshakes: Subcontracting in the Japanese Automobile Industry*, Cambridge University Press, 1992.

[61] David Collis, "The Machine Tool Industry and Industry Policy, 1955–82," in A. Michael Spence and Heather A. Hazard, eds., *International Competitiveness*, Ballinger, 1988,

Even then, the very fact that one strong vertically related enterprise has emerged out of the development of another creates a continuing basis for cooperative investment policies while each builds its own internal organization. The organizational capability developed through intercompany cooperation within groups enhances the ability of firms from different groups to engage in cooperative research and development projects, as has been the case in the emergence of an internationally competitive Japanese computer industry.[62]

The ability to organize cooperative investment strategies across enterprises is enhanced by the structure of managerial decision making within enterprises. Consensus decision making – the ringi system – emphasizes the two-way flow of ideas and information up and down the corporate hierarchy. Consensus decision making grew out of the need of the rapidly growing zaibatsu of the early twentieth century to lure college graduates – products of a concerted effort by the state to create an educated elite – away from prestigious government posts. Considerable technical information was required from, and considerable authority had to be delegated to, these professional managers. Even in the cotton textile industry, which in Japan as in Britain and the United States played a major role in early industrialization, the recruitment of college graduates to serve as mechanical engineers was central to modification of imported machinery to achieve high levels of productivity on the basis of inexpensive cotton and unskilled labor.[63]

The institutional basis for the devolution of decision-making power from chief executives to a wider group that extends further down the

75–114; Seiichiro Yonekura and Hans-Jürgen Clahsen, "Innovation by Externalization: A New Organizational Strategy for High-Tech Industries – Fuji Denki, Fujitsu, and Fanuc," in Takeshi Yuzawa, ed., *Japanese Business Success: The Evolution of a Strategy*, Routledge, 1994, 39–64.

[62] Marie Anchordoguy, *Computers Inc: Japan's Challenge to IBM*, Harvard University Press, 1989; Martin Fransman, *The Market and Beyond: Cooperation and Competition in Information Technology Development in the Japanese System*, Cambridge University Press, 1990.

[63] Shin'ichi Yonekawa, "University Graduates in Japanese Enterprises before the Second World War," *Business History*, 26, July 1984, 193–218; Hidemasa Morikawa, "The Increasing Power of Salaried Managers in Japan's Large Corporations," in William D. Wray, ed., *Managing Industrial Enterprise: Cases from Japan's Prewar Experience*, Harvard University Press, 1989, 27–51; Morikawa, "Increasing Organizational Capabilities"; William Mass and William Lazonick, "The British Cotton Industry and International Competitive Advantage: The State of Debates," *Business History*, 32, October 1990, 9–65; William Lazonick and William Mass, 'Indigenous Innovation and Economic Development: Foundations of Japanese Development and Advantage," in Association for Japanese Business Studies, *Best Papers 1995*, Association for Japanese Business Studies, 1995.

formal hierarchy is permanent, or lifetime, employment. Japanese managers typically rise out of the ranks of "white-collar workers" who enter the firm after graduating from college. Like consensus decision making, the policy of permanent employment was extended to managerial personnel in the early twentieth century in order to attract them away from government service and to create the long-term attachments that would make it worthwhile for the business enterprises to invest further in the training of the recruits.[64]

Over time, however, the offer of permanent employment has been extended further down the organizational hierarchy. Before World War I permanent employment was used as a strategy to transform "key" skilled workers (*oyakata*) who, as highly mobile labor contractors, had recruited, trained, and supervised shop-floor labor, into permanently employed foremen who now performed the same functions, but with a long-term commitment to one particular company.[65] In the early 1950s, a strategy of substituting cooperative enterprise unions for the militant industrial unions that had arisen after World War II resulted in the extension of permanent employment status to all male blue-collar workers in the larger enterprises.[66]

The recent success of Japanese mass-producers in introducing flexible manufacturing systems owes much to the fact that, for decades before the introduction of the new automated technologies, blue-collar workers were granted considerable discretion to monitor and adjust the flow and quality of work on the shop floor.[67] Moreover, the ability of Japanese managers to develop the skills of blue-collar workers owes much to the existence for over a century of a national system of mass education designed specifically to ensure that the work forces of the future will possess the general cognitive competences that advanced production technology requires.[68]

Japanese practice is in marked contrast to the U.S. managerial concern

[64] E. Daito, "Recruitment and Training of Middle Managers in Japan, 1900–1930," in Kesaji Kobayashi and Hidemasa Morikawa, eds., *Development of Managerial Enterprise*, University of Tokyo Press, 1986, 151–79.

[65] Reiko Okayama, "Japanese Employer Policy: The Heavy Engineering Industry, 1900–1930," in Howard Gospel and Craig Littler, eds., *Managerial Strategies and Industrial Relations*, Heinemann, 1983, 157–70; Andrew Gordon, *The Evolution of Labor Relations in Japan: Heavy Industry, 1853–1955*, Harvard University Press, 1985.

[66] Michael Cusumano, *The Japanese Automobile Industry*, Harvard University Press, 1985, ch. 3.

[67] Cusumano, *The Japanese Automobile Industry*, chs. 5–6.

[68] Odagiri and Goto, "Japanese System of Innovation"; Ronald P. Dore and Mari Sako, *How the Japanese Learn to Work*, Routledge, 1989.

with using technology to take skills and initiative off the shop floor, a practice that goes back to the late nineteenth century when the success of U.S. mass production was dependent upon breaking the power of craft workers and transferring to management the sole right to plan and coordinate the development and utilization of technology. Despite the existence of militant unions in Japan at various points in the first half of the twentieth century, there was never any attempt by Japanese workers or their organizations to establish craft control on the shop floor.[69] As a result, Japanese employers never had to confront established craft positions of workers as was the case with U.S. manufacturers around the turn of the century, nor did they have to resign themselves simply to leaving skills on the shop floor in the hands of autonomous craftsmen as was the case in Britain.

Historically, the problem facing Japanese employers was not to rid themselves of skilled workers who might use their scarce skills to establish craft autonomy on the shop floor. Rather their problem coming into the twentieth century was the absence of a self-generating supply of workers with industrial skills. To overcome this constraint, industrial employers had to make the investments that would transform unskilled workers into skilled workers and then retain them by integrating them into the organization. To be sure, these same employers generally only accepted the institutionalization of permanent employment, enforced by enterprise unions, when compelled to do so by the threat of militant unionism after World War II. In practice, however, out of the exigencies of developing and utilizing workers with industrial skills, the social foundations for the current permanent employment system were laid in Japan decades before the long-term commitment of the enterprise to the blue-collar worker became an institutional feature of Japanese industry.

SKILL FORMATION AND COMPETITIVE ADVANTAGE

In terms of the organizational integration of management and labor, the Japanese system of skill formation is most similar to that of Germany. In both nations, skill formation on the shop floor is integral to the strategy and structure of skill formation in the enterprise as a whole. In Germany, however, the skill-formation structure of the enterprise derives from an industrywide strategy to set high-quality product standards, whereas in

---

[69] Gordon, *Evolution of Labor Relations*, part 1.

Japan the skill-formation structure derives from an enterprise strategy to engage in continuous problem solving to cut costs. In Germany shop-floor workers are trained to perform to precise occupational standards, whereas in Japan shop-floor workers are trained to perform many tasks that will enable them to recognize and confront production problems as they arise. In historical perspective, the German system of skill formation reflects a tradition of producing for markets that demand high quality, whereas the Japanese system reflects a tradition of producing for markets that demand low costs.

The German and Japanese systems of skill formation also differ in the ways in which they are shaped by and diffuse to large and small manufacturing companies. In Japan, large and small companies tend to be vertically linked through enterprise groups, with the strategy for skill formation issuing from the dominant enterprise but extending to smaller subcontracting firms. In Germany, the industrywide, and even nationwide, character of the strategy and structure of skill formation means that the system extends to both larger and smaller companies, whether they are vertically linked or not. Notwithstanding regional variations within Germany, the German system of skill formation appears to be driven as much by the needs of the Mittelstand – Germany's medium-sized enterprises – as by those of major industrial corporations such as Siemens, BMW, and BASF.

Although shaped by different product–market orientations, by making skill formation on the shop floor central to their investment strategies both the German and Japanese systems differ markedly from the American system. In the American case, the shop-floor investment strategy has been to substitute machines and materials for the skills of workers. What all three systems have in common, however, is investment in managerial structures as the historical precondition for the shop-floor investment strategy, whether it be skill-creating as in Germany and Japan or skill-destroying as in the United States.

What are the implications of these different systems of skill formation for changes in international competitive advantage? In the post–World War II decades, Japanese enterprises gained competitive advantage over American enterprises in those industries such as steel, consumer electronics, and automobiles in which an integrated system of skill formation within the managerial structure was critical for product innovation, but also in which the evolution of process technology made an integrated system of skill formation that included shop-floor workers and suppliers critically important for process innovation. In industries in which, from the 1960s, a system of skill formation that focused on the managerial structure alone continued to suffice in global competition – industries such as pharmaceuticals and chemicals – the Americans continued to be leading innovators, and Japanese companies were unable to mount an effective competitive challenge.[70]

Indeed, in industries such as pharmaceuticals and chemicals, the system of skill formation that generates organizational learning and innovation includes tight research and development linkages with universities, a set of relationships that has long prevailed in Germany and the United States, but not in Japan. In Germany, these industry–university linkages are part of a national system of skill formation designed to generate high-quality products without the achievement of low unit costs being a primary concern. In machine-based industries, however, where process innovation has been important in driving down costs, the Japanese have been able to use their highly integrated systems of skill formation to generate the organizational learning that has permitted them over time to move into high-quality market segments at lower unit costs than their high-quality competitors. Some two decades ago, the Japanese used their process innovations to displace Germans in the high-quality camera and binocular markets. Recently, Japanese companies have been mounting similar competitive challenges to Germany in the precision machine tool and luxury automobile markets.[71]

In the United States, the dominant response to the Japanese challenge has been to seek to remain competitive by restraining wage increases and increasing labor effort (in large part as a concomitant to downsizing), with a neglect of investments in skill formation that are essential for raising living standards and improving employment conditions over the long term. As the Japanese challenge has begun to make itself felt in Germany (as well as in other economies of continental Europe), similar adverse pressures on wages, effort, and investments in skill formation are becoming manifest.

The American experience has shown that, in response to the pressures of global competition, strategic decision makers have a tendency to turn from making value-creating investments in skill formation that can

---

[70] For an elaboration of this argument, see William Lazonick and Jonathan West, "Organizational Integration and Competitive Advantage: Explaining Strategy and Performance in American Industry," *Industrial and Corporate Change*, 4, 1, 1995, 229–270.

[71] See O'Sullivan, "Innovation, Industrial Development, and Corporate Governance," ch. 6.

generate higher-quality, lower-cost products in the future to implementing value-extracting strategies that permit those who control resources to live off the value-creating investments made in the past.[72] Financial interests exert much more pressure on American strategic decision makers in industry to treat the process of skill formation not as a productive investment that can generate returns in the future but as an operating expense that depresses returns in the present.

An understanding of the importance of the process of skill formation to economic development and international competitive advantage raises critical questions about the valuation of human-capital investments in capitalist economies, who have an interest in making these investments, and in whom these investments are made. Especially when, as is the case in the United States, and increasingly in Germany, existing systems of skill formation are under intense competitive pressure, policies for industrial restructuring must consider the modes of corporate governance (and underlying changes in political alignments) that are required to put new, more innovative systems of skill formation in place.

Acknowledgments

We acknowledge helpful comments from the editors of this book. Space limitations have compelled us to keep documentation of the arguments in this chapter to a minimum. For an elaboration with more complete documentation, see William Lazonick and Mary O'Sullivan, "Organization, Finance, and International Competition," *Industrial and Corporate Change 5*, 1 (1996); and Mary O'Sullivan, "Innovation, Industrial Development, and Corporate Governance," Ph.D. dissertation, Harvard University, 1996.

---

[72] William Lazonick, "Creating and Extracting Value: Corporate Investment Behavior and American Economic Performance," in Michael Bernstein and David Adler, eds., *Understanding American Economic Decline*, Cambridge University Press, 1994.

18

Government, big business, and
the wealth of nations

THOMAS K. MCCRAW

THE INTELLECTUAL BACKGROUND: SMITH AND LIST

In his famous formulation of the proper role of government in promoting the wealth of nations, Adam Smith limited public activities to three
functions:

1. "protecting the society from the violence and invasion of other societies";
2. "protecting, as far as possible, every member of the society from the
   injustice or oppression of every other member of it, or the duty of establishing an exact administration of justice";
3. "erecting and maintaining those publick institutions and those publick
   works, which, though they may be in the highest degree advantageous to
   a great society, are, however, of such a nature, that the profit could never
   repay the expence to any individual or small number of individuals."[1]

Throughout *The Wealth of Nations*, an occasional exception to Smith's
limited functions appears, but by and large he sees little role for the state.
He also saw little role for corporations, particularly those receiving any
type of government support. He had little use for public education or for
many types of public works – he advocated private operation of roads
and waterworks, for example. So we can see in a nutshell the fundamental
attitude not only of Adam Smith but also of the classical and neoclassical
traditions that have followed in his formidable wake. The market will
suffice to almost all things, so the role of government is to create the
minimal facilitative conditions, then step back. Treat market imperfec-
tions on an ad hoc basis, as they arise.

---

[1] Adam Smith, *An Enquiry into the Nature and Causes of the Wealth of Nations* (1776),
Book V.

Some of the countries in this study (the United Kingdom, the United States, a few others) have done pretty well by most of Smith's prescriptions: limited government, high individual liberty, and a good if never "exact" administration of justice. It is arguable in a prima facie sense that the considerable wealth of these nations is related largely to their policies of economic and political liberalism. I leave aside as an unfortunate anachronism Smith's hostility to corporations.

But if Smith was correct, what are we to make of the performance of the Soviet Union during most of the twentieth century? To the economic historian, the interesting question about the Soviet Union is not why it ultimately failed, but rather how it survived for so long, and how it industrialized so remarkably during the seventy years between the Bolshevik Revolution and the breakup of 1989. Equally extraordinary in the light of Adam Smith's prescriptions, how are we to understand the success of the German economy in the decades after the unification of 1871? Or, most strikingly of all, how can we explain the spectacular post–World War II performance of the economies of Japan and South Korea? Whatever else we know or do not know about the economic history of the Soviet Union, Japan, and South Korea – plus those of other late industrializers such as Taiwan, Czechoslovakia, Brazil, Argentina, and the rest – we know for certain that the essence of their development was not Smithian laissez-faire. As a general proposition, the later the industrialization, the larger the role of the state.[2]

Leaving aside command economies, we also know that the market process lies at the heart of all successes of the Japanese and Korean sort. Yet in every case of late industrialization (and in several of early, such as Germany), it has not quite been a Smithian market process. For most such countries it has been a guided market. It's been shaped. It's been planned. And in some places it has worked far better than the most optimistic planners in those countries would have dared to predict.

To understand some of the processes by which these economies grew, we might turn to the German economist Friedrich List (1789–1846), one of Adam Smith's most effective early critics. Consider these comments made by List in the 1840s about the role of government in developing national wealth:

<hr>

[2] This point has been emphasized by many scholars who have examined the historical record of development; see, for example, Alexander Gerschenkron, *Economic Backwardness in Historical Perspective* (Cambridge, MA: Harvard University Press, 1962).

Nowhere do the advocates of that [Smithian] system care to point out by what means those nations which are now prosperous have raised themselves to that stage of power and prosperity which we see them maintain. . . . [List adds that deliberate state development of manufacturing and commerce was the secret, even in England, but that Adam Smith had camouflaged it in *The Wealth of Nations*.]

It would be more correct to describe the limbs of men (the head, hands, and feet) as the causes of wealth (we should thus at least approach far nearer to the truth), and the question then presents itself, what is it that induces these heads, arms, and hands to produce, and calls into activity these exertions? [List here anticipates a host of writers, from Marx and Marshall to Coase and Chandler.]

Everywhere [the Smithian system] seeks to exclude the action of the power of the State. . . . Statistics and history, however, teach on the contrary, that the necessity for the intervention of legislative power and administration is everywhere more apparent, the further the economy of the nation is developed.[3]

Both Adam Smith and Friedrich List were correct interpreters of the nature and causes of the wealth of nations. Both were shrewd, penetrating analysts. They differed about the role of the state, but the area of their agreement on almost all other matters was far greater than one might imagine – on the order, I would estimate, of about 95 percent. They both held that without the market mechanism, no economic process could work well for very long. They both placed competition at the center of the ideal economic system. They both abhorred heavy and inefficient taxation. They both valued individual entrepreneurship and innovation.

Smith and List represent the foundations of two important traditions of analyzing economic growth and the role of the state. Of course, there are others, such as that pioneered by Karl Marx, who read Smith and List carefully and learned a great deal from both. But I will focus on the latter two in the discussion that follows.

WHAT DO WE KNOW NOW THAT SMITH AND LIST DID NOT KNOW?

First, we know that for analytical purposes we should separate macroeconomic tools, doctrines, and policies from the microeconomic ones that preoccupied Smith and List. Microeconomic policies did affect the rise of big business in all countries, but in a different way from macroeconomic and industry-specific measures. In promoting aggregate demand, especially during the post–World War II period, macro policies were undeniably

[3] Friedrich List, *The National System of Political Economy* (1841, English translation by Sampson S. Lloyd, London: Longman, Green, 1885, 1916).

important. In the formative years of big business, however, other categories of policy may have been more important. But even then a stable microeconomic environment seems to have been a necessary (but not sufficient) condition for economic development.

Thus, whether government activity in any industry, or in any national economy, should have been greater or less is almost never the correct question to ask. Instead, the first question to ask is, Did the government manage to erect and maintain a suitable macroeconomic environment? (If the answer is no, then the story line languishes until the answer becomes yes.) Considering the historical record, one might then identify a few general types of government policy regimes:

1. Extremely liberal (late Victorian Britain)
2. Liberal but moderately protectionist (the United States until the 1930s)
3. Moderately protectionist and moderately developmental (Germany until the 1960s)
4. Powerfully protectionist and powerfully developmental (Japan from the 1950s to the 1970s, Korea more recently)

The next question is which of these policy regimes worked best. The statistical record of economic performance indicates that all of these economies (Britain, the United States, Germany, Japan, Korea) worked very well indeed. Some, of course, have done and are now doing better or worse than others. Each one, however, at one time or other has led the other four in sheer growth performance, and that is a very interesting phenomenon. All are fundamentally market economies. All have installed a mixture of Smithian and Listian policies in various proportions at different times, according to culture, ideology, and political or military necessity. And all have been the home of large companies that we would do well to study in close detail if we are better to understand the nature and causes of the wealth of nations.

A second thing we know that Smith and List did not is that the study of particular institutions can be very revealing. Smith and List lived in the age before "Big Government," so they could not have foreseen the importance of the national economic bureaucracy in fostering economic growth. By "national economic bureaucracy," I refer to such institutions as the ministry of finance, the central bank, the mobilization agency funnelling research and development funds to companies for new products, or a bureau of economic development, such as Japan's MITI.

Also, in spite of Smith's notorious hostility to the corporation, neither he nor List witnessed the rise of "Big Business." They could not appreciate the significance of the major business corporation, another key institution to study if we are to understand the modern growth of the wealth of nations. Because the large corporation lives in a world partially defined and regulated by government institutions, in studying it we automatically study those public institutions. To understand the history of Krupp or Thyssen in Germany, we must know about universal banks, cartel policies, protective tariffs, and, eventually, co-determination. When we examine the history of Toyota in Japan, we learn about the transition from making textile machinery to making – under definitive pressure from a militarizing government in the 1930s – trucks and automobiles. When we study the history of Du Pont and IBM in the United States, we learn about antitrust policy, and about the government as a customer, an early market for sophisticated new products involving chemicals and computers.

In many of these examples, we see government policy influencing the structure of the markets in which large companies operate. This is true to some extent even for the manufacturing industries that form the focal core of this book and have always been the salient unit of analysis in the Chandlerian framework. It is applicable to a much greater degree for those highly regulated infrastructural industries such as banking, transportation, energy, and telecommunications, most of which do not form the focus of this book but loom extremely important historically as loci of big businesses.[4]

For the general subject of industry structure and the role of big business in economic growth, we now know one more enormously important fact that Smith, List, and thousands of other analysts and policy makers over the past 200 years did not know. That transcendent fact is that in the absence of very strong and specifically targeted government policy, *industry structure in every country is determined largely by basic industry conditions – that is, by the underlying technology and demand conditions of the industry.* It is for this reason that big business tends to arise only in certain industries, no matter what the country or national culture might be. In other industries (by far the majority, as measured in total employment), small and medium-sized businesses prevail.

---

[4] For almost all industrial countries, the scholarly literature on regulated industries is vast. For the United States, see Thomas K. McCraw, *Prophets of Regulation* (Cambridge, MA: Harvard University Press, 1984); and Richard H. K. Vietor, *Contrived Competition: Regulation and Deregulation in America* (Cambridge, MA: Harvard University Press, 1994), which focuses specifically on the way in which public policy can define market structures in which large companies must operate.

We know this fact primarily from the work of Alfred D. Chandler, Jr., and his followers. We know from Chandler's book *The Visible Hand* (1977) that in the history of the American economy, certain industries always hatched large enterprises: railroads, telephone and telegraph, steel, aluminum, copper, automobiles, heavy machinery, electrical equipment, chemicals, pulp and paper. In other industries, seldom if ever did large-scale firms evolve: boots and shoes, apparel, printing, auto repair, hotels, restaurants. (In a few of these industries, such as the last three just named, systems of franchising developed in the post–World War II years, resulting in a blend of big and small businesses: Midas Muffler in auto repair, Holiday Inn in hotels, McDonald's in food service.) The very same pattern generally prevails in other major market economies, as a host of studies have shown. The most noteworthy of these studies is Chandler's own *Scale and Scope* (1990), which covers the United Kingdom and Germany as well as the United States.

The fact that industry structure depends largely on underlying market conditions has immense and largely underappreciated implications for public policy. Knowledge of this fact should influence, far more than has actually been the case, the role governments take in promoting or discouraging large or small business. It means that most such attempts are severely delimited, and consequently that they should be undertaken only in extreme circumstances. To be more specific, for early industrializers antitrust laws and other antimonopoly measures seldom had much chance of stopping the growth of big business unless the government was prepared to take truly draconian measures that in turn would curtail national economic efficiency. The internal logic and dynamic of market forces proved far too strong even for such vigorous legislation as the Sherman Antitrust Act (the United States, 1890) to have had much effect in preventing the evolution of giant firms. Consequently, the principal result of such legislation proved to be their anticartel provisions. These measures sometimes had the ironic effect of promoting large mergers. That is, antitrust enforcement (and, more importantly, the threat of it) sometimes promoted bigness. It usually happened in the following manner: groups of companies, when denied the opportunity to collude in loose horizontal combinations, took the next step impelled by the logic of market pressures and merged into tight, horizontally integrated giant firms. This process was most conspicuous in the American economy during the years from about 1895 to 1915.

In other early industrializers such as the United Kingdom and Germany, monopoly policy took longer to catch up, and did not become parallel to the American pattern until the post–World War II period. (The British counterpart to the Sherman Act was passed in 1948, the relevant German laws in the 1950s.) Earlier, British law had been agnostic on the subject of monopolies and mergers, neither preventing nor encouraging cartel behavior. German law, in contrast to both American and British, was long hospitable to cartelization, a policy that was coordinated with protectionism and an intense drive for industrial efficiency. The way in which all this was done clashed with many tenets of classical and neoclassical economic theory, but it proved effective nonetheless. It also contained ample lessons for late industrializers.

For late industrializers, the predetermined nature of industry structure had somewhat more complicated results. Because first-mover advantages in the industries that gave birth to big business were so inordinately powerful, and because barriers to entry remained so overwhelming, the usual route late industrializers took toward the acquisition of large companies was through hospitality to American or European multinational firms. But this was partly a matter of government policy, as the case of Japan's hostility toward multinationals shows.

The alternative route to big business was substantially more difficult. Any late-developing industrializer that wished to become the *home base* of firms in an industry characterized by large enterprise would likely require a staged program of development involving protection of the home market, financial and other subvention of the industry, and – in those countries with a home market whose size fell below the minimal efficient scale of plants in such industries – export promotion. Many, many countries found it irresistibly tempting at least to try this kind of coordinated development program. Only a tiny number succeeded. The quintessential example is post–World War II Japan. In this book, however, it is the chapter on South Korea that best exemplifies both the process itself and the extraordinary difficulty of pulling it off.

For a third category of countries, the command economies, the authorities often went to almost desperate lengths to promote bigness, sometimes working against basic industry conditions which were conducive to small enterprises. The chapter in this book on the Soviet Union delineates the extreme measures and distortions that accompany and result from a relentless drive to bring big business to industries (not to mention collectivized agriculture) that more naturally gravitate toward small firms.

WHAT THE DATA TELL US ABOUT GOVERNMENT
POLICY AND ECONOMIC PERFORMANCE

Unlike Smith and List, we can draw on an enormous amount of know-ledge concerning the performance of different countries and companies over the last two centuries. We have huge data banks of statistics. We have thousands of volumes of historical and economic analysis. And we have somewhat better theory, although we still do not fully understand the process of economic growth or the role of big business in promoting or retarding it.

One of the things neither Smith nor List nor any other pre-1850 analyst of note anticipated was the phenomenal economic growth that was about to occur in certain countries. The records of the industrialized countries over the last 170 years exhibit far, far higher performance than Smith or List would ever have predicted. According to Angus Maddison's data, between 1820 and 1989 per capita GDP increased anywhere from eight times (United Kingdom) to twenty-six (Japan) among the four leading industrial powers (United Kingdom, United States, Germany, Japan).[5] This corresponds to compound annual growth rates of 1.27 percent (United Kingdom) to 1.83 percent (Japan). Compared to the extremely slow growth that prevailed for hundreds of years before this period – one estimate is that the average annual growth rate was no greater than 0.11 percent over the ten centuries since A.D. 700 – the recent growth record of these countries is astounding.[6]

While the industrialized countries exhibited strong economic perform-ance, many "developing" countries failed to develop at all, resulting in a vast gap between the industrialized countries on the one hand and the developing countries on the other. Real per capita income in the advanced industrialized countries today is *six times* the average for the rest of the world.[7] Many countries have not only failed to catch up with the industrialized nations, but have even fallen further behind. Consider Table 18.1, which shows per capita GDP (using purchasing power parity)

---

[5] Angus Maddison, *Dynamic Forces in Capitalist Development: A Long-Run Comparative View* (Oxford: Oxford University Press, 1991), pp. 6–7.

[6] This estimate comes from William J. Baumol, Sue Anne Batey Blackman, and Edward N. Wolff, *Productivity and American Leadership: The Long View* (Cambridge, MA: MIT Press, 1989), p. 12.

[7] Maddison, *Dynamic Forces*, p. 1.

Table 18.1. *Index of GDP per capita in 1990 (on the basis of PPP), a sample of 125 countries, United States = 100 (absolute amount in current dollars = $21,360)*

High-income economies	
United States	100.0
Japan	79.4
West Germany	76.3
France	71.2
UK	70.0
Italy	68.1
Middle-income economies	
Greece	34.4
South Korea	33.7
Brazil	22.4
Argentina	21.9
Thailand	21.6
Poland	21.2
Lower-income economies	
Indonesia	11.0
China	9.1
Pakistan	8.3
Nigeria	6.6
India	5.4
Ethiopia	1.5

Source: World Development Report 1992 (New York: World Bank, Oxford University Press, 1992), pp. 276–277.

for eighteen representative countries in 1990, with the United States as the index country at 100.

How are we to explain these wildly divergent numbers? Did the presence or absence of big business make a major difference? Was government policy the determining factor? Have the rich countries been blessed with superior factor endowments? Are they located in advantageous latitudes? Have they benefited from distinctively wise public policies? Have they simply had better luck?

These questions are very challenging, to put it mildly. As the economist

Robert Lucas had noted, the consequences for human welfare involved in questions like these are simply staggering: once one starts to think about them, it is hard to think about anything else.[8] But for many years most economists largely ignored such questions. It is only recently with the development of "new growth theory," spearheaded by scholars such as Robert Lucas, Paul Romer, and Robert Barro, that these questions have again become an active area of research for economists. Still, as I discuss later, the questions remain largely unanswered.

Although I take a very different approach from that of the new growth theorists, I hope to examine some of the same issues. In particular, I consider the countries included in this volume with regard to the following questions:

1. What has been the overall degree of importance of big business in the growth of the national economy?
2. What has been the degree of government intervention in industrial life? (I exclude, to the extent possible, macroeconomic interventions.)
3. How market-conforming has that intervention been, on the whole? That is, did public policy tend to work against market forces, or to accelerate them?
4. What has been the level of economic performance in each country?
5. What is the relationship, if any, between political democracy and economic growth?

In Table 18.2, I present schematically some very rough answers to these questions for each of the countries.

I emphasize that these answers are extremely tentative and in some cases arbitrary. The table itself is a lamentably crude and clumsy device. But it does facilitate a quick comparative analysis. The answers to each question show variety of experiences among countries, a summary of the things we now know that Adam Smith and Friedrich List did not.

However crude and tentative the characterizations in Table 18.2, several points stand out.

1. In almost every category, an extraordinary range of results is evident. The answer to nearly every question ranges from low for one or two countries, to medium for some, and to high for others. So the historical experience of these countries over the past hundred years has ranged all over the lot.

---

[8] Robert Lucas, "On the Mechanics of Economic Development," *Journal of Monetary Economics*, 22, no. 1, July 1988, pp. 2–42.

Table 18.2.

Country	Overall degree of importance of big business in industry	Degree of government intervention in industry		Degree of market-conformity in interventions		Degree of political democracy[a]		Level of economic performance[b]	
		Pre-WWII	Since WWII	Pre-WWII	Since WWII	Pre-WWII	Since WWII	Pre-WWII (1870–1950)	Since WWII (1950–1989)
Early industrializers									
United States	High	Med	Med	Med-high	Med	Very high	Very high	Very high	Low to 1973 med since
United Kingdom	Med	Low	Med	Low-med	Med	High	Very high	Low-med	Low to 1973 high since
Germany	Med-high	Med-high	Med	Med	High	Low	High	Med	High
France	Med	Med-high	Med-high	Low-med	Med	Med	High	Med	Med-high
Small European Developing countries	Med	Med-high	Med-high	Med	Med	Med	High	Med[c]	Med-high[c]
Late European industrializers									
Italy	Med	Med-high	Med	Med	Med	Low	High	Med	High
Spain	Low	Med-high	Med since 1970s	Low to 1970s	Med since 1970s	Low to 1970s	High since 1970s	Low	High before 1973 med since
Other late industrializers									
Japan	High	High	High	Med	Very high	Low	High	Med	Very high
South Korea	Very high	High	Very high	Low	Very high	Very low	Low-med	Very low	Very high
Argentina	Low	High	Med-high	Low-med	Med	Low-med	Med	Very high before 1913, low after	Very low
Command economies									
USSR	Very high	Very high	Very high	Very low	Very low to 1989	Very low	Very low to 1989	Very low to 1913 very high after	Med to 1973 very low since
Czechoslovakia	Med	Med	High to 1987	Med	Low to 1980s med since	Med	Low to 1980s med since	High	Low

Average Compound Rate of Growth

Country	1820–1870	1870–1913	1913–1950	Prewar	1950–1973	1973–1989	Postwar
USA	1.2	1.8	1.6	1.71	2.2	1.6	1.95
UK	1.2	1.0	0.8	0.91	2.5	1.9	2.25
Germany	0.7	1.6	0.7	1.18	5.0	1.9	3.73
France	0.8	1.3	1.1	1.21	4.0	1.9	3.14
Netherlands	0.9	1.0	1.1	1.05	3.4	1.3	2.54
Italy	0.4	1.3	0.8	1.07	5.0	2.6	4.02
Spain	0.6	1.4	0.2	0.85	5.1	1.8	3.75
Japan	0.1	1.4	0.9	1.17	8.0	3.0	5.95
South Korea			-0.2	-0.20	5.2	6.4	5.69
Argentina		1.9	0.7	1.35	2.1	-1.2	0.75
USSR		0.8	2.3	1.49	3.6	1.0	2.53
Czechoslovakia	0.6	1.4	1.4	1.40	3.1	1.3	2.36

Rank Order (Highest to Lowest)

Country	1820–1870	1870–1913	1913–1950	1950–1973	1973–1989
USA	1	2	2	11	8
UK	1	9	7	10	4
Germany	5	3	9	4	4
France	4	7	4	6	4
Netherlands	3	9	4	8	9
Italy	8	7	7	4	3
Spain	6	4	11	3	7
Japan	9	4	6	1	2
South Korea			12	2	1
Argentina		1	10	12	12
USSR		11	1	7	11
Czechoslovakia	6	4	3	9	10

[a] The post-WWII rankings correspond closely to those compiled by Freedom House in Raymond D. Gastil, *Freedom in the World 1991–1992.* (New York: Freedom House, 1992).

[b] Data from Angus Maddison, *Dynamic Forces in Capitalist Development: A Long-Run Comparative View* (New York: Oxford University Press, 1991). Prepared by Jeffrey Bernstein. The rate of economic growth is used as the measure of performance, and the countries are ranked relative to each other (not relative to all nations). Also, the rankings are relative within each time period; that is, "very high" performance in the pre-WWII period corresponds to a much lower rate of growth than "very high" in the post-war period.

[c] In this ranking, the Netherlands is used as a proxy for the small European developing countries.

2. *Levels* of government intervention mean virtually nothing in their effect on economic performance. Most of the rhetoric about governments being best that govern least is not borne out by the economic experience of these countries.

3. *Types* of intervention, especially in the category of market-conformity, mean much more than do levels. Only in the case of the Soviet Union were non–market-conforming interventions associated with high economic performance over a long period of time. And, as we know, that performance was associated with murderous political oppression. Also, the Soviet economy itself deteriorated in the 1970s and collapsed in the 1980s. By contrast, market-conforming developmental interventions in Japan and Korea in the postwar period seem to have helped produce wildly successful economic performances. What exactly are "market conforming" policies and interventions? Certainly they are *not* measures such as rent control and agricultural subsidies that arrest or retard market forces. Yet the distinction is sometimes quite subtle, contingent on the specific context. For example, protection and subsidy are usually non–market-conforming measures, but not always. A vivid example of the use of such tools to promote market forces appears in this book's chapter on South Korea. There, protection and subsidized financing accelerated the development of new industries. These measures were market-conforming in two senses. First, they channeled resources into industries with high growth potential. Second, they were proffered by the state only on a quid pro quo basis. They had to be earned by the corporate recipients through competitive performance with other Korean companies.

In the United States, much antitrust action has been market-conforming. In particular, the credible threat of prosecution has intensified competition, and thereby has enhanced the market process without interfering unduly with the operations of big business.[9] Similarly, the very intricate American system of securities regulation is a market-conforming policy that has undergirded and given legitimacy to the American capital markets, helping to make them the largest and most efficient in the world. Securities legislation since the 1930s has deliberately aimed at this result. Its architects eschewed punitive measures and emphasized disclosure and openness. The authorities chose cooperative approaches that enlisted the participants themselves in the enforcement of the laws. Legions of accountants,

---

[9] Of course, one can think of numerous exceptions to this statement, but I think it is an accurate generalization.

corporate executives, lawyers, and stock exchange officials are enmeshed in an elaborate system of reporting, all designed to maximize the smooth functioning of the securities laws and preserve legitimacy of the capital markets. Within the United States, this whole process has become quite difficult to see for what it actually is, because readers of the financial and popular press are fed a steady diet of sensational stories about fraud and other abuses. Yet the regulatory system on the whole is unquestionably market-conforming. Its goal is to make the capital markets work better by preserving their integrity. In the absence of faith in that integrity, the flow of investment funds from small and large investors would simply dry up. It often does just that in countries without such systems, and it sometimes did in the United States as well before the creation of this system.[10]

4. Therefore, on the whole, it is the timeliness, appropriateness to the industry concerned, degree of market conformity, and practicality of the intervention – in a word, the *wisdom* of each particular intervention – that has mattered for economic growth, regardless of political system, stage of national development, or any other variable.

Although it is not the focus of either this chapter or of the book as a whole, I might parenthetically note one other aspect of Table 18.2. That aspect is this: no direct, consistent relationship is observable between a high degree of political democracy on the one hand and high economic performance on the other. In some cases, the United States for example, the connection is there. Elsewhere, as with South Korea, it is not. And in the case of the rapid industrialization of the Soviet Union after 1920 and its good economic performance during World War II, the relationship seems inverse.

GOVERNMENT AND BIG BUSINESS IN THE UNITED STATES AND JAPAN

This book includes essays on each of the several countries by an expert on that country. The authors of each chapter say something about the relationship of public policy to big business. In a few cases, such as the treatments of the Soviet Union by Professor Andrei Yudanov and of Korea by Professor Alice H. Amsden, this relationship is the primary concern of the essay. I need add nothing here to their analyses.

For eight other countries in the study (the United Kingdom, France,

---

[10] On the design of the system of securities regulation, see McCraw, *Prophets of Regulation*, chapter 5.

Germany, Italy, Spain, Czechoslovakia, Argentina, and the group of small European developed countries), I have neither the space in this essay nor the requisite expertise to comment much beyond the coverage provided by each of the authors of the eight essays. I will say that most of these authors cannot in the nature of this project provide a fully satisfactory analysis of the role of government. Their assignment has been to focus on the growth and functions of big business itself, not of government. The project is entitled *Big Business and the Wealth of Nations*, not *The Role of the Relationship of Government to Big Business in the Wealth of Nations*.

The chapters by Chandler on the United States and Morikawa on Japan also pay little attention to public policy and its role in the rise of big business and in the economic performance of the country. In focusing so sharply on the morphology of big business, Chandler and Morikawa necessarily understate the importance of government in the economic experience of the United States and Japan, the two largest economies today. As a supplement to these two chapters and as a way of illustrating some of the ideas presented earlier, my remaining remarks concentrate on the relationship between government and big business in the United States and Japan.

The United States[11]

Broadly speaking, both federal and state governments were active in the economic sphere during the first half of the nineteenth century, passive in the second half, and then active again throughout the twentieth century. The legal order of the United States was shaped, over the course of the nineteenth century, so as to lubricate the operations of private enterprise. The federal government generally kept its hands off, leaving commercial law and regulation to the states. Decade by decade, the states relaxed requirements for the privilege of incorporation, far in advance of parallel developments in Europe. In nineteenth-century bankruptcy law, incentives were fashioned so as to favor debtors more than creditors, a reversal of common European practice. Contract law became highly refined in America, facilitating commerce among the disparate populations of strangers who came to America and pushed westward. Federal direct and excise taxes remained remarkably light, a policy made possible by ample revenues from public land sales and customs duties on European imports. State and

---

[11] These comments on the United States are adapted from my essay, "Government and the Economy," in *Reader's Encyclopedia of American History* (Boston: Houghton Mifflin, 1992), pp. 459–62.

local taxation was based much more on wealth, primarily real estate, than on commerce.

All of these circumstances added up to a situation uncommonly friendly to what Alexis de Tocqueville called (and the legal scholar Willard Hurst developed into a major historiographical theme) "the release of [economic] energy." Policy makers systematically designed a fertile setting for private entrepreneurship, a greenhouse for business. Within this hospitable setting, big business first appeared in the 1840s, in the form of railroads. That industry flowered in the 1850s, and by the 1870s it had developed an intricate coast-to-coast communication network that made possible the rise of big business in manufacturing and marketing as well. Once established, big business grew faster in the United States, and to larger size, than it did anywhere else in the world.

That phenomenon, which originated in the 1880s, remains true in the 1990s. The sheer size of the American market, then and now, is perhaps the most important single variable, and it may even be a necessary condition. But it is still only a part of the whole story. For at least a hundred years, there has been something about the Untied States – the size of the market, the culture, the legal system, the overall level of affluence – that has promoted big business in this country as in no other. It is still possible today for a firm to grow to very large size very fast, as the experiences of such companies as Microsoft and Compaq attest.

Largely because of the American nation's individualistic ideology, almost no government ownership of business enterprise developed at any time. This too was in distinct contrast to substantial public undertakings in other market economies in the twentieth century, not to mention socialist ones. Throughout American history, the total tax bite of all governmental units has typically been less than in comparable industrial countries such as Germany, France, and the United Kingdom. Today among the major industrialized nations, only the Japanese government takes as small a tax bite. Of the OECD countries, the bottom five in taxation as a percentage of GDP are Switzerland, Australia, Japan, Spain, and the United States.

Alone in the United States of all major market economies, the rise of big business preceded that of big government.[12] And when big business

---

[12] Some of the important implications of this different pattern in the United States as compared with other countries are explored in Alfred D. Chandler, Jr., "Government versus Business: An American Phenomenon," in John T. Dunlop, ed., *Business and Public Policy* (Boston: Harvard University Graduate School of Bushiness Administration, 1980), pp. 1–11; and Thomas K. McCraw, "Business and Government: The Origins of the Adversary Relationship," *California Management Review*, 26 (Winter 1984), pp. 33–52.

did come, no countervailing force resisted its initial impact. Thus, its arrival in the 1880s and the manifold problems it raised provoked a powerful public response that immediately moved out of the realm of administrative management (there being no European- and Japanese-style public bureaucracies to deal with it) and into the realm of partisan politics. In the closing years of the nineteenth century, the United States became the only major industrial power to enact systematic legislation designed to curb the power of large corporations. Congress passed the Interstate Commerce Act in 1887, the Sherman Antitrust Act in 1890, and the Federal Trade Commission and Clayton Acts in 1914. Although many other industrialized countries eventually adopted antimonopoly laws, mostly during the post–World War II period, the Sherman Act remains today probably the most stringent such law in the world.

American regulatory practice during the twentieth century was shaped by three outbursts of legislation: during the Progressive Era (1901–1914), the New Deal (1933–1938), and the later period of focused concern for safety, social justice, and environmental protection (1964–1971). Although several exceptions might be noted, this legislation and the administrative agencies it created generally were designed to restrain the power of business, and especially big business. An appropriate symbol is the giant statuary outside the Federal Trade Commission Building in Washington, D.C., which depicts powerful and unruly horses being held in check by human hands. Agencies with direct authority over business practices, such as the Securities and Exchange Commission, remain much stronger than their foreign counterparts. In the United States, then, regulatory behavior in the twentieth century has typically been restrictive. This is not to say that it has been necessarily antimarket, or non–market-conforming, as the preceding examples regarding antitrust and securities regulation illustrate. Public policy in America has often been restrictive, but sometimes indirectly promotional.

In many other countries, though by no means all, regulatory behavior has more often been directly promotional. In some ways this represents a reversal of nineteenth-century practice, when the United States was the most hospitable of all countries to the conduct of free-wheeling business enterprise. The more precise point is that during the twentieth century, the promotional activities of the American government have differed in kind from those elsewhere. In America, such activities have focused primarily on indirect legal frameworks such as antitrust and securities regulation, heavy developmental assistance through tax-supported funding of research to new industries (aviation, electronics, chemicals), plus macroeconomic demand management through fiscal policy.

In other countries, promotional measures often have focused on industrial planning, sectoral growth, and targeted key industries. Best exemplified in the post–World War II activities of agencies such as Britain's Neddie and Japan's MITI, industrial planning had many counterparts elsewhere: in French indicative planning of the 1950s and 1960s; in the corporatist interlocks of German banks, labor unions, and large firms; and in the breathtaking promotions of big business represented by the *chaebol* in South Korea. None of these practices, all of which fall under the rubric "industrial policy," has taken firm root in America, with the sole exception of what pejoratively is called Pentagon capitalism (R&D support of and huge purchases from defense industries).

In America, nearly all promotional management of the macroeconomy has been a post–New Deal phenomenon and until the 1980s was Keynesian in outlook. It looked not to individual firms, industries, or sectors – with the exceptions of agriculture and defense – but rather to aggregates of the major national income accounts: consumption, investment, and government spending. It operated primarily on the demand side, through management of fiscal policy. Its general aim was to stimulate consumption and counteract violent swings of the business cycle such as those that brought severe depressions in the 1890s and 1930s. The ideas that motivated it are complex, involving as they do such Keynesian arcana as equations designed to compute the "autonomous spending multiplier" as a tool for setting tax policy. At the height of Keynesian influence during the 1960s, some economists spoke with rash confidence of "fine tuning" the entire economy. Subsequent events, including the Vietnam War, the stagflation of the 1970s, and a revolution in macroeconomic theory, have brought an embarrassed silence on the subject of fine tuning.[13]

Yet the American government did explicitly accept the principle of a mixed economy, and with it responsibility for national economic well-being. This acceptance began formally with the Employment Act of 1946

---

[13] This "revolution" encompasses several different strands of thought, including the discrediting of the Phillips curve by Milton Friedman and Edmund Phelps, the incorporation of "rational expectations" into models by Robert Lucas, Thomas Sargent, and Neil Wallace, and the attacks on big government by public choice theorists such as James Buchanan and by supply siders such as Arthur Laffer.

and continued through all postwar presidencies, even that of Ronald
Reagan, who, though no Keynesian, oversaw the most dramatic peacetime expansion of the federal government debt in U.S. history.

Attitudes of the American government toward big business, meanwhile,
remained and are to this day of the love–hate variety. Despite continual
rhetoric about how many jobs are "created" by the small business sector, and how few by the Fortune 500 companies (which have indeed been
divesting jobs along with divisions since the 1970s), not many scholars
seriously question the importance of large firms to overall American industrial power and success. So the anomaly remains: the biggest companies
in the biggest economy in the world exist within a culture that enjoys
celebrating their failures. Yet, up to this point in American history, popular animosity has never become sufficiently strong to interfere with the
success of big business and its role in helping to create the wealth of
the nation.

What, exactly, has been that role, and how should we think about
it? The academic record in answering these questions has been dismal,
redeemed by only a few beacons of insight such as those of Chandler and
his school. For the most part, scholars have not yet figured out how to
measure the role of big business with any precision. Their failure derives
in large measure from a glaring lack of theoretical success in relating the
role of the large business corporation to microeconomic theory, and from
a more general failure in economic theory to connect microeconomic
phenomena with macroeconomic performance.

Japan

More than any other economy analyzed in this book, with the exception
of the Soviet and South Korean, that of Japan is characterized by numerous big businesses. In the years since 1960, the names of large Japanese
companies have gradually become familiar all over the world. In addition
to firms within the six major horizontal enterprise groups – Mitsubishi,
Mitsui, Sumitomo, Fuyo, Sanwa, and Dai-ichi Kangyo – new giants have
emerged to maturity in the last thirty years. Some are closely affiliated
with industrial groups (*keiretsu*), others loosely. Some are in automobiles, trucks, or motorcycles: Toyota, Nissan, Mazda, Subaru, Mitsubishi,
Honda, Suzuki, Kawasaki. Some are electronics giants: Sony, Hitachi,
Matsushita, NEC, Canon, Sanyo, Sharp, Ricoh. In heavy equipment, there
is Komatsu. In finance, there are the immense banks and insurance

companies affiliated with keiretsu, plus the four big securities firms. Many of these companies, particularly those in manufacturing, are involved in dense webs of relationships involving primary, secondary, and tertiary contractors of varying sizes and dependence on the core firm.

How did Japan develop these big businesses, and what was the role of government? The Japanese experience, like that of other major industrial powers, is not easily summarized. But as with the American story, the dependence of industry structure on basic demand and technological conditions is manifest. There are no small automobile firms in Japan or any other country, with the unimportant exception of custom shops and limited edition luxury manufacturers, such as Lamborghini in Italy. Conversely, there are no really large apparel companies in Japan or elsewhere, with the occasional exception of a firm such as Levi Strauss (the United States) or Benneton (Italy). In Japan as elsewhere, big businesses by and large are to be found in a small number of easily identifiable industry groups: utilities, primary metals, automobiles and other transportation machinery, electrical equipment, electronics, and chemicals (less prominent in Japan than in Germany and the United States).

The role of the Japanese state in the evolution of these large companies was fundamentally different from that of the American government. Whereas the American story, like the British, owes more to a Smithian market characterized by government restraint, the Japanese example is a classic Listian development, with deliberate promotion by the government of big businesses. This can be seen most clearly in MITI's coordinating efforts in industries such as steel. It is less clear in automobiles and electronics, but it is there nonetheless.

In most of the important manufacturing industries, the Japanese government has assiduously protected the home market, reserving it for Japanese manufacturers. Much more than any other major industrial power, Japan has restricted the activities of foreign multinational corporations. Far more thoroughly (and more intelligently) than any other power, it has planned the nation's industrial development in specific stages: primary manufacture first, then gradually up the value-added chain to more and more sophisticated products. And more than any other great industrial power, the Japanese government has relentlessly promoted exports of manufactured goods. Japanese consumers have paid a heavy price for this strategy, and they continue to do so down to the present time, as every index of purchasing power parity shows. Even in the era since 1985 of the very strong yen, Japanese consumers continue to pay more for some goods manufactured in Japan than foreigners pay for the same Japanese goods in markets thousands of miles from the great Japanese factories of Tokyo, Osaka, Nagoya, and Toyota City.

These are rather broad generalizations, to be sure, but only someone who is willing to ignore the actual history of the Japanese economy, or who wishes to analyze its development without reference to comparative frameworks, will maintain otherwise. The important point is precisely to see Japan and the other countries in comparative perspective.

In absolute terms, it would be incorrect to assert that the Japanese economic miracle was a child of the Ministry of International Trade and Industry, the Ministry of Finance, or the Japanese government as a whole. The miracle had many parents, and the great companies did the actual rearing of the child through infancy and adolescence to robust adulthood. But the government was always there, a powerful background presence. The government protected the home market. It provided administrative guidance through the difficult years of the 1950s and 1960s, when a shortage of capital necessitated a type of credit rationing. It engaged in ceaseless and usually informal cajoling. Much in the Korean pattern described in Amsden's chapter in this book, it permitted companies to do what they wished to do only if those companies demonstrated high competence. (Unlike the Korean government, the Japanese state and the central bank provided little direct financing.) In hundreds of ways both big and small, the elite economic ministries systematically shaped market-conforming incentive structures, all the while encouraging saving and investment in every conceivable way. At the same time, the Liberal Democratic Party and the ministerial bureaucrats held the country's social fabric together by essentially buying off powerful interest groups (farmers, small shopkeepers) whose votes might otherwise have impeded Japan's overall drive to industrial development.

Analytically, it is especially revealing to explore the issue of what the Japanese government did *not* do. Most strikingly, the Japanese government did not do what the governments of many other late-industrializing countries tried to do. For example, the Japanese government, despite the country's severe shortage of capital, explicitly rejected the option of heavy borrowing from abroad. This strategy was in fact followed in the post–World War II period by such countries as Brazil, Mexico, Poland, South Korea – and, in the pre–World War I era, by the United States. Similarly, the Japanese government consistently deterred foreign direct investment in Japan by American and European multinationals. The only important exceptions were high-tech companies such as IBM and Texas Instruments, and energy companies such as Caltex. And even these few companies were admitted on much harsher terms than they received almost anywhere else. Third, the Japanese government explicitly rejected a strategy of state-owned enterprise. This kind of development plan was followed with at least some success by some sophisticated industrializers such as France and Italy. But the Japanese rejected it as insufficiently market-conforming. In this brief list of negative counterfactuals, one can see clearly a sort of satellite photograph of the nature of the Japanese strategy.

But the real key to Japanese success must be viewed through the close-up lens. That perspective would focus on the structure of market-conforming competition among Japanese firms. It would look deep inside the companies themselves. If there is any one key to the Japanese economic miracle, it lies in the maintenance of a fever pitch of interfirm competition that by the 1990s had persisted without abatement into its fourth decade. This remarkable aspect of Japanese capitalism is insufficiently understood in the West, and its importance is often underestimated even by Japanese scholars. It is a competition that emphasizes market share as much as profit, if not more. It is a ceaseless, almost obsessive drive to uphold the status of the company – not for the purpose or with the aim of driving domestic competitors out of business, but of maintaining position and corporate honor, and of avoiding shame.

The phenomena of which I have written can be traced through many sources: Chalmers Johnson's influential history of MITI, Karel van Wolferen's savage critique of unlimited Japanese industrial expansion, James Fallows' books on Asian capitalism, Clyde Prestowitz's lament about how the United States gave away its markets. These Western "revisionists," who are typically political scientists and journalists, often give unbalanced or exaggerated accounts. Nevertheless, they have a better grasp of the essence of the story than do the orthodox economists whose works they have criticized, and whose version of the Japanese miracle looks more to Adam Smith than to Friedrich List.[14]

But the truest index of the nature of the miracle, and of Japanese capitalism as a whole, is to be found in the individual histories of the

[14] Chalmers Johnson, *MITI and the Japanese Miracle: The Growth of Industrial Policy, 1925–1975* (Stanford, CA: Stanford University Press, 1982); Karel von Wolferen, *The Enigma of Japanese Power* (New York: Alfred A. Knopf, 1989); James Fallows, *Looking at the Sun* (New York: Pantheon, 1994); Clyde Prestowitz, *Trading Places* (New York: Basic Books, 1988); Thomas K. McCraw, ed., *America versus Japan*, (Boston: Harvard Business School Press, 1986).

several hundred companies that led the miracle. Here the experiences of the companies as compared with their American and European counterparts is best understood. Here too the differential role of the national government appears most clearly. It is nearly always a background role. There is very little direct involvement. It is a story of the iron fist in the velvet glove. But without the government it is a story of Hamlet without the prince, or at the very least without the queen.

CONCLUSION: TOWARD A BETTER UNDERSTANDING

Though we have much more information about the nature of economic development and the roles of government and big business in this process than did Adam Smith or Friedrich List, there is still much that we do not know. Numerous first-rate economists, from Smith, List, and Marx to Joseph Schumpeter, Arthur Lewis, Albert Hirschman, Robert Solow, Robert Barro, and Paul Romer, have produced some insights, but their overall understanding of the process of economic development is quite limited.[15] One can similarly point to scholars of business administration, such as Alfred Chandler, Michael Porter, and Bruce Scott, whose work has shed some light on these questions.[16] But their analyses, too, provide only partial answers and leave much unexplained.

No doubt the enormity of the questions, coupled with the almost infinite number of variables, has hampered our ability to find definitive answers. One cannot deny that untangling the relations between government, big business, and the wealth of nations is a difficult task. Still,

---

[15] Two good survey articles on the relative ignorance surrounding the sources of economic growth are Robert M. Solow and Peter Temin, "Introduction: The Inputs for Growth," chapter 1 of The Cambridge Economic History of Europe, vol. 7, The Industrial Economies: Capital, Labor, and Enterprise, pt. 1, Britain, France, Germany, and Scandinavia, ed. Peter Mathias and M. M. Postan (Cambridge: Cambridge University Press, 1978); and Moses Abramovitz, "The Search for the Sources of Growth: Areas of Ignorance, Old and New," Journal of Economic History, 53 (June 1993), pp. 217–243.

[16] Alfred Chandler has produced an enormous amount of literature on the rise and development of big business; see Thomas K. McCraw, ed., The Essential Alfred Chandler: Essays toward a Historical Theory of Big Business (Boston: Harvard Business School Press, 1988), pp. 505–517 for a partial list. By virtue of its comparative nature, Scale and Scope: The Dynamics of Industrial Enterprise (Cambridge, MA: Harvard University Press, 1990) is probably the most relevant to this subject. Michael Porter's main work on the "competitiveness" of various nations is The Competitive Advantage of Nations (New York: Free Press, 1990), along with some subsequent country studies based on the general framework contained in this book. Bruce Scott's views are most succinctly summarized in Economic Strategy and Economic Performance, Harvard Business School Case #N9–792–086 (Boston, 1992).

I think that we can do better than we have done so far. Crucial to finding more satisfactory explanations is greater communication between academic disciplines, each of which has tended to occupy itself with only one aspect of these relations. Economists have focused on the wealth of nations, while giving little consideration to the roles of government or big business. In many growth models, the existence of firms and governments is essentially omitted. Business historians, by contrast, have focused on specific companies and industries, drawing conclusions from case studies that, while relevant to those examples, may not be generally applicable. Political scientists have tended to overestimate the role of government and underestimate that of businesses and individuals. In short, the balkanization of disciplines serves as a barrier to a better understanding of these issues. The rigid lines separating disciplines would no doubt be unfamiliar to Smith and List, who considered their subject to be the political economy, not just politics or economics in isolation. We still have much to learn, therefore, from the old masters.

19

Constructing big business:
The cultural concept of the firm

JEFFREY R. FEAR

INTRODUCTION

The chapters in this book allude to a number of potential research directions that can help clarify the effect of culture on the rise of big business
and the wealth of nations. Although culture can be maddeningly difficult
to define, culture's consequences have shaped national economic policies
and business strategies to a greater extent than has been generally acknowledged by present economic and business historiography. Alexander
Gerschenkron's stance on ideology reflects the difficulty of integrating
culture into a historical explanation. He posited a successively important
role to national ideologies for late developers, but failed to develop the
idea to any great extent. In his postscript, the impact of ideology fades
out of the analysis. Culture, much like Gerschenkron's argument about
ideology, has largely been ignored by economic historians, less "because
it is irrelevant but because it is intractable."

Culture does matter. The often protean quality of ideology or culture
should not frighten off attempts to identify its specific impact on big business and the wealth of nations. The organizing principle of this book, in
fact, orients itself around the development of big business in a national
context. As "imagined communities," nations and nationalism have significantly affected the global environment for business, yet they are *cultural*
constructs of the first order, built around some notion of a people united
by a common heritage. This apparently timeless heritage is an invented
tradition of rather recent vintage, which helps to legitimize the existence of
nation-states, one of the main organizing principles of our modern world.
Culture may be intractable (and the problem of national identity has
spawned a vast academic industry), but it cannot be made irrelevant.

But how does one develop an effective cultural explanation for business history? In this chapter, I would like to advocate an approach that establishes relatively firm intermediate analytical links between culture and economic practices so that an effective historical *explanation* can be generated. Culture is not outside business and economy, but permeates its practices. Instead of beginning with, and relying on, an ahistorical and worn-out notion of Confucianism or Protestantism or national character, we should take the opposite tack and take the appearance of corporate capitalism, its institutional framework, its practices and technologies as cultural *artifacts*, as expressions of deeply held values and assumptions, as meaningful symbols of cultural change itself. Practices express how values of a given society are operationalized meaningfully and legitimately.

Here I would like to focus on four intersecting areas of culture and business suggested by the preceding chapters. The scope of this commentary precludes a broader discussion. The first section focuses on the legitimacy of big business itself. The second discusses the cultural values underlying legitimate competitive or cooperative behavior. The third concentrates on the role of the family and big business. The last section combines the previous insights into a brief synthesis. Overall, I want to argue how one *conceives* of a firm as a *unified whole* is critical for understanding the construction of corporations and their organizational capabilities.

THE LEGITIMACY OF BIG BUSINESS

Culture helps to establish limits to the socially acceptable, between the legitimate and illegitimate, the natural and the unnatural, the abnormal and the normal, the good versus the bad. Widely shared values legitimize institutions. Yet the contributions in this volume hardly begin to discuss the legitimacy of big business itself. These large business organizations were widely despised and were at the center of some of the most heated controversies of their time. Making the transition into a brave new world of industrial society, which divorced people from the land, the "natural" source of wealth and power for millennia, was by no means immediately desirable. A few of the central issues surrounding these new forms of business were their "bigness," their anonymity, their market behavior (section 2), their threat of dividing family ownership from control (section 3), their bureaucracies, and their centralization of political power. How individual societies came to terms with these issues decisively affected the existence and trajectories of big business.

In the United States, the great entrepreneurs of business history were "robber barons." The rise of big trusts was probably the number one issue in American politics in the late nineteenth century. Whether John D. Rockefeller's Standard Oil grew large by ruthlessly undercutting competitors or through superior, long-run cost-effectiveness was not immediately clear. The very size of Standard Oil or U.S. Steel left economists of both classical and Marxist persuasion with one word in their vocabulary – monopoly. For very different reasons, monopoly was bad. Standard Oil was broken up. U.S. Steel lost market share in order to "win" its continuing existence. Other countries also had trouble with big business. The Italian Confederation of Industry expressly promoted and rescued small, family-run businesses in order to avoid the "threat" of big business. Enrico Mattei's goal of unifying Italy's energy enterprises into one large corporation was defeated, but on what grounds? How did Italians discuss this threat, in what terms? Was it the same as in the United States?

As in Spain and France, Italian big business apparently could only be promoted if it was deemed in the national interest. In spite of its liberal nineteenth-century policies, Spain did not develop a positive attitude toward business until after the "national and psychological crisis" of 1898. These big businesses, however, developed less in the name of private enterprise than in the name of state nationalism and autarky. The contrast between Japan and Spain is most instructive. Spanish import substitution policies were designed less to promote industry than to protect Spanish society from insidious outside influences. "Fired by a desire to catch up," Japan felt that it had to fundamentally transform itself, incorporating and adapting foreign ideas, in order to perpetuate its national culture. Spain hid behind "Chinese walls." Much like Italy, Argentina promoted small and medium-sized firms through government policies, but more in the interests of income redistribution to labor-intensive sectors after 1943. All of these countries were probably no less nationalistic, but they did have different notions about the role of business in society. At heart, it is a question of how the role of business and entrepreneurship in a national context is conceived. Italian, French, Argentinian, and Spanish versions of a national champions policy often seem to be characterized less by creative, adaptive entrepreneurship than by conservative entrepreneurship with the goal of preserving some vision of national culture.

How that national culture was defined made a difference in countries' respective strategies. Big business was considered a particular problem in all these countries because it destroyed family competencies, hindered job creation, and threatened to monopolize national markets and drive out smaller businesses. How public policy institutionalized these different value-laden reasonings regarding big business dramatically affected the regulatory environment in which big business operated.

Other countries had less of a problem with bigness; they were more than willing to bestow favors on large firms, especially national champions. The smaller European states and Czechoslovakia did not have the same problem of bigness because they did not conceive of their firms in terms of market concentration inside national markets precisely because they were small countries; the *nation* was not necessarily the proper framework for evaluating the legitimacy of size. The Škoda Works alone controlled most of the Czech engineering and armaments industry by 1935. The Soviet Union and South Korea positively basked in bigness. Magnitogorsk was less a successful enterprise than a symbol of Soviet industrial might and its arrival into modernity. In both South Korea and Japan, size was tolerated (at least by government bureaucrats who held power) in the name of international competition.

This bigness, however, still drew considerable heat from public opinion in both Japan and South Korea. The term *zaibatsu* or financial clique hardly rings of wholehearted endorsement. The zaibatsu engendered quite a bit of resentment from both the right and left symbolized by the assassinations of Yasuda and Mitsui executives in the 1920s and 1930s. Park Chung Hee thought that "mammoth" business was "indispensable" to economic growth as long as it remained "guided" by state goals. This guidance set limits to corporate behavior. Park's statement even intimates a note of defensiveness (a defensiveness that is especially obvious in the hypersensitive reaction to Amsden's article, "The Specter of Anglo-Saxonization Is Haunting South Korea"). What were those limits to corporate behavior. On what assumptions were the limits drawn? With the recent rise of political democracy, this cosy guidance has come under fire in Korean domestic politics. American notions of competition have recently penetrated into Korean politics, indicating a cross-cultural exchange of values perhaps much like Western Europe after 1945.

It would be of great interest to have cross-national studies comparing specific issues dealing with the legitimacy of large-scale corporations. Those public attitudes toward bigness, rightly or wrongly, shaped its legal status, its property relations, its ability to carry out business, and its very existence. Standard Oil no longer exists as a single corporation. Considerable legal contortions were also needed to view "societies" of investors or a massive corporation with hundreds of subsidiaries and employees as one judicial person. What makes an array of legally independent subsidiaries one corporation?

In Germany, for instance, the legal conception of a firm still betrays its modest origins as a "merchant." The supervisory board, the managing board, and the shareholder assembly are considered the agents (*Organ*) of the firm. Before the 1920s, agents of a firm had to be natural persons. This original conception of a firm (section 4) also reproduced a set of cultural assumptions unreflectively institutionalized into legal practice. However, the growth of large-scale *Konzerne*, multisubsidiary operations under the financial control of a person or corporation, called this conception of a firm into question. After 1919 when turnover taxes were introduced based on individual firms, the internal sales of Konzerne were suddenly external and subject to taxes, inadvertently accelerating the post–World War I merger movement. The ensuing mergers contradicted a general preference of German managers for corporate flexibility (especially needed for vertically integrated operations ranging from coal to machine engineering), multiplied the inherent problems involved with mergers in general, and worried a strongly skeptical public. German lawyers had to reinvent the legal concept of agent to include judicial persons and the legal notion of *one* corporation. The unintended consequences of the original, seemingly natural notion of a firm had tremendous implications for management strategy. The new business forms called into question the older legal definition of the firm, which in turn was difficult to alter without destroying the integrity of corporate law and the legitimacy of big business itself.

The debates surrounding the legitimacy of big business and the development of corporate law would provide a rich field of cultural comparisons, whose unconscious assumptions could be read from the terms of the debates. Americans debated the trust problem in terms of their overwhelming concentration levels, prices, economic power, labor policies, safety, and political power. In Italy, it seems to be an issue of size and family control; in Argentina, a problem of job creation. Each of these value judgments, if institutionalized in law and public policy, would have very different impacts on the growth of big business. These values informed the way legal sanctions and public policy were codified into practice, thus establishing the basic "rules of the game." In summary, one could establish intermediate links between cultural values, legal principles, state policies, and then their effects on business structures and growth.

LA MANIÈRE DE VOIR

Nowhere does a society's business climate, its *manière de voir*, become more manifest than in its consideration of legitimate market behavior, the social preference for competition or cooperation. The post-1945 era of remarkable growth is impossible to explain without noting the shift toward *intra*national market competition and *inter*national free trade. This sea change called into question the previous use of tariffs, informal trade barriers, cartels, and other varieties of collusion as legitimate means of market behavior (which is not to argue that they do not still exist). Of utmost importance for understanding the rise of business around the world would be a comparative intellectual history of the value of competition and/or cooperation in various countries over time.

Harm Schröter comes the closest to analyzing explicitly this *manière de voir*. A social preference for cooperative capitalism found its most salient indicator in the legitimacy of cartels, which found "general acceptance" in Europe and Japan before 1945. The French were at least the equals of the most notorious colluder, the Germans. The Czechs seem to be an extreme version of the European norm, allowing monopolies, cartels, and foreign direct investment with little inhibition on all fronts. They had a business culture of "bigness" and collusion, organizing the "tightest monopoly structure within the International Steel Cartel." Even the shoe industry exhibited a high degree of concentration. At the opposite pole in Europe, free-trade Britain still tolerated conventions and cartels, but did not effectively enforce them, rendering them less effective than elsewhere. Hard competition was viewed as something ungentlemanly or vulgar.

As elsewhere, the German rationale behind such agreements usually included avoiding ruinous competition, allocating resources and markets among industry firms, coordinating supply and demand, smoothing out price swings, promoting rationalization, regulating industrial activity through *private* self-governing associations, and promoting the national interest. Wengenroth argues that German business was permeated by a "vision of an organic economy." Schröter attributes the European resistance to competitive capitalism to the "tradition of how business was run." The hidden values of this "vision" or "tradition" need to be examined more closely, especially to explain the mysterious "mental changes" alluded to by Wengenroth after 1945.

In order for this mental "paradigm" to change, another subculture, another *generation* of managers had to come into power. Who did this generation consist of and what new sort of values did they hold? What was needed to retool and rethink notions of economy, competition, and regulation? Decartelization or "Americanization" (note the conflation of the concepts) was especially slow in coming to Switzerland. Despite Norway's progressive anticartel legislation, a single individual held up its enforcement after the war. Italy "forgot" to deal with antitrust legislation until recently. Would this paradigm shift have taken place without American military intervention and power? How much was due to American pressure for free trade? Wengenroth states that this change was "politically enforced." How much change was due to a voluntary imitation of a successful model? In the end, the "conviction that competition offers more advantages than cooperation, needed many years to mature in the heads of people." Why did it take so long to "mature"? What advantages did they accrue from cooperation? The link between cultural values and economics could be made quite explicit here. Such questions would be as much in the realm of intellectual–social history as economic–business history.

From a global perspective, the United States was the clear exception before 1945. It would be a far better *historical* question to ask why Americans could *not* accept cartels, rather than why Europeans or Japanese encouraged them. This refusal to sanction cartels helped to accelerate the development of oligopoly capitalism in the United States – only in retrospect the way of doing business in the late twentieth century.

A comparative discussion about the legitimacy of cartels would accomplish much to illuminate countries' cultural preferences that could generate intermediate links to the development of industry structure and business strategy, and then, to changes in economic performance and the concept of the firm. Schröter is tentative in establishing these connections. For instance, German or French cartels were particularly adept at organizing syndicates, which integrated marketing functions. These operations, however, were internalized into one corporate structure in America. The cartels thus tended to reinforce the engineering/technical perspective of French and German firms. While the high degree of vertical integration of German Konzerne, ranging from coal mining to machine engineering, is unthinkable without the existence of cartels, the technical innovations inside German steel firms should not be reduced to "market failure," as Wengenroth argues. The cartel quotas were less expressions of "delicate" technological balance of multiples or "defensive investment to protect [them]" than the result of fierce market competition translated by higgling and bargaining into formal cooperative structures. The cartel agreements were short-lived and continually renegotiated. Much like the Japanese, a considerable amount of competition still remained inside these cooperative arrangements. Despite admittedly less than efficient allocation of resources across the industry as a whole, Germans still managed to set up some of the premier and innovative steel firms in the world. The Anglo-Saxon notion that cartels *inevitably* lead to disastrous economic performance may need to be differentiated. It is quite paradoxical that in most fields of human endeavor – except modernist economics – cooperation is considered "good."

The cartel question is also a much more interesting question than just its degree of deviance from ideal free-market competition. There is much more at stake. First, two different cultural assumptions clashed in the cartel question. As Schröter hints, cartels were essentially *private* contracts. European governments tended to emphasize the legal right of freedom of association over an abstract freedom of competition that only brought "wild competition." The decision affirming the legitimacy of cartels in Germany was based on freedom of association. A similar conflict of legal principles and social values occurred in the United States, but was resolved in favor of freedom of competition. This stance also helped to legitimize collective labor movements in Europe and delegitimize them in the United States.

Ironically, prohibiting cartels promoted *state* regulation of economic life, a practice opposed determinately for at least a century by proponents of cooperative capitalism. The state had to create a regulatory agency to "intervene" in the market in order to preserve open competition. Germans were quite proud that the state did not have to intervene in their self-governing cartels. Somewhat counterintuitively, laissez-faire was practiced in this respect more by those countries who let industry collude than by those with open competition policies that had to be state-enforced. State regulation drove a potential wedge into the freedom of "the economy" and its self-government. A fundamental question about the boundaries between the public and the private was involved.

Second, how a country conceives of market power also illuminates cultural presuppositions. How does a country conceive of legitimate competition? What sort of market behavior is sanctioned or permitted? What are the "barriers to cooperation"? When is market power excessive and how should it be measured: absolute size, market share, the ability to raise prices, the degree of deviation from "perfect" competition, monopoly rents to innovations, concentrations of property, or other reasons? Germans, for instance, viewed cartels as a means of preventing excessive concentration of property – as a "dike" against American trustification – less as a problem of collusive market power. From the Germans' perspective, the "clumsy" Sherman Act promoted property, financial, and market concentration. Cartels *reduced* concentration levels and allowed smaller firms to stay in business. Firms where family ownership and control could remain more tightly entwined were valued more than abstract questions of allocative efficiency.

In the end, the Sherman Act was more an anticartel law than an antitrust act. In the words of the German historical economist, Gustav Schmoller, only "fanatics of individualism" would want to prohibit cartels. Thus, the cartel question involved value questions about power, size, family ownership, individualism, the right of association, and the boundaries between the public and the private.

In Japan, cooperation and competition were organized quite differently, so differently that it is still quite controversial to conclude if cooperation or competition predominates. According to Morikawa, the zaibatsu organized whole enterprise groups, each of whose enterprises competed vigorously with one another so that Japan developed a type of competitive managerial capitalism. Collusive agreements among zaibatsu could also be activated, but competition remained "dominant." The postwar period saw even greater "concerted effort" to ensure coordination of processes and information *within* the enterprise group but without dictating a single unified strategy. *Keiretsu* firms were not formally required to adhere to an overall strategy but were highly discouraged from deviating from it so as to avoid making other members "uncomfortable." The longstanding experience, knowledge, personnel relationships, quality controls, and trust built up within each group did create a barrier to entry to outsiders. The decisive question is whether these informal "biases," which tend to keep insiders inside and outsiders outside, should be considered cooperative or competitive. Clearly, one country's competition is another country's cooperation.

Furthermore, both Japanese and Korean "groups" simply do not fit the cooperative–competitive framework of understanding, which is built around the concept of a firm as an *individual* – one of the deep cultural assumptions of many Western countries. Again, what makes a firm, one firm? Why should that be the unit of analysis? Why not a network of firms?

Third, cartels and collusion also played a key role in most countries as a protectionist or development device. Germany's Imperial Court reasoned that cartels could not be outlawed even if they artificially raised prices because tariffs did the same. Tariffs were considered a legitimate part of a country's economic policy arsenal. In South Korea, the extremely exclusive nature of manufacturing and marketing networks, the tight symbiosis of state/*chaebol* relations, and finally, the high degree of family control in chaebol has led to a top-heavy, if not repressive, entrepreneurial framework, but has been deemed in the interests of national economic development.

In conclusion, these two issues of "competition abroad, cooperation at home" need to be connected with one another. Cooperation may have been a more appropriate strategy in states without wide-open markets – a product of the cultural *nationalism* of pre–World War II politics. All of the contributions indicate the crucial shift away from the virtues of national autarky after 1945. The international division of labor, comparative advantages, and specialization among countries is dependent on some degree of trust and cooperation across nations. Cooperation based on a relatively shared set of values needed first to be established in the postwar world so that larger markets could be generated – one of the basic preconditions of big business. The most striking aspect of the U.S. experience is the presence of a wide-open, relatively uncontested, and peaceful domestic market. In this sense, the United States and its antitrust policies should not necessarily be used as a model or yardstick for evaluating smaller countries in the midst of considerable military, political, and economic rivalries. It is not surprising, then, that nationalized cooperative capitalism slowly lost ground to competitive capitalism as the international trading regime expanded. This connection between international free trade and intranational competition illustrates once again the importance of understanding cultural nationalism for the rise of big business.

THE ROLE OF THE FAMILY

Wrapped up in questions about bigness and competitive behavior is the role of the family. Competition policies were often formulated to avoid problems with the separation of (family) ownership and control. However, the contributions in this book show little consensus on the (dys)functionality of family involvement in big business. Often the same author has contradictory conclusions. To make matters more confusing, the contributions slip between Alfred Chandler's *Visible Hand* and *Scale and*

Scope classifiction schemes. The implications of family values and family involvement in big business are thus not clearly articulated.

The impact of the family on big business was quite diverse. According to the chapters in this book, families seem to be largely dysfunctional in America, generally but not completely disadvantageous in Britain (especially in manufacturing), yet highly advantageous in Japan and South Korea (especially in manufacturing). It is not clear if families were helpful or harmful in Argentina, France, or Germany, although they obviously played a major role. Fridenson largely defines the reduction of French exceptionalism, its reliance on personal or family capitalism, as the substitution of family members by salaried entrepreneurs in strategic decision making. Ironically, state nationalization did the most to promote managerial capitalism. Still, Peugeot, Renault, and Michelin competed internationally as family firms with strong organizational capabilities for a long period of time. Against a long tradition of French historiography, Fridenson concludes that family firms were not a "real obstacle to growth." In Germany, single entrepreneurs and family members continued to play a decisive role in Europe's most successful *managerial* economy as late as 1969. According to one estimate, 60 of Germany's 150 largest firms were still owned by family members. Moreover, the role of family-run, export-oriented *Mittelstand* business in Germany is still legendary. In Argentina, European immigrants developed the family financial/commercial *Grupos*, who invested in a diverse array of unrelated areas much like the zaibatsu or chaebol. Argentinians, however, seemed to invest with a personal, financial portfolio strategy like the British more than the manufacturing competency strategy like the Japanese or Koreans.

In Italy, however, family business acted as the national paradigm, but at the cost of developing organizational capabilities for large firms. Italian family–big business relationships were "tormented." Like many German companies, large-scale Italian companies tended to be dominated by single men: Agnelli, Cini, Volpi, Pirelli, Falck, Olivetti, Gardini, Berlusconi. Although Montecatini was the "giant of the Italian economy," Guido Donegani managed it as an "entrepreneurial company" with little discussion about formal organization. Amatori attributes this torturous relationship to the notion of a company as a family domain.

At the other end of the spectrum, Japan's early success is wrapped up considerably, but not exclusively, in the history of zaibatsu, which were "diversified enterprise groups exclusively owned and controlled by a single wealthy family." Mary Rose has recently pointed out that their successes contradict much of Chandler's assessment about the dysfunctions of family control. Morikawa even warns the reader not to overestimate the development of managerial enterprises before World War II. By 1930, only a quarter of the largest 158 enterprises in Japan had filled more than half of their top management positions with salaried managers. As in Europe, the postwar period saw a greater separation of ownership and control; a new generation of managers imbued Japanese management with a new sense of "vitality." At the same time, Morikawa is quick to emphasize that top salaried managers inside zaibatsus "showed a marked tendency to give priority to the reinforcement of corporate organizational capabilities, rather than expanding the wealth of the owners." Although the zaibatsu were family-owned, they were not necessarily family-operated as at Mitsui or Sumitomo. These managers and families ensured that zaibatsu firms reinvested in their competitive advantages.

Morikawa thus concludes ambivalently about family involvement. On the one hand, the separation of ownership and control is good, but Japan's early success did not depend on it. On the other hand, managers tended to be oriented more toward the long-term, but families could be effective as well. In joint-stock companies with broadly held stock ownership – presumably where family ownership was more separate from management – the companies were less capable over the long-term because shareholders tended to maximize short-term shareholder value. Families thus helped to anchor a long-term commitment to reinvestment in their firms. Morikawa thus ends on an ambiguous but generally positive note about the role of the family.

South Korea's industrial businesses were also dominated by families. Amsden even concedes that the chaebol formally resembled Great Britain's personal capitalism because they remained family-owned and managed. Except for two chaebol (KIA, Samyang), forty-eight of fifty top managers of the top fifty chaebol were family relatives! Based on previous criticisms about family and personal capitalism, this arrangement would not bode well for future South Korean economic development.

There is, however, little consistent criteria for judging the impact of families in strategic decision making. This can be seen most dramatically by the example of the Pilkington family which served as a devastating critique of British personal capitalism in Chandler's *Scale and Scope*. Despite its rather quaint decision-making process, the new "family" hire did create the float glass technique that kept Pilkington on the postwar industrial map. Geoffrey Jones argues that Pilkington's being a family firm may have been an advantage because it did not have to answer to shareholders. In Italy, family firms ranged from myriad small businesses, to Martini and Rossi, to the relatively successful Fiat, Italy's largest company at present. In brief, eliminating family members from strategic decision making does not make an end to personal capitalism, nor does it necessarily make a successful company.

Amatori's tendency to set up family *versus* management is not the proper approach. Strong family involvement in La Rinascente did not stop it from developing "one of the best managerial groups in the world in the retailing industry" until the mid-1960s. The question is not "family versus management," but how does a family, manager, or a state run a large business? Is the family or CEO willing to delegate responsibility to others (even family members) and judge them on their performances? How does a family define its control over a company – by ownership, by absolute majority, or minority shareholding, by its ability to intervene at all points in the firms' operations (micromanaging), or by simply maintaining a voice in strategic decision making? Enrico Cuccia of the Italian merchant bank, Mediobanca, believed that only those who own could properly maintain control over management.

Morikawa's contribution points to one way out of the family versus big business dilemma. If founders did not instrumentalize or conceive of the company as a source of personal wealth – as a kind of personal treasure chest – they could be just as successful as managerial enterprises (section 4). They could anchor a company's reinvestment policies. The difference with the zaibatsu, chaebol, and the largest German enterprises (Konzerne) was the willingness of families to delegate control to professional management, judge them on their performance, and develop firm-specific capabilities. Amsden makes this point central to her interpretation. All of the major chaebol developed significant managerial capabilities particularly in planning and coordination functions. The firm did not seem to be conceived mainly as family domain, but as a bundle of technological and organizational capacities.

In effect, family capitalism is not necessarily personal capitalism.

We must go back to Alfred Chandler to clarify some terminology. Like Max Weber, Chandler sets up "ideal types" to describe differences in business organization. In the *Visible Hand*, Chandler's typology divides firms into three types: family enterprises, entrepreneurial or personal enterprises, and managerial enterprises. A family enterprise refers to a firm owned and controlled entirely by a family or single figure. An entrepreneurial or personal enterprise refers to a firm in which the owner still holds significant control, but hires a staff; the owner still personally manages the firm in varying degrees. The managerial enterprise refers to a firm in which salaried managers make the strategic investment decisions; the separation of control from ownership has been completed. These classifications shade over into explanations. In the *Visible Hand*, the weakness of entrepreneurial enterprises was that they failed to develop "systematic, impersonal techniques" of management and had slightly different goals than managerial enterprises. They "assured income rather than appreciation of assets," paid out dividends rather than reinvesting, and opted to retain personal control over the enterprise – thus inhibiting the competitive advantages of a managerial hierarchy. Obviously, the managerial enterprise did just the opposite.

The *Visible Hand* formulation actually describes very little. It asks whether the top person in the firm is a family member, an owner-manager with other salaried managers, or a salaried manager. In "ideal-type fashion," a whole slew of qualities followed from this shorthand. But, as can be seen by the previous discussion, these imputed set of qualities do *not* necessarily follow. Chandler confirms as much in *Scale and Scope* (1990). A strict version of the *Visible Hand* classification scheme broke down – less for Britain than for Germany.

After a decade-long study of the British and German experiences Chandler critically revised the old classification to incorporate the German case. The first redefinition, which corresponded to a family enterprise in the *Visible Hand*, is personal management, that is, a firm run without a broad administrative hierarchy. The second category encompasses entrepreneurial or family firms, those who run their firms *with* managerial hierarchies; they are not personally operated. *Note that personal management has been detached from entreprenurial or family firms.* Managerial enterprises refer to firms *with* hierarchies but without owner control.

In *Scale and Scope*, the critical factor is the size and competency of managerial staffs. The question is not whether the chief executive of the firm was a family member, entrepreneur, or manager, but whether the firm itself creates, maintains, and improves its organizational capabilities. Nevertheless, the old and the new classifications do slip into one another and are misleading. Therefore, it might be more useful to label the type or qualities of managerial hierarchies more forcefully rather than those top-level decision makers. We need to view and define organizations as a whole more effectively rather than as extensions of the owner or CEO.

The career of one German entrepreneur, August Thyssen, shows up the weaknesses in both classifications and clearly delineates how family capitalism is not personal capitalism. Thyssen founded his first firm in 1871. By 1882, he employed around 1,000 workers and had hired numerous salaried managers who essentially ran the company on a day-to-day basis. Thyssen built up one of the largest industrial complexes in Germany by 1913, roughly comparable to Krupp (the largest) in total assets. Although he maintained complete control over all strategic decision making (he rarely issued shares and was not beholden to banks), he relied on managers. At the time of his death in 1926, his Konzern employed roughly 50,000 employees and was widely considered to be the most efficient steel firm in Germany. Classifying the Thyssen-Konzern as a family enterprise (*Visible Hand*) cannot distinguish the changes in a 72-employee firm in 1872 with that of a 1,000-employee firm in 1882 with that of a 50,000-employee Konzern in 1925. Describing the Thyssen-Konzern as entrepreneurial (*Scale and Scope*) is somewhat better, but again leads to the problem of distinguishing the tremendous changes in industrial organization between 1882 and 1925 in an effective manner. In fact, Thyssen constructed one of the more sophisticated management systems among German firms, complete with an independent auditing and organizational planning office. It was a managerial enterprise with an entrepreneur at its head.

Personal capitalism is thus less the result of entrepreneurial or family involvement in management than the *reluctance to invest in firm-specific capabilities*. The basic problem with this "naive" classification scheme (in Dosi's term) is its tendency to focus on the person responsible for the entrepreneurial moment (Is there just one?) and not the structure of the firm, its scale or scope, its decision-making process, its management system or culture, or its organizational capabilities. These should not be reduced to one person, however important that person may be. Typical problems may arise though. For family-run enterprises, the typical problem would be one of succession as shown by Olivetti, Brustio/Borletti, Fiat, or Thyssen. For state-run enterprises, it would be the politicized nature of change or innovation. But we should not be so quick to attribute a set of business qualities to entrepreneurs, families, CEOs, various trainings, nationalities, the state, or managerial hierarchies. We need to concentrate on the development of a firm's internal manner of coordination and cooperation – not just the top people, who are at best rough proxies and at worst red herrings.

The question is whether a family can disavow personalized control for systematic control and develop firm-based competencies that allow the enterprise to grow and sustain itself over time – beyond family time. What makes a family able to grow and manage a successful large-scale firm? Which values work and which ones do not? A major but not exclusive component of organizational capabilities is the development of a managerial hierarchy, which should not be reduced to the bare bones of organizational design (U-form, M-form, or whatever). Management does not automatically create coherent policies either. The state-controlled ENI at the beginning of the 1960s, the state-owned Renault and family-controlled Peugeot since the 1980s, the development of a "cohesive, competent, aggressive managerial team (which was familiar with American industrial practices)" for ILVA after World War II, and the continuing success of Japanese alliance capitalism – each of these examples illustrates that under certain conditions, state and family-run firms can compete, *if* their organizational capabilities are effective. We need to define more precisely the manner in which people work together inside a business firm.

One critical way to link a cultural approach with business history is to pay close attention to how families, managers, or nations talk about their firms. In what terms? Under what assumptions should the "management system" of a firm work? What is the concept of the firm? If the family or national culture conceives of a firm as a personal domain, this could effectively hinder its long-term growth. Here a cultural approach to big business could be most insightful.

THE CONCEPT OF THE FIRM

The development of organizational capabilities is deeply dependent on the familiar (pun intended) or dominant national idea of the business firm itself. The critical question is how the enterprise (or enterprise system) is conceived as a *unified whole*. What is the concept of the corporation? This concept of the firm refers to an unreflected, seemingly "natural" preunderstanding of what a business is, what it should do, and who it should work for. How national cultures "think" what a firm "is" affects its strategy, structure, and managerial practices; how management perceives its mission and possibilities; what qualities it chooses to develop in its organization (possibly at the expense of others); how it analyzes corporate performance; and how it chooses to develop a firm's organizational capabilities.

The contributions reflect a considerable diversity in the national concept of the corporation. In Britain, the firm tends to be conceived as a profit-maximizing agent designed to return the highest level of commercial profits to shareholders. Jones goes so far as to describe British and American firms after the 1970s as "commodities that were bought and sold." Not surprisingly, they were run by accountants and marketing managers. For Chandler, the American firm until the 1980s has been conceived as a bundle of general managerial capabilities, binding together manufacturing, marketing, and management for investment purposes. Wengenroth's article certainly testifies to the engineering orientation of German business culture that has maintained itself in spite of a 100-year Americanization process. Not until the 1980s was a nonchemist appointed to the managing board of one of the Big Three chemical compaines. While "British managers think industry is about making money," Germans feel that firms are "about making three-dimensional artefacts." German firms have been conceived as a type of engineer that makes good products. In France, firms have been either intimate family enterprises or huge bureaucracies patterned on the French royal state. French managers were administrative "generalists" who slipped easily between state and business spheres. In Italy, a national culture of "familism" viewed companies as "private domains" governed by a "political culture of smallness." Even those firms run by salaried managers were still run by strong autocratic, paternal figures on a "limited suffrage" model. Spanish firms conceived their firms less as profit-making enterprises than as nationalized bulwarks against internationalism. Not surprisingly, the military suffused its influence throughout Spanish business and prevented a managerial culture from developing until the early 1960s.

Managerial models differed significantly across these countries. In England, managers seem to be cut from a merchant or financier capitalist cloth; in the United States from that of a general manager with an eye toward return on investment; in France, from that of an administrative generalist; in Germany, from that of a production engineer; in Italy, from that of a *paterfamilias*; and in Spain, from that of a military/civil engineer.

In the former Czechoslovakia and USSR, firms under Communist planning were conceived as heavy industrial output factories. The control over the means of production reduced enterprises to modes of production, that is production sites. Marketing became "detached" from enterprises and controlled through syndicates. After 1931/1932, Soviet enterprises could no longer manage their own wage and salary levels. As such they had a "role of user, but not creator, of core producer capacities." Communist

planning tended to reinforce an already strong emphasis on heavy industrial engineering so that a kind of perverted Gerschenkronian approach
toward industrialization arose. Service sector businesses were ranked as
"nonproductive" – the term itself speaks volumes. In these planned economies, a manager was either a state planner or a production engineer.
Even the bureaucratic planning agencies organized themselves according
to a distinct conception of a firm as a producer of discreet things – not
as a united system of technological, personnel, financial, and marketing
operations.

Yudanov also makes an important point that firms cannot be viewed
in isolation, but within a "natural community of companies" that provide
flexibility and choice. Nowhere else in the world are firms conceived of
so explicitly as enterprise communities as in Japanese and South Korean
"relational capitalism." The relatively new idea of clustering in Western
management literature only begins to take this into consideration. The
groups are conceived of as concentric and hierarchical relations of familiarity. Note the metaphors for two types of enterprise groups: brethren and
parent–child. The parent company's relationship to its subsidiary could
be conceived of as a guardian or teacher – for quality control, technical
guidance, and a type of guarantor for bank loans. Group managers feel
personally close to other "brethren" group managers – a sense reinforced
by personnel policies, information sharing, confidence in the group's skills,
and product quality, experience, and knowledge. The groups also tend to
draw from the same universities so that fraternal (and there have been
very few female) connections are systematically promoted. This relational
capitalism extends to enterprises' organizational capabilities, which are
expressly conceived of as both physical facilities and human skills in practice. These human skills are considered neither as the "soft" side of business as in the United States (a very gendered conception of management
in itself) nor as "human resources" or "human capital," whose phrasing
implies the instrumentalization of humans *as* resources, capital, or
functions, not humans as active agents endowed with skill, intellect, and
knowledge. Paradoxically, the East Asian "imitator" countries emphasize
human skill creativity more than Western "inventive," "creative" countries
in this regard.

To be perfectly clear about the role of culture, I am not arguing that
these cultural values single-handedly caused zaibatsu/chaebol corporate
forms – the late development thesis based on unrelated risk diversification
strategy seems to be a much more convincing explanation – but rather

helped to *construct* them as a "way of running a business," which, once proved successful and legitimate, generated their own momentum as model business formations.

What difference do these national images of management make? These models are reproduced in corporate practices, creating a national business culture based on certain implicit assumptions and not others. Charles Hampden-Turner and Alfons Trompenaars set up a series of "dilemmas" to get at these cultural presuppositions. One such question asked whether a company was more a system designed to perform functions and tasks in an efficient way, or more a group of people working together whose social relations with other people outside and inside the organization made those functions work. Seventy-four percent of United States managers chose the first preference; only 35 percent of French and 29 percent of Japanese managers chose the first preference. Another dilemma asked (in somewhat loaded fashion) whether the "only real goal" of a company is making a profit or whether a company has other goals, besides making a profit, directed to other stakeholders such as employees or customers. Again the Anglo-Saxon countries were most likely to agree with the first preference, while the French and Japanese were least likely to agree with the first. Moreover, the consistent ranking of France among the Pacific Rim countries along this spectrum of dilemmas indicates that something other than "Eastern" or "Western" ideas is at stake here.

The concept of a firm subtly biases business operations toward certain organizational capabilities and strategic choices. If a company's business is to make profits rather than make three-dimensional things, or be responsible to its employees or family, or its nation's interests, then that company would tend to downplay those other options in practice although all may be desirable in principle.

The concept of a firm affects how the company is coordinated as a *whole*. Any industrial business firm has to coordinate – *account for* – at least four distinct areas: production, finance, sales, and personnel. None of these areas can be said to have internally consistent objectives and the goals of one can contradict those of another. Engineers may want a production process that cannot be financed or manufacture a product that marketing managers will not sell. People may not want to work for a company. Management may want to reinvest but shareholders may want higher dividends. By its very nature, then, a business firm is a contested terrain that can be "rationalized, economized, maximized, optimized" in any number of directions. Different strategies can be proposed that all have the same goal of earning profits. Although all firms may want to maximize profits, the more interesting question is *how* they should go about earning them. Formulating a profit-maximizing strategy is the question, not the answer. Moreover, the different rationales for the various operational areas need to be coordinated with one another into a more or less coherent overall policy. Trade-offs are in some way inevitable. Since it is extremely difficult to "optimize" each of these areas simultaneously, corporate or national cultures bias the strategic direction of companies. One of the best indicators for the dominant strategy and concept of the corporation is the type of actors in a position of leadership. Are they engineers, salespersons, accountants, financial officers, lawyers, or personnel managers? Each would also tend to draw on a different educational and training experience to make decisions.

If one views the firm more as a forum of contesting rationales, that is, of legitimate but possibly conflicting reasons and goals, then these (cultural) preferences based on national, corporate, historical, and personal experience inform and shape strategic decisions. It is particularly in the realm of legitimate trade-offs, informational ambiguity, uncertain choices – those gray areas of decision making that bet on the future yet draw on past experience – that culture, values, models, mentalities, preferences, and the implicit concept of the firm matter most. The disputes over strategy should not just be seen as disruptive forces blocking the "one best way" or even as a type of Machiavellian office politics, but as a legitimate part of the decision-making process of a corporation that creates a companywide policy from diverse perspectives. Those discussions are usually reasoned arguments backed up by *informed* practices. Those debates are also shaped by generalized models of management or corporate behavior that reflects prevalent mental and perception patterns designed to simplify a highly complicated environment and interpret it, signify the most important aspects, and create meaning. These mental models of the firm and its management help to shape corporate development and decision making; but they can also create potential blindspots. Hence it would be of great interest to analyze the implicit metaphors, terms, ideologies, and models used by families, states, and managers to describe firms and corporations across cultures.

But to make culture work as an explanation, one must go beyond metaphors – after all both Italian and Japanese companies employ family-oriented metaphors for their businesses. The dominant metaphor acts more as a signpost than an explanation.

The concept of a firm should be used as some free-floating cultural metaphor, but lies embedded in companies' practices which *construct* how managers view their business. This formal/informal decision-making process and information system can be seen as a fifth business area that synthesizes the other four areas of business into some sort of coherent corporate policy that coordinates, monitors, assesses, and controls the performance of the company. This fifth area is central to managing complexity. It does little good to have good production, financing, sales, and personnel operations if they work at cross-purposes and coordination suffers. An effective unified organization is needed that *makes sense* of the business firm as a whole.

The accounting and information system is the single most important representation of a business firm as a unified whole. The accounting and information system figuratively tells a "story" about the progress and condition of the firm. These accounts form the basis for decisions or at least reasoned arguments based on them. The accounting and information system helps to inform action, transform decision making, and create organizational reality.

But what types of information are taken most seriously in decision making? Any number of criteria can be used to evaluate the success of a complex organization, but some are more compelling than others in given business cultures. Japanese managers of large corporations tend to define performance in terms of a ruthless drive for market share, while American managers tend to define performance in terms of share price, dividends, and their fiduciary responsibility to shareholders. How do participants, shareholders, managers, bureaucrats, or employees across cultures evaluate their company and its managerial performance? What is "performance"? How is performance measured? Is it defined in the name of the family, dividends to shareholders, long-term growth, profitability, sales, market share, production costs, the level of technological learning, the ability of a firm to provide steady employment, or its ability to represent the country abroad as a national champion? Which performance standards are given priority by a given corporate culture or national culture? What version of profitability or performance is of utmost importance? Does the firm emphasize profit margins, production costs, return on sales, earnings per share, return on assets, return on investment, cash flow ratios, market share?

These representations of company performance become institutionalized in the standard operating procedures and the culture of the firm itself.

Most tellingly, Jones points out that British firms focused on financing the commercial activity of the firm and tended to define success as a return on sales – not net assets or investment. British companies ranked among the most profitable in Europe as late as the 1980s, but continued to lose competitive advantage in terms of market share. In the United States, return on investment (ROI) became the standard, but this too has recently come under fire. In Germany, making highly engineered products by German craftsmanship with an emphasis on manufacturing efficiency was strongly emphasized; profits should eventually follow. A German company was considered as something more than its book value; managers valued the long-term stability of their companies. In Spain, they were judged as public enterprises to "address national problems and not to expand through the world" (i.e., not very "business-oriented" at all). In the Soviet Union and Czechoslovakia after 1948, producer goods industries' output was both a sign and symbol of success; maximum output instead of optimum output became the main criteria. Quantitative targets had to be matched or surpassed based on mechanical, physical quantities. Prices became a bureaucratic transfer procedure. While Soviet firms were certainly scale-oriented, they were not cost- or price-oriented – in either economic or human terms.

Japanese zaibatsu/keiretsu developed a notion of performance and control built extensively, but not exclusively, around human skills and personnel practices. This type of policy is no less systematic but based more on formalized behavior rather than presumably universal statistical or financial procedures. The Japanese placed real stress on market share and international cost and quality competitiveness. The Korean state also measured Korean firms less on their absolute profitability than on progress in their technological and organizational learning capacity, even after setbacks. Export targets were set, reinforcing an orientation toward international market share.

I would argue that the hierarchy of relevant information and measures is intimately tied to the dominant notion of the firm in a given culture. A loosely coupled link between the dominant conception of a company, its strategies, the key types of players involved in strategy formulation, and its information system can be forged. One critical area of research could focus on particular "formative periods" for a nation's big business, in which the patterns of business culture, practices, and institutions were established. For instance, the formative period for British capitalism seems to be situated in the 1850s to 1890s of merchant capitalism. The "mentality and rationale of German management for most of this century has to depart from the formative years in the late 19th century." These formative periods set countries' big businesses on trajectories or path dependencies that were not easily overcome. These formative periods also tended to crystallize a business culture that was not easily changed, for "this is how we do business here."

CONCLUSION

Culture does not lie outside of economy and business, but permeates it. Cultural values are embedded in symbolic meaningful systems and institutionalized in business practices. How do managers make sense of their activities and their world? What are legitimate business practices and what are not? In this respect, it is not a question of rationality or irrationality, but the reasons and meanings given to actions. Culture is nonrational in this respect, but rather based on *conventions* that are more or less sensible and meaningful. A good cultural explanation does not necessarily exclude other motivations or lines of reasoning. Human actions are often mediated by a mixture of economic scarcity, cultural values, and power relations, but they are always mediated by culture, institutions, conventions, practices, symbols, values, meanings, and, above all, by language. All economic and cultural practices depend somehow on symbolic representations of some sort that make sense to the people involved.

There are two ways to establish the intermediate connections between culture and business practice. One way, as practiced by Geert Hofstede, is to isolate dimensions of culture (such as power distance, collectivism versus individualism, femininity versus masculinity, and uncertainty avoidance, long-term versus short-term orientation), and then show how they correlate or cluster along various lines with one another. However, it is often difficult to show how these dimensions translate into historical explanations rather than descriptions. We can easily agree that East Asian cultures are more group-oriented and Anglo-Saxon cultures are more individualistic, but how does this observation help as an explanation for industry/business systems and economic performance? How do those values affect the building and the success of a steel or shoe company in 1890, 1920, 1960, or 1990? Those general values, as true as they may be, have to confront considerably different economic and political conditions so that they either remain unchanged but have dramatically different effects, or are heavily modified themselves through time and situation.

Another way is to work outward by a close and comparative reading of *how* the house of capitalism was built with an eye toward the values embedded in regulatory and business practices themselves, and then move outward to establish firm intermediate links between culture and economy. Listening closely to the type of language used to describe corporations and managerial decision making, the criteria used to form strategy, the type of information reaching those in power, and how managers conceive of their objectives are all crucial indicators of culture in practice. These institutionalized practices simultaneously express unconscious values and shape decisions. This approach, moreover, can capture the dynamic interaction between culture and economy. Values can be reshaped by calculative reasoning; calculative reasoning can be affected by subtle or unconscious cultural conventions. A systematic and historical study of the concept of the firm and managerial decision making would do much to pinpoint how cultural values affected the growth of big business around the world.

In conclusion, if the notion of organizational capabilities will grow in theoretical stature, then it must also integrate managerial values and interpersonal communication, that is, the structure and creation of the means of coordination, cooperation, control, and trust inside business firms. *How* that coordination through communication and knowledge has been carried out inside the "black box" of corporations over the past 100 years and across national cultures should be highlighted by more research. Such questions may be particularly important for understanding large-scale service-sector industries. While there may be a "logic" to a particular technological innovation in terms of capital investment and marketing apparatus, if knowledge and service are the product, then culture may become even more of an issue.

Bibliographic Essay

All discussions regarding various countries derive from the country chapters presented in this volume. Gerschenkron's use of culture is discussed in Alexander Gerschenkron, *Economic Backwardness in Historical Perspective* (Cambridge, Mass.: Belknap Press of Harvard University Press, 1962). David S. Landes, "Does It Pay to be Late?" in *Economy and Society: European Industrialisation and Its Social Consequences*, ed. Colin Holmes and Alan Booth (Leicester: Leicester University Press, 1991), 3–23. Richard Sylla and Gianni Toniolo (eds.), *Patterns of European Industrialization: The Nineteenth Century* (London: Routledge, 1991), especially the introduction and William Parker's contribution.

Classic works that deal explicitly with culture as an explanation include David S. Landes, *The Unbound Prometheus: Technological Change and Industrial Development in Western Europe from 1750 to the Present* (Cambridge: Cambridge University Press, 1969); Thomas C. Cochran, *Frontiers of Change: Early Industrialism in America* (Oxford: Oxford University Press, 1981); Sidney M. Greenfield, Arnold Strickon, and Robert T. Aubey (eds.), *Entrepreneurs in Cultural Context* (Albuquerque: University of New Mexico Press, 1979). Jonathan Brown and Mary B. Rose (eds.), *Entrepreneurship, Networks and Modern Business* (Manchester: Manchester University Press, 1993). For an example of the dysfunctional implications of following an inappropriate model of industrialization, see Stephen H. Haber, *Industry and Underdevelopment: The Industrialization of Mexico, 1890–1940* (Stanford: Stanford University Press, 1989). For overviews, arguments, and bibliographies on the relationship between Confucianism and economic growth, see Anis Chowdhury and Iyanatul Islam, *The Newly Industrialising Economies of East Asia* (London: Routledge, 1993); Ezra F. Vogel, *The Four Little Dragons: The Spread of Industrialization in East Asia* (Cambridge, Mass.: Harvard University Press, 1991); Michio Morishima, *Why Has Japan "Succeeded"?: Western Technology and the Japanese Ethos* (Cambridge: Cambridge University Press, 1982); Kim Kyong-Dong, "Confucianism and Capitalist Development in East Asia," in *Capitalism and Development*, ed. Leslie Sklair (London: Routledge, 1994), 87–106.

Not surprisingly, culture's consequences has found its most heated point of debate to be British economic decline: Martin J. Wiener, *English Culture and the Decline of the Industrial Spirit, 1850–1980* (Cambridge: Cambridge University Press, 1981), and Correlli Barnett, *The Audit of War: The Illusion and Reality of Britain As a Great Nation* (London: Macmillan, 1986). Bruce Collins and Keith Robbins (eds.), *British Culture and Economic Decline* (New York: St. Martin's Press, 1990), especially the article by Harold James which compares the German case. Robert R. Locke, "Education and Entrepreneurship: An Historian's View," in *Entrepreneurship, Networks and Modern Business*, ed. Jonathan Brown and Mary B. Rose (Manchester: Manchester University Press, 1993), 55–75 and the rebuttal by W. D. Rubinstein, *Capitalism, Culture and Decline in Britain 1750–1990* (London: Routledge, 1993), for an overview and critique of the debate.

Works that deal explicitly with the classic problem of explanation in general and culture in economic history are Donald McCloskey, *If You're*

So Smart: The Narrative of Economic Expertise (Chicago: University of Chicago Press, 1990), and *Knowledge and Persuasion in Economics* (Cambridge: Cambridge University Press, 1994). See as well the lucid discussion in Carlo Cipolla, *Between Two Cultures: An Introduction to Economic History* (New York: W.W. Norton Company, 1991). Angus Maddison, "Explaining the Economic Performance of Nations 1820–1989," in *Convergence of Productivity: Cross-National Studies and Historical Evidence*, ed. William J. Baumol, Richard R. Nelson, Edward N. Woff (New York: Oxford University Press, 1994), 20–61. Joseph Melling and Jonathan Barry (eds.), *Culture in History: Production, Consumption and Values in Historical Perspective* (Exeter: University of Exeter Press, 1992). John A. James and Mark Thomas (eds.), *Capitalism in Context: Essays on Economic Development and Cultural Change* (Chicago: University of Chicago Press, 1994). Culture's impact has been neatly discussed for technological change using a "social systems" of "social construction" approach: for example see Wiebe E. Bijker, Thomas P. Hughes, and Trevor Pinch (eds.), *The Social Construction of Technological Systems: New Directions in the Sociology and History of Technology* (Cambridge, Mass.: MIT Press, 1987). For a theoretical approach that seeks to combine new cultural and language theory with rational choice theory in historical explanations, see William H. Sewell, Jr., "Toward a Post-Materialist Rhetoric for Labor History," in *Rethinking Labor History*, ed. Lenard R. Berlanstein (Urbana: University of Illinois Press, 1993), 15–38. Sewell casts his net more widely than the article's title indicates.

For culture as it relates to organizational and business behavior, see Geert Hofstede, *Cultures and Organizations: Software of the Mind* (London: McGraw-Hill, 1991). Edgar Schein, *Organizational Culture and Leadership* (San Francisco: Jossey-Bass, 1992), which supplies a list of different definitions of culture and an extensive bibliography. Terri Morrison, Wayne A. Conaway, and George A. Borden, *Kiss, Bow, or Shake Hands: How to Do Business in Sixty Countries* (Holbrook, Mass.: Bob Adams, Inc., 1994). John P. Kotter and James L. Heskett, *Corporate Culture and Performance* (New York: The Free Press, 1992). Charles Hampden-Turner and Alfons Trompenaars, *The Seven Cultures of Capitalism: Value Systems for Creating Wealth in the United States, Japan, Germany, France, Britain, Sweden, and the Netherlands* (New York: Doubleday, 1993). Theodore D. Weinshall (ed.), *Societal Culture and Management* (Berlin: W. de Gruyter, 1993). Tomoko Hamada, *American Enterprise in Japan* (Albany, N.Y.: State University of New York Press, 1991). Günter Dlugos and Klaus Weiermair (eds.), *Management under Differing Value Systems: Political, Social and Economical Perspectives in a Changing World* (Berlin: W. de Gruyter, 1981). David Granick, *The European Executive* (Garden City, N.Y.: Doubleday, 1962). Sidney M. Greenfield and Arnold Strickon (eds.), *Entrepreneurship and Social Change* (Lanham, Md: University Press of America, 1986). The effect of business and economic development on culture and social history should also not be neglected. For a few outstanding examples, see Wolfgang Schivelbusch, *The Railway Journey: The Industrialization of Time and Space in the 19th Century* (Berkeley: University of California Press, 1986), and *Disenchanted Night: The Industrialization of Light in the Nineteenth Century* (Berkeley: University of California Press, 1988); Michael B. Miller, *The Bon Marché: Bourgeois Culture and the Department Store, 1869–1920* (Princeton, N.J.: Princeton University Press, 1981); Stephen Kern, *The Culture of Time and Space, 1880–1918* (Cambridge, Mass.: Harvard University Press, 1983); David Harvey, *The Condition of Postmodernity* (Oxford: Blackwell, 1989). A recent theoretical overview on the important but relatively neglected field of consumption can be found in Ben Fine and Ellen Leopold, *The World of Consumption* (London: Routledge, 1993).

How and why people identify themselves as a national community (and are willing to die for it) is an immensely important topic that has implications for understanding national economic policy and the context in which business operates. The literature on nationalism has recently grown into a cottage industry unto itself. A brief and useful overview can be found in the journal *Daedalus: Reconstructing Nations and States*, 122, 3 (Summer 1993). Benedict Anderson's book *Imagined Communities: Reflections on the Origin and Spread of Nationalism* (London: Verso, 1991), has been immensely influential. For the relationship between nations and big business, see Martin Carnoy, "Multinationals in a Changing World Economy: Whither the Nation-State," in *The New Global Economy in the Information Age: Reflections on Our Changing World*, ed. Martin Carnoy, Manuel Castells, Stephen S. Cohen, and Fernando Henrique Cardoso (University Park, Pa.: Pennsylvania State University Press, 1993), 45–96, with its bibliography. On the problem of the legitimacy of big business inside nations, see Matthew Josephson, *The Robber Barons: The Great American Capitalists, 1861–1901* (New York: Harcourt, Brace and Co., 1934). Louis Galambos, *The Public Image of Big Business in America, 1880–1940: A Quantitative Study in Social Change* (Baltimore: Johns Hopkins University Press, 1975). Thomas P. Hughes, *American Genesis:*

A Century of Invention and Technological Enthusiasm 1870–1970 (New York: Viking Press, 1989), esp. 249–284. Kenneth D. Barkin, *The Controversy over German Industrialization, 1890–1902* (Chicago: University of Chicago Press, 1970).

On how national laws and values affect regulation and legitimate market behavior, see Tony Freyer, *Regulating Big Business: Antitrust in Great Britain and America, 1880–1990* (Cambridge: Cambridge University Press, 1992). Herbert Hovenkamp, *Enterprise and American Law, 1836–1937* (Cambridge, Mass.: Harvard University Press, 1991). Leigh Hancher and Michael Moran (eds.), *Capitalism, Culture, and Economic Regulation* (Oxford: Clarendon Press, 1989). Richard Whitley (eds.), *European Business Systems: Firms and Markets in Their National Context* (London: Sage Publications, 1992), and *Business Systems in East Asia: Firms, Markets and Societies* (London: Sage Publications, 1992). The last two offer sophisticated discussions on the role of institutions and values in structuring market behavior. For Germany, a series of books dealing with changes in economic thought and policy and the transition from cooperative to competitive capitalism are Volker R. Berghahn, *The Americanisation of West German Industry, 1945–1973* (Cambridge: Cambridge University Press, 1986); A.J. Nicholls, *Freedom with Responsibility: The Social Market Economy in Germany 1918–1963* (Oxford: Clarendon Press, 1994); Martin F. Parnell, *The German Tradition of Organized Capitalism: Self-Government in the Coal Industry* (Oxford: Clarendon Press, 1994).

My comments on the family refer only to the impact of the family for big business, not small-business enterprises. As a guide to this vast literature, see Mary B. Rose, "The Family Firm in British Business, 1780–1914," in *Business Enterprise in Modern Britain*, ed. Maurice W. Kirby and Mary B. Rose (London: Routledge, 1994), 61–87, and "Beyond Buddenbrooks: The Family Firm and the Management of Succession in Nineteenth-Century Britain," in *Entrepreneurship, Networks and Modern Business*, ed. Jonathan Brown and Mary B. Rose, 127–143. See the contributions in Akio Okochi and Shigeaki Yasuoka (eds.), *Family Business in the Era of Industrial Growth* (Tokyo: Tokyo University Press, 1984), especially that of Maurice Lévy-Leboyer. David S. Landes, "Religion and Enterprise: The Case of the French Textile Industry," in *Enterprise and Entrepreneurs in Nineteenth- and Twentieth-Century France*, ed. Edward C. Carter II, Robert Forster, and Joseph N. Moody (Baltimore: Johns Hopkins University Press, 1976), 41–86. Larissa Lomnitz, *Family and Enterprise: The History of a Mexican Elite Kinship Group* (Princeton,

N.J.: Princeton University Press, 1987). For a brilliant exposition on how old-style family enterprise could fuse with modern, rationalized business practices, see Miller, *Bon Marché*, 86–112. For South Korea, see Alice H. Amsden, *Asia's Next Giant* (New York: Oxford University Press, 1989). Hidemasa Morikawa, *Zaibatsu: The Rise and Fall of Family Enterprise Groups in Japan* (Tokyo: University of Tokyo Press, 1992). Alfred D. Chandler, Jr., *The Visible Hand* (Cambridge, Mass.: Belknap Press of Harvard University Press, 1977), and *Scale and Scope* (Cambridge, Mass.: Belknap Press of Harvard University Press, 1990). See as well the response to Frank Church by Chandler in "Scale and Scope: A Review Colloquium," *Business History Review* 64 (Winter 1990), 690–735. The Thyssen examples are drawn from my own work: Jeffrey R. Fear, *Thyssen & Co., Mülheim/Ruhr, 1871–1934: The Institutionalization of the Corporation* (Ph.D. dissertation: Stanford University, 1993).

The discussion on the conception of the firm is loosely based on the following works. Peter Drucker, *Concept of the Corporation* (New York: John Day Co., 1972). The criticism of Chandler's *Scale and Scope* by Hidemasa Morikawa, "The View from Japan," *Business History Review* 64 (Winter 1990), 716–725. Peter Lawrence, *Managers and Management in West Germany* (New York: St. Martin's Press, 1980). Michael L. Gerlach, *Alliance Capitalism: The Social Organization of Japanese Business* (Berkeley: University of California Press, 1992). Mauro F. Guillén, *Models of Management: Work, Authority, and Organization in a Comparative Perspective* (Chicago: University of Chicago Press, 1994). Gareth Morgan, *Images of Organization* (Newbury Park, Calif.: Sage Publications, 1986). On the relationship between accounting, information, conceptions of control, and organization, see Walter W. Powell and Paul J. DiMaggio (eds.), *The New Institutionalism in Organizational Analysis* (Chicago: University of Chicago Press, 1991). John Roberts, "The Possibilities of Accountability," *Accounting, Organizations and Society* 16, 4 (1991), 355–368. H. Thomas Johnson and Robert S. Kaplan, *Relevance Lost: The Rise and Fall of Management Accounting* (Boston, Mass.: Harvard Business School Press, 1991). Neil Fligstein, *The Transformation of Corporate Control* (Cambridge, Mass.: Harvard University Press, 1990).

Index of Company Names

General Index

cartels (*cont.*)
  small European nations, 189–202
  Switzerland, 189, 194–5
Casson, Mark, 111
cement industry, France, 242
CEOs (chief executive officers), corporate
  France
    educational levels and experience,
      219
    selection, career, and mobility of, 219
    training as engineers, 220
  Germany, educational levels (1990), 219
chaebol, South Korea
  capital-intensive focus, 348
  diversification of, 340–1
  as exporters, 353–6
  family influence, 557
  general trading companies of, 355
  government discipline of, 363–4, 494
  government role in development, 19–20
  Hyundai, 350
  managerial hierarchy in, 483
  personal capitalism of, 357–8
  postwar, 19, 20
  Samsung, 350–1
  size and resource concentration, 340–1
  as state entrepreneurial capitalism, 336
  three-pronged investments, 351–7
Chandler, Alfred D., 102, 108, 110, 128,
    155, 176–8, 180, 197, 207, 222,
    302–3, 482–3, 490, 527, 558–9
Channon, Derek F., 119–20
Chapman, Stanley D., 106
chemical industry, *see also* dyestuff
    industry; petrochemical industry
  Argentina, 378–9
  Britain, 133
  Czechoslovakia, 445–6
  France
    ententes in, 226
    large firms in, 212–13
    post-1945 product realignment, 234
  Germany
    chemical engineering approach, 155
    coal consumption, 143
    factors in international success of,
      143–4
    foreign investment from, 145
    industry-university links, 520
    post–World War I trusts, 152
    pre–World War I performance, 145
  West Germany, U.S. firms' investment
    in, 164–5
  Italy, 252–3
  United States
    industry-university links, 520
    leadership in, 99
    oil-based, 85
    polymer/petrochemical revolution, 84

post–World War II polymer and
    petrochemical, 84–8
  productivity and growth, 80
  as science-based industry
    (1880–1950), 73–6, 80–2
chief executive officers, *see* CEOs
Church, Roy, 186
Ciborra, Claudio, 272
coal industry
  Germany, 141, 143
  West Germany, 163–4
Coleman, Donald, 108
commercialization of technologies
  basis for, 25
  in Third Industrial Revolution, 54
  Britain, 14
  Germany, 14–15
  United States
    of new technologies, 13, 64
    of polymer products, 85
commodity exchanges, post-Soviet Russia,
    425–6
comparative advantage, *see also*
    competitive advantage
  Germany, 148
  Spain, 303–4
competition
  enterprises losing out to, 35
  of oligopolistic firms, 31–2, 34
  Britain
    food and drink industries, 135
    pharmaceutical industry, 134
  France, interfirm, 225
  German electric power industry, 149
  Japan, interfirm, 19, 543
  South Korean interchaebol rivalry,
    494
  United States, electronics industry,
    89–98
competition, international, *see also*
    markets, international
  among capital- and knowledge-intensive
    industries, 54
  among pharmaceutical firms, 89
  effect of, 52
  products of Japan's labor-intensive
    industries, 308–9
  South Korea, 366
competitive advantage, *see also*
    comparative advantage
  of enterprises in capital-intensive
    industries, 484
  exploiting scale economies, 54
  in new technologies, 29
  post-1945 European manufacturing,
    161
  Britain
    complex-production manufacturing,
      113, 137

electronics industry
  France
    Japanese investment in consumer,
      232
    SAGEM's economies of scope, 223–4
  West Germany
    consumer mass market, 168–70
    takeovers by foreign firms, 168
  Japan, 95, 99
  United States, 89–98
embeddedness, institutional, 471–2
employers
  Germany
    benefits of apprenticeship system to,
      512
    investment in worker training, 509
    opposition to unions, 509
    restrictions on power of, 511
  Japan, investment in worker training,
    518
  United States, opposition to unions,
    502–3
employment
  Japan's system of, 323
  Russian Empire, in industrial enterprises
    (1901–11), 431t
  Soviet Union, in industrial enterprises
    (1925), 431t
energy sector, Germany, 153
engineering
  Germany
    as academic field, 504–5
    chemical, 155
    concentration of heavy, 148
    engineers in pre- and post-1914
      industries, 142
    recruitment and contributions of
      engineers, 506–7
    strength of, 170–1
  Japan
    education of engineers, 514
    zaibatsu recruitment of engineers,
      516
  United States, research and development
    by engineers, 38
ententes, France, 225–6
enterprise groups, see chaebol, South
    Korea; keiretsu, Japan; zaibatsu,
    Japan
enterprises
  clustering under personal capitalism,
    186
  concept of, 564–6
  differences in national concept, 562–4
  entrepreneurial, 482–3, 558–9
  family, 558–60
  organization with new industrial
    technologies, 8
  personal, 482–3, 558–9

Britain, post–World War II structure,
    118–36
Germany, American technology in
    manufacturing, 140
Italy, role of capital-intensive, 17
enterprises, large industrial
  change in geographic location
    (1962–93), 52–4
  contributions of, 25–6, 37
  distribution worldwide by industry
    (1962–93), 50–2
  empirical and practical knowledge,
    484–5
  network activities, 36
  role during Second Industrial
    Revolution, 24
  role in economic growth, 5–8
  Argentina
    domestic, foreign, and state-owned,
      388
    ranking (1929, 1975), 389–93
    types of, 21
  Belgium and Luxemburg, 180–4
  Britain
    diversified conglomerates, 125–6
    under pre-1945 personal capitalism,
      103–12
  Czechoslovakia
    sectoral distribution and number
      (1918–38), 439–42
    sectoral distribution and number
      (post-1948), 441, 443–4
    under Soviet-style central planning,
      23
    structure and production of, 22
    war production under German
      occupation, 23, 447
  Denmark, 181–4
  Finland, 181–4
  France
    after World War II, 230–43
    emergence and growth, 209–17
    factors in small number of, 214
    financing and credit arrangements,
      227–8
    interaction with mid- and small-size
      forms, 224–5
    interfirm markets, 222–30
    investment abroad, 232
    limits to growth of, 16
    merger waves (1920s, 1960s), 222
    post–World War II convergence, 233
    publicly traded equity, 228–9
  Germany, during Nazi regime, 155–60
  Italy
    government support for innovation
      in, 259–62
    in private sector, 265–70
    before World War II, 249–54

government role
Britain (cont.)
voluntarist attitude toward education,
131–2
Czechoslovakia
State Planning Office, 448–51
France, 220–1
creating and promoting national
champions, 16, 230, 233–5
critical nature of, 234
effect of, 244–5
investment (1914–50), 15–16
post–World War II intervention, 230
against restriction of competition, 226
in selection of corporate CEOs, 218
in stock market, 229
Germany, during Nazi regime, 155–7;
155–60
West Germany, 160–71
Italy
in banking system, 275
failures of intervention, 262–5
intervention to rescue large
corporations, 256–9
investment (1914–50), 15–16
in nineteenth-century
industrialization, 255–7
support for industrial innovation,
259–62
in support of large enterprises, 256
Japan
to develop industry competence, 328
in development of big business, 541–2
MITI, 326–8
trade policy and performance
standards, 18–19
South Korea
in development of chaebol, 20
in discipline of business, 363–4
disciplining of firms, 363–5
in encouraging general trading
companies, 353, 494
in industrialization, 336–7
intervention in price mechanism, 362
subsidies to business, 361
targeting of specific industries, 362–3
trade policy and performance
standards, 18–19
Soviet Union
intervention in industrial production
and investment decisions, 401–2
in management of production
association, 410
in price setting, 403
in support of large enterprises, 422
Spain
intervention to create large
corporations, 294
investment (1914–50), 15–16

United States, 538
investment in industrial research, 38
promotional, 538–9
related to nineteenth-century business,
536–7
grain processing technology, 65–6
Granovetter, Mark, 472
Gualino, Riccardo, 253
gun manufacture, Germany, 146

Hall, Bronwyn, 490
Hampden-Turner, Charles, 564
Hattori, Tamio, 365
Hendry, John, 123
Hinterhuber, H., 412
Hofstede, Geert, 111
holding companies
Belgium, 187–8
France, 211
Germany, 163
Italy, 271
Italy's government-owned, 17, 257
Spain's government-owned, 18
Houssiaux, Jacques, 209
human capital
cultivated by large industrial enterprises,
26
Britain
inadequate interwar, 110
underinvestment in, 130, 136
Japan's human skills network, 323

IG (Interessengemeinschaften), Germany,
144
import penetration
Germany (1980s), 113
post-1945 British, 113–14
import substitution, Argentina
characteristics of enterprises with,
380–1
encouragement of, 21
second stage (1952–76), 382–4
industrialization
government role in late, 523
Czechoslovakia, 433–5
Germany
apprenticeship system with, 508–10
nineteenth-century, 140
Italy
effect of World War I, 247
pre-1914 industrial revolution, 246–7
pre–World War II military build-up,
247–8
role of capital-intensive industries, 17
Japan, 307–8
Soviet Union
development of basic industries
(1930s–1950s), 403
rapid pace of, 421

industry groups, clustered
  capital-intensive (1962–93), 50–2
  concentration of large firms in United
    States (1917–88), 40–6
  world-wide capital-intensive, 50–2
information, *see also* knowledge
  asymmetry in managerial capitalism,
    481
  distribution to stakeholders, 489
  hazard of asymmetric, 489
  from large industrial enterprises, 25
  mobility of, in U.S. firms, 123
  required by top management, 481–2
infrastructure, Germany, 505–6
INI (Industrial National Agency), Spain,
    278–9
innovations, *see also* Industrial
    Revolution, First; Industrial
    Revolution, Second; Industrial
    Revolution, Third
  absence in Soviet enterprises, 419
  late nineteenth century technological, 8
  new products and processes in
    technological, 6
  role of American and European firms in
    technological, 9–10
  slowdown in technological (1970s), 11
  Argentina, between wars (1920–40), 379
  France, 214
integration
  France, 224
  Germany
    pre-1914 backward, 141
    vertical technological, 141
  Italy, 266–7
  West Germany
    of chemical producers, 165
    factors influencing vertical, 162
internal-combustion engine, 77, 79
investment
  foreign direct investment, capital market
    role in, 483
  of industries with scale-dependent
    technologies, 30–1
  research and development (1965–88),
    54–6
  with new industrial technologies, 8
  Britain, 103–12
  Czechoslovakia, 437–8
  Japan
    cooperative strategies for, 516
    factors behind growth of equipment
      investment, 312–21
    industrial restructuring through
      equipment investment, 314, 321–2
  Soviet Union
    centralized state (1918–75), 401–2
    during economic reform (1960s), 401
    NEP period, 400–1

Spain, 296–9
United States
  capital-intensive industries
    (1880s–1914), 63–4
  in industrial research and
    development (1990), 46, 48–9t
  substituting machines for worker
    skills, 519
West Germany, 162–3
investment, three-pronged
  for big business to succeed, 351
  of managerial enterprises, 178
  France, 232
  Italy, 266
  Japan, 315
  South Korea, 351–7
IRI (Istituto di Recostruzione Industriale),
    Italy, 17, 257, 260, 263–5, 269
Iwasaki family, 19, 316

Jensen, Michael, 486–7, 490
joint-stock companies
  Argentina, 377
  Japan
    influence of managers in, 310
    as managerial enterprises, 318
    prewar, 308
  Russia (prerevolution), 397–8
joint ventures, France, 233, 234
Jorgenson, Dale, 27

keiretsu, Japan, *see also* zaibatsu, Japan
  competition among, 326
  corporations with interlocking
    shareholdings (brethren-type),
    328–30, 333–5, 563
  corporations with subsidiaries (parent-
    child), 329–35, 563
  horizontal and vertical, post-war, 19,
    515
  linking of large and small companies
    through, 519
  post-war emergence, 515–16
Kilby, Jack, 95
knowledge, *see also* industries, knowledge-
    based; learning, organizational
  company- and industry-specific, 34–5
  developed by industrial enterprises, 25
  distribution to stakeholders, 489
  empirical and practical, 485
  in managerial capitalism, 483–5, 495–6
  required by top management, 481–2
  Germany, 506
knowledge-based industries, *see* industries,
    knowledge-based
Kocka, Jürgen, 216, 387
Kogut, Bruce, 129, 209, 470
Korean War, 313
Kornai, Janos, 493

Ministry of International Trade and
Industry (MITI), Japan
as arm of government, 541–2
relations with business, 328
role of, 326–8
Mitsui family, 19
monetary system, international, 11
Montgomery, Arthur, 198
Morikawa, Hidemasa, 351, 361
Morita, Akio, 418
Mowery, David, 109
multinational enterprises, *see* enterprises,
multinational
Mussolini, Benito, 268, 274

national champion policy, France, 222,
230, 233–5, 237–49
nationalization
Argentina, 381
Britain, 120, 124
Czechoslovakia, 447
France, 231, 233
in electrical equipment and electronics
industry, 235–6
Pechiney (1982), 235
Rhône-Poulenc (1982), 234–5
Saint-Gobain (1982–6), 241
Thomson, 236
South Korea, 362
Soviet Union, 398–9
Spain
of foreign and domestic companies,
18
management in state-owned firms,
300
Nelson, Richard, 28, 356
networks
developed by large industrial
enterprises, 26
of related industrial activities, 36–7
France
industrial and commercial entents,
225
relationships among large-, mid-, and
small-sized companies, 224–5
Japan, of unique skills, 310, 321–6
New Economic Policy (NEP), Soviet
Union, 398–9
Noyce, Robert, 95
nuclear power plant technology, West
Germany, 169

occupation forces, postwar Japan
effect of changed policies, 312
effect of managerial changes, 319–20
tax and land reforms, 313, 318–19
oil industry
Argentina, 383
Britain, 114, 133

Italy, 260–2
small European nations, 184–5
United States
development of, 68–70
oil-refining technology, 69–70
vertical integration in, 79
Olds, Ransom E., 77
oligopolies
emergence in industrial economies, 31–2
oil industry as, 70, 79
in prerevolution Russia, 398
Olivetti, Adriano, 272
Olivetti family, 272
Olsen, Kenneth, 92
O'Mahony, Mary, 114–15
organizational capabilities, *see* capabilities,
organizational
Our Nation's Path (Park), 364–5
Owens, Michael, 66

Panfilov, M. P., 408
paper technology, 67
Park Chung Hee, 36–5
Pavan, Robert J., 270–1
Pavitt, Keith, 472–3
Payno, Juan A., 301
perestroika (Soviet Union), 425
Perrone, Mario, 258
Perrone, Pio, 258
personal capitalism, *see* capitalism,
personal
petrochemical industry
Italy, 254, 261–2
West Germany, 164–5
pharmaceutical industry
Argentina, 378–9
British, 133–4
France
foreign direct investment in, 232
merger, 212–13
Germany
industry-university links, 520
institutional cooperation, 144
United States
alliances with biotech firms, 89
with development of antibiotics,
88–9
industry-university links, 520
investment in recombinant DNA, 89
leadership in, 99
Pilkington, Alastair, 132
politicization, West Germany, 164
polymers, 84–6
Pompidou, Georges, 234
Porsche, Ferdinand, 159
Porter, Michael, 207, 412
primary metals industries
impact of motor vehicle production, 80
scale economies, 67